GIVE ME LIBERTY OR GIVE ME OBAMACARE

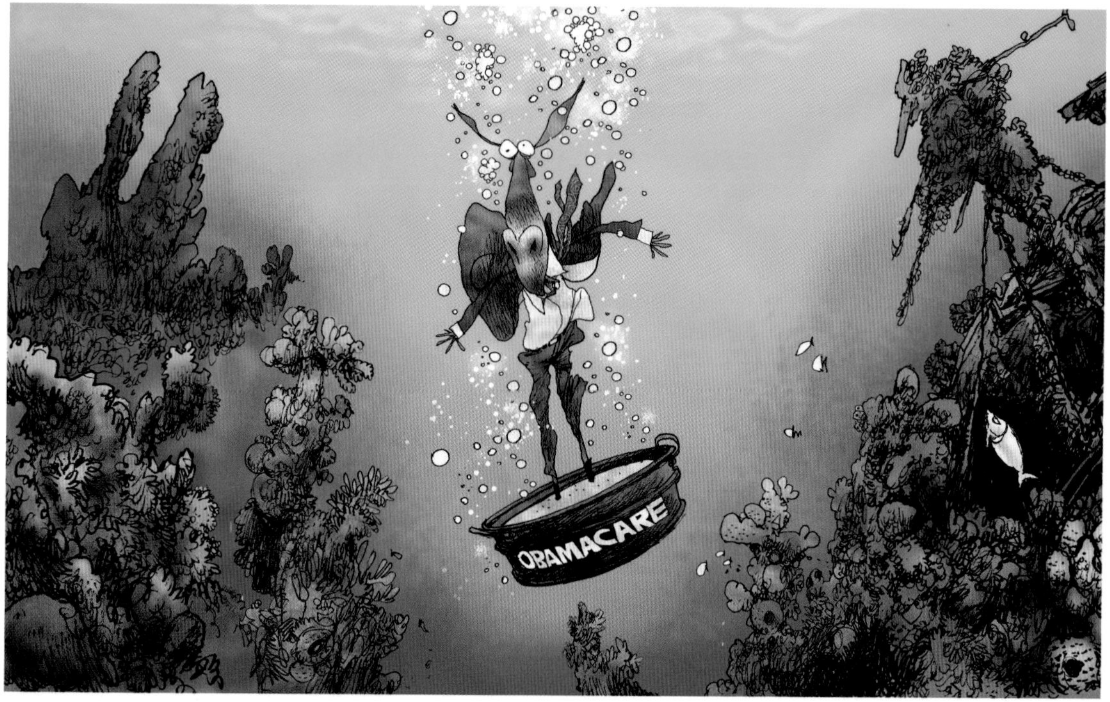
OBAMACARE

MICHAEL RAMIREZ

THRESHOLD EDITIONS
NEW YORK LONDON TORONTO SYDNEY NEW DELHI

Threshold Editions
An Imprint of Simon & Schuster, Inc.
1230 Avenue of the Americas
New York, NY 10020

First Threshold Editions hardcover edition October 2015

Interior design by Davina Mock-Maniscalco

Manufactured in the United States of America

10 9 8 7 6 5 4 3 2 1

Library of Congress Cataloging-in-Publication Data is available.

ISBN 978-1-5011-1025-2
ISBN 978-1-5011-1027-6 (ebook)

DEDICATION

To the world's best parents, I. Edward and Fumiko Ramirez; to the entire Ramirez Clan; to my beloved Deborah, whose love, devotion and support has been my inspiration; to my darling Clementine, who fills me with joy; to all our brave soldiers whose heroism, dedication, and sacrifice keep our country safe, and who defend the freedom that so many strive for and too many take for granted; to all you patriots whose support, perseverance, and selfless hard work in defense of liberty nourish and sustain me; and last, to those self-serving politicians who put their political interests before their duty to country—I couldn't have done it without you.

Acknowledgments

Any book is an enormous undertaking and cannot be put together without the help and support of others. Frankly, this book may never have been published if it were not for the encouragement and dedication of so many.

I want to thank my mother and father for their boundless love, unconditional support, and absolute belief in me. You made me the man I am today. The best advice I ever received in my life was from you. You taught me to never allow anyone's actions define my own, to always be my own man and make my own choices, and to do all I can to make this world a better place. Your words of wisdom and your love have served me well, and I will always be grateful to you. I was blessed with the most wonderful parents in the world.

I have the best family a man can have. I thank my best friend and my love, Deborah, for your love, devotion, and patience, and for always being there when I've needed you most. I am thankful for our sweet Clementine, who brings me endless joy and has given me a whole new perspective on life. To my family, who have always surrounded me with love and support, thank you: my brother Ed; his wife, Jane; their daughter, Julia; my sister Victoria—my own personal health consultant; her husband, Denley; and their daughter, Alexandra; my brother Alexander; his wife, Lori; their daughters, Ke'ea and Ellie; my sister Liz; her husband, Bryan; their son, Bryson, and their daughter, Amelie; and Bryan's brother, Hannibal, who is like a brother to me.

I want to thank Vice President Dick Cheney. You are a true hero and an inspiration to me as well as to millions of other Americans. You provided us with strong, unapologetic leadership when America needed it most. We love you, Lynne, and your entire family. Thank you for your service. Thank you for your generosity and your time. I am so very honored to know you and to count you as a friend.

I want to thank Rush Limbaugh for his generous contribution to this book. Rush, you influence millions every day, though I can't listen to you all the time because I'm afraid you'll come up with better ideas than me! You may have single-handedly saved the conservative movement. I thank you for all that you do, for all that you are, and for having the courage to tell it like it is. I am proud to know you and call you my friend.

There are so many people who have been instrumental in putting this book together and whose generosity of time and significant contributions enrich it. Among them are Bill O'Reilly, Sean Hannity, Governor Mike Huckabee, Governor Pete Wilson, Michelle Malkin, Walter Williams, Ambassador John Bolton, Michael Barone, and Greg Gutfeld; special thanks go to my dear friend Ann Coulter, who made this book possible.

I thank my friends, who help me keep my head on straight and who also fight the good fight: my lifelong friend Ray Gonzalez (it's hard to believe we've been talking politics now for more than twenty-five years—you are a good man, despite what everyone says about you); his wife, Lisa, and their son, Alex; Mark Joseph, who is my spiritual conscience and my brother-in-arms in the culture war; Paul Shanklin, one of my dearest friends and the guy who always makes me laugh, and his dear wife, Angie; and Chip Saltsman, "two thumbs-up close together" (what more can I say?).

I want to thank my book agent, Eric Lupfer, and the entire gang at William Morris Endeavor, whose great work made this book a reality. I look forward to future projects together.

Special thanks to my boss, William J. O'Neil, whose support, vision, wisdom, and dedication to good journalism allow *Investor's Business Daily* to be the beacon of truth for millions of readers with the best editorial page in the country. And thanks to Scott O'Neil, who is leading *IBD* into the twenty-first century. I am so proud to be part of the *IBD* family.

I want to thank the *IBD* editorial page team, led by editor Wes Mann, and my colleagues Terry Jones, Kerry Jackson, Monica Showalter, John Merline, Tom McArdle, Matt Galgani, and Stephen Moore for making me laugh—you make me think and you make me smarter. Thanks also to Chris Gessel, Susan Warfel, Mary Ann Edwards (who fixes all my errors), and the rest of the staff at *Investor's Business Daily*. I'm honored to be on the *IBD* team.

The goal of every editorialist is to reach as many people as possible. Nobody does it better than my syndicate, Creators. I want to thank my friend Rick Newcombe for your help on this book and your friendship and support all these years, and to my friend Jack Newcombe for your friendship, support, and leadership. Hats off to the great staff at Creators for all the hard work you do on my behalf. I appreciate you all. Please keep the hate mail coming.

Thanks to Mitchell Ivers, Vice President and Editorial Director at Threshold Editions; Natasha Simons, Assistant Editor, for her work on this book (and for trying to keep me on deadline); and all the team at Threshold and Simon and Schuster. Thanks for believing in this project.

I thank God for all the blessings in my life.

And I want to thank all my readers, fans, Facebook page friends, and Twitter followers. Keep the faith. The truth will prevail.

God bless America.

I believe there are more instances of the abridgement of freedom of the people by gradual and silent encroachments by those in power than by violent and sudden usurpations.

—James Madison

CONTENTS

FOREWORD
BY DICK CHENEY

I have heard that Darth Vader never smiles. If that's true, it is only because he's never seen Michael Ramirez's cartoons. Even a Dark Lord of the Sith would find the skewering that Michael gives to hypocrites funny, whether it's President Obama proclaiming himself to be a humble man or Hillary Clinton saying she and Bill were "dead broke" when they left the White House.

One of the things I most appreciate about Michael is his deep understanding of politics. He's not fooled by office-holders who try to hide the truth, calling acts of terrorism "man-caused disasters," "workplace violence," or, in the case of Benghazi, "a spontaneous protest." And Michael's memory is long. He doesn't forget when Barack Obama tells us that if we like our health care plan, we can keep it, and he calls the president to account for selling his programs with untruths—or "lies," as Michael would say. He is nothing if not blunt.

Michael also knows the high stakes involved. Obamacare isn't just a scam, it violates the Constitution. Big government isn't just an annoyance, it's a threat to our liberty.

Michael doesn't close his eyes to tragedies, whether Americans bring them on themselves, by drug abuse, for example, or whether enemies inflict them upon us, as most notably on 9/11. His dramatic and unforgettable drawings are a prod to action, to do something to better our culture—and to do everything we can to prevent another mass-casualty attack on our country.

Michael has won two Pulitzer Prizes—and he deserves a dozen more.

Keep at it, Michael. The Republic needs you.

Dick Cheney
August 2015

INTRODUCTION

BY MICHAEL RAMIREZ

If the phrase "the Peter Principle" is used to describe what happens when a person is elevated to their level of incompetence, then the "Obama Principle" should be used to describe what happens when that incompetent person becomes president of the United States.

It didn't start out that way. In 2009, America was brimming with anticipation. America had made history. According to liberal pundits, America had finally dispossessed itself of its racial enmity by electing our first African-American president. Barack Obama was called a unifier. America had hope. And change.

What then, I wondered, would I, as an editorial cartoonist, find to draw cartoons about?

Then the illusion of hope and change began to unravel. As a candidate, Barack Obama had denounced the Bush administration for their lack of diplomacy. He had claimed to be an expert in negotiation and said he was prepared for that "three-call." And then, as president-elect, Obama, although short on experience, was brimming over with confidence. He would rise to any challenge.

Then we found out, during the Benghazi attack, that the 3:00 a.m. call came and Presidend Obama was nowhere in sight.

Many were disappointed, deeply disappointed. In my own disappointment, cartoon ideas began to come to me. . . .

What might have happened when the 3:00 a.m. call came in? Perhaps an answering machine? "You've reached the office of President Barack Hussein Obama. I'm not here right now. If you have an anti-Islam video I can use for political cover, press 1. If you want me to go to Las Vegas for a fundraiser right after the killing of three brave Americans and the first assassination of a U.S. ambassador in thirty-three years, press 2. For golf after beheadings, press 3."

In 2009, the newly inaugurated President Obama claimed to be a centrist and offered a vision of unity and reasonable moderation. America was ready for change. With Obama came the promise of transparency and a return to the rule of law. He promised a sound fiscal policy. He promised to bring America back together.

But he didn't. More ideas.

And then he promised Americans, "If you like your health plan, you can keep it."

But they couldn't. More ideas.

We soon found that the president had a big flaw: a pathological addiction to prevarication. More ideas. This flaw, however, turned out to be relatively minor, compared to the size of his ego. More ideas. What we didn't realize until later was that *everything* is relatively small compared to the size of his ego. And that oversize ego and those pathological lies became an abundance of cartoon ideas.

He was a president with a majority in the House and a supermajority in the Senate, and the power to implement his vision. *That* was the essential problem. He was never a centrist. His centrism was a fable conjured up by his campaign and repeated ad nauseam by a complicit media. But many of us knew there was never anything moderate about Barack Obama. He was a far-left politician with a far-left agenda. His real vision for America was its radical transformation: the first step, like limbo, the first circle of Dante's hell. "Abandon all hope, ye who enter here."

There was no hope; it was all about change.

President Obama believes government is not the problem; he believes it is the solution.

He believes our enemies are not bad; he believes they are simply misunderstood.

He believes that corporations create inequality, not jobs.

He sees America as the "land of plenty," but in his mind this is a bad thing.

All these realizations created cartoon ideas.

In Obama's world, America is a land of excess, of immoderate indulgences, of intemperance and gluttony, with a lack of restraint and a rapacious appetite for everything. In Obama's world, American capitalism is responsible for the subjugation of the worker. American consumption is responsible for creating ecological destruction and global warming. American greed is responsible for creating the poor. American ingenuity is responsible for exploitation of the masses. American exceptionalism is the reason for global hostility against America. President Obama believes, to borrow a phrase from Walt Kelly, that "we have met the enemy. He is us."

That's why the media loves him. They *agree* with him.

Thomas Jefferson once said: "Educate and inform the whole mass of the people. . . . They are the only sure reliance for the preservation of our liberty." Unfortunately, the American media is too immersed in adulation of the president to educate and inform the masses of the president's shortcomings.

In 2009, following Obama's speech in Cairo, *Newsweek* editor Evan Thomas, appearing on MSNBC, promoted the president from the rank of commander in chief to deity in chief, declaring, "I mean, in a way Obama's standing above the country, above—above the world, he's sort of God." *New York Times* columnist Judith Warner wrote in her column that "many women . . . were dreaming about sex with the president." Meanwhile, the entire mainstream media in America seemed to be having virtual sex with the president in print.

The only person who loved the president more than the media was the president himself. In 2007, he bragged: "I think that I'm a better speechwriter than my speechwriters. I know more about policies on any particular issue than my policy directors. And I'll tell you right now that I'm gonna think I'm a better political director than my political director." But somehow he was going to heal the nation. In 2008, he said he was going to heal this *planet*. Obama proclaimed, "I face this challenge with profound humility, and knowledge of my own limitations . . . this was the moment when the rise of the oceans began to slow and our planet began to heal. . . ."

He is a dangerous combination of ignorance and arrogance, and both are fertile ground for my cartoons.

Don't get me wrong. I'm an equal-opportunity cartoonist, but with this administration, editorial cartooning is more like stenography than a creative process. When people ask me, "How do you come up with your ideas?" I simply reply, "I have the best gag writer in the world working for me in the Oval Office every day . . . well, every day he's not on vacation or on the golf course. His policies are the joke, his speeches are the setup, and their failure are the punch lines, except, nobody is laughing. It hurts too much to laugh."

Albert Einstein once said, "Intellectuals solve problems. Geniuses prevent them."

Obama creates them.

Obama's first chief of staff, Rahm Emanuel, in preparation for taking over the White House, notoriously stated, "You never want a serious crisis to go to waste."

Taking those words to heart, this administration has spent two terms *creating* crisis after crisis.

I have spent those two terms memorializing how they did that. This book tells that story.

THE OBAMA "GREEN" ECONOMY was in 2012 called the worst economic recovery in American history. Under Obamanomics, the national debt increased $7.4 trillion in just six years. At the beginning of 2015, our national debt was more than $18 trillion, six times the annual federal revenue. A 2013 Federal Reserve Survey of Consumer Finance report, released in 2014, showed that U.S. household median income level dropped 12% in the six years between 2007 and 2103. By 2013, incomes had dropped twice as much during the recovery than they had during the recession. A Census Bureau Report released in October of 2014 showed more than 48 million Americans living in poverty, including 1 in 5 young adults. The same report showed 65% of children living in households receiving one or more forms of federal aid. At the same time, the USDA reported that 46.4 million Americans were receiving food stamps Also, the BLS reported that the labor participation rate was at its lowest rate since 1978 while the U6 unemployment rate was 11.5%.

During the Obama administration, we witnessed the first ever credit downgrade in U.S. history in 2011, and the second in 2012. We have seen a substantial growth in government regulations, subsidies, and programs under this administration. The result has been a dramatic increase in income inequality, with black and minority families being hit the hardest. An analysis by Pew Research of data from the Federal Reserve's Survey of Consumer Finances, released in December of 2014, shows that in 2013, the wealth of white households was thirteen times the median wealth of blacks in 2013, which is seven times greater than in 2010.

While the list of economic failures to date is long, the administration's list of excuses for the weak economic recovery is even longer. The president has blamed: George W.

Bush, Congress (when it was controlled by Democrats); the "GOP" Congress (when the GOP controlled neither House nor Senate); the "GOP" Congress (when it controlled only the House); the European debt crisis; the Japan tsunami; ATMS; the rich; Wall Street; Main Street; millionaires; those who make more than $250,000; the Iraq War; the war in Afghanistan; the Arab Spring; tax breaks; global warming; globalization; automation; the Euro; bad luck; Superposes; the Supreme Court; the Tea Party; airport ticket kiosks; oil companies; oil speculators; soft and lazy Americans; businesses; the U.S. Constitution; Fox News; Rush Limbaugh; corporations; Dick Cheney; "Joe the Plumber"; the "worst economy since the Great Depression"; the weather; not enough of stimulus; Paul Ryan; Mitt Romney; Mitch McConnell; John Boehner; messy democracy; not enough spending; too much spending; the media; Ronald Reagan: the Gulf oil spill; outsourcing; Bain Capital; Wall Street "fat cats"; Washington, D.C.; the top 2%; the top 1%; Washington insiders; Washington outsiders; tax cuts; the Middle East crisis; Israel; George W. Bush and George W. Bush. This has been a president who refuses to take responsibility for anything.

Fortunately, the U.S. economy is resilient. Our recovery plods along, not because of Obama economic policies but in spite of them. The same could not be said for U.S. foreign policy.

Obama believes America is not a shining city on the hill. Rather, he believes America is and should be just one nation among many, many nations. His foreign policy was designed to rein in American global leadership, to bring us back into the fold and temper our imperious stature in the world. (The psychological term for this is "projection.") He succeeded.

Obama's foreign policy of appeasement and "Leading from Behind" has diminished our global reputation, alienated our allies, and emboldened our enemies. It left a power vacuum that has quickly filled with chaos and malefaction. Islamic extremism and the prospect of terrorism in our post-9/11 world has expanded and continues to do so. Radical Islamic groups control more territory than ever. Iran has come ever closer to developing a nuclear weapon and to starting a nuclear arms race in a region awash in oil money but lacking reverence for human life. China has begun flexing its muscles and threatens its neighbors. Russia has invaded hers. Under President Obama, the world has become a more dangerous place, particularly for Americans.

The architecture of policy, the setting of artificial timetables, the micro-management and conclusion of the wars in both Iraq and Afghanistan were designed by the Obama administration for political advantage, not for strategic victory. Relinquishing those countries to terrorists, releasing terrorists to close Gitmo and giving Cuba to communists was, in the president's mind, a small price to pay in order to fulfill his political promises. But, Obama could proclaim "mission accomplished" and, naturally, he did.

In President Obama's mind, this made perfect sense. The threat was not external; it was internal. America is the threat, and Obama is at war with America. American "exceptionalism" is the disease, and Obamacare was just the first step toward a cure. Saul Alinsky's "third rule of ethics of means and ends" in *Rules for Radicals* is that "in war, the end justifies almost any means."

Ignoring the law has never seemed to be a problem for this administration. There is a long list of scandals proving that: Fast and Furious, possible Holder perjuries, the GM bailout, Obamacare, Solyndra, National Intelligence leaks, Benghazi, using the IRS to target political enemies, the VA, the DOJ investigation of Fox Reporter James Rosen, monitoring AP phone calls, NSA data collection expansion, executing the Dream Act, illegal Executive Appointments during Congressional recess, Gruber, and Executive Amnesty. Yet these were just the ones the president "discovered" while he was "reading the newspaper." Any one of these scandals would have crippled a Republican administration and sent scores of investigative teams in pursuit of a Pulitzer Prize and maybe, just maybe the truth. But largely because they agree with this administration's political agenda, the media have turned a blind eye as the president acts with impunity.

This is a lawless administration. We have seen it taken to new levels with the launch of Obamacare. The administration's unilateral actions of deciding which aspects of the new law were applicable, applying its own exemptions and exclusions, and making postponements should have raised red flags for a former constitutional law professor. It didn't. The president's circumvention of the Constitution was audacious, but with each new step and every election loss during the process, he grew bolder. In January 2014, Obama even went so far as to declare: "I've got a pen and I've got a phone, and I can use that pen to sign executive orders and take executive actions and administrative actions that move the ball forward." Liberal constitutional scholar and George Washington University law professor Jonathan Turley later called President Obama "the president Richard Nixon always wanted to be."

In Federalist Paper number 47, James Madison quoted Charles Montesquieu: "When the legislative and executive powers are united in the same person or body, there can be no liberty, because apprehensions may arise lest the same monarch or senate should enact tyrannical laws to execute them in a tyrannical manner." With immigration, the president showed he was keenly aware of his executive limitations. Dating as far back as March 2008, he stated twenty-two times that he did not have the constitutional authority to create law without Congress. On January 30, 2013, when asked about executing a moratorium on deportation, President Obama said, "I am not a king. I am head of the executive branch of government. I am required to follow the law." Despite this awareness, he reversed himself.

By November of 2014, President Obama had declared war on the U.S. Constitution and claimed an imperial right to execute Executive Amnesty. The *New York Times* defended this action, stating, "*The right* will falsely label Mr. Obama's actions lawless. They are a victory for problem-solving over posturing, common sense over cruelty, and lawful order over a chaotic status quo."

This attitude was no real surprise, since most of the so-called watchdogs of mainstream journalism were already drooling lapdogs or had long since rolled over and were still playing dead. This complacent media, coupled with the administration's penchant for deception and lack of transparency, left most of the scandals unexplored—a shameful display of obsequious acquiescence and the evacuation of the fourth estate.

The most damning criticism of the Obama administration has surprisingly come from *the left*. It was Jonathan Turley who said, "What the president is suggesting is tearing at the very fabric of the constitution. We have a separation of powers that gives us balance and that doesn't protect the branches. It's not there to protect the executive branch or the legislative branch, it's there to protect liberty."

This was a constitutional crisis and no one was really covering it. As it turns out, the only people more incompetent than those in the Obama administration are the Washington press corps.

IN 2008, Barack Obama promised hope and change. By 2015, all that he has delivered is doubt and division. This book is a record of the misdeeds, unconstitutional overreaching, scandals, policy failures, unlawful executive actions, and pathological behavior of an imperial presidency. It is a chronicle of global and domestic events and policy failures that transpired during the presidency of Barack Obama. Its importance is predicated by the absence of quality, objective reporting in what can only be characterized as journalistic complicity or neglect during the entirety of his two terms. The fact is that when an editorial cartoonist has to take on the responsibility of exposing the truth because the mainstream media refuses to do so—to do its job—or is simply unwilling to do so be-cause it agrees with the broader political agenda, the state of journalism is quite sad.

There are those who want to eliminate the freedom of information. On January 7, 2015, terrorists attacked the offices of a satirical weekly newspaper, *Charlie Hebdo*, in Paris, France, killing twelve and injuring ten for publishing cartoons depicting Muhammed.

This despicable act of terror was not just an attack on cartoonists. It was an attack on freedom and liberty. The cowards who committed this crime should be condemned for the evil they represent. The right to freedom of expression preserves our liberty.

John Milton in 1644 said, "Give me the Liberty to know, to utter, and to argue freely according to conscience, above all liberties." John Stuart Mill in 1859 argued in "On Liberty" that without freedom and free expression, there can be no progress made, that arguments need to be pushed to their logical limits to advance thinking.

"Such being the reasons which make it imperative that human beings should be free to form opinions, and to express their opinions without reserve; and such the baneful consequences to the intellectual, and through that to the moral nature of man, unless this liberty is either conceded, or asserted in spite of prohibition."

Thomas Jefferson once wrote, "Our Liberty depends on the freedom of press, and that cannot be limited without it being lost."

The reason our Founding Fathers included the right to a free press in our Constitution was because they knew the communication of ideas and information, the right to inform and be informed, the dissemination of ideas, and the expression of opinion are all necessary components in a political system based on self-governance and individual liberty.

The U.S. Supreme Court, in the 1988 *Hustler Magazine, Inc. v. Falwell* case, even affirmed the right to parody public figures regardless of how crude or boorish the portrayal, because the contributions of free expression to the public interest outweighed those of prurient interest. Judge William Rehnquist wrote for the majority: "At the heart of the First Amendment is the recognition of the fundamental importance of the free flow of ideas and opinions on matters of public interest and concern.

"The freedom to speak one's mind is not only an aspect of individual liberty—and thus a good unto itself—but also is essential to the common quest for truth and the vitality of society as a whole."

We have therefore been particularly vigilant to ensure that individual expressions of ideas remain free from governmentally imposed sanctions. The First Amendment recognizes no such thing as a "false" idea.

As Justice Holmes wrote: "When men have realized that time has upset many fighting faiths, they may come to believe even more than they believe the very foundations of their own conduct that the ultimate good desired is better reached by free trade in ideas—that the best test of truth is the power of the thought to get itself accepted in the competition of the market. . . ."

Imagine a world that did not have the freedom, or the journalists, the editorial cartoonists, and a free and unrestrained press to point out the injustices, iniquity, tyranny, evil misdeeds, and transgressions of the world. As the light of liberty is dimmed, so are prospects for a peaceful and safer world.

Editorial cartoons are a check on the erosion of our liberties and a first line of defense against the unrestrained power of government and those who attack our freedom.

The tragedy in Paris demonstrates the need to expose those who subvert religion to justify barbarism. Only when the world can see these emissaries of death and destruction for what they are will the world unite against them.

Whether you agree with the cartoons or not is immaterial. Freedom must endure. The attack on *Charlie Hebdo* might have silenced a few pens, but evil will never extinguish the light of liberty.

James Madison once wrote, "Knowledge will forever govern ignorance; and a people who mean to be their own governors must arm themselves with the power which knowledge gives."

It is the duty of good editorial cartooning to inform. It is the job of the good citizen to be informed.

I hope you find this book, at the very least, entertaining but more so serving as a catalyst for thought. I hope it will inspire you as a call to action, a call to serve and to get involved in the process of self-governance, because "who" controls your destiny is up to you.

In the Beginning

"I face this challenge with profound humility, and knowledge of my own limitations . . . this was the moment when the rise of the oceans began to slow and our planet began to heal."

—President Barack Obama,
St. Paul, Minnesota, June 3, 2008

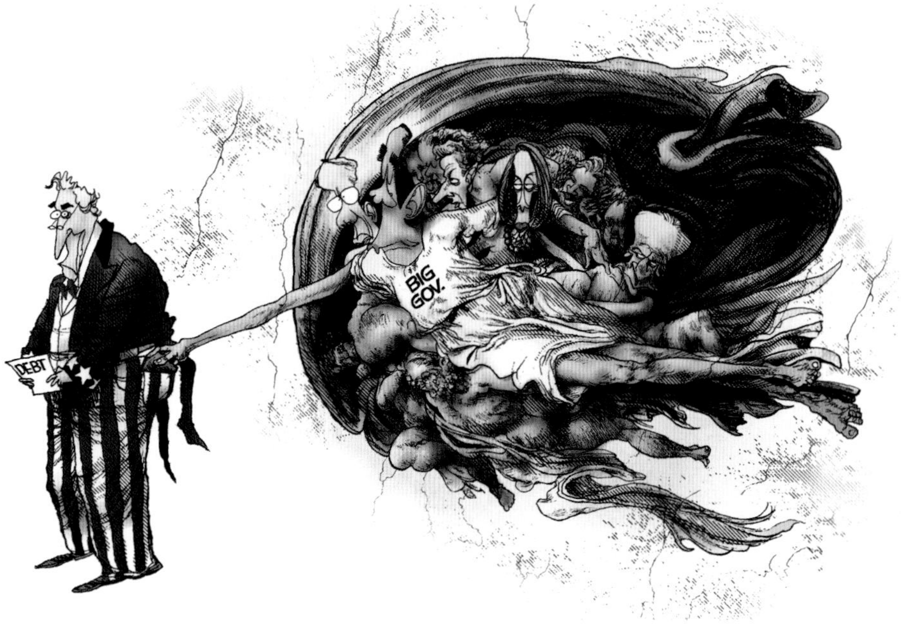
DEBT
BIG GOV.

It was a time of great expectations and anticipation of a new direction for America, but what was delivered was the old politics of division, big-government spending, and big-government solutions.

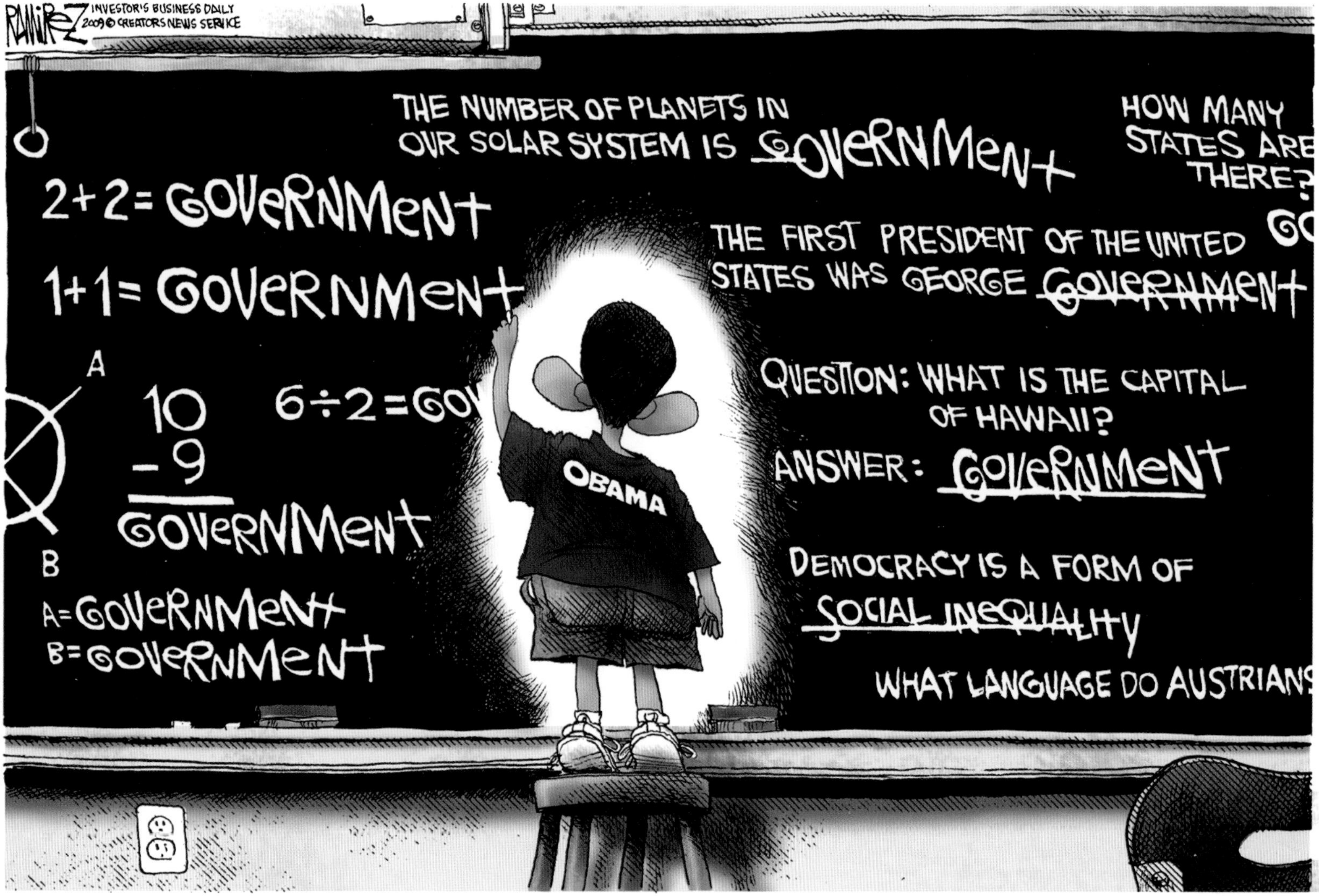
RAMIREZ INVESTOR'S BUSINESS DAILY 2009 © CREATORS NEWS SERVICE
THE NUMBER OF PLANETS IN OUR SOLAR SYSTEM IS GOVERNMENT
HOW MANY STATES ARE THERE?
2+2= GOVERNMENT
1+1= GOVERNMENT
THE FIRST PRESIDENT OF THE UNITED STATES WAS GEORGE GOVERNMENT
A
10
-9
GOVERNMENT
6÷2=GOV
QUESTION: WHAT IS THE CAPITAL OF HAWAII?
ANSWER: GOVERNMENT
OBAMA
B
A=GOVERNMENT
B=GOVERNMENT
DEMOCRACY IS A FORM OF SOCIAL INEQUALITY
WHAT LANGUAGE DO AUSTRIANS

A YOUNG BARACK OBAMA.

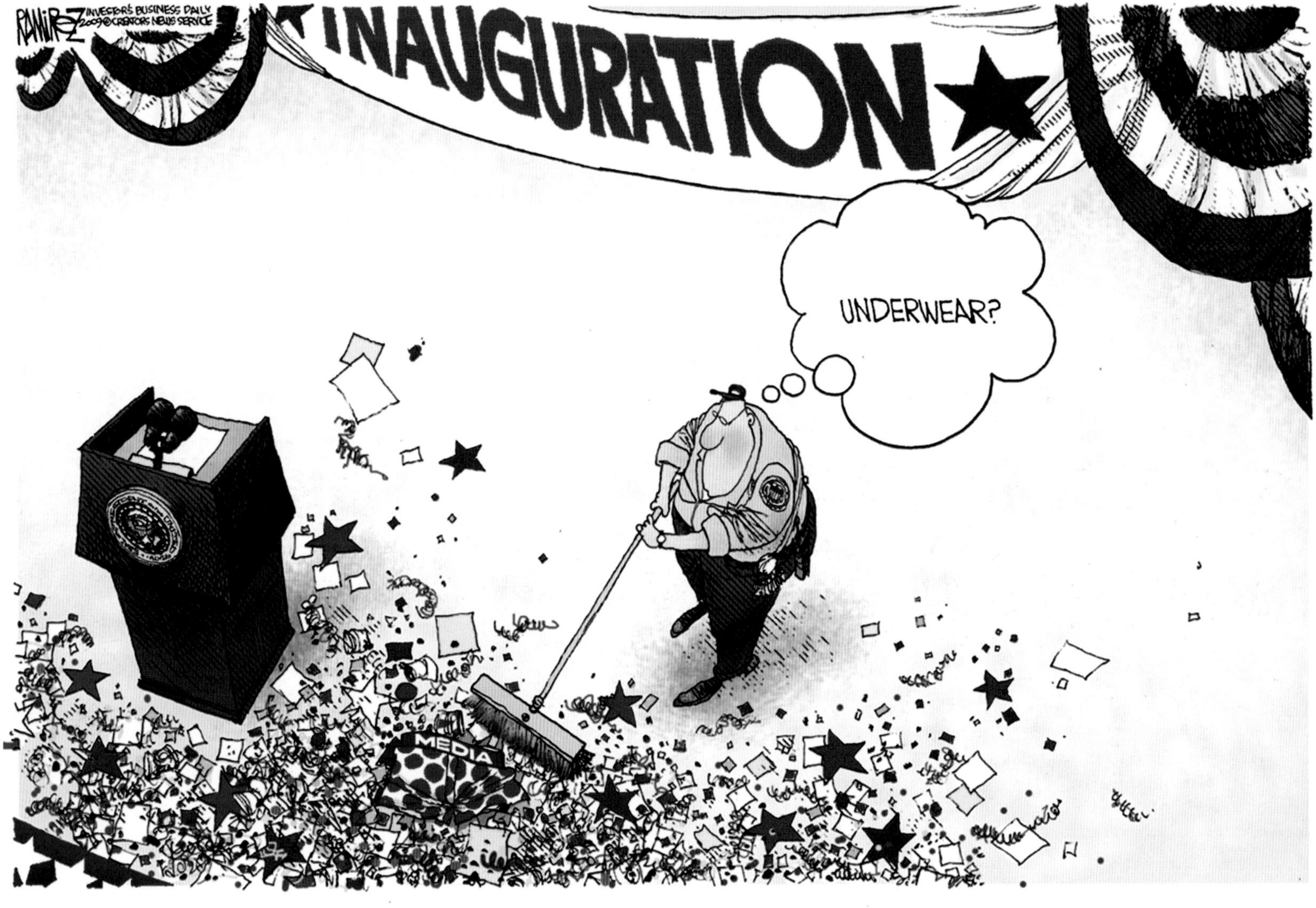
RAMIREZ INVESTOR'S BUSINESS DAILY 2009 © CREATORS NEWS SERVICE
INAUGURATION
UNDERWEAR?
MEDIA

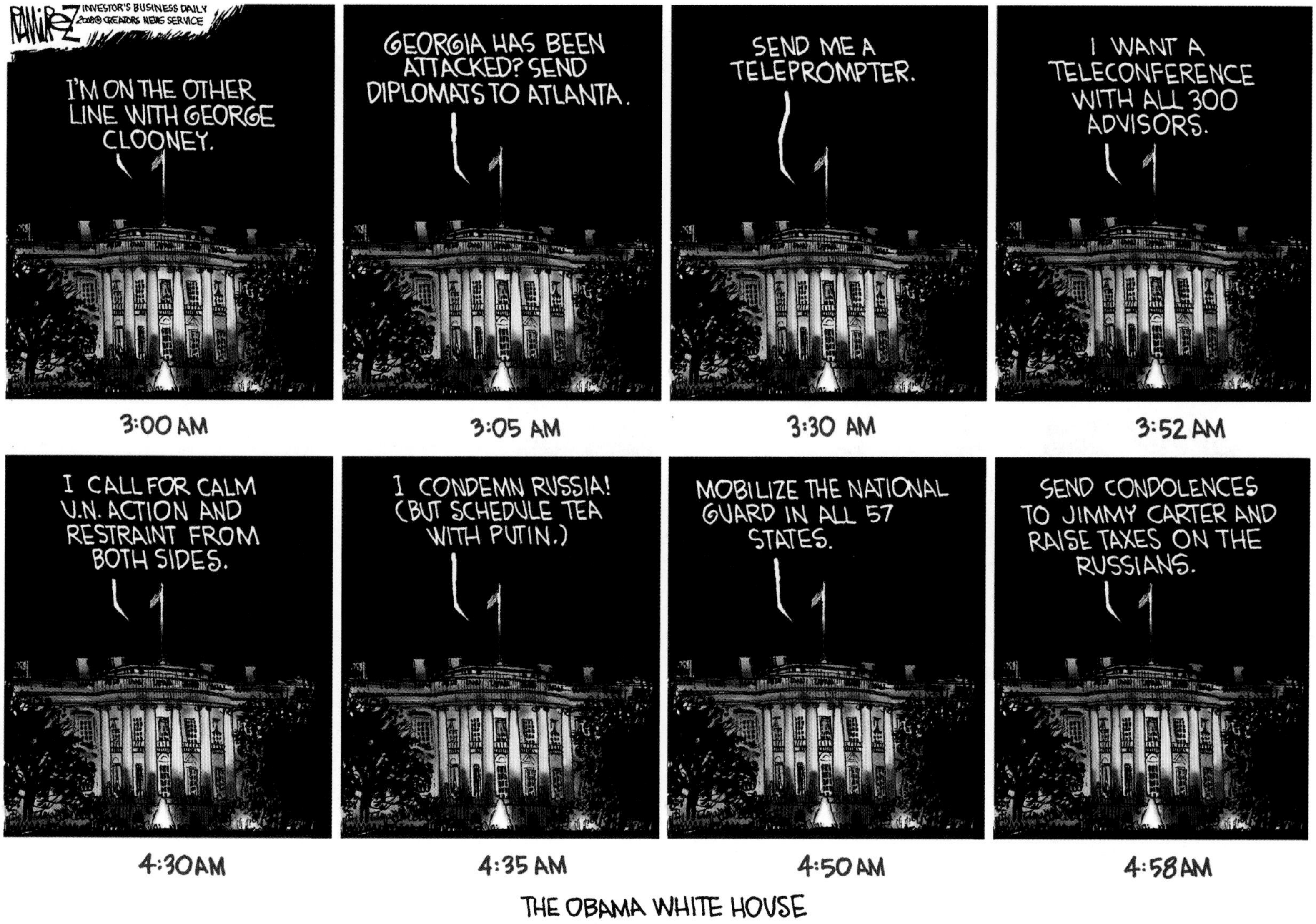
RAMIREZ INVESTOR'S BUSINESS DAILY 2008© CREATORS NEWS SERVICE
I'M ON THE OTHER LINE WITH GEORGE CLOONEY.
3:00 AM
GEORGIA HAS BEEN ATTACKED? SEND DIPLOMATS TO ATLANTA.
3:05 AM
SEND ME A TELEPROMPTER.
3:30 AM
I WANT A TELECONFERENCE WITH ALL 300 ADVISORS.
3:52 AM
I CALL FOR CALM U.N. ACTION AND RESTRAINT FROM BOTH SIDES.
4:30 AM
I CONDEMN RUSSIA! (BUT SCHEDULE TEA WITH PUTIN.)
4:35 AM
MOBILIZE THE NATIONAL GUARD IN ALL 57 STATES.
4:50 AM
SEND CONDOLENCES TO JIMMY CARTER AND RAISE TAXES ON THE RUSSIANS.
4:58 AM
THE OBAMA WHITE HOUSE

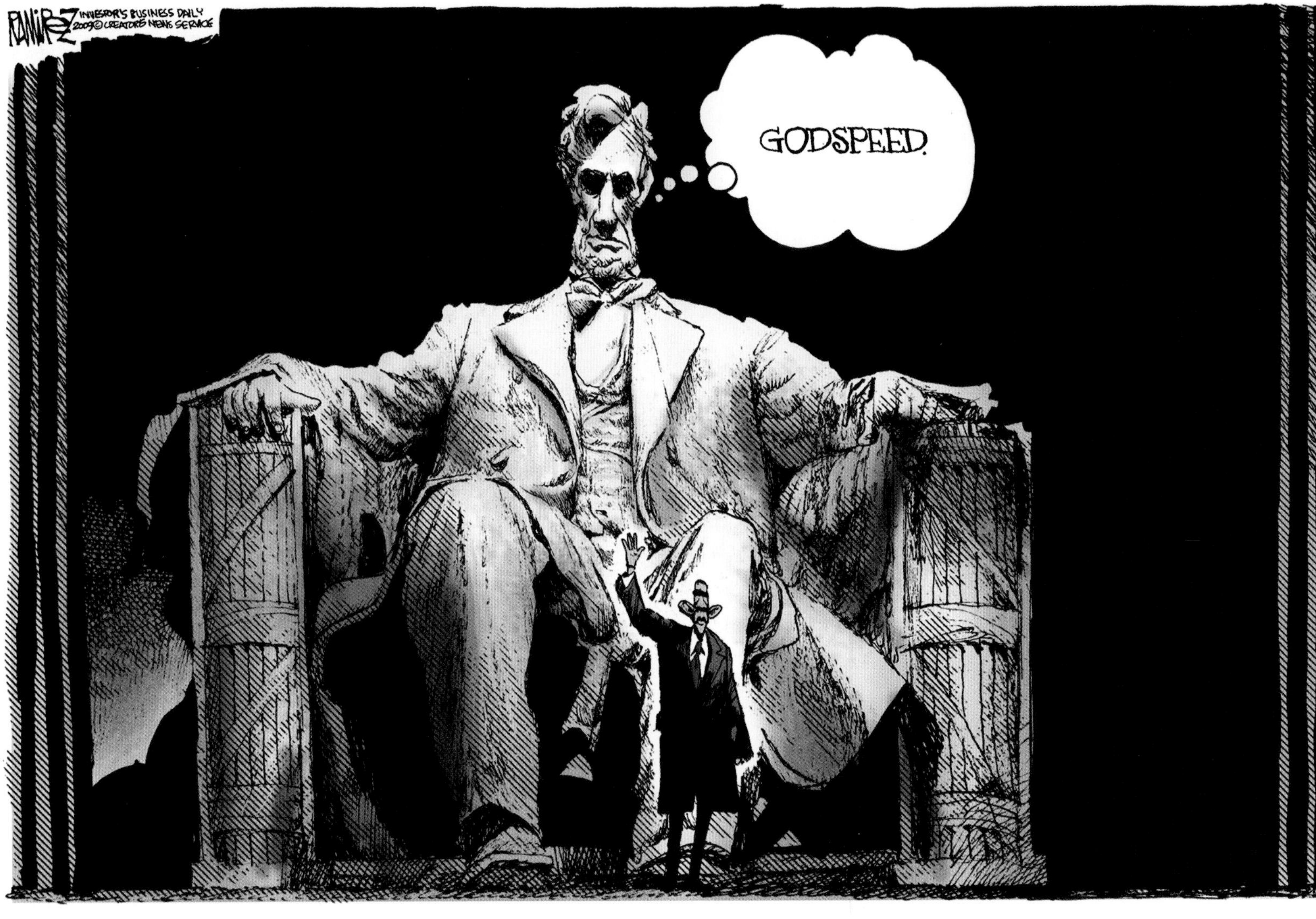
RAMIREZ
INVESTOR'S BUSINESS DAILY
2009 © CREATORS NEWS SERVICE
GODSPEED.

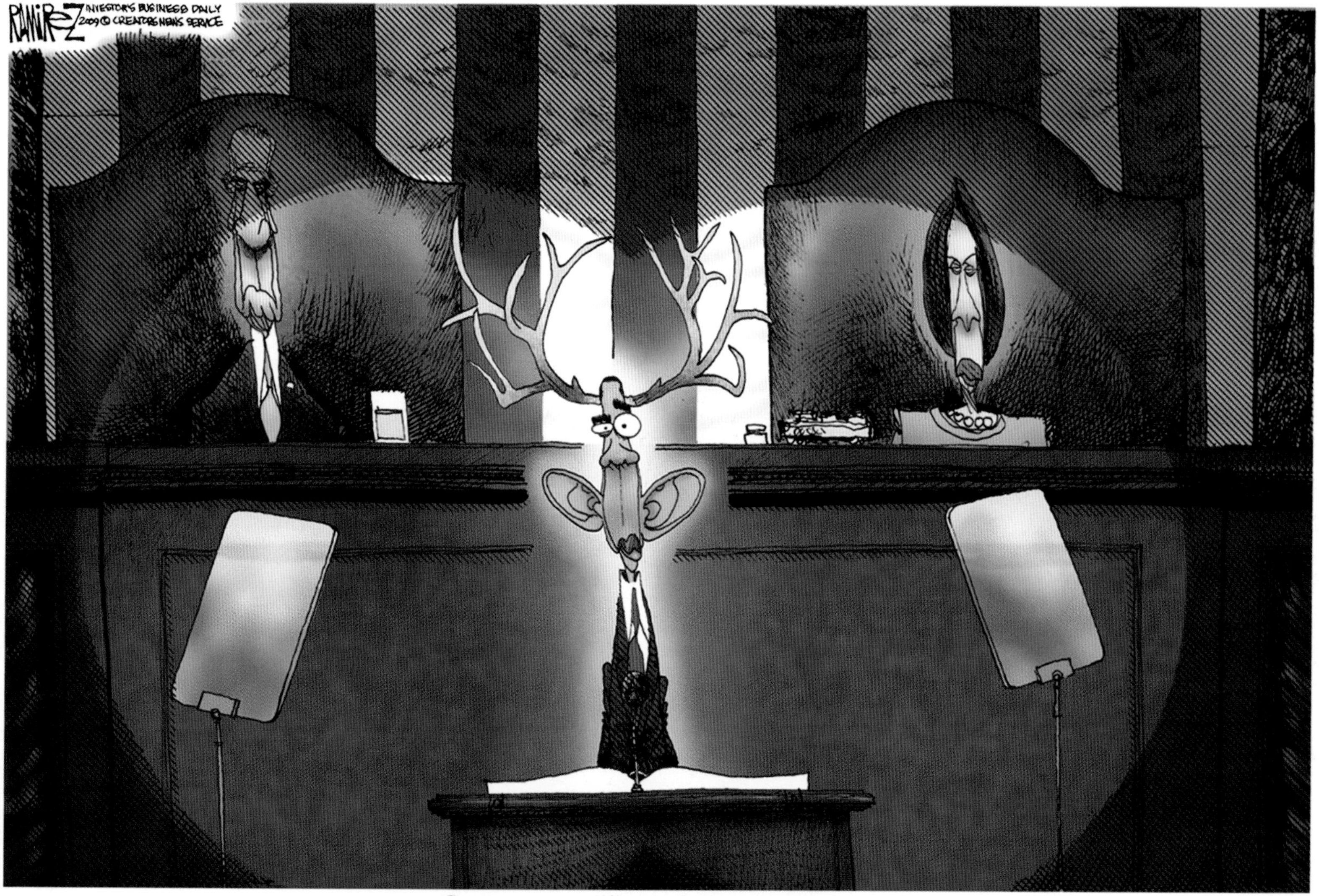
RAMIREZ
INVESTOR'S BUSINESS DAILY
2009 © CREATORS NEWS SERVICE

DEER IN THE HEADLIGHTS

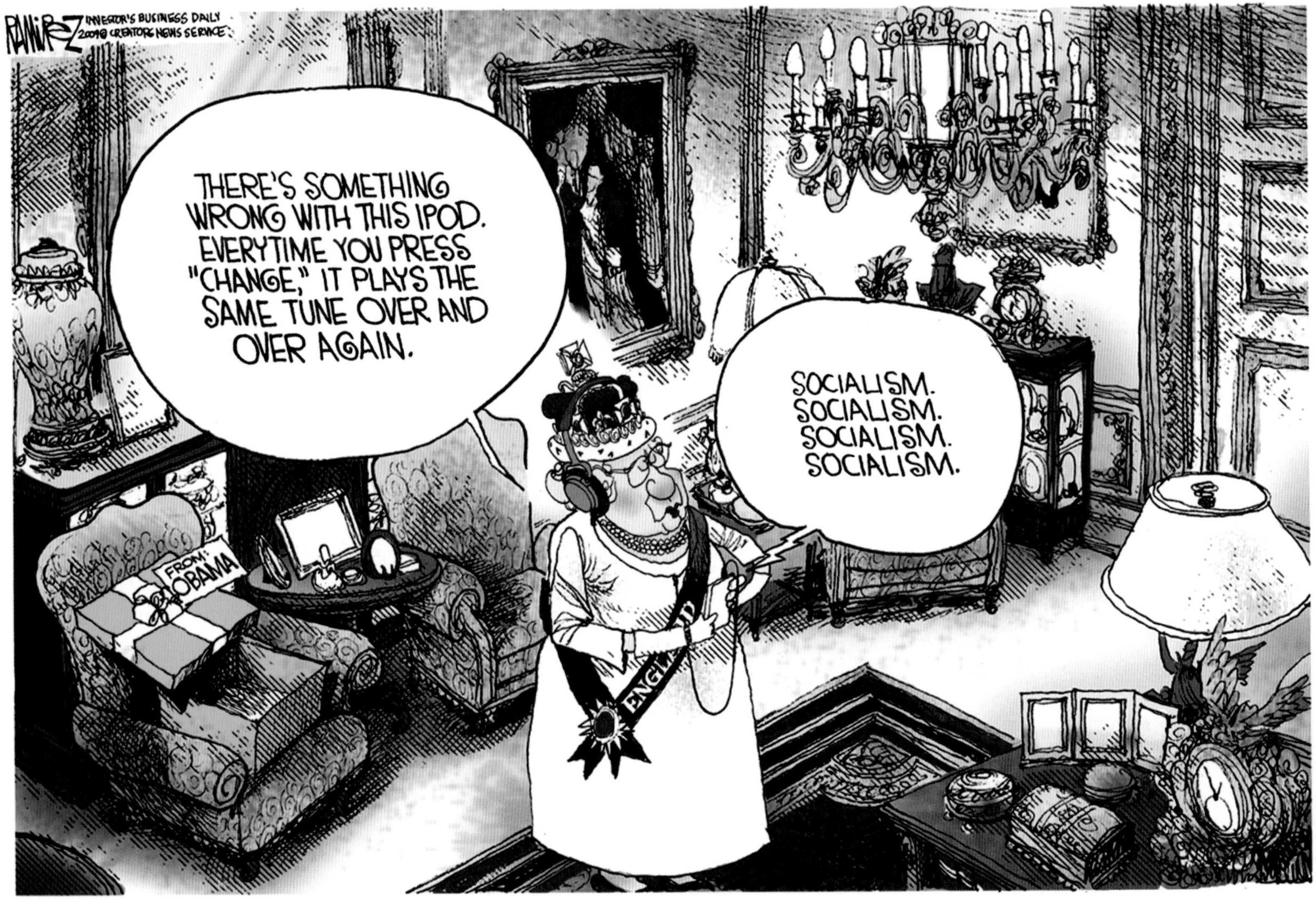
RAMIREZ
INVESTOR'S BUSINESS DAILY
2009© CREATORS NEWS SERVICE
THERE'S SOMETHING WRONG WITH THIS IPOD. EVERYTIME YOU PRESS "CHANGE," IT PLAYS THE SAME TUNE OVER AND OVER AGAIN.
SOCIALISM. SOCIALISM. SOCIALISM. SOCIALISM.
FROM: OBAMA
ENGLAND

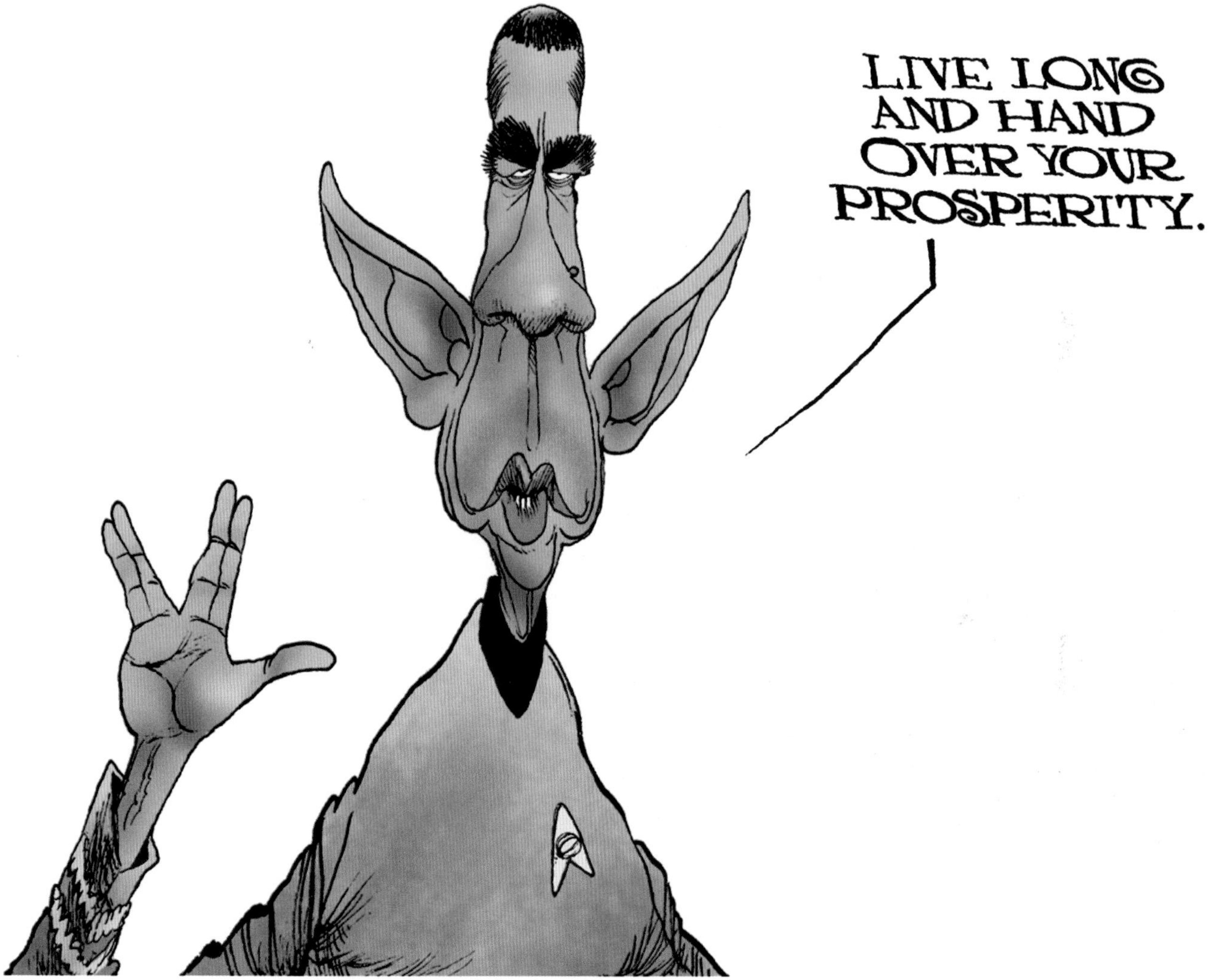
LIVE LONG AND HAND OVER YOUR PROSPERITY.

BARACK SPOCK

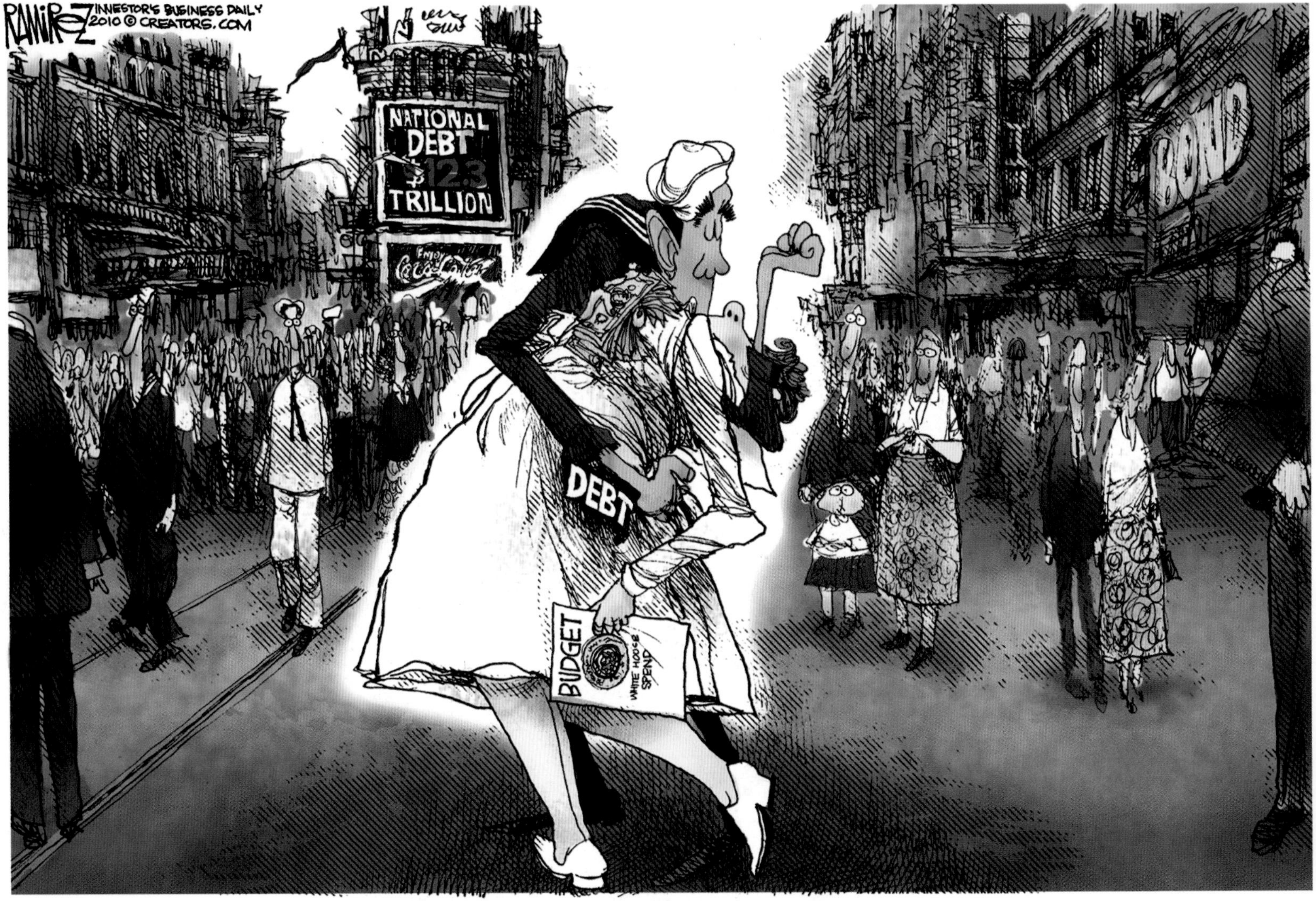
RAMIREZ
INVESTOR'S BUSINESS DAILY
2010 © CREATORS.COM
NATIONAL
DEBT
$12.3
TRILLION
BOND
DEBT
BUDGET
WHITE HOUSE
SPEND

LIKE A DRUNKEN SAILOR....

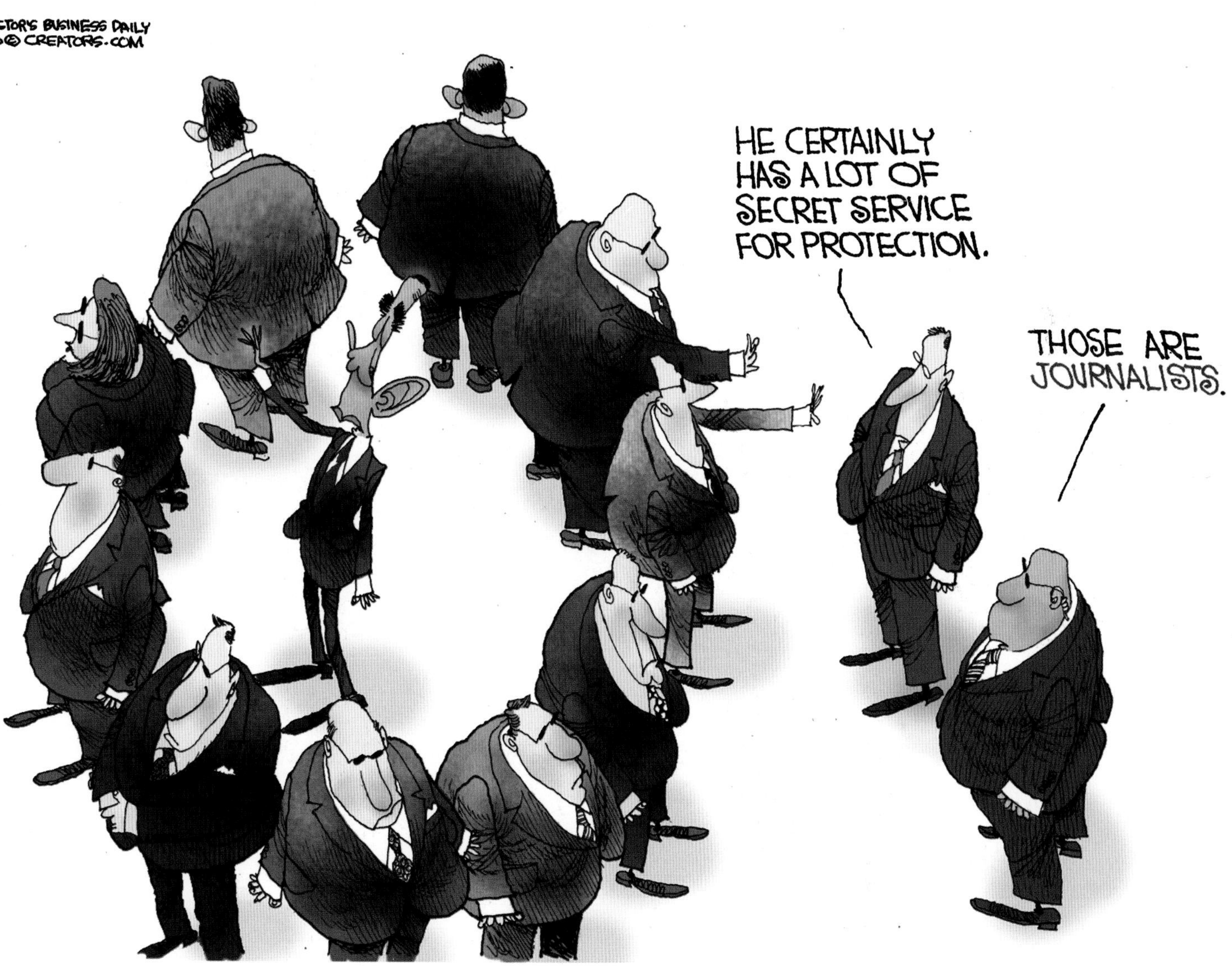
RAMIREZ INVESTOR'S BUSINESS DAILY 2010 © CREATORS.COM
HE CERTAINLY HAS A LOT OF SECRET SERVICE FOR PROTECTION.
THOSE ARE JOURNALISTS.

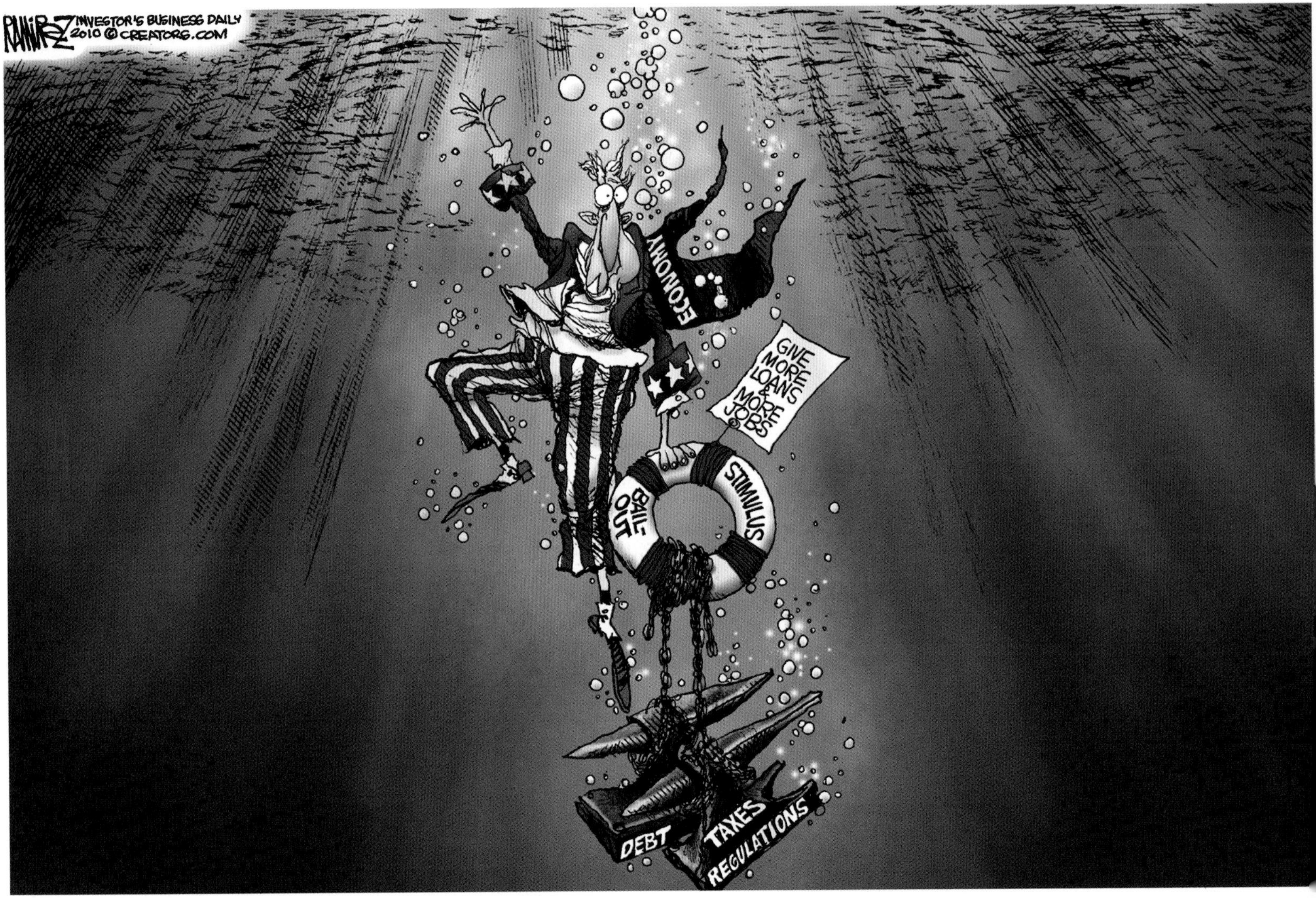
RAMIREZ INVESTOR'S BUSINESS DAILY
2010 © CREATORS.COM
ECONOMY
GIVE MORE LOANS & MORE JOBS
STIMULUS
BAIL-OUT
DEBT
TAXES
REGULATIONS

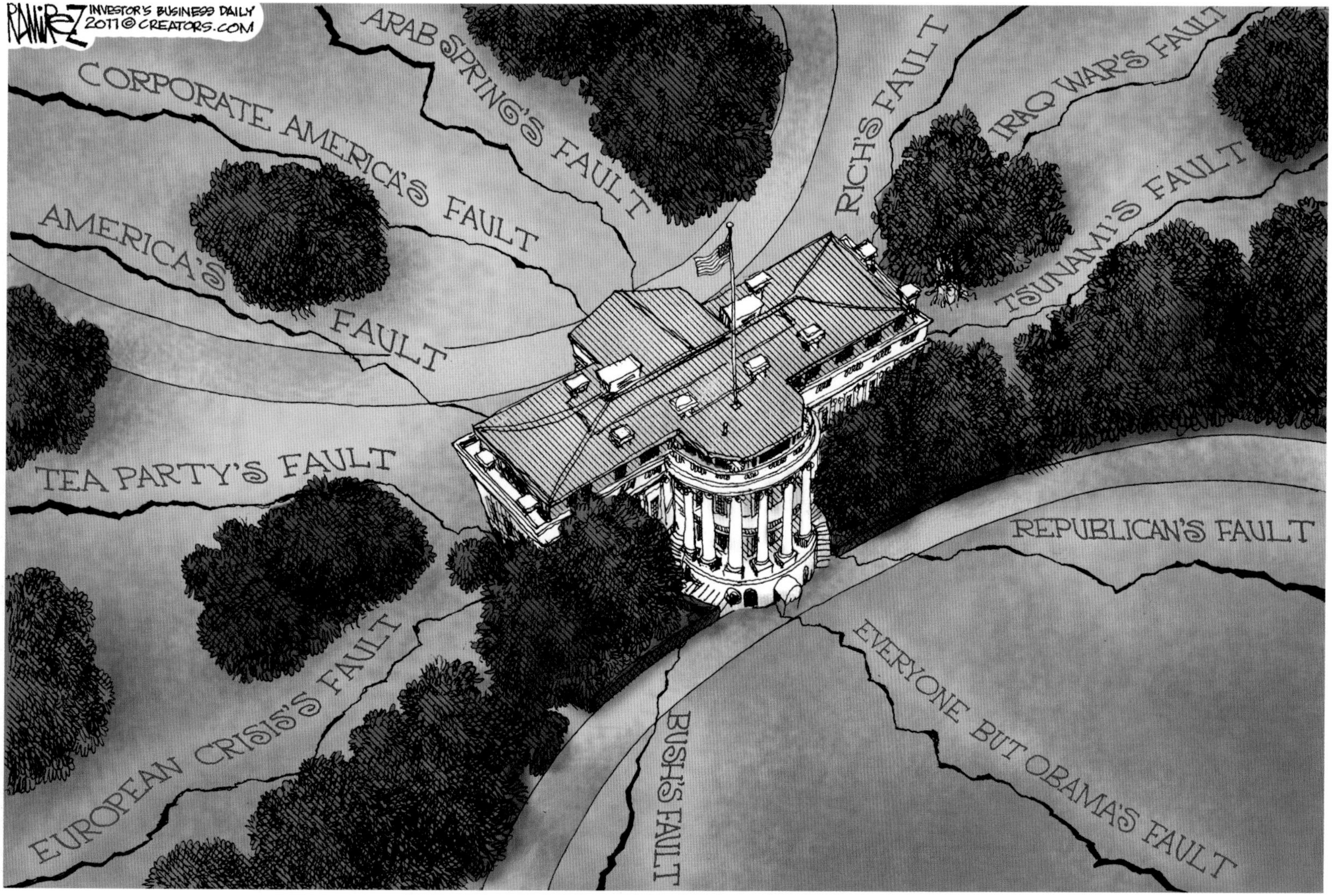
RAMIREZ INVESTOR'S BUSINESS DAILY 2011 © CREATORS.COM
CORPORATE AMERICA'S FAULT
ARAB SPRING'S FAULT
RICH'S FAULT
IRAQ WAR'S FAULT
TSUNAMI'S FAULT
AMERICA'S FAULT
TEA PARTY'S FAULT
REPUBLICAN'S FAULT
EUROPEAN CRISIS'S FAULT
BUSH'S FAULT
EVERYONE BUT OBAMA'S FAULT

THE EPICENTER OF EXCUSES

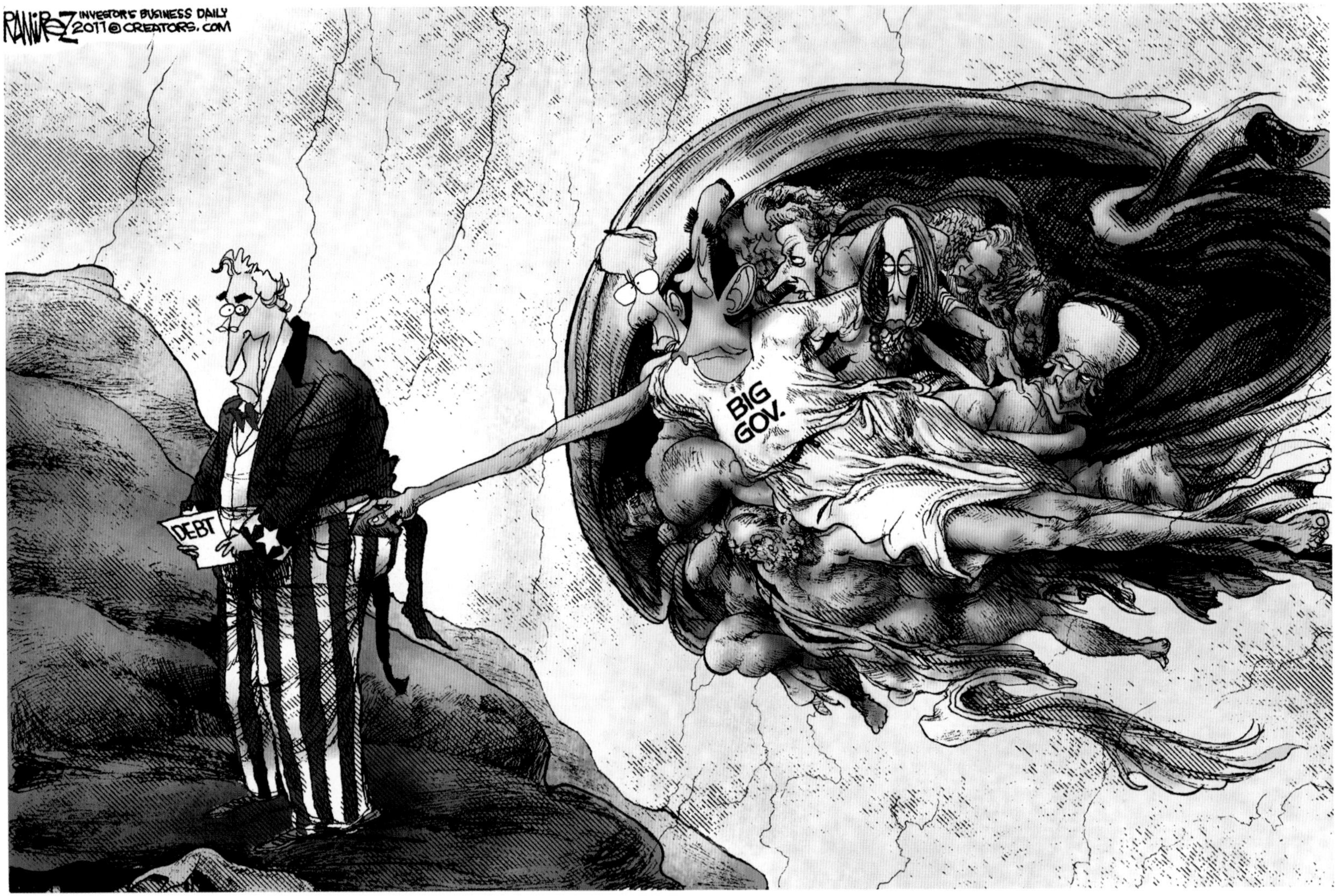
RAMIREZ INVESTOR'S BUSINESS DAILY
2011 © CREATORS.COM
DEBT
BIG GOV.

ON THE DEBT CEILING.

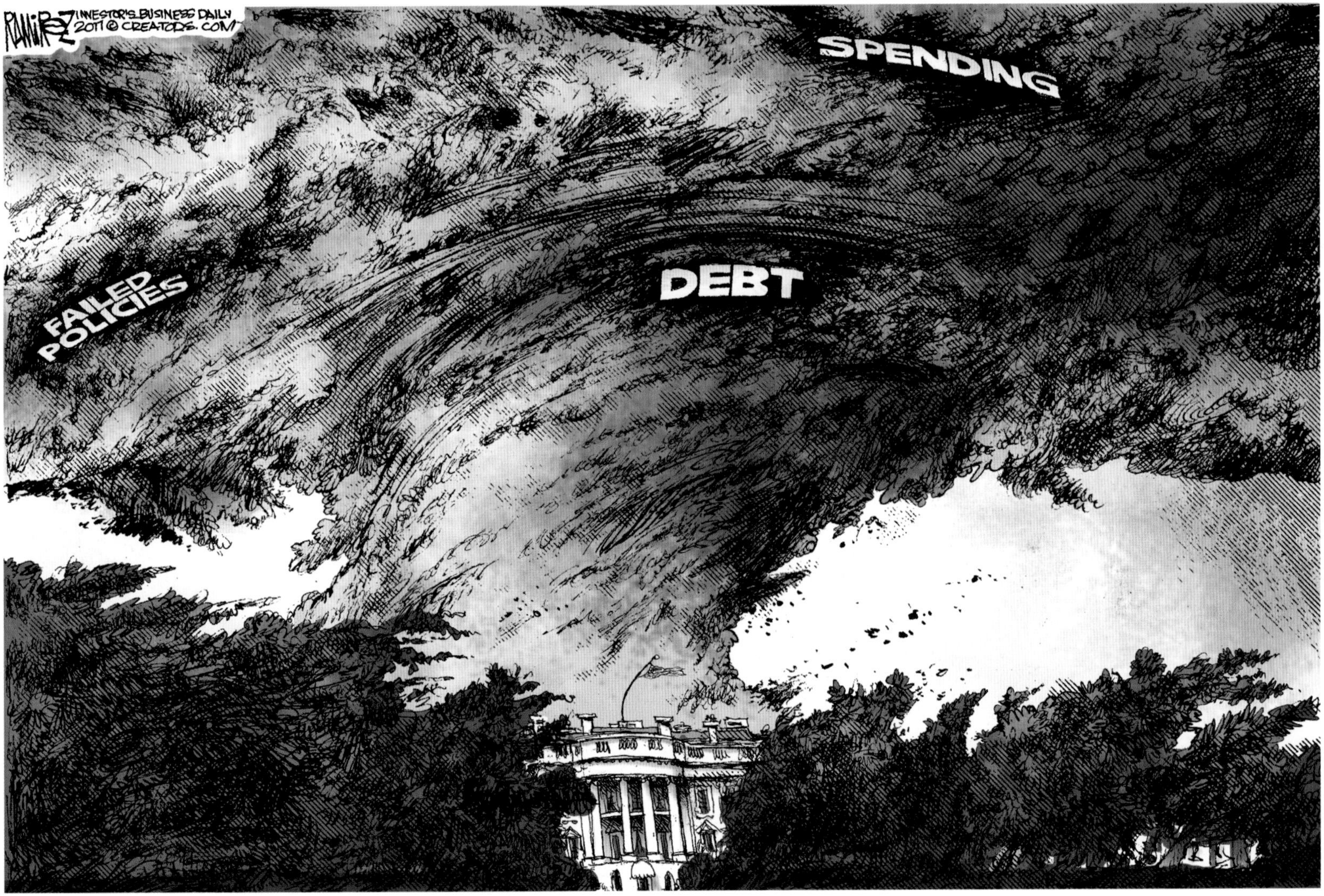
RAMIREZ INVESTOR'S BUSINESS DAILY
2011 © CREATORS.COM
SPENDING
DEBT
FAILED POLICIES

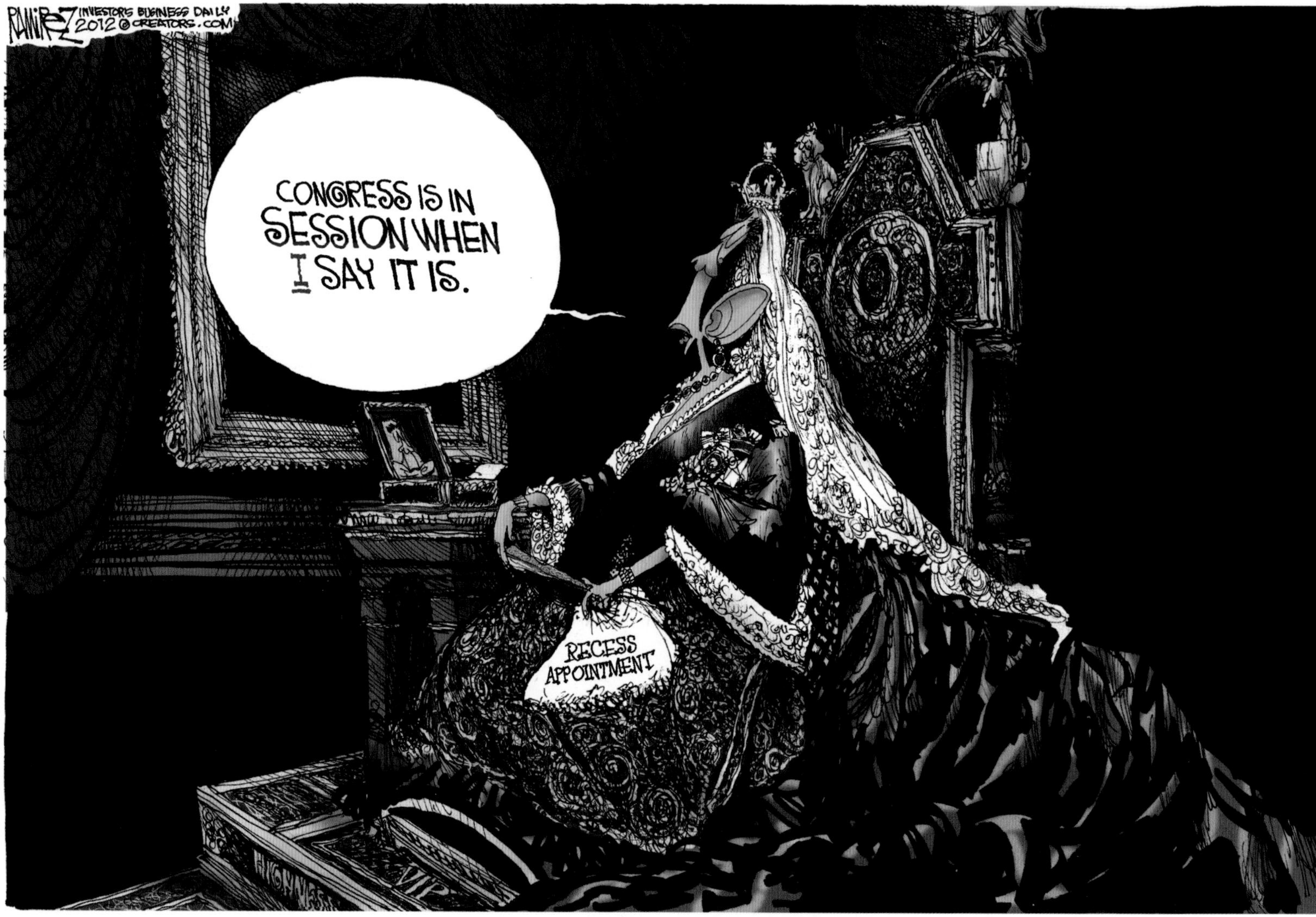
RAMIREZ INVESTOR'S BUSINESS DAILY 2012 © CREATORS.COM
CONGRESS IS IN SESSION WHEN I SAY IT IS.
RECESS APPOINTMENT
VIP

THE IMPERIAL PRESIDENT

OBAMACARE

"If you like your doctor, you can keep your doctor. If you like your private health insurance plan, you can keep your plan. Period."

—President Barack Obama, Weekly Presidential Address, August 22, 2009

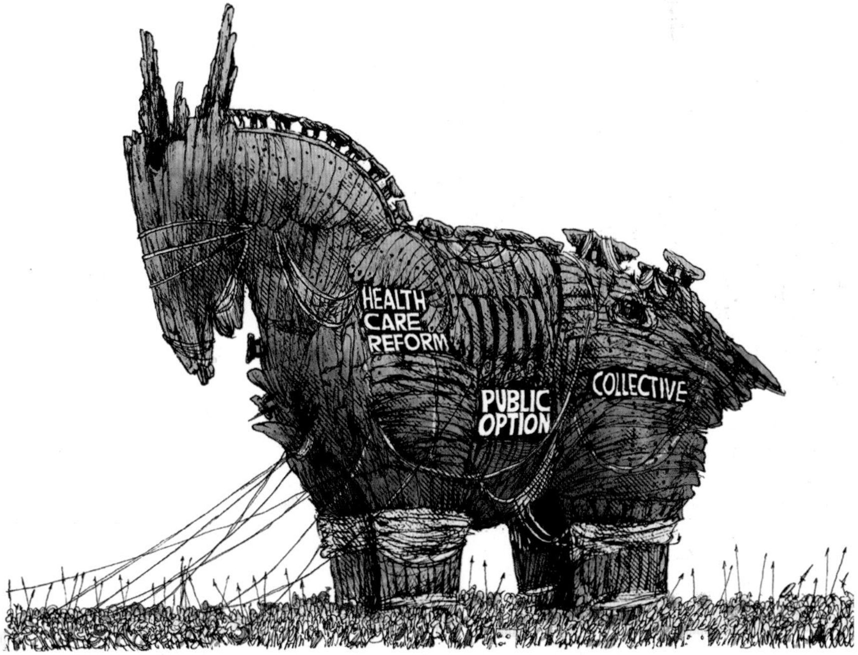
HEALTH CARE REFORM
PUBLIC OPTION
COLLECTIVE

Obamacare was built on a foundation of lies, false promises, and unrealistic goals. It was sold through deception and passed through bribery, chicanery, and a subversion of the normal legislative process. The dismantling of the world's most advanced medical system had begun.

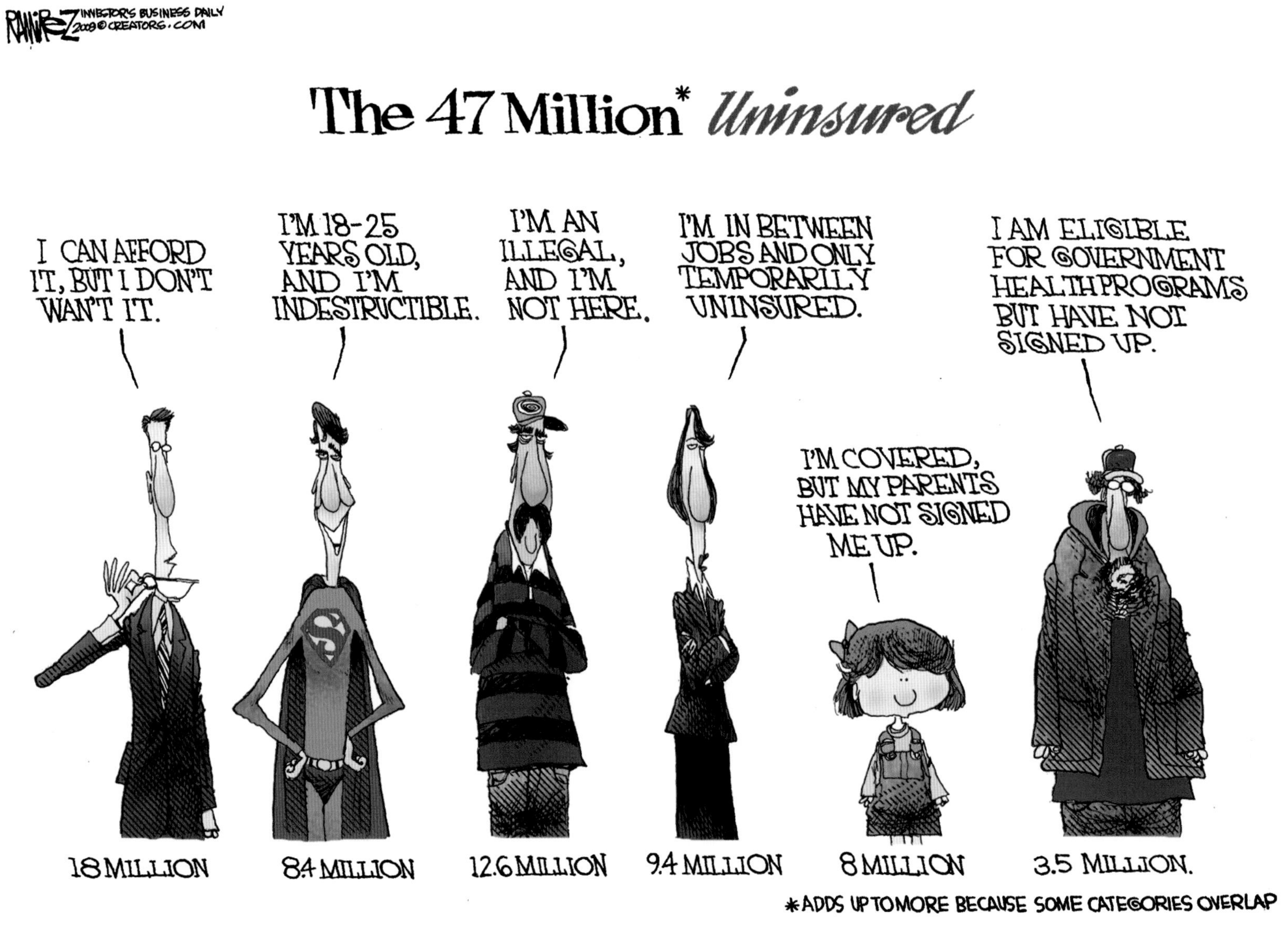
RAMIREZ INVESTOR'S BUSINESS DAILY 2009 © CREATORS.COM
The 47 Million* Uninsured
I CAN AFFORD IT, BUT I DON'T WANT IT.
I'M 18-25 YEARS OLD, AND I'M INDESTRUCTIBLE.
I'M AN ILLEGAL, AND I'M NOT HERE.
I'M IN BETWEEN JOBS AND ONLY TEMPORARILY UNINSURED.
I'M COVERED, BUT MY PARENTS HAVE NOT SIGNED ME UP.
I AM ELIGIBLE FOR GOVERNMENT HEALTH PROGRAMS BUT HAVE NOT SIGNED UP.
18 MILLION
8.4 MILLION
12.6 MILLION
9.4 MILLION
8 MILLION
3.5 MILLION.
*ADDS UP TO MORE BECAUSE SOME CATEGORIES OVERLAP

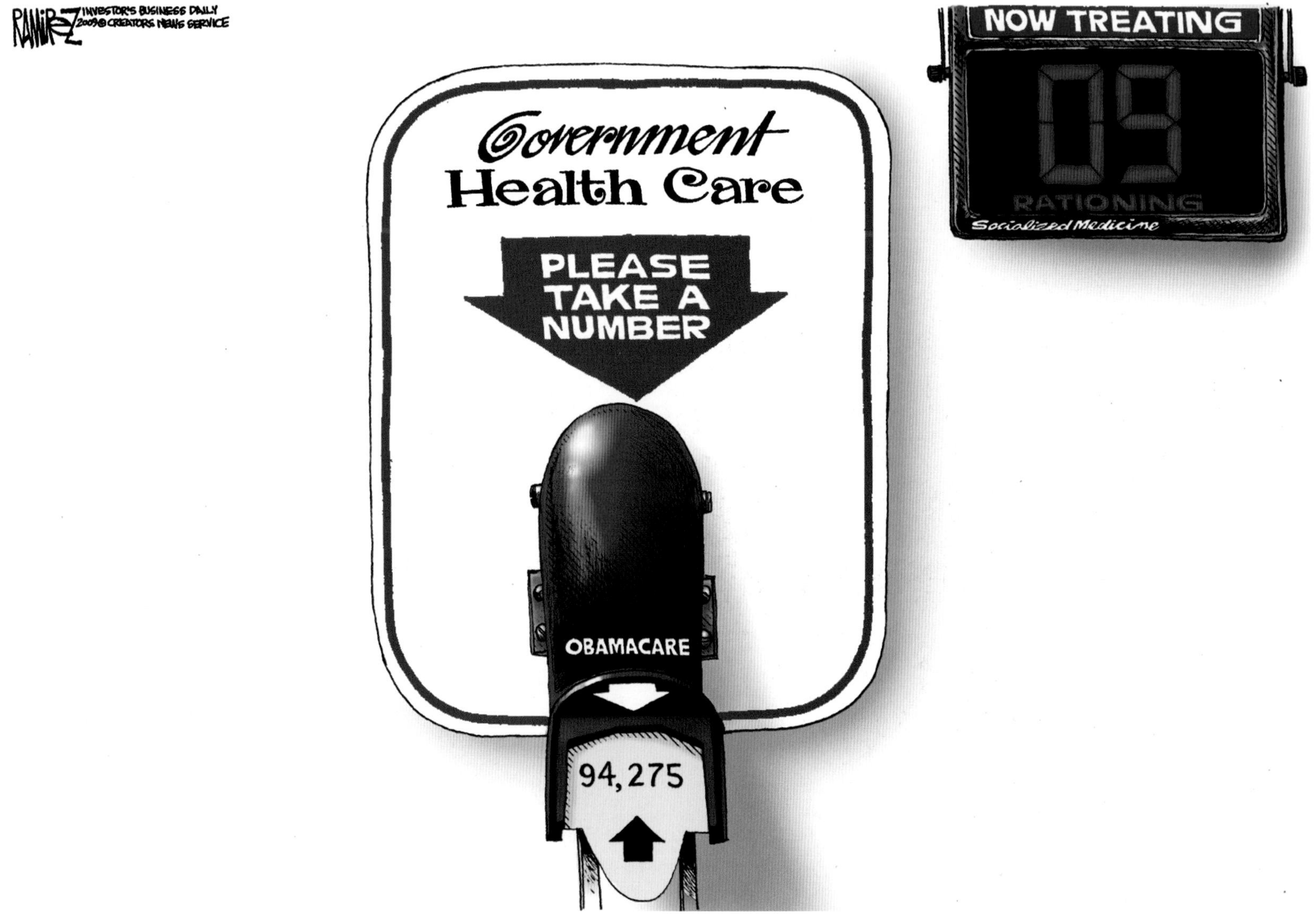
RAMIREZ
INVESTOR'S BUSINESS DAILY
2009© CREATORS NEWS SERVICE
NOW TREATING
09
RATIONING
Socialized Medicine
Government
Health Care
PLEASE TAKE A NUMBER
OBAMACARE
94,275

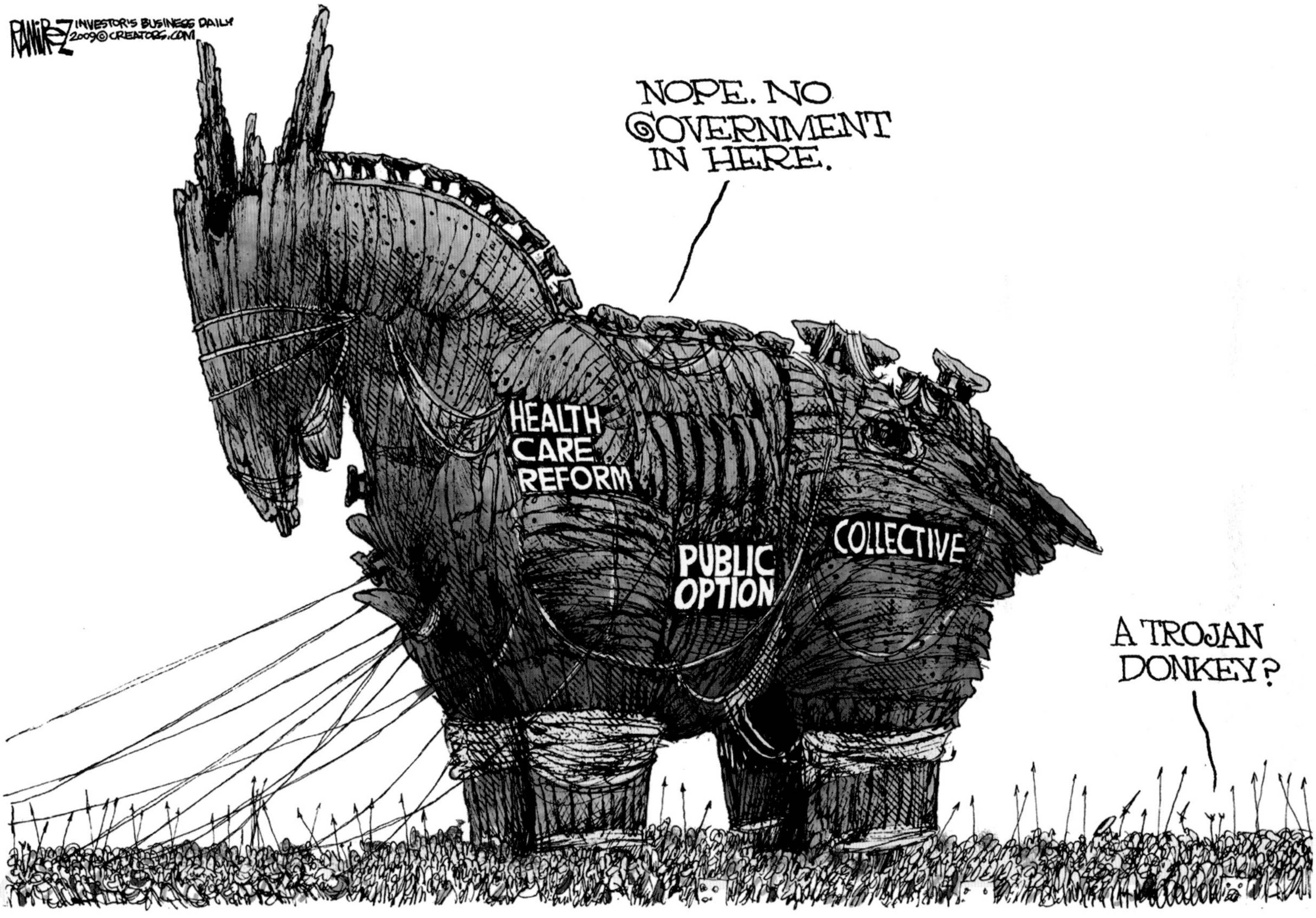
RAMIREZ INVESTOR'S BUSINESS DAILY 2009© CREATORS.COM
NOPE. NO GOVERNMENT IN HERE.
HEALTH CARE REFORM
PUBLIC OPTION
COLLECTIVE
A TROJAN DONKEY?

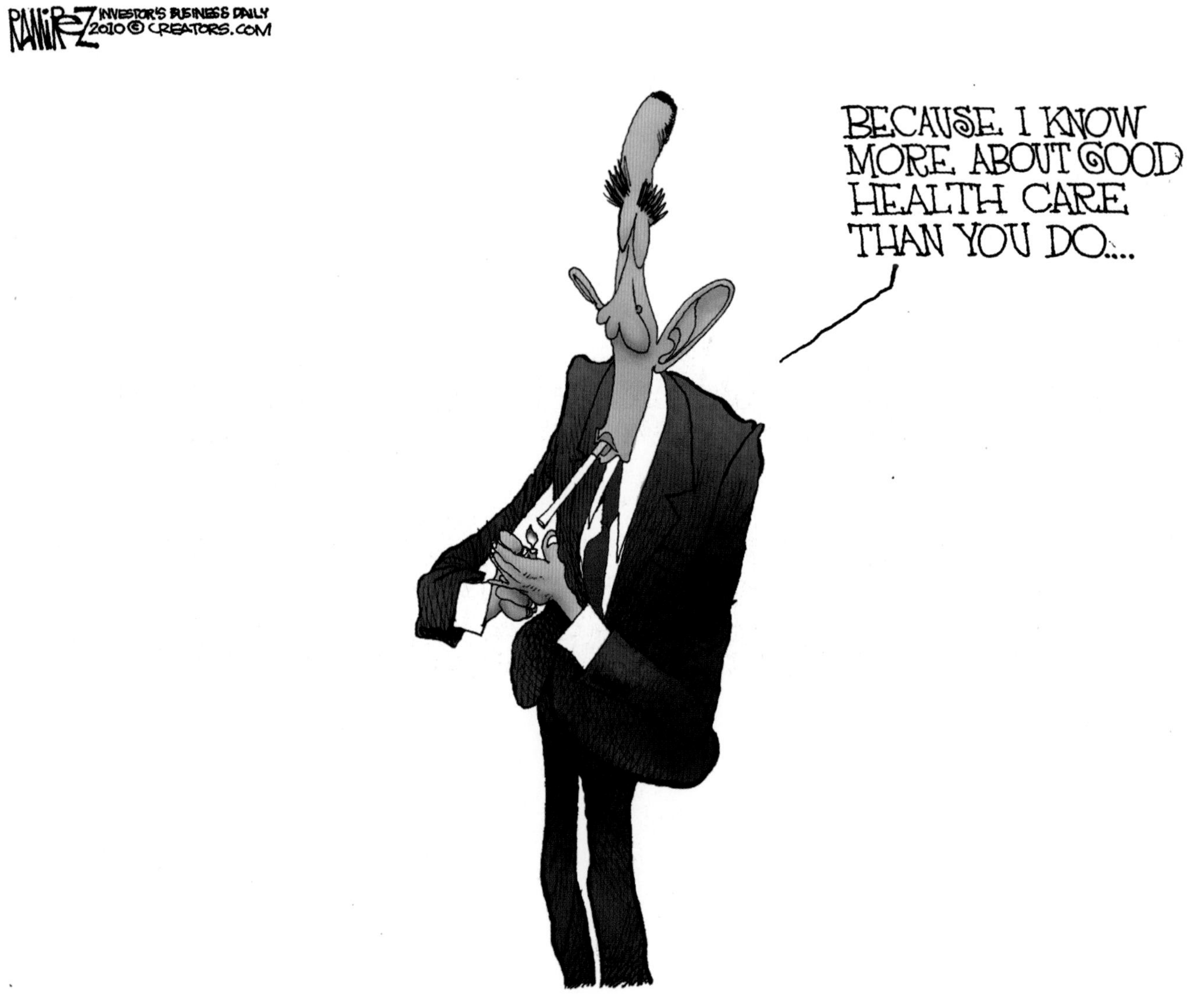
RAMIREZ INVESTOR'S BUSINESS DAILY 2010 © CREATORS.COM
BECAUSE I KNOW MORE ABOUT GOOD HEALTH CARE THAN YOU DO....

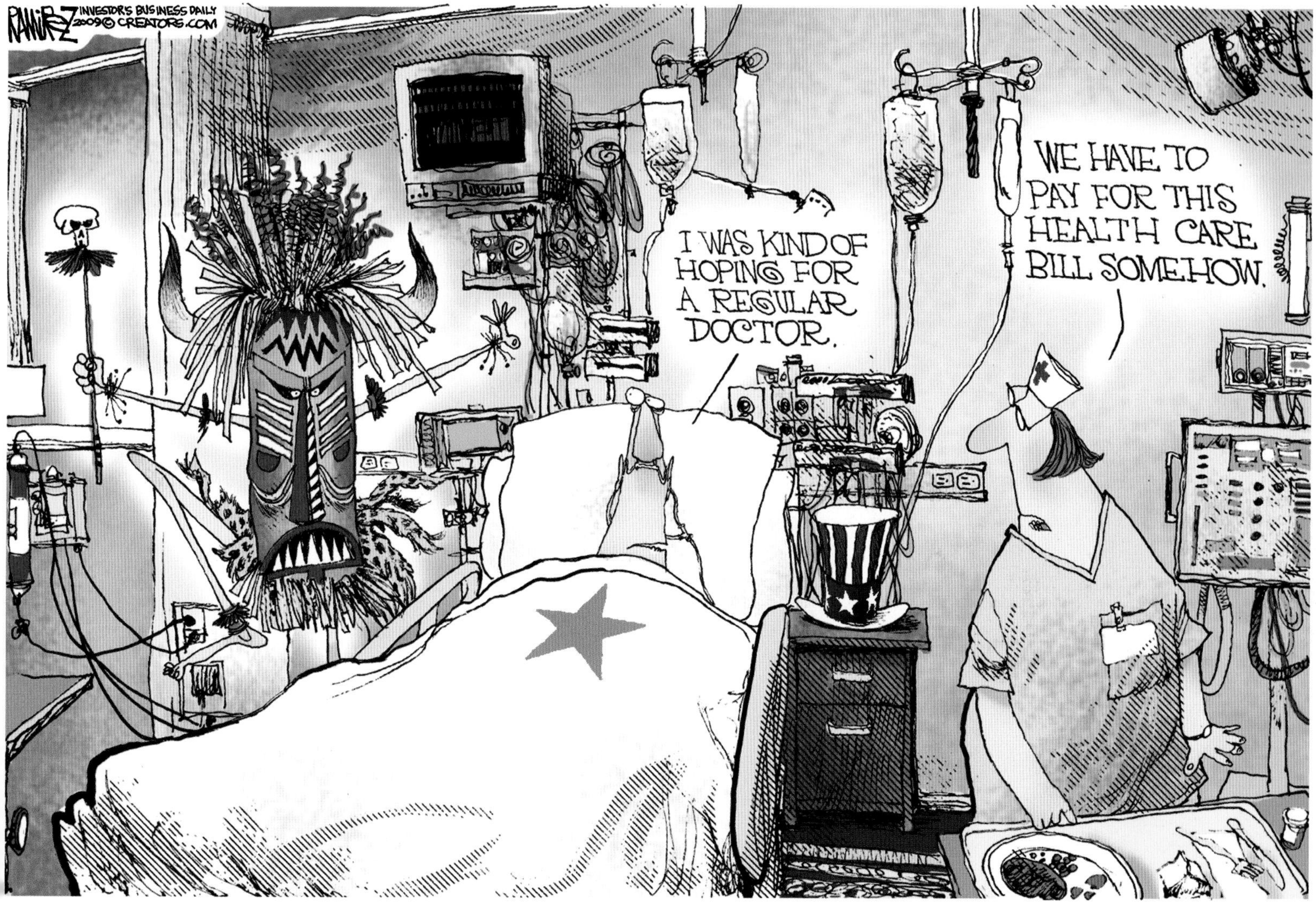
RAMIREZ INVESTOR'S BUSINESS DAILY 2009 © CREATORS.COM
I WAS KIND OF HOPING FOR A REGULAR DOCTOR.
WE HAVE TO PAY FOR THIS HEALTH CARE BILL SOMEHOW.

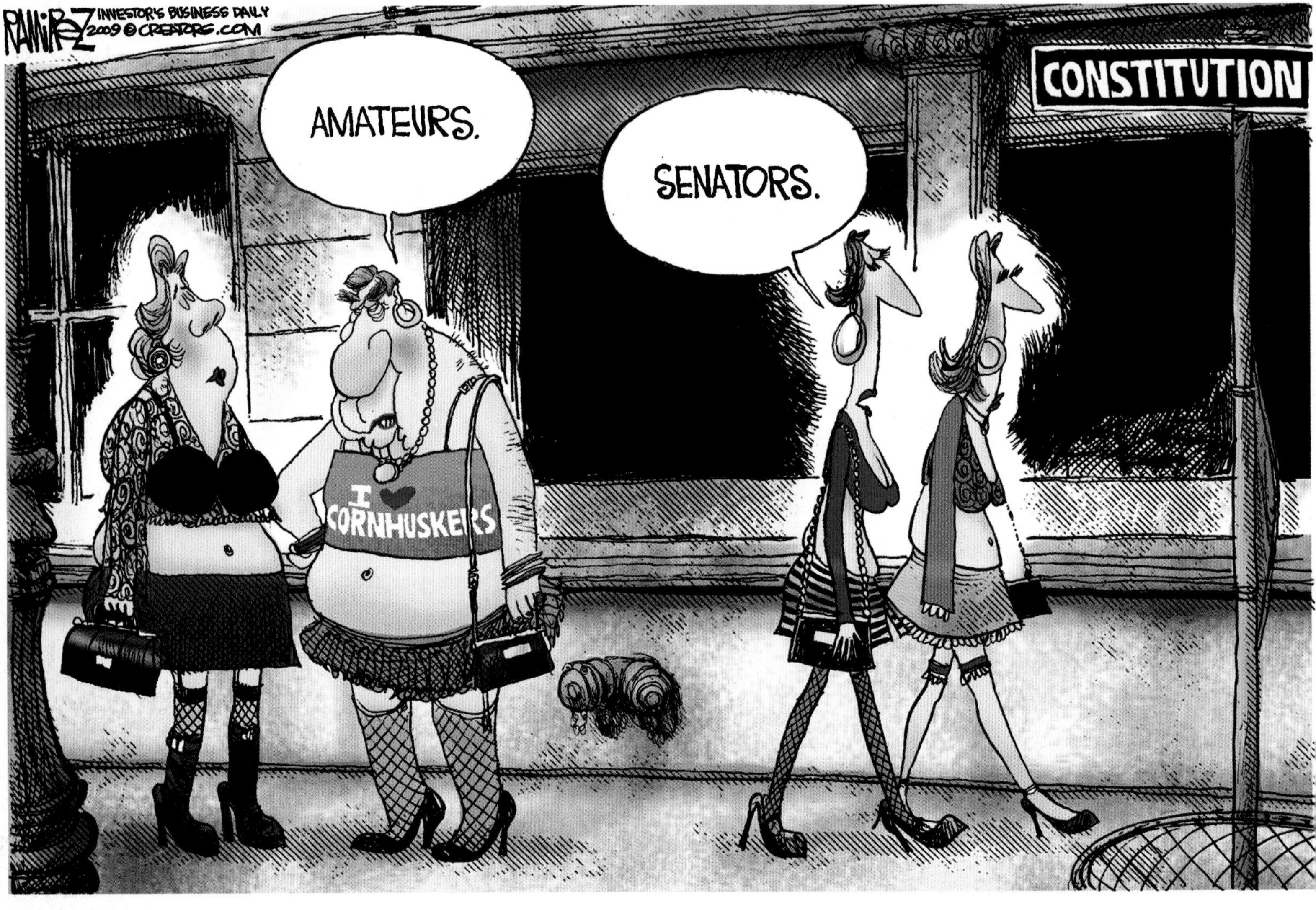
RAMIREZ INVESTOR'S BUSINESS DAILY 2009 © CREATORS.COM
CONSTITUTION
AMATEURS.
SENATORS.
I ♥ CORNHUSKERS

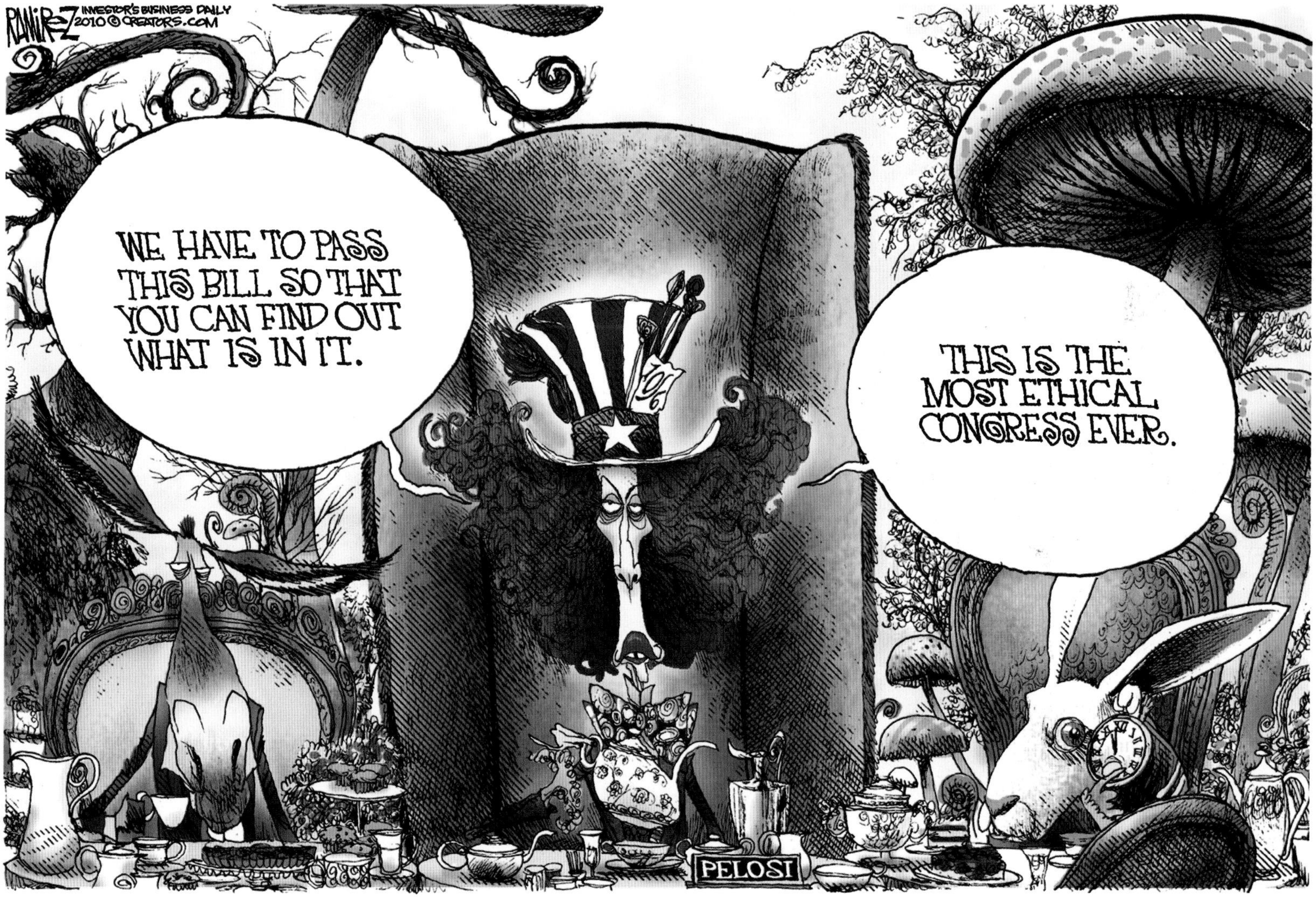
RAMIREZ INVESTOR'S BUSINESS DAILY 2010 © CREATORS.COM
WE HAVE TO PASS THIS BILL SO THAT YOU CAN FIND OUT WHAT IS IN IT.
THIS IS THE MOST ETHICAL CONGRESS EVER.
PELOSI

THE MAD HATTER

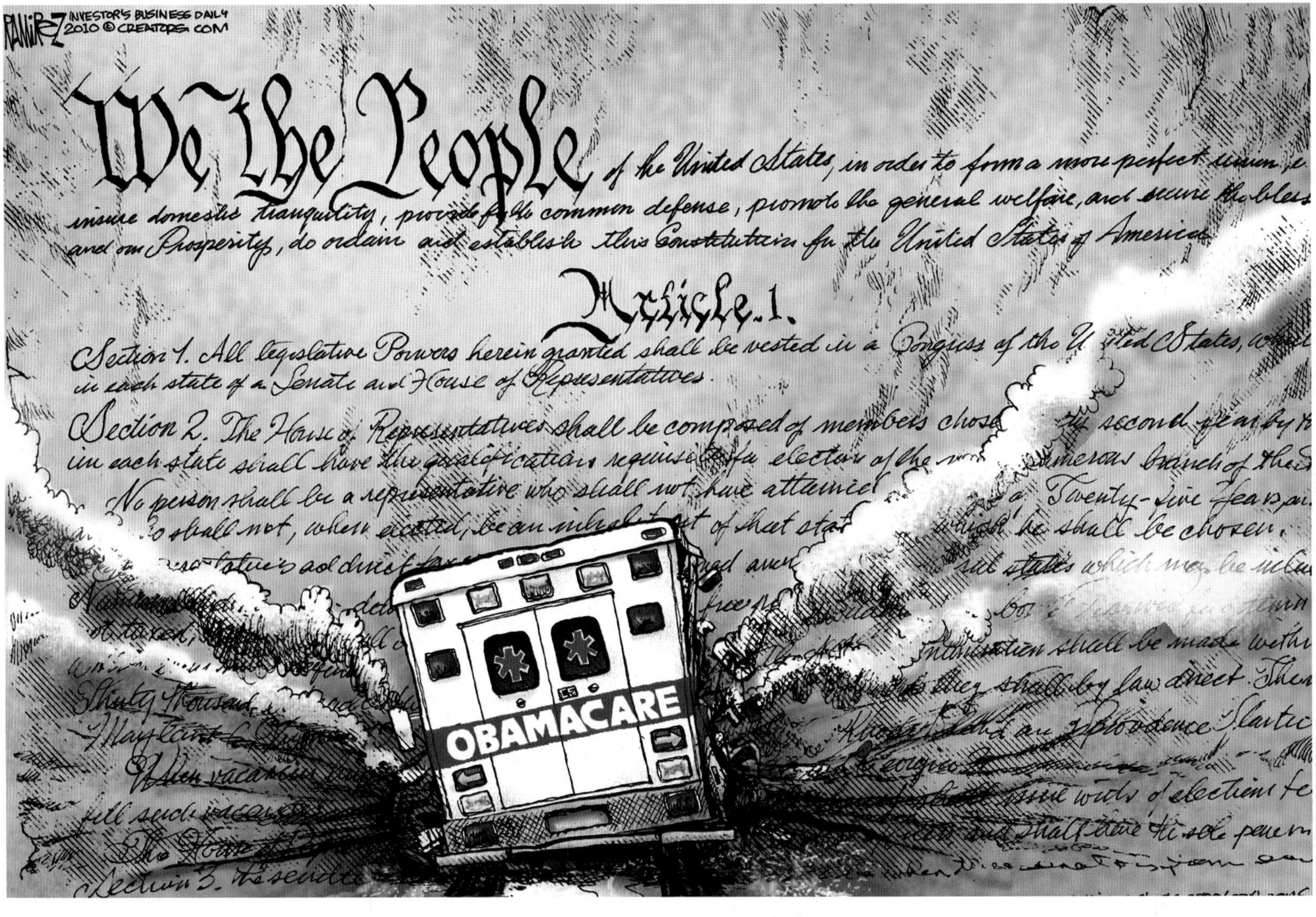
RAMIREZ INVESTOR'S BUSINESS DAILY 2010 © CREATORS.COM
We the People
Article. 1.
OBAMACARE

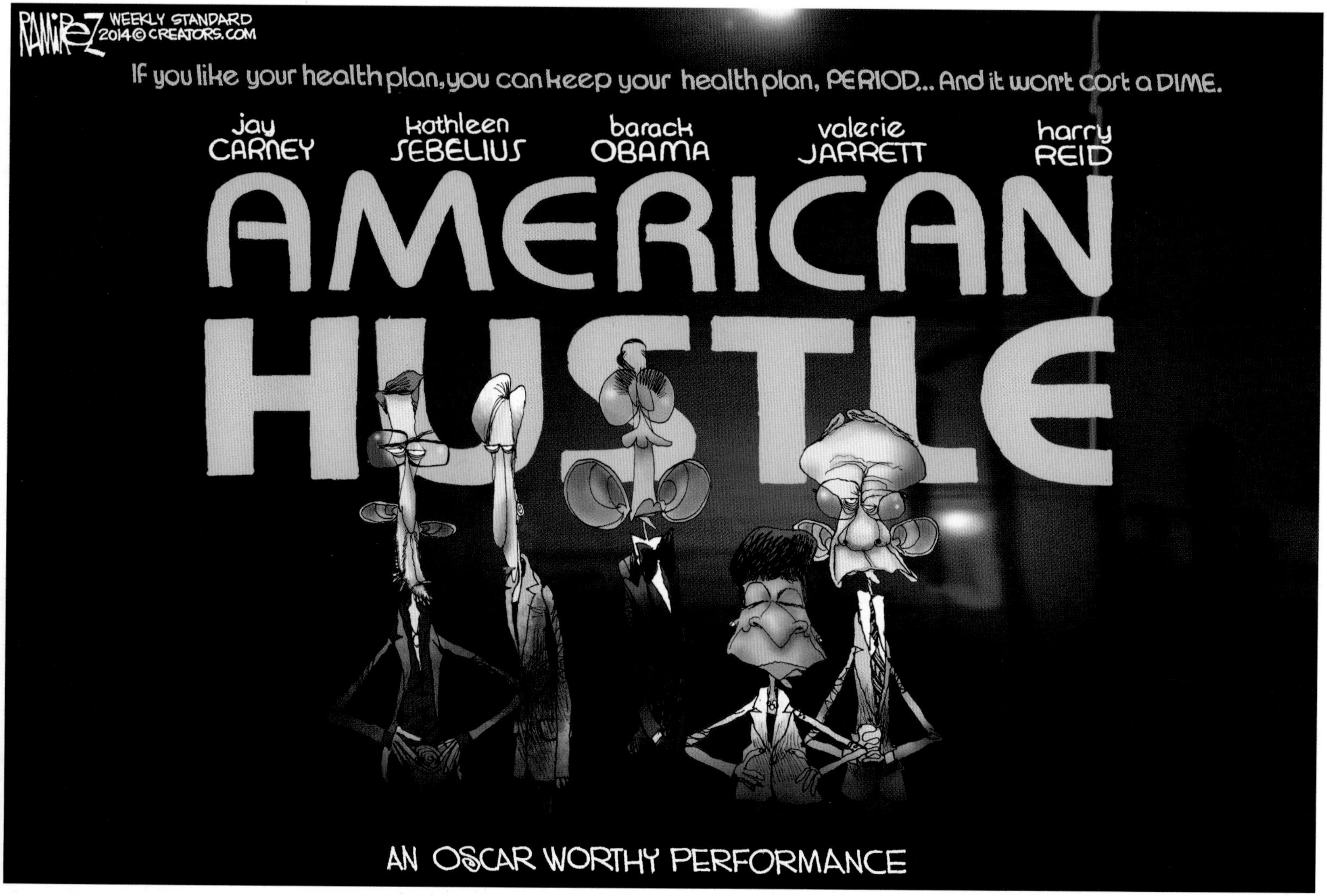

RAMIREZ
WEEKLY STANDARD
2014 © CREATORS.COM
If you like your health plan, you can keep your health plan, PERIOD... And it won't cost a DIME.
jay CARNEY
kathleen SEBELIUS
barack OBAMA
valerie JARRETT
harry REID
AMERICAN HUSTLE
AN OSCAR WORTHY PERFORMANCE

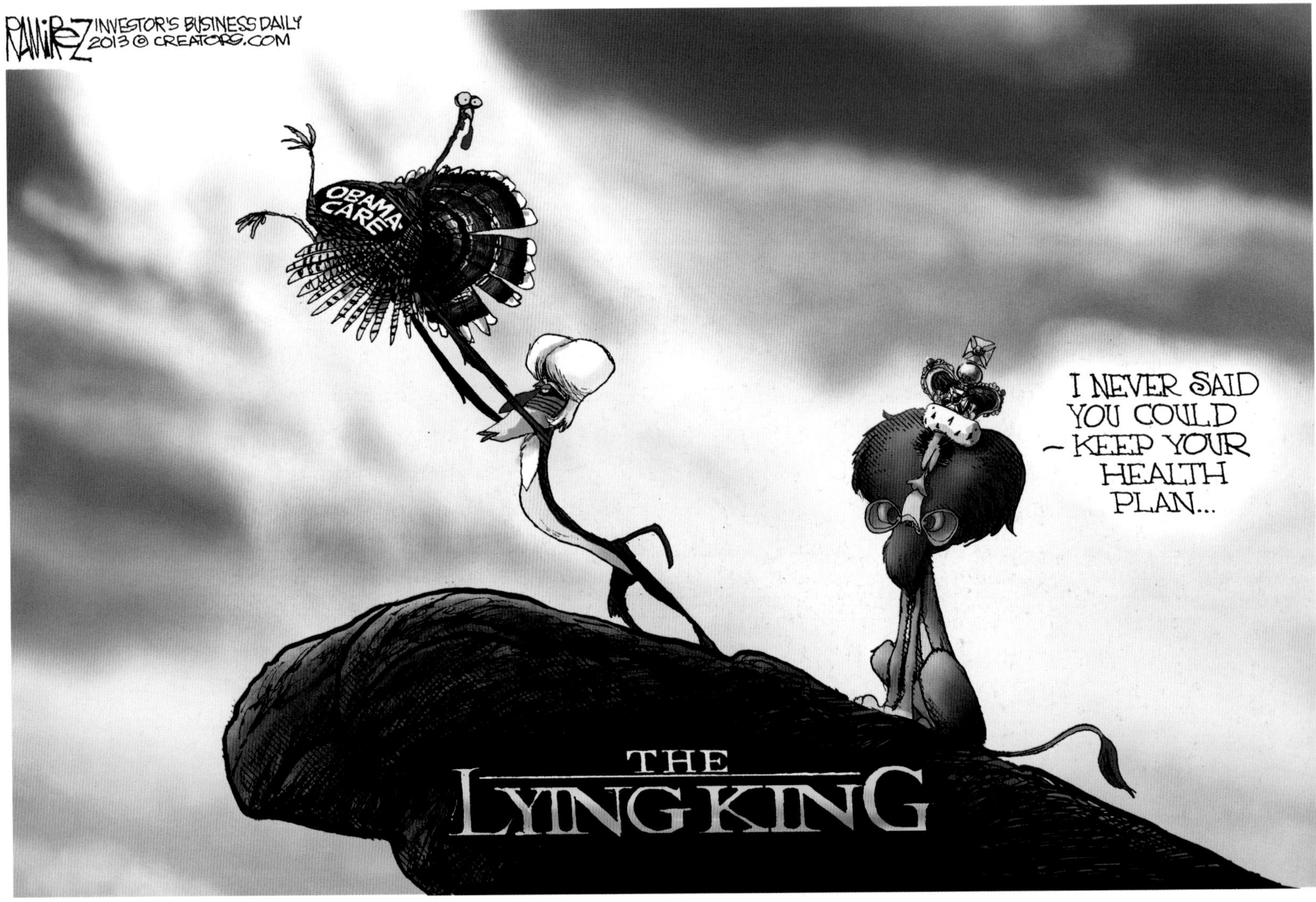
RAMIREZ INVESTOR'S BUSINESS DAILY
2013 © CREATORS.COM
OBAMA-CARE
I NEVER SAID YOU COULD ~ KEEP YOUR HEALTH PLAN...
THE LYING KING

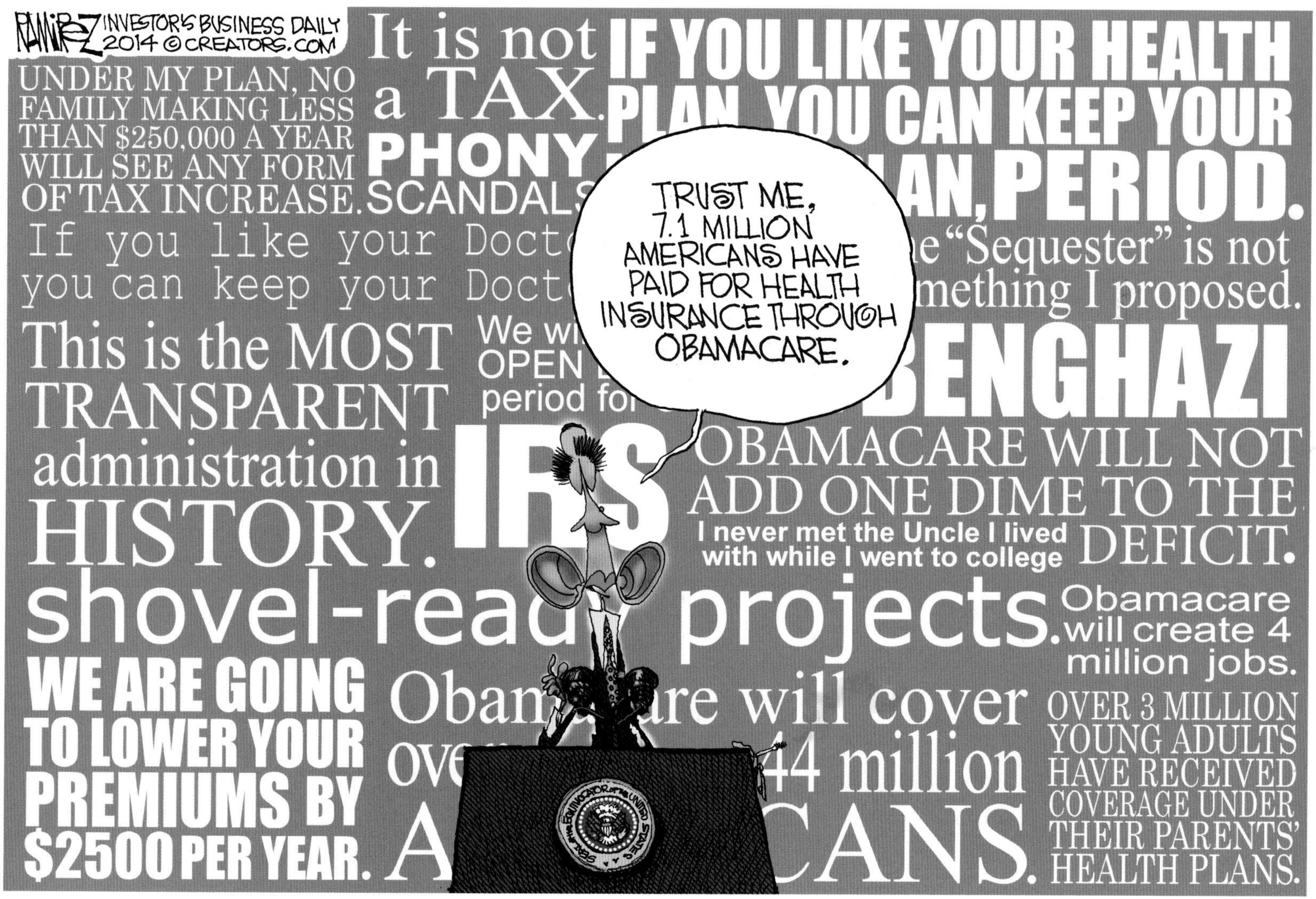
RAMIREZ INVESTOR'S BUSINESS DAILY 2014 © CREATORS.COM
UNDER MY PLAN, NO FAMILY MAKING LESS THAN $250,000 A YEAR WILL SEE ANY FORM OF TAX INCREASE.
It is not a TAX.
PHONY SCANDALS
IF YOU LIKE YOUR HEALTH PLAN, YOU CAN KEEP YOUR
AN, PERIOD.
If you like your Docto
you can keep your Docto
TRUST ME, 7.1 MILLION AMERICANS HAVE PAID FOR HEALTH INSURANCE THROUGH OBAMACARE.
e "Sequester" is not
mething I proposed.
This is the MOST TRANSPARENT administration in HISTORY.
We wi
OPEN
period fo
BENGHAZI
IRS
OBAMACARE WILL NOT ADD ONE DIME TO THE DEFICIT.
I never met the Uncle I lived with while I went to college
shovel-read projects.
Obamacare will create 4 million jobs.
WE ARE GOING TO LOWER YOUR PREMIUMS BY $2500 PER YEAR.
Obam re will cover
ove 44 million
A CANS.
OVER 3 MILLION YOUNG ADULTS HAVE RECEIVED COVERAGE UNDER THEIR PARENTS' HEALTH PLANS.

APRIL FOOLS

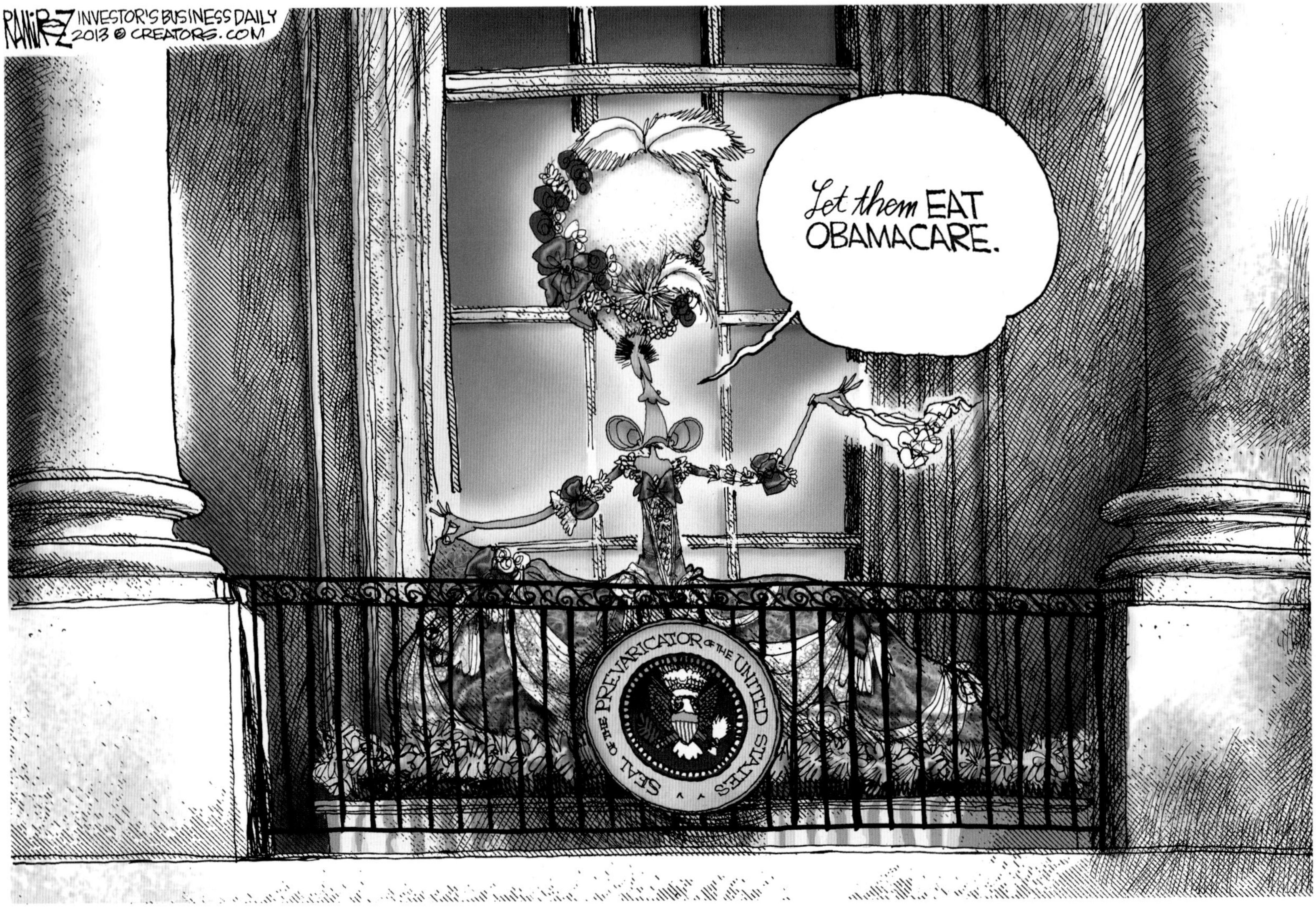
RAMIREZ INVESTOR'S BUSINESS DAILY
2013 © CREATORS.COM
Let them EAT OBAMACARE.
SEAL OF THE PREVARICATOR OF THE UNITED STATES

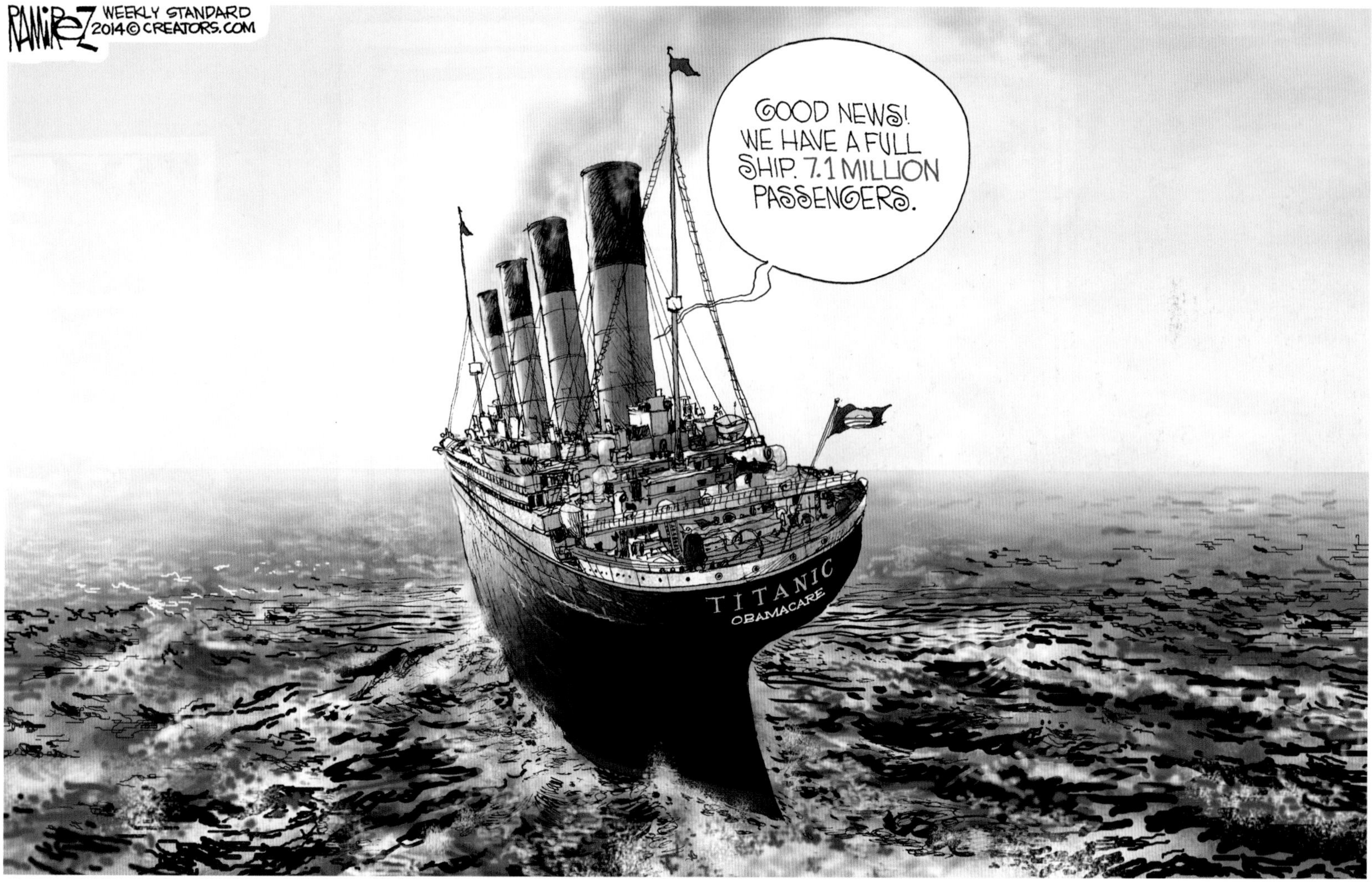
RAMIREZ WEEKLY STANDARD 2014 © CREATORS.COM
GOOD NEWS! WE HAVE A FULL SHIP. 7.1 MILLION PASSENGERS.
TITANIC
OBAMACARE

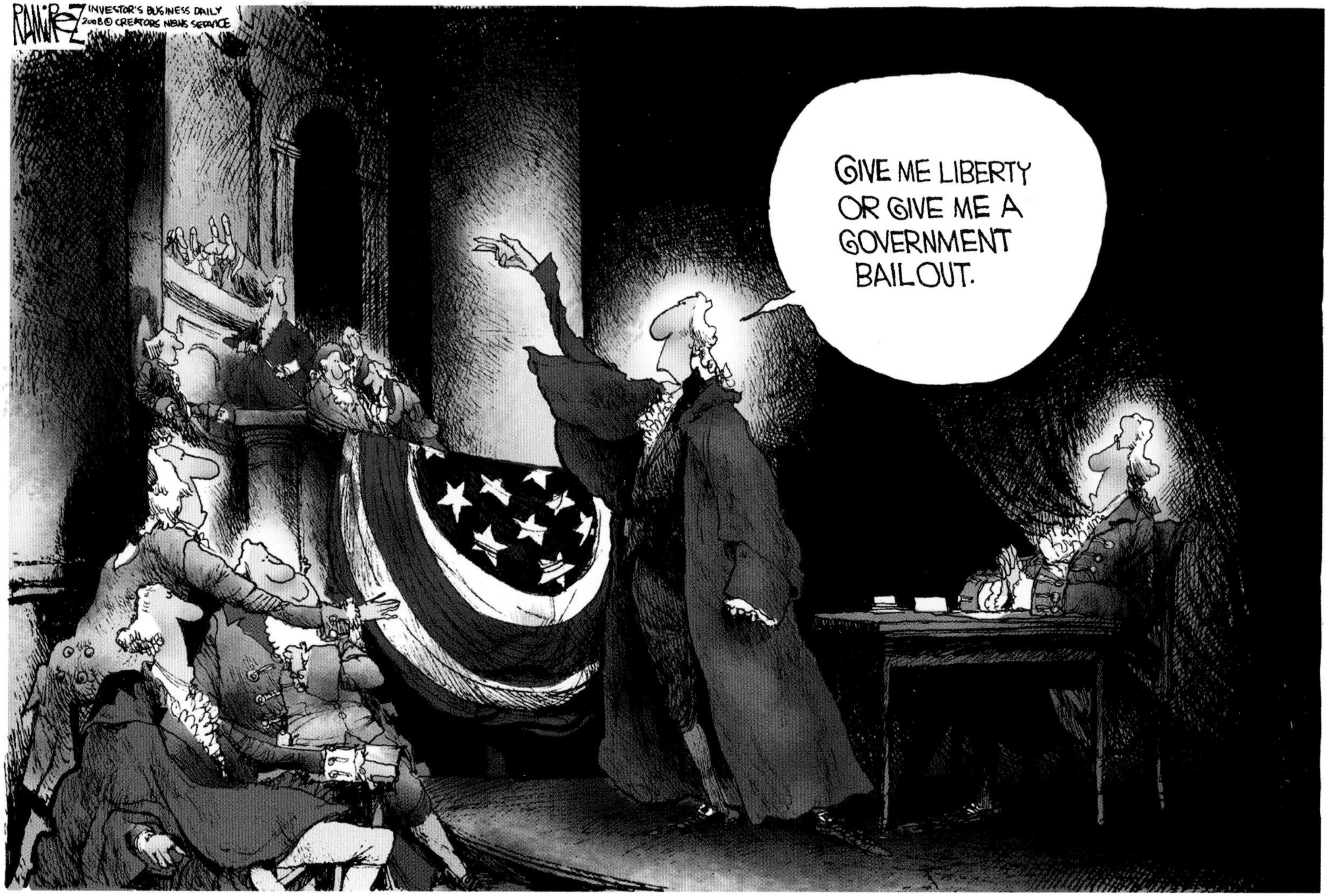
RAMIREZ INVESTOR'S BUSINESS DAILY 2008 © CREATORS NEWS SERVICE
GIVE ME LIBERTY OR GIVE ME A GOVERNMENT BAILOUT.

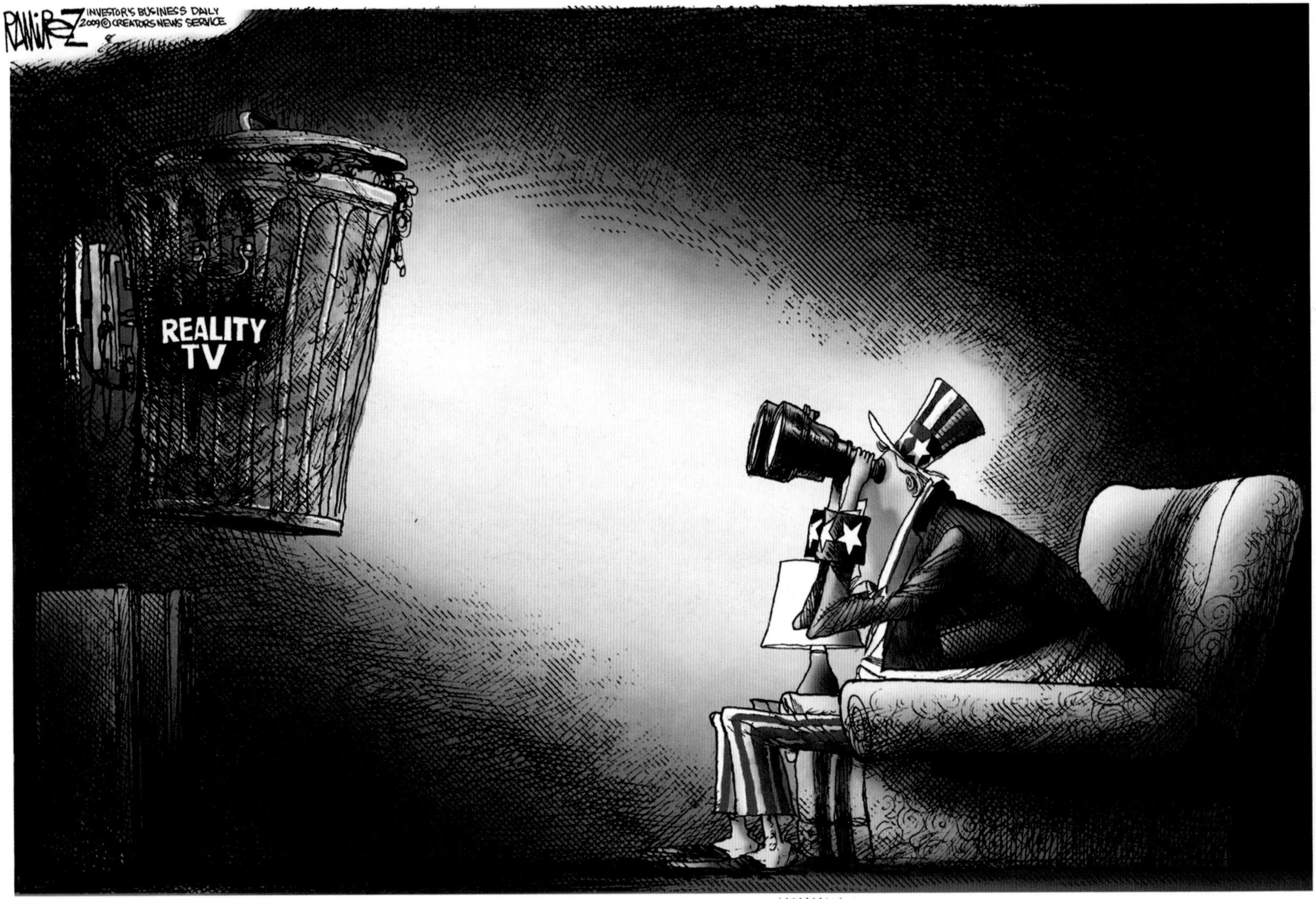
RAMIREZ INVESTOR'S BUSINESS DAILY 2009 © CREATORS NEWS SERVICE
REALITY TV

THE VOYEUR

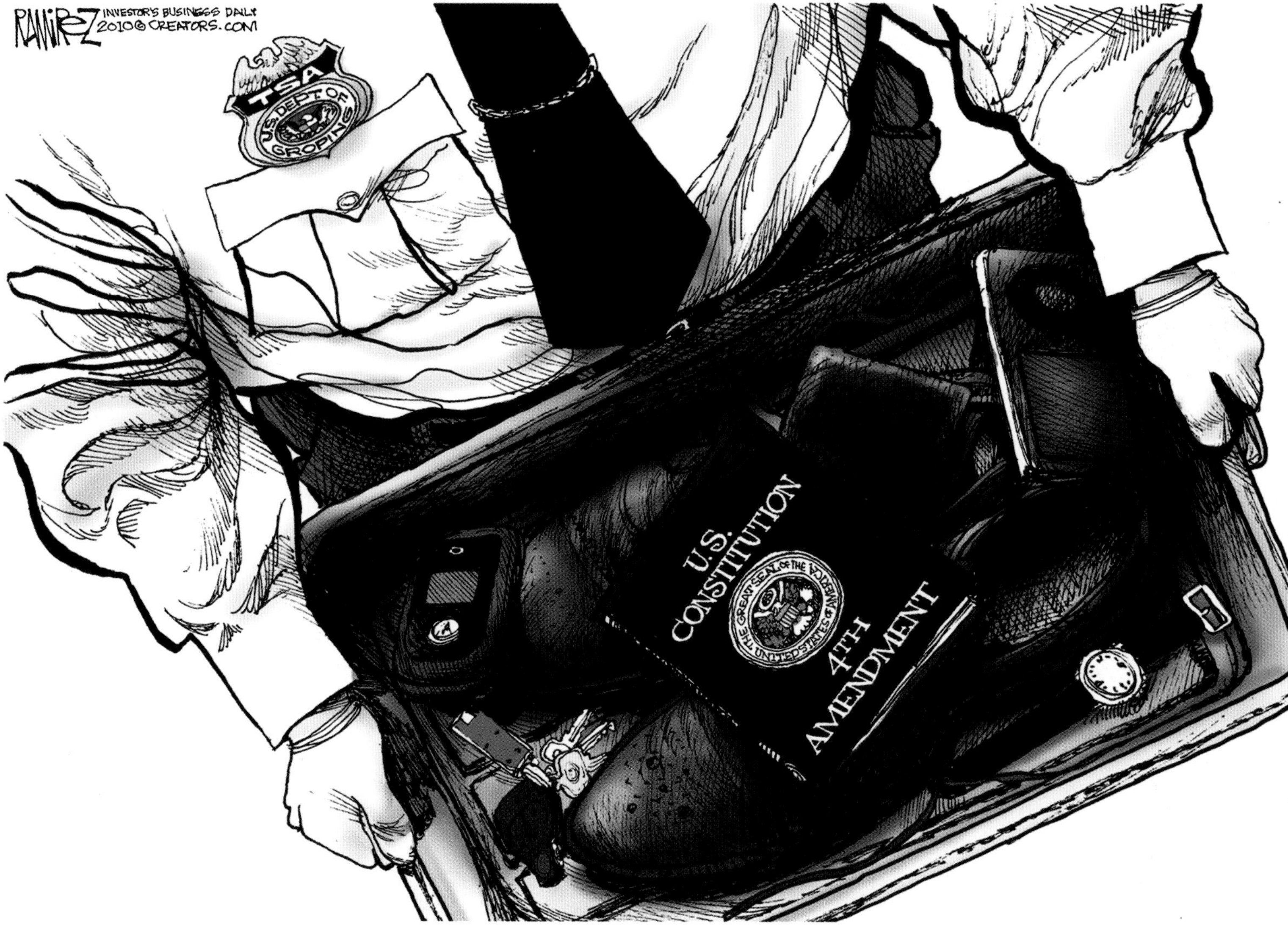
RAMIREZ INVESTOR'S BUSINESS DAILY 2010 © CREATORS.COM
TSA
U.S. DEPT OF GROPING
U.S. CONSTITUTION
THE GREAT SEAL OF THE UNITED STATES OF AMERICA
4TH AMENDMENT

PLEASE REMOVE THESE ITEMS FROM YOUR PERSON.

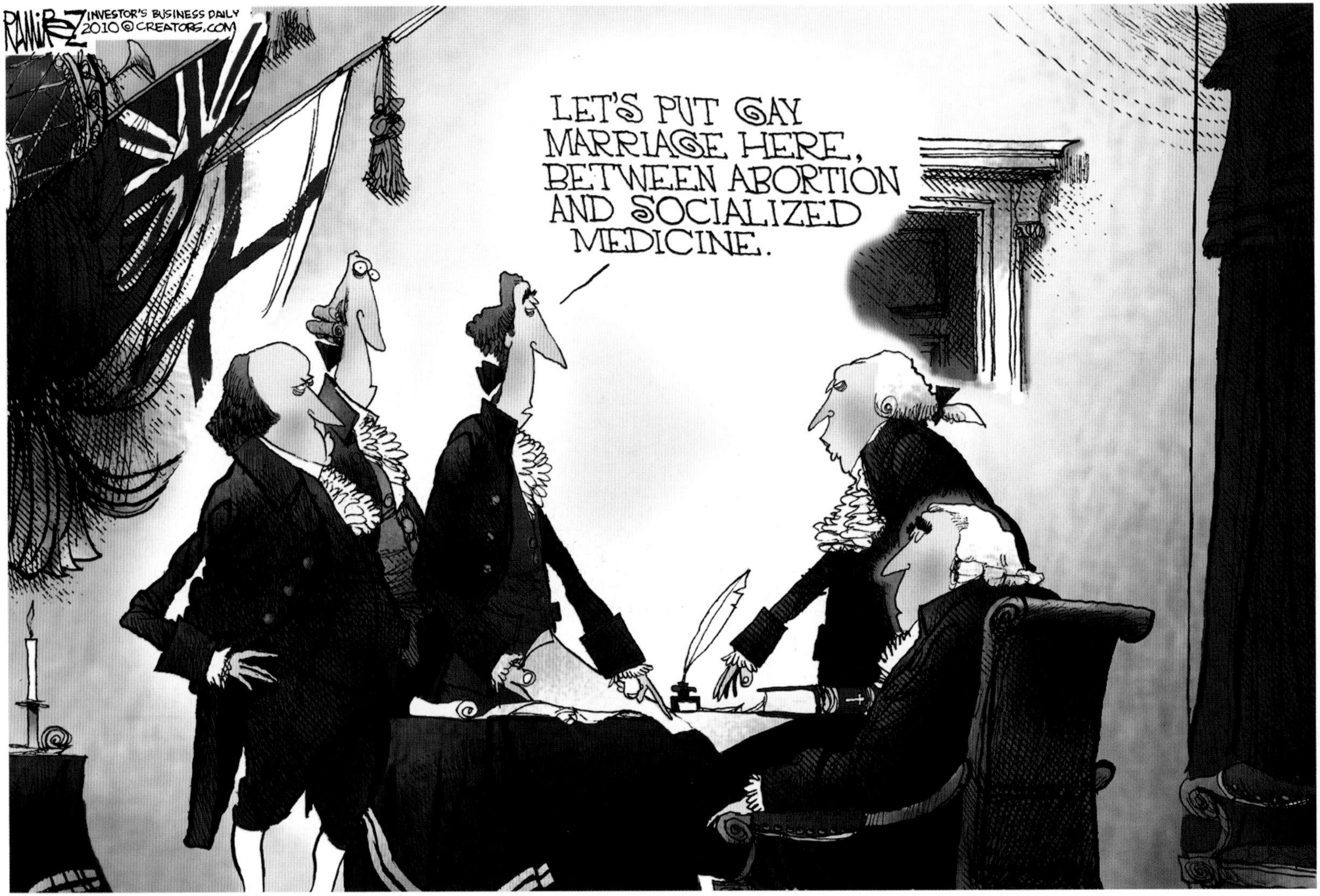
RAMIREZ INVESTOR'S BUSINESS DAILY 2010 © CREATORS.COM
LET'S PUT GAY MARRIAGE HERE, BETWEEN ABORTION AND SOCIALIZED MEDICINE.

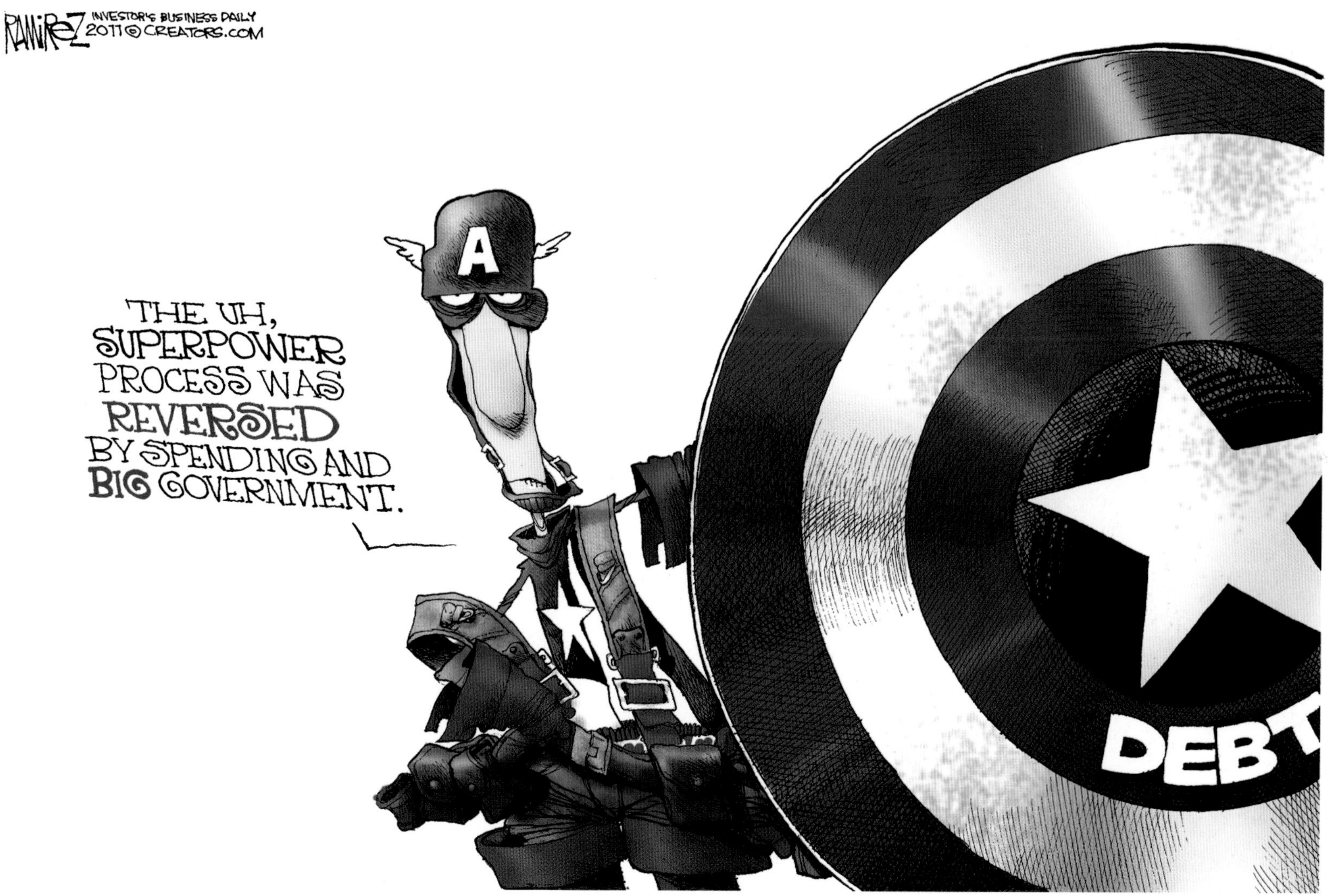
RAMIREZ INVESTOR'S BUSINESS DAILY 2011 © CREATORS.COM
THE UH, SUPERPOWER PROCESS WAS REVERSED BY SPENDING AND BIG GOVERNMENT.
A
DEBT

CAPTAIN AMERICA 2011

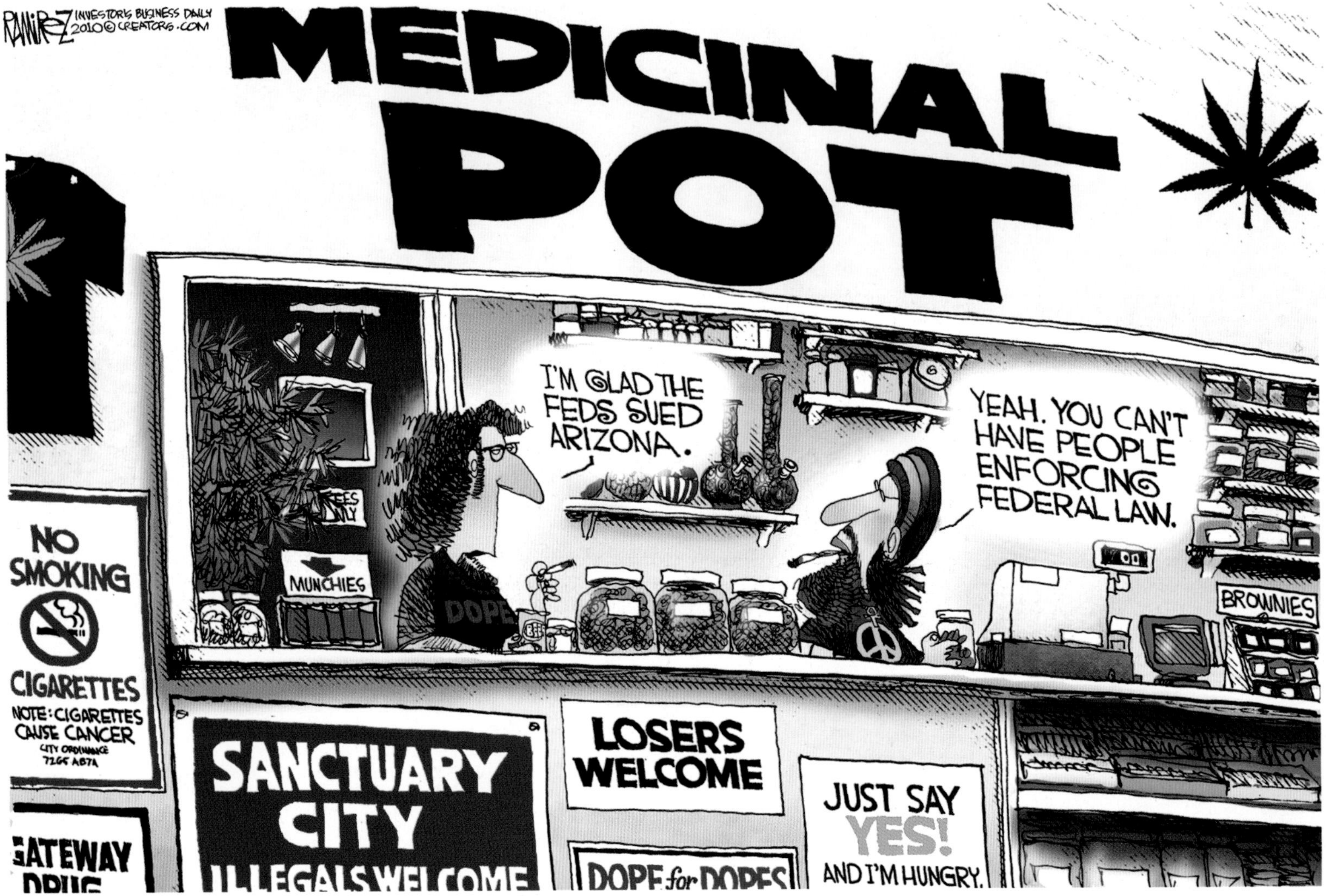

RAMIREZ INVESTOR'S BUSINESS DAILY 2010 © CREATORS.COM
MEDICINAL POT
I'M GLAD THE FEDS SUED ARIZONA.
YEAH. YOU CAN'T HAVE PEOPLE ENFORCING FEDERAL LAW.
MUNCHIES
DOPE
BROWNIES
NO SMOKING
CIGARETTES
NOTE: CIGARETTES CAUSE CANCER
SANCTUARY CITY
ILLEGALS WELCOME
LOSERS WELCOME
DOPE for DOPES
JUST SAY YES!
AND I'M HUNGRY.

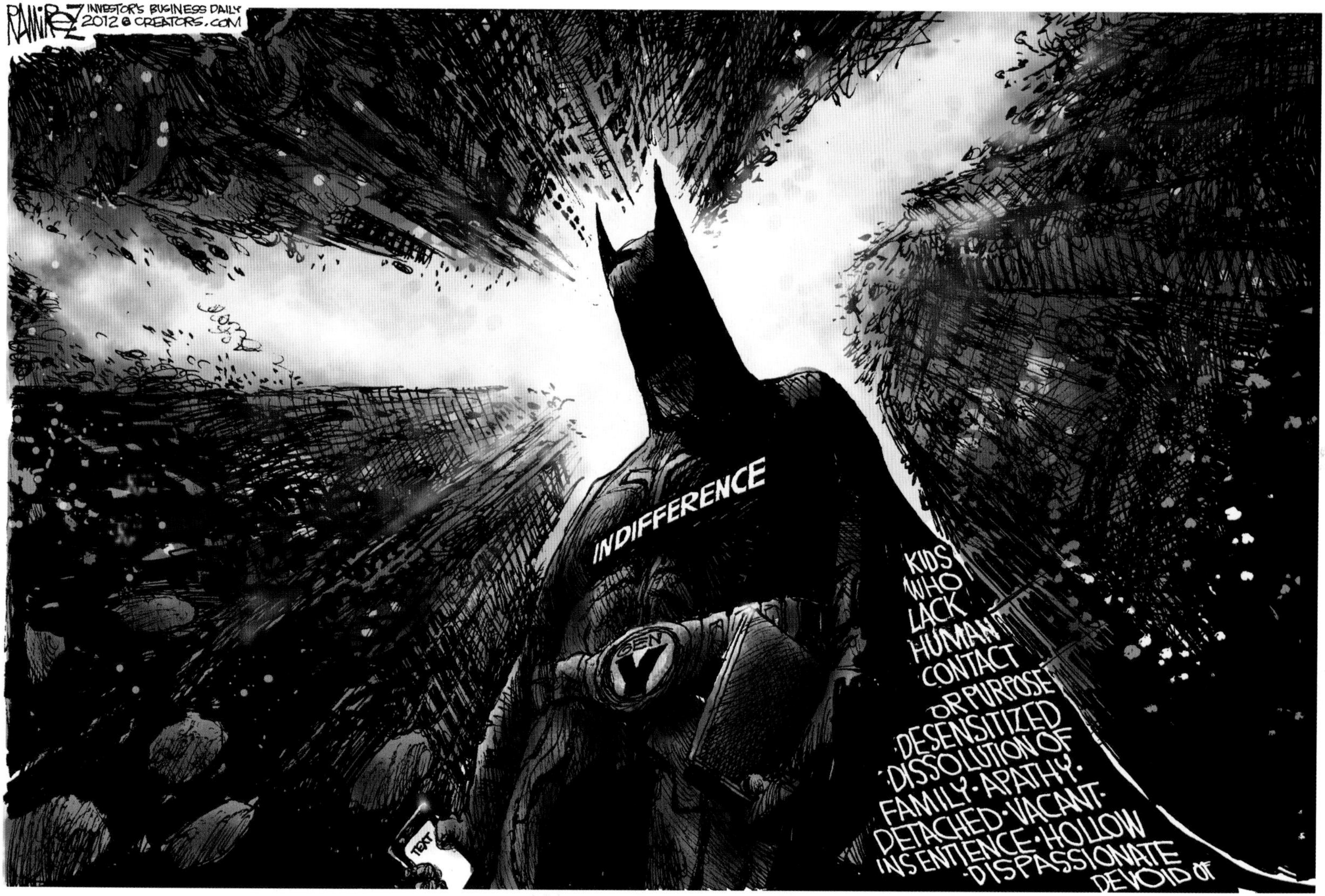
RAMIREZ
INVESTOR'S BUSINESS DAILY
2012 © CREATORS.COM
INDIFFERENCE
GEN Y
TEXT
KIDS
WHO
LACK
HUMAN
CONTACT
OR PURPOSE
·DESENSITIZED
·DISSOLUTION OF
FAMILY·APATHY·
DETACHED·VACANT·
INSENTIENCE·HOLLOW
·DISPASSIONATE
DEVOID OF

A DARKNESS RISING.

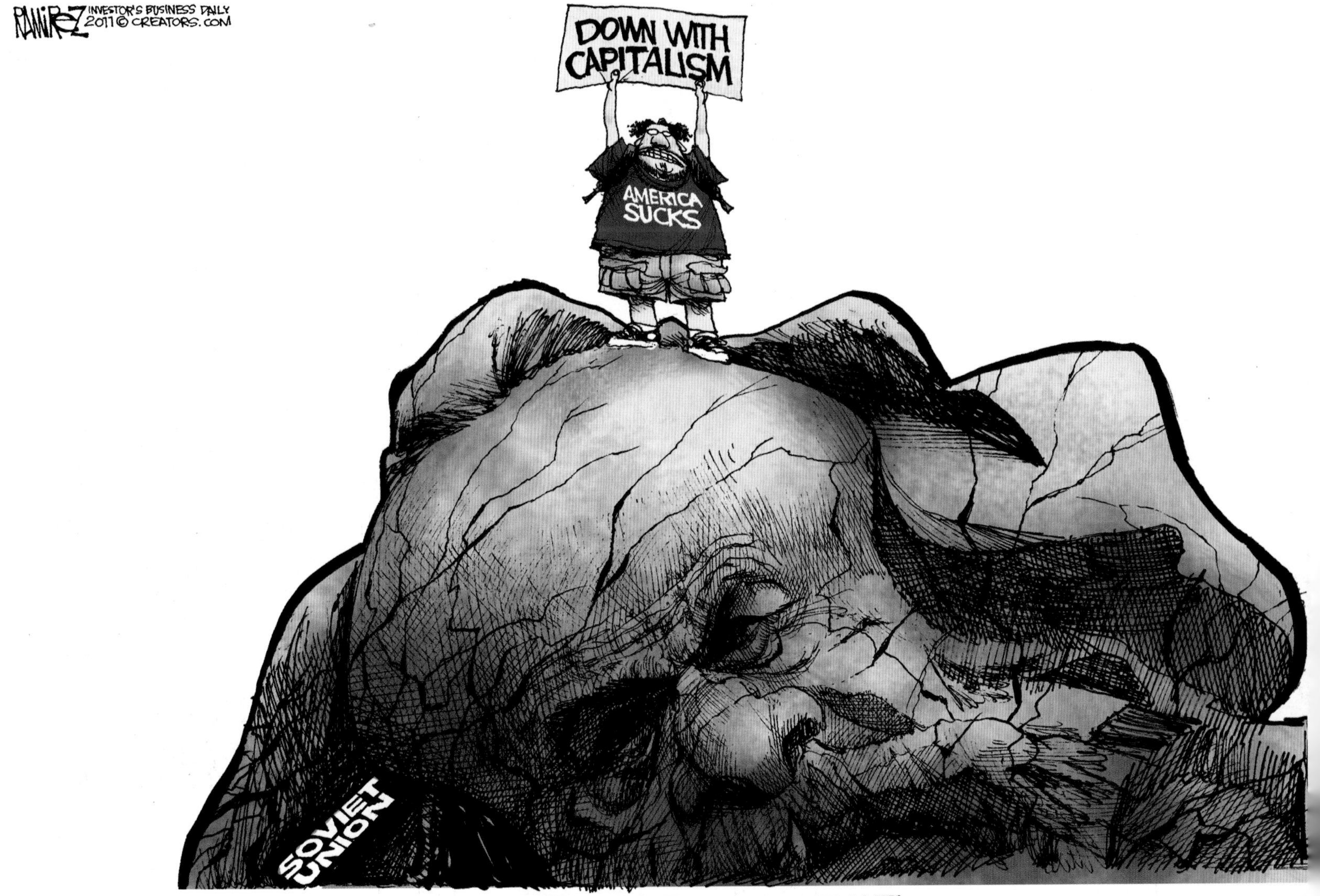
RAMIREZ INVESTOR'S BUSINESS DAILY 2011 © CREATORS.COM
DOWN WITH CAPITALISM
AMERICA SUCKS
SOVIET UNION

BEEN THERE, DONE THAT.

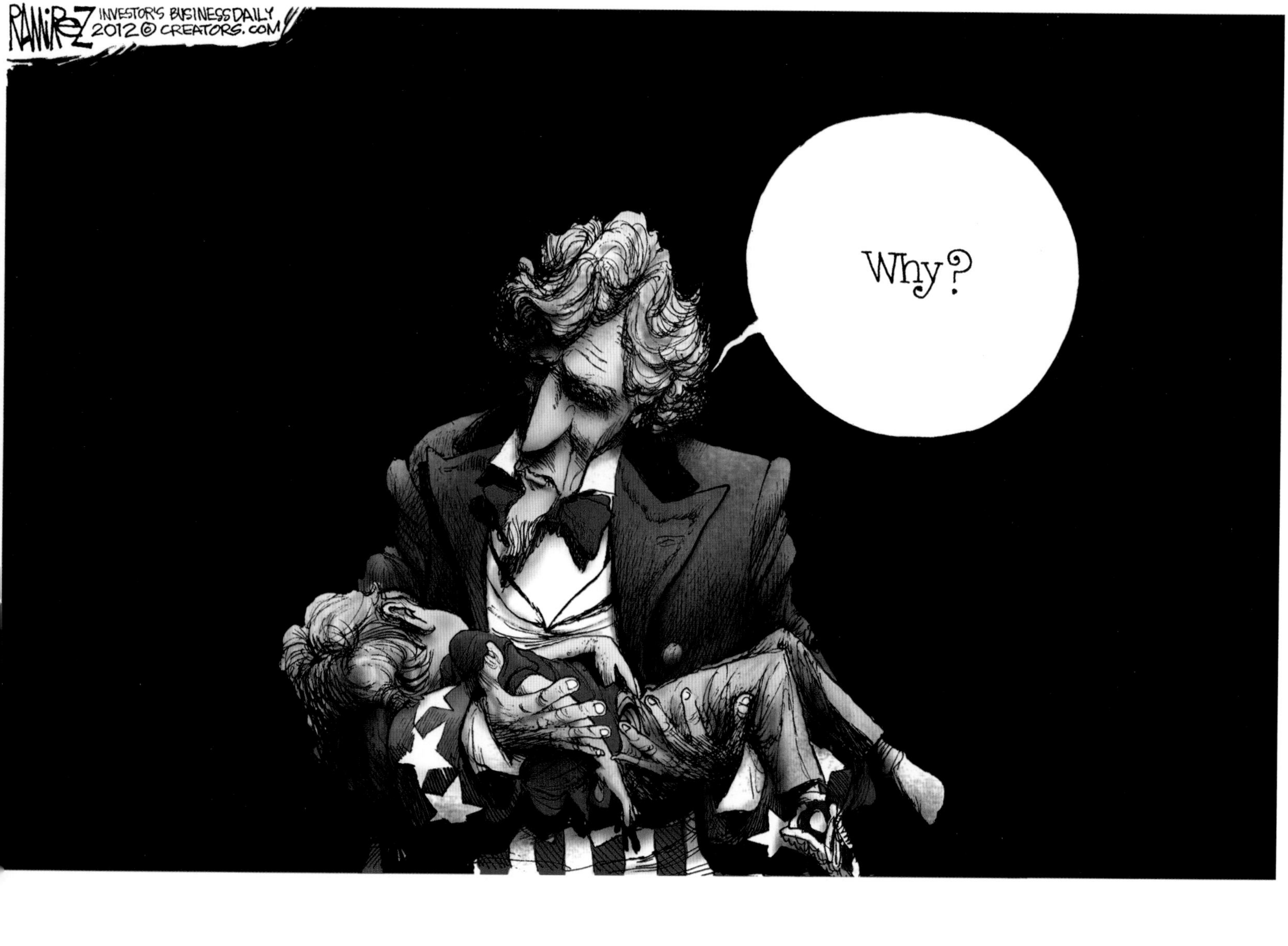
RAMIREZ
INVESTOR'S BUSINESS DAILY
2012 © CREATORS.COM
Why?

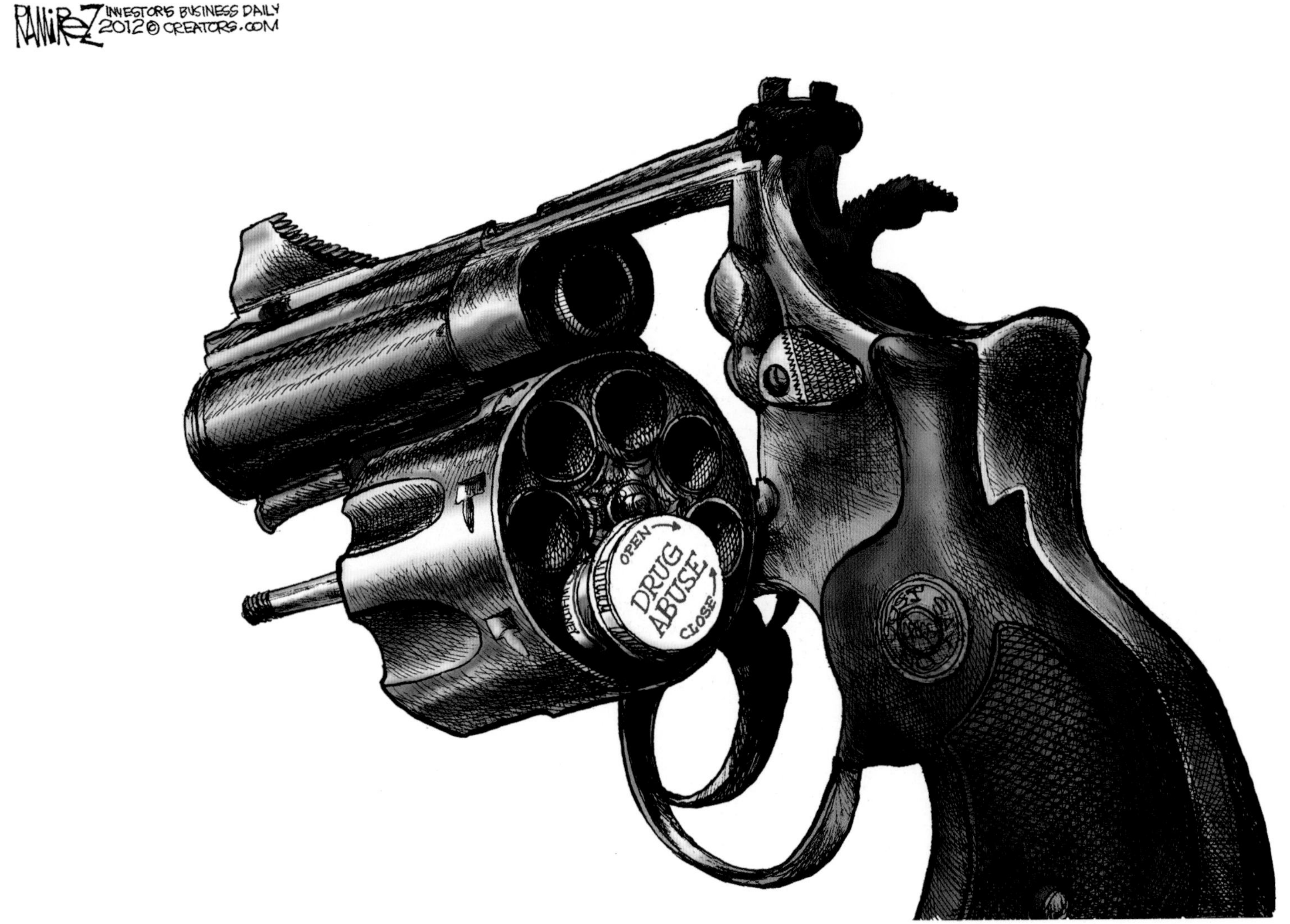
RAMIREZ
INVESTOR'S BUSINESS DAILY
2012 © CREATORS.COM
OPEN
DRUG ABUSE
CLOSE

RUSSIAN ROULETTE

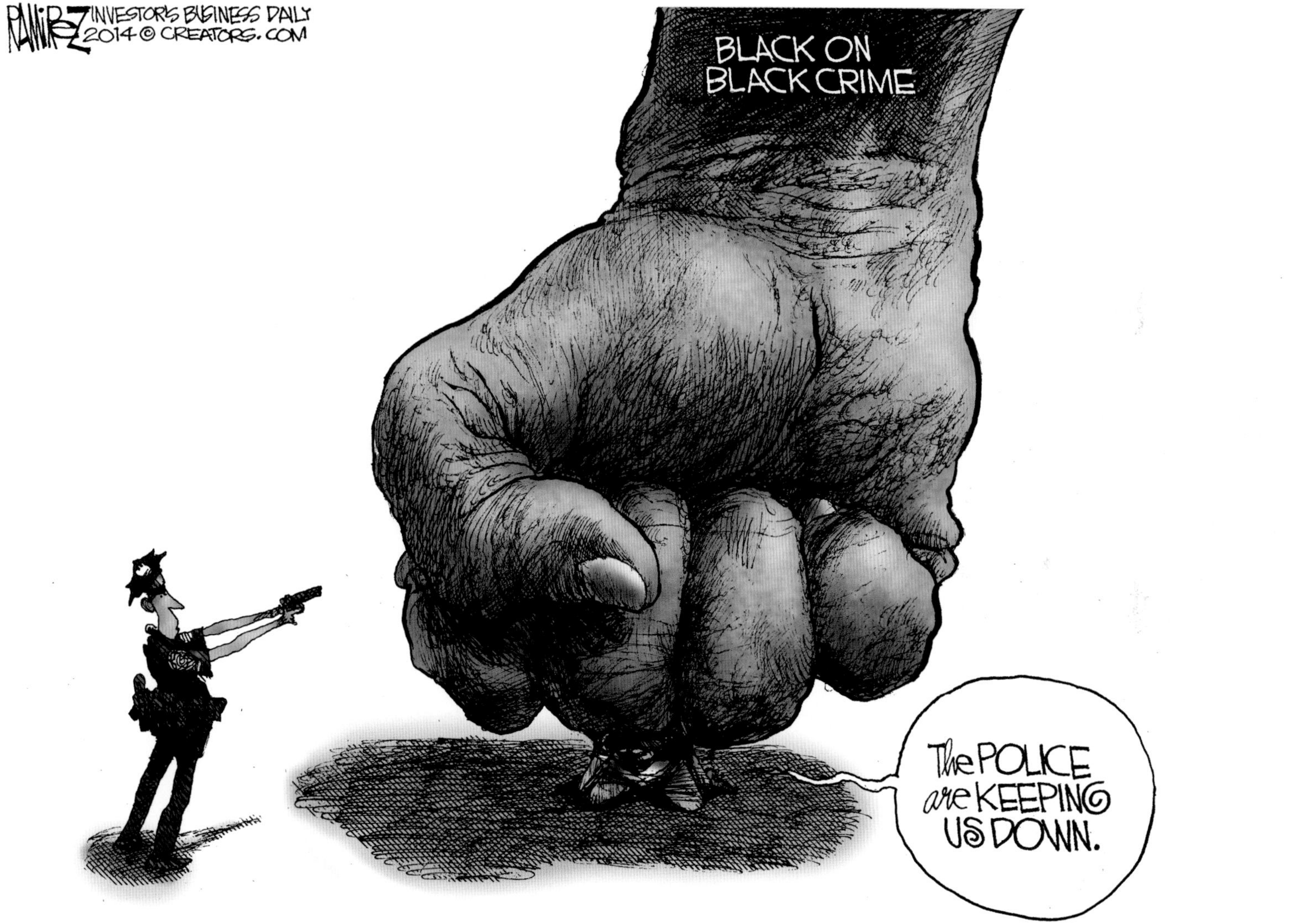
RAMIREZ INVESTOR'S BUSINESS DAILY 2014 © CREATORS.COM
BLACK ON BLACK CRIME
The POLICE are KEEPING US DOWN.

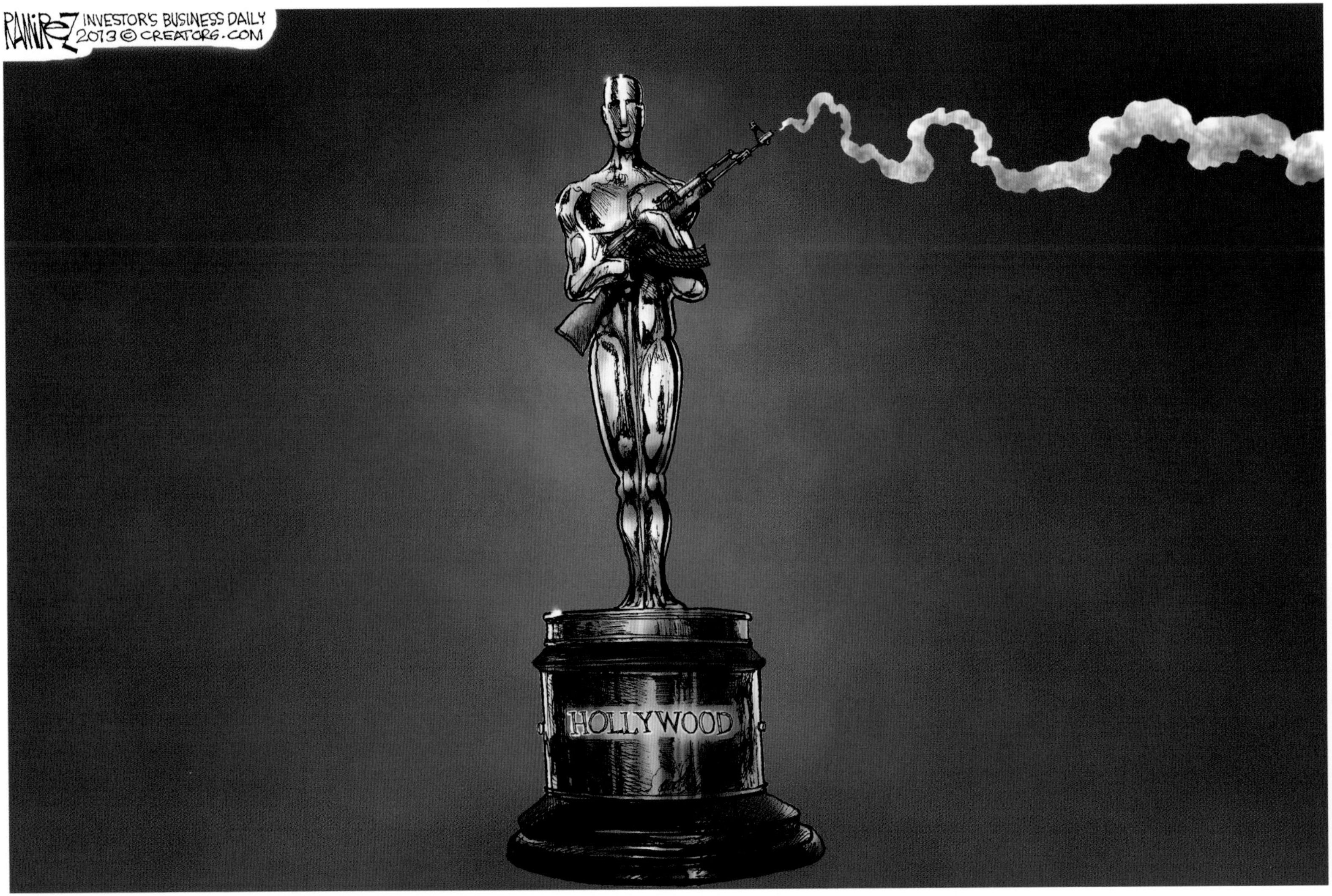
RAMIREZ INVESTOR'S BUSINESS DAILY 2013 © CREATORS.COM
HOLLYWOOD

AND FOR LEADING ACTOR IN THE PROMOTION OF VIOLENCE...

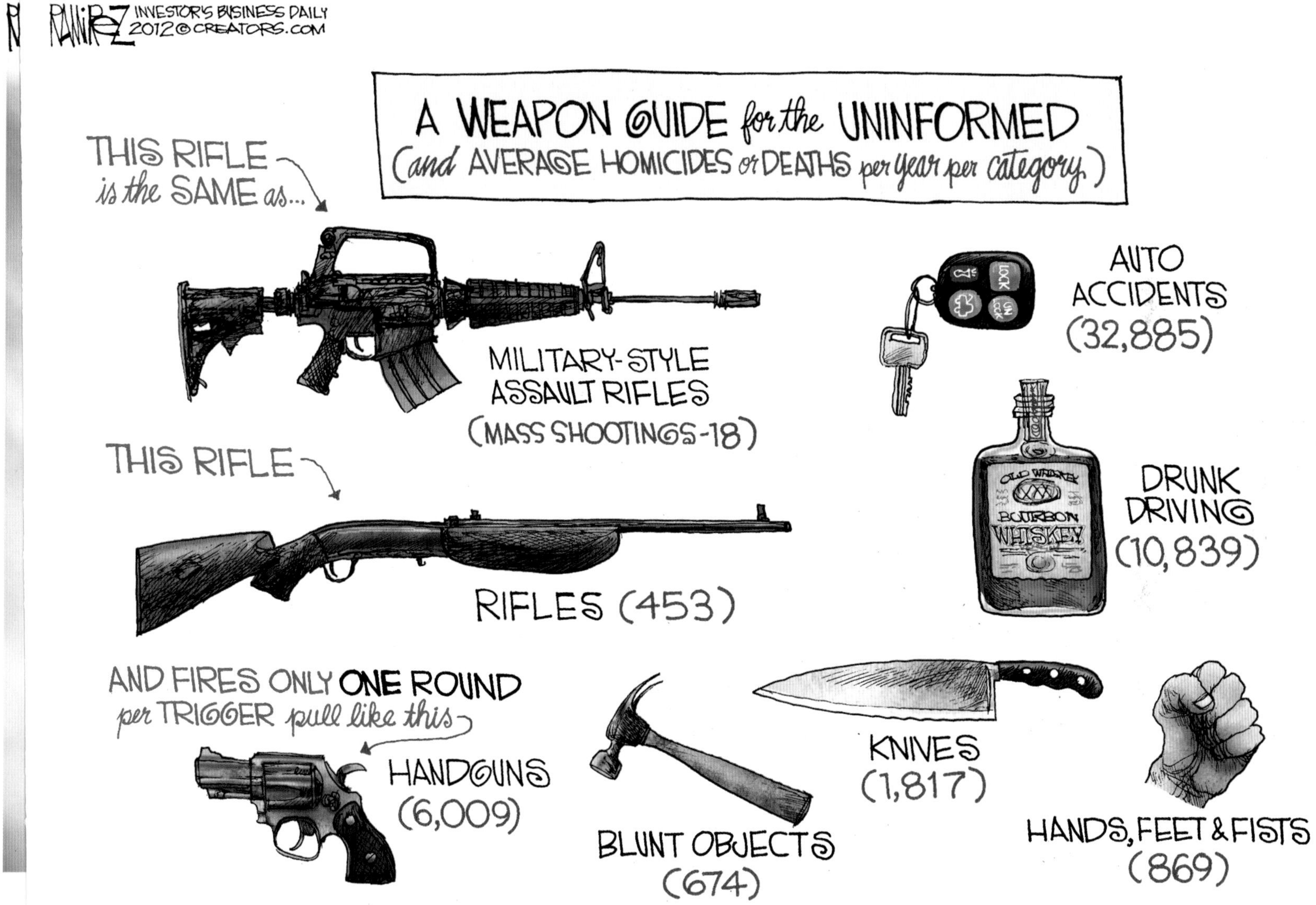
RAMIREZ INVESTOR'S BUSINESS DAILY 2012 © CREATORS.COM
A WEAPON GUIDE for the UNINFORMED
(and AVERAGE HOMICIDES or DEATHS per year per category)
THIS RIFLE is the SAME as...
MILITARY-STYLE ASSAULT RIFLES (MASS SHOOTINGS-18)
THIS RIFLE
RIFLES (453)
AND FIRES ONLY ONE ROUND per TRIGGER pull like this
HANDGUNS (6,009)
BLUNT OBJECTS (674)
KNIVES (1,817)
AUTO ACCIDENTS (32,885)
DRUNK DRIVING (10,839)
HANDS, FEET & FISTS (869)
LOCK
UNLOCK
OLD WHISKEY
XXX
BOURBON WHISKEY

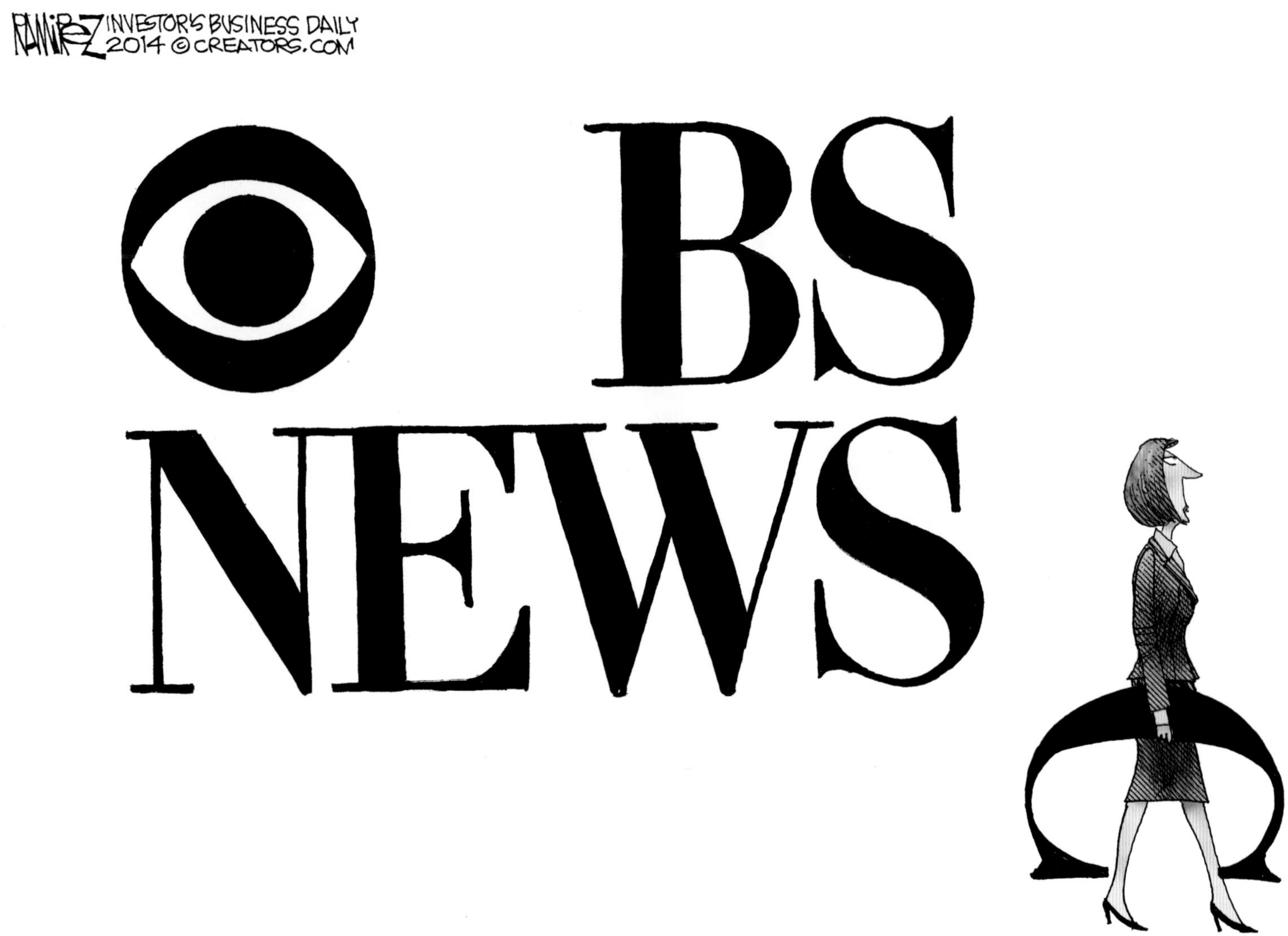
RAMIREZ INVESTOR'S BUSINESS DAILY
2014 © CREATORS.COM
BS
NEWS

SHARYL ATTKISSON LEAVES CBS NEWS

Domestic Affairs

"I've now been in 57 states—I think one left to go."

—President Barack Obama,
Beaverton, Oregon, May 9, 2008

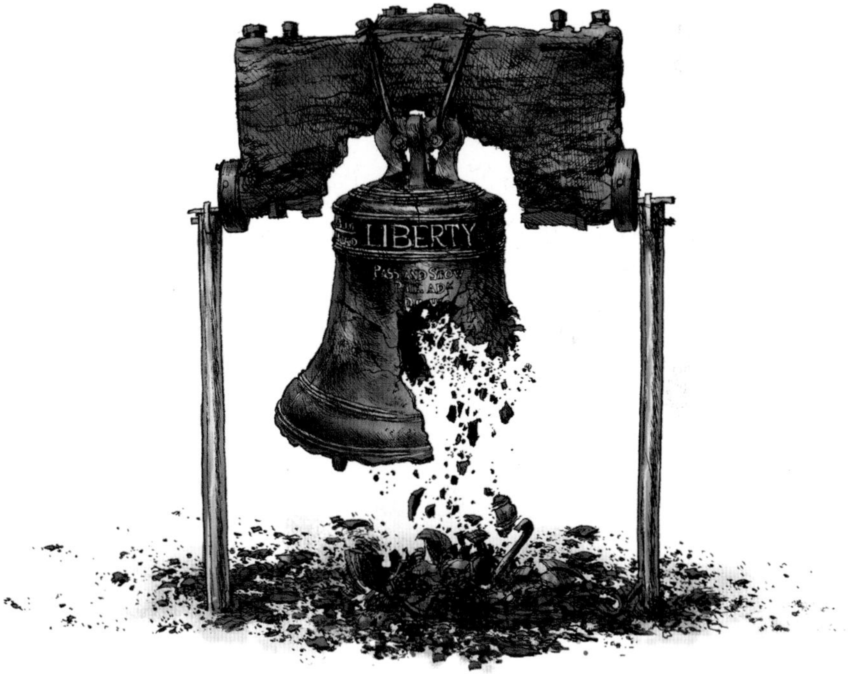
LIBERTY

The strategy used to "change" America was federalization of power and a plan to divide and conquer. Washington traded handouts for liberty. The politics of envy blamed achievers for inequality, and the transition of America from a nation of achievement to a nation of entitlement had begun in earnest.

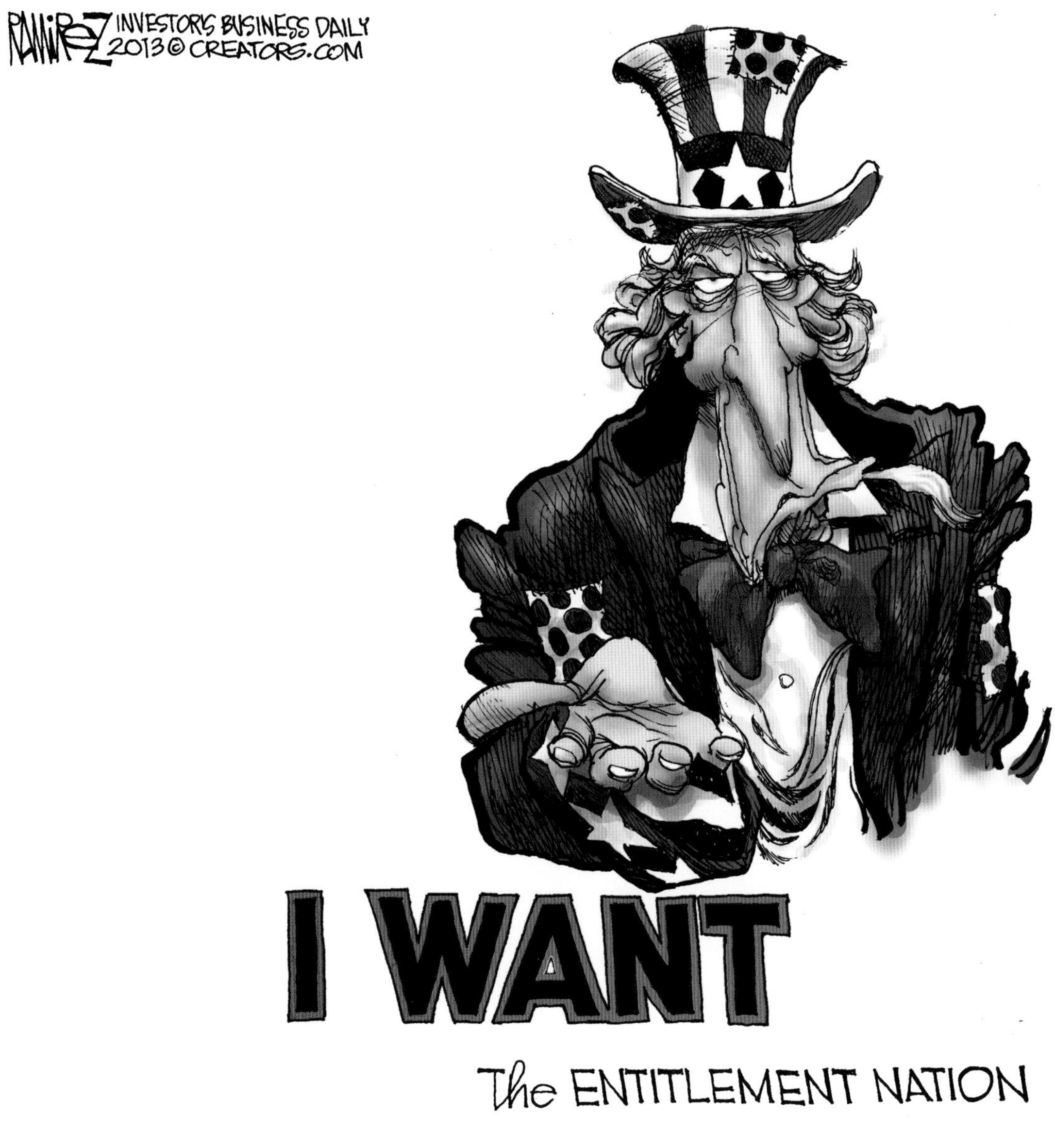
RAMIREZ INVESTOR'S BUSINESS DAILY
2013 © CREATORS.COM
I WANT
The ENTITLEMENT NATION

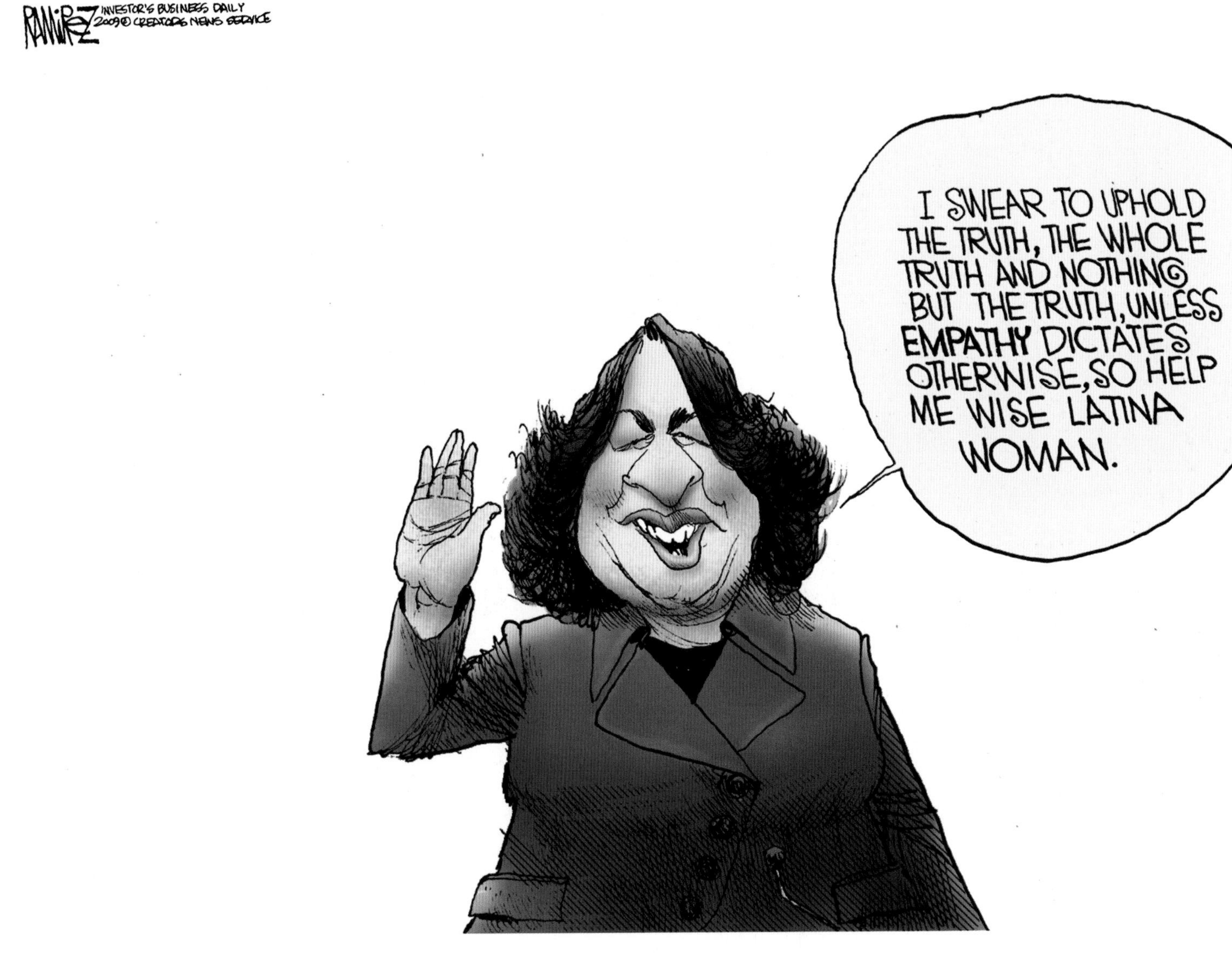
RAMIREZ
INVESTOR'S BUSINESS DAILY
2009© CREATORS NEWS SERVICE
I SWEAR TO UPHOLD THE TRUTH, THE WHOLE TRUTH AND NOTHING BUT THE TRUTH, UNLESS **EMPATHY** DICTATES OTHERWISE, SO HELP ME WISE LATINA WOMAN.

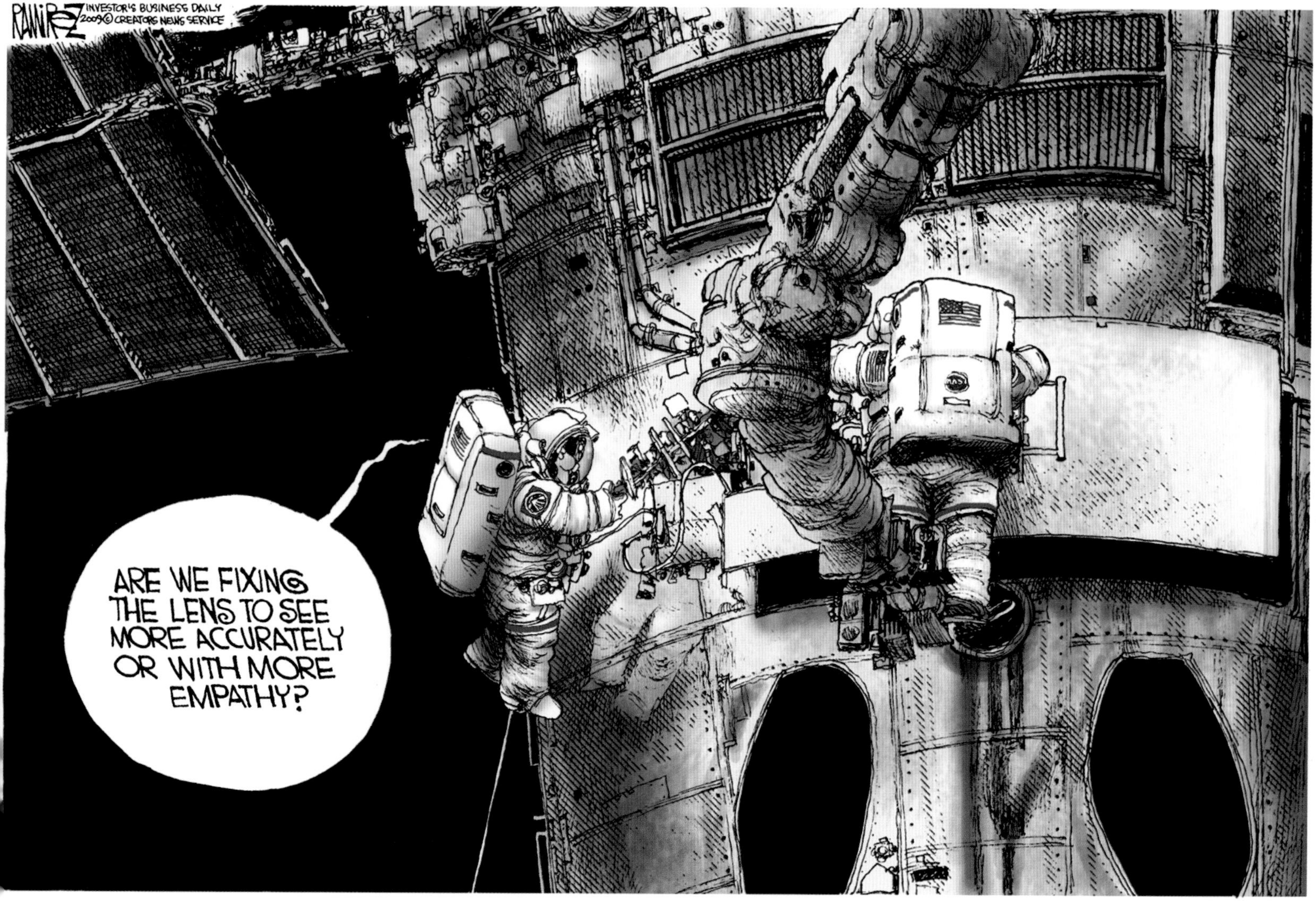
RAMIREZ
INVESTOR'S BUSINESS DAILY
2009 © CREATORS NEWS SERVICE
ARE WE FIXING THE LENS TO SEE MORE ACCURATELY OR WITH MORE EMPATHY?

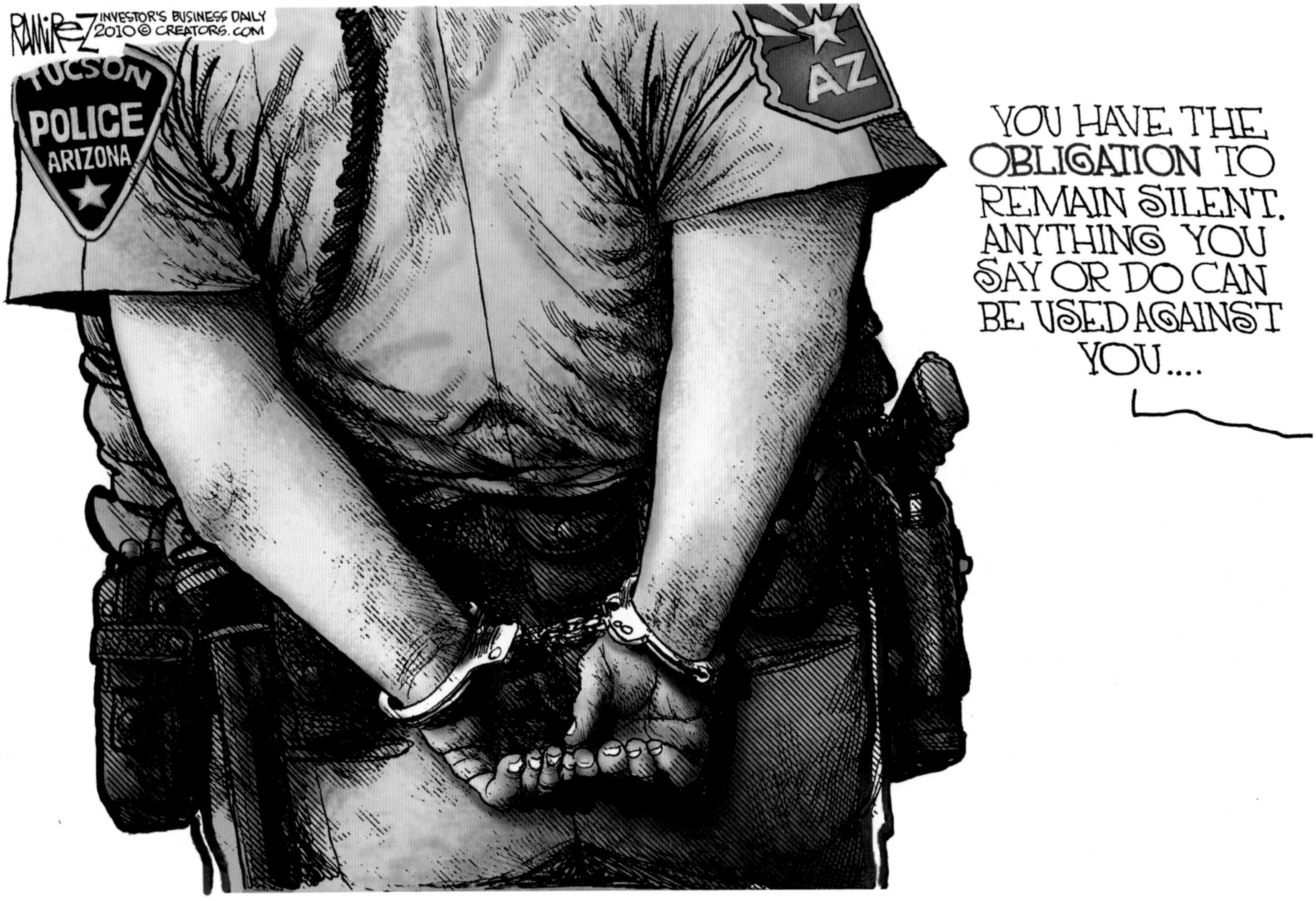
RAMIREZ INVESTOR'S BUSINESS DAILY 2010 © CREATORS.COM
TUCSON POLICE ARIZONA
AZ
YOU HAVE THE OBLIGATION TO REMAIN SILENT. ANYTHING YOU SAY OR DO CAN BE USED AGAINST YOU....

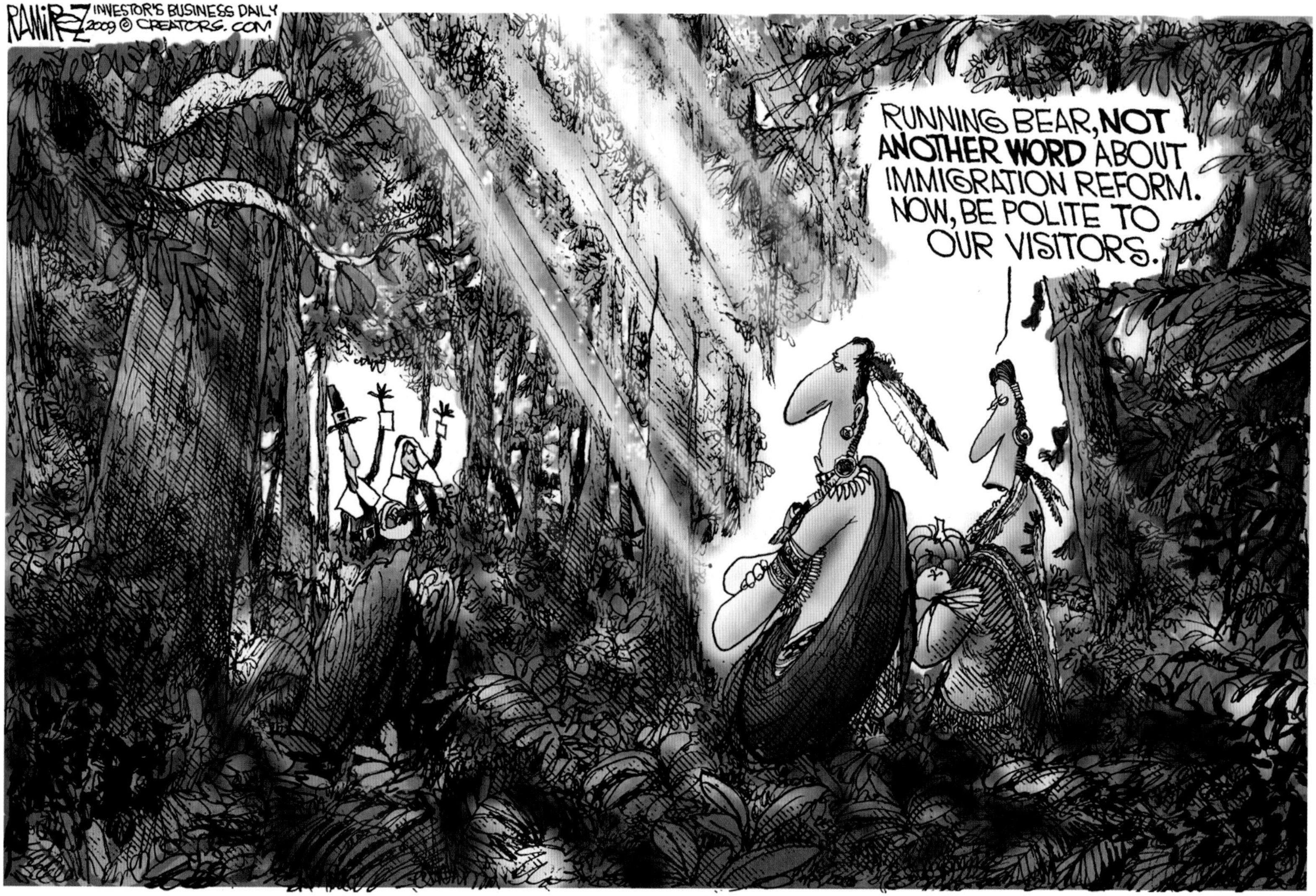
RAMIREZ INVESTOR'S BUSINESS DAILY 2009 © CREATORS.COM
RUNNING BEAR, **NOT ANOTHER WORD** ABOUT IMMIGRATION REFORM. NOW, BE POLITE TO OUR VISITORS.

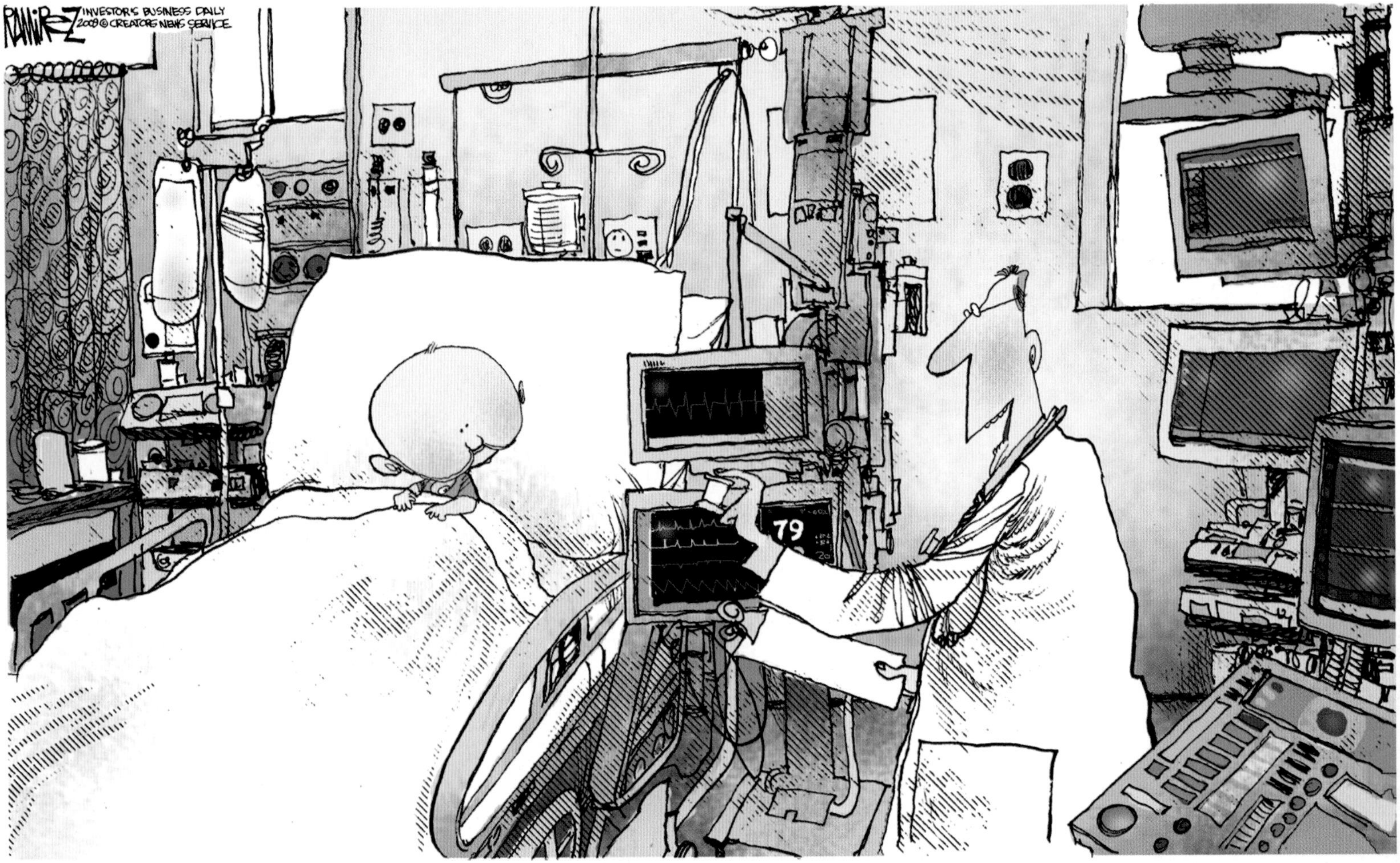
RAMIREZ
INVESTOR'S BUSINESS DAILY
2009 © CREATORS NEWS SERVICE
79

BECAUSE OF LOOMING PRICE CONTROLS, STRATOSPHERIC DRUG DEVELOPMENT COSTS, EXTENSIVE CLINICAL TRIALS, AND THE THREAT OF LAWSUITS, WE CAN NO LONGER TREAT YOU. THE GOOD NEWS IS, CHEAP GENERIC VIAGRA.

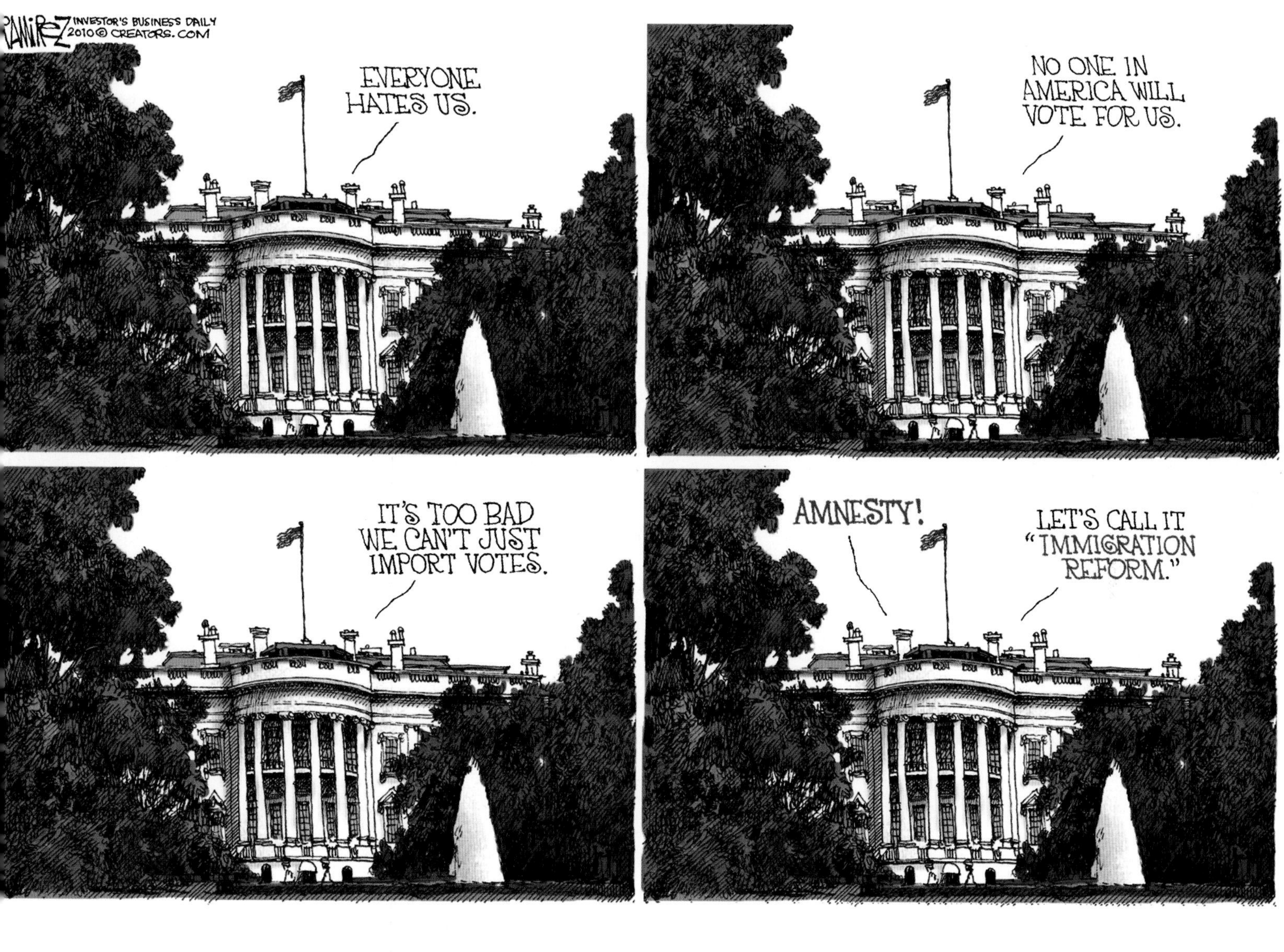
RAMIREZ INVESTOR'S BUSINESS DAILY 2010 © CREATORS.COM
EVERYONE HATES US.
NO ONE IN AMERICA WILL VOTE FOR US.
IT'S TOO BAD WE CAN'T JUST IMPORT VOTES.
AMNESTY!
LET'S CALL IT "IMMIGRATION REFORM."

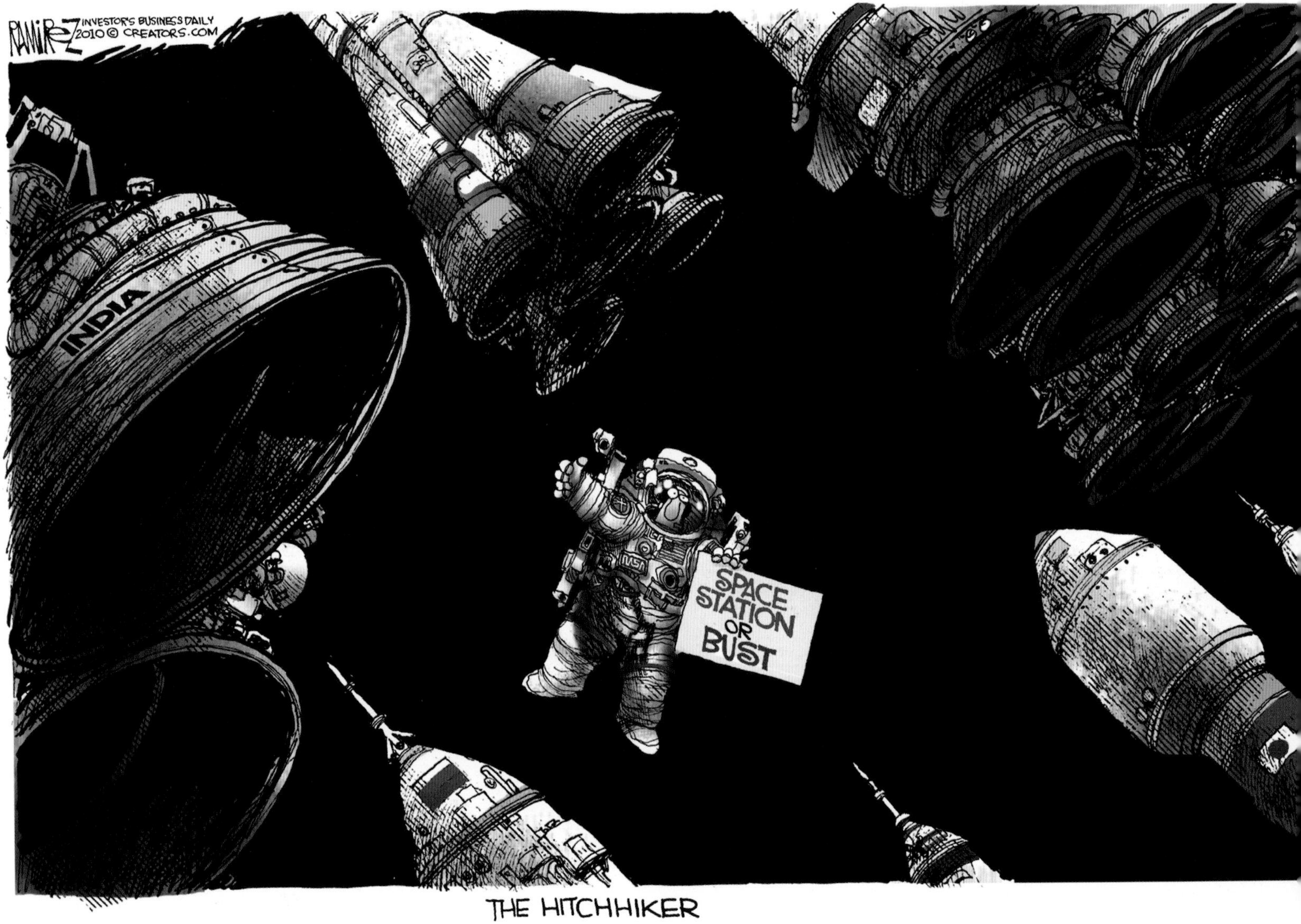
RAMIREZ INVESTOR'S BUSINESS DAILY 2010 © CREATORS.COM
INDIA
SPACE STATION OR BUST

THE HITCHHIKER

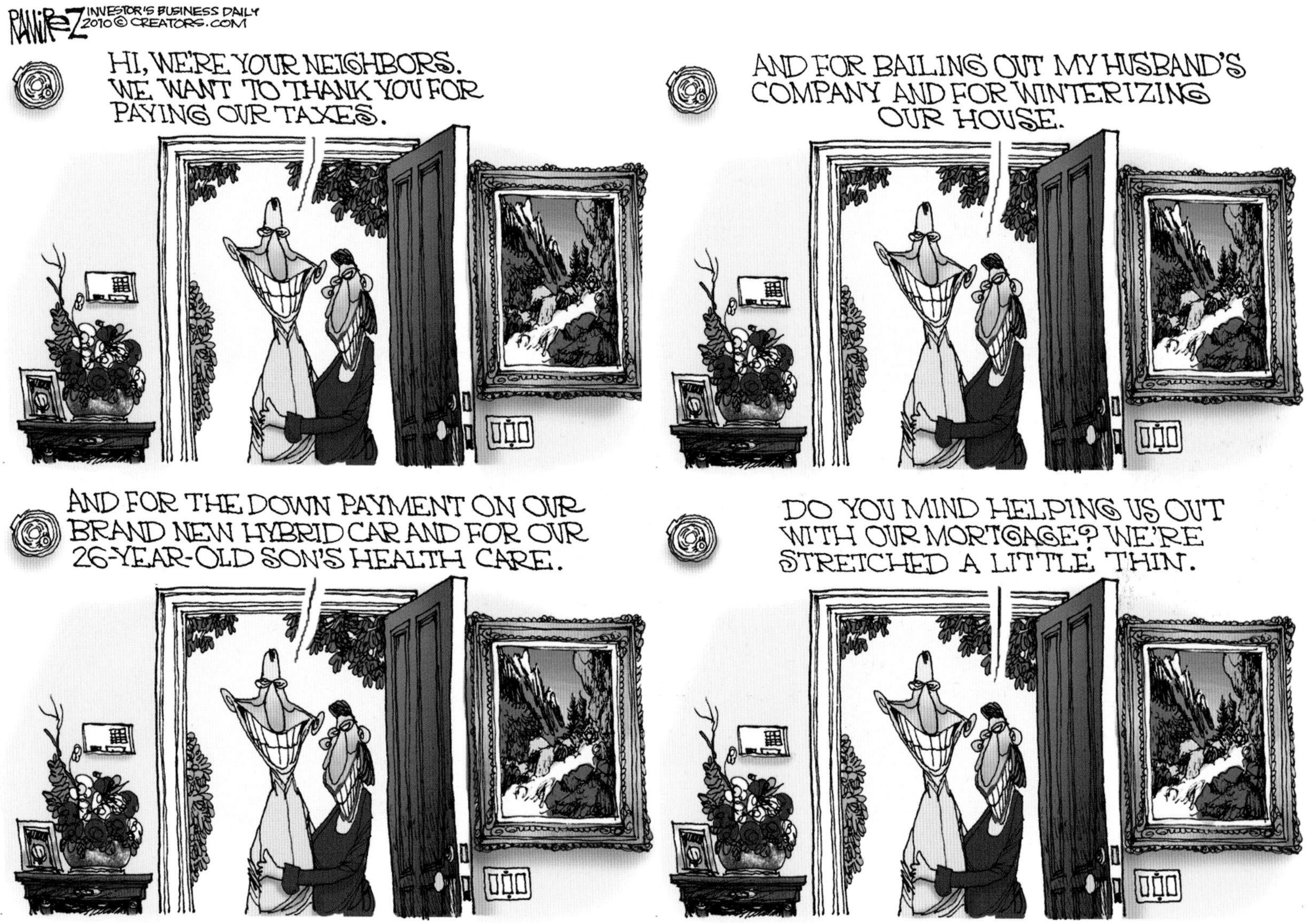
RAMIREZ INVESTOR'S BUSINESS DAILY 2010 © CREATORS.COM
HI, WE'RE YOUR NEIGHBORS. WE WANT TO THANK YOU FOR PAYING OUR TAXES.
AND FOR BAILING OUT MY HUSBAND'S COMPANY AND FOR WINTERIZING OUR HOUSE.
AND FOR THE DOWN PAYMENT ON OUR BRAND NEW HYBRID CAR AND FOR OUR 26-YEAR-OLD SON'S HEALTH CARE.
DO YOU MIND HELPING US OUT WITH OUR MORTGAGE? WE'RE STRETCHED A LITTLE THIN.

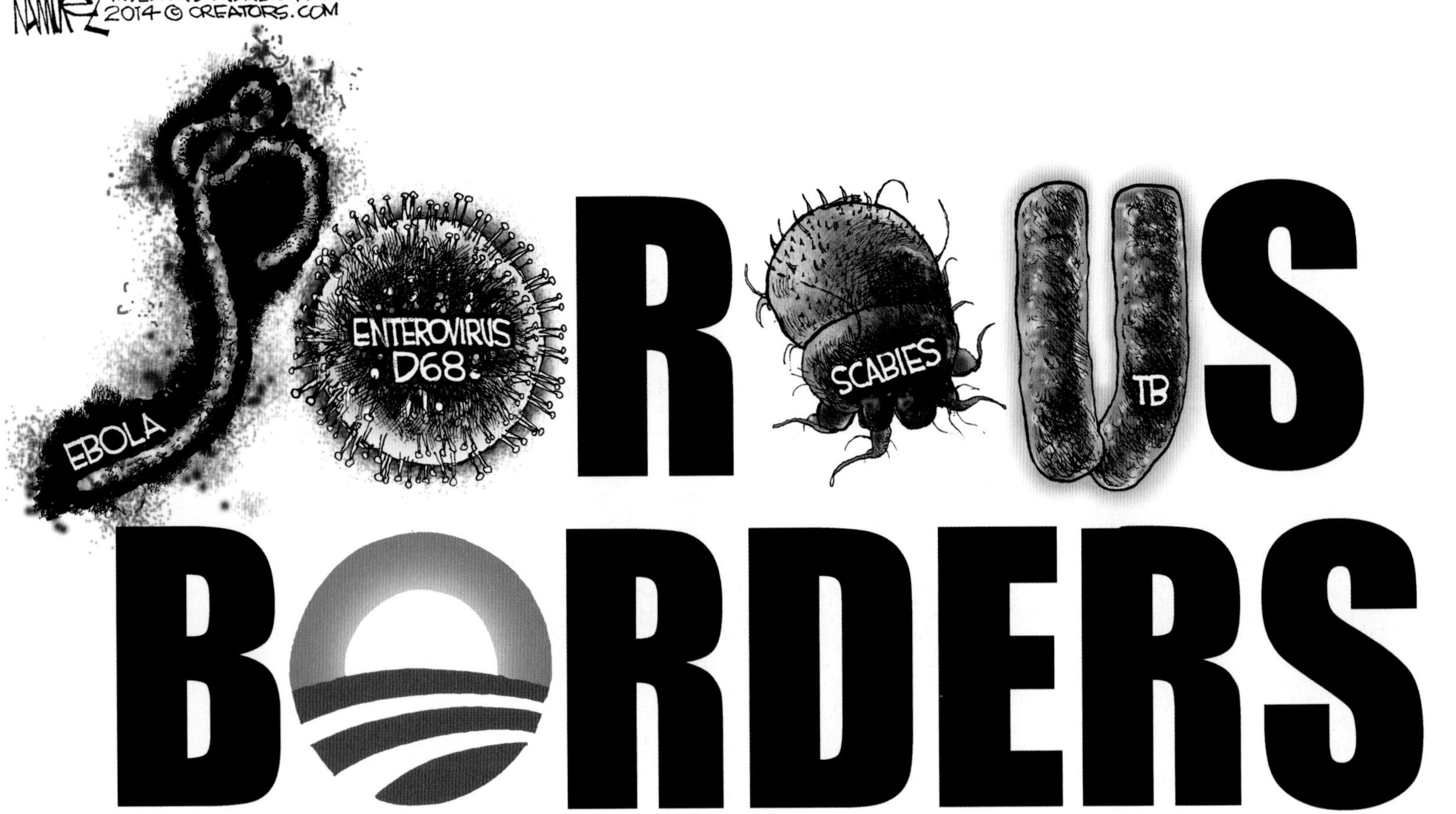
RAMIREZ INVESTOR'S BUSINESS DAILY 2014 © CREATORS.COM
EBOLA
ENTEROVIRUS D68
R
SCABIES
TB
S
B
RDERS

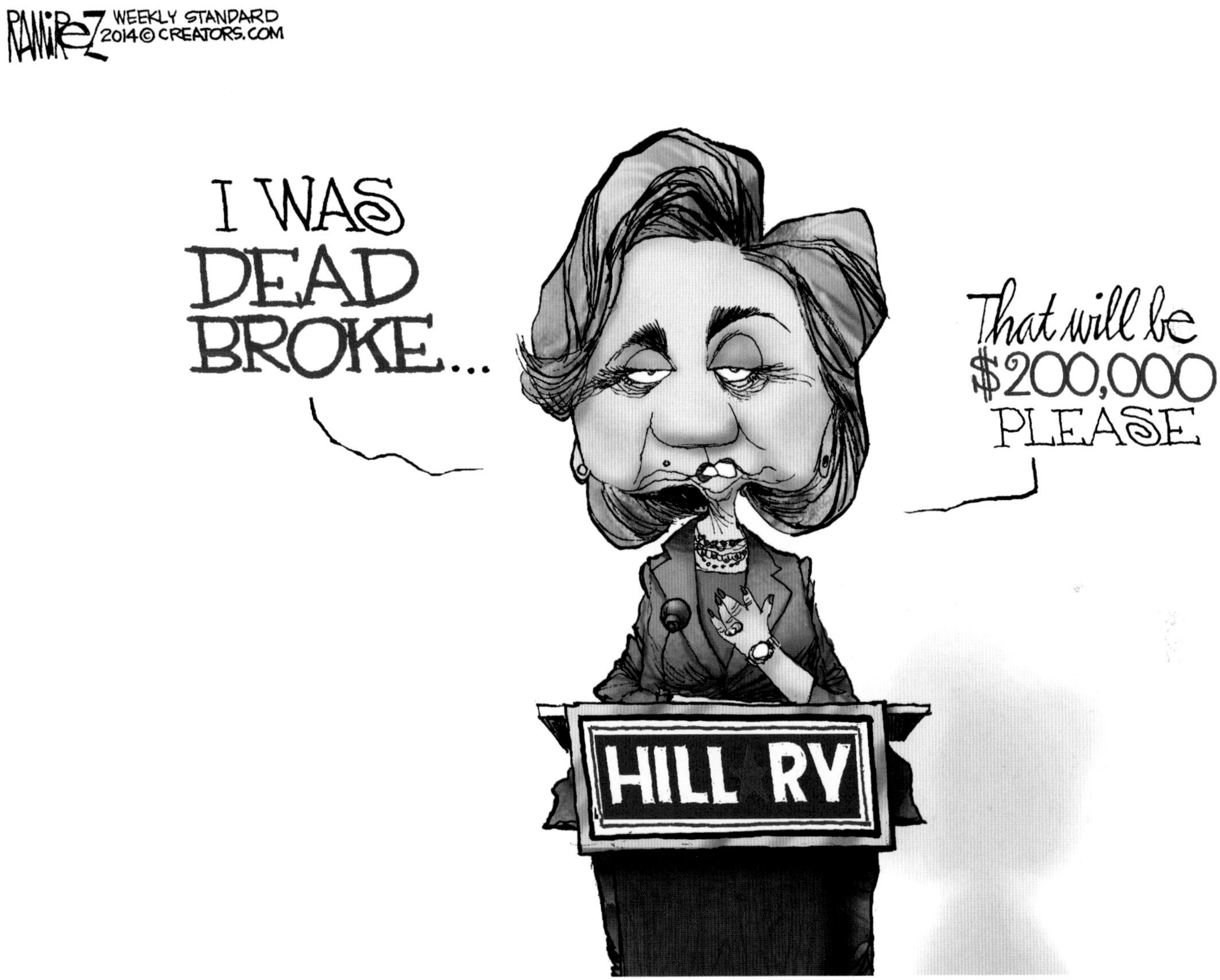
RAMIREZ WEEKLY STANDARD 2014 © CREATORS.COM
I WAS DEAD BROKE...
That will be $200,000 PLEASE
HILL RY

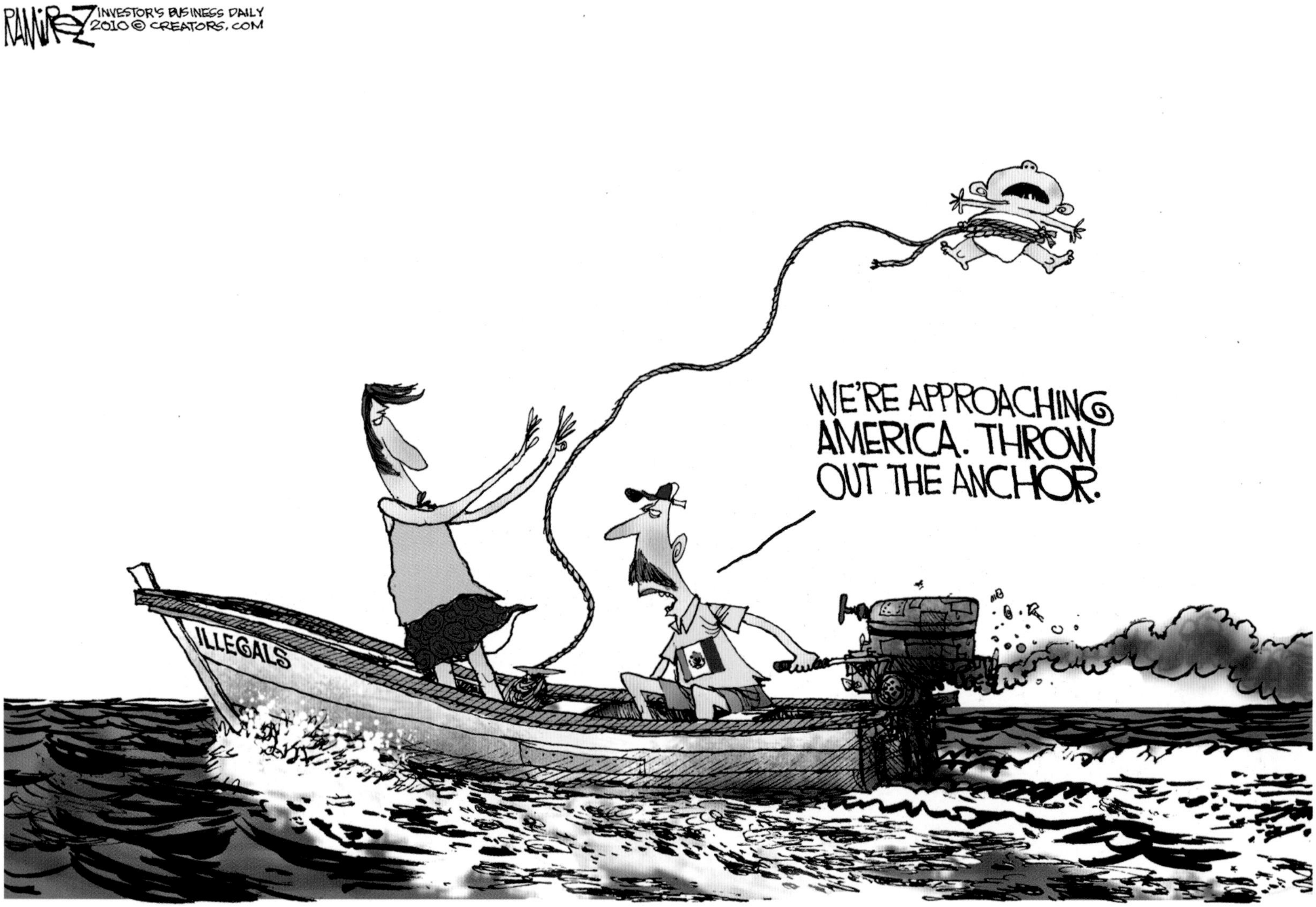
RAMIREZ INVESTOR'S BUSINESS DAILY 2010 © CREATORS.COM
WE'RE APPROACHING AMERICA. THROW OUT THE ANCHOR.
ILLEGALS

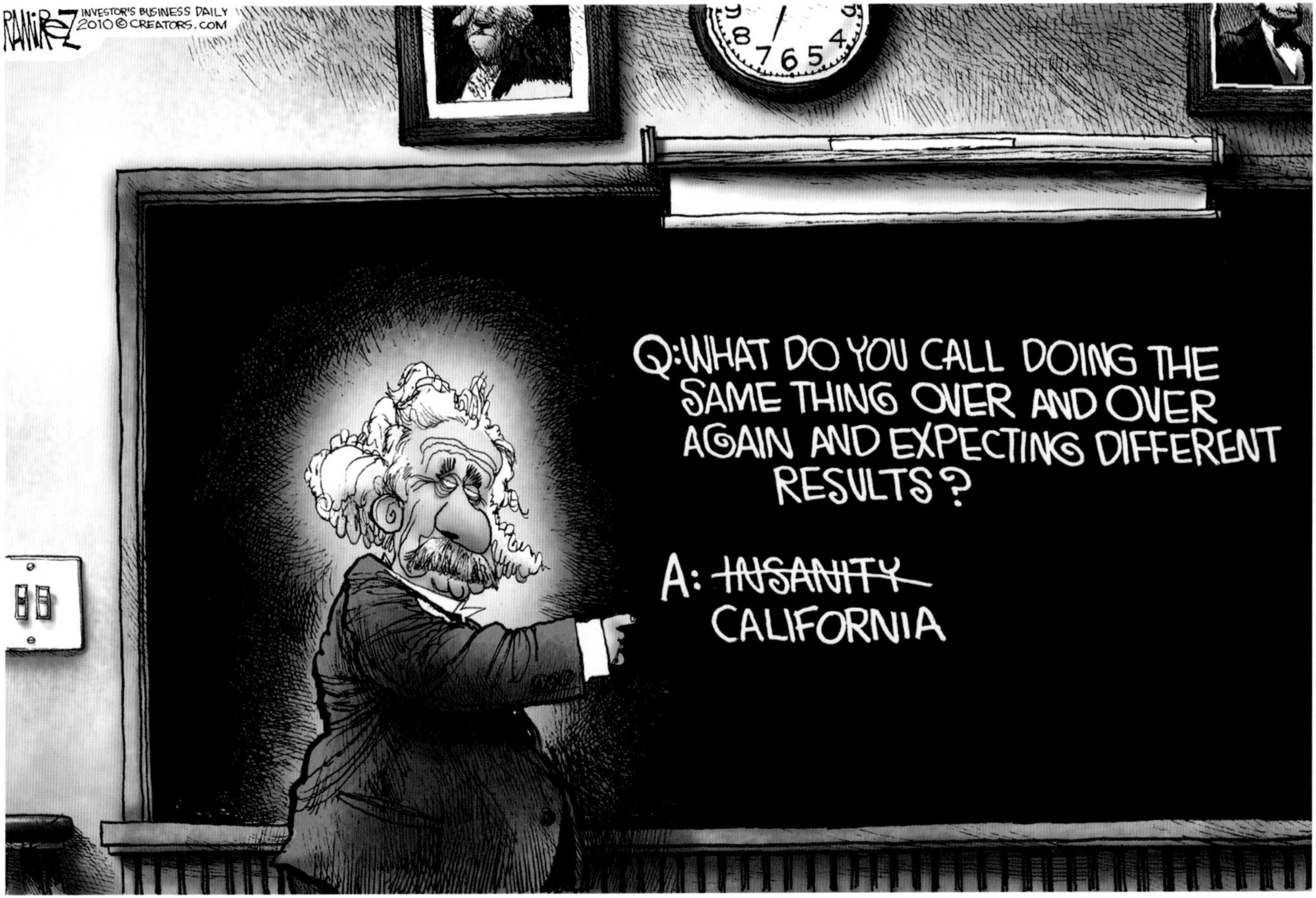
RAMIREZ
INVESTOR'S BUSINESS DAILY 2010 © CREATORS.COM
Q: WHAT DO YOU CALL DOING THE SAME THING OVER AND OVER AGAIN AND EXPECTING DIFFERENT RESULTS?
A: ~~INSANITY~~ CALIFORNIA

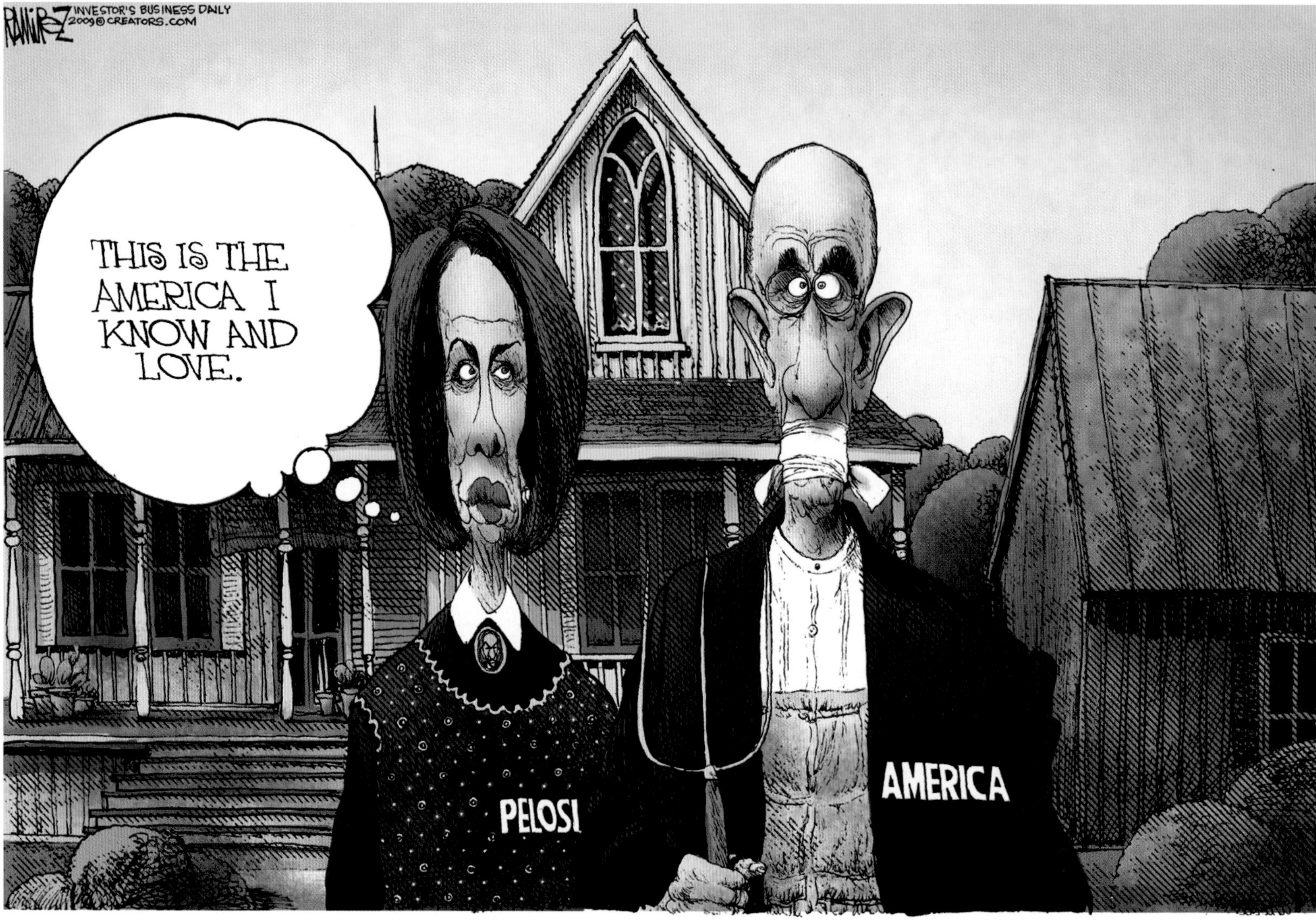
RAMIREZ INVESTOR'S BUSINESS DAILY
2009 © CREATORS.COM
THIS IS THE AMERICA I KNOW AND LOVE.
PELOSI
AMERICA
AMERICAN BOLSHEVIK

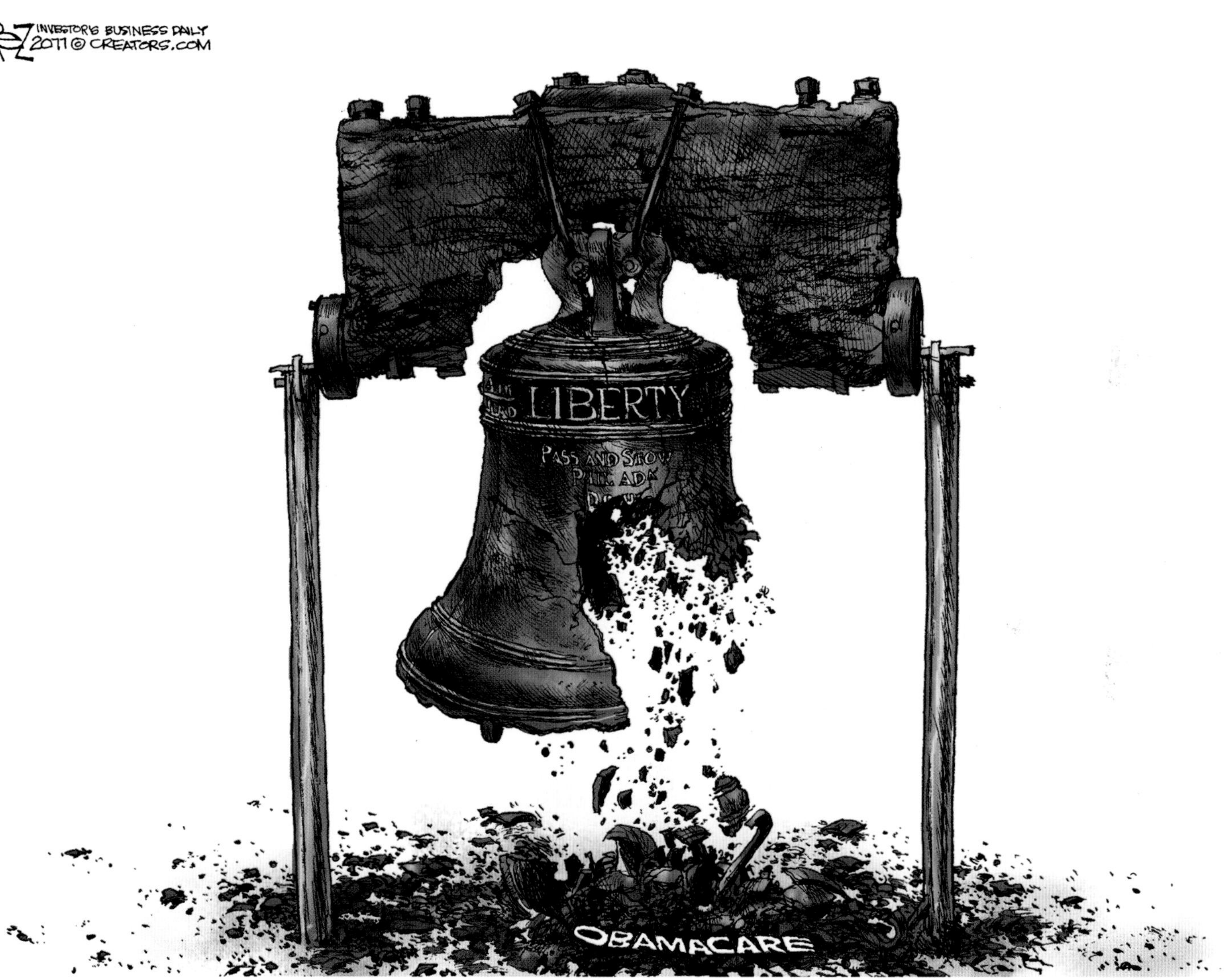

RAMIREZ
INVESTOR'S BUSINESS DAILY
2011 © CREATORS.COM
LIBERTY
PASS AND STOW
OBAMACARE

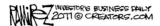

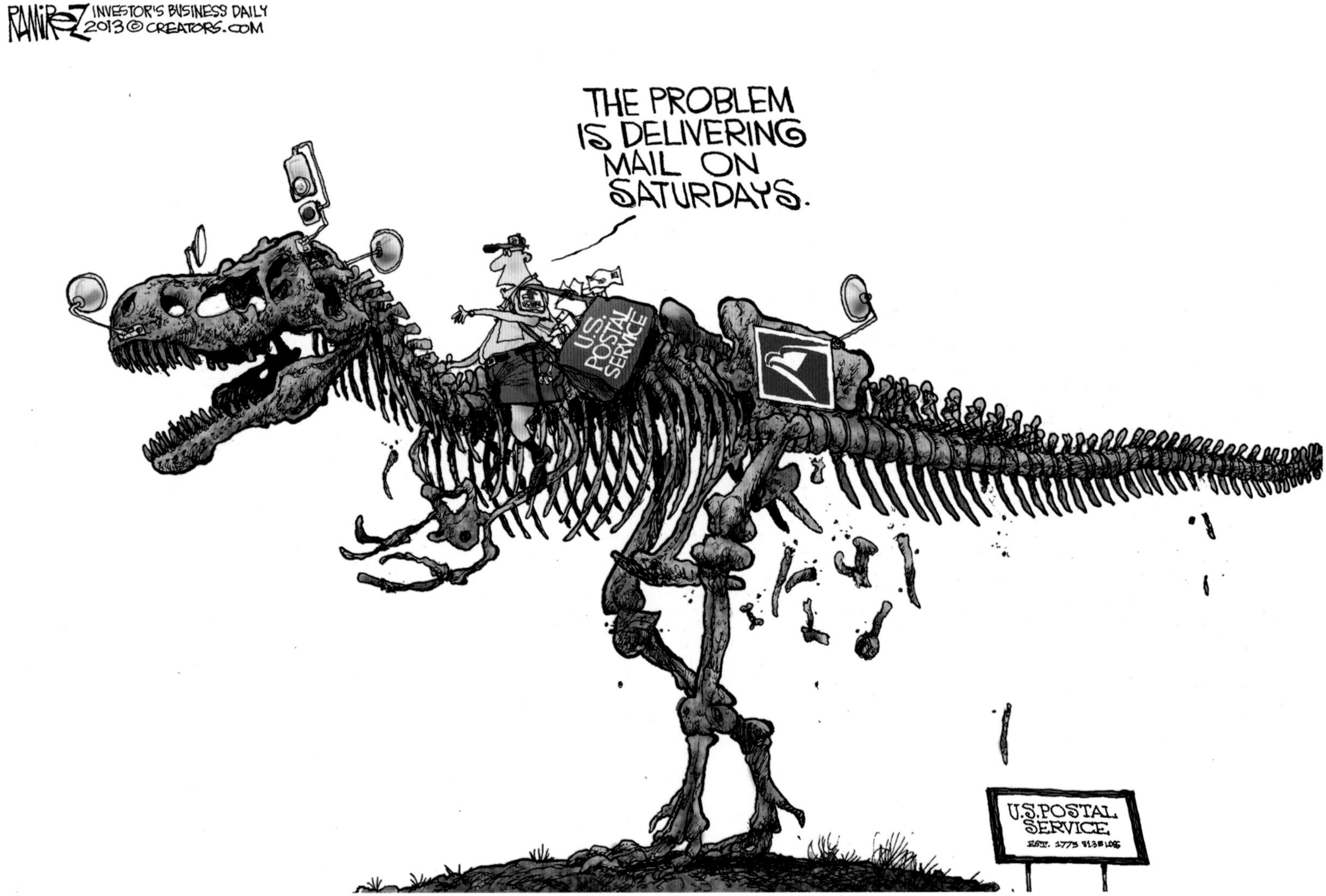
RAMIREZ
INVESTOR'S BUSINESS DAILY
2013 © CREATORS.COM
THE PROBLEM IS DELIVERING MAIL ON SATURDAYS.
U.S. POSTAL SERVICE
U.S.POSTAL SERVICE
EST. 1775 $13B LOSS

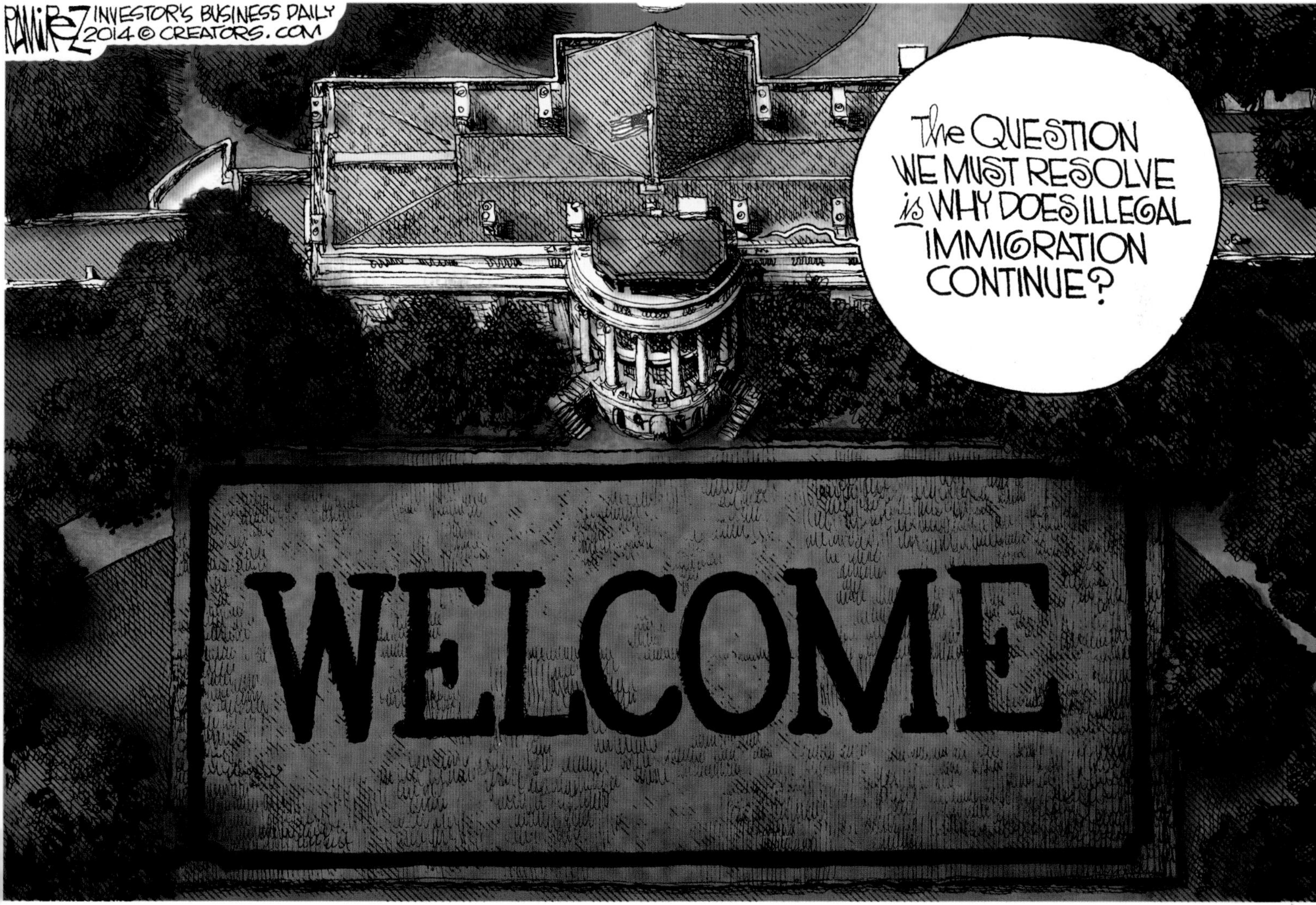
RAMIREZ INVESTOR'S BUSINESS DAILY
2014 © CREATORS.COM
The QUESTION WE MUST RESOLVE is WHY DOES ILLEGAL IMMIGRATION CONTINUE?
WELCOME

www.investors.com/cartoons

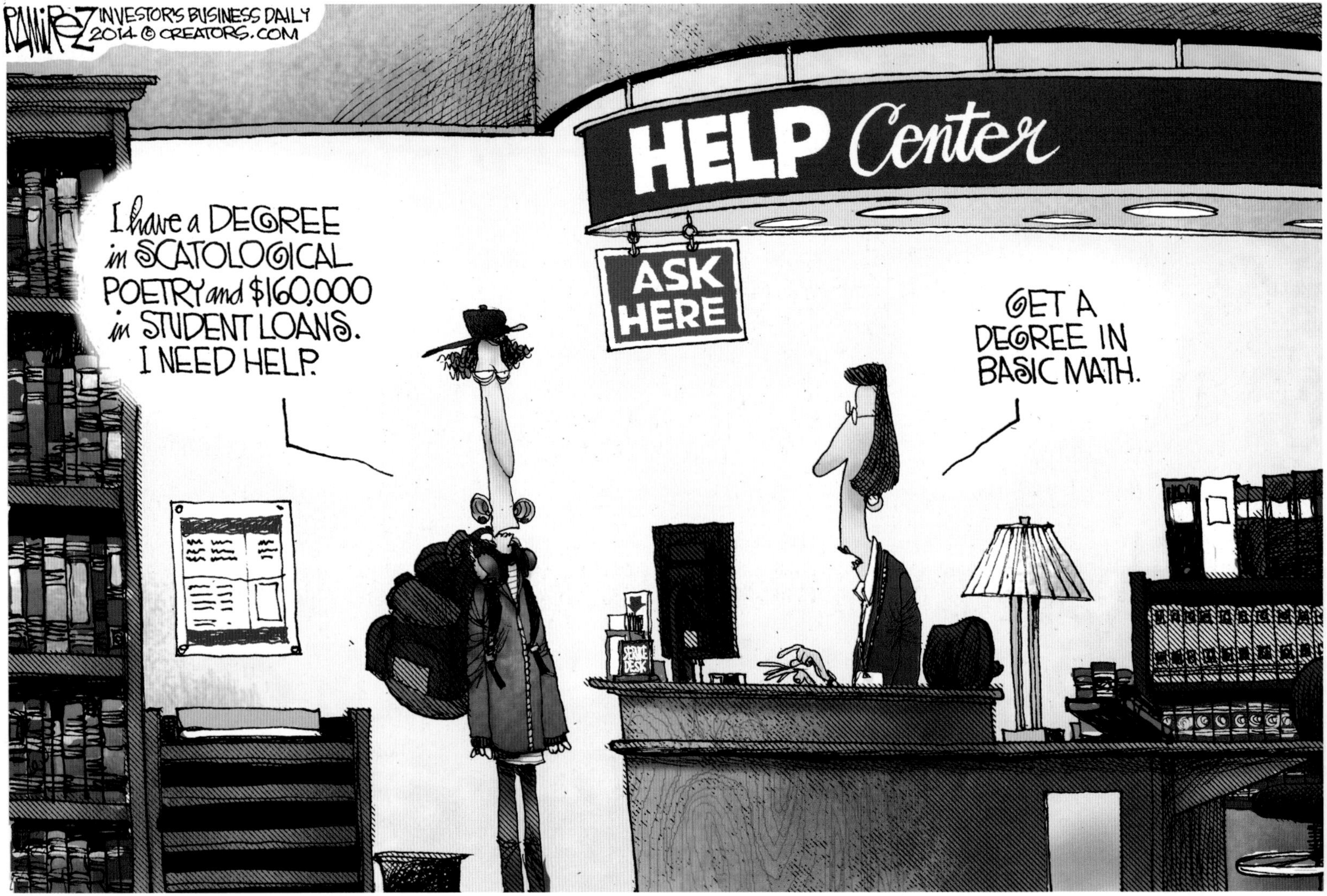
RAMIREZ INVESTOR'S BUSINESS DAILY 2014 © CREATORS.COM
HELP Center
ASK HERE
I have a DEGREE in SCATOLOGICAL POETRY and $160,000 in STUDENT LOANS. I NEED HELP.
GET A DEGREE IN BASIC MATH.
SERVICE DESK

www.investors.com/cartoons

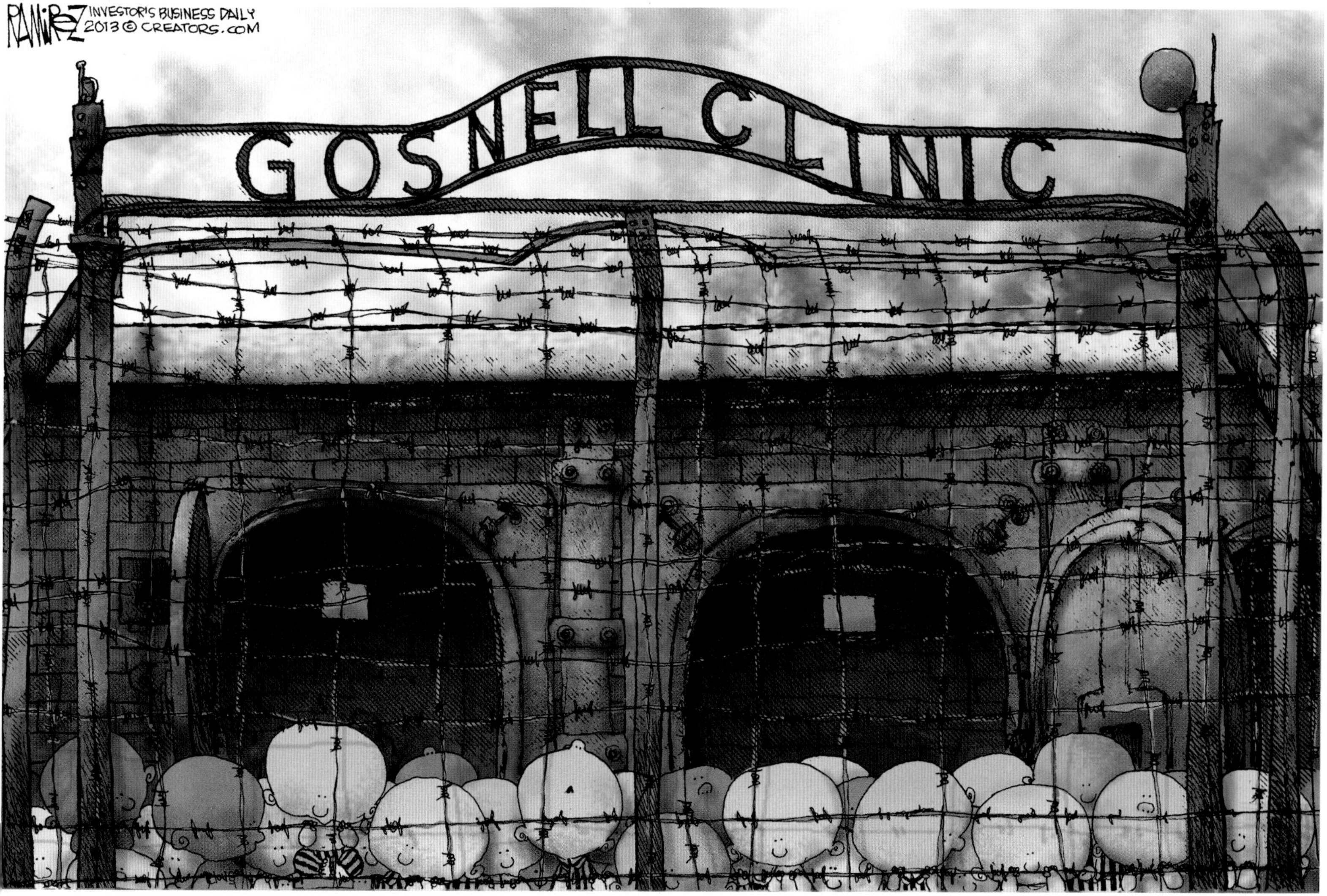
RAMIREZ INVESTOR'S BUSINESS DAILY 2013 © CREATORS.COM
GOSNELL CLINIC
NEVER AGAIN.

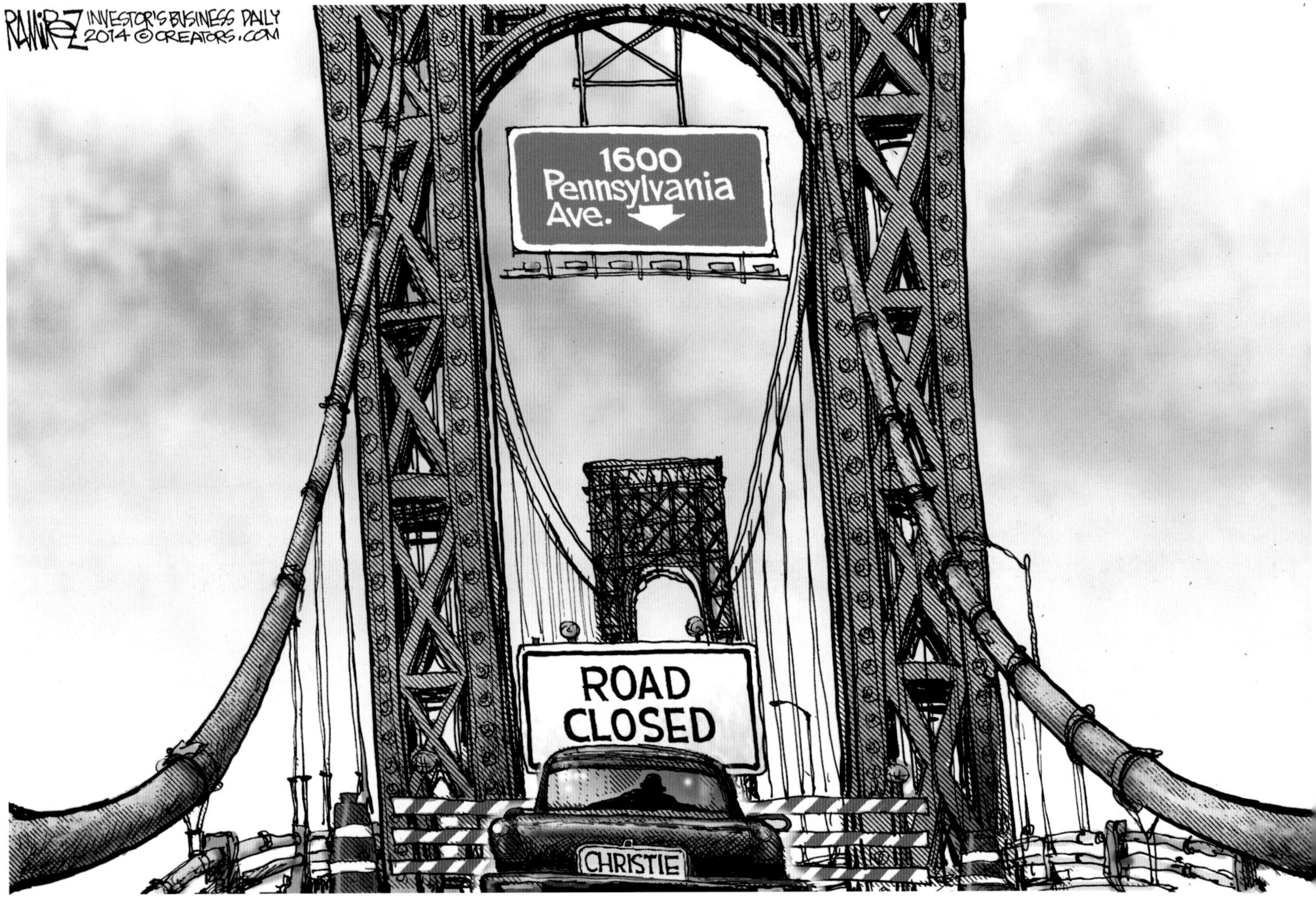
RAMIREZ INVESTOR'S BUSINESS DAILY
2014 © CREATORS.COM
1600
Pennsylvania
Ave.
ROAD
CLOSED
CHRISTIE

OBAMANOMICS

"If you've got a business—you didn't build that. Somebody else made that happen."

—President Barack Obama,
Roanoke, Virginia, July 13, 2012

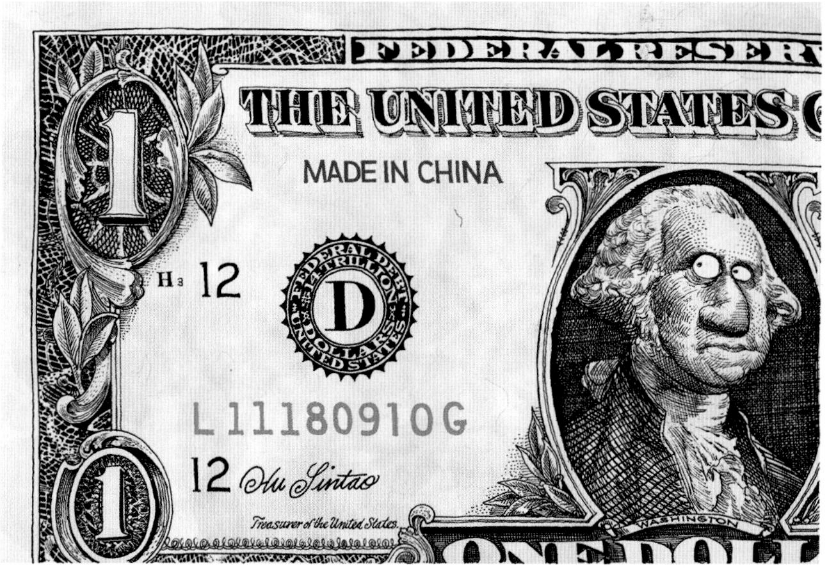

FEDERAL RESERV
THE UNITED STATES
MADE IN CHINA
H3 12
FEDERAL DEBT
TRILLION
D
DOLLARS
UNITED STATES
L11180910G
12
Hu Jintao
Treasurer of the United States
WASHINGTON

A strange mix of Keynesian theory, wishful thinking, and economic illiteracy, coupled with socialism and sprinkled with social justice, was the Obama administration's answer to capitalism. President Obama took the tail end of an economic downturn and turned it into the Great Recession and produced the slowest economic recovery in history.

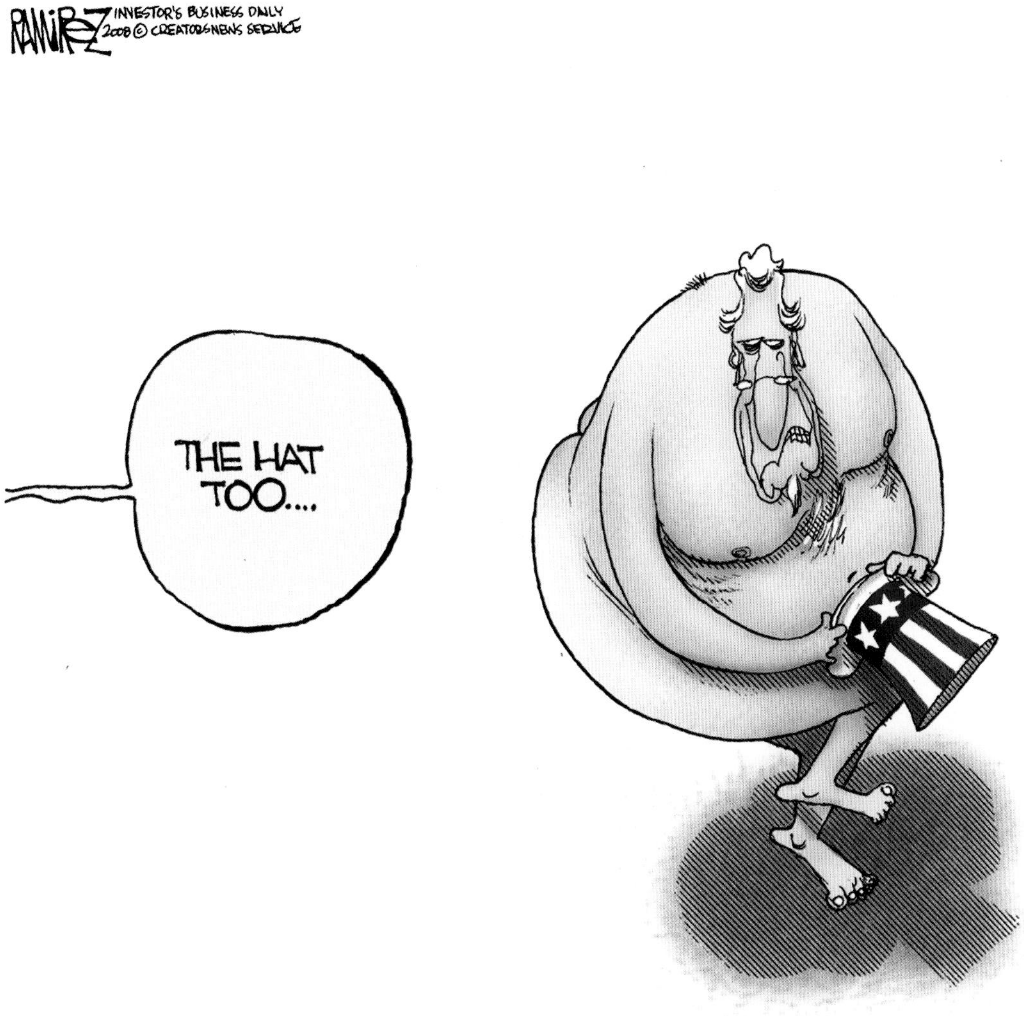
RAMIREZ INVESTOR'S BUSINESS DAILY 2008 © CREATORS NEWS SERVICE
THE HAT TOO....
THE BARE MARKET.

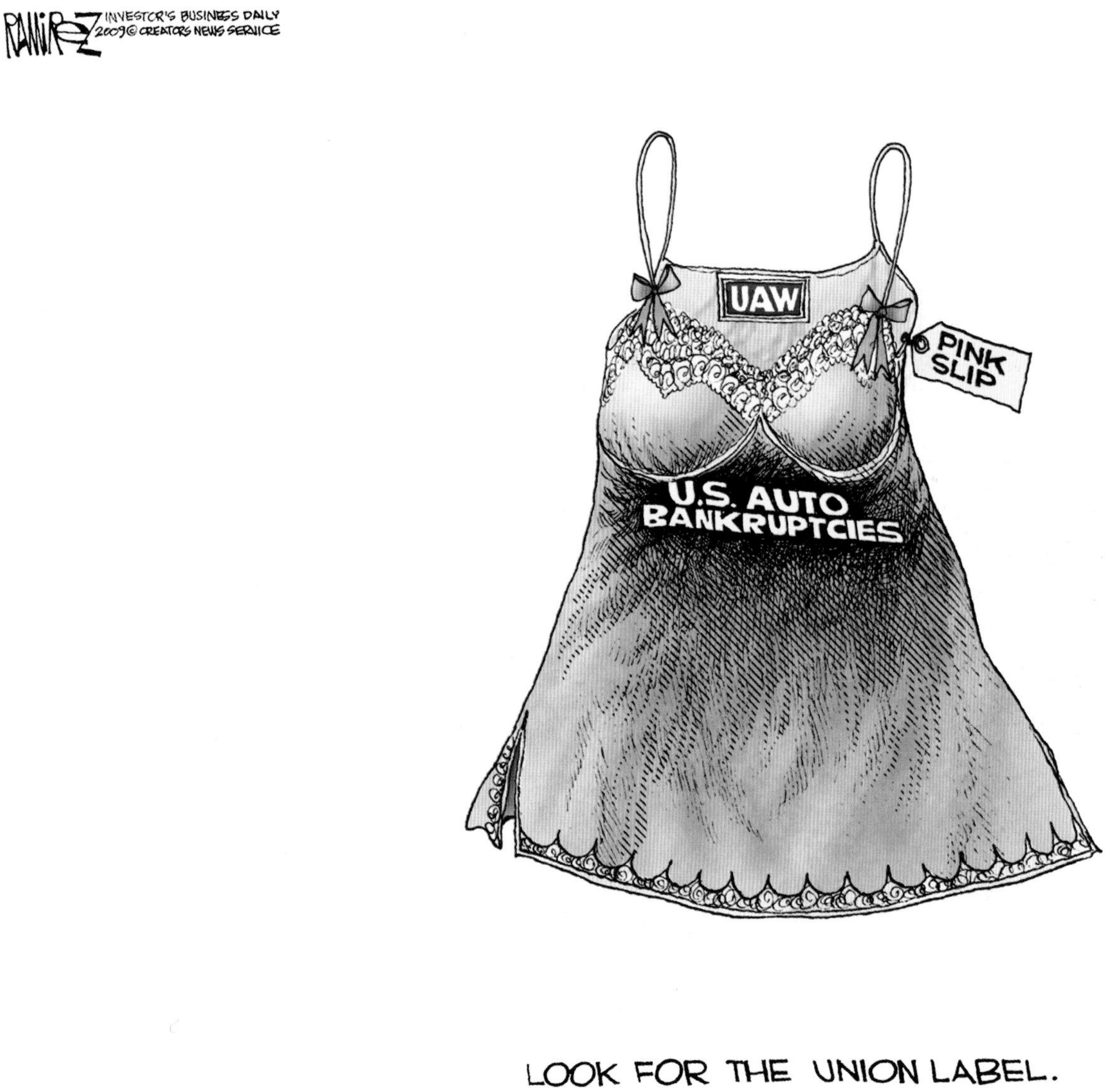
RAMIREZ INVESTOR'S BUSINESS DAILY 2009 © CREATORS NEWS SERVICE
UAW
PINK SLIP
U.S. AUTO BANKRUPTCIES
LOOK FOR THE UNION LABEL.

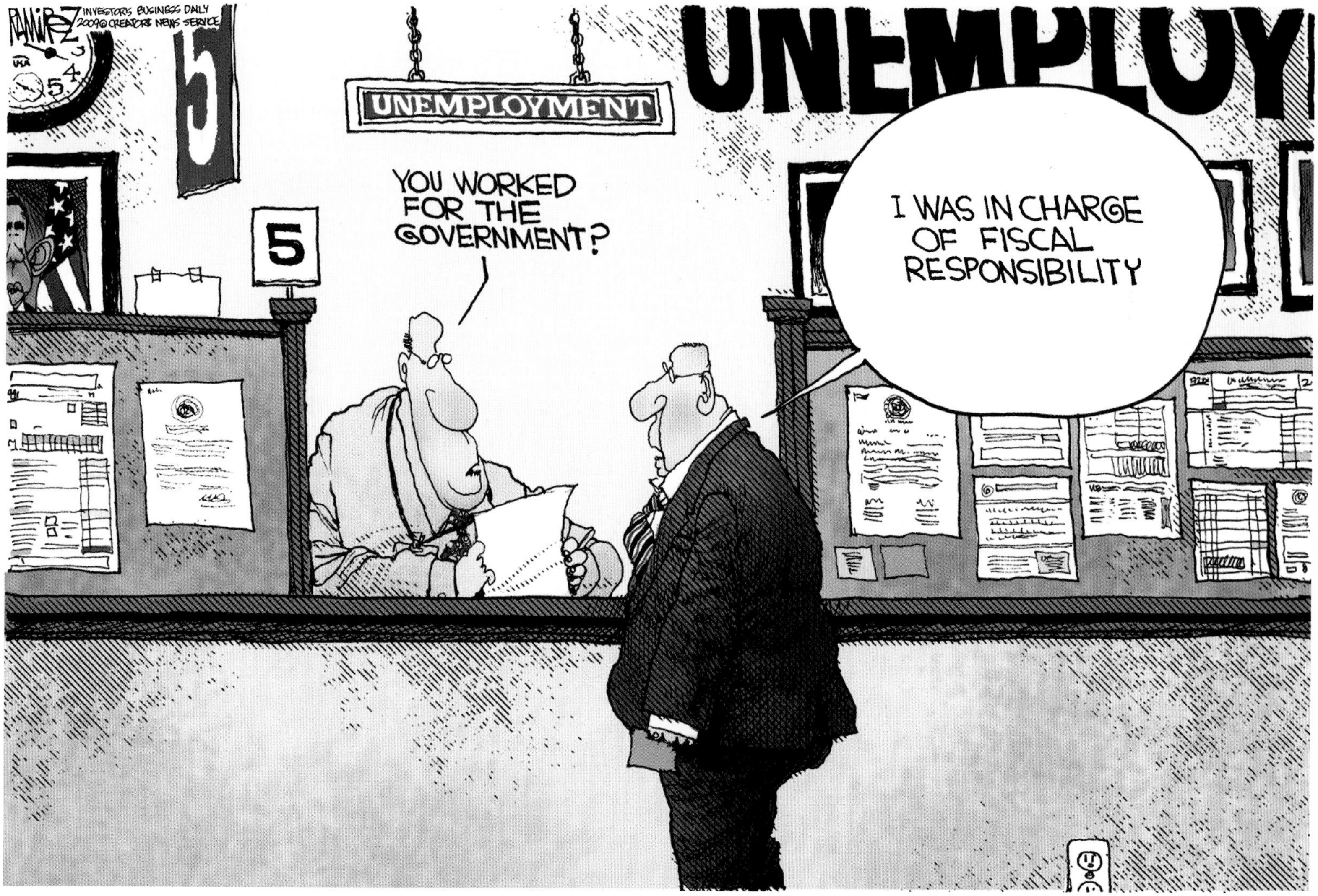
RAMIREZ INVESTOR'S BUSINESS DAILY 2009© CREATORS NEWS SERVICE
UNEMPLOYMENT
UNEMPLOY
5
YOU WORKED FOR THE GOVERNMENT?
I WAS IN CHARGE OF FISCAL RESPONSIBILITY

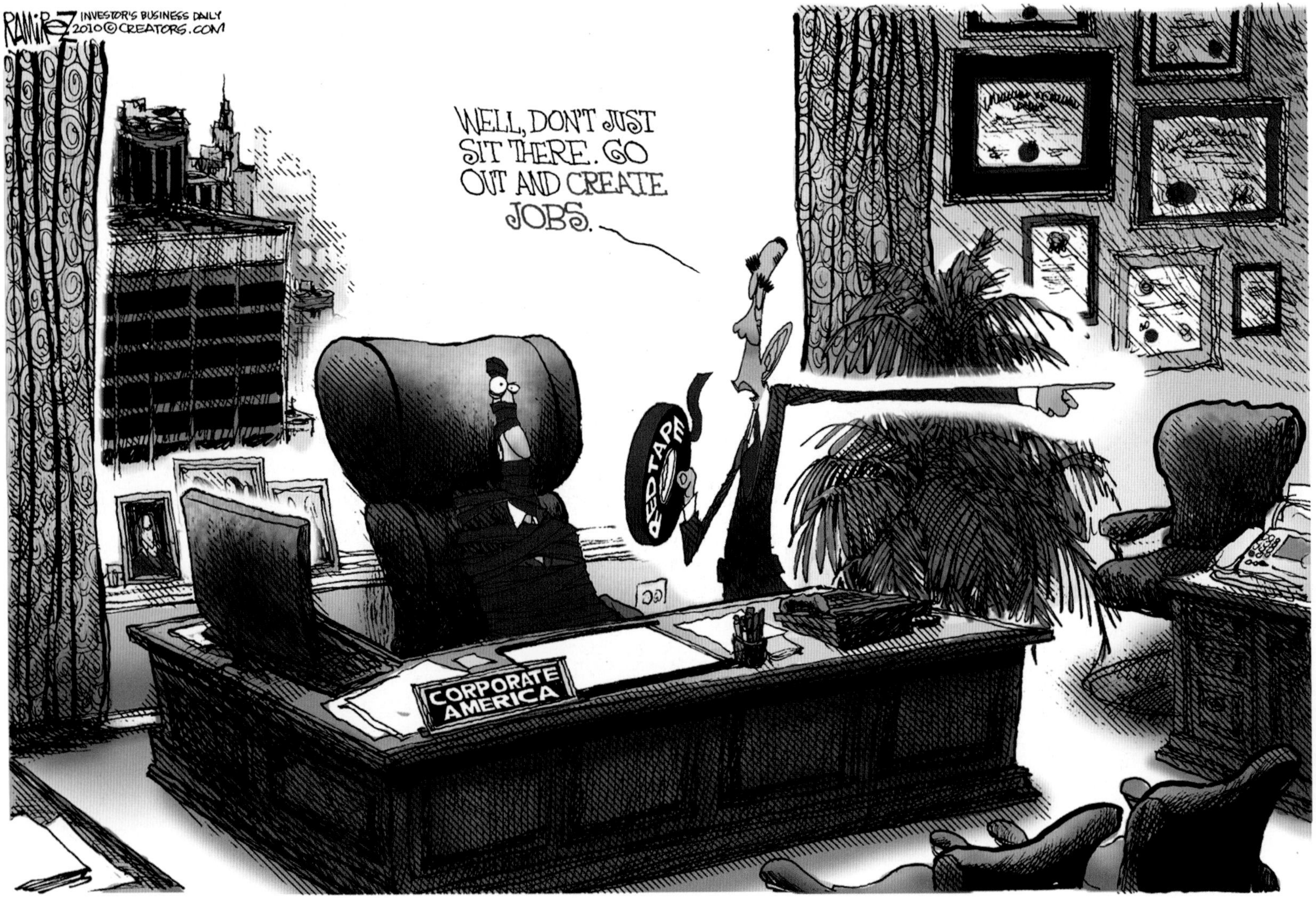
RAMIREZ INVESTOR'S BUSINESS DAILY 2010 © CREATORS.COM
WELL, DON'T JUST SIT THERE. GO OUT AND CREATE JOBS.
RED TAPE
CORPORATE AMERICA

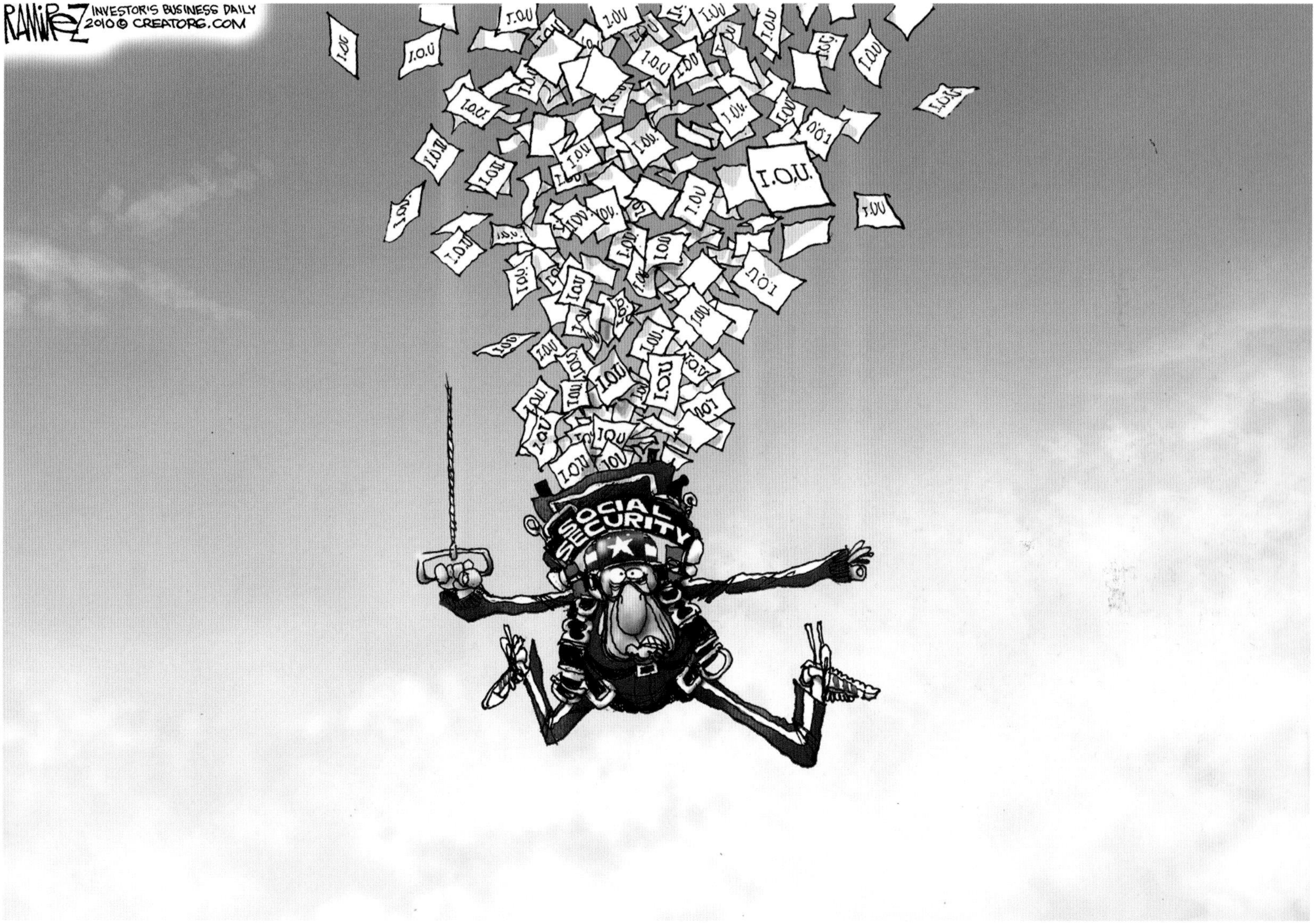
RAMIREZ INVESTOR'S BUSINESS DAILY 2010 © CREATORS.COM
SOCIAL SECURITY
I.O.U.

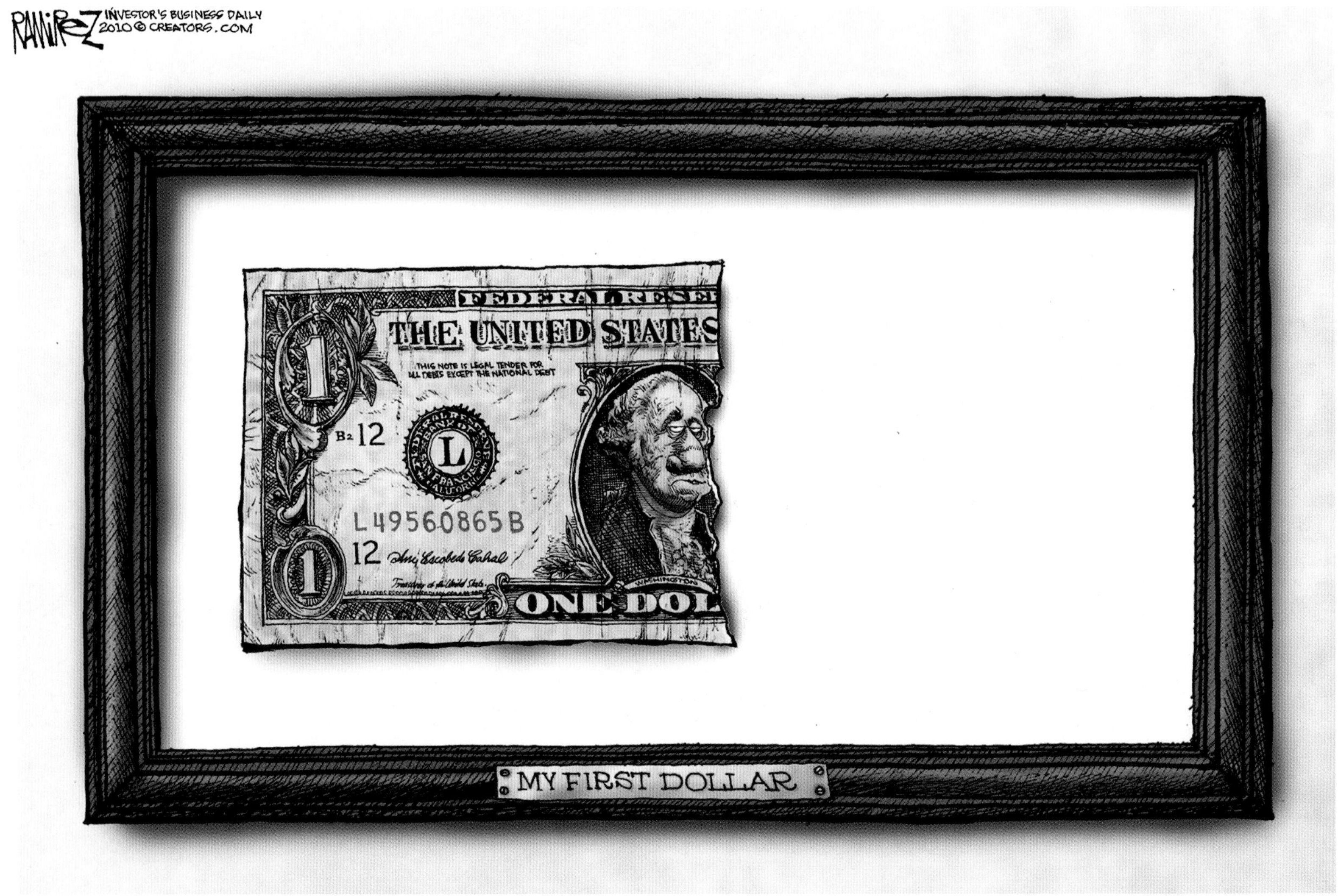
RAMIREZ
INVESTOR'S BUSINESS DAILY
2010 © CREATORS.COM
THE UNITED STATES
THIS NOTE IS LEGAL TENDER FOR ALL DEBTS EXCEPT THE NATIONAL DEBT
B2 12
L
L49560865B
12
ONE DOL
MY FIRST DOLLAR

QUANTITATIVE EASING

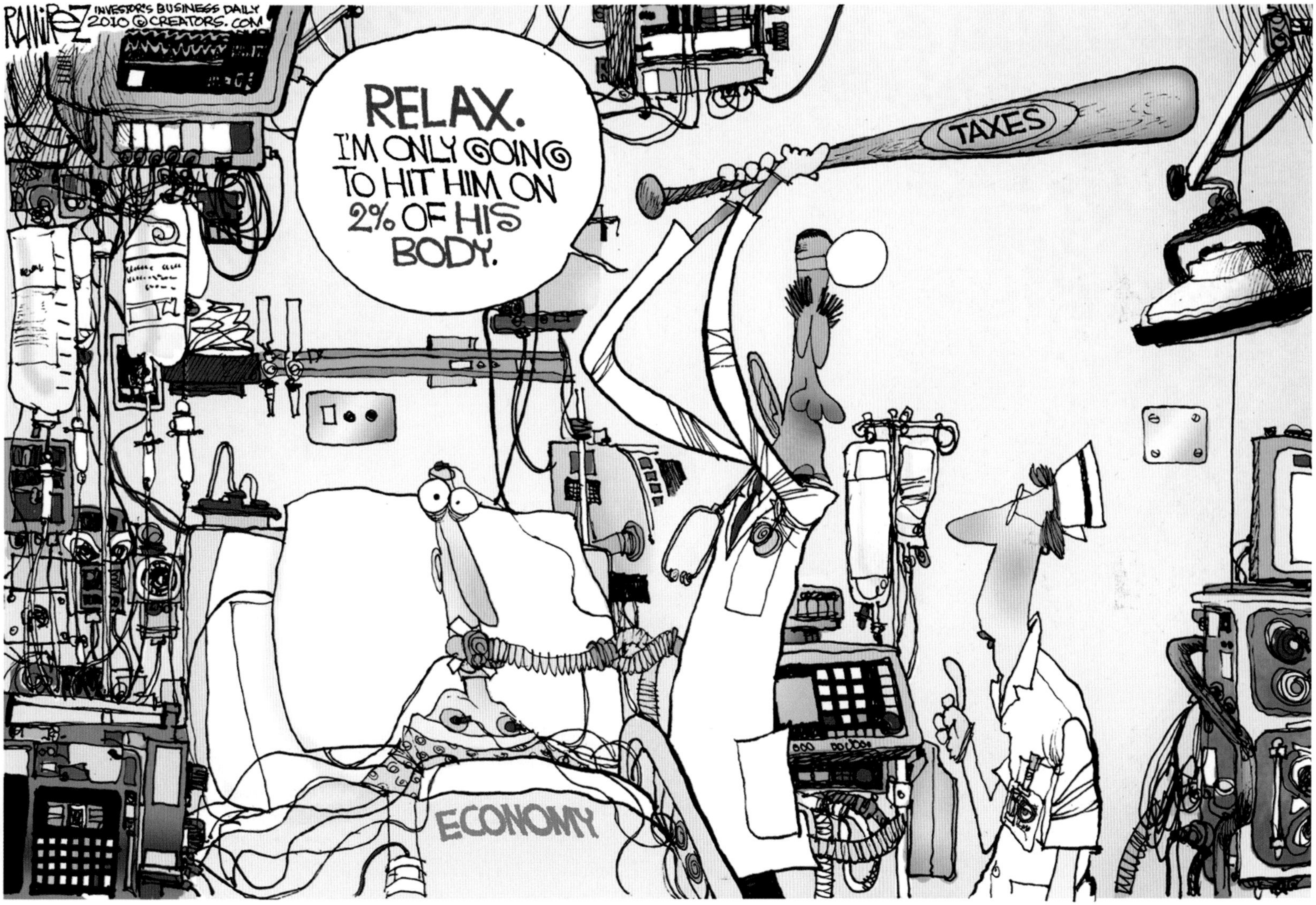
RAMIREZ INVESTOR'S BUSINESS DAILY 2010 © CREATORS.COM
RELAX. I'M ONLY GOING TO HIT HIM ON 2% OF HIS BODY.
TAXES
ECONOMY

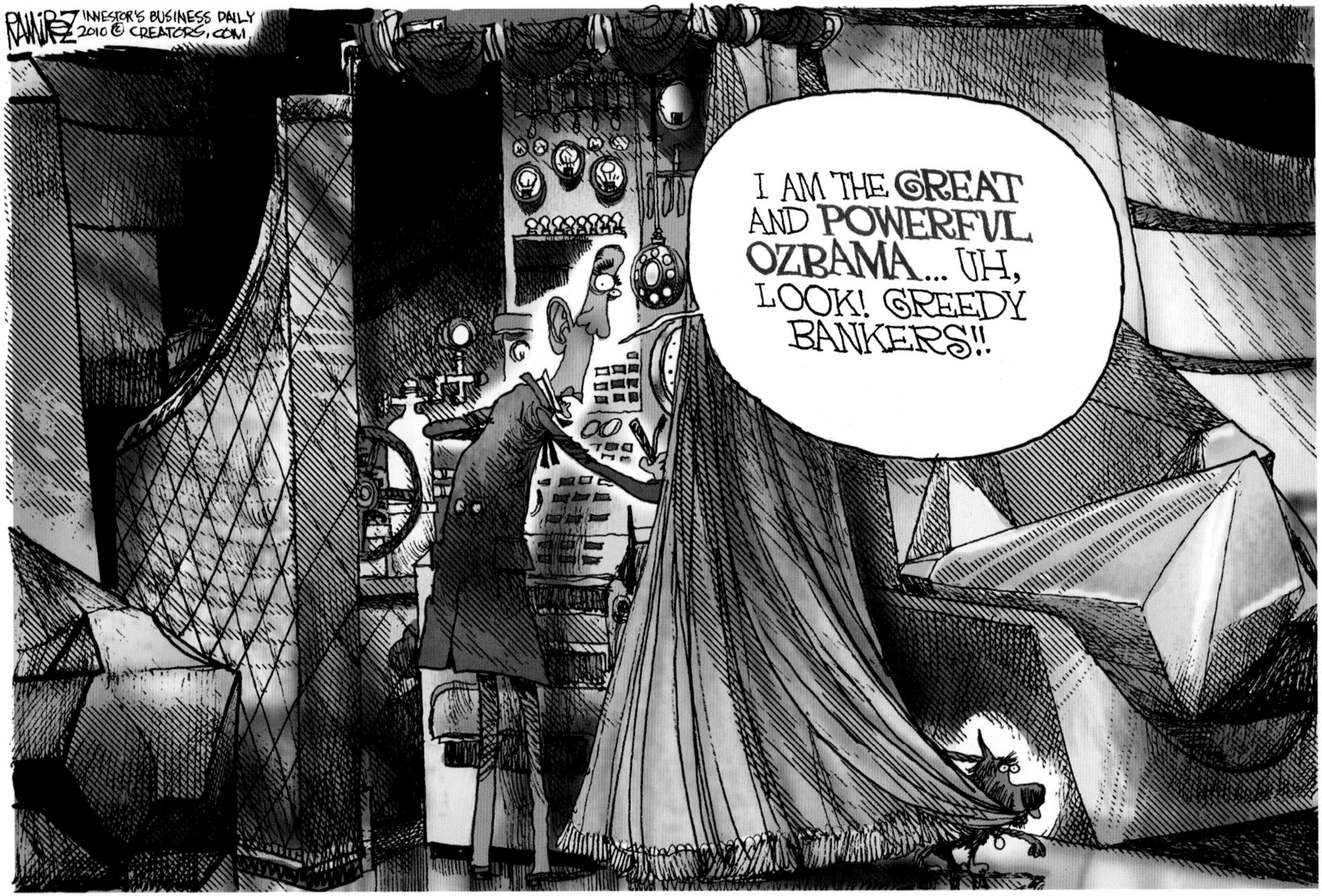
RAMIREZ INVESTOR'S BUSINESS DAILY 2010 © CREATORS.COM
I AM THE GREAT AND POWERFUL OZBAMA... UH, LOOK! GREEDY BANKERS!!

PULLING THE CURTAIN BACK ON THE WIZARD.

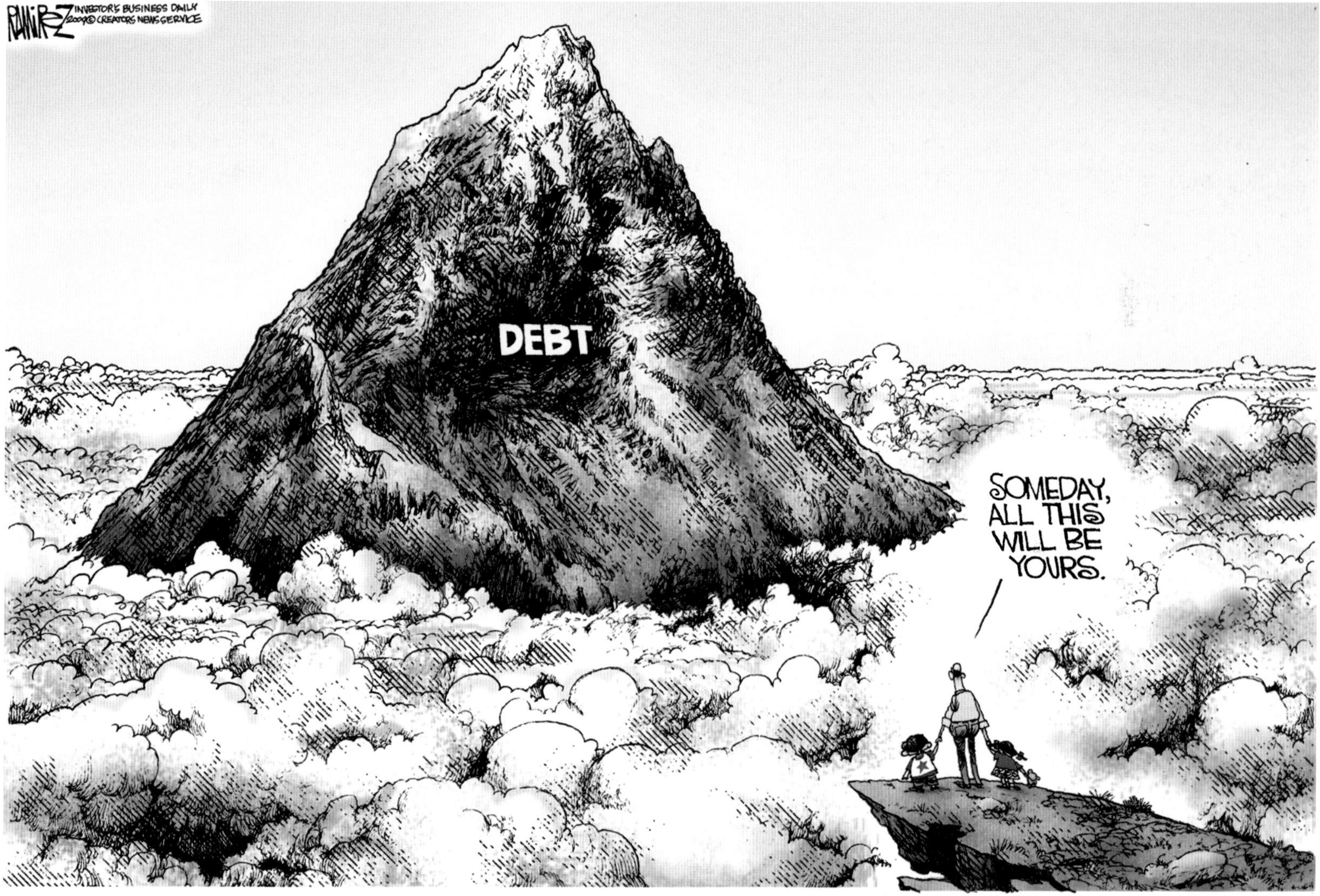
RAMIREZ INVESTOR'S BUSINESS DAILY ©2009 CREATORS NEWS SERVICE
DEBT
SOMEDAY, ALL THIS WILL BE YOURS.

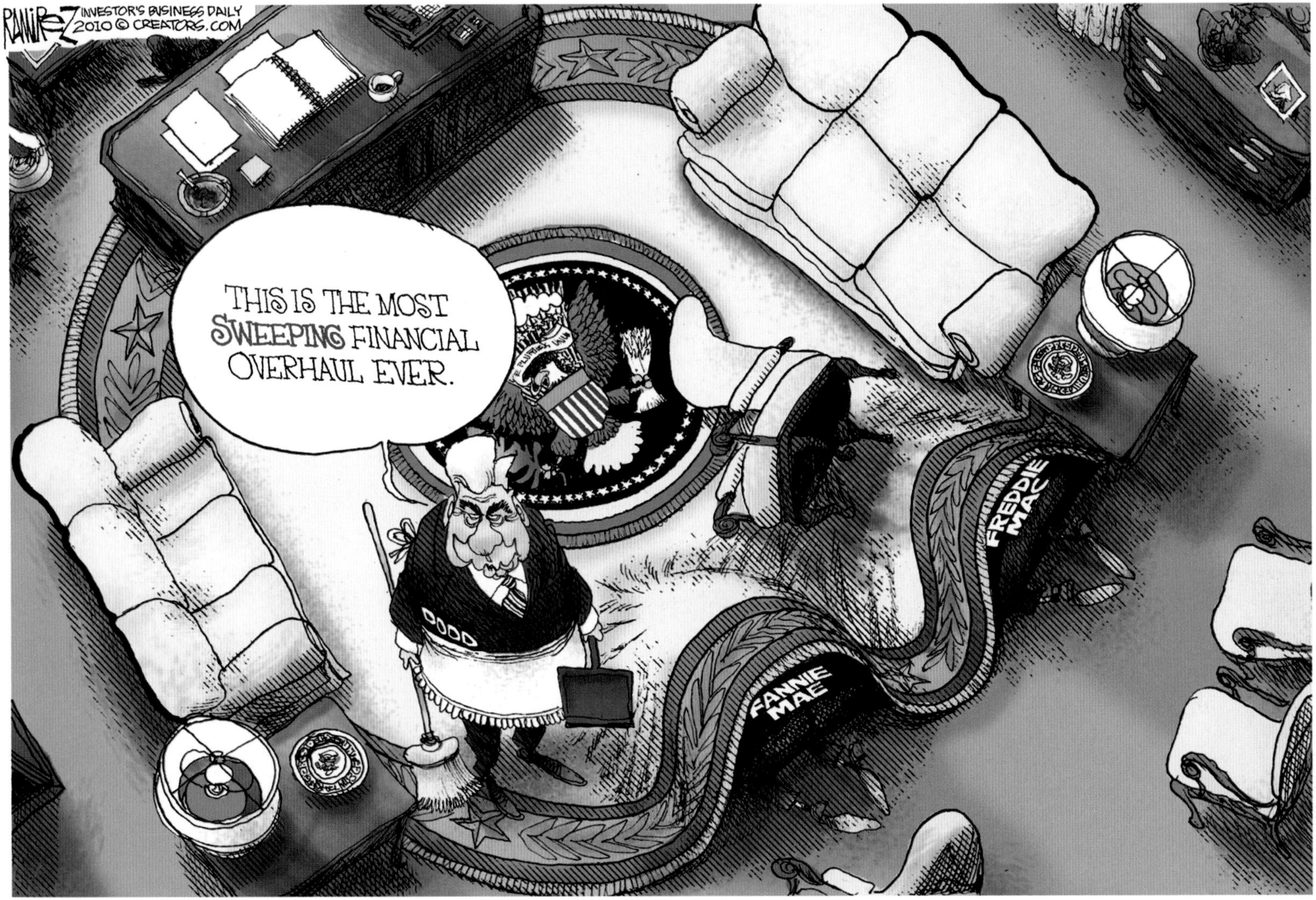
RAMIREZ INVESTOR'S BUSINESS DAILY 2010 © CREATORS.COM
THIS IS THE MOST SWEEPING FINANCIAL OVERHAUL EVER.
DODD
FREDDIE MAC
FANNIE MAE

SWEPT

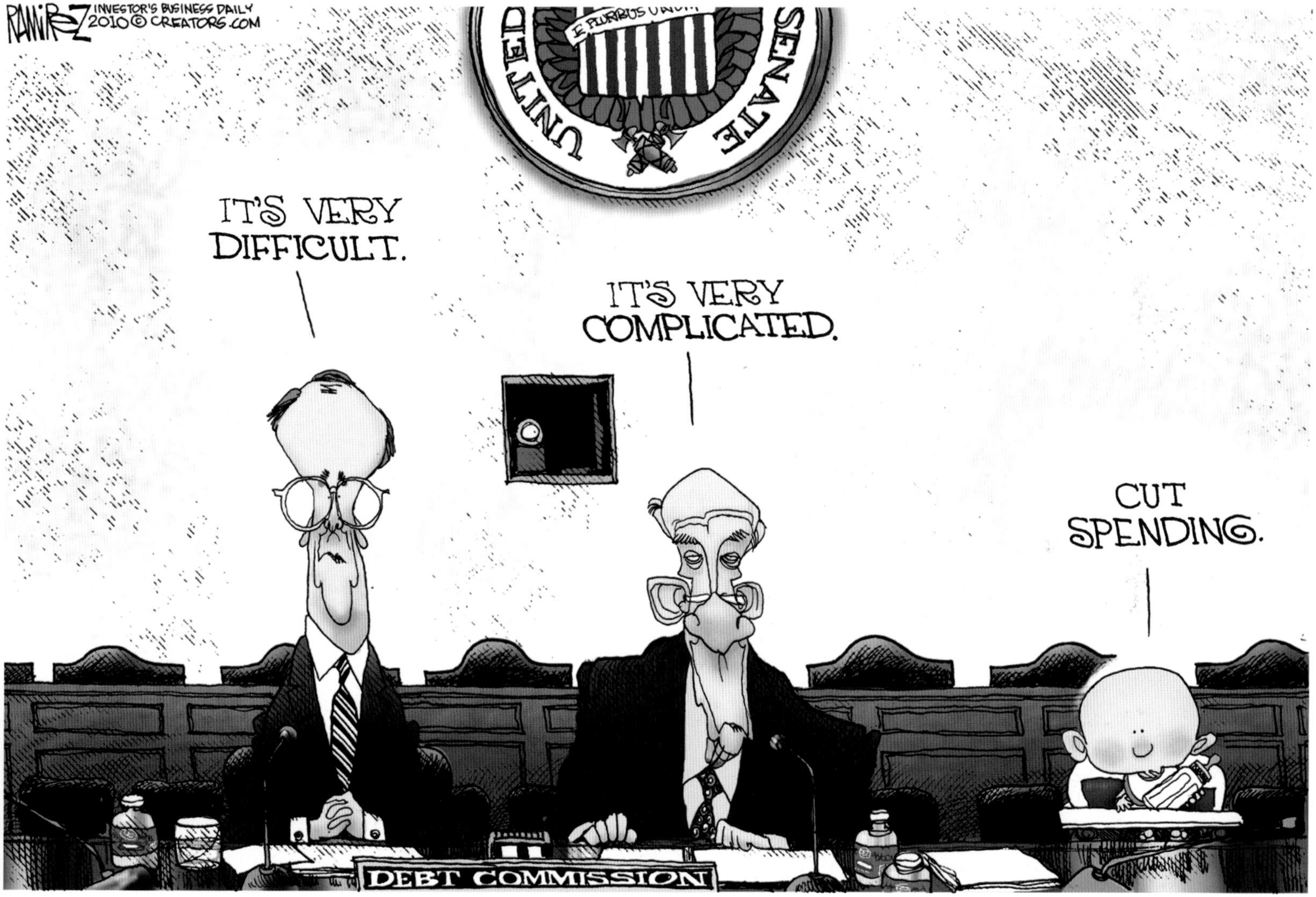
RAMIREZ INVESTOR'S BUSINESS DAILY 2010 © CREATORS.COM
E PLURIBUS UNUM
UNITED SENATE
IT'S VERY DIFFICULT.
IT'S VERY COMPLICATED.
CUT SPENDING.
DEBT COMMISSION

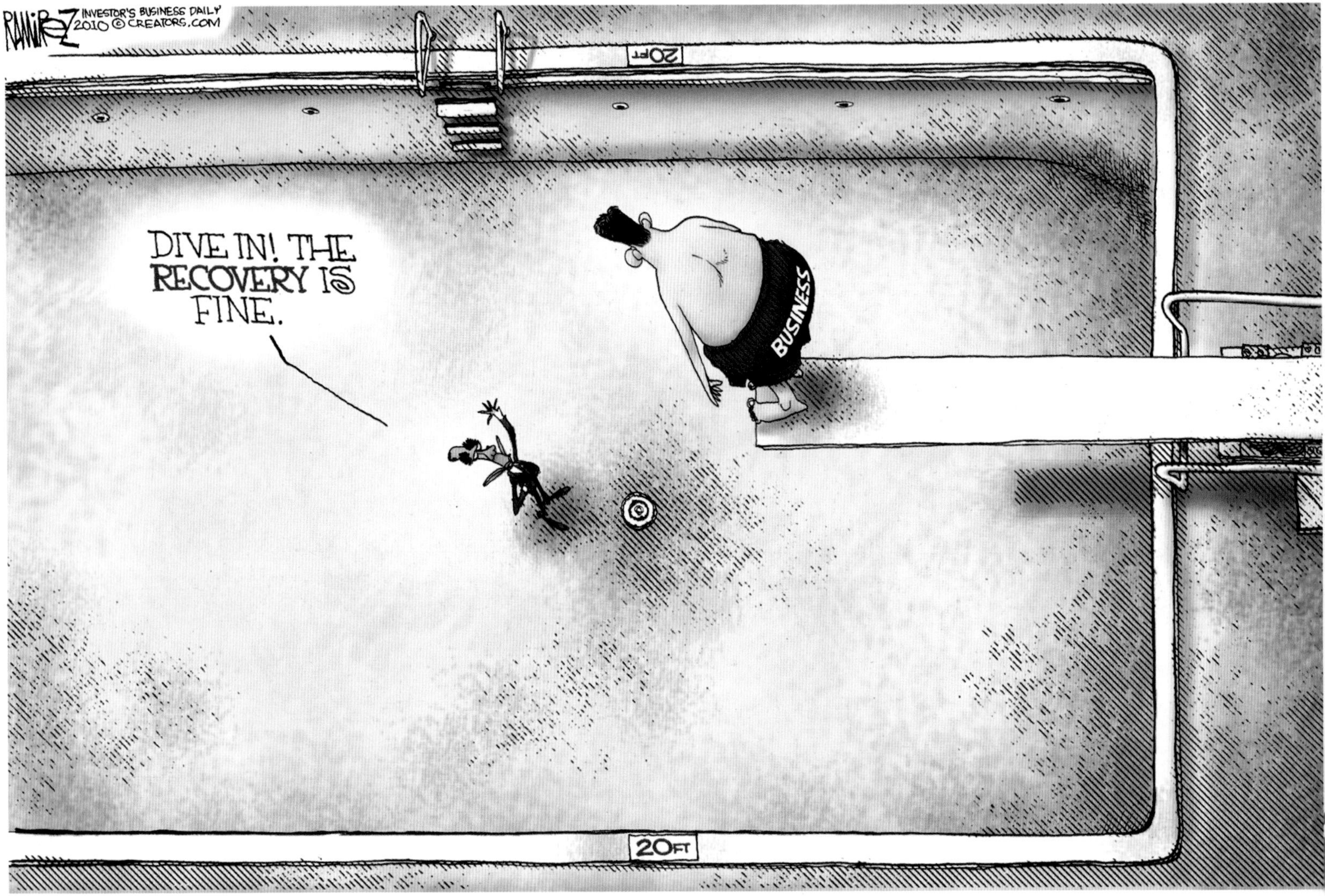
RAMIREZ INVESTOR'S BUSINESS DAILY 2010 © CREATORS.COM
20FT
DIVE IN! THE RECOVERY IS FINE.
BUSINESS
20FT

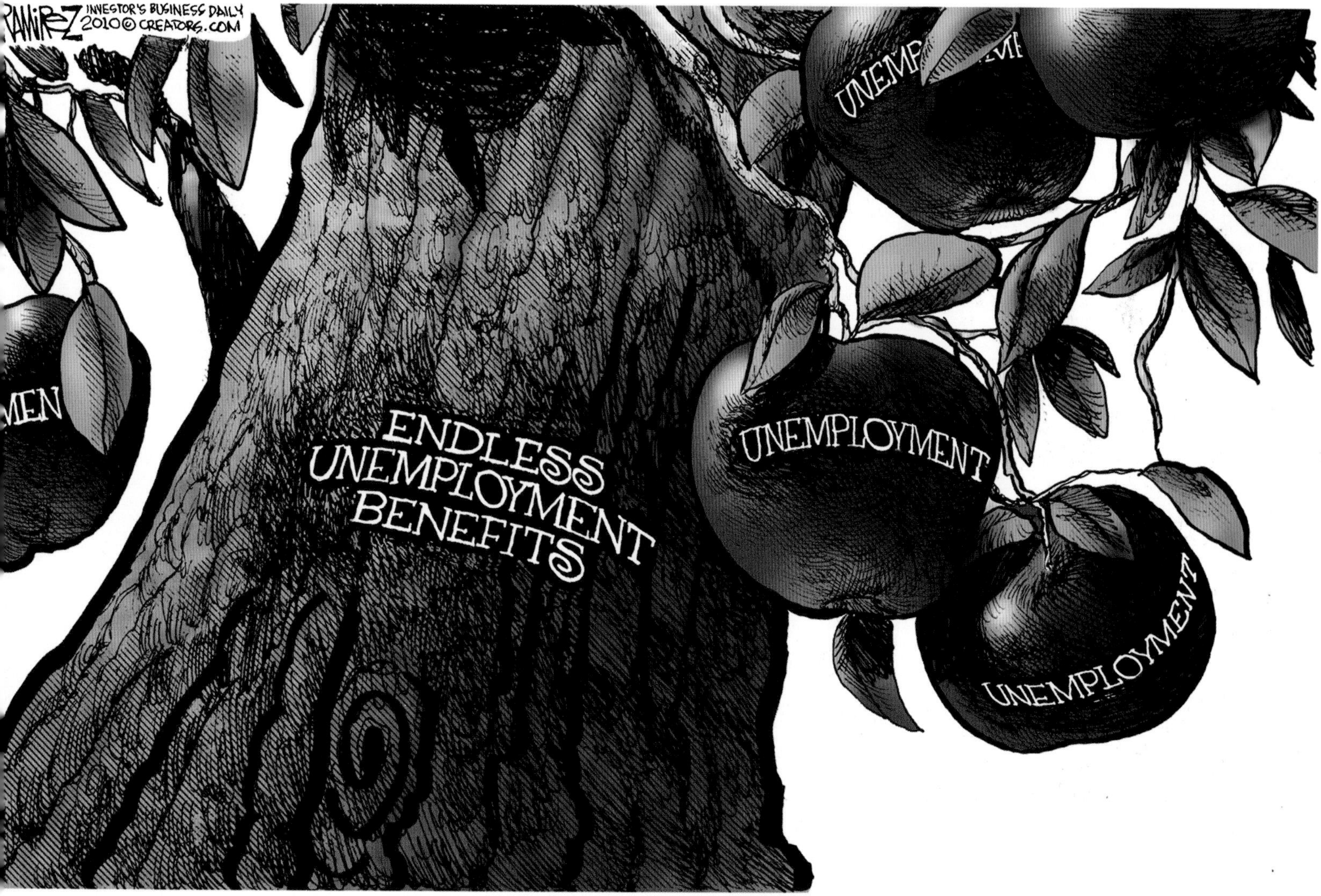
RAMIREZ INVESTOR'S BUSINESS DAILY 2010© CREATORS.COM
ENDLESS UNEMPLOYMENT BENEFITS
UNEMPLOYMENT
UNEMPLOYMENT
MEN

BEARING FRUIT

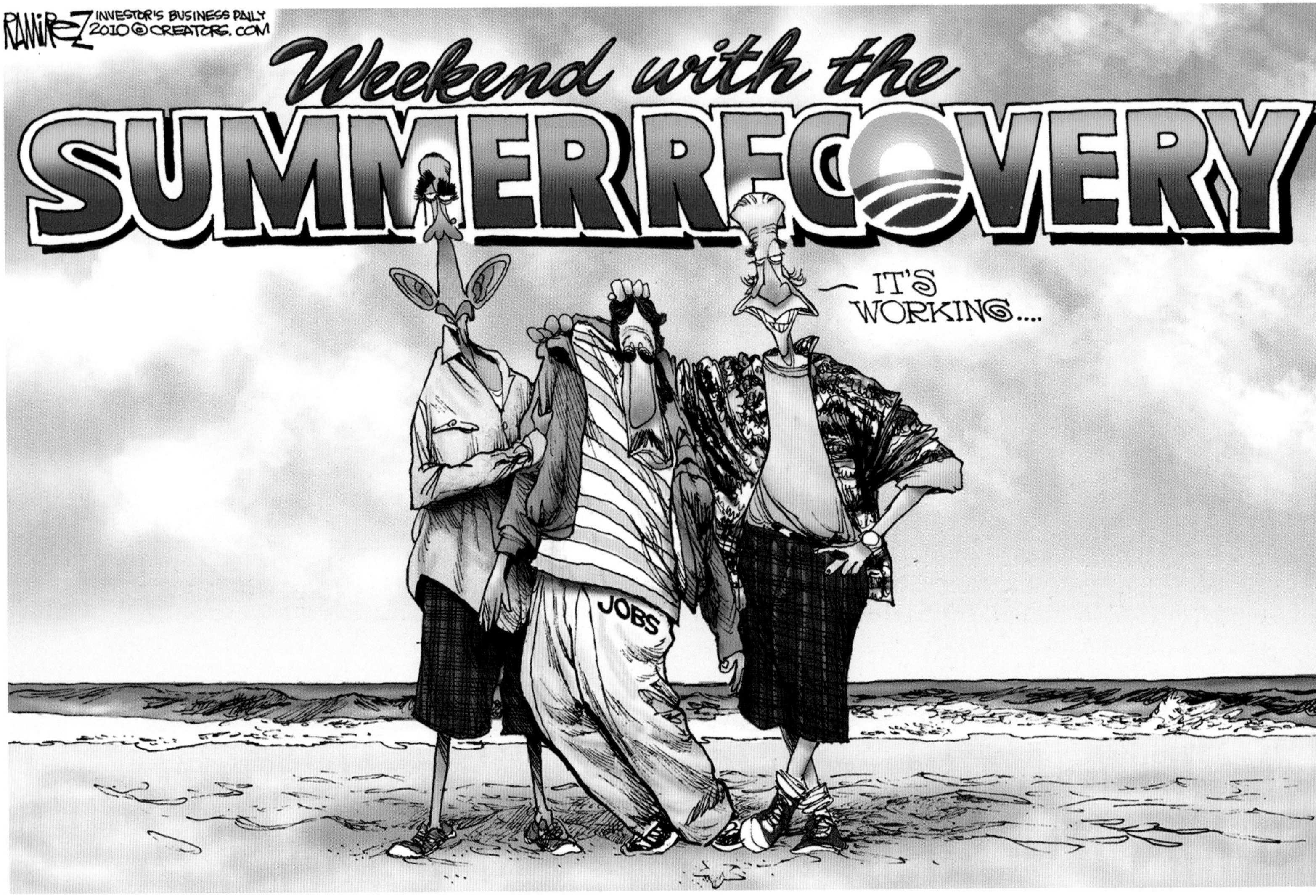
RAMIREZ INVESTOR'S BUSINESS DAILY 2010 © CREATORS.COM
Weekend with the
SUMMER RECOVERY
IT'S WORKING....
JOBS

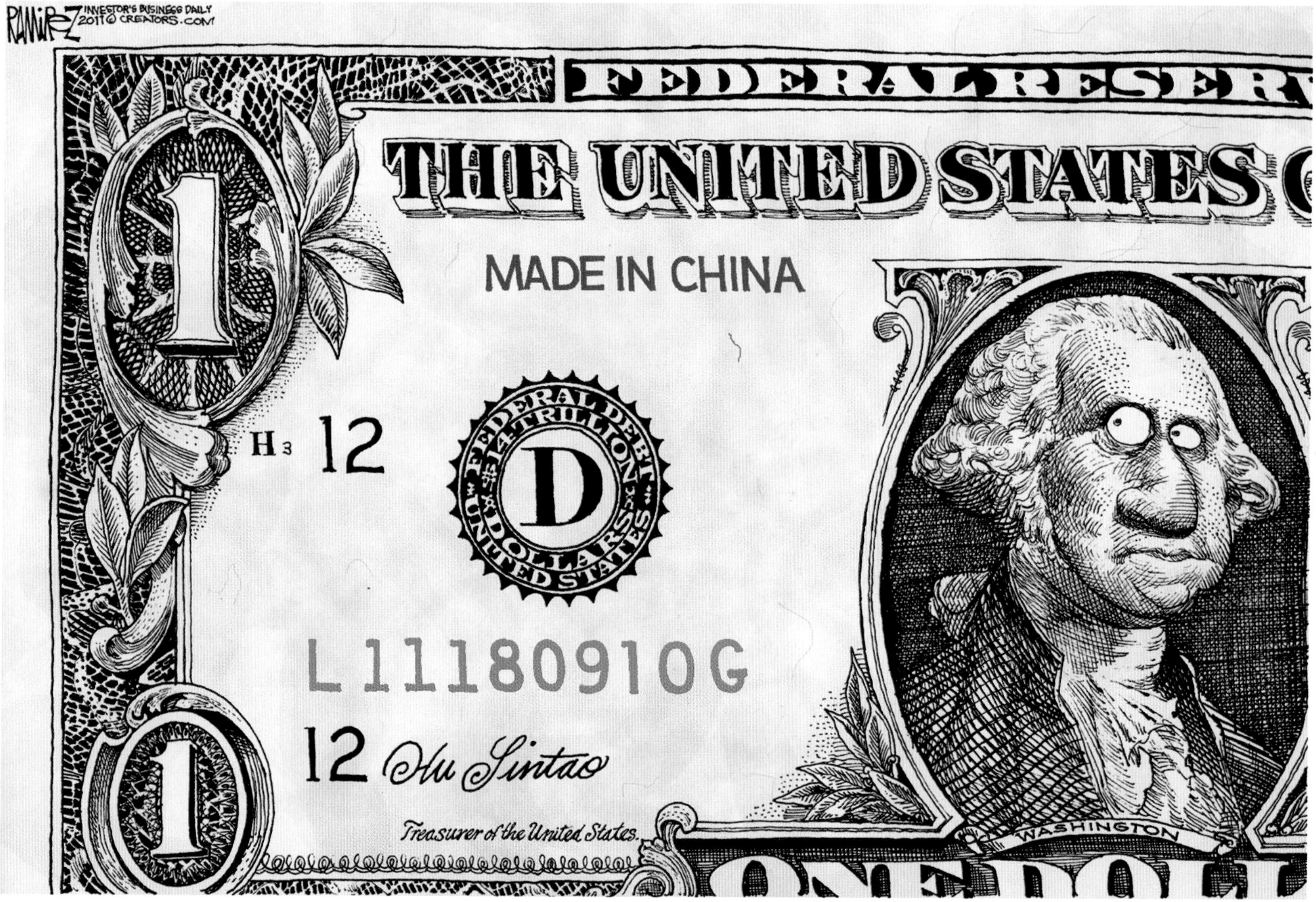
RAMIREZ
INVESTOR'S BUSINESS DAILY
2011 © CREATORS.COM
THE UNITED STATES
MADE IN CHINA
H3 12
FEDERAL DEBT
$14 TRILLION
DOLLARS
UNITED STATES
D
L 11180910 G
12
Hu Jintao
Treasurer of the United States.
WASHINGTON

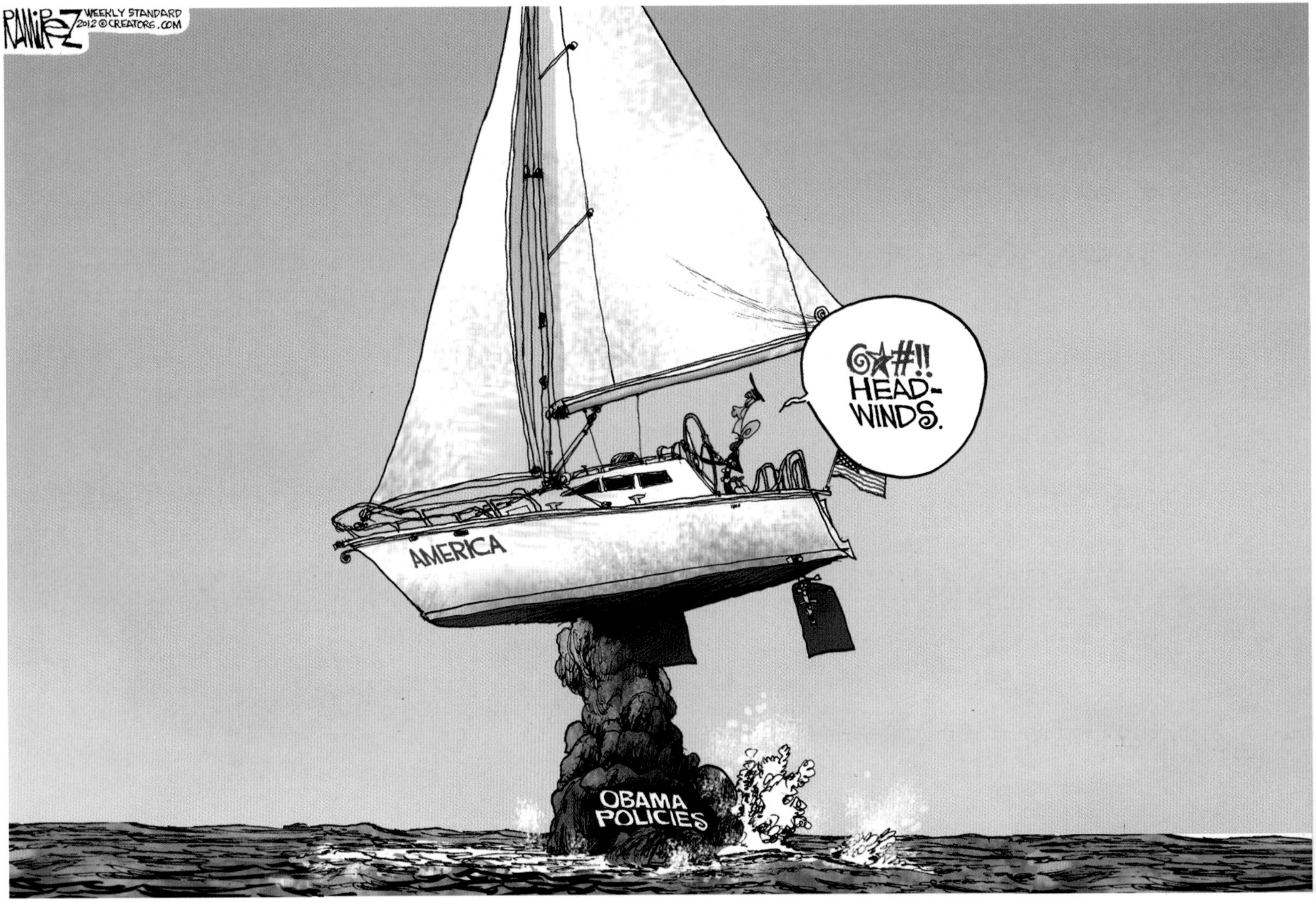
RAMIREZ WEEKLY STANDARD 2012 © CREATORS.COM
G☆#!! HEAD-WINDS.
AMERICA
OBAMA POLICIES

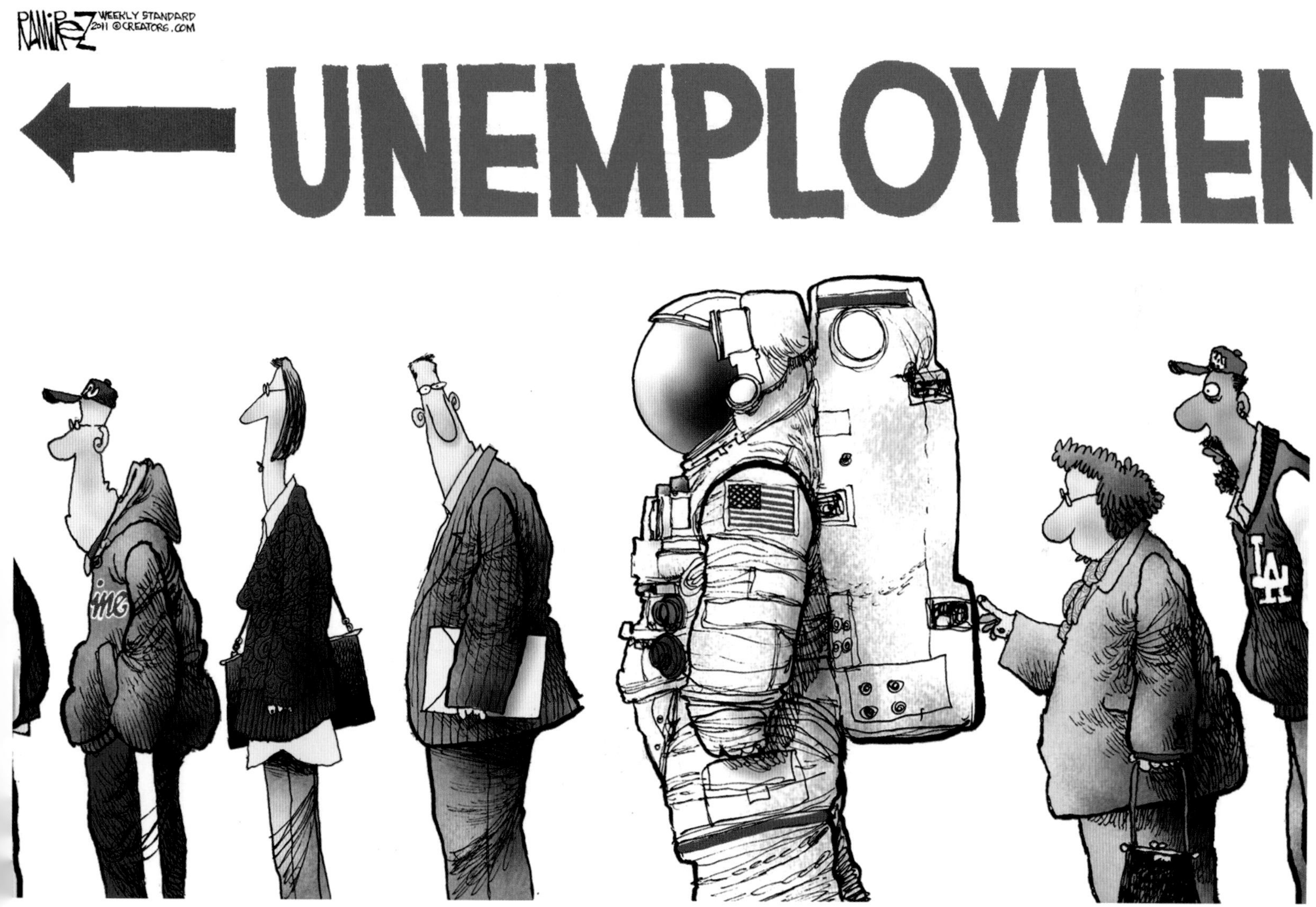
RAMIREZ WEEKLY STANDARD 2011 ©CREATORS.COM
UNEMPLOYMEN
LA

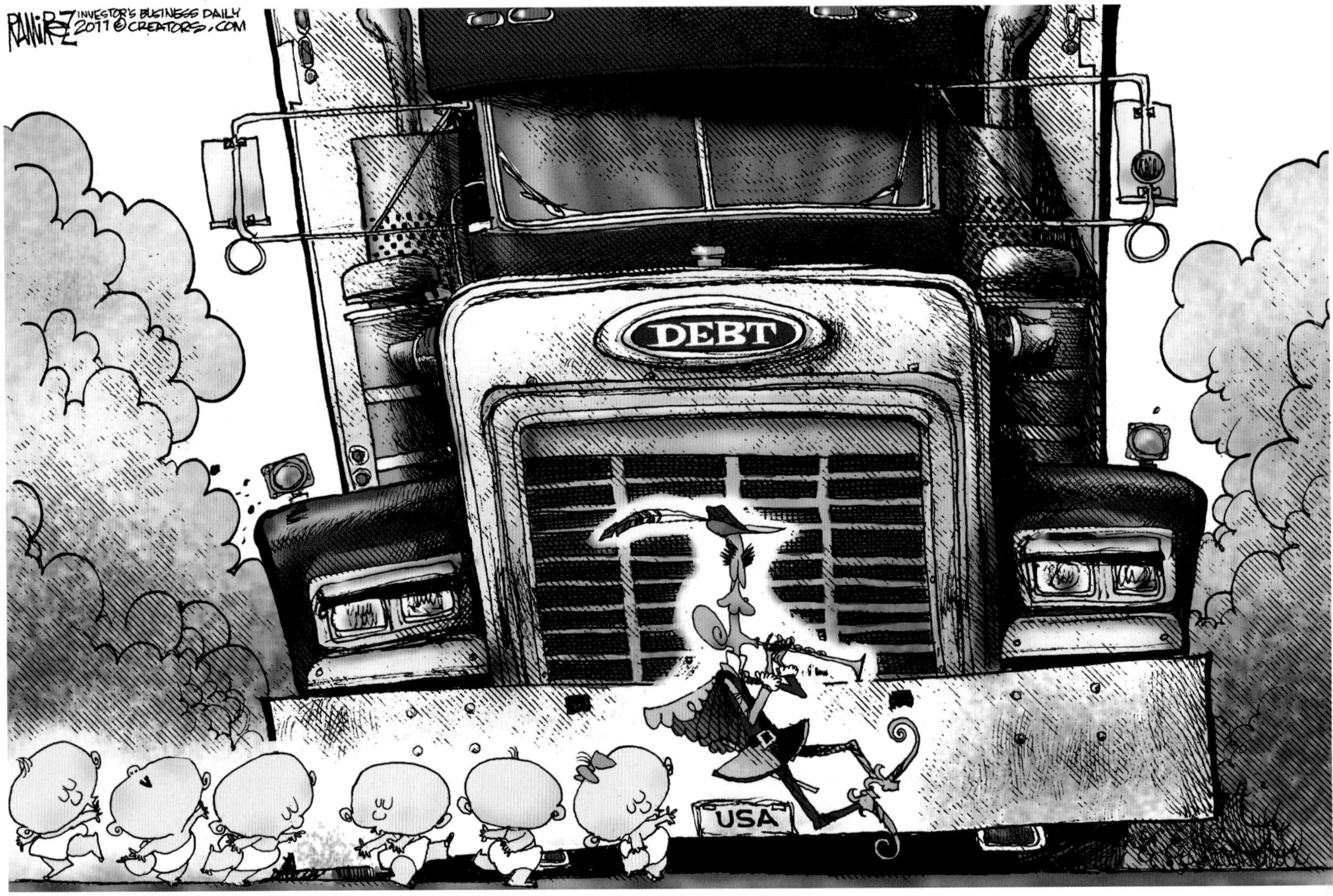
RAMIREZ INVESTOR'S BUSINESS DAILY 2011 © CREATORS.COM
DEBT
USA

THE PIED PIPER

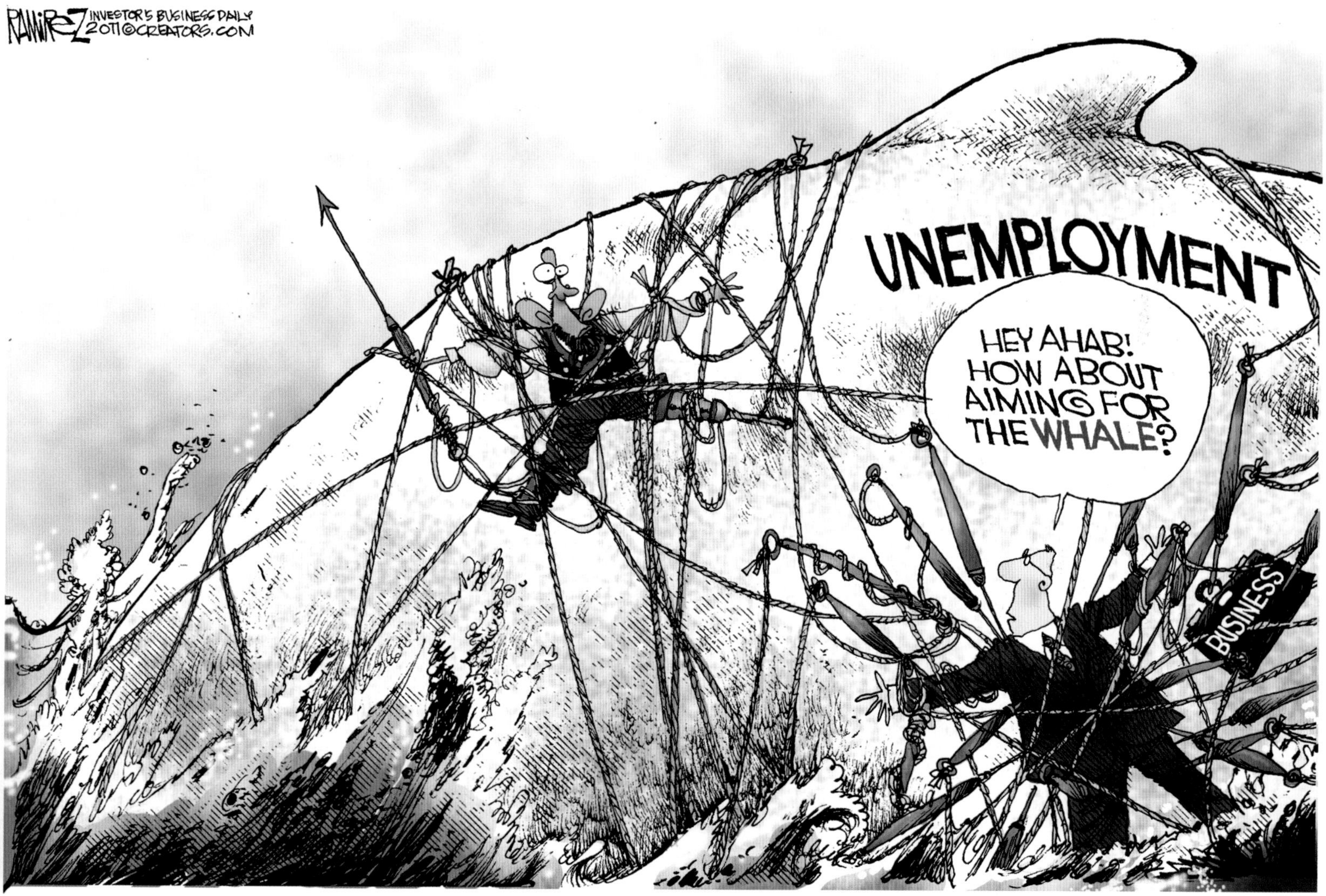
RAMIREZ INVESTOR'S BUSINESS DAILY 2011 ©CREATORS.COM
UNEMPLOYMENT
HEY AHAB! HOW ABOUT AIMING FOR THE WHALE?
BUSINESS

THE GREAT WHITE WHALE

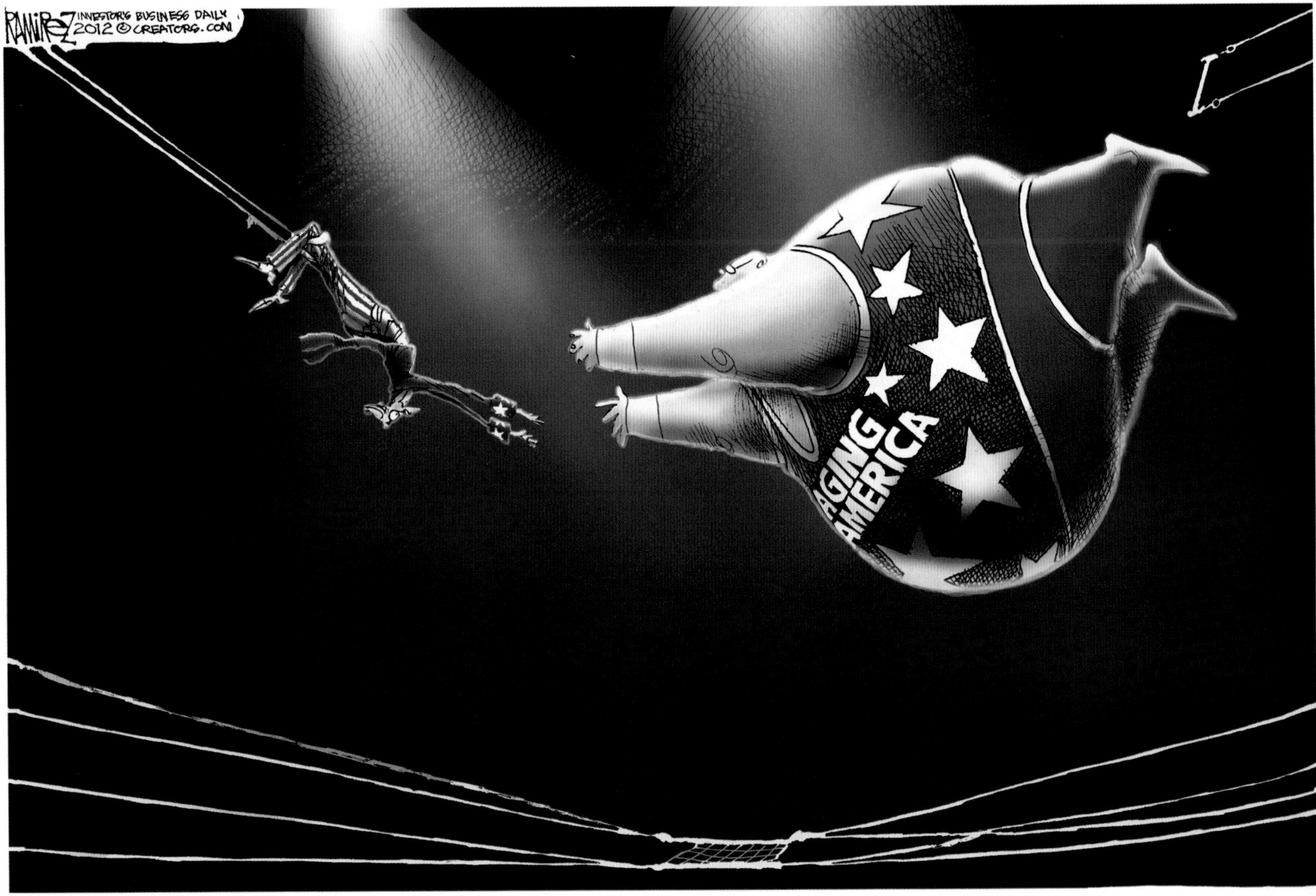
RAMIREZ
INVESTOR'S BUSINESS DAILY
2012 © CREATORS.COM
AGING AMERICA

THE SAFETY NET

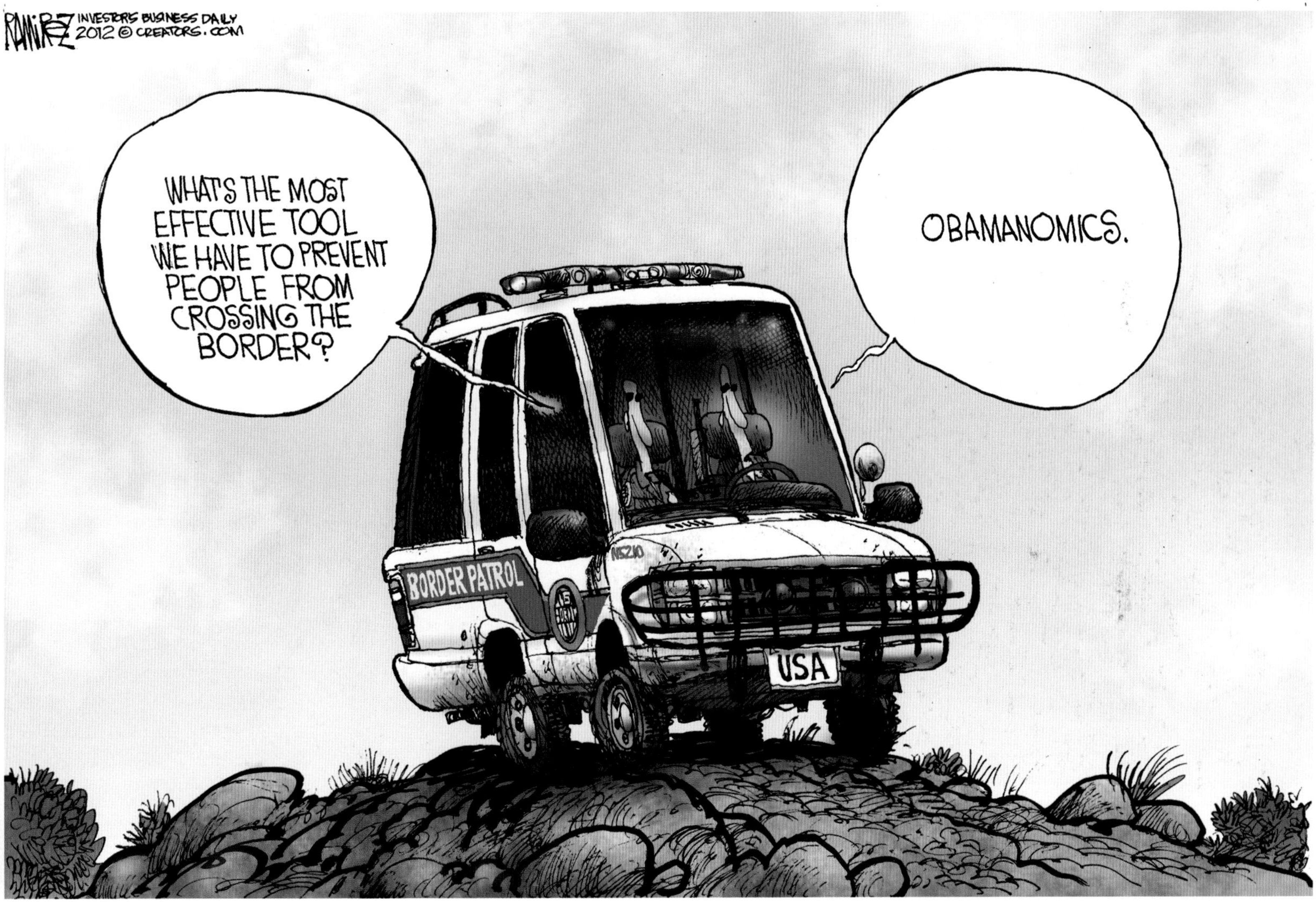
RAMIREZ INVESTOR'S BUSINESS DAILY 2012 © CREATORS.COM
WHAT'S THE MOST EFFECTIVE TOOL WE HAVE TO PREVENT PEOPLE FROM CROSSING THE BORDER?
OBAMANOMICS.
BORDER PATROL
USA

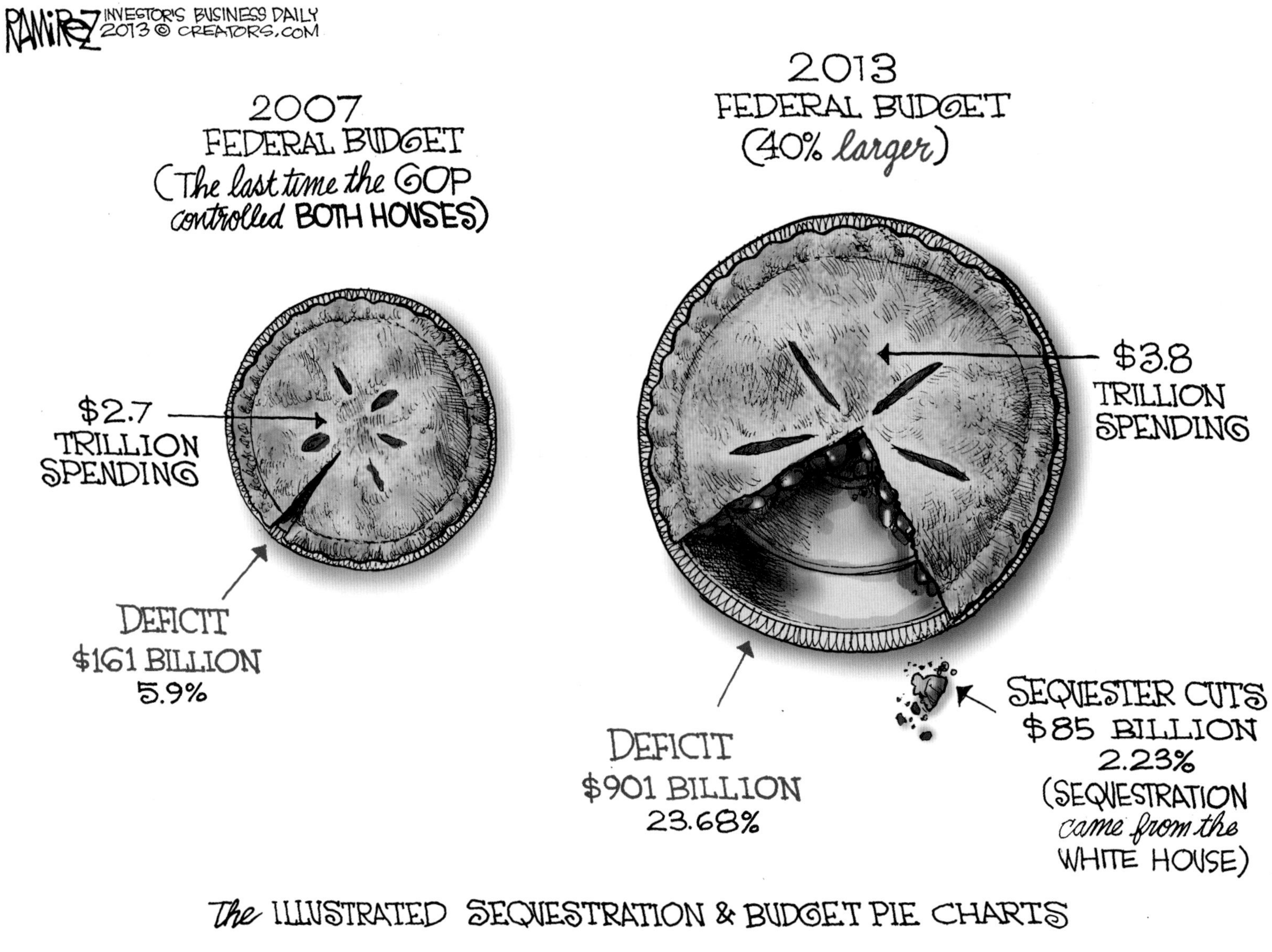

RAMIREZ INVESTOR'S BUSINESS DAILY 2013 © CREATORS.COM
2007 FEDERAL BUDGET (The last time the GOP controlled BOTH HOUSES)
$2.7 TRILLION SPENDING
DEFICIT $161 BILLION 5.9%
2013 FEDERAL BUDGET (40% larger)
$3.8 TRILLION SPENDING
DEFICIT $901 BILLION 23.68%
SEQUESTER CUTS $85 BILLION 2.23% (SEQUESTRATION came from the WHITE HOUSE)
The ILLUSTRATED SEQUESTRATION & BUDGET PIE CHARTS

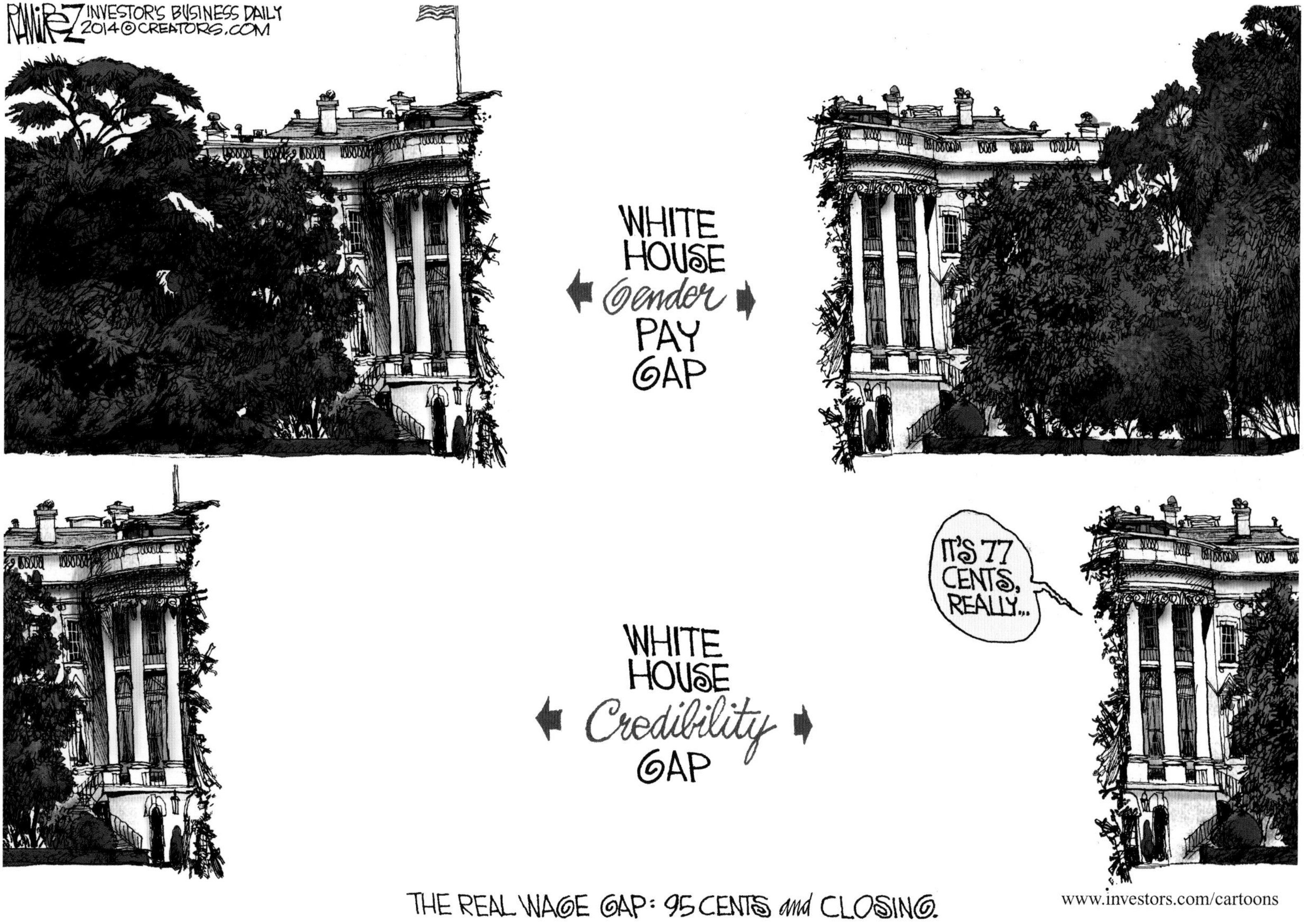
RAMIREZ INVESTOR'S BUSINESS DAILY 2014 © CREATORS.COM
WHITE HOUSE Gender PAY GAP
WHITE HOUSE Credibility GAP
IT'S 77 CENTS, REALLY...
THE REAL WAGE GAP: 95 CENTS and CLOSING.
www.investors.com/cartoons

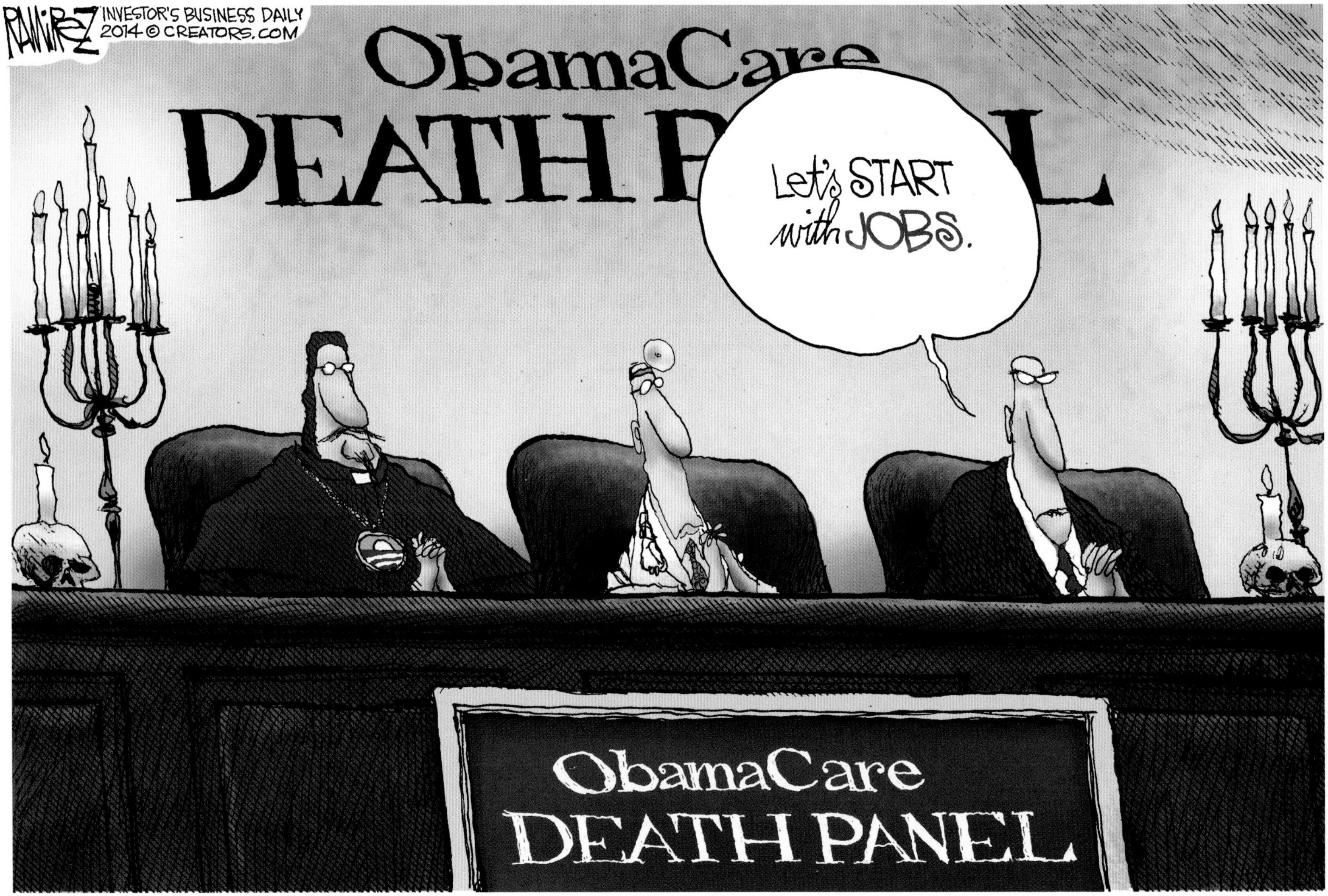
RAMIREZ INVESTOR'S BUSINESS DAILY 2014 © CREATORS.COM
ObamaCare
DEATH P
L
Let's START with JOBS.
ObamaCare
DEATH PANEL

THE STATE OF THE UNION

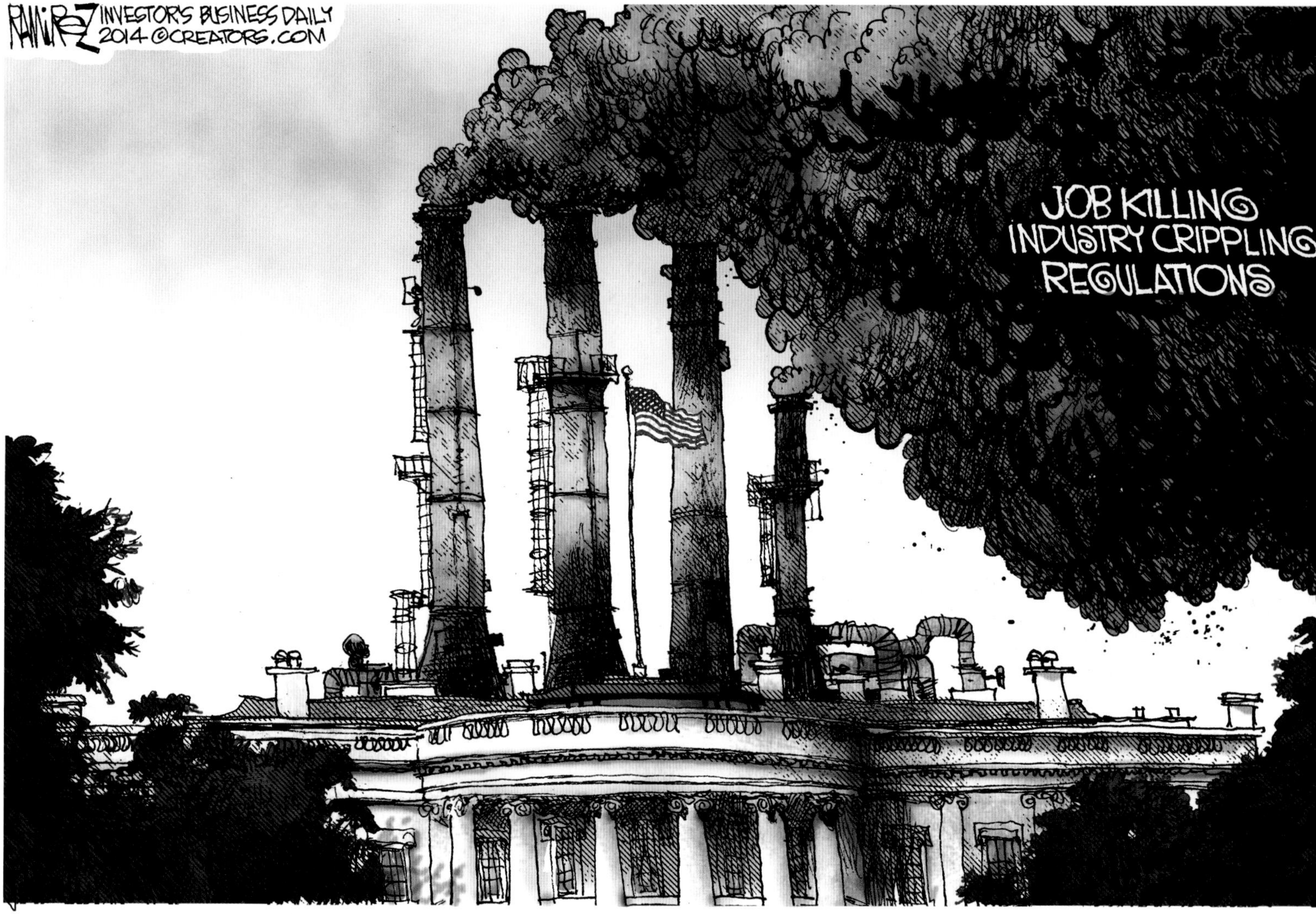
RAMIREZ INVESTOR'S BUSINESS DAILY
2014 ©CREATORS.COM
JOB KILLING
INDUSTRY CRIPPLING
REGULATIONS

SPEAKING of releasing TOXIC EMISSIONS.

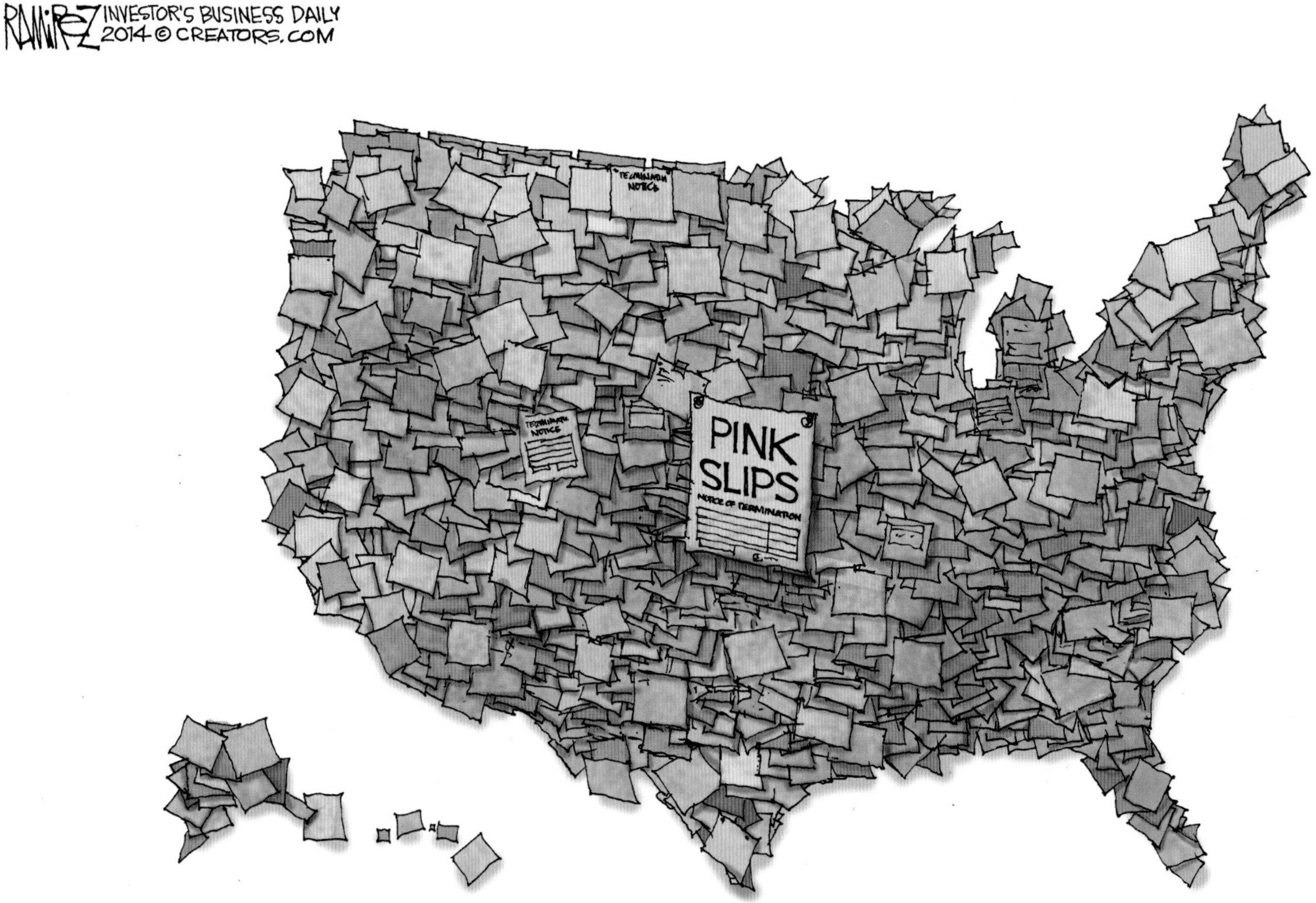
RAMIREZ
INVESTOR'S BUSINESS DAILY
2014 © CREATORS.COM
PINK SLIPS
NOTICE OF TERMINATION

THE STATE OF THE UNION

GREEN ENERGY

"The true engine of economic growth will always be companies like Solyndra."

—President Barack Obama,
at Solyndra in Fremont, California, May 26, 2010

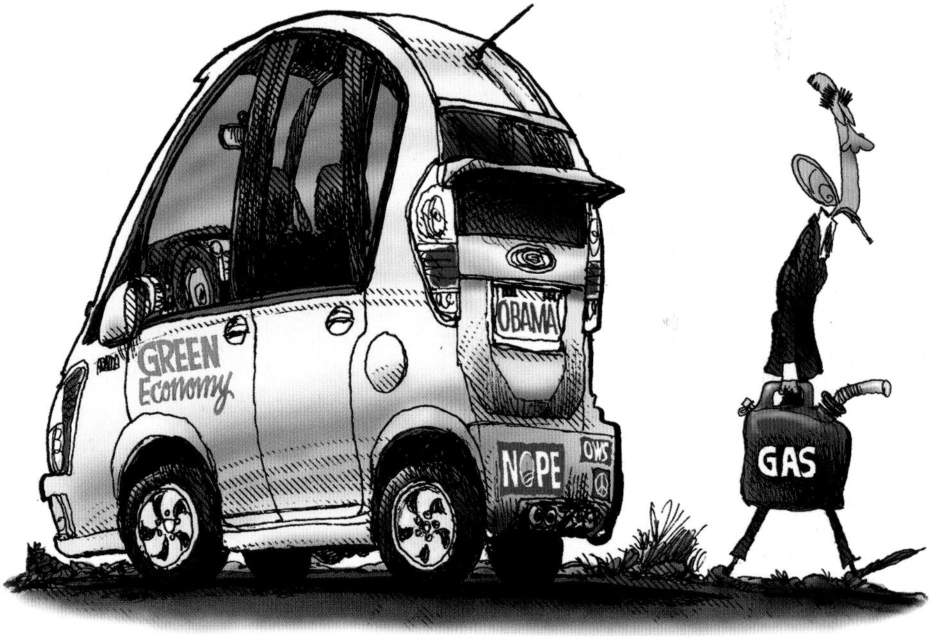
GREEN
Economy
OBAMA
NOPE
OWS
GAS

Green energy was to be the engine for economic growth. Unfortunately, because of the lack of viable alternatives to fossil fuels, it ran out of gas. Green energy never caught fire. The Chevy Volt did. Obama environmental policy was more effective at reducing jobs than greenhouse gases.

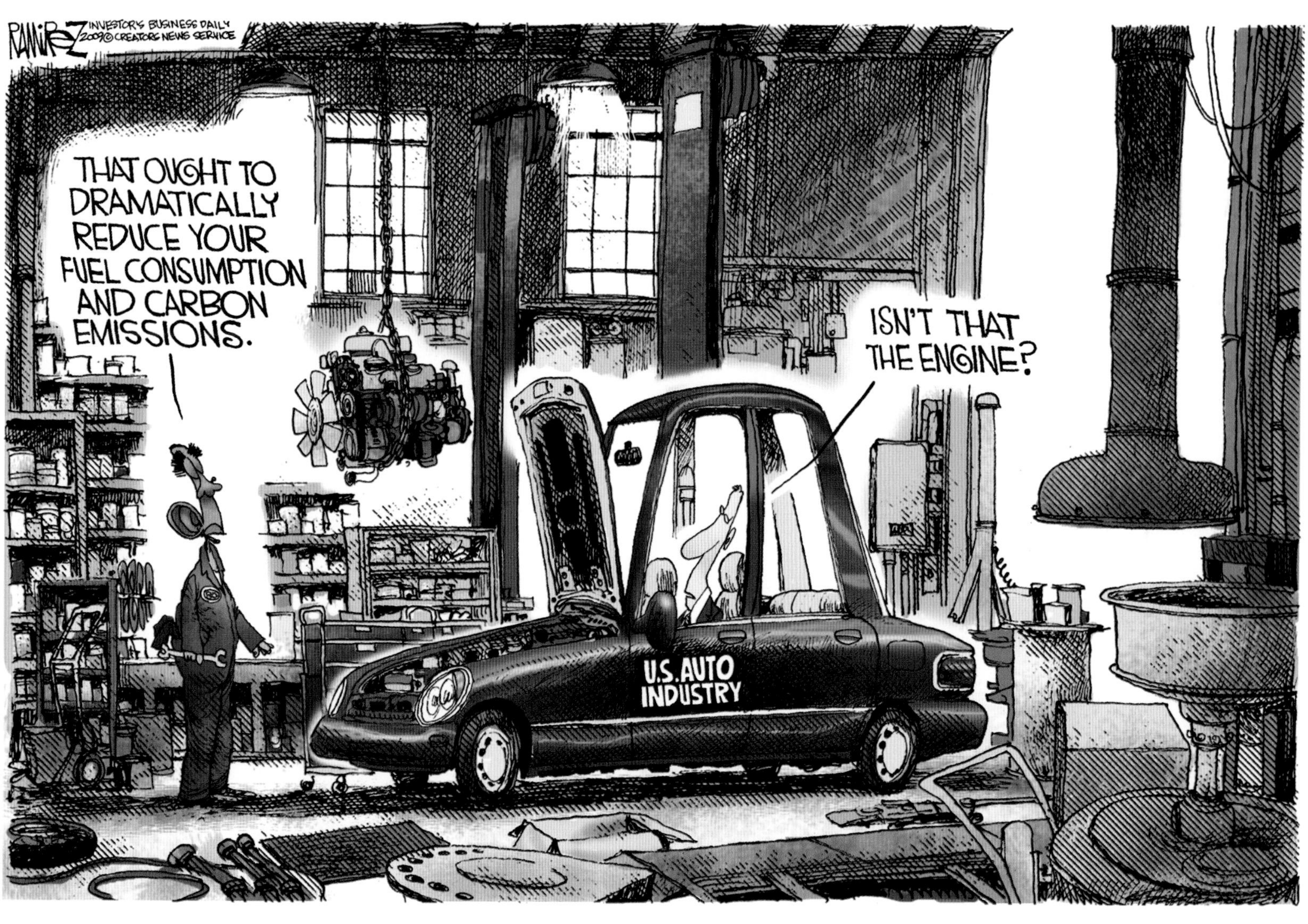
RAMIREZ INVESTOR'S BUSINESS DAILY 2009 © CREATORS NEWS SERVICE
THAT OUGHT TO DRAMATICALLY REDUCE YOUR FUEL CONSUMPTION AND CARBON EMISSIONS.
ISN'T THAT THE ENGINE?
U.S. AUTO INDUSTRY

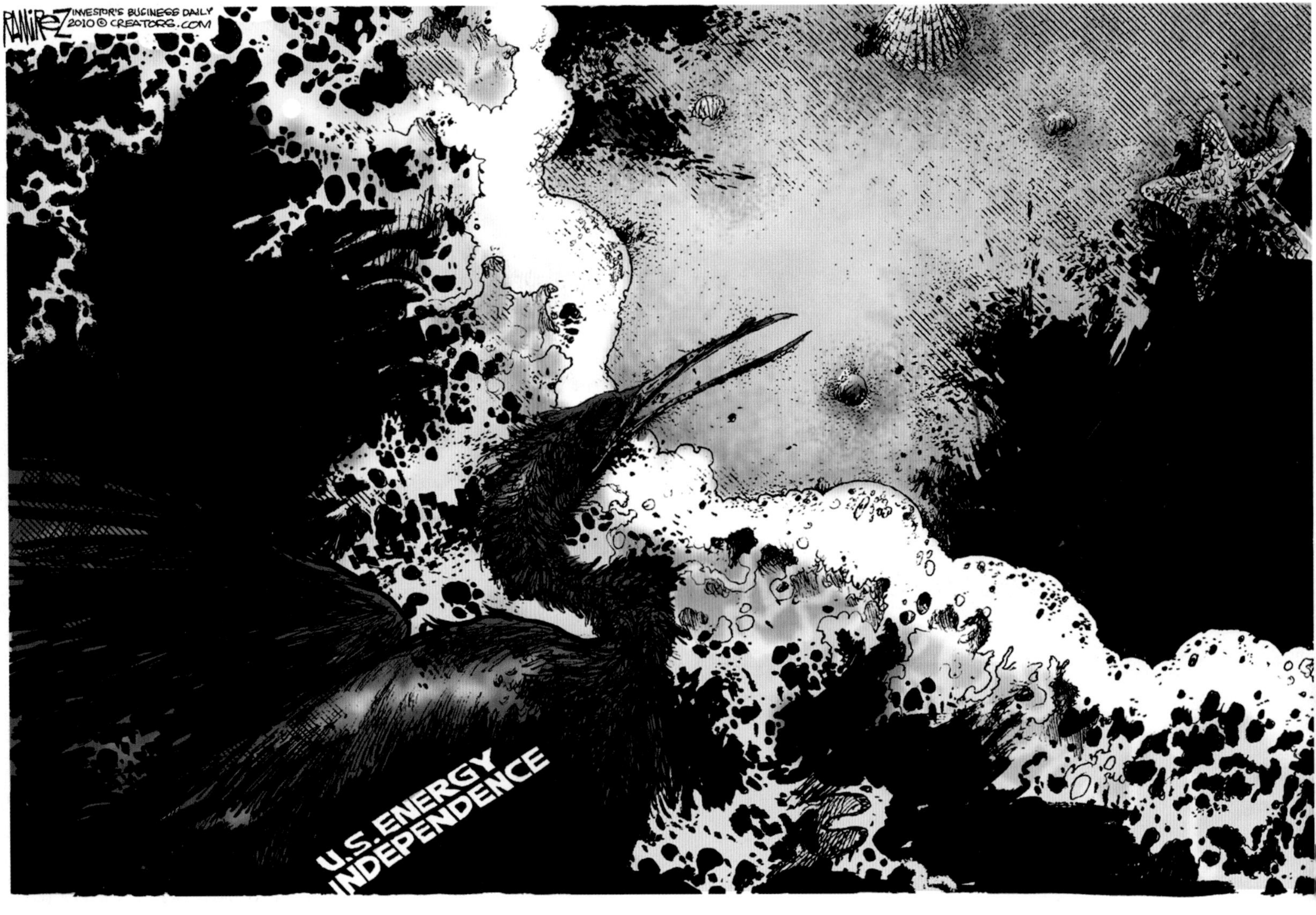
RAMIREZ
INVESTOR'S BUSINESS DAILY
2010 © CREATORS.COM
U.S. ENERGY
INDEPENDENCE

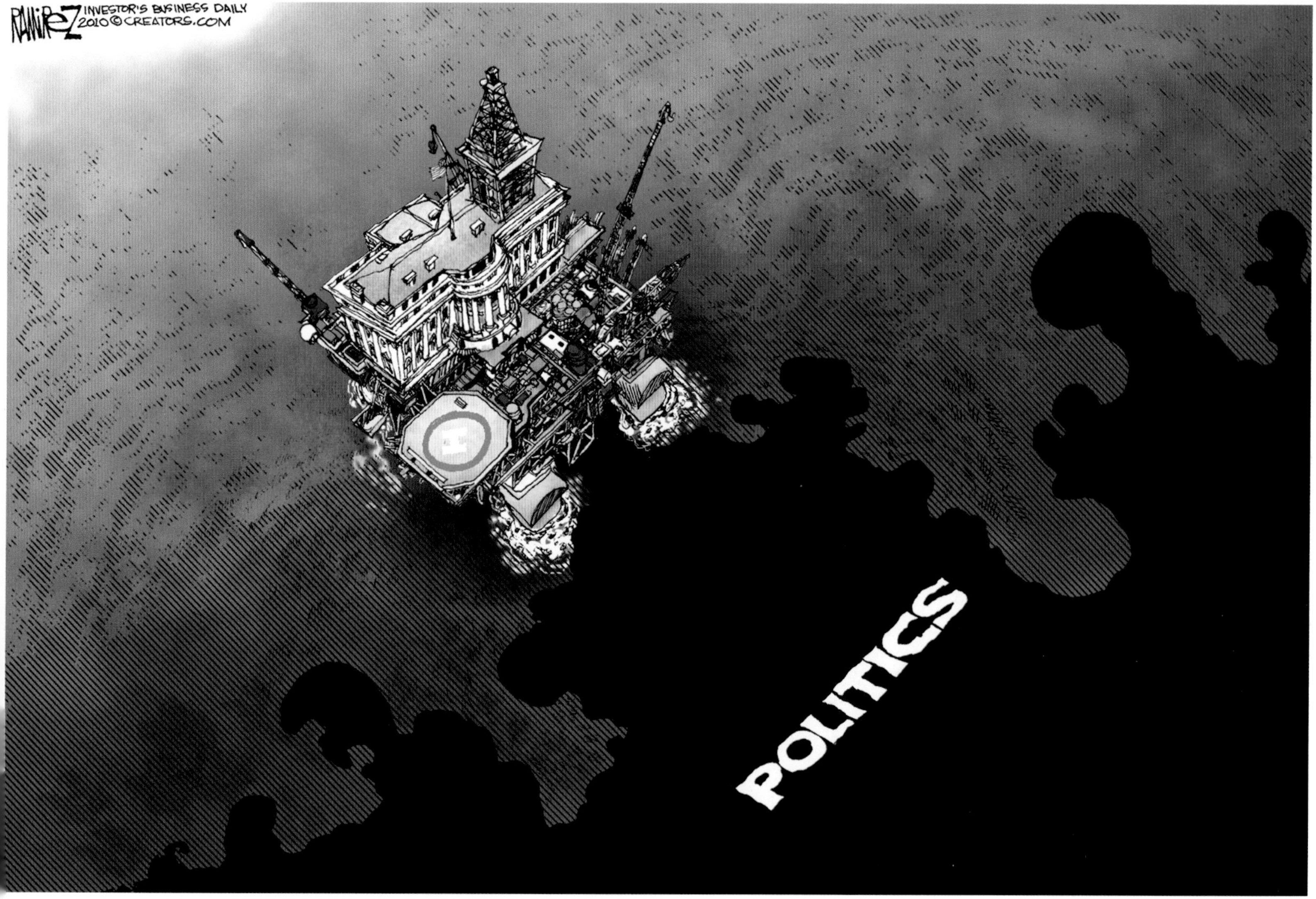
RAMIREZ
INVESTOR'S BUSINESS DAILY
2010 © CREATORS.COM
POLITICS

WHERE THE MORATORIUM IS NEEDED.

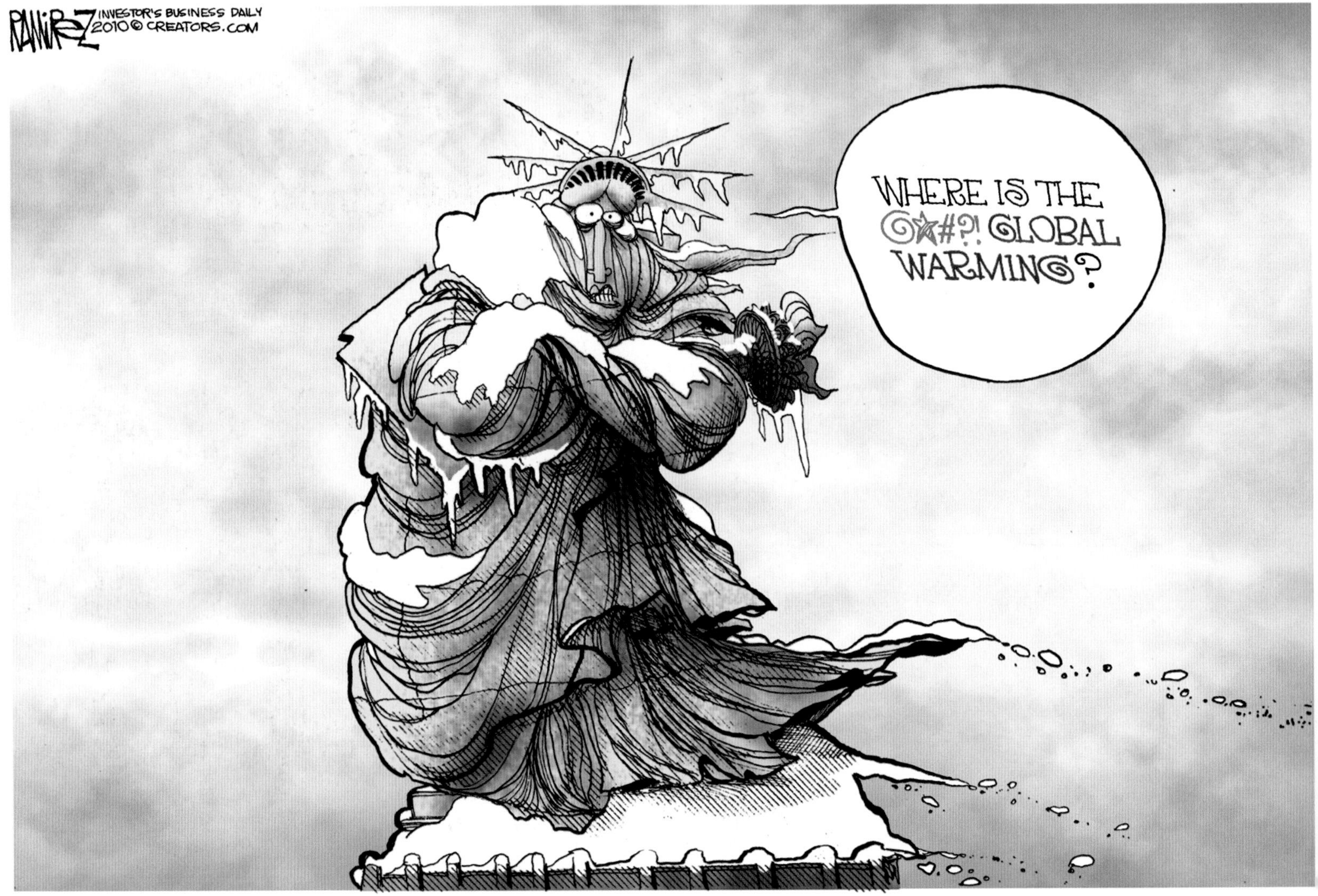
RAMIREZ INVESTOR'S BUSINESS DAILY 2010 © CREATORS.COM
WHERE IS THE @☆#?! GLOBAL WARMING?

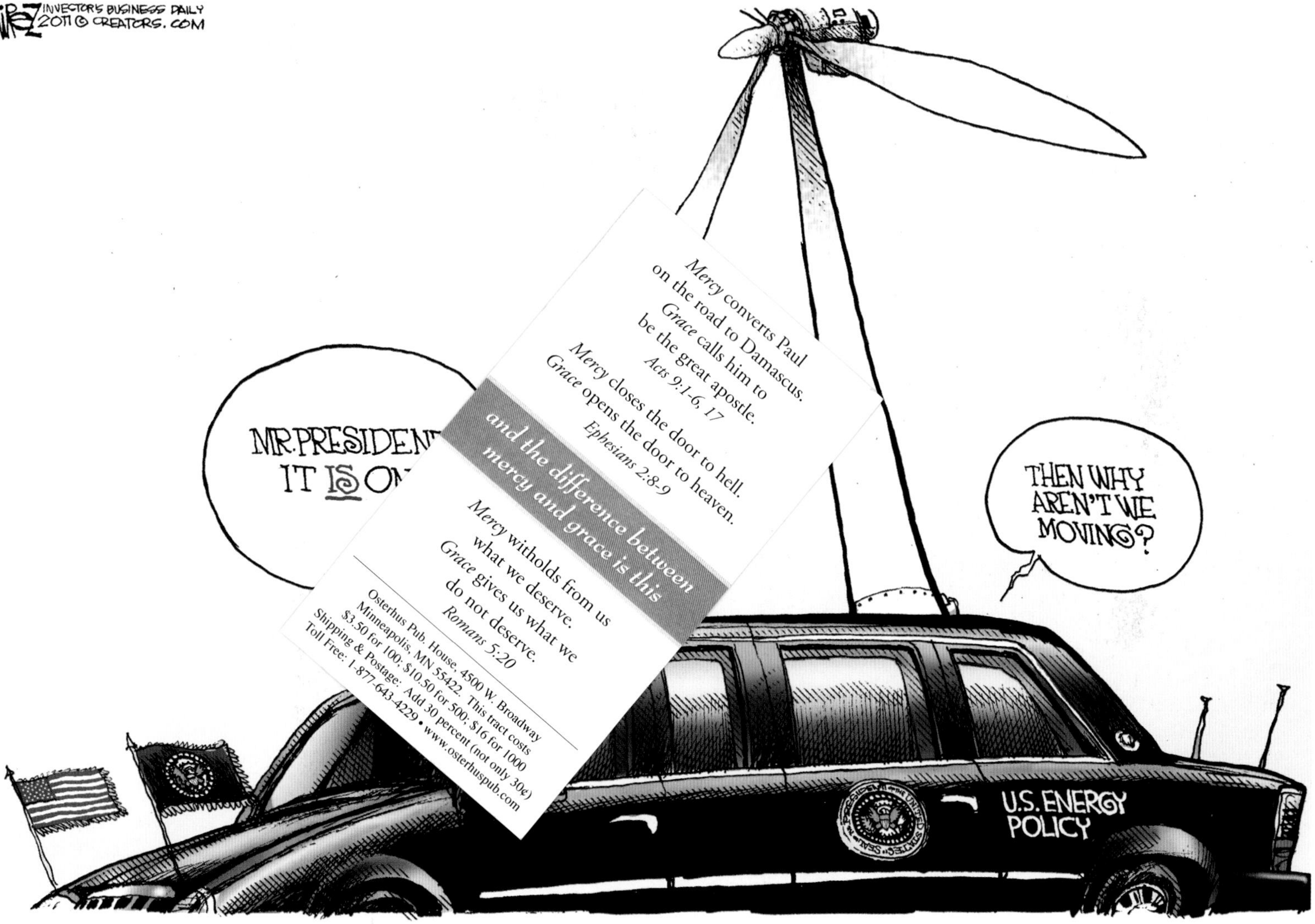
RAMIREZ INVESTOR'S BUSINESS DAILY 2011 © CREATORS.COM
MR.PRESIDEN
IT IS O
THEN WHY AREN'T WE MOVING?
U.S. ENERGY POLICY

Mercy converts Paul
on the road to Damascus.
Grace calls him to
be the great apostle.
Acts 9:1-6, 17

Mercy closes the door to hell.
Grace opens the door to heaven.
Ephesians 2:8-9

and the difference between
mercy and grace is this

Mercy witholds from us
what we deserve.
Grace gives us what we
do not deserve.
Romans 5:20

Osterhus Pub. House, 4500 W. Broadway
Minneapolis, MN 55422. This tract costs
$3.50 for 100; $10.50 for 500; $16 for 1000
Shipping & Postage: Add 30 percent (not only 30¢)
Toll Free: 1-877-643-4229 • www.osterhuspub.com

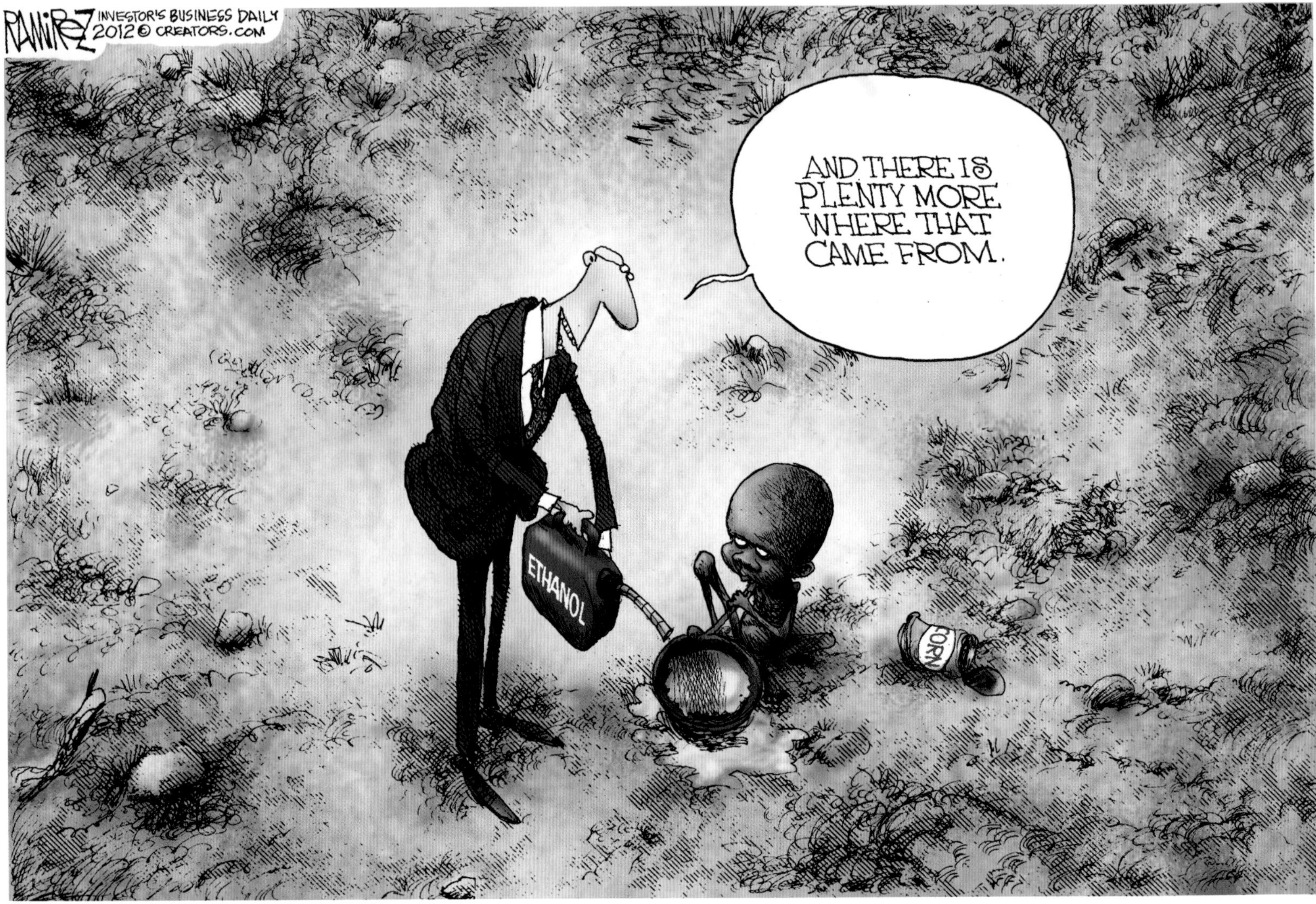
RAMIREZ INVESTOR'S BUSINESS DAILY 2012 © CREATORS.COM
AND THERE IS PLENTY MORE WHERE THAT CAME FROM.
ETHANOL
CORN

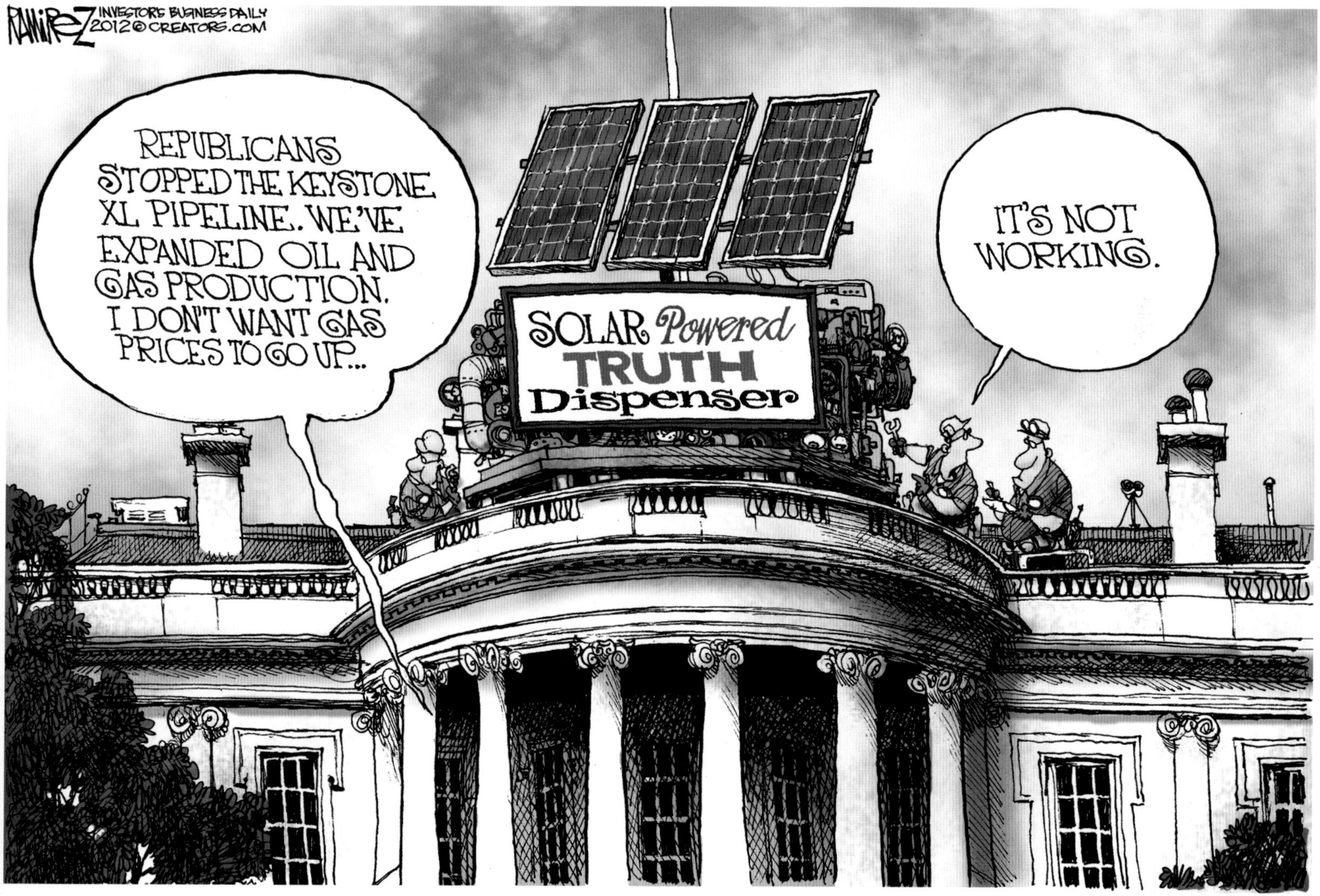
RAMIREZ INVESTOR'S BUSINESS DAILY 2012 © CREATORS.COM
REPUBLICANS STOPPED THE KEYSTONE XL PIPELINE. WE'VE EXPANDED OIL AND GAS PRODUCTION. I DON'T WANT GAS PRICES TO GO UP...
SOLAR Powered TRUTH Dispenser
IT'S NOT WORKING.

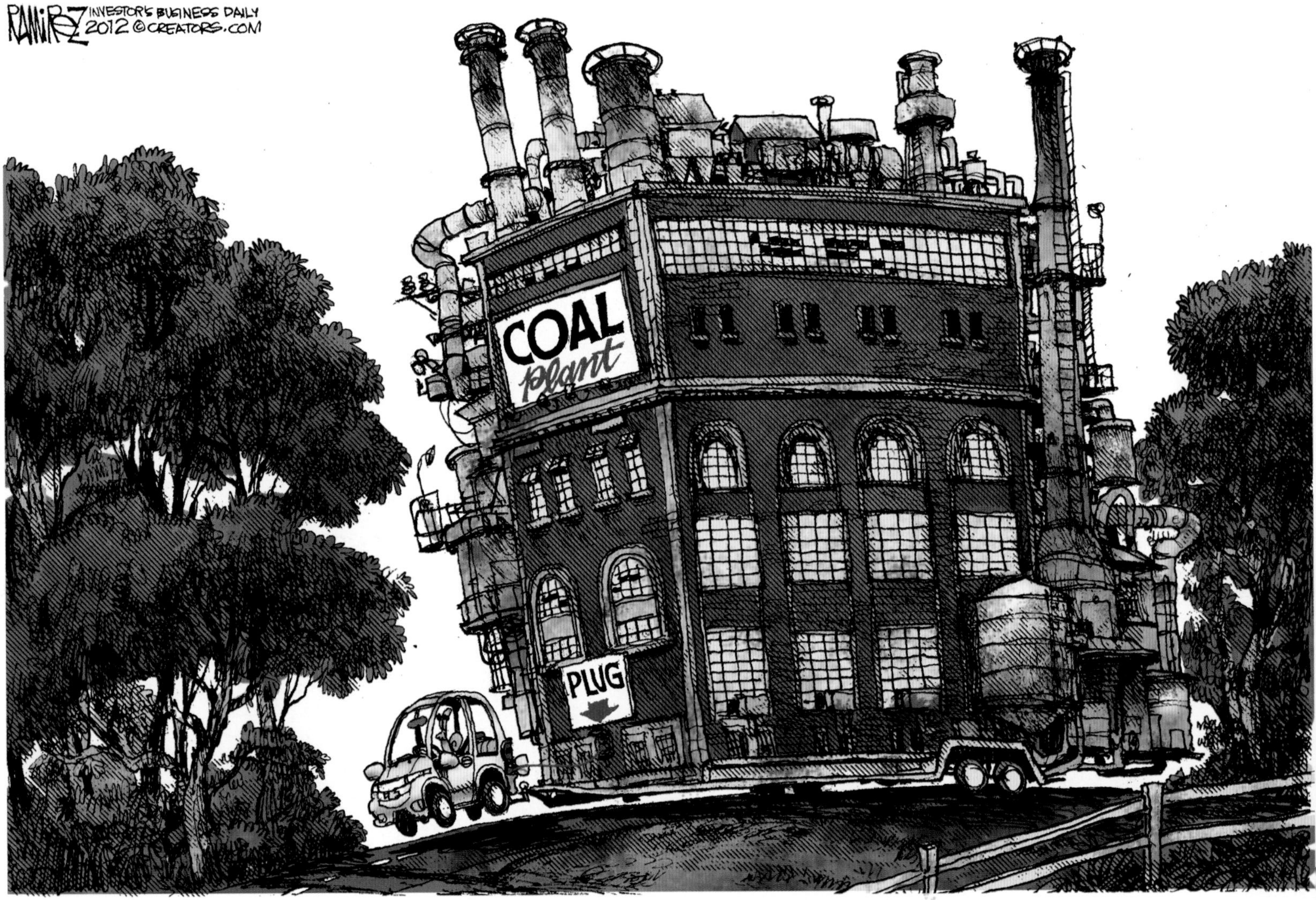
RAMIREZ
INVESTOR'S BUSINESS DAILY
2012 ©CREATORS.COM
COAL
plant
PLUG

HOW ELECTRIC CARS WORK

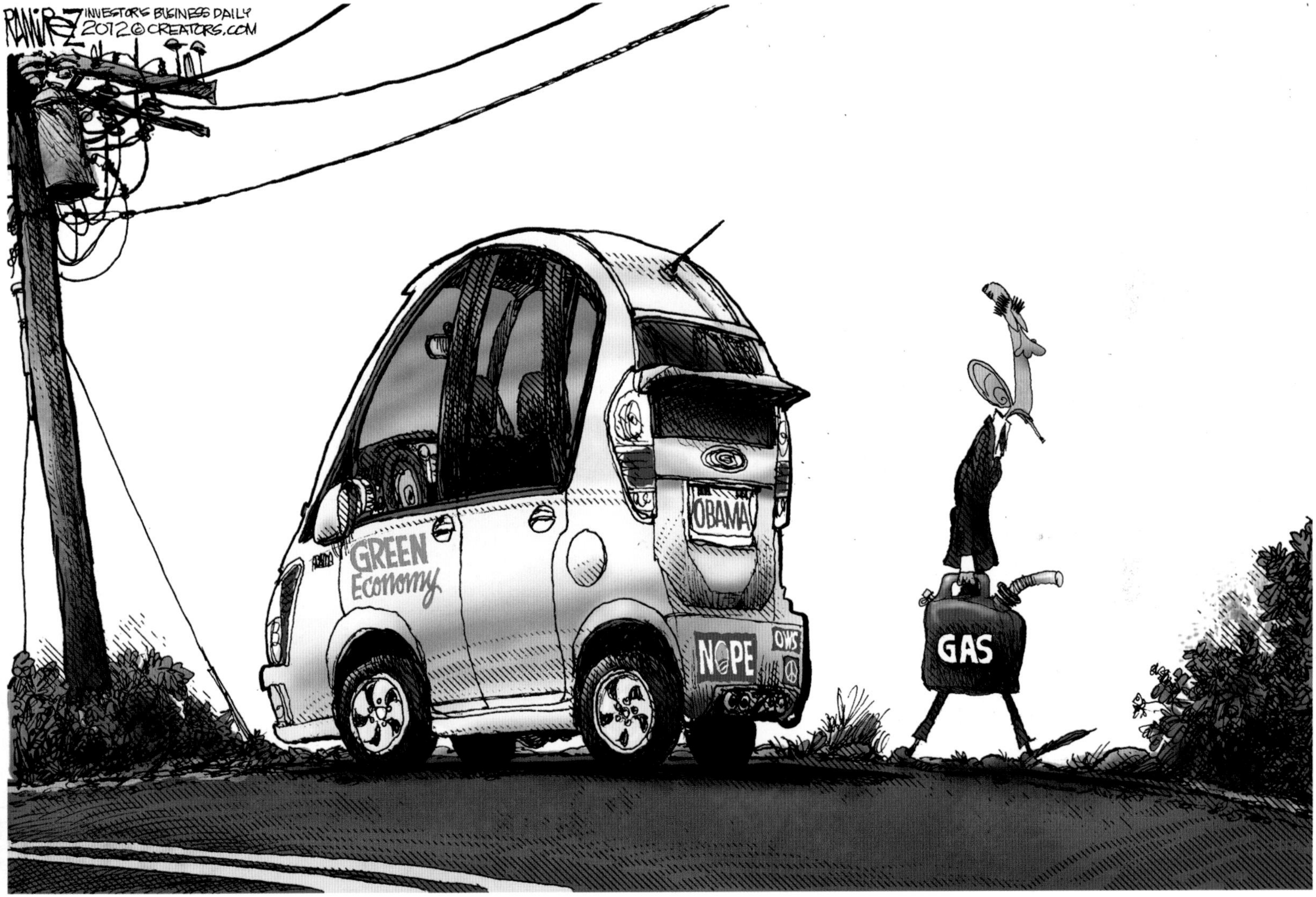

RAMIREZ
INVESTOR'S BUSINESS DAILY
2012 © CREATORS.COM
GREEN
Economy
OBAMA
NOPE
OWS
GAS

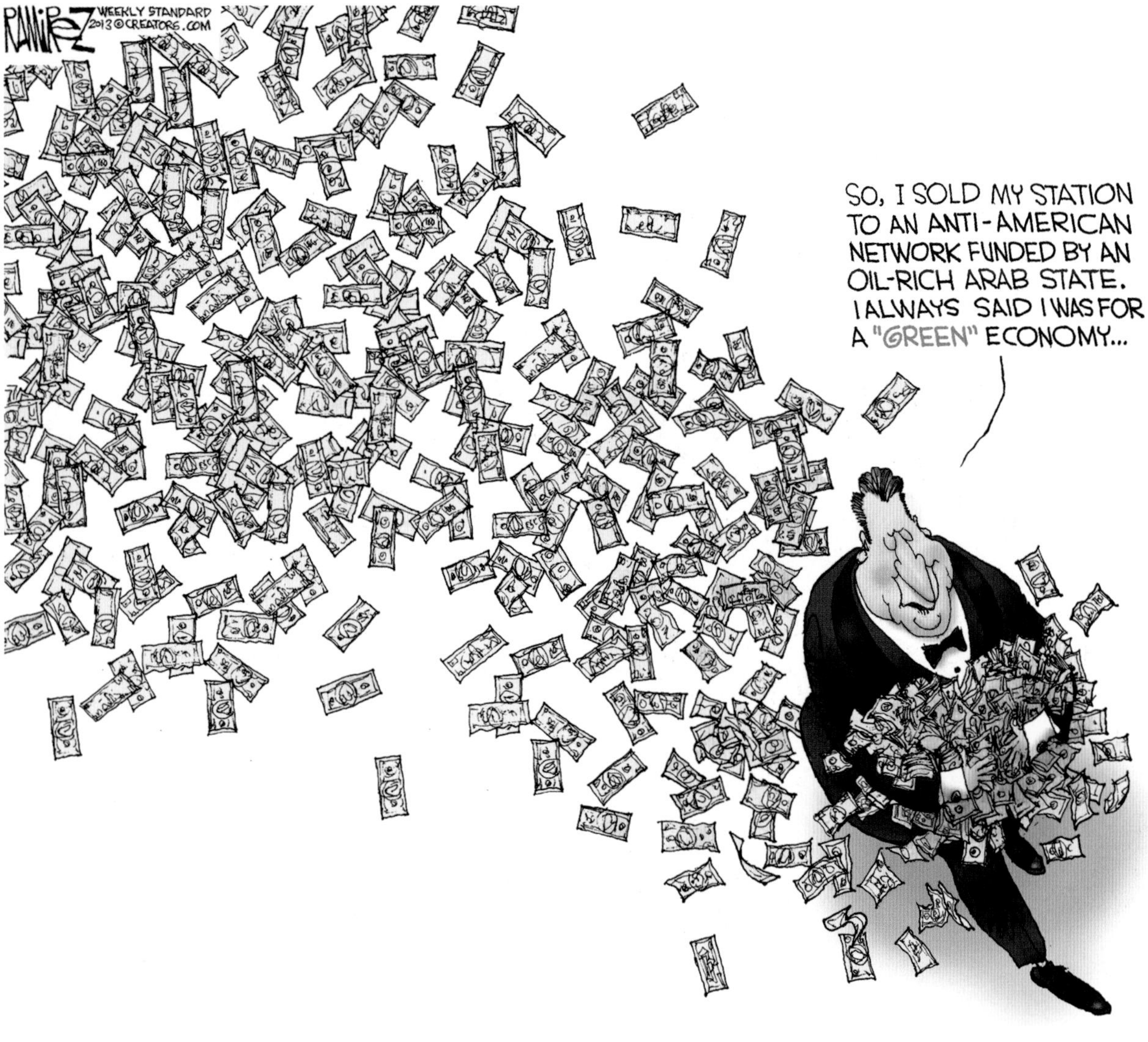
RAMIREZ WEEKLY STANDARD 2013 © CREATORS.COM
SO, I SOLD MY STATION TO AN ANTI-AMERICAN NETWORK FUNDED BY AN OIL-RICH ARAB STATE. I ALWAYS SAID I WAS FOR A "GREEN" ECONOMY...

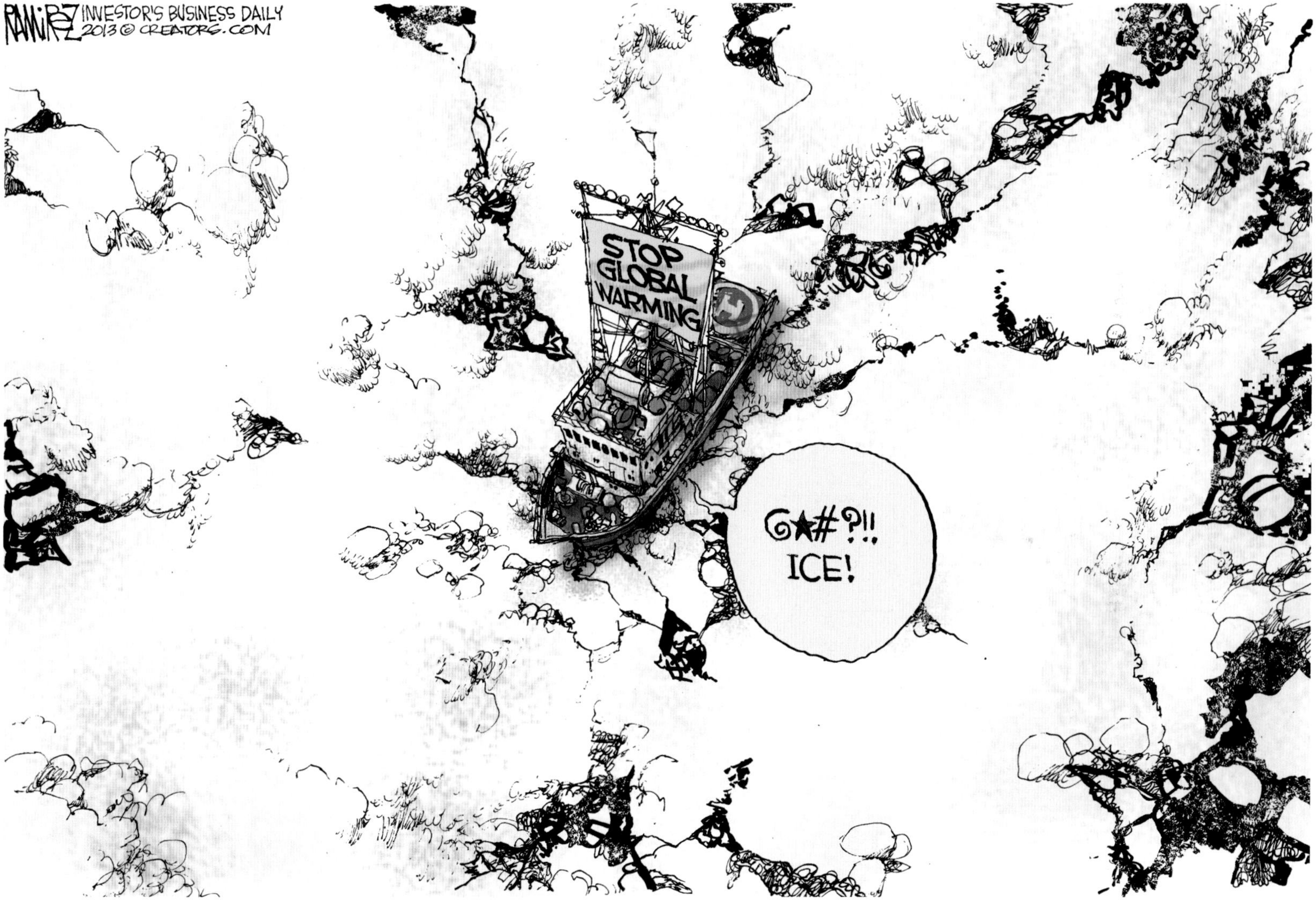
RAMIREZ INVESTOR'S BUSINESS DAILY
2013 © CREATORS.COM
STOP GLOBAL WARMING
G★#?!! ICE!

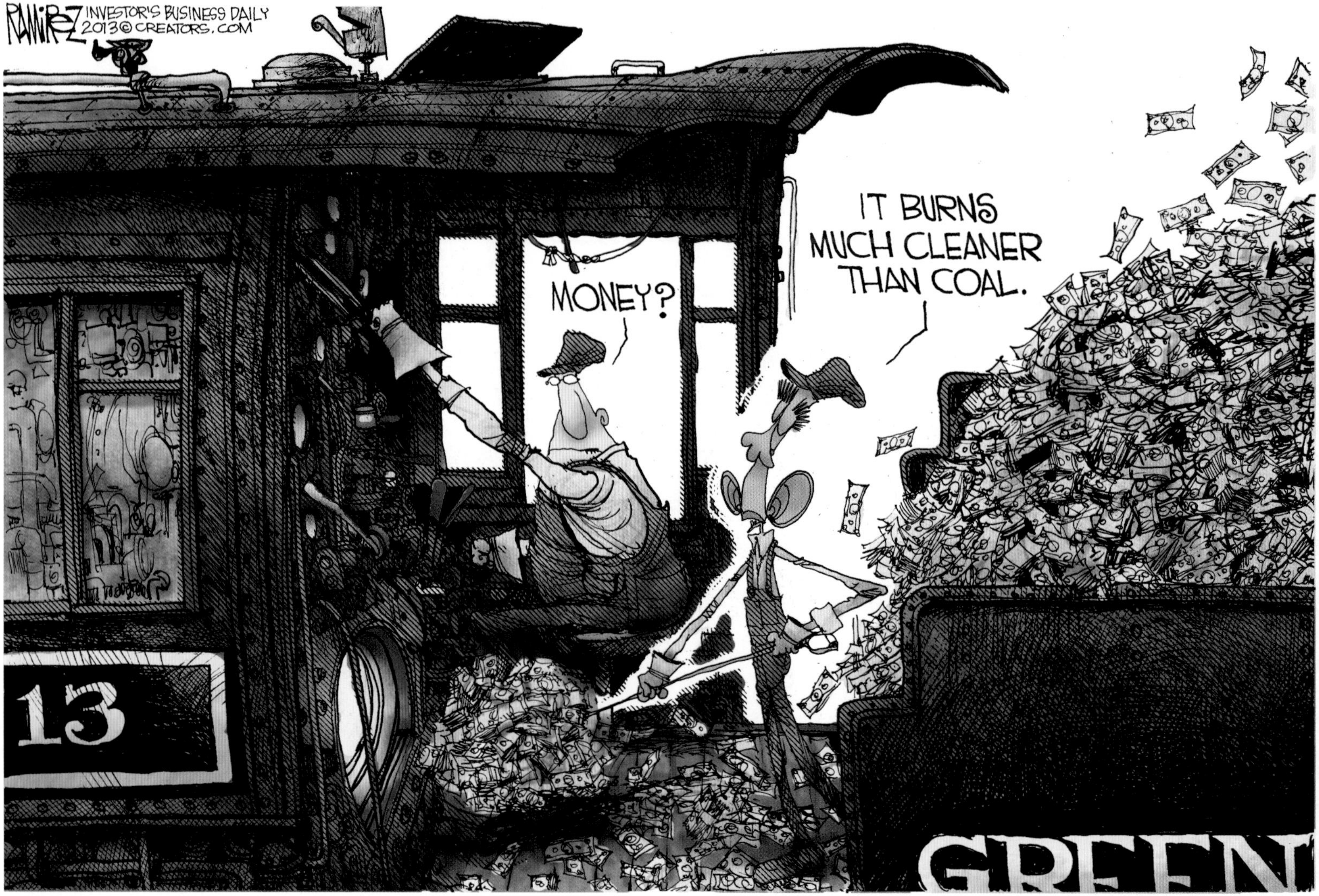
RAMIREZ INVESTOR'S BUSINESS DAILY
2013© CREATORS.COM
MONEY?
IT BURNS
MUCH CLEANER
THAN COAL.
13
GREEN

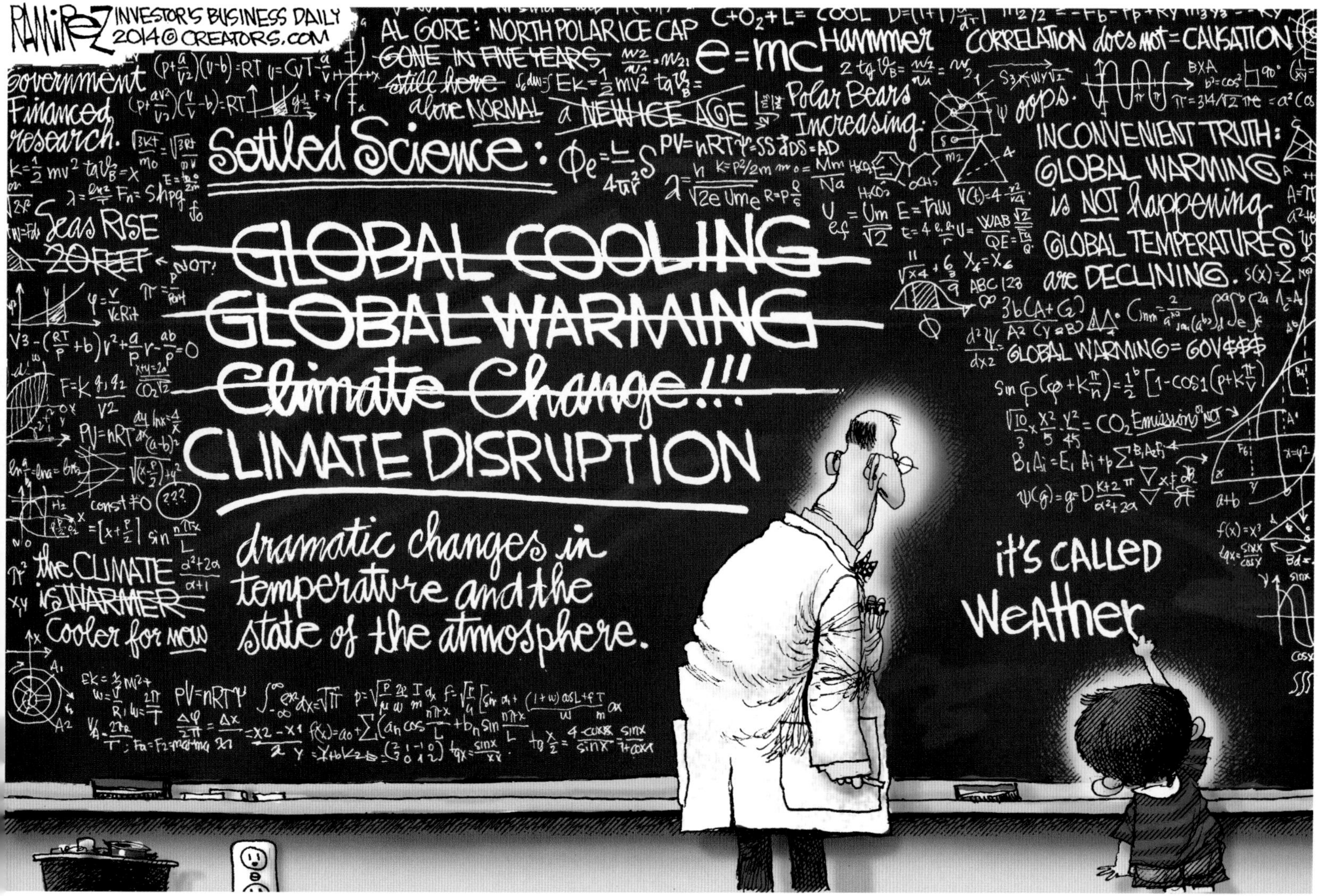
RAMIREZ INVESTOR'S BUSINESS DAILY 2014 © CREATORS.COM
AL GORE: NORTH POLAR ICE CAP GONE IN FIVE YEARS still here
above NORMAL
a NEW ICE AGE
E=MC Hammer
Polar Bears Increasing
CORRELATION does NOT = CAUSATION
oops.
Government Financed research.
Settled Science:
INCONVENIENT TRUTH: GLOBAL WARMING is NOT happening GLOBAL TEMPERATURES are DECLINING.
Seas RISE 20 FEET NOT!
GLOBAL COOLING
GLOBAL WARMING
Climate Change!!!
CLIMATE DISRUPTION
GLOBAL WARMING = GOV$$$
CO2 Emission NOT
the CLIMATE is WARMER Cooler for NOW
dramatic changes in temperature and the state of the atmosphere.
it's CALLED Weather

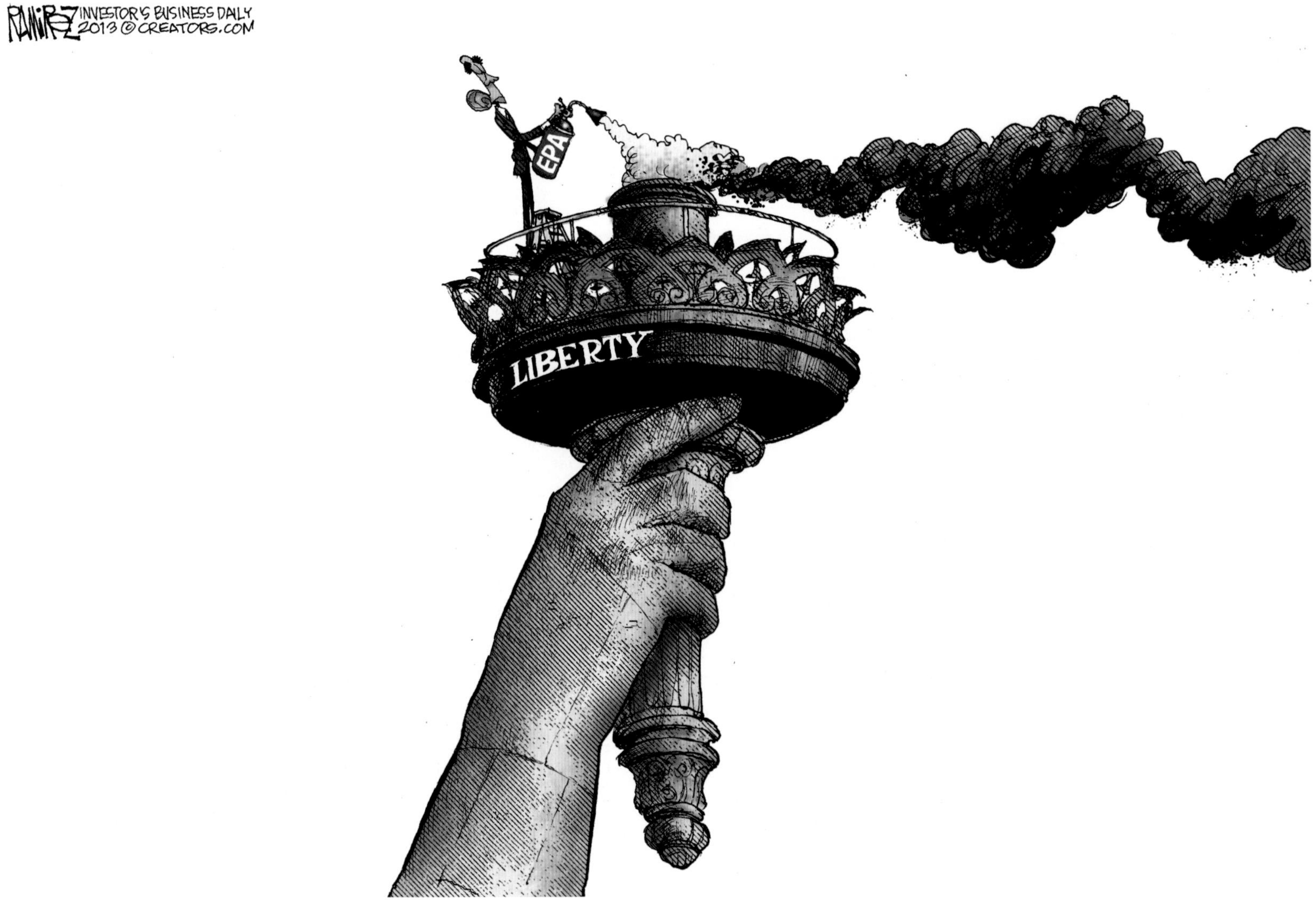
RAMIREZ INVESTOR'S BUSINESS DAILY
2013 © CREATORS.COM
EPA
LIBERTY

RES PUBLICA

"The problem is, is that the way Bush has done it over the last eight years is to take out a credit card from the Bank of China in the name of our children, driving up our national debt.... That's irresponsible. It's unpatriotic."

—President Barack Obama,
Fargo, North Dakota, July 3, 2008

Washington, D.C., continued to be the problem instead of the solution. Democrats pushed forward on legislation with a proven track record of failure. Republicans fought among themselves. Politics won the day, and America lost.

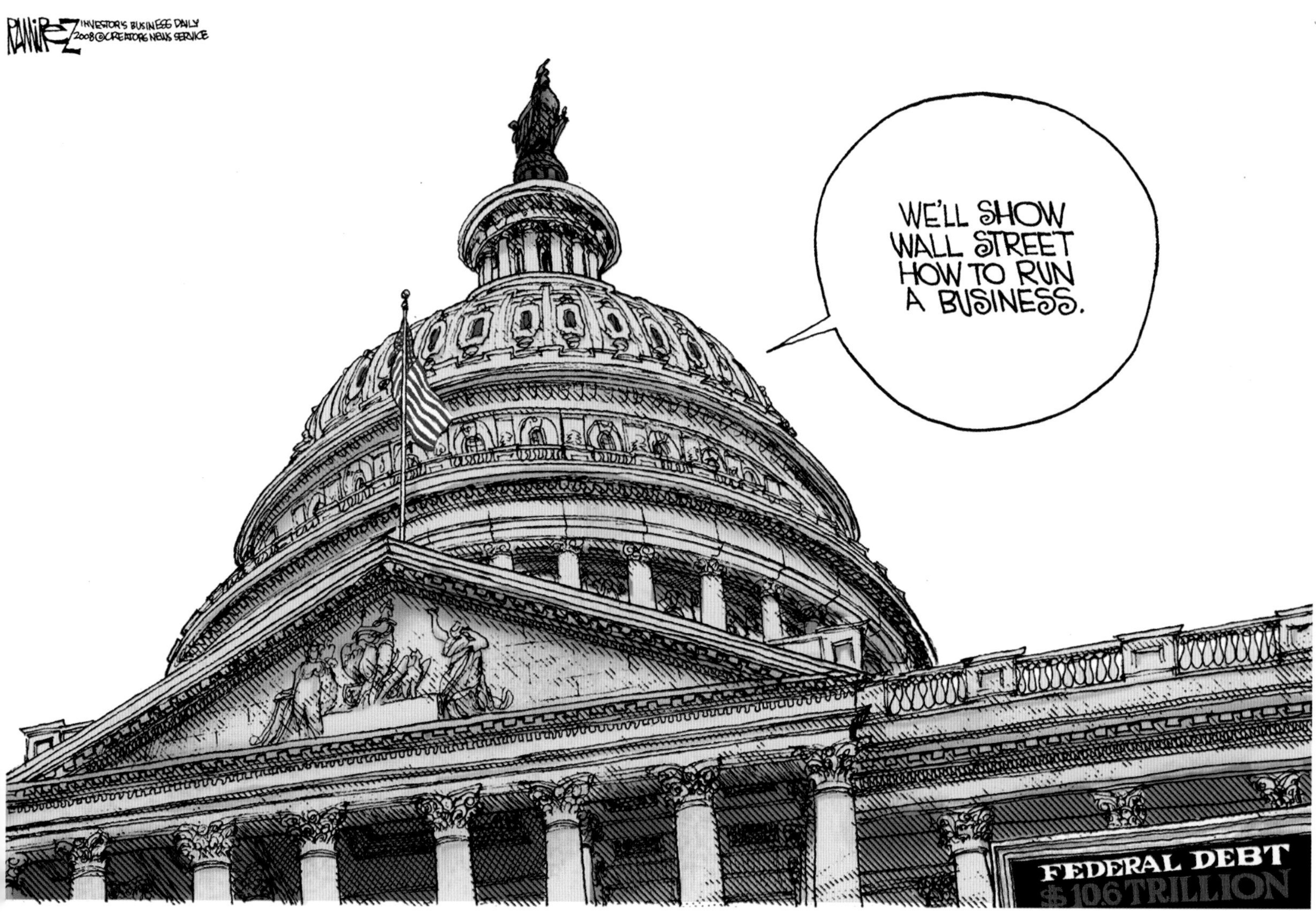
RAMIREZ INVESTOR'S BUSINESS DAILY 2008 ©CREATORS NEWS SERVICE
WE'LL SHOW WALL STREET HOW TO RUN A BUSINESS.
FEDERAL DEBT
$10.6 TRILLION

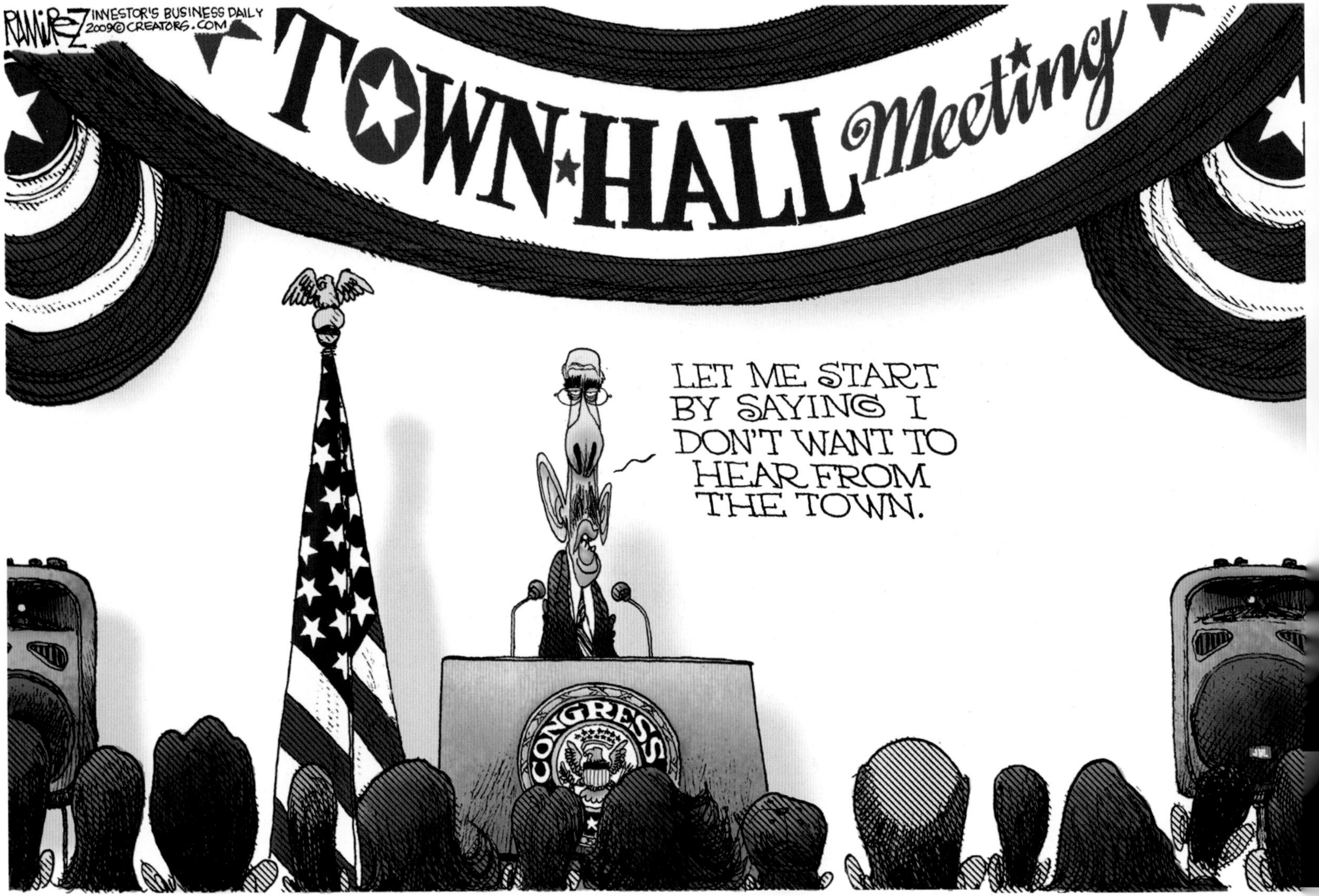
RAMIREZ
INVESTOR'S BUSINESS DAILY
2009© CREATORS.COM
TOWN★HALL Meeting
LET ME START BY SAYING I DON'T WANT TO HEAR FROM THE TOWN.
CONGRESS

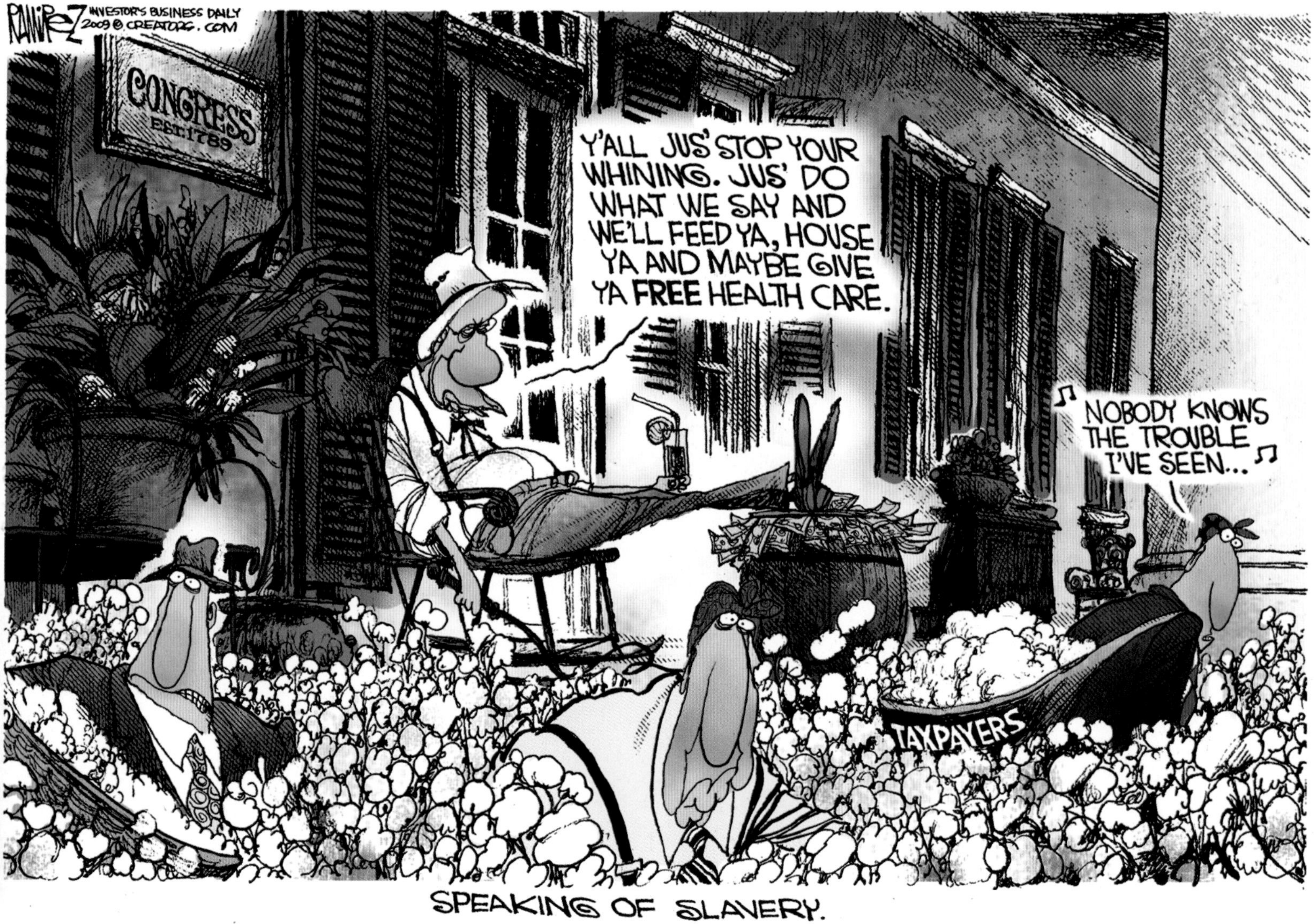
RAMIREZ INVESTOR'S BUSINESS DAILY 2009 © CREATORS.COM
CONGRESS EST. 1789
Y'ALL JUS' STOP YOUR WHINING. JUS' DO WHAT WE SAY AND WE'LL FEED YA, HOUSE YA AND MAYBE GIVE YA **FREE** HEALTH CARE.
NOBODY KNOWS THE TROUBLE I'VE SEEN...
TAXPAYERS
SPEAKING OF SLAVERY.

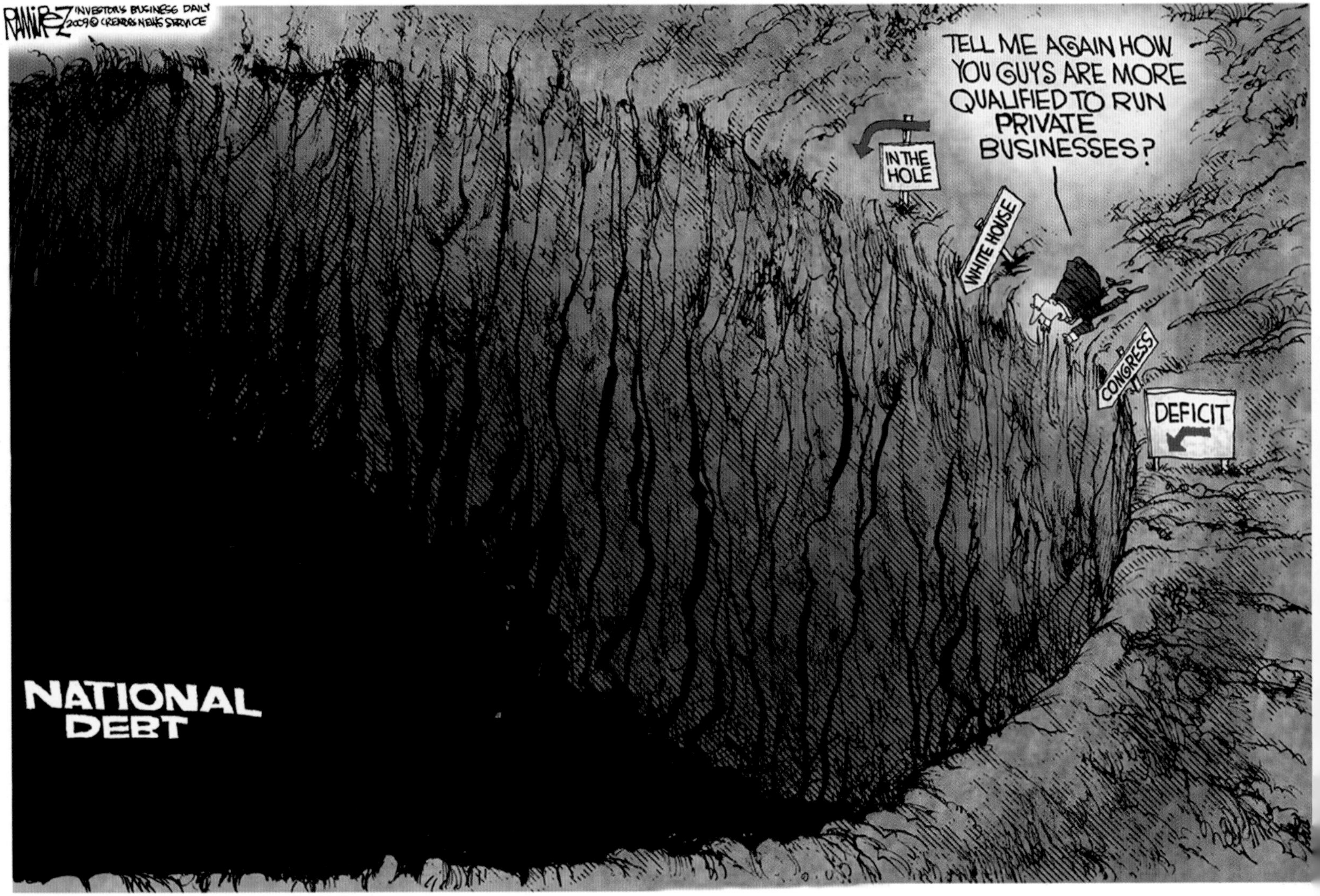
RAMIREZ INVESTOR'S BUSINESS DAILY
2009 © CREATORS NEWS SERVICE
TELL ME AGAIN HOW YOU GUYS ARE MORE QUALIFIED TO RUN PRIVATE BUSINESSES?
IN THE HOLE
WHITE HOUSE
CONGRESS
DEFICIT
NATIONAL DEBT

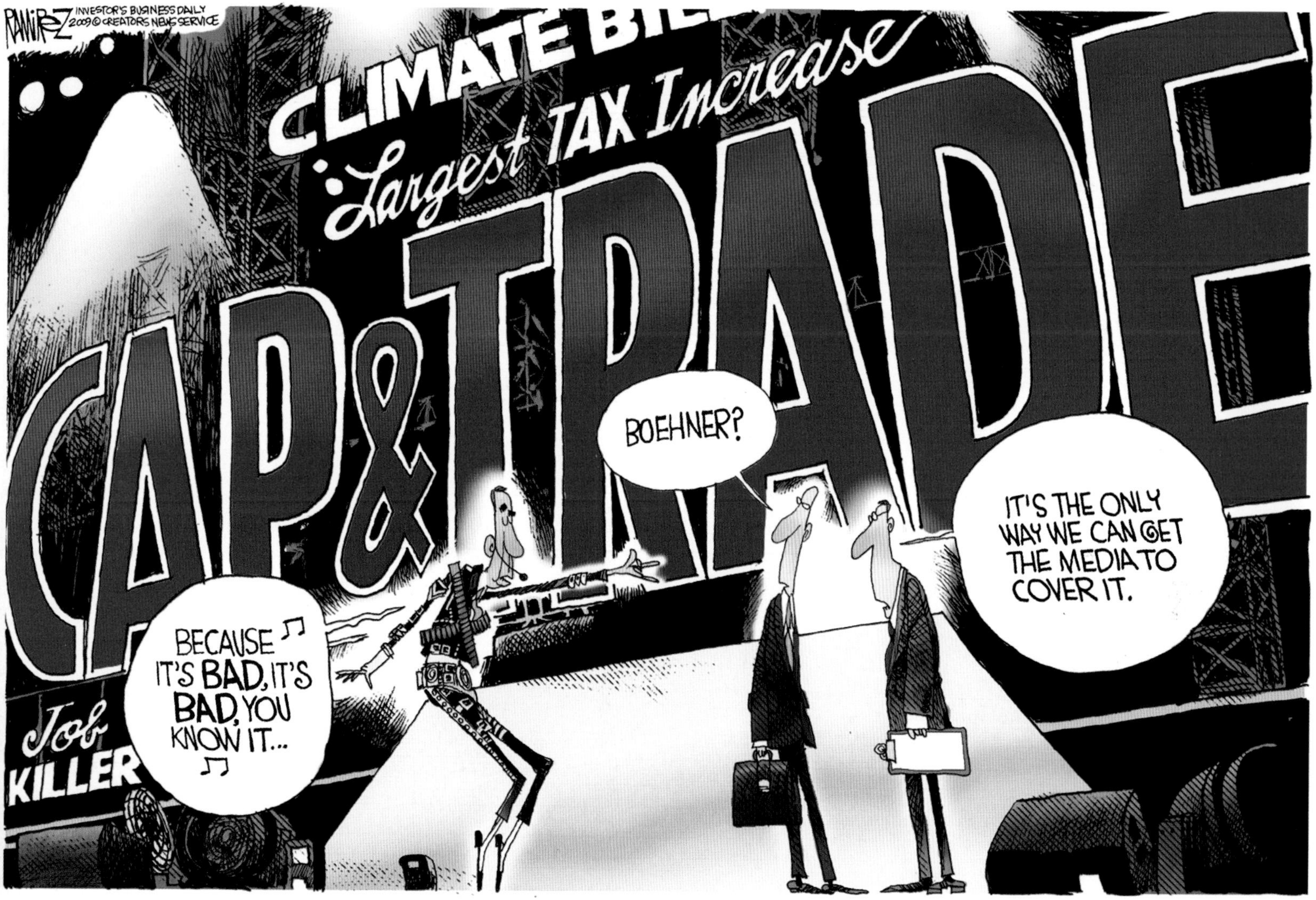
RAMIREZ INVESTOR'S BUSINESS DAILY 2009 © CREATORS NEWS SERVICE
CLIMATE BI
Largest TAX Increase
CAP&TRADE
Job KILLER
BECAUSE IT'S BAD, IT'S BAD, YOU KNOW IT...
BOEHNER?
IT'S THE ONLY WAY WE CAN GET THE MEDIA TO COVER IT.

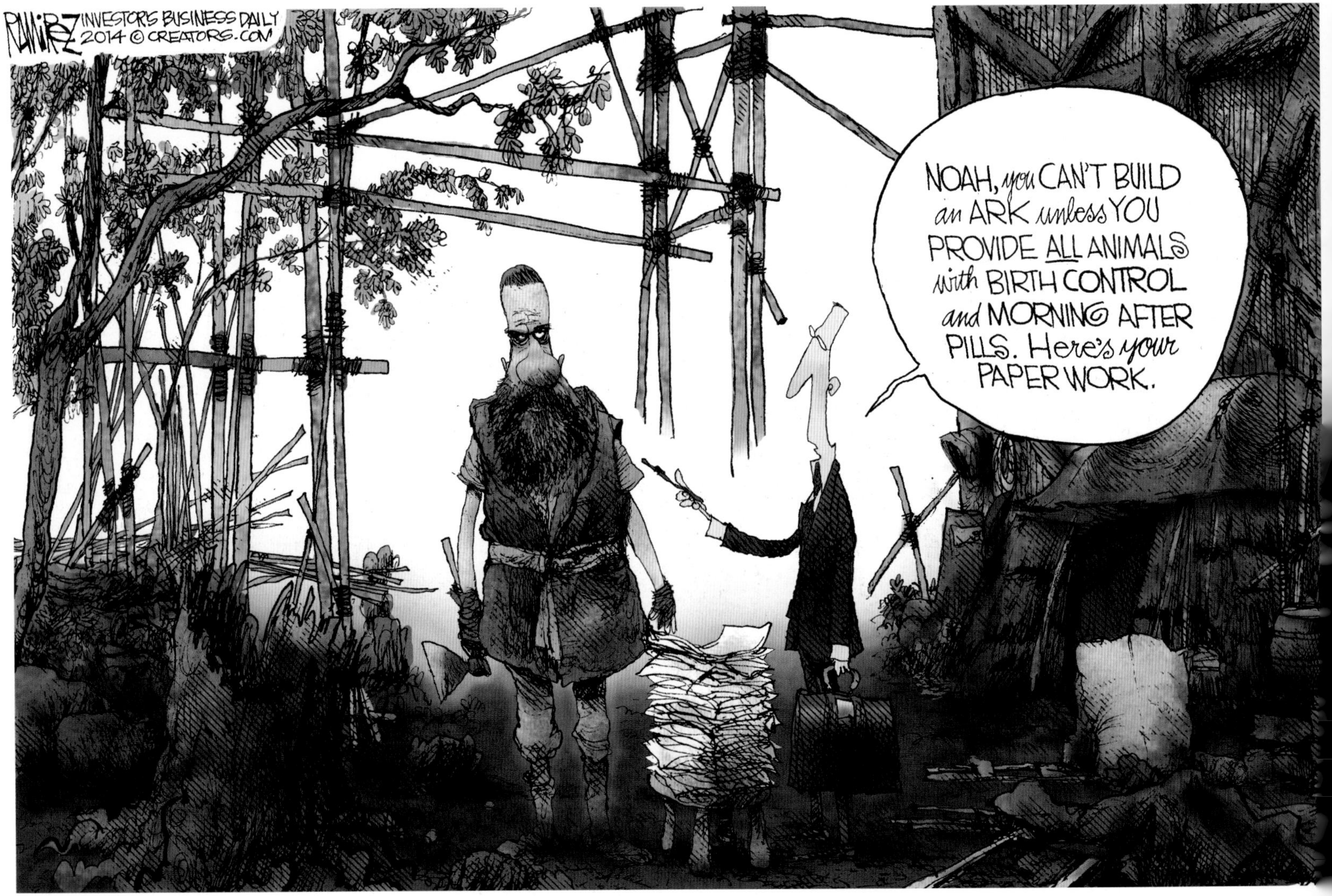
RAMIREZ INVESTOR'S BUSINESS DAILY
2014 © CREATORS.COM
NOAH, you CAN'T BUILD an ARK unless YOU PROVIDE ALL ANIMALS with BIRTH CONTROL and MORNING AFTER PILLS. Here's your PAPER WORK.

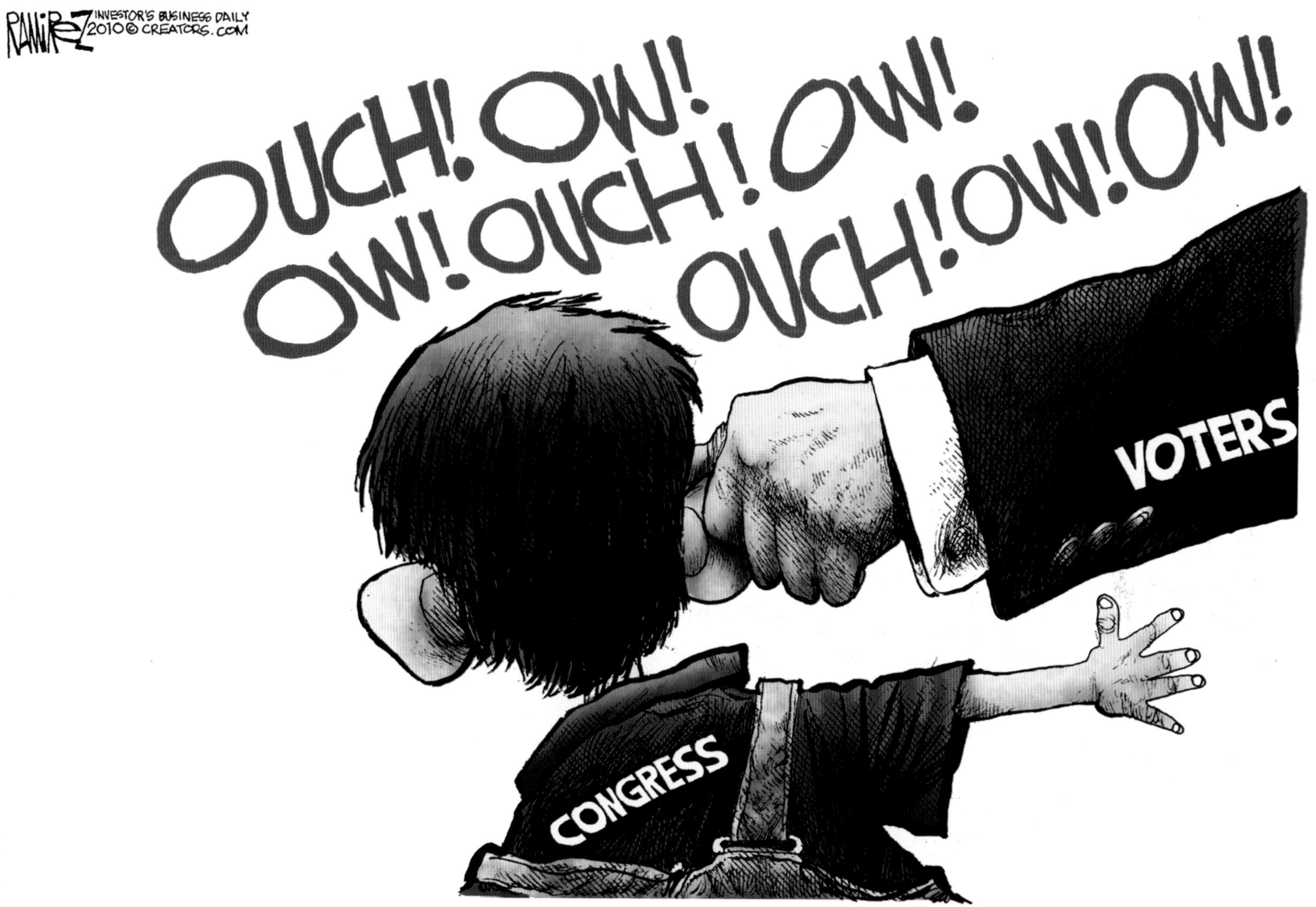
RAMIREZ INVESTOR'S BUSINESS DAILY 2010 © CREATORS.COM
OUCH! OW! OW! OUCH! OW! OUCH! OW! OW!
VOTERS
CONGRESS

EARMARKS

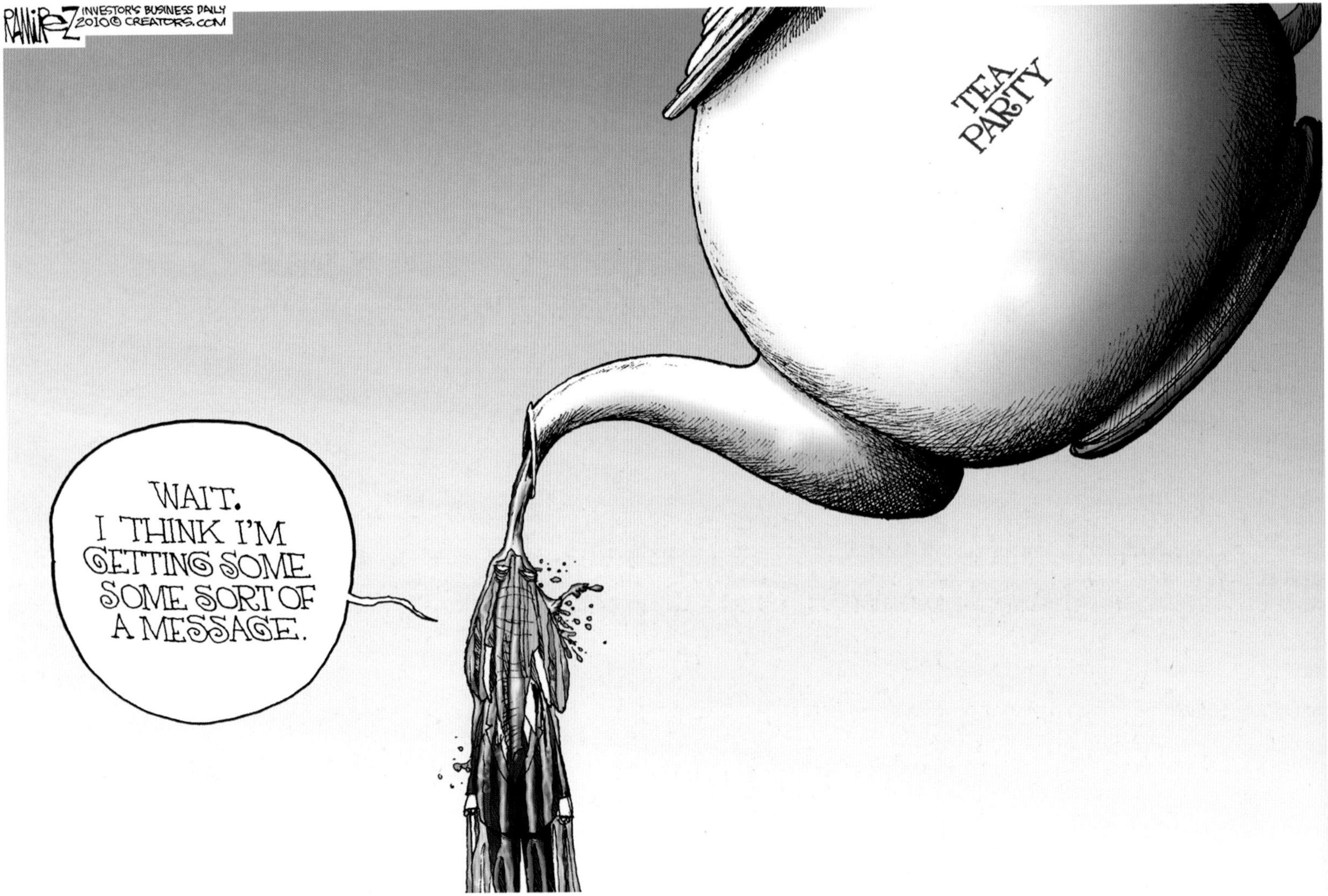
RAMIREZ INVESTOR'S BUSINESS DAILY 2010© CREATORS.COM
TEA PARTY
WAIT. I THINK I'M GETTING SOME SOME SORT OF A MESSAGE.

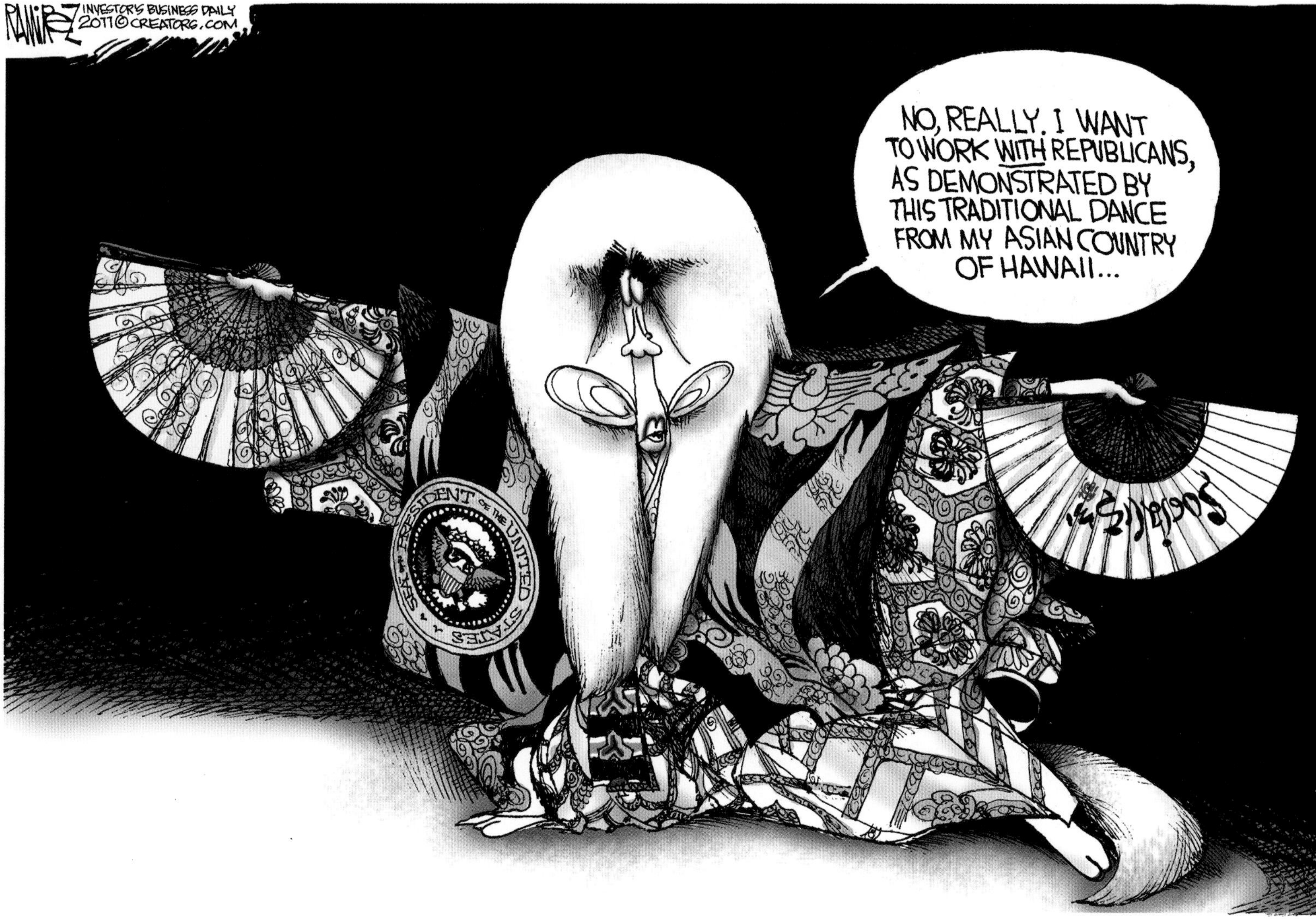
RAMIREZ
INVESTOR'S BUSINESS DAILY 2011 © CREATORS.COM
NO, REALLY. I WANT TO WORK WITH REPUBLICANS, AS DEMONSTRATED BY THIS TRADITIONAL DANCE FROM MY ASIAN COUNTRY OF HAWAII...
SEAL OF THE PRESIDENT OF THE UNITED STATES

KABUKI THEATER

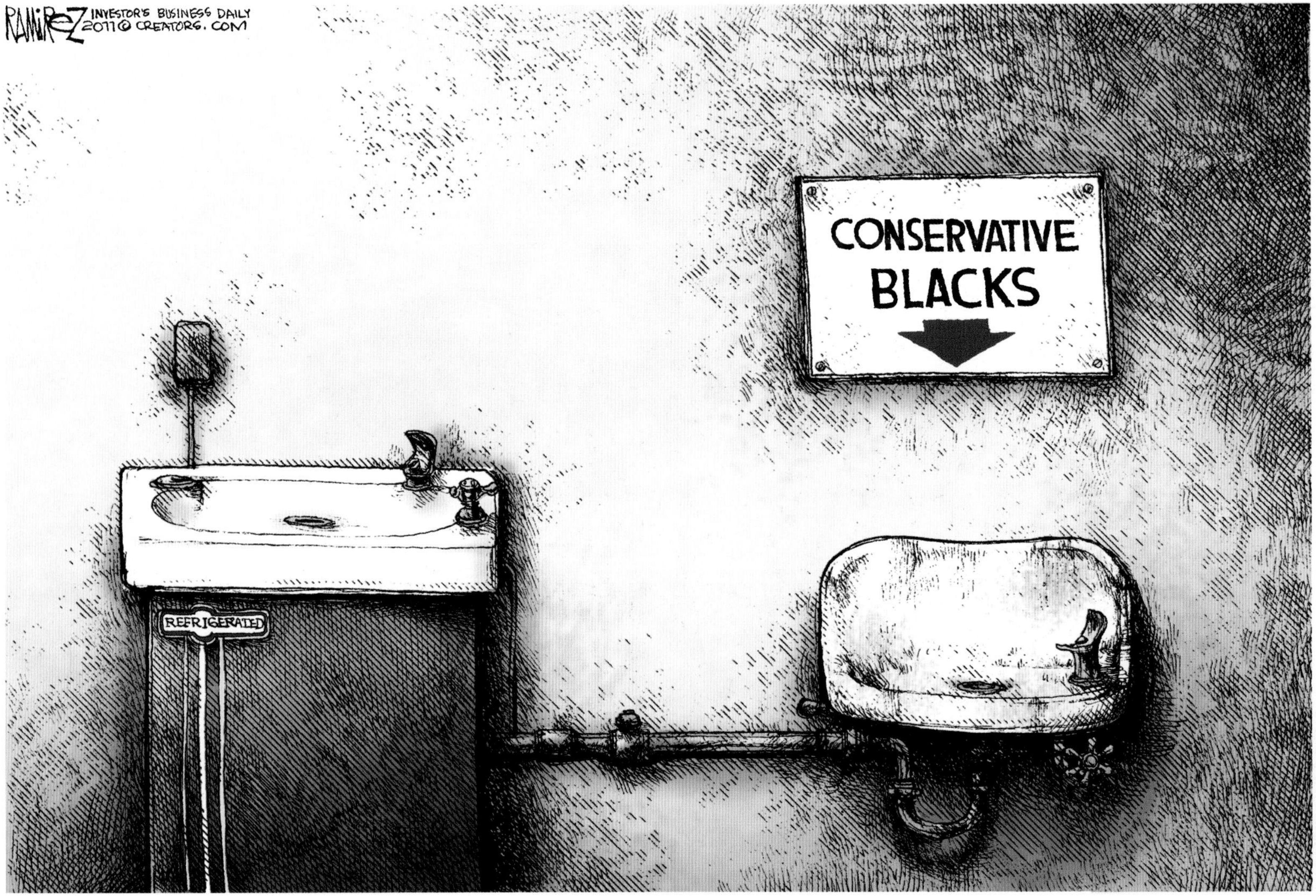
RAMIREZ INVESTOR'S BUSINESS DAILY
2011 © CREATORS.COM
CONSERVATIVE
BLACKS
REFRIGERATED

* 1991 REVISTED

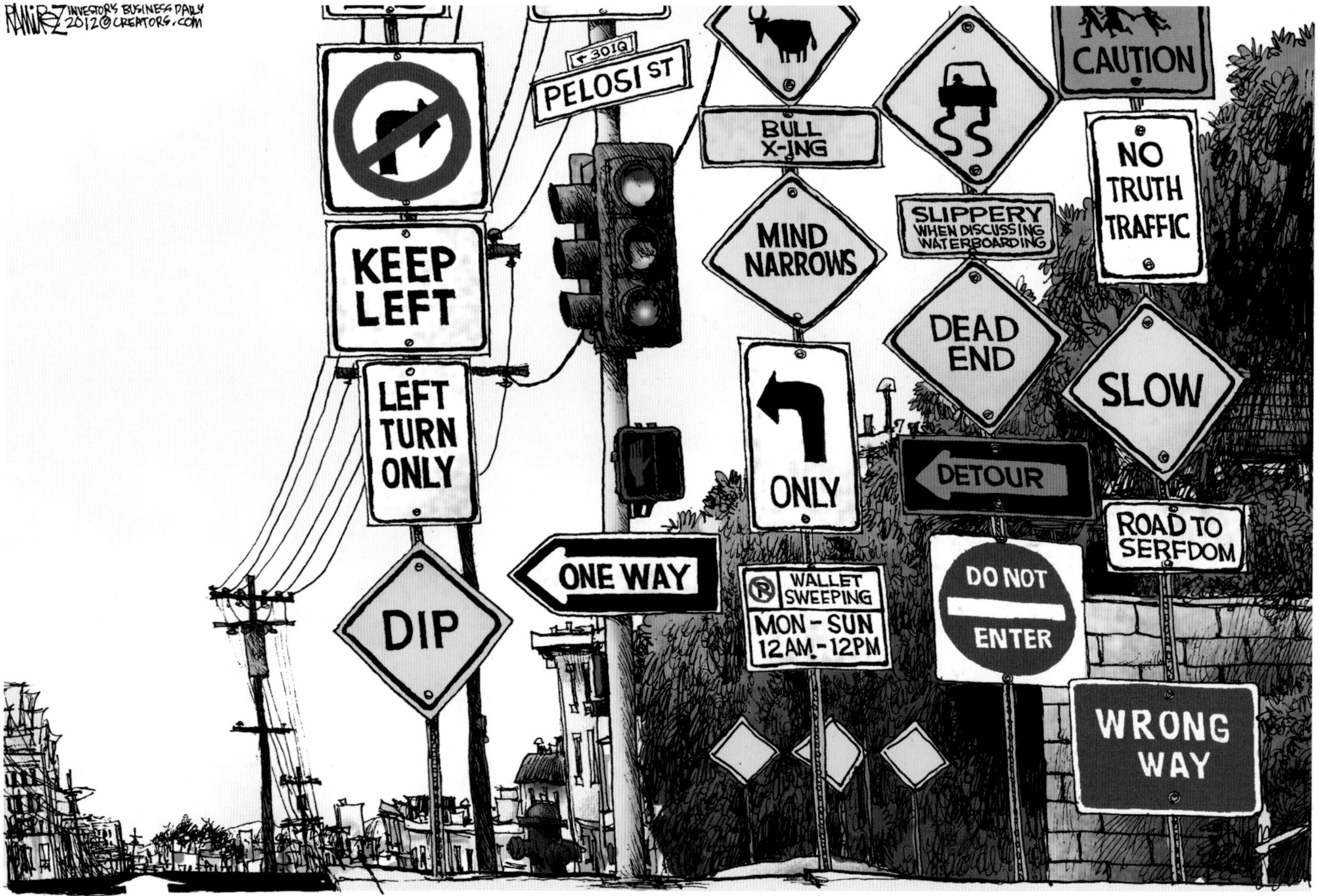
RAMIREZ INVESTOR'S BUSINESS DAILY 2012 © CREATORS.COM
PELOSI ST
BULL X-ING
CAUTION
NO TRUTH TRAFFIC
SLIPPERY WHEN DISCUSSING WATERBOARDING
KEEP LEFT
MIND NARROWS
DEAD END
LEFT TURN ONLY
SLOW
ONLY
DETOUR
ROAD TO SERFDOM
ONE WAY
WALLET SWEEPING MON - SUN 12AM - 12PM
DO NOT ENTER
DIP
WRONG WAY

SAN FRANCISCO TO RENAME STREET AFTER NANCY PELOSI

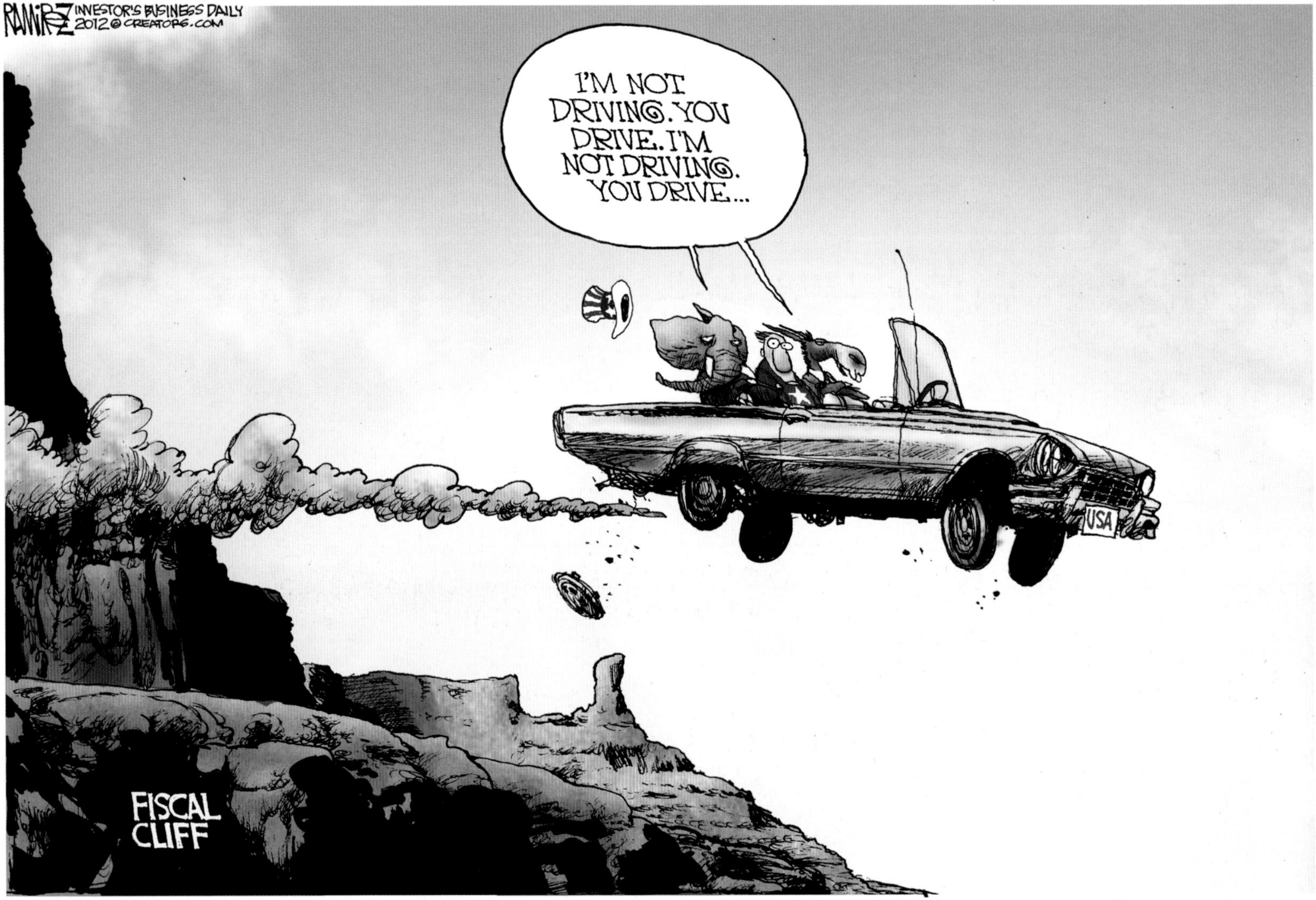
RAMIREZ INVESTOR'S BUSINESS DAILY 2012 © CREATORS.COM
I'M NOT DRIVING. YOU DRIVE. I'M NOT DRIVING. YOU DRIVE...
USA
FISCAL CLIFF

THELMA, UNCLE SAM & LOUISE

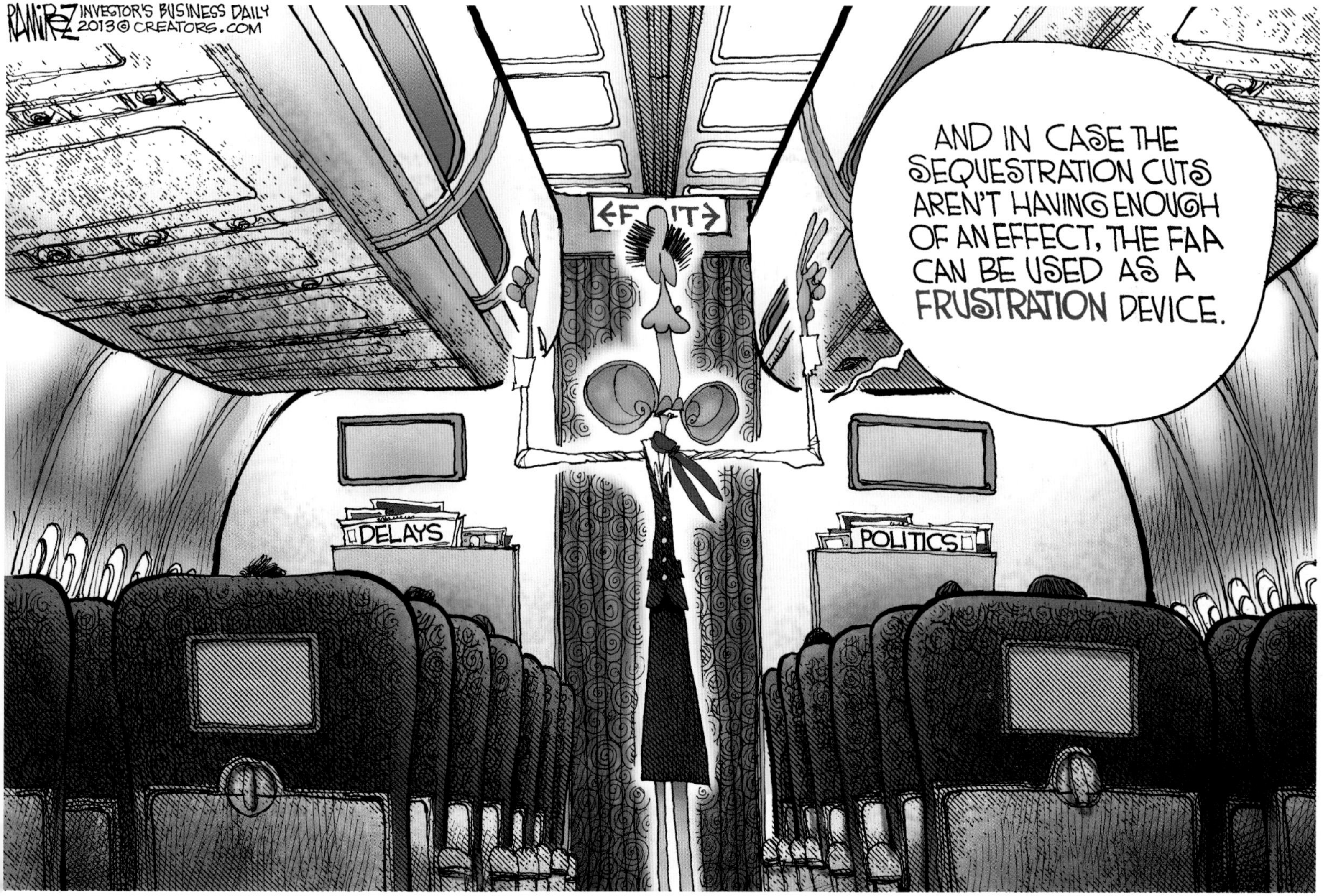
RAMIREZ INVESTOR'S BUSINESS DAILY 2013 © CREATORS.COM
AND IN CASE THE SEQUESTRATION CUTS AREN'T HAVING ENOUGH OF AN EFFECT, THE FAA CAN BE USED AS A FRUSTRATION DEVICE.
DELAYS
POLITICS

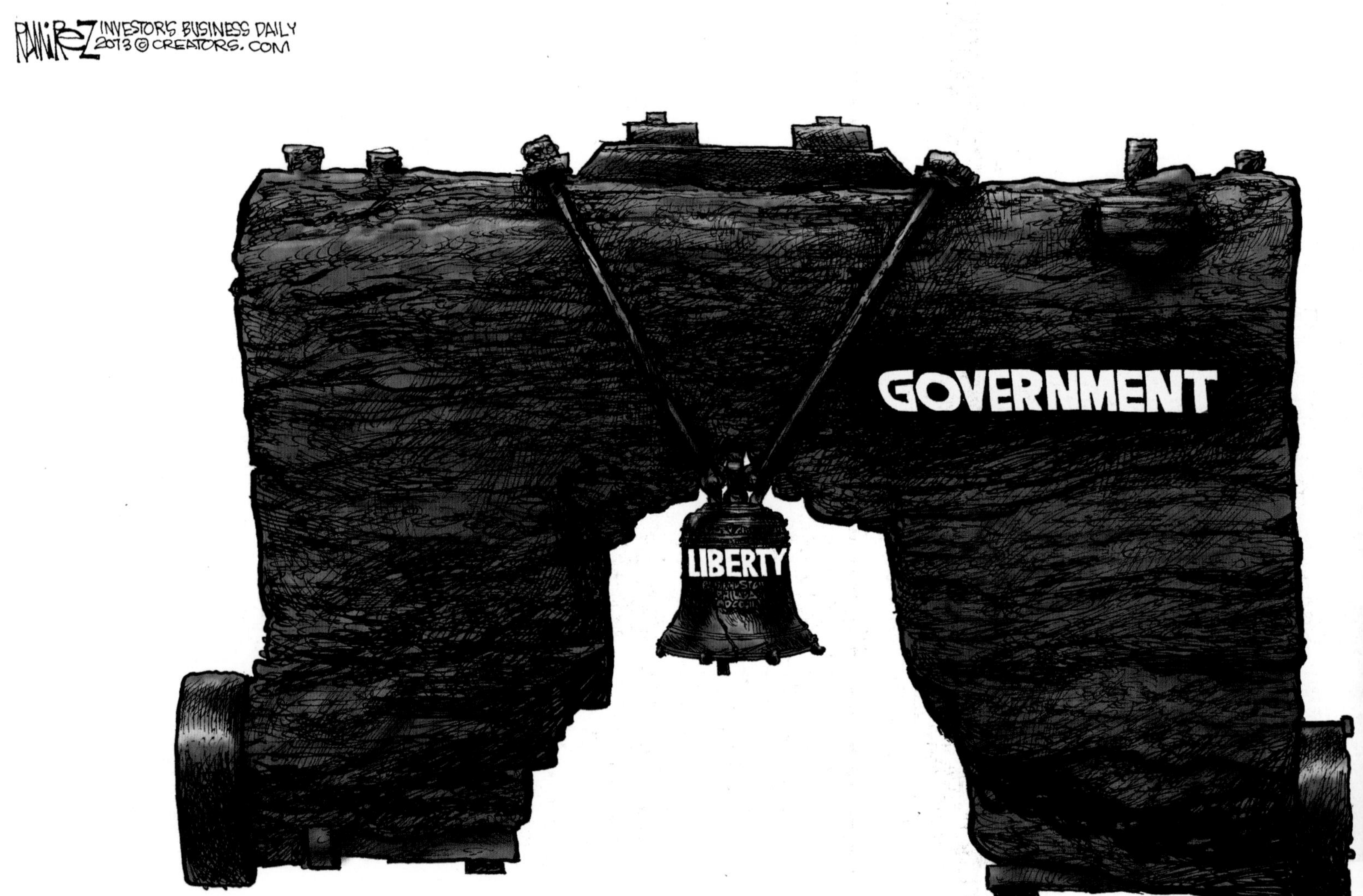
RAMIREZ
INVESTOR'S BUSINESS DAILY
2013 © CREATORS.COM
GOVERNMENT
LIBERTY

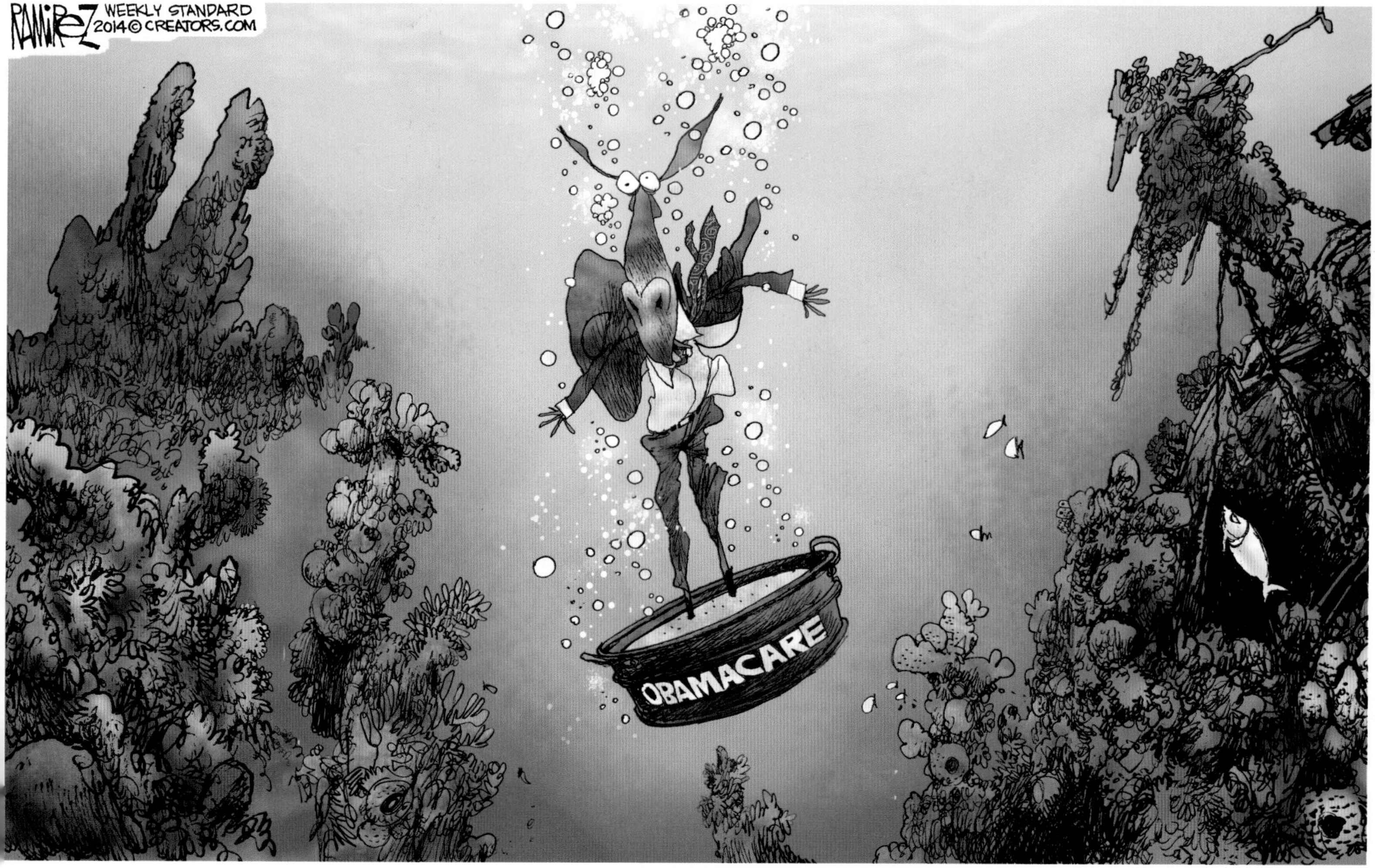
RAMIREZ
WEEKLY STANDARD
2014 © CREATORS.COM
OBAMACARE

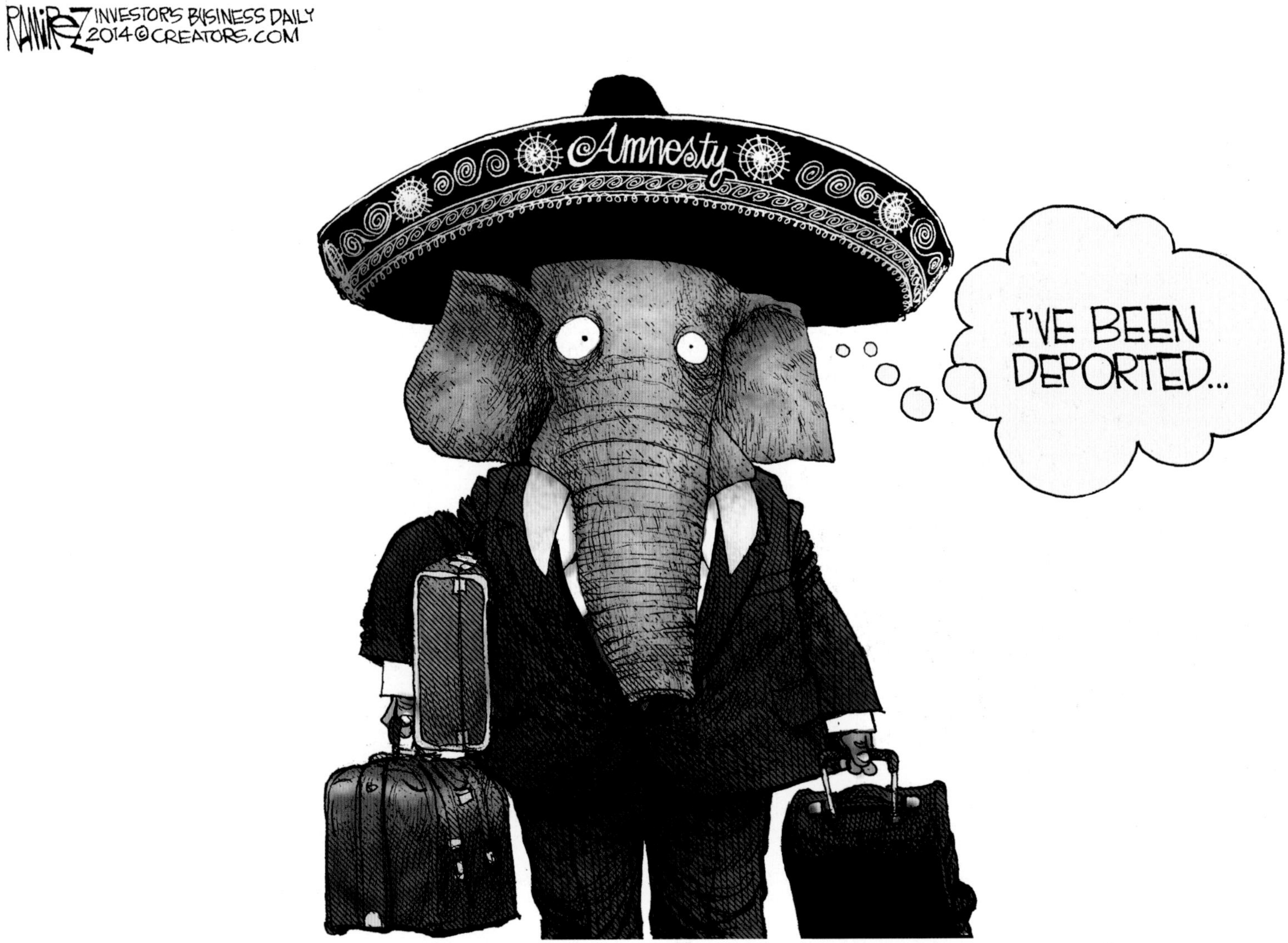
RAMIREZ INVESTOR'S BUSINESS DAILY
2014 © CREATORS.COM
Amnesty
I'VE BEEN DEPORTED...

The ONLY ACTION CONGRESS should take on IMMIGRATION this year.

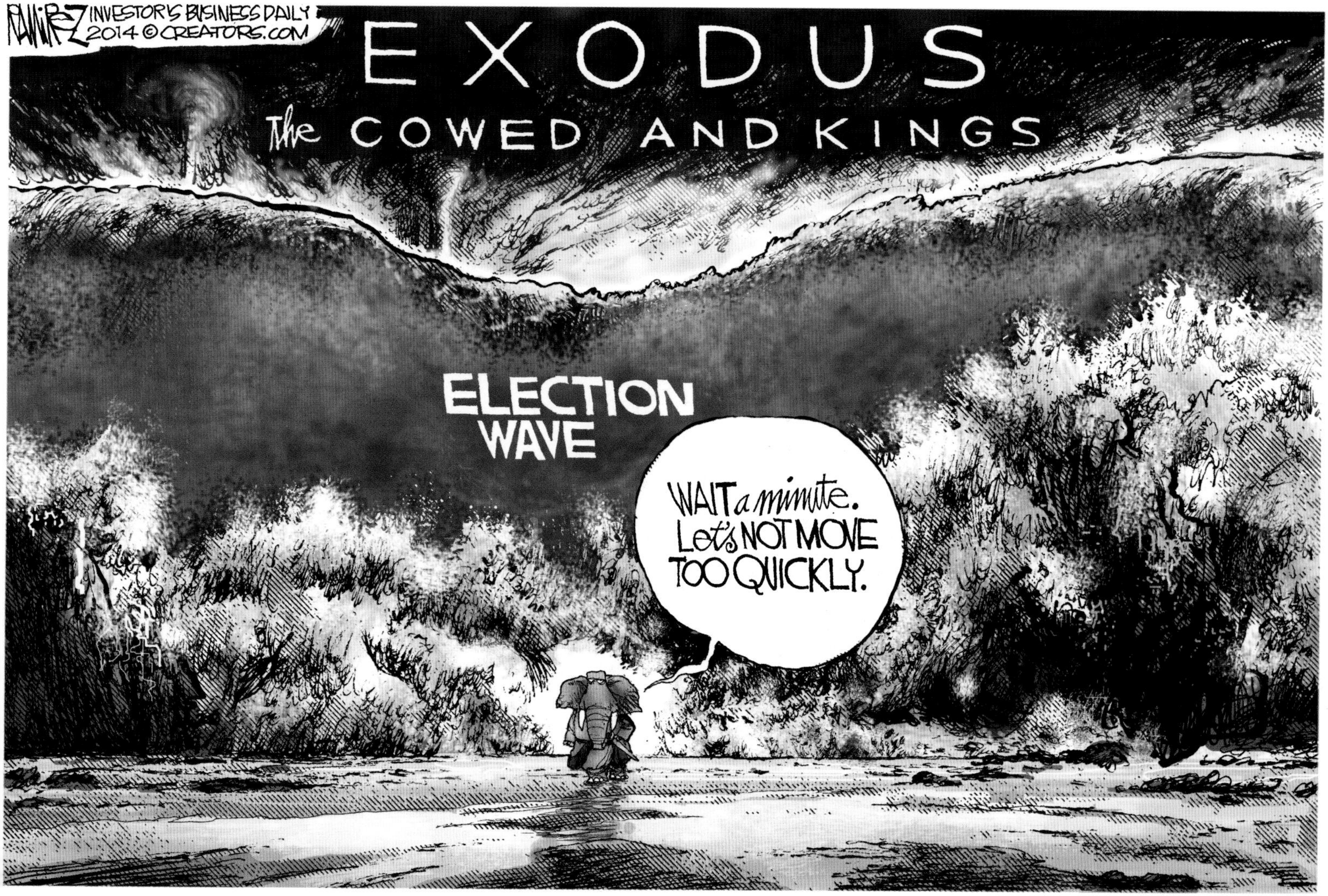
RAMIREZ INVESTOR'S BUSINESS DAILY 2014 © CREATORS.COM
EXODUS
The COWED AND KINGS
ELECTION WAVE
WAIT a minute. Let's NOT MOVE TOO QUICKLY.

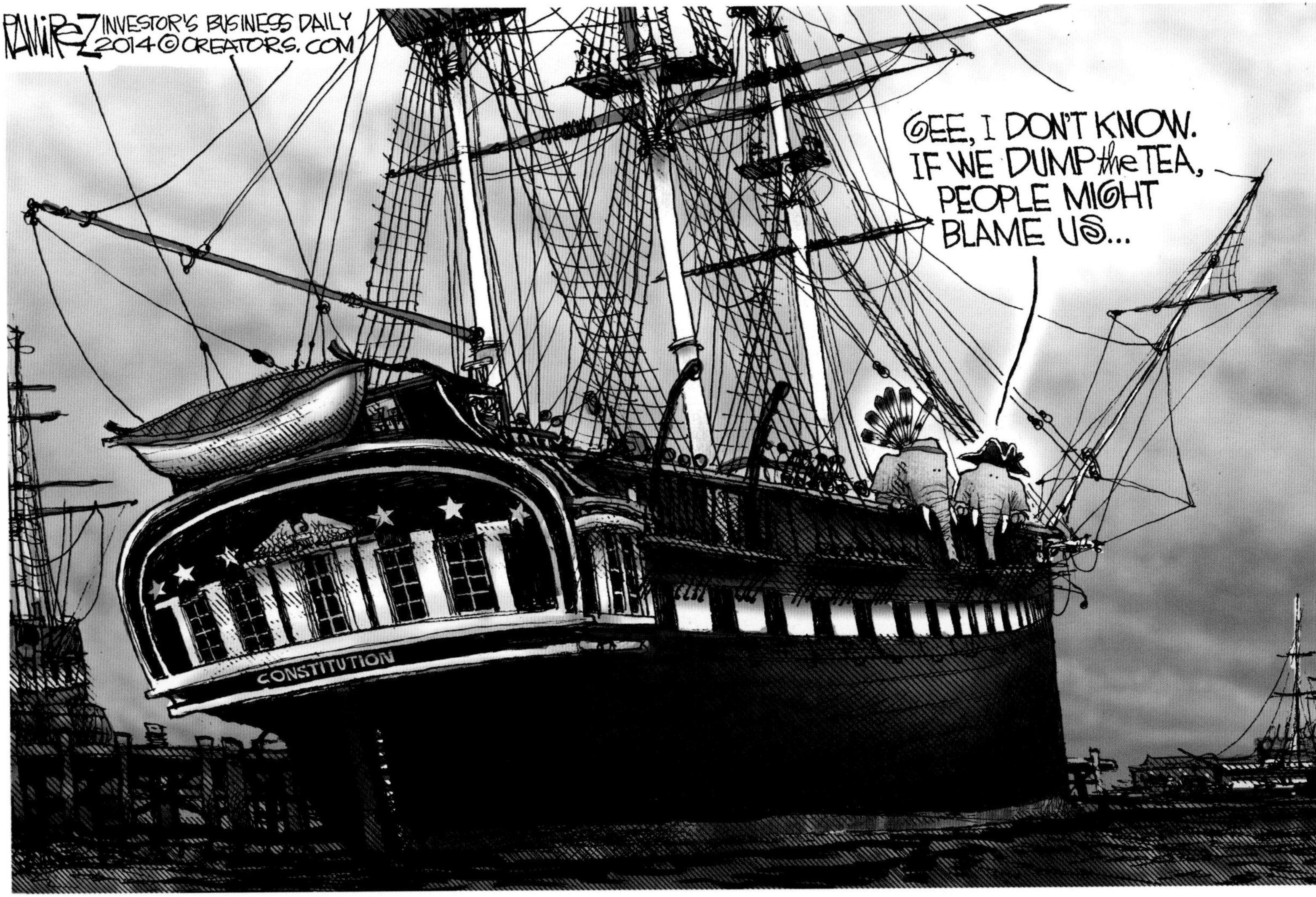
RAMIREZ INVESTOR'S BUSINESS DAILY
2014 © CREATORS.COM
GEE, I DON'T KNOW. IF WE DUMP the TEA, PEOPLE MIGHT BLAME US...
CONSTITUTION

IF the GOP was in CHARGE during the AMERICAN REVOLUTION...

SCANDAL

"Not even a smidgen of corruption."

—President Barack Obama,
Washington, D.C., February 2, 2014

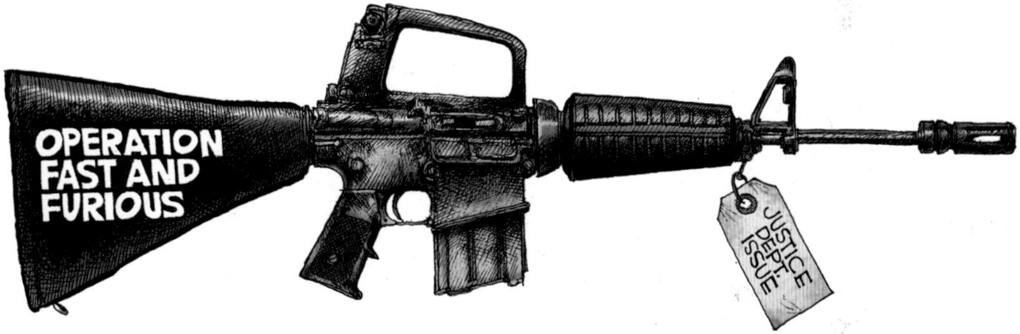
OPERATION FAST AND FURIOUS
JUSTICE DEPT. ISSUE

Scandals plagued the Obama administration: Obamacare, Fast and Furious, the VA, the IRS, Solyndra, Benghazi, DOJ investigations of the press, releasing Gitmo detainees, releasing illegal immigrant felons, national intelligence leaks, spying on foreign leaders, NSA data collection, the unconstitutional overreach by the president. These were just a few that could not be ignored unless, of course, you were in the media. While a national nightmare, it was an editorial cartoonist's dream.

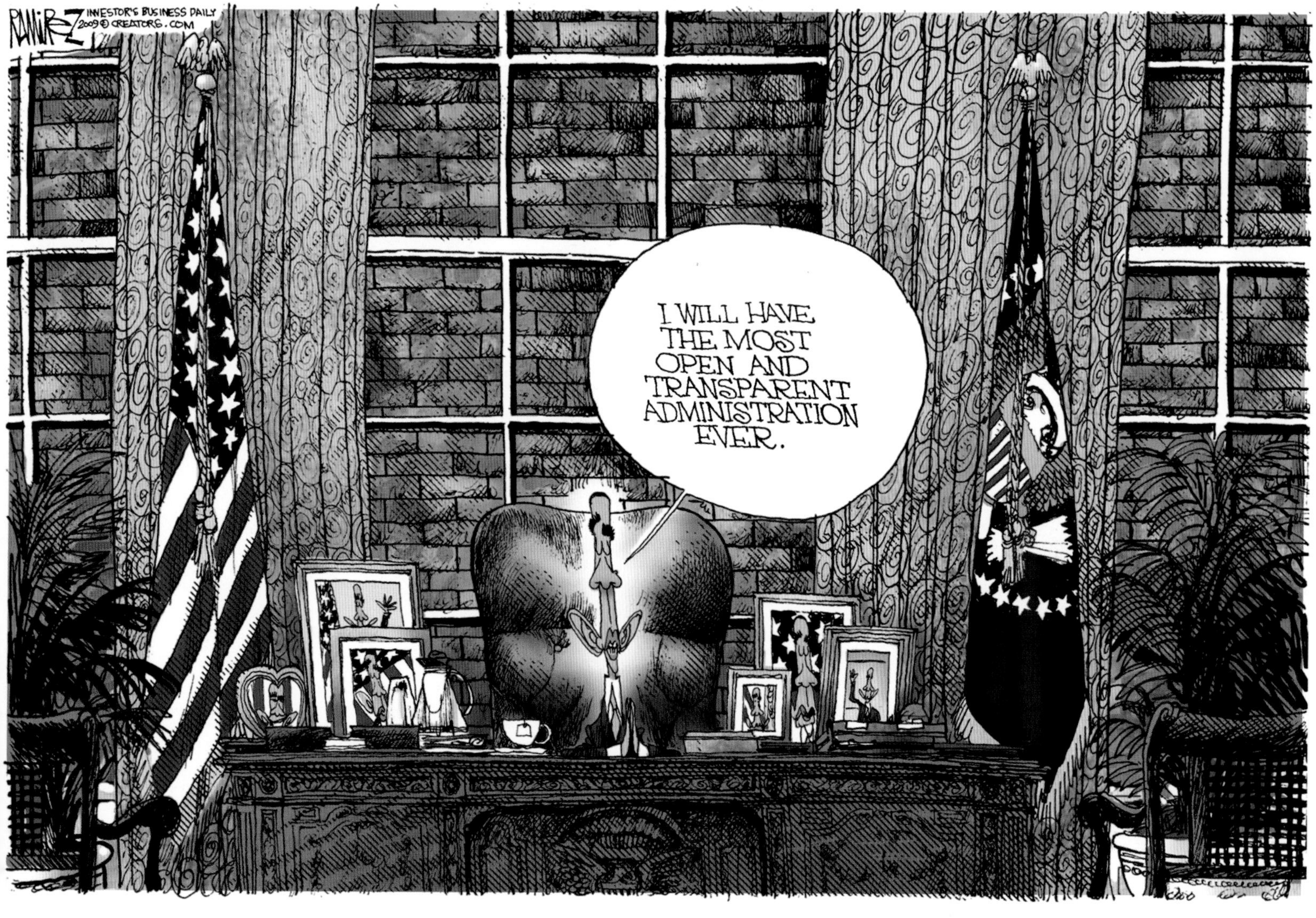
RAMIREZ
INVESTOR'S BUSINESS DAILY
2009 © CREATORS.COM
I WILL HAVE THE MOST OPEN AND TRANSPARENT ADMINISTRATION EVER.

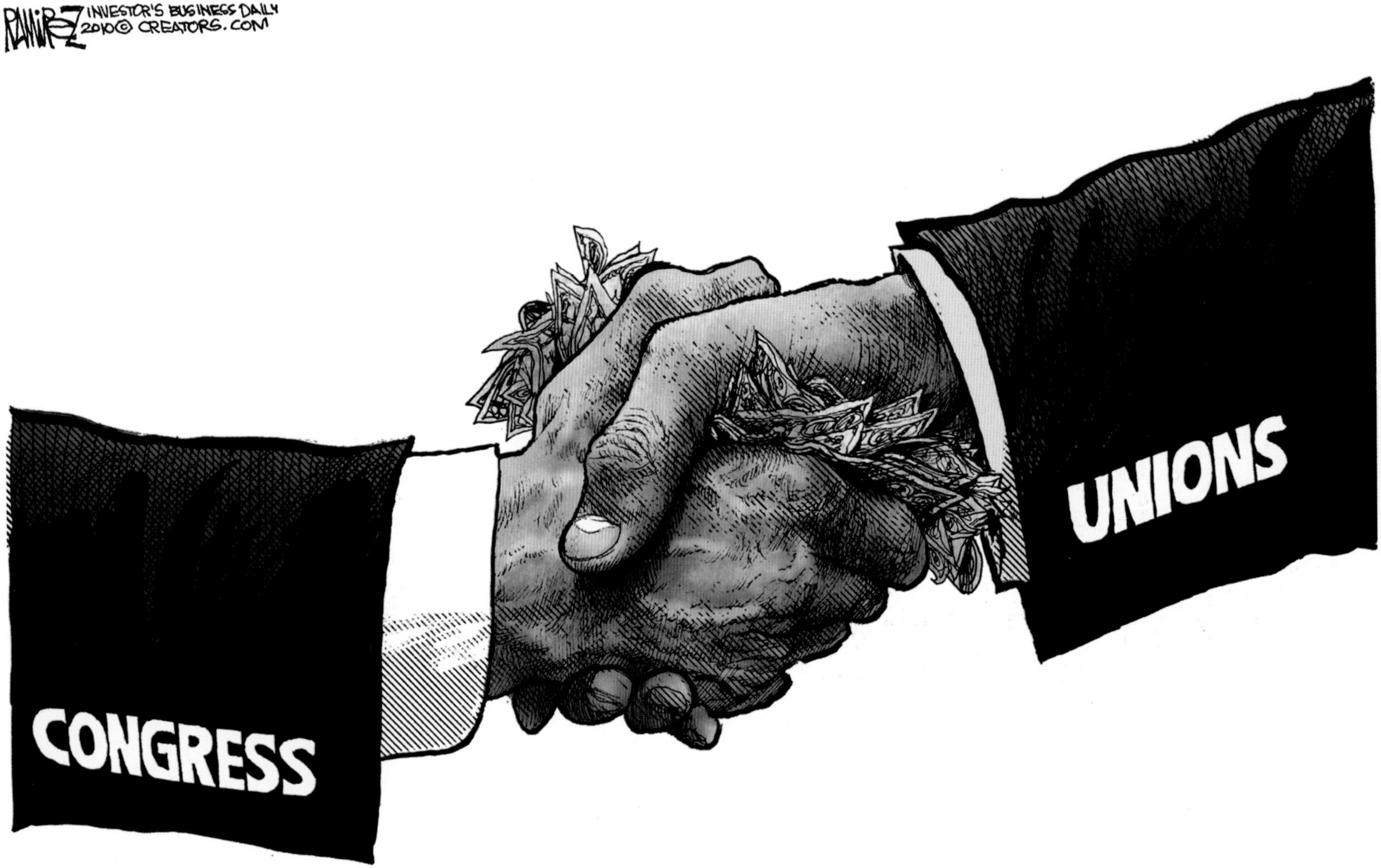
RAMIREZ INVESTOR'S BUSINESS DAILY 2010© CREATORS.COM
UNIONS
CONGRESS

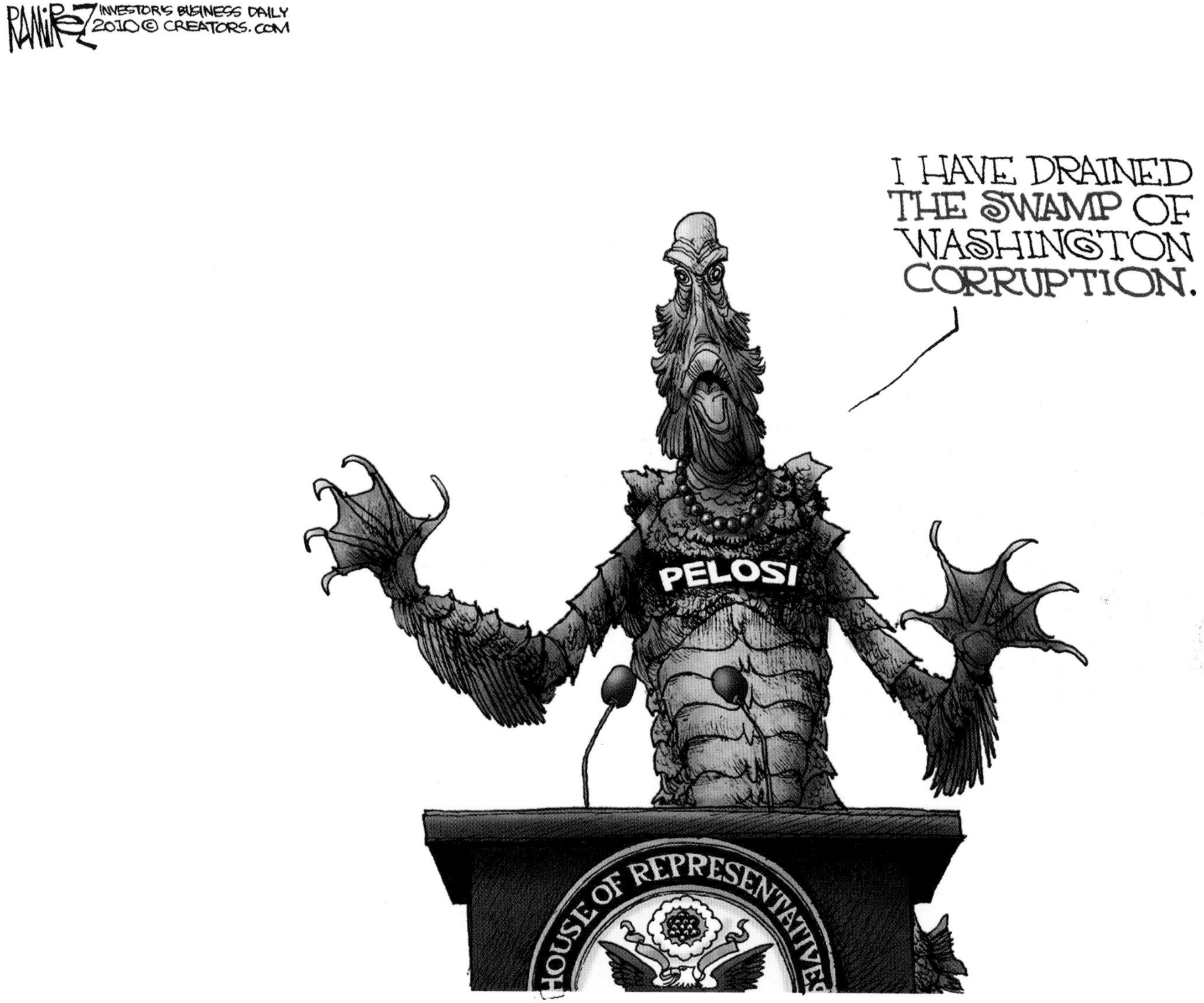
RAMIREZ INVESTOR'S BUSINESS DAILY 2010 © CREATORS.COM
I HAVE DRAINED THE SWAMP OF WASHINGTON CORRUPTION.
PELOSI
HOUSE OF REPRESENTATIVES

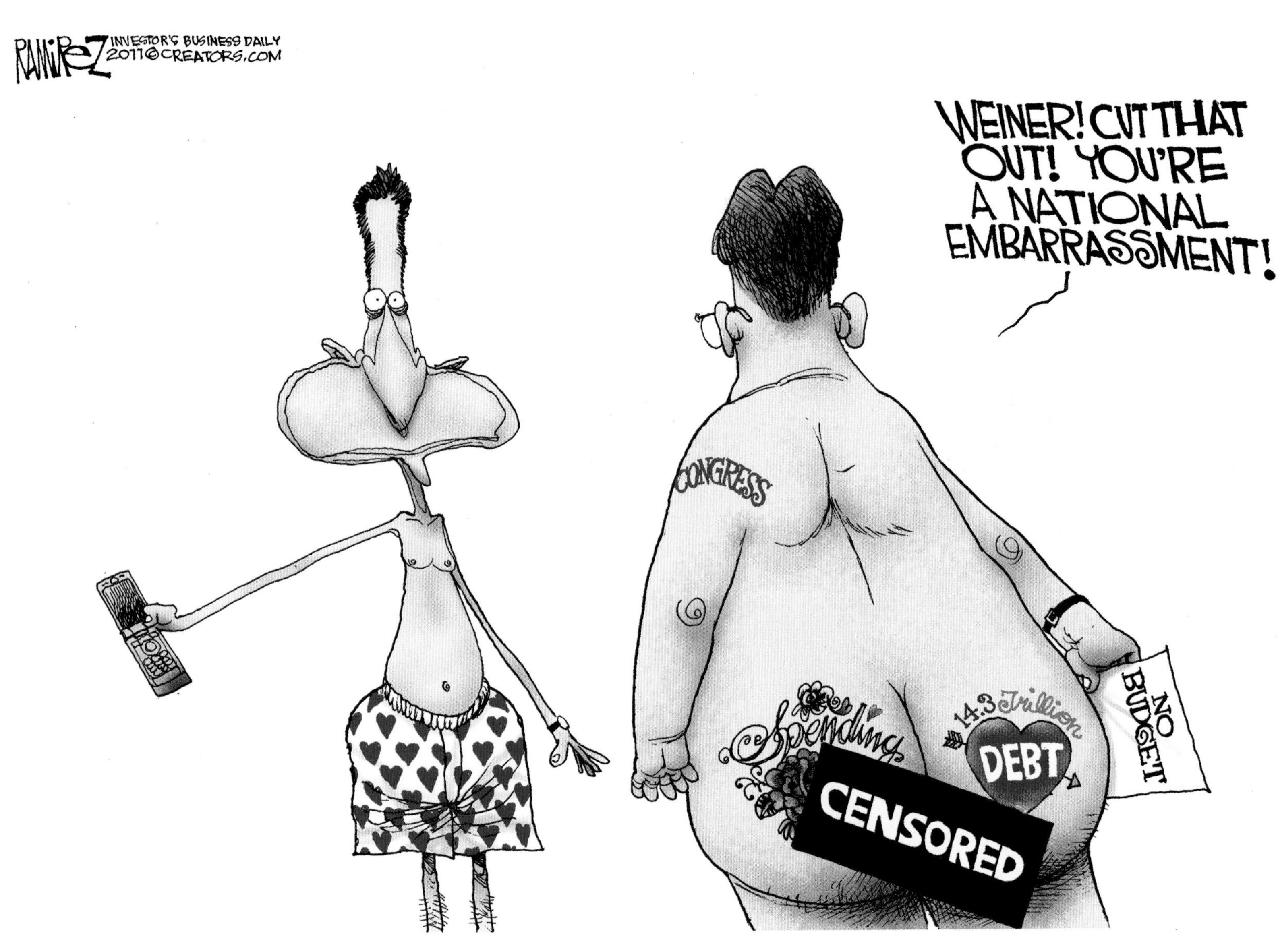
RAMIREZ
INVESTOR'S BUSINESS DAILY
2011©CREATORS.COM
WEINER! CUT THAT OUT! YOU'RE A NATIONAL EMBARRASSMENT!
CONGRESS
Spending
14.3 Trillion
DEBT
CENSORED
NO BUDGET

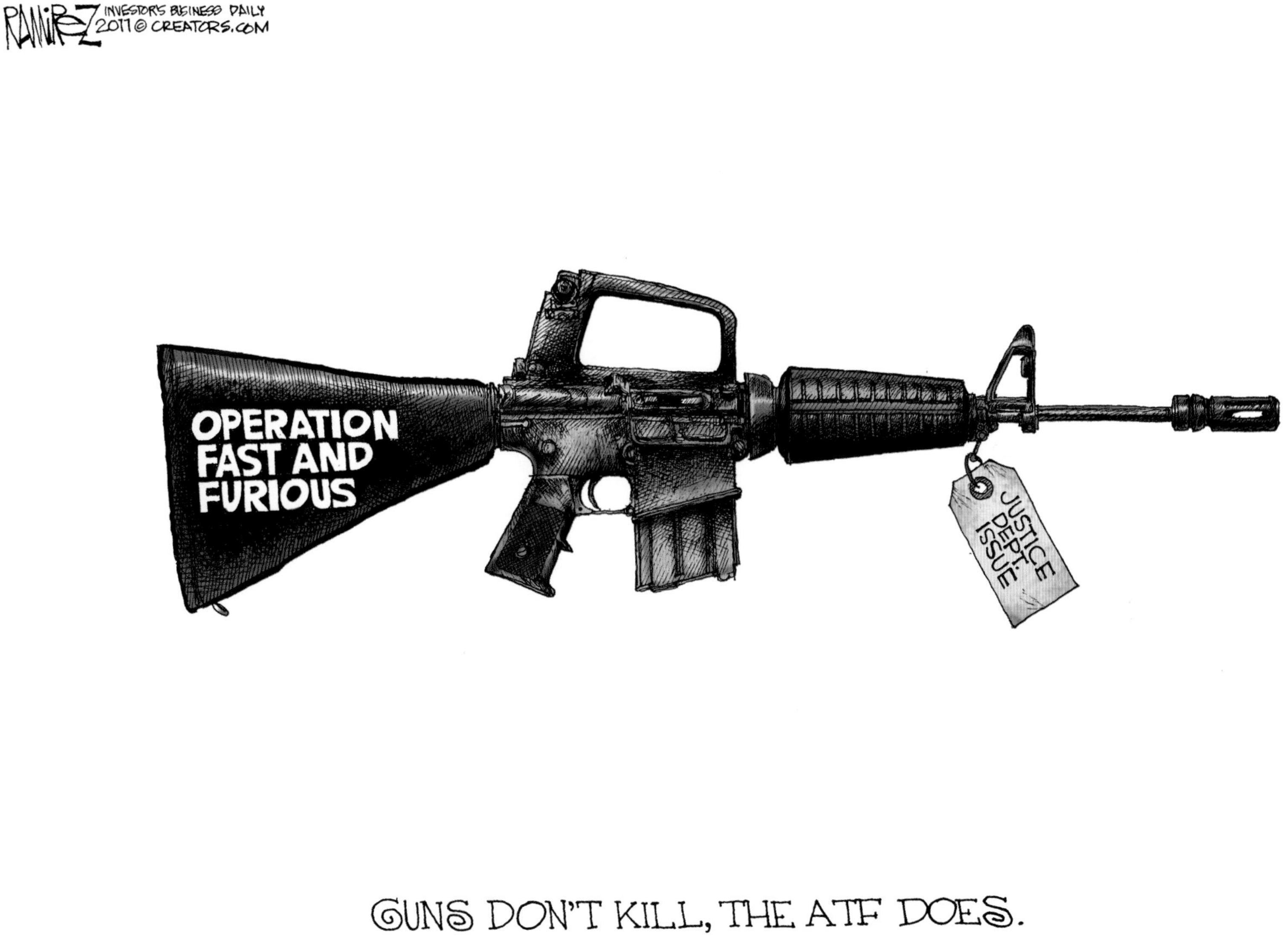
RAMIREZ INVESTOR'S BUSINESS DAILY 2011 © CREATORS.COM
OPERATION FAST AND FURIOUS
JUSTICE DEPT. ISSUE
GUNS DON'T KILL, THE ATF DOES.

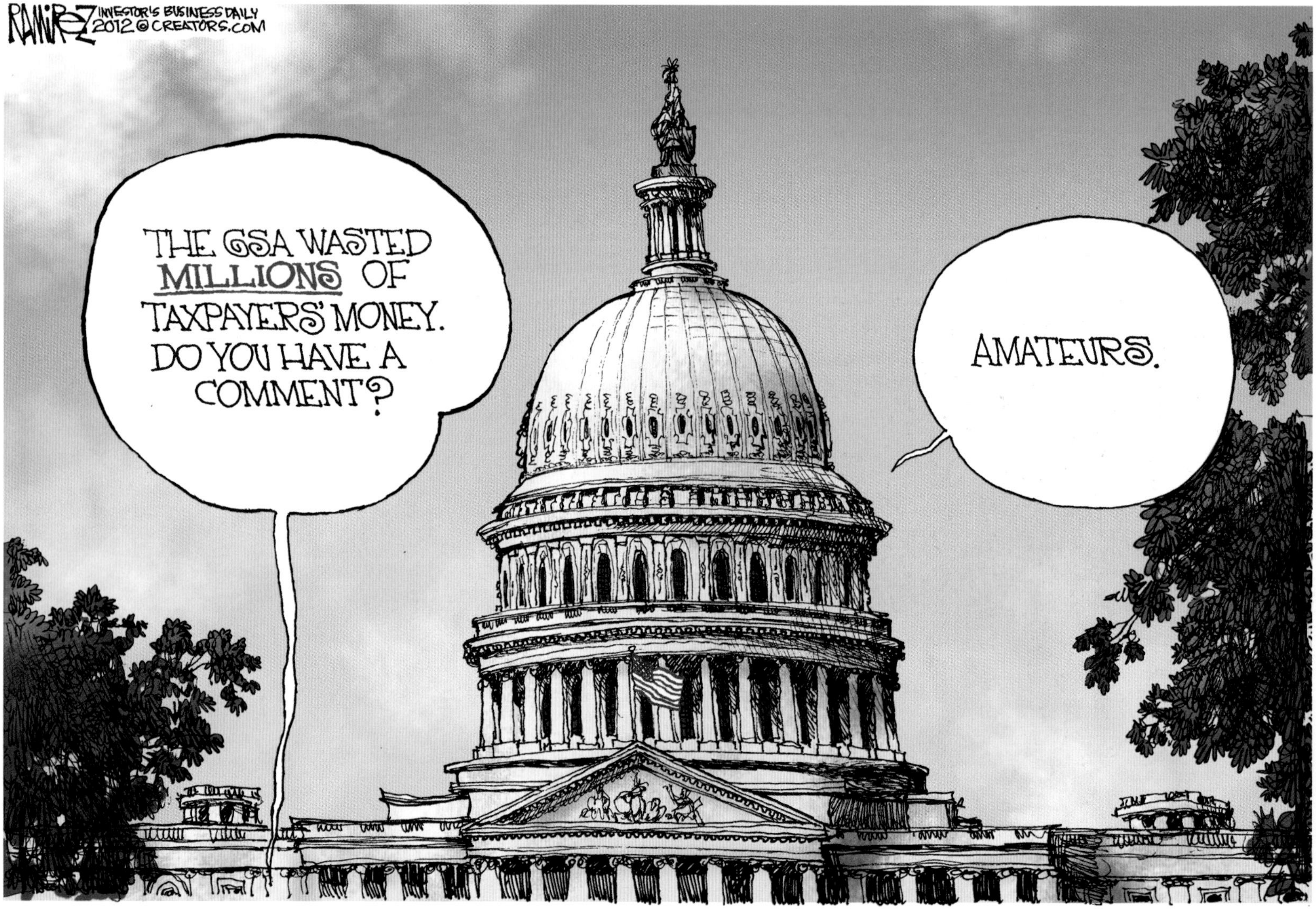
RAMIREZ INVESTOR'S BUSINESS DAILY 2012 © CREATORS.COM
THE GSA WASTED MILLIONS OF TAXPAYERS' MONEY. DO YOU HAVE A COMMENT?
AMATEURS.

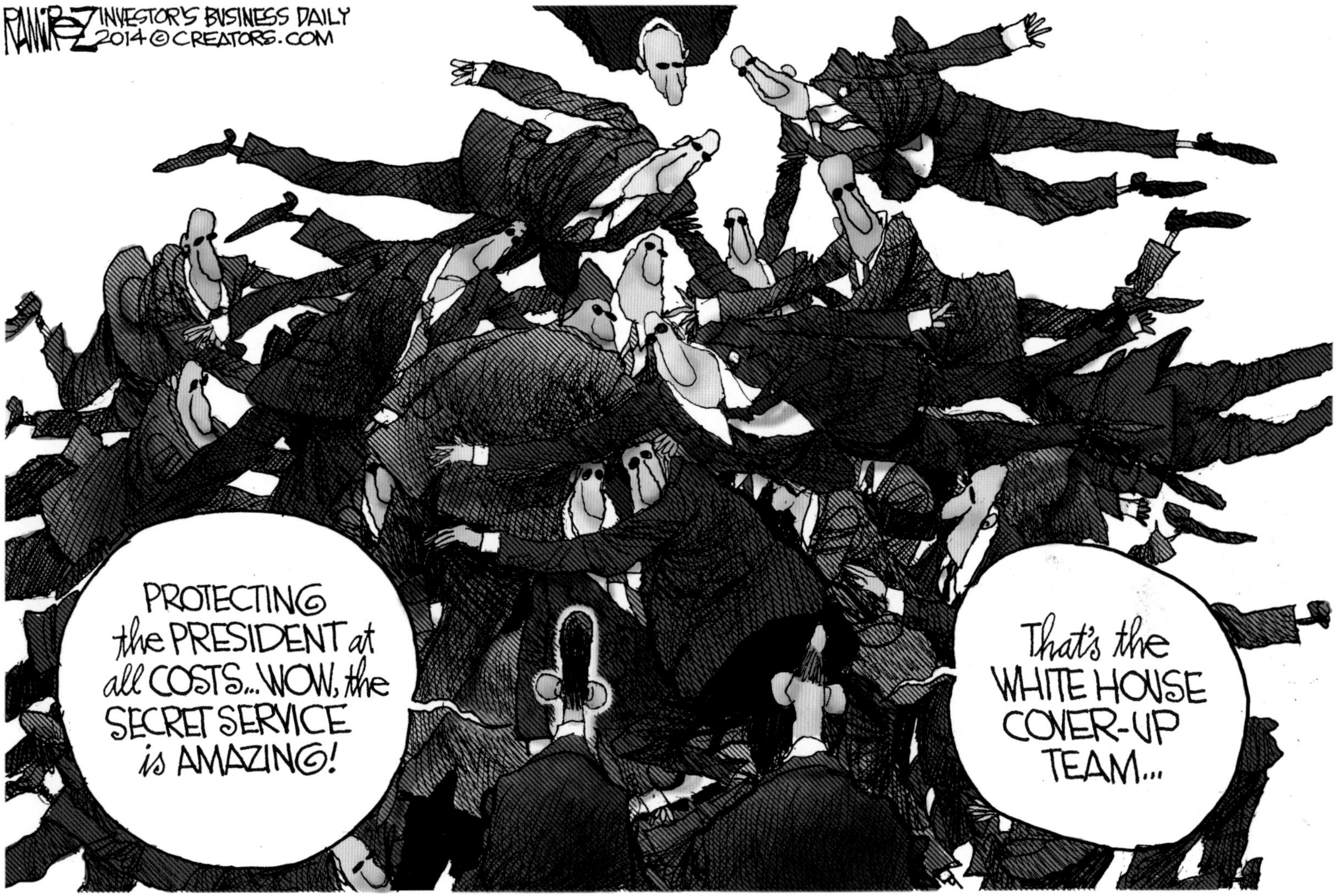
RAMIREZ INVESTOR'S BUSINESS DAILY 2014 © CREATORS.COM
PROTECTING the PRESIDENT at all COSTS... WOW, the SECRET SERVICE is AMAZING!
That's the WHITE HOUSE COVER-UP TEAM...

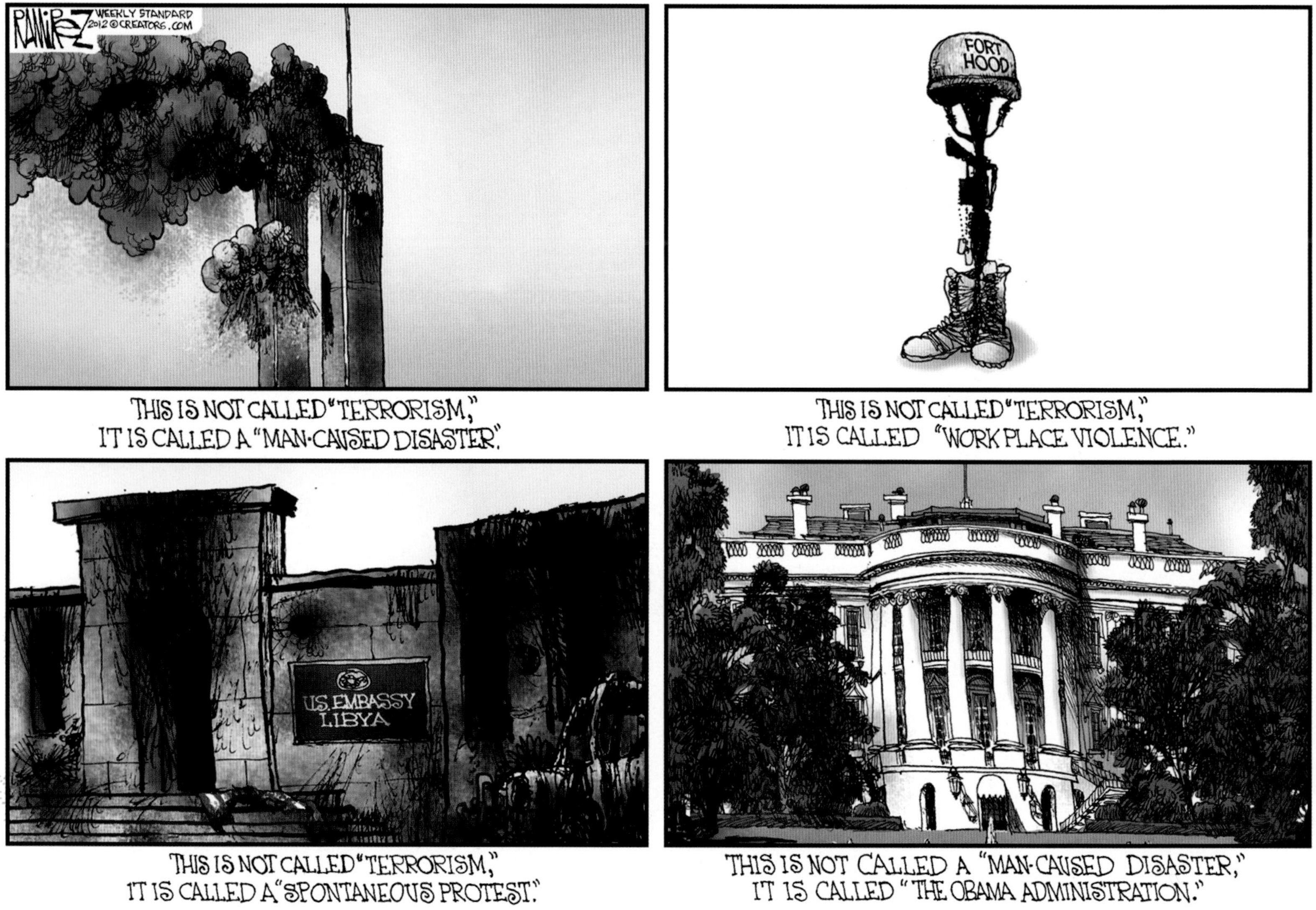
RAMIREZ
WEEKLY STANDARD
2012 © CREATORS.COM
THIS IS NOT CALLED "TERRORISM," IT IS CALLED A "MAN-CAUSED DISASTER."
FORT HOOD
THIS IS NOT CALLED "TERRORISM," IT IS CALLED "WORK PLACE VIOLENCE."
U.S. EMBASSY LIBYA
THIS IS NOT CALLED "TERRORISM," IT IS CALLED A "SPONTANEOUS PROTEST."
THIS IS NOT CALLED A "MAN-CAUSED DISASTER," IT IS CALLED "THE OBAMA ADMINISTRATION."

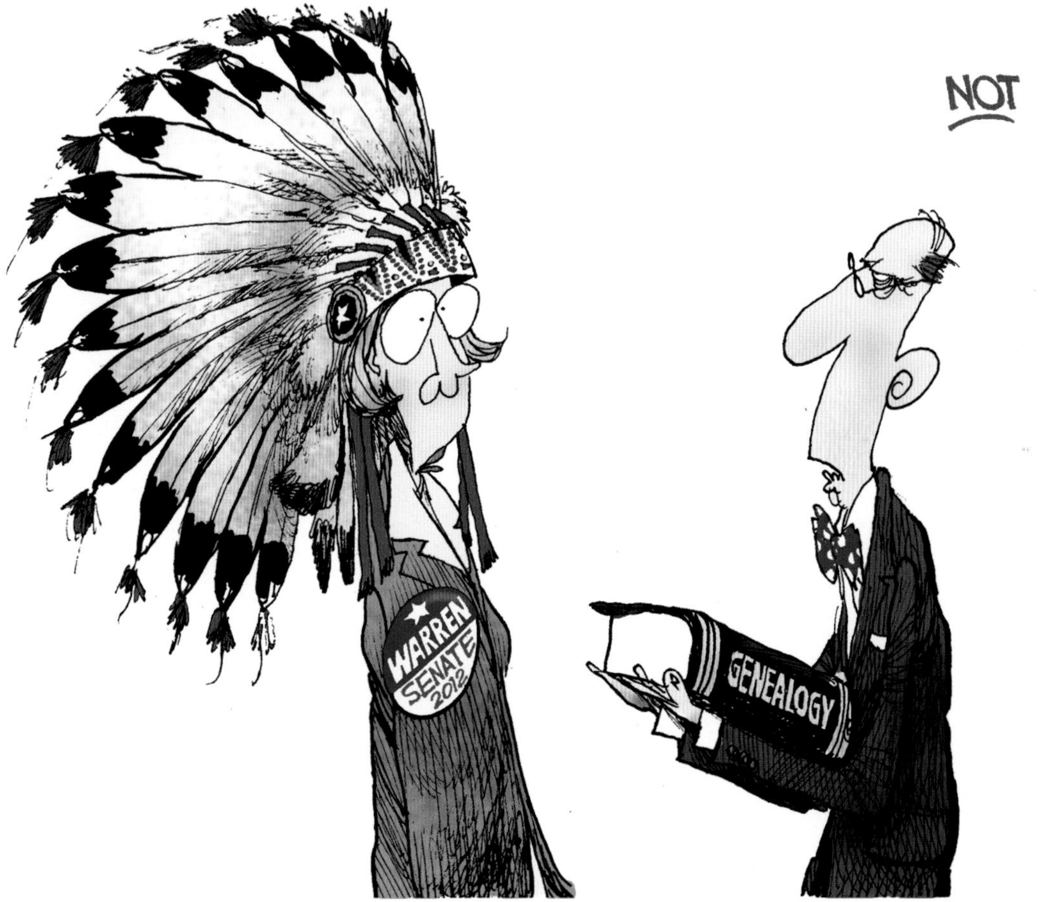
NOT
WARREN
SENATE
2012
GENEALOGY

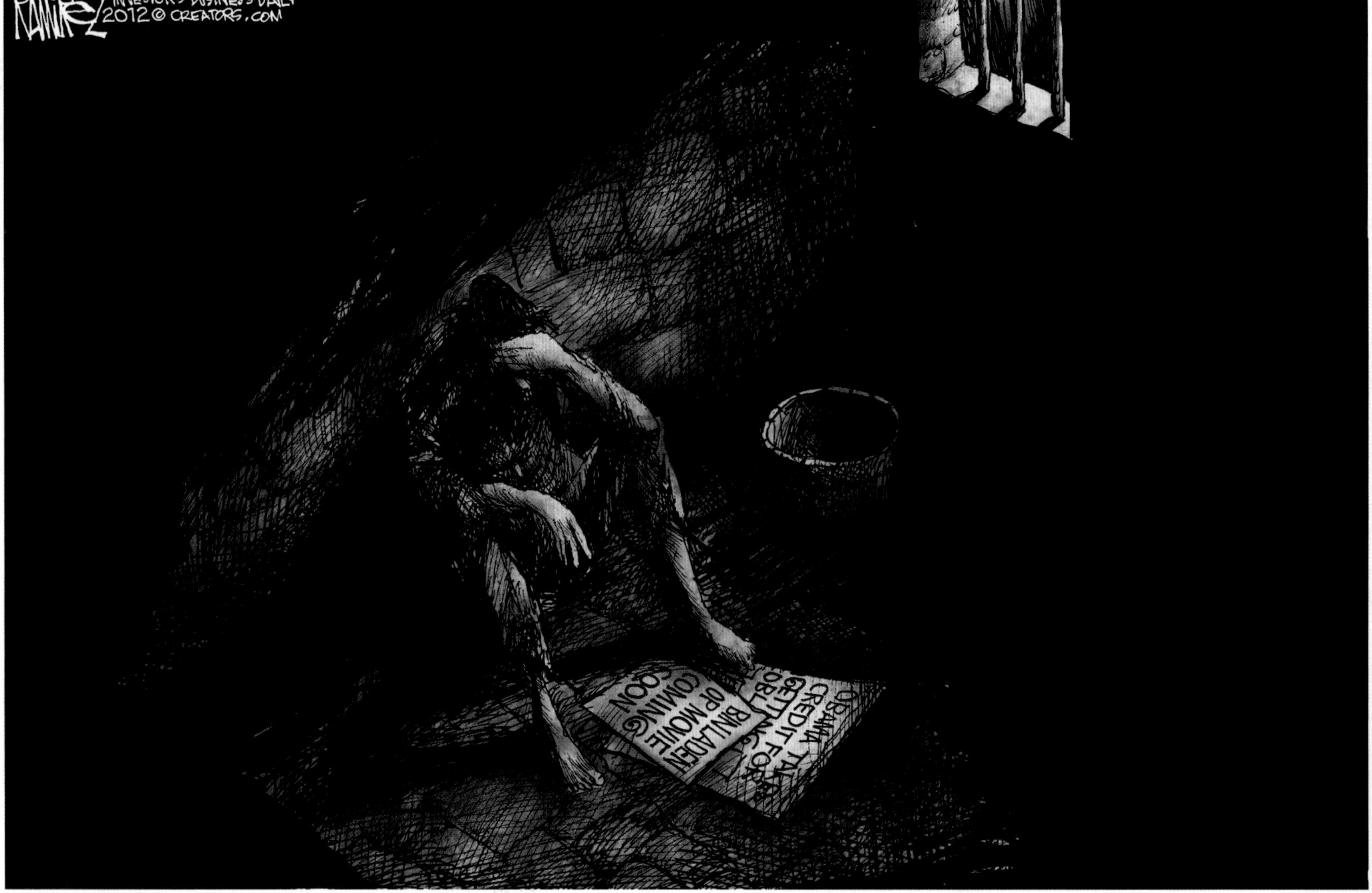
RAMIREZ
INVESTOR'S BUSINESS DAILY
2012 © CREATORS.COM
OBAMA
CREDIT FOR
BIN LADEN
OP MOVIE
COMING
SOON

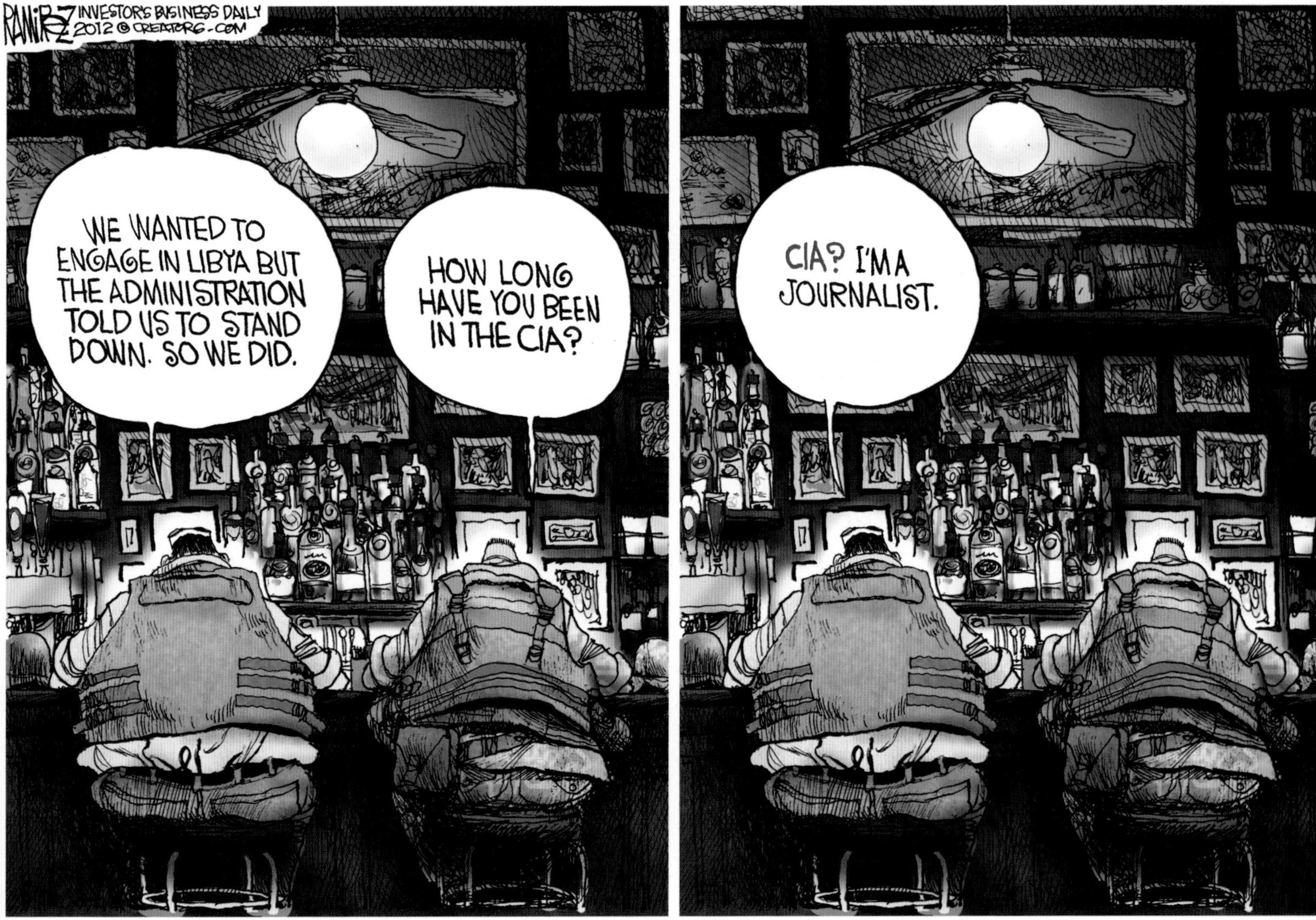
RAMIREZ INVESTOR'S BUSINESS DAILY 2012 © CREATORS.COM
WE WANTED TO ENGAGE IN LIBYA BUT THE ADMINISTRATION TOLD US TO STAND DOWN. SO WE DID.
HOW LONG HAVE YOU BEEN IN THE CIA?
CIA? I'M A JOURNALIST.

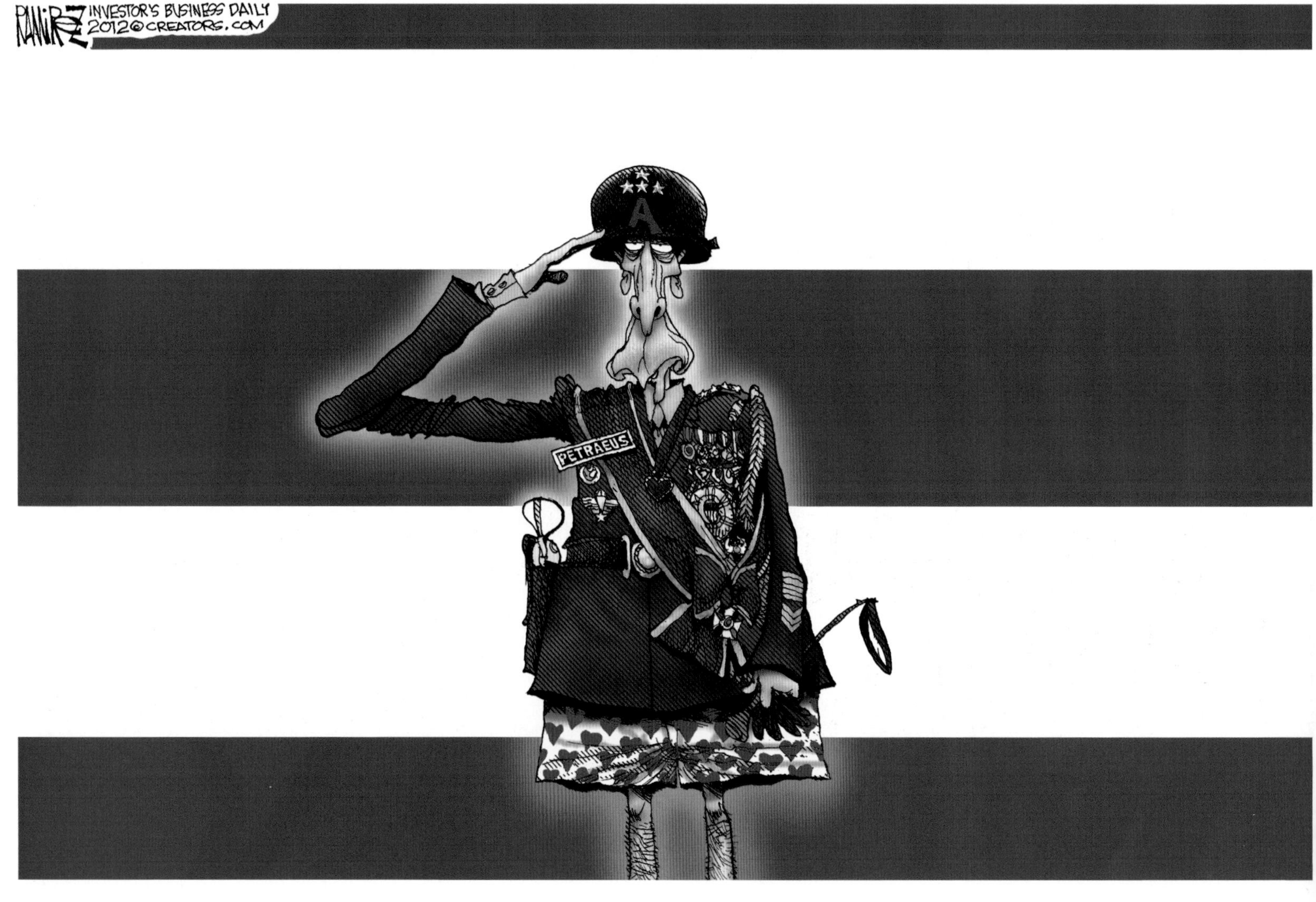
RAMIREZ
INVESTOR'S BUSINESS DAILY
2012 © CREATORS.COM
A
PETRAEUS

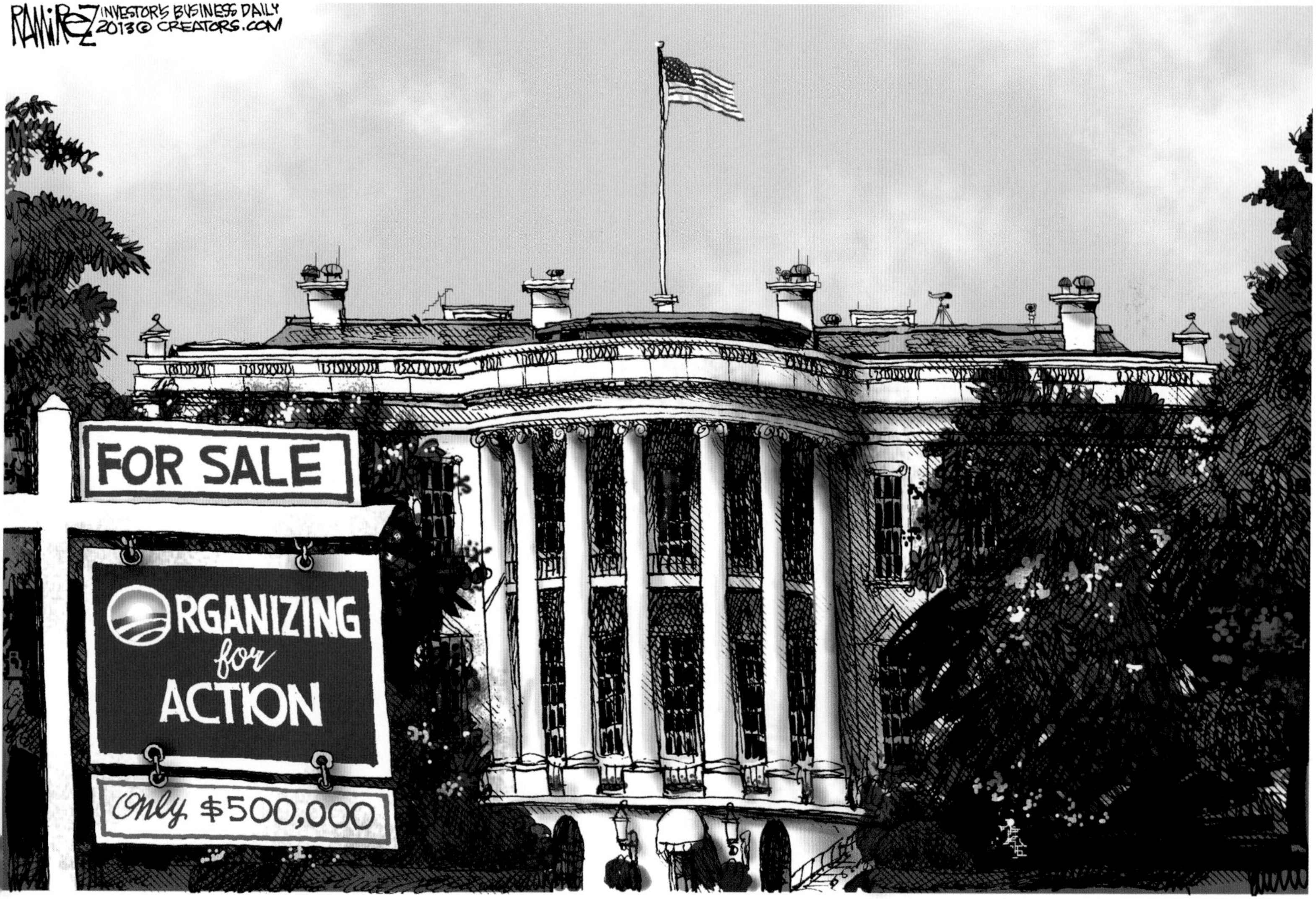
RAMIREZ INVESTOR'S BUSINESS DAILY 2013 © CREATORS.COM
FOR SALE
ORGANIZING for ACTION
Only $500,000

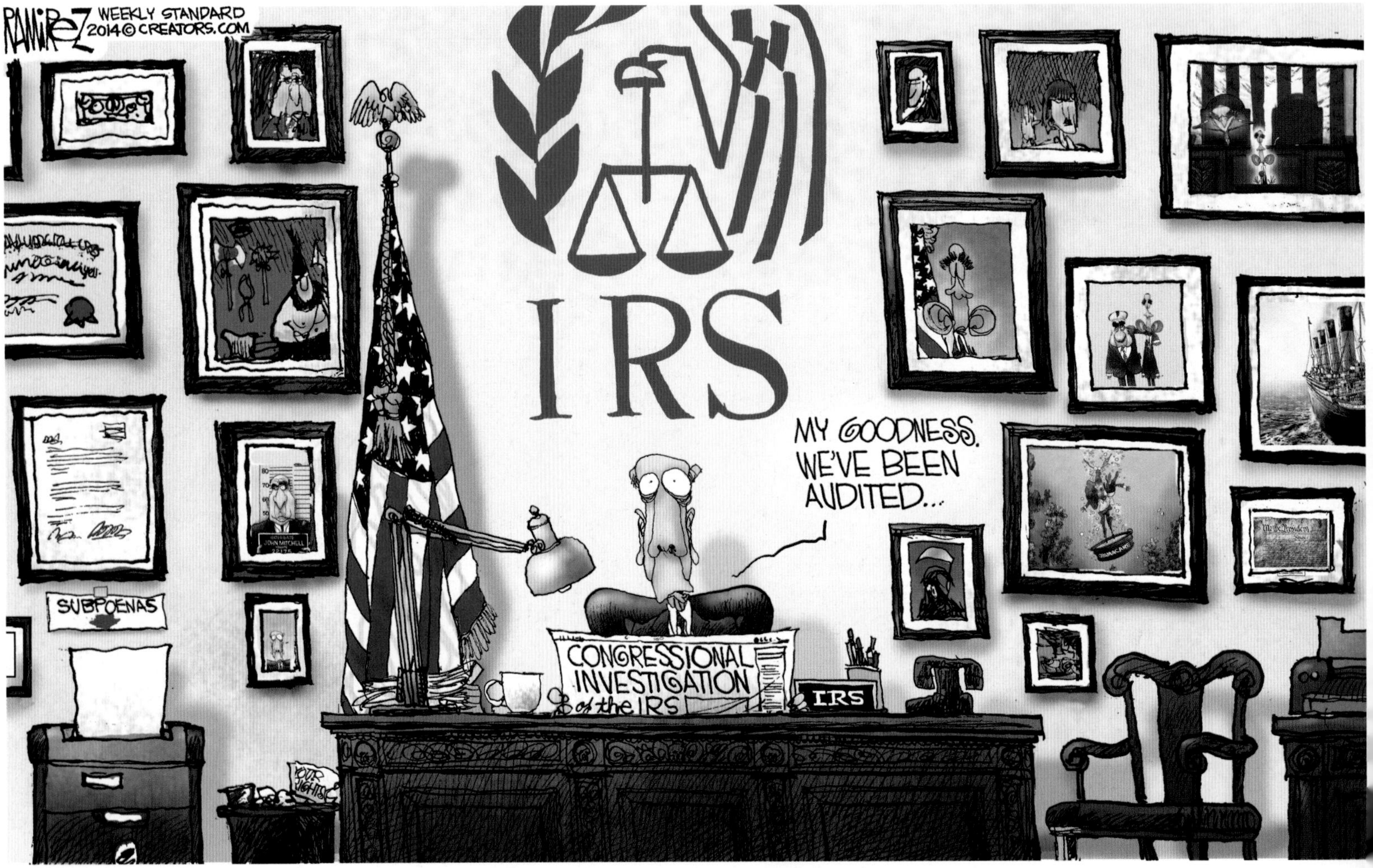
RAMIREZ WEEKLY STANDARD 2014 © CREATORS.COM
IRS
MY GOODNESS. WE'VE BEEN AUDITED...
CONGRESSIONAL INVESTIGATION of the IRS
IRS
SUBPOENAS
JOHN MITCHELL

NOW YOU KNOW HOW WE FEEL.

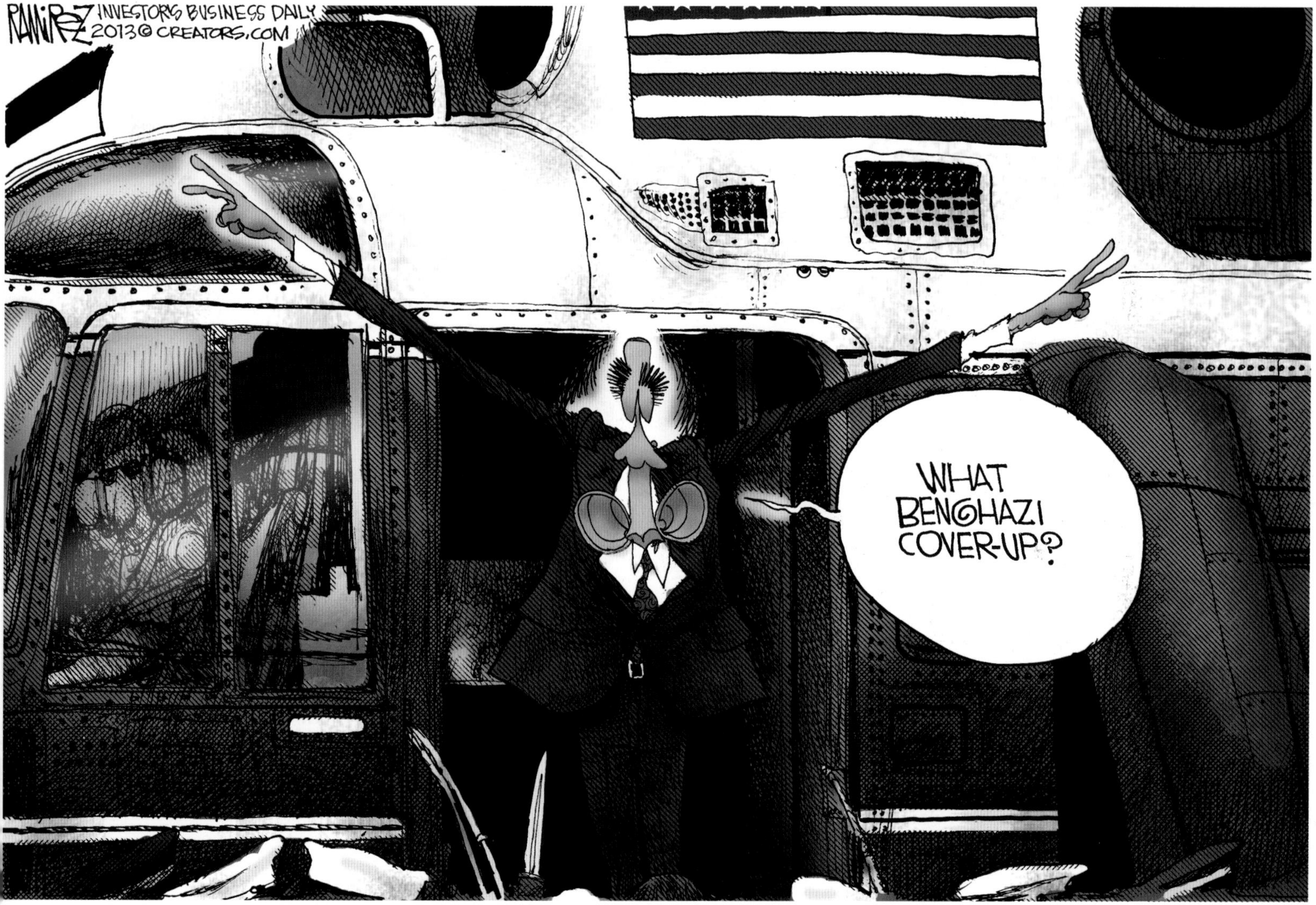
RAMIREZ INVESTOR'S BUSINESS DAILY 2013© CREATORS.COM
WHAT BENGHAZI COVER-UP?

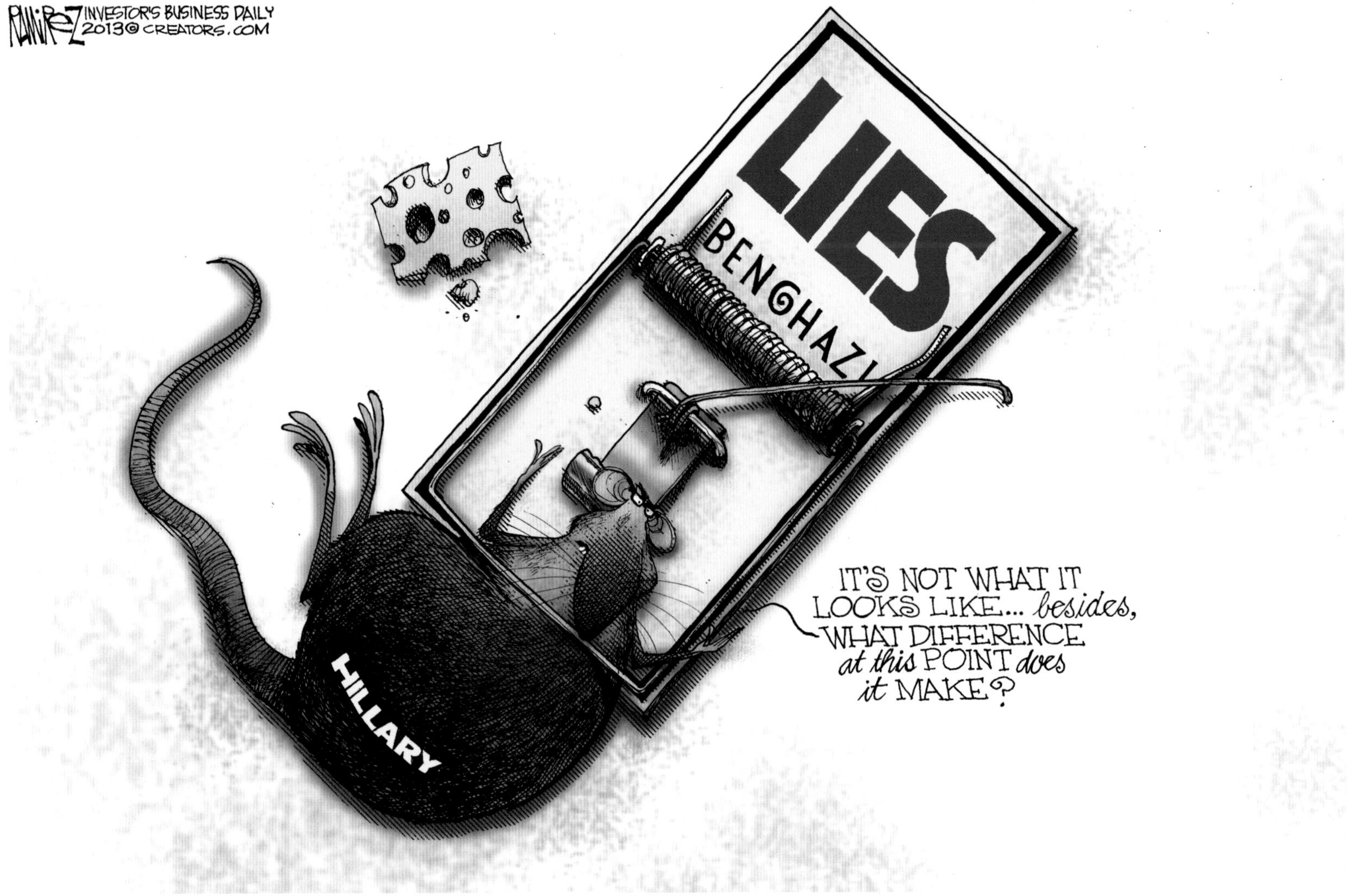
RAMIREZ INVESTOR'S BUSINESS DAILY
2013© CREATORS.COM
LIES
BENGHAZI
HILLARY
IT'S NOT WHAT IT LOOKS LIKE... besides, WHAT DIFFERENCE at this POINT does it MAKE?

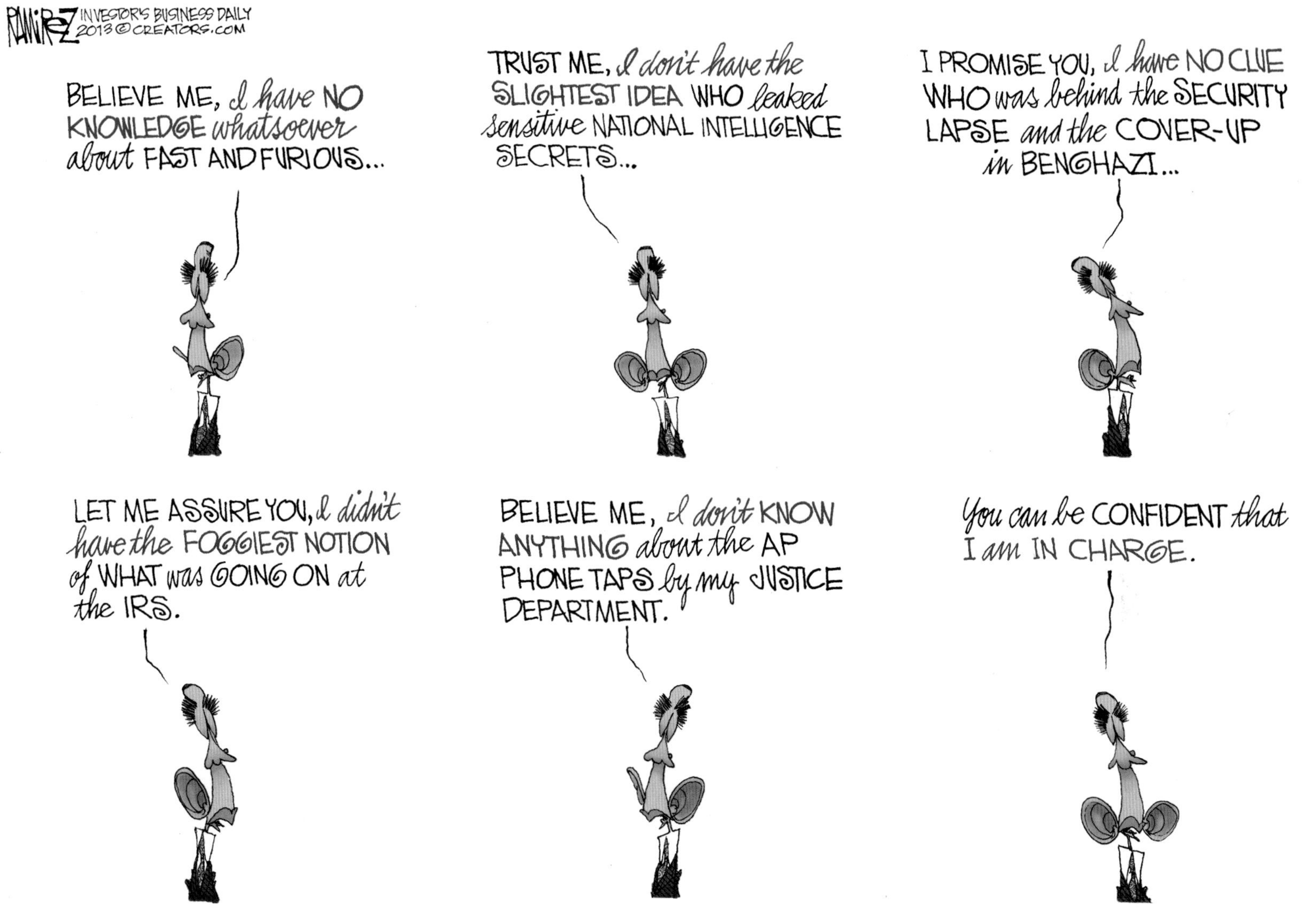

RAMIREZ INVESTOR'S BUSINESS DAILY 2013 © CREATORS.COM
BELIEVE ME, I have NO KNOWLEDGE whatsoever about FAST AND FURIOUS...
TRUST ME, I don't have the SLIGHTEST IDEA WHO leaked sensitive NATIONAL INTELLIGENCE SECRETS...
I PROMISE YOU, I have NO CLUE WHO was behind the SECURITY LAPSE and the COVER-UP in BENGHAZI...
LET ME ASSURE YOU, I didn't have the FOGGIEST NOTION of WHAT was GOING ON at the IRS.
BELIEVE ME, I don't KNOW ANYTHING about the AP PHONE TAPS by my JUSTICE DEPARTMENT.
You can be CONFIDENT that I am IN CHARGE.

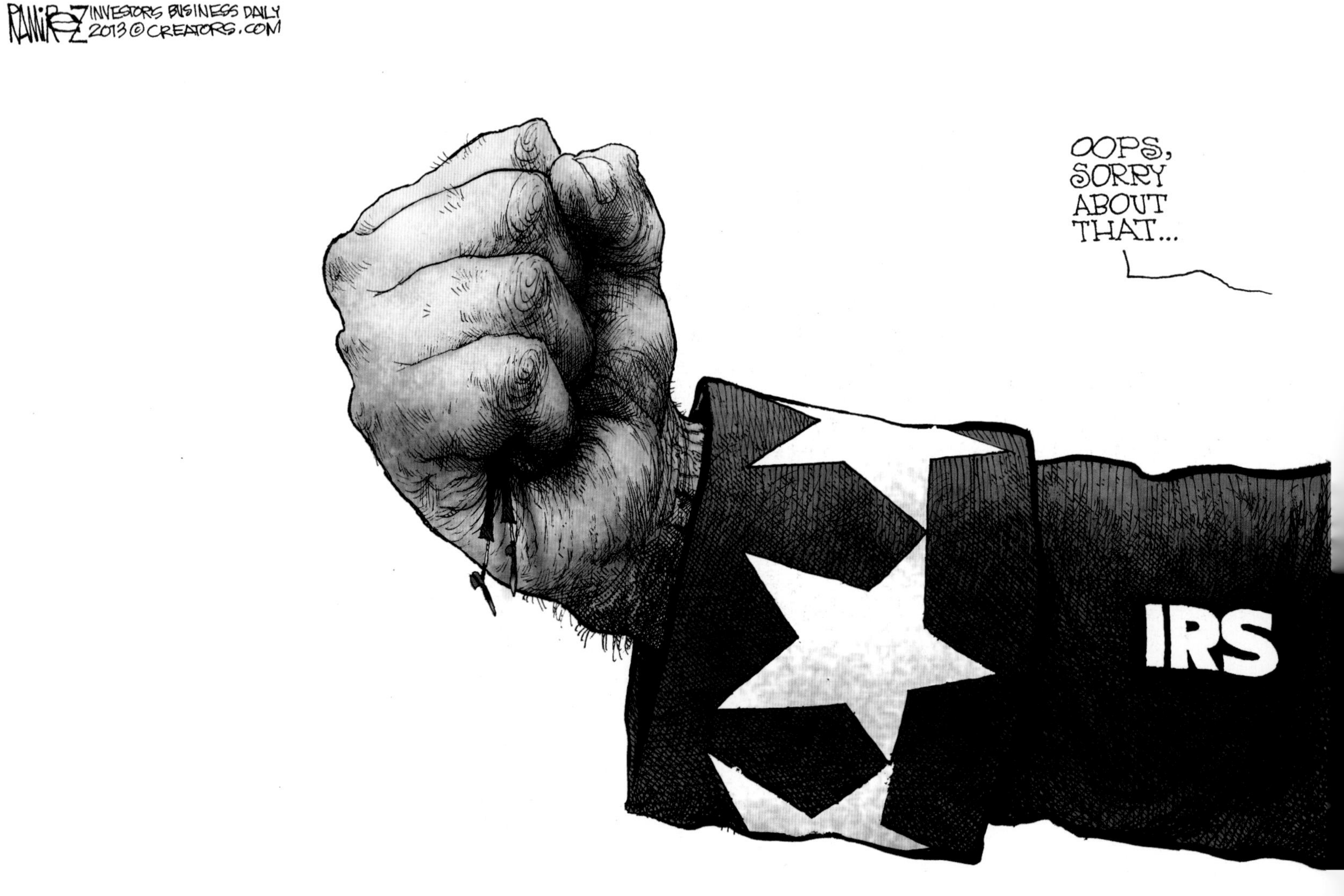
RAMIREZ INVESTOR'S BUSINESS DAILY
2013 © CREATORS.COM
OOPS, SORRY ABOUT THAT...
IRS

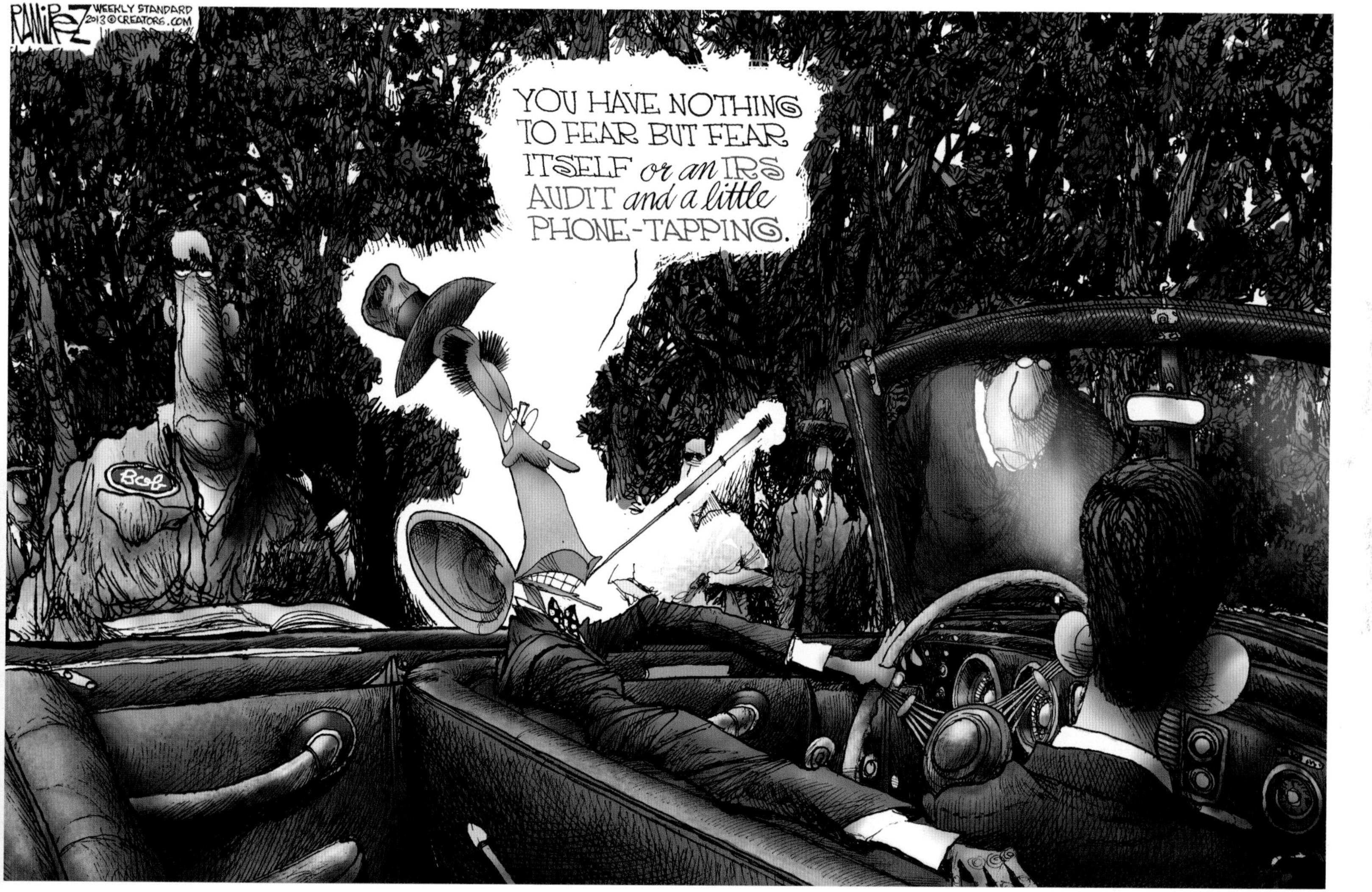
RAMIREZ WEEKLY STANDARD 2013 © CREATORS.COM
YOU HAVE NOTHING TO FEAR BUT FEAR ITSELF or an IRS AUDIT and a little PHONE-TAPPING.
BOB

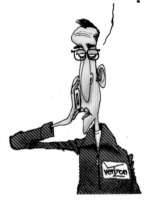

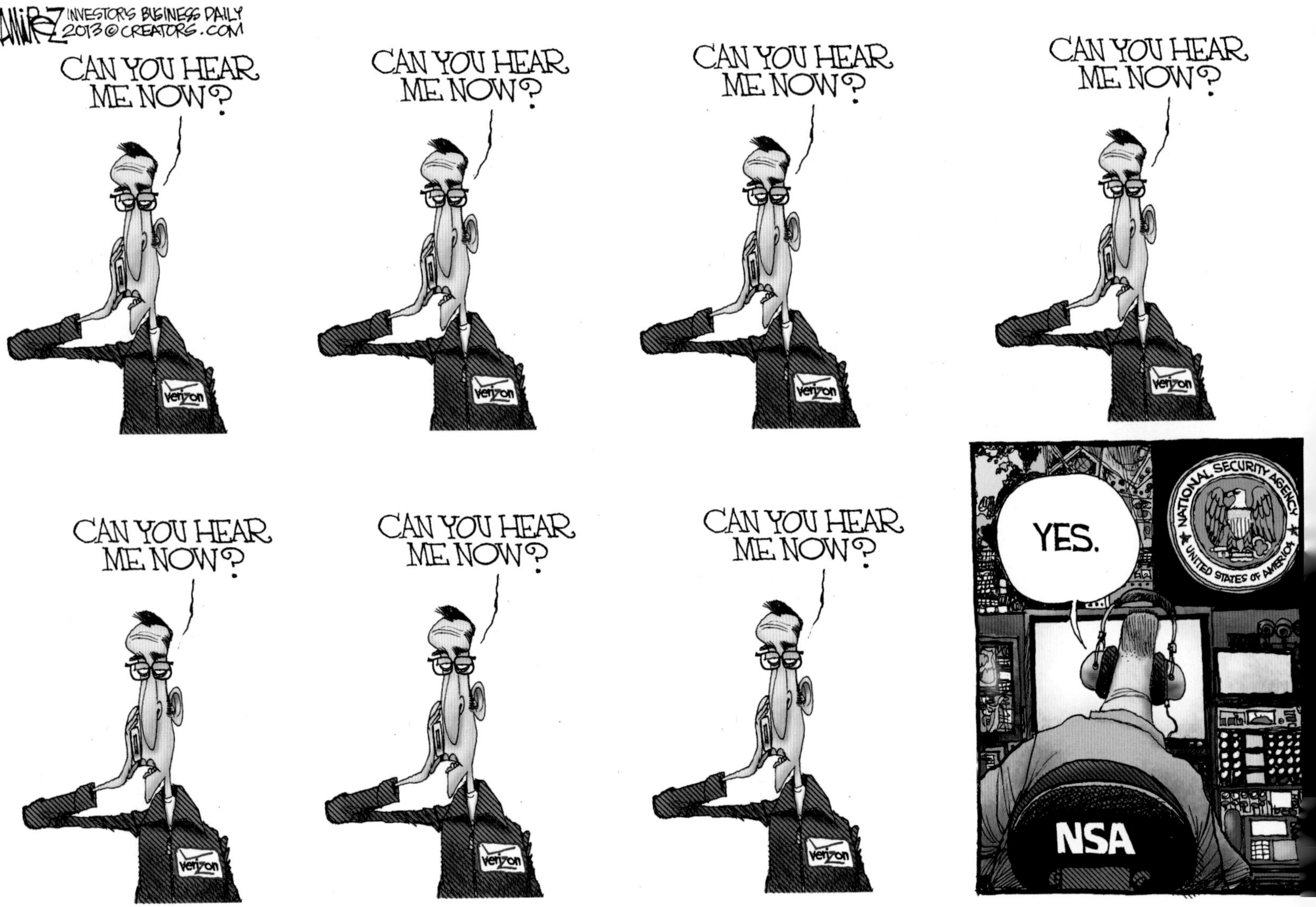
RAMIREZ INVESTOR'S BUSINESS DAILY 2013 © CREATORS.COM
CAN YOU HEAR ME NOW?
verizon
CAN YOU HEAR ME NOW?
verizon
CAN YOU HEAR ME NOW?
verizon
CAN YOU HEAR ME NOW?
verizon
CAN YOU HEAR ME NOW?
verizon
CAN YOU HEAR ME NOW?
verizon
CAN YOU HEAR ME NOW?
verizon
NATIONAL SECURITY AGENCY UNITED STATES OF AMERICA
YES.
NSA

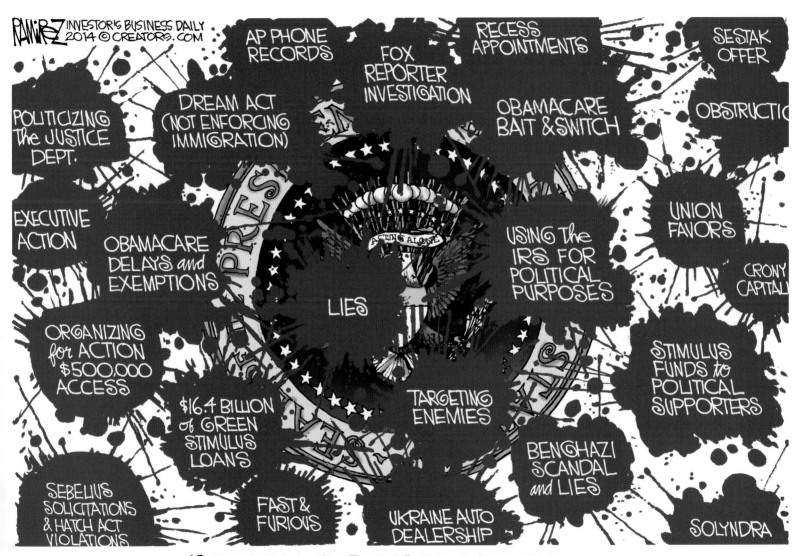

AP PHONE RECORDS

FOX REPORTER INVESTIGATION

RECESS APPOINTMENTS

SESTAK OFFER

DREAM ACT (NOT ENFORCING IMMIGRATION)

OBAMACARE BAIT & SWITCH

OBSTRUCTIO[N]

POLITICIZING the JUSTICE DEPT.

EXECUTIVE ACTION

OBAMACARE DELAYS and EXEMPTIONS

PRES

ACTING ALONE

LIES

USING The IRS FOR POLITICAL PURPOSES

UNION FAVORS

CRONY CAPITALI[SM]

ORGANIZING for ACTION $500,000 ACCESS

$16.4 BILLION of GREEN STIMULUS LOANS

TARGETING ENEMIES

STIMULUS FUNDS to POLITICAL SUPPORTERS

SEBELIUS SOLICITATIONS & HATCH ACT VIOLATIONS

FAST & FURIOUS

UKRAINE AUTO DEALERSHIP

BENGHAZI SCANDAL and LIES

SOLYNDRA

NOT EVEN A SMIDGEN OF CORRUPTION

RAMIREZ INVESTOR'S BUSINESS DAILY 2014 © CREATORS.COM

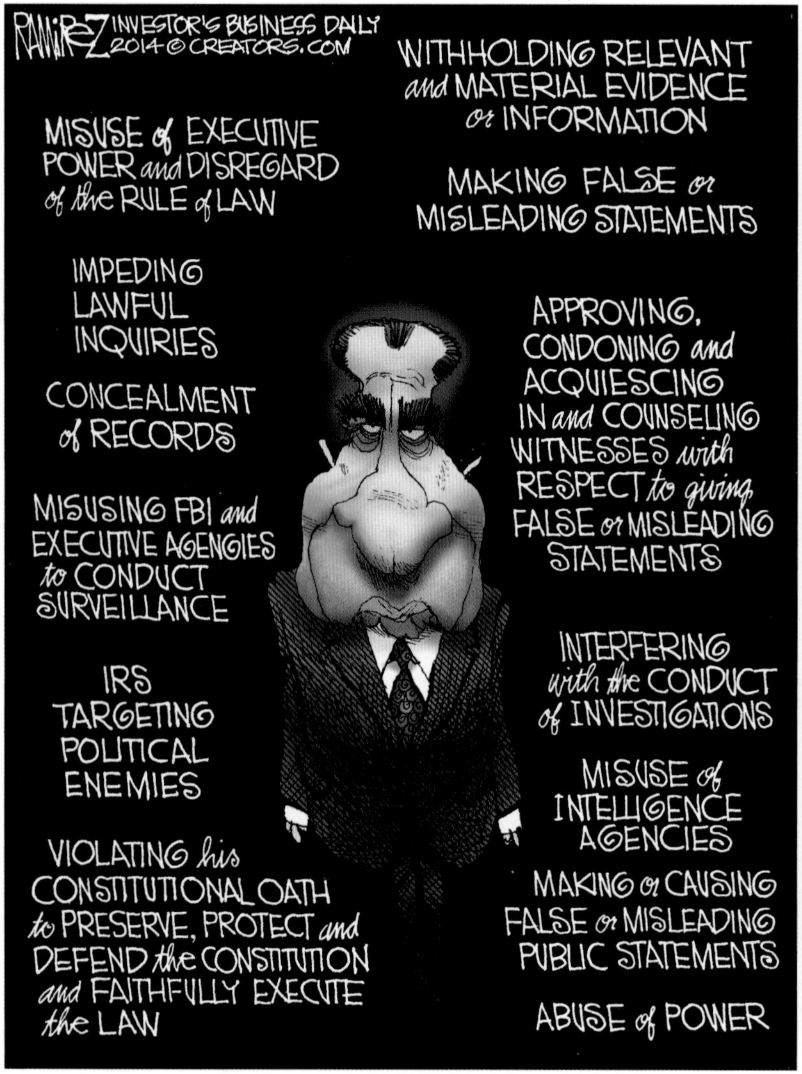
RAMIREZ INVESTOR'S BUSINESS DAILY 2014 © CREATORS.COM
WITHHOLDING RELEVANT and MATERIAL EVIDENCE or INFORMATION
MISUSE of EXECUTIVE POWER and DISREGARD of the RULE of LAW
MAKING FALSE or MISLEADING STATEMENTS
IMPEDING LAWFUL INQUIRIES
APPROVING, CONDONING and ACQUIESCING IN and COUNSELING WITNESSES with RESPECT to giving FALSE or MISLEADING STATEMENTS
CONCEALMENT of RECORDS
MISUSING FBI and EXECUTIVE AGENCIES to CONDUCT SURVEILLANCE
INTERFERING with the CONDUCT of INVESTIGATIONS
IRS TARGETING POLITICAL ENEMIES
MISUSE of INTELLIGENCE AGENCIES
VIOLATING his CONSTITUTIONAL OATH to PRESERVE, PROTECT and DEFEND the CONSTITUTION and FAITHFULLY EXECUTE the LAW
MAKING or CAUSING FALSE or MISLEADING PUBLIC STATEMENTS
ABUSE of POWER

ARTICLES of IMPEACHMENT

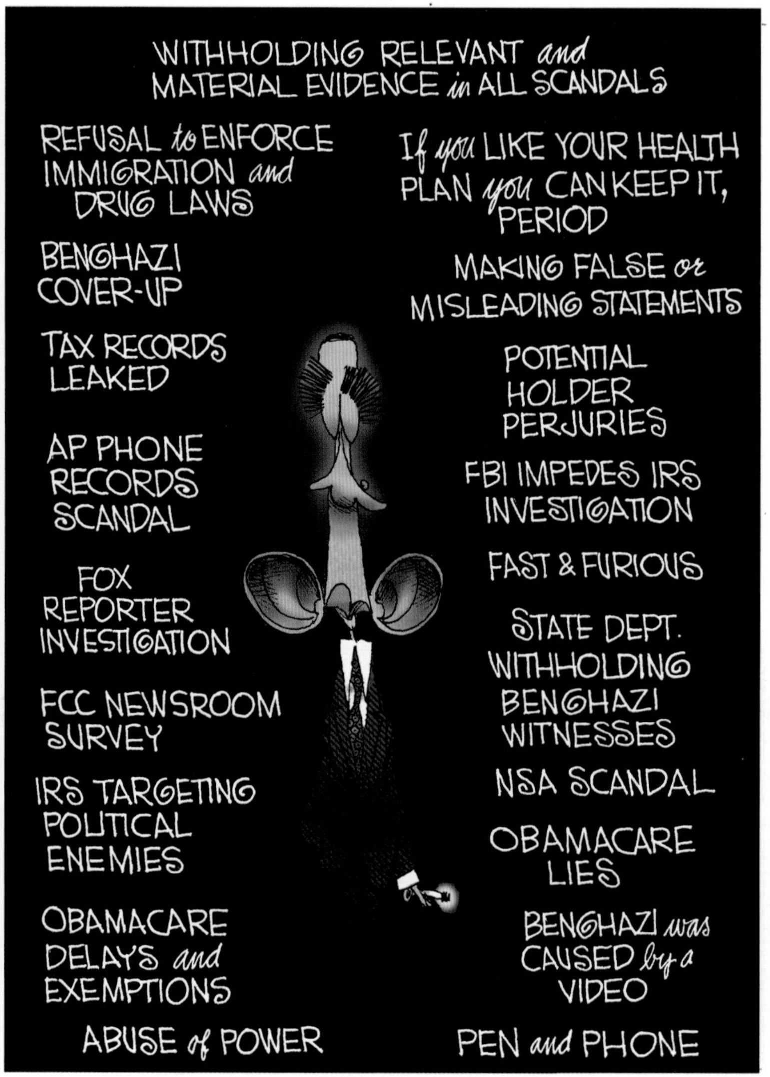
WITHHOLDING RELEVANT and MATERIAL EVIDENCE in ALL SCANDALS
REFUSAL to ENFORCE IMMIGRATION and DRUG LAWS
If you LIKE YOUR HEALTH PLAN you CAN KEEP IT, PERIOD
BENGHAZI COVER-UP
MAKING FALSE or MISLEADING STATEMENTS
TAX RECORDS LEAKED
POTENTIAL HOLDER PERJURIES
AP PHONE RECORDS SCANDAL
FBI IMPEDES IRS INVESTIGATION
FOX REPORTER INVESTIGATION
FAST & FURIOUS
STATE DEPT. WITHHOLDING BENGHAZI WITNESSES
FCC NEWSROOM SURVEY
IRS TARGETING POLITICAL ENEMIES
NSA SCANDAL
OBAMACARE LIES
OBAMACARE DELAYS and EXEMPTIONS
BENGHAZI was CAUSED by a VIDEO
ABUSE of POWER
PEN and PHONE

ARTICLES IGNORED by the PRESS

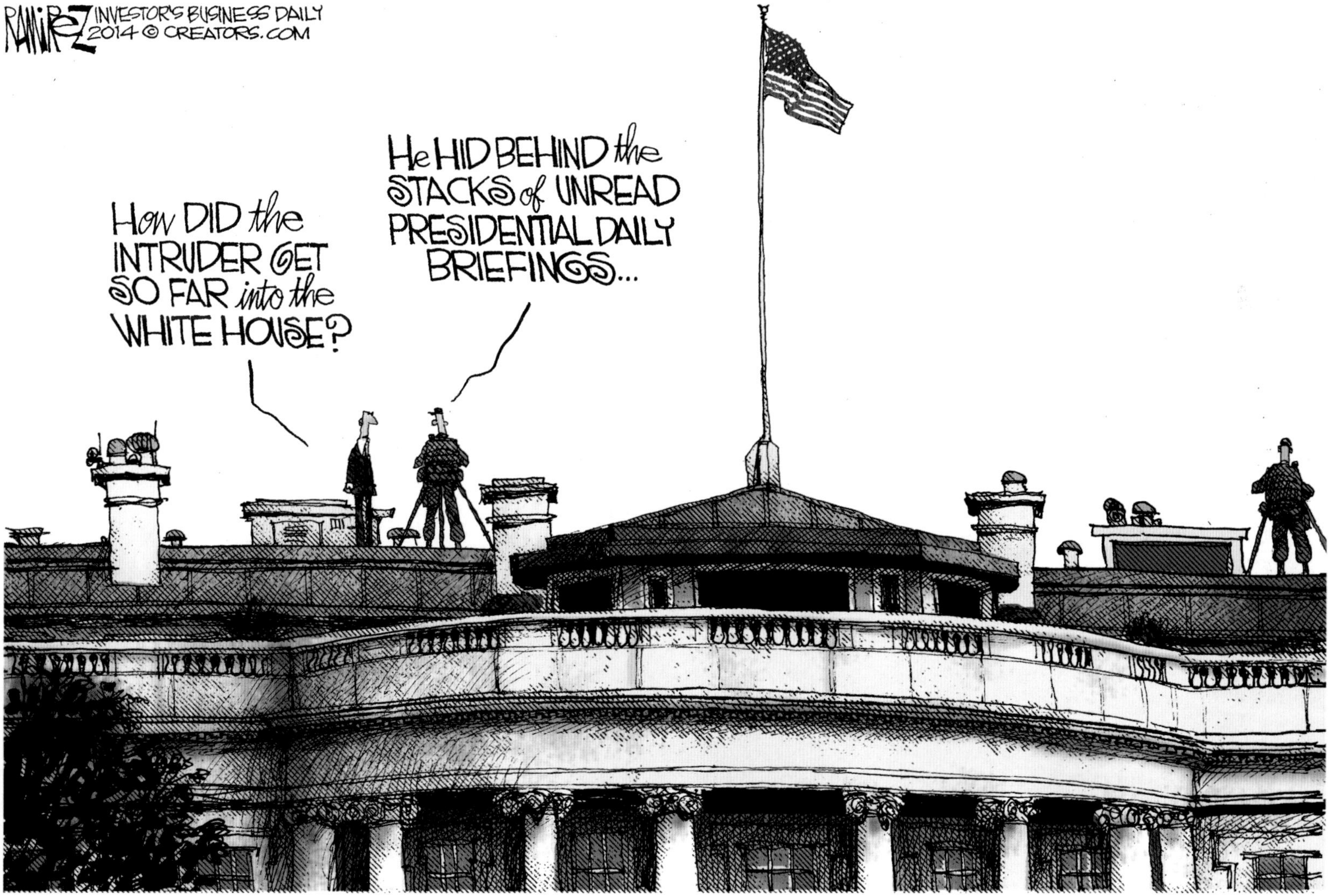
RAMIREZ INVESTOR'S BUSINESS DAILY
2014 © CREATORS.COM
How DID the INTRUDER GET SO FAR into the WHITE HOUSE?
He HID BEHIND the STACKS of UNREAD PRESIDENTIAL DAILY BRIEFINGS...

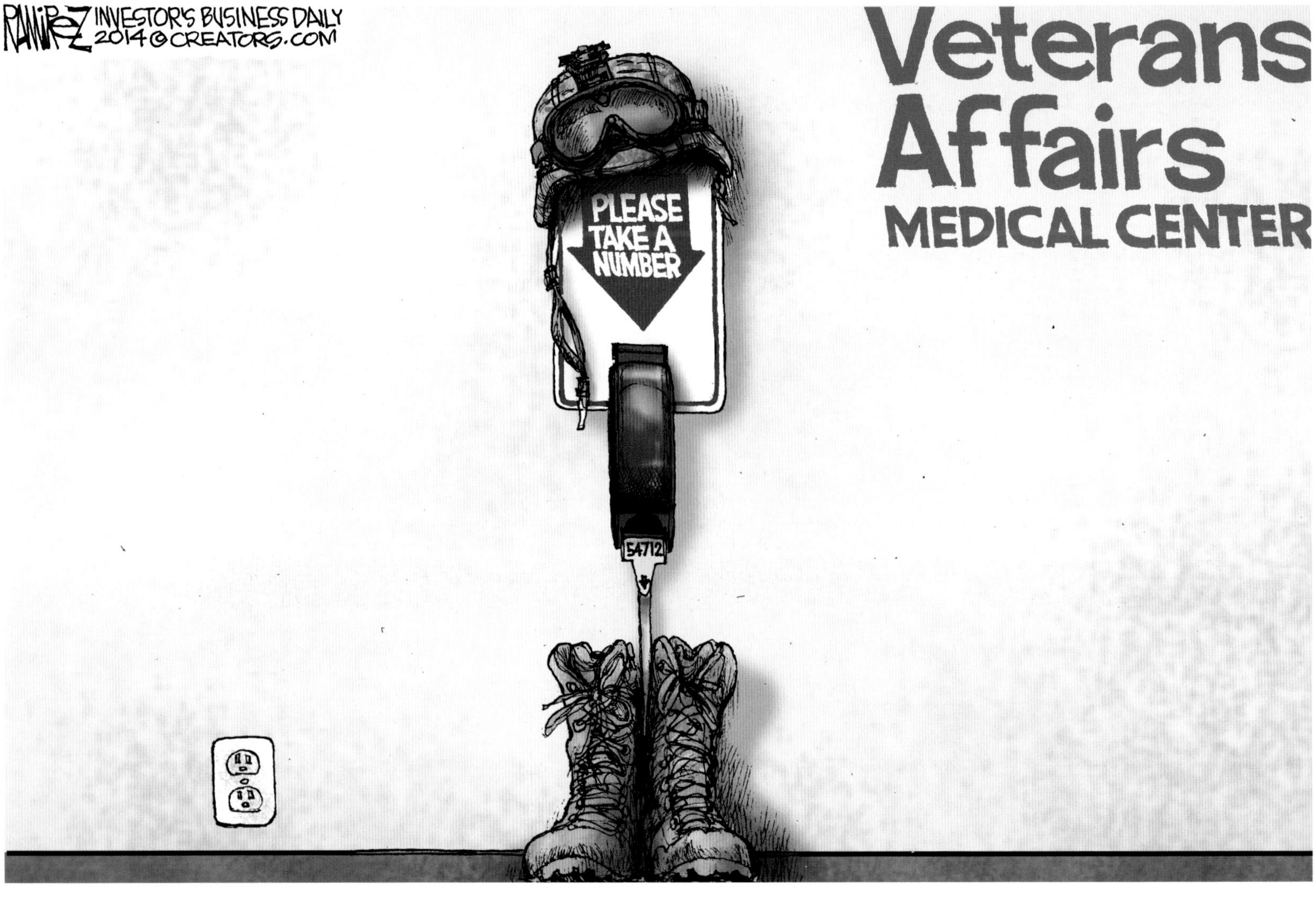
RAMIREZ INVESTOR'S BUSINESS DAILY 2014 © CREATORS.COM
Veterans Affairs MEDICAL CENTER
PLEASE TAKE A NUMBER
54712

WORLD AFFAIRS

"The world is less violent than it has ever been. It is healthier than it has ever been. It is more tolerant than it has ever been. It is better fed than it's ever been. It is more educated than it's ever been."

—President Barack Obama,
Washington, D.C., June 11, 2014

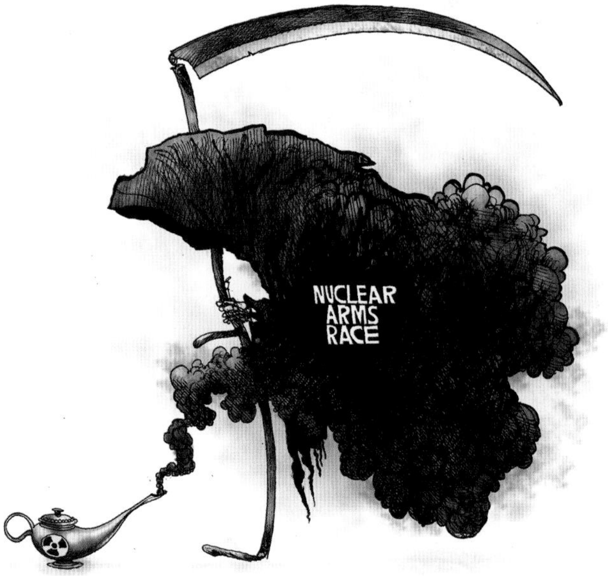
NUCLEAR
ARMS
RACE

The Obama doctrine of "Leading from Behind" created a vacuum of leadership that was quickly filled in with chaos. This failed policy emboldened our enemies and alienated our friends. It led to the rise of ISIS, Russian invasions, Iranian hegemony, and Chinese aggression. It generated a nuclear arms race in one of the most dangerous and unstable regions on earth. But according to our president, the world "is a safer place."

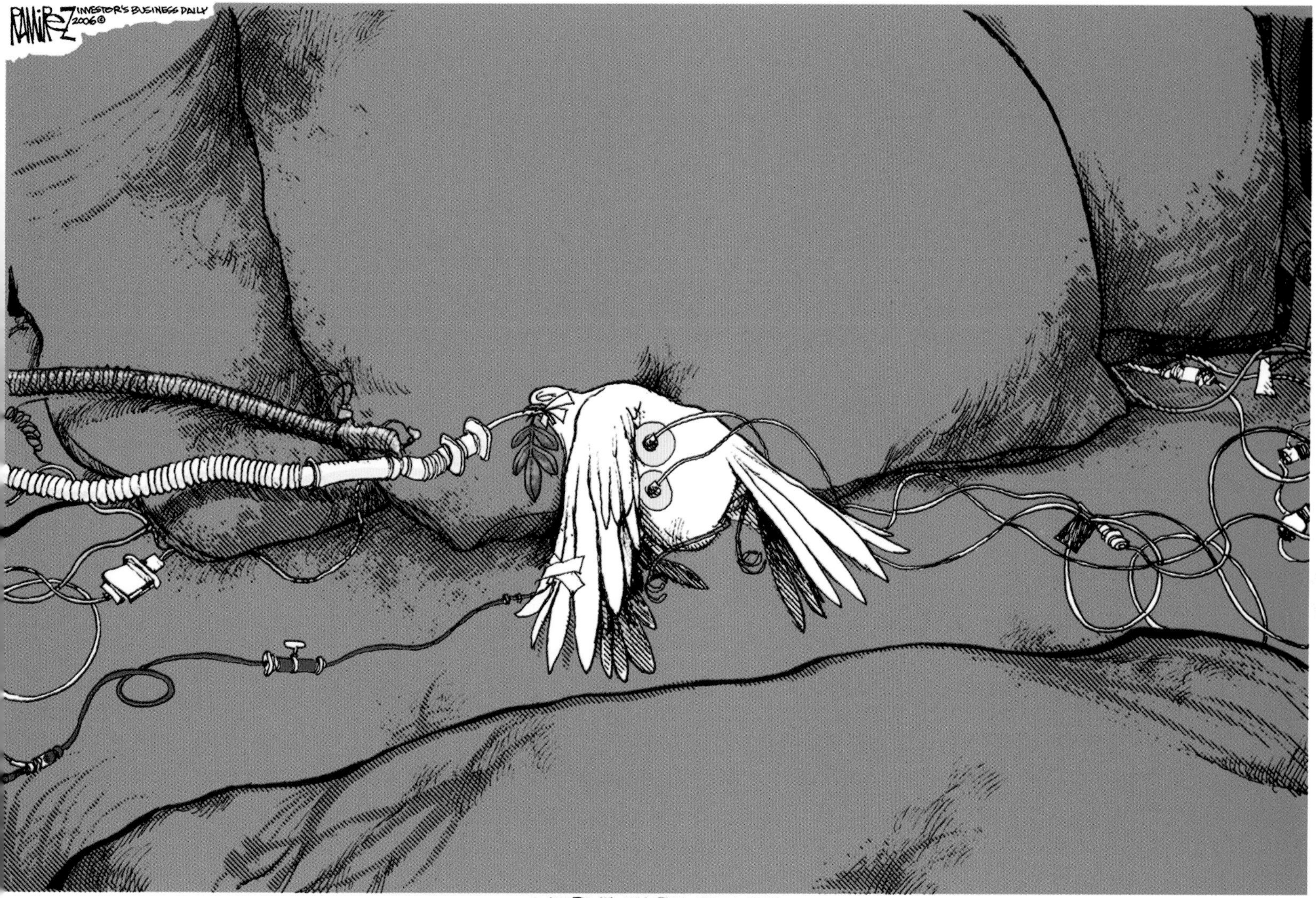
RAMIREZ INVESTOR'S BUSINESS DAILY 2006©

MIDDLE EAST PEACE

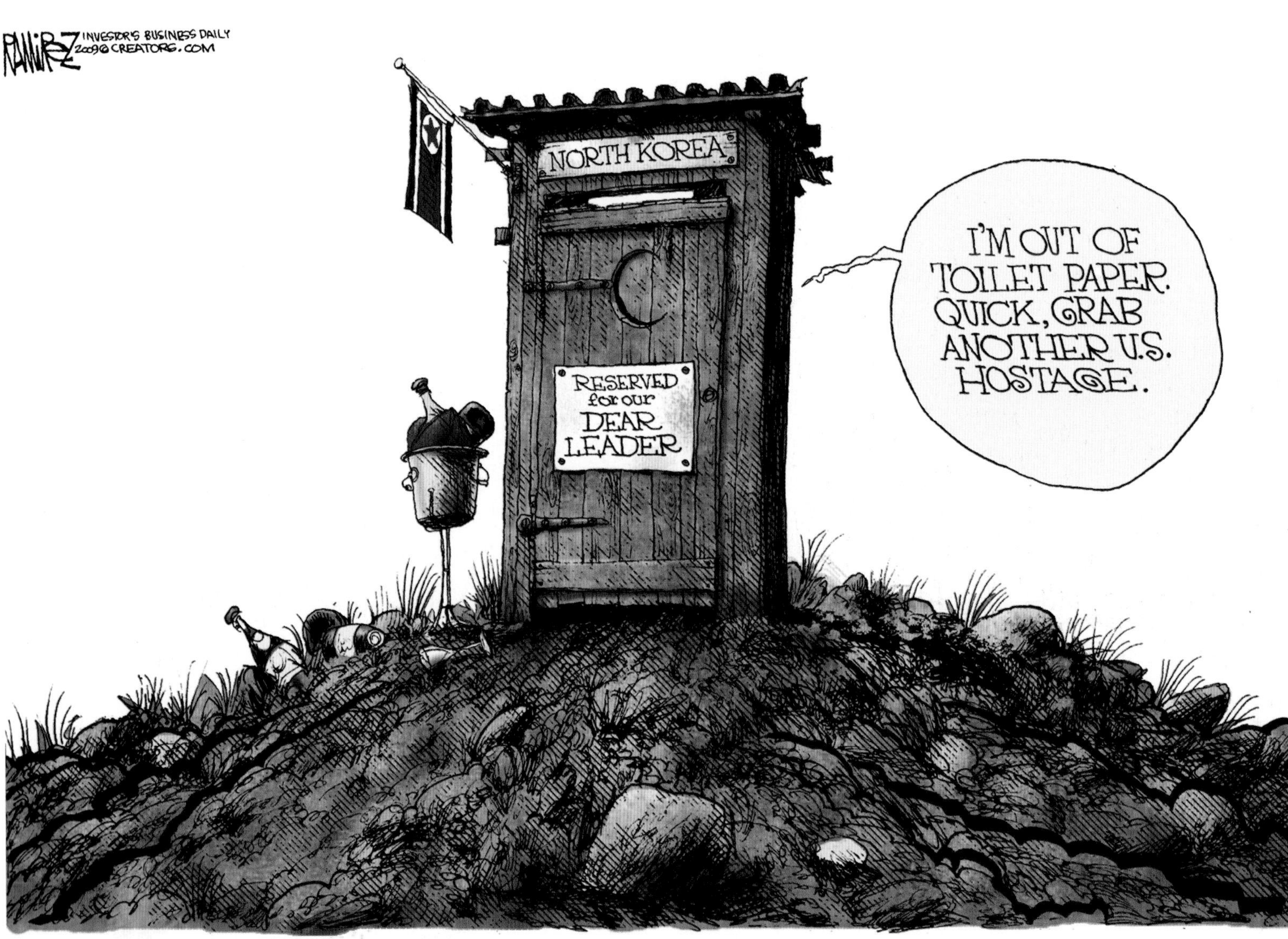
RAMIREZ INVESTOR'S BUSINESS DAILY 2009 © CREATORS.COM
NORTH KOREA
RESERVED for our DEAR LEADER
I'M OUT OF TOILET PAPER. QUICK, GRAB ANOTHER U.S. HOSTAGE.

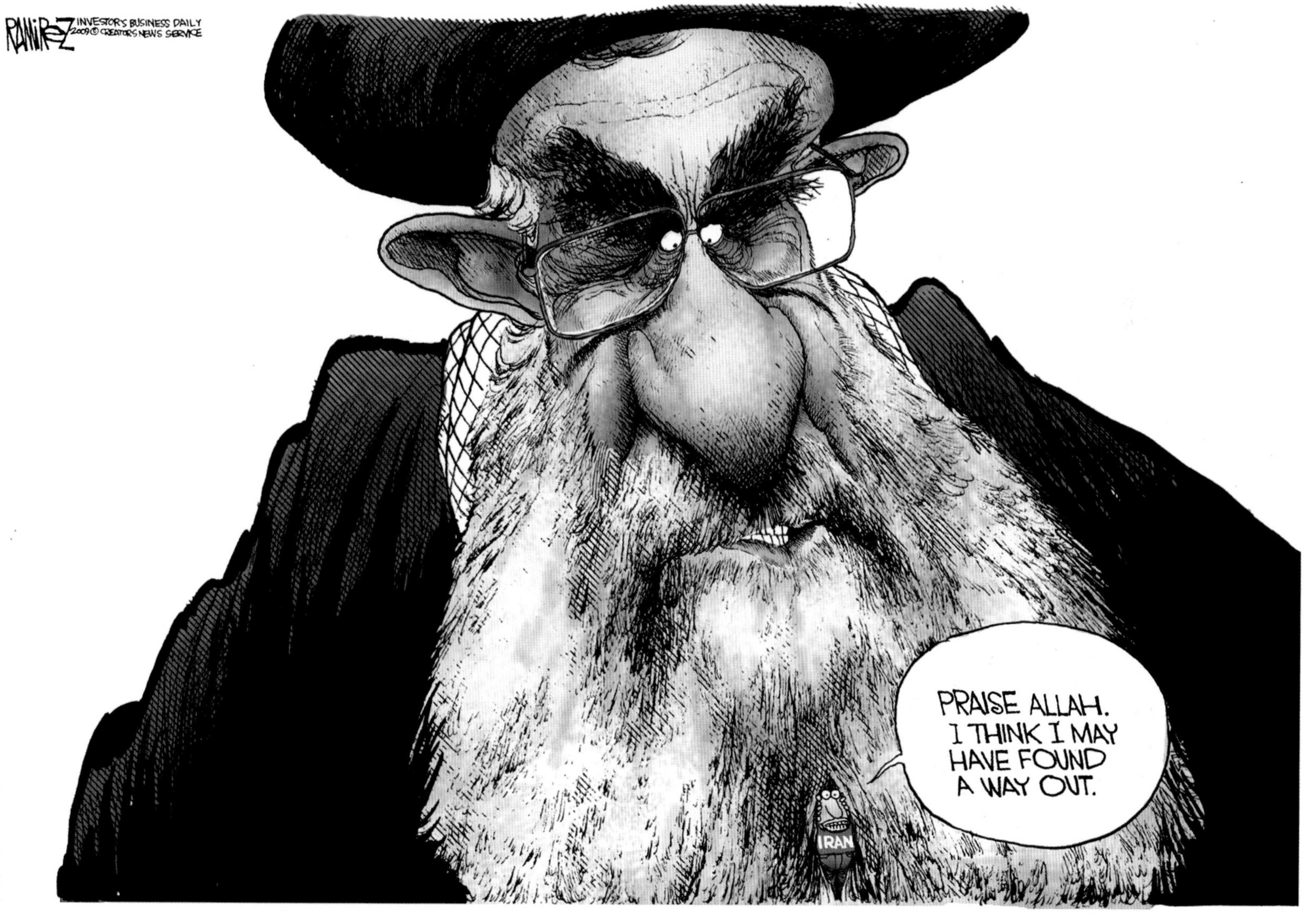
RAMIREZ
INVESTOR'S BUSINESS DAILY
2009 © CREATORS NEWS SERVICE
PRAISE ALLAH. I THINK I MAY HAVE FOUND A WAY OUT.
IRAN

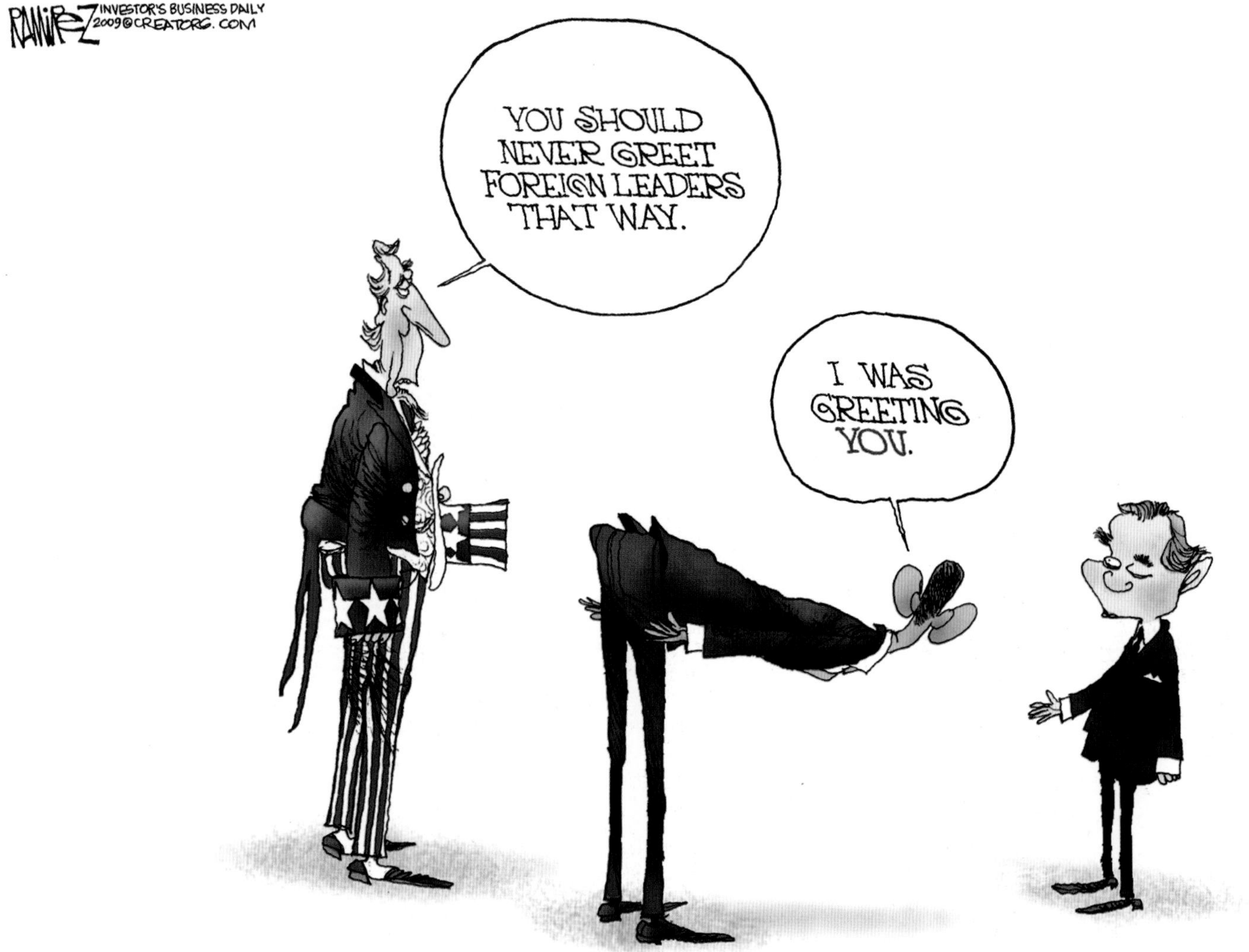
RAMIREZ INVESTOR'S BUSINESS DAILY 2009©CREATORS.COM
YOU SHOULD NEVER GREET FOREIGN LEADERS THAT WAY.
I WAS GREETING YOU.

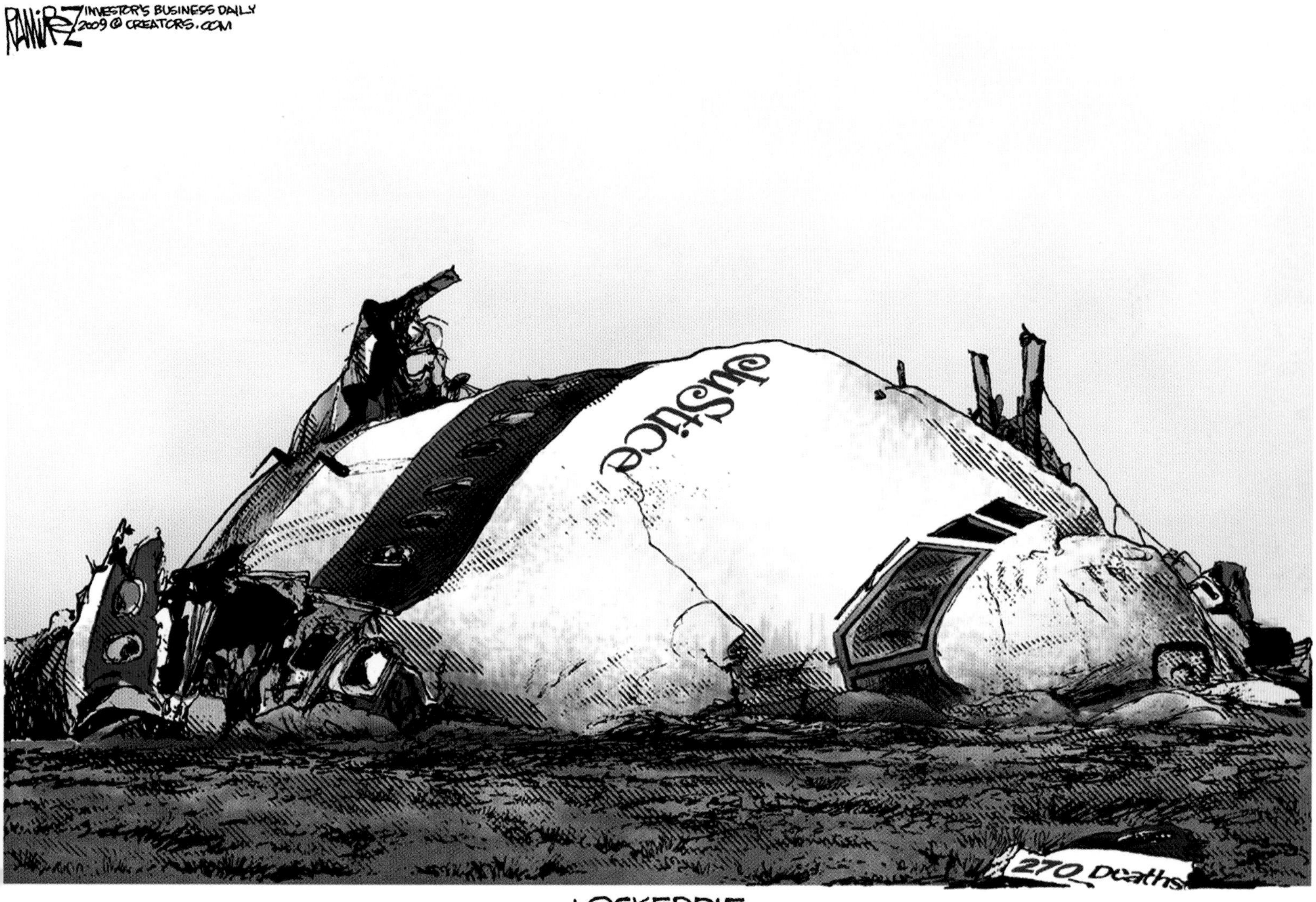
RAMIREZ INVESTOR'S BUSINESS DAILY
2009 © CREATORS.COM
Justice
270 Deaths

LOCKERBIE

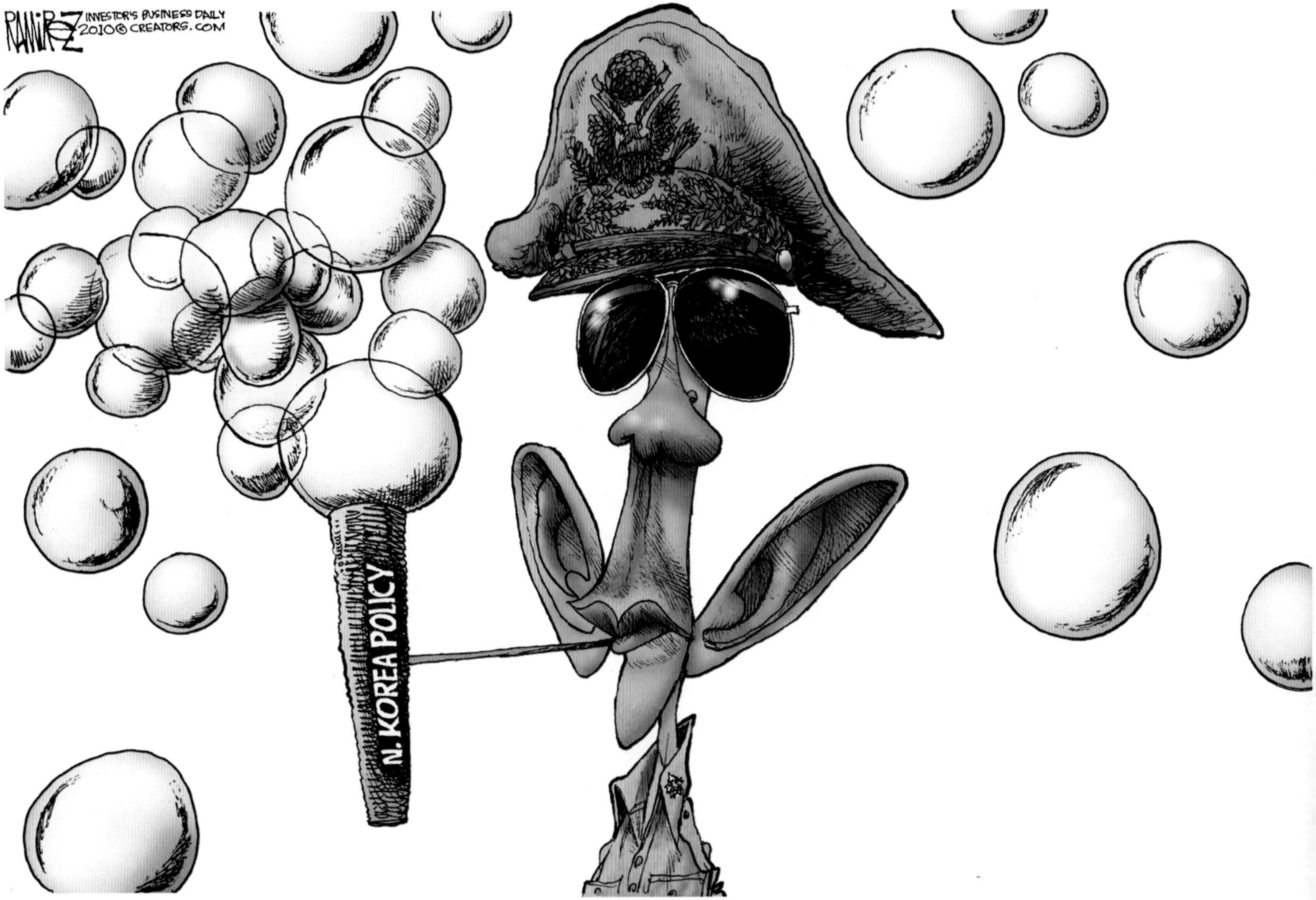
RAMIREZ
INVESTOR'S BUSINESS DAILY
2010© CREATORS.COM
N. KOREA POLICY

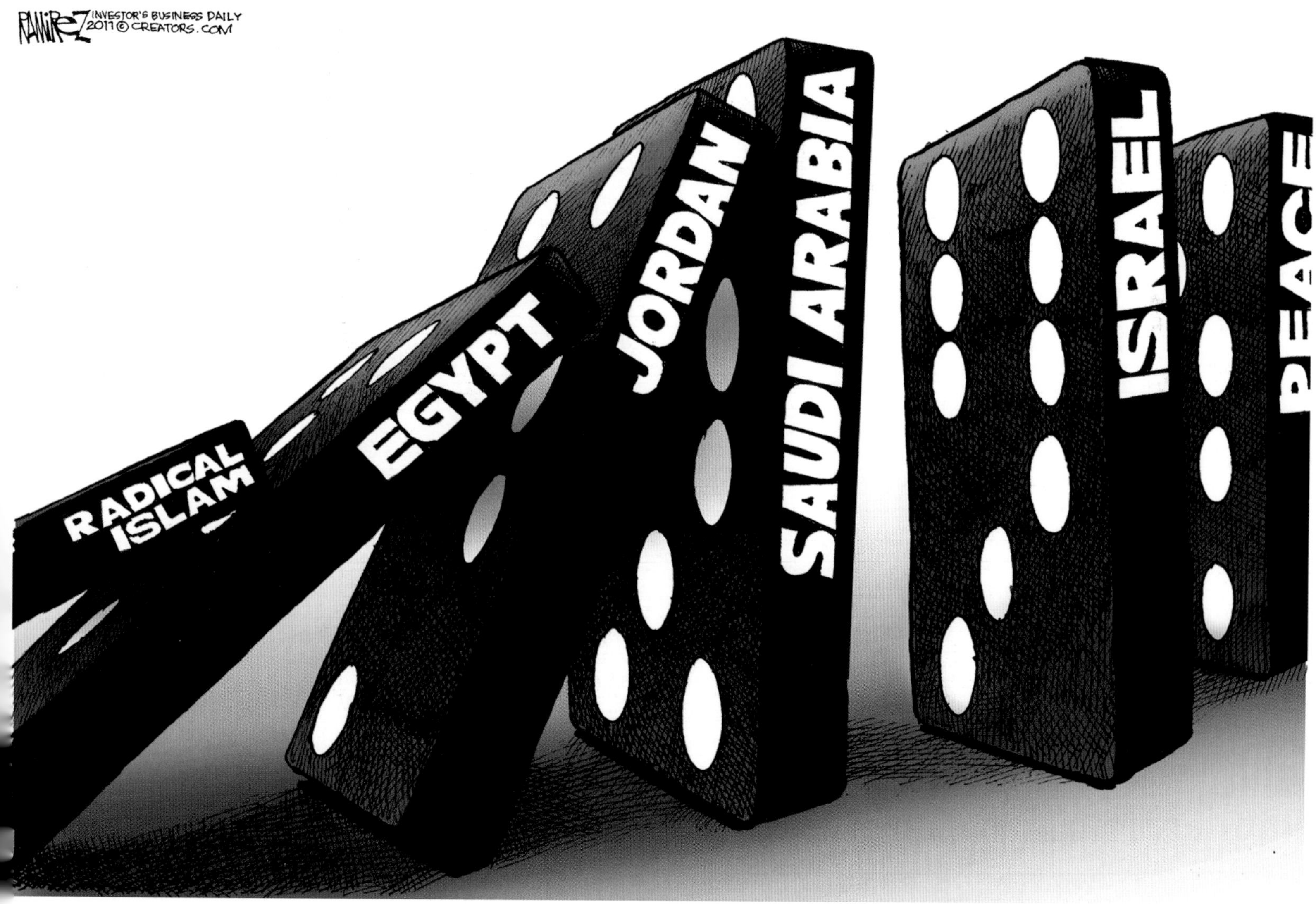
RAMIREZ INVESTOR'S BUSINESS DAILY 2011 © CREATORS.COM
RADICAL ISLAM
EGYPT
JORDAN
SAUDI ARABIA
ISRAEL
PEACE

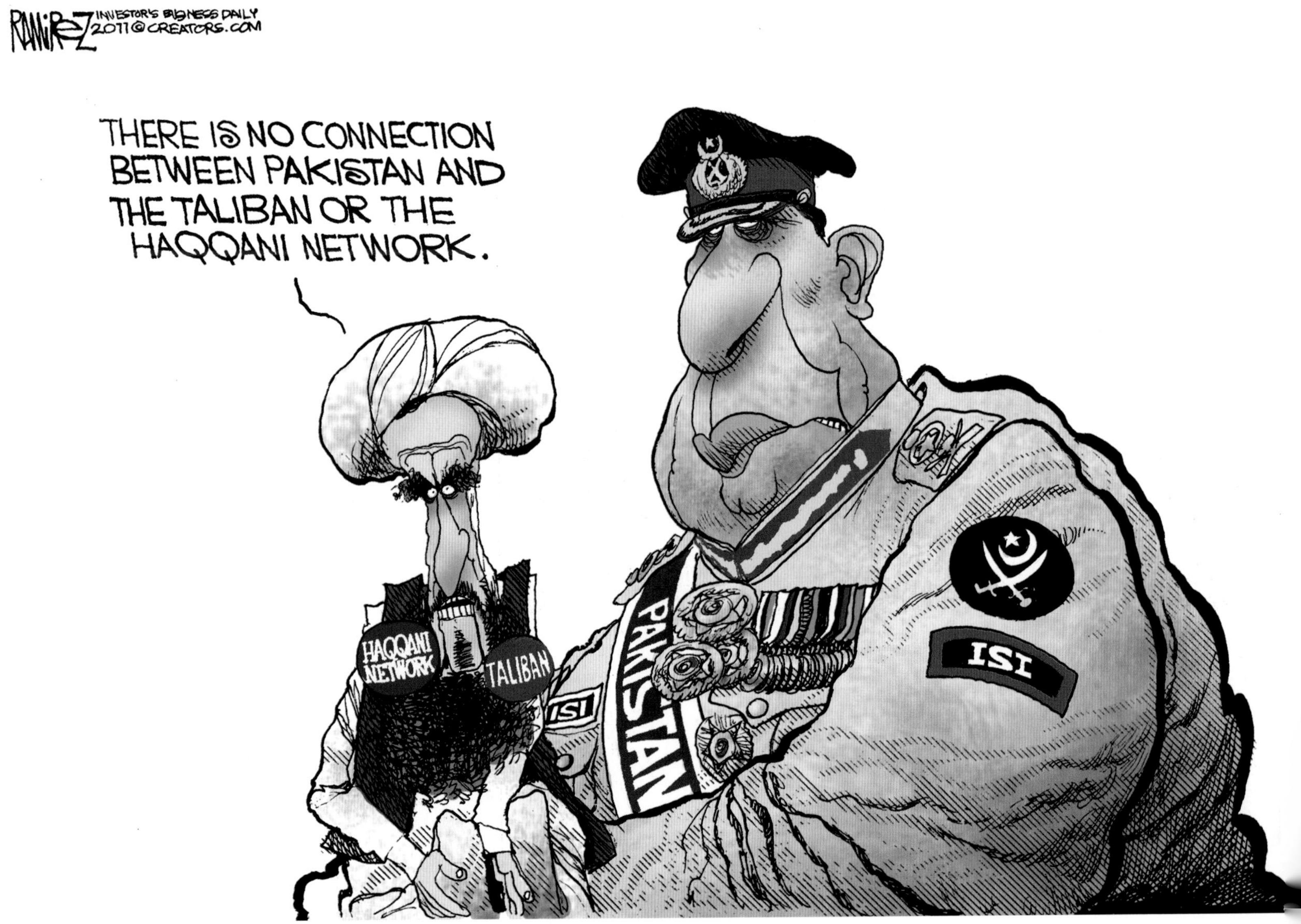
RAMIREZ INVESTOR'S BUSINESS DAILY 2011 © CREATORS.COM
THERE IS NO CONNECTION BETWEEN PAKISTAN AND THE TALIBAN OR THE HAQQANI NETWORK.
HAQQANI NETWORK
TALIBAN
ISI
PAKISTAN
ISI

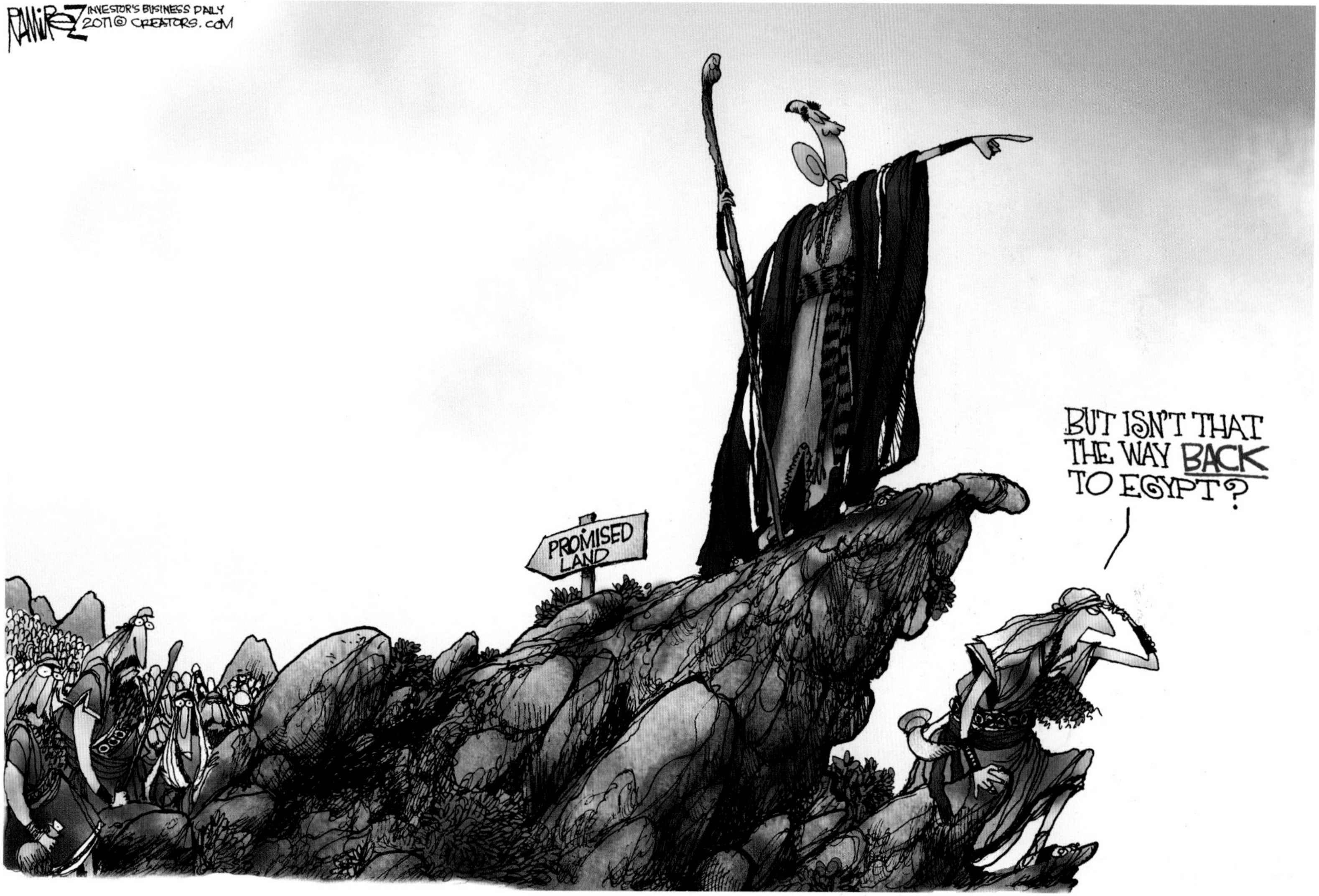
RAMIREZ INVESTOR'S BUSINESS DAILY 2011 © CREATORS.COM
PROMISED LAND
BUT ISN'T THAT THE WAY BACK TO EGYPT?

OBAMOSES

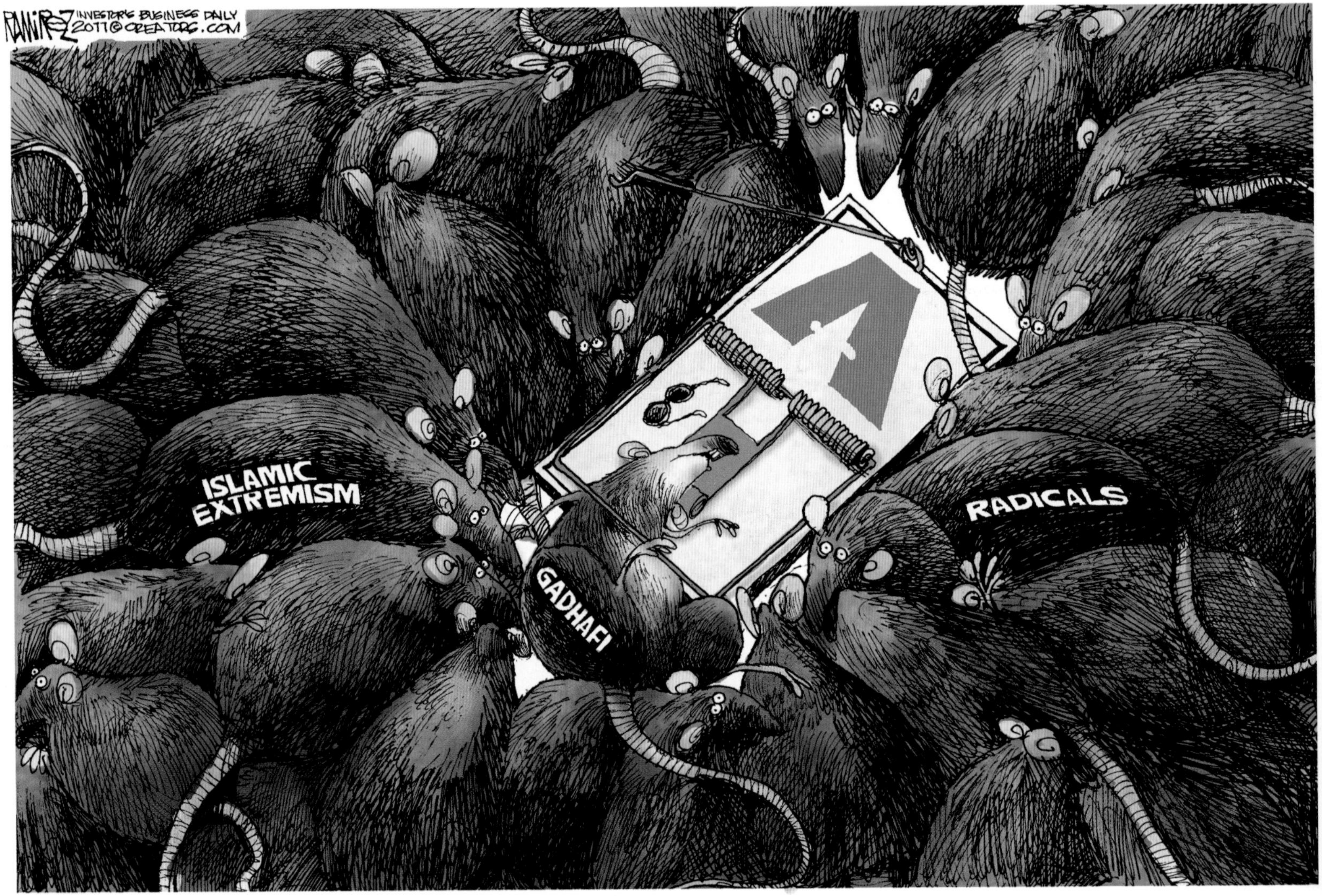
RAMIREZ INVESTOR'S BUSINESS DAILY 2011 © CREATORS.COM
ISLAMIC EXTREMISM
RADICALS
GADHAFI

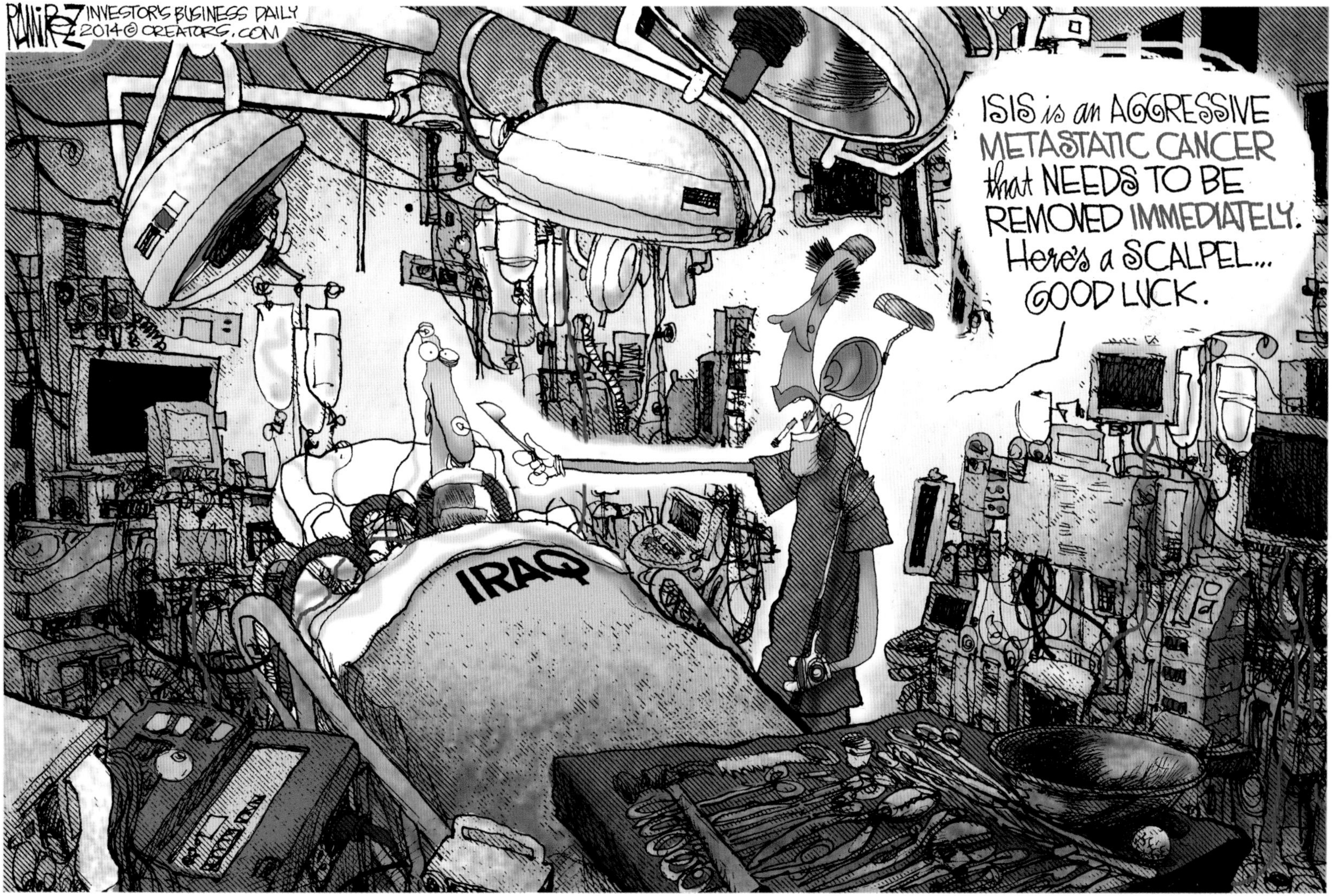
RAMIREZ INVESTOR'S BUSINESS DAILY
2014 © CREATORS.COM
ISIS is an AGGRESSIVE METASTATIC CANCER that NEEDS TO BE REMOVED IMMEDIATELY. Here's a SCALPEL... GOOD LUCK.
IRAQ

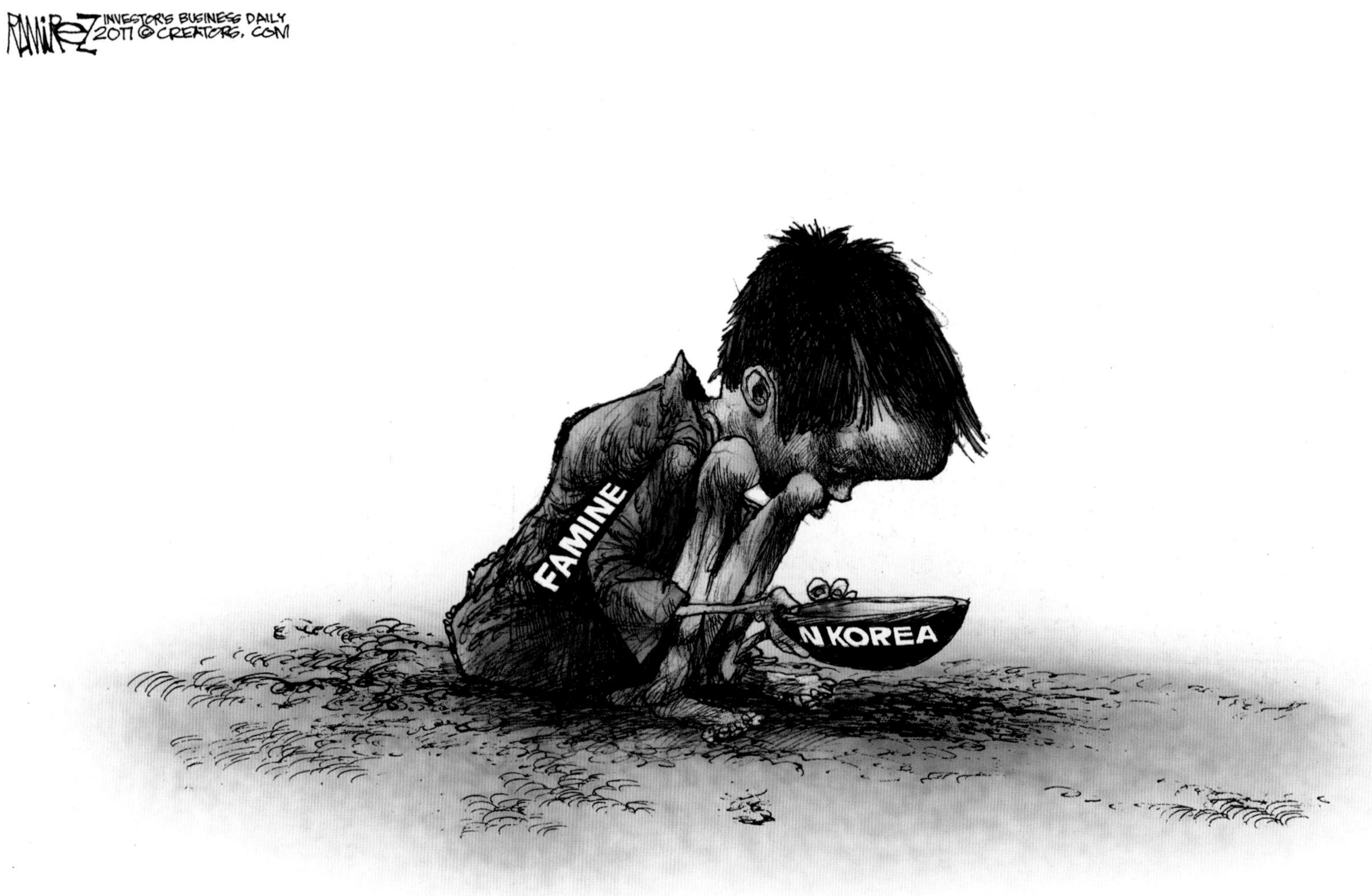
RAMIREZ INVESTOR'S BUSINESS DAILY 2011 © CREATORS.COM
FAMINE
N KOREA

THE GREAT SUCCESSOR.

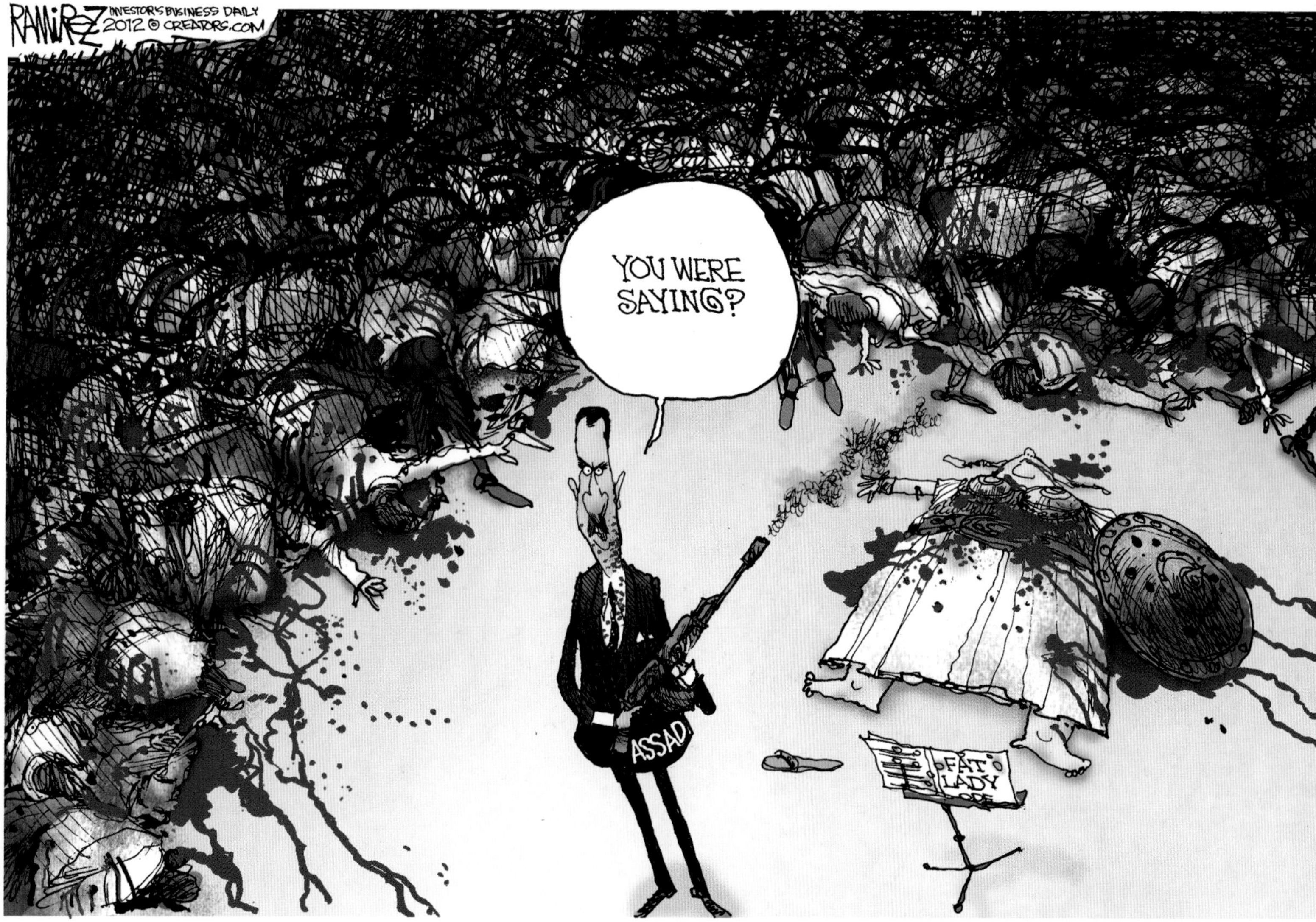
RAMIREZ INVESTOR'S BUSINESS DAILY 2012 © CREATORS.COM
YOU WERE SAYING?
ASSAD
FAT LADY

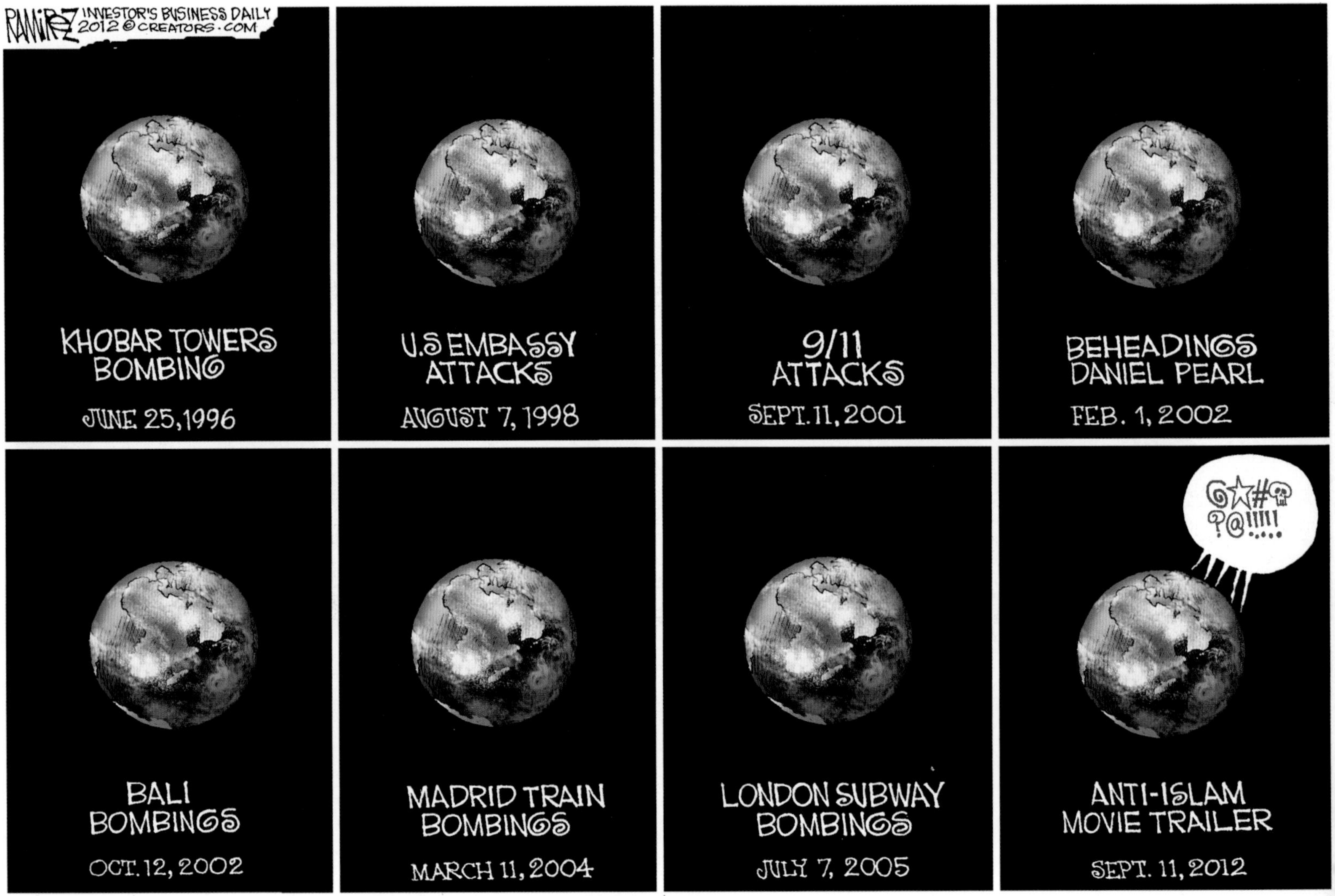
RAMIREZ INVESTOR'S BUSINESS DAILY 2012 © CREATORS.COM
KHOBAR TOWERS BOMBING
JUNE 25, 1996
U.S EMBASSY ATTACKS
AUGUST 7, 1998
9/11 ATTACKS
SEPT. 11, 2001
BEHEADINGS DANIEL PEARL
FEB. 1, 2002
BALI BOMBINGS
OCT. 12, 2002
MADRID TRAIN BOMBINGS
MARCH 11, 2004
LONDON SUBWAY BOMBINGS
JULY 7, 2005
ANTI-ISLAM MOVIE TRAILER
SEPT. 11, 2012

A BRIEF *History of* MUSLIM OUTRAGE.

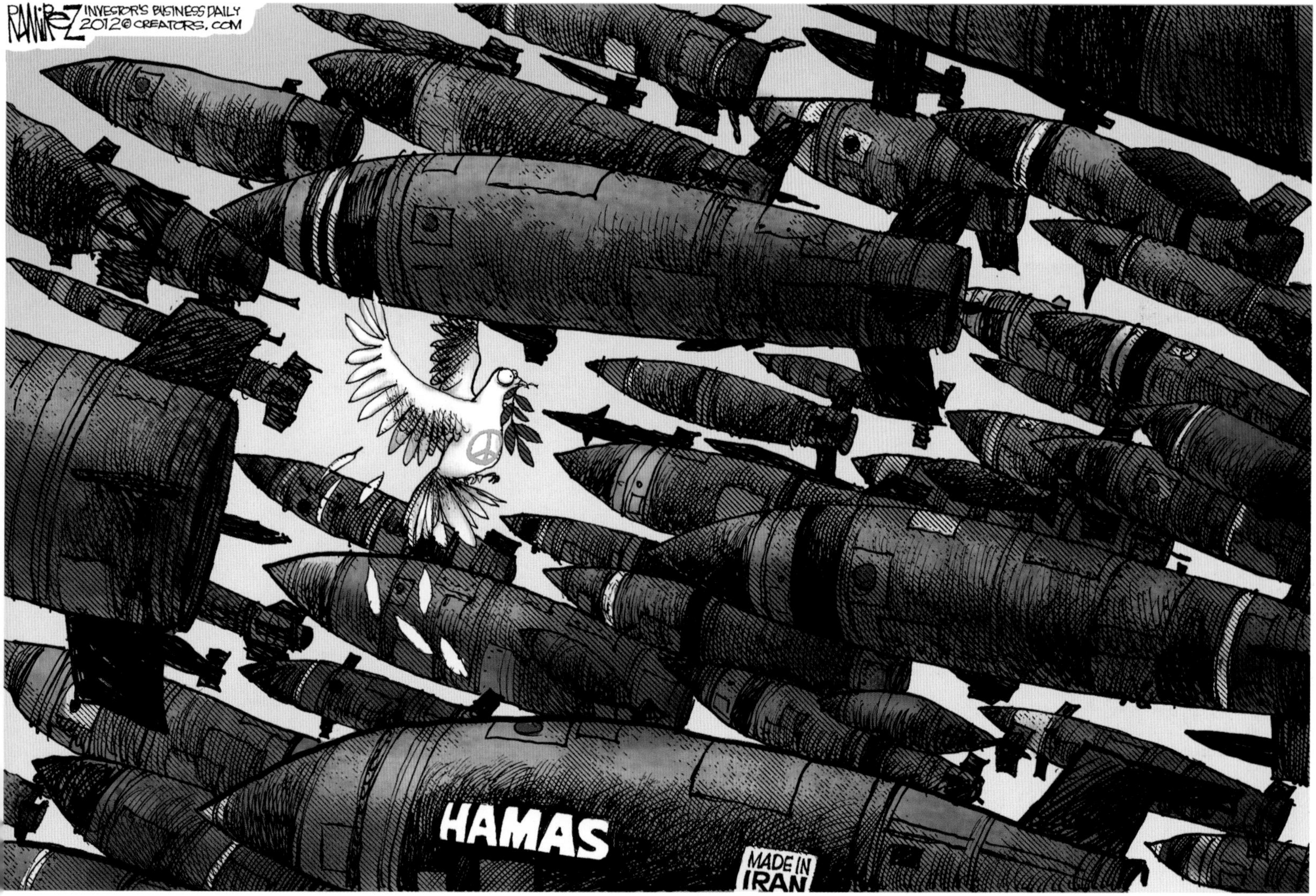
RAMIREZ INVESTOR'S BUSINESS DAILY 2012© CREATORS.COM
HAMAS
MADE IN IRAN

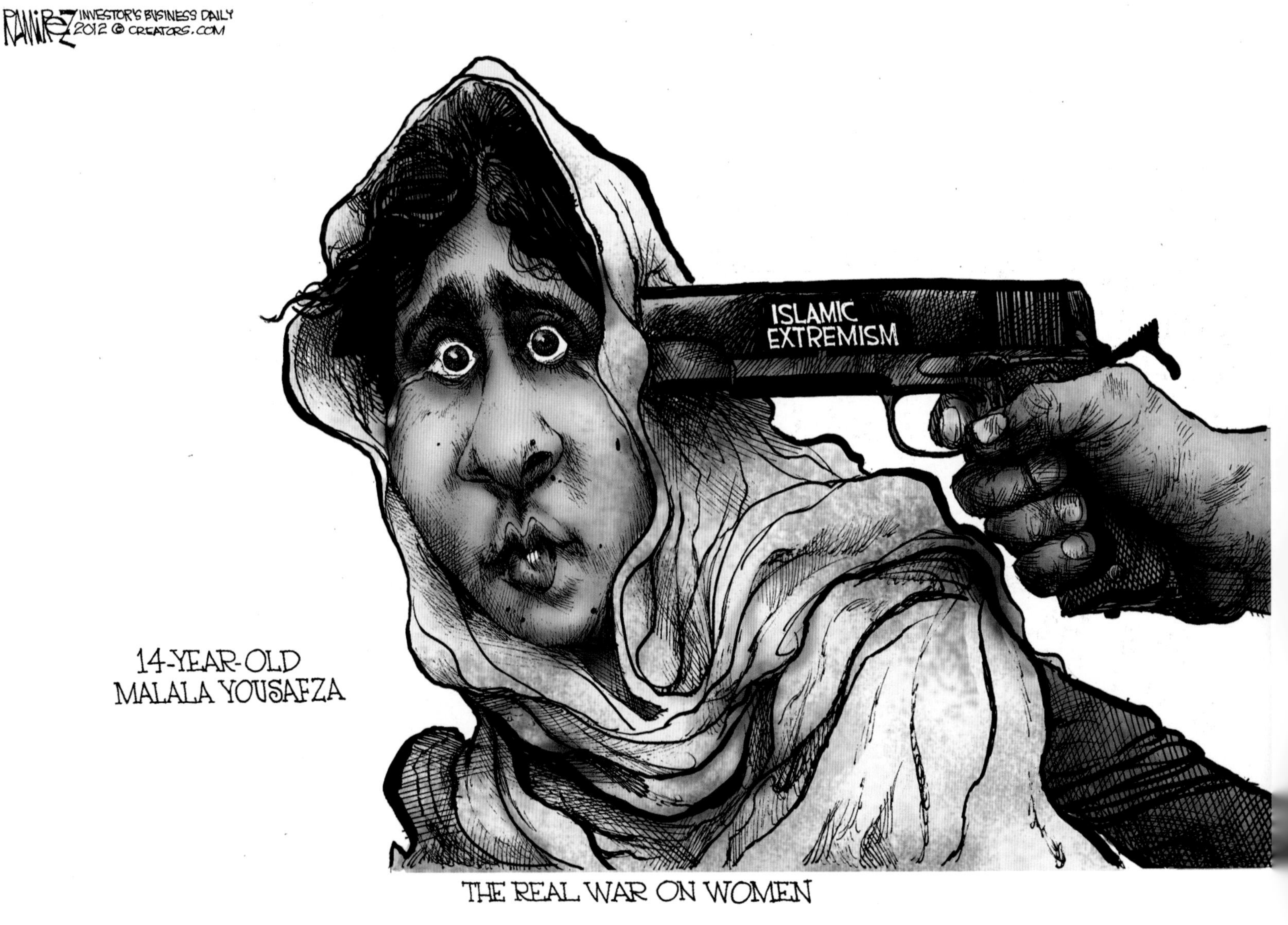
RAMIREZ
INVESTOR'S BUSINESS DAILY
2012 © CREATORS.COM
ISLAMIC
EXTREMISM
14-YEAR-OLD
MALALA YOUSAFZA
THE REAL WAR ON WOMEN

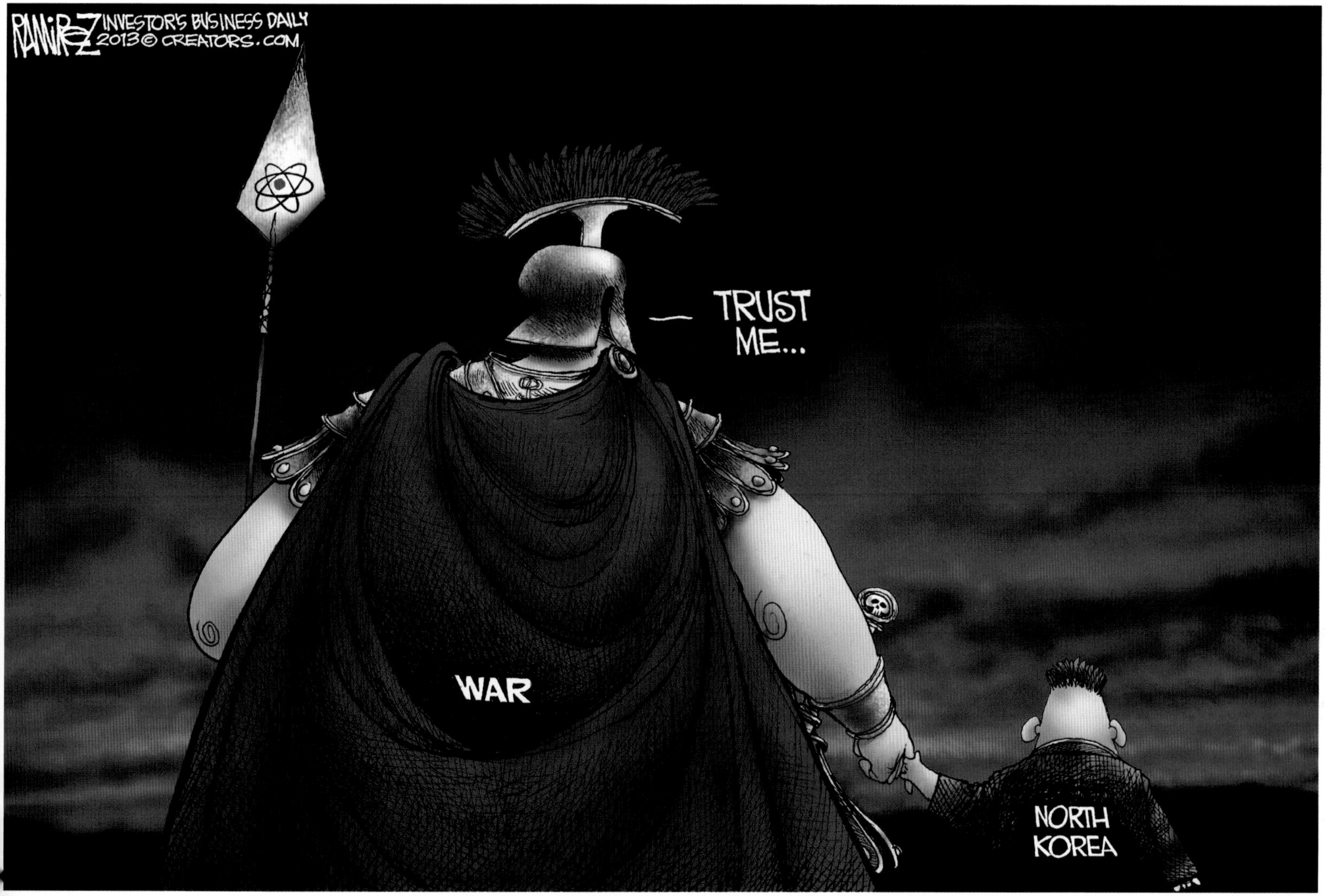
RAMIREZ INVESTOR'S BUSINESS DAILY
2013 © CREATORS.COM
TRUST ME...
WAR
NORTH KOREA

THE "FAT MAN" *and* THE "LITTLE BOY."

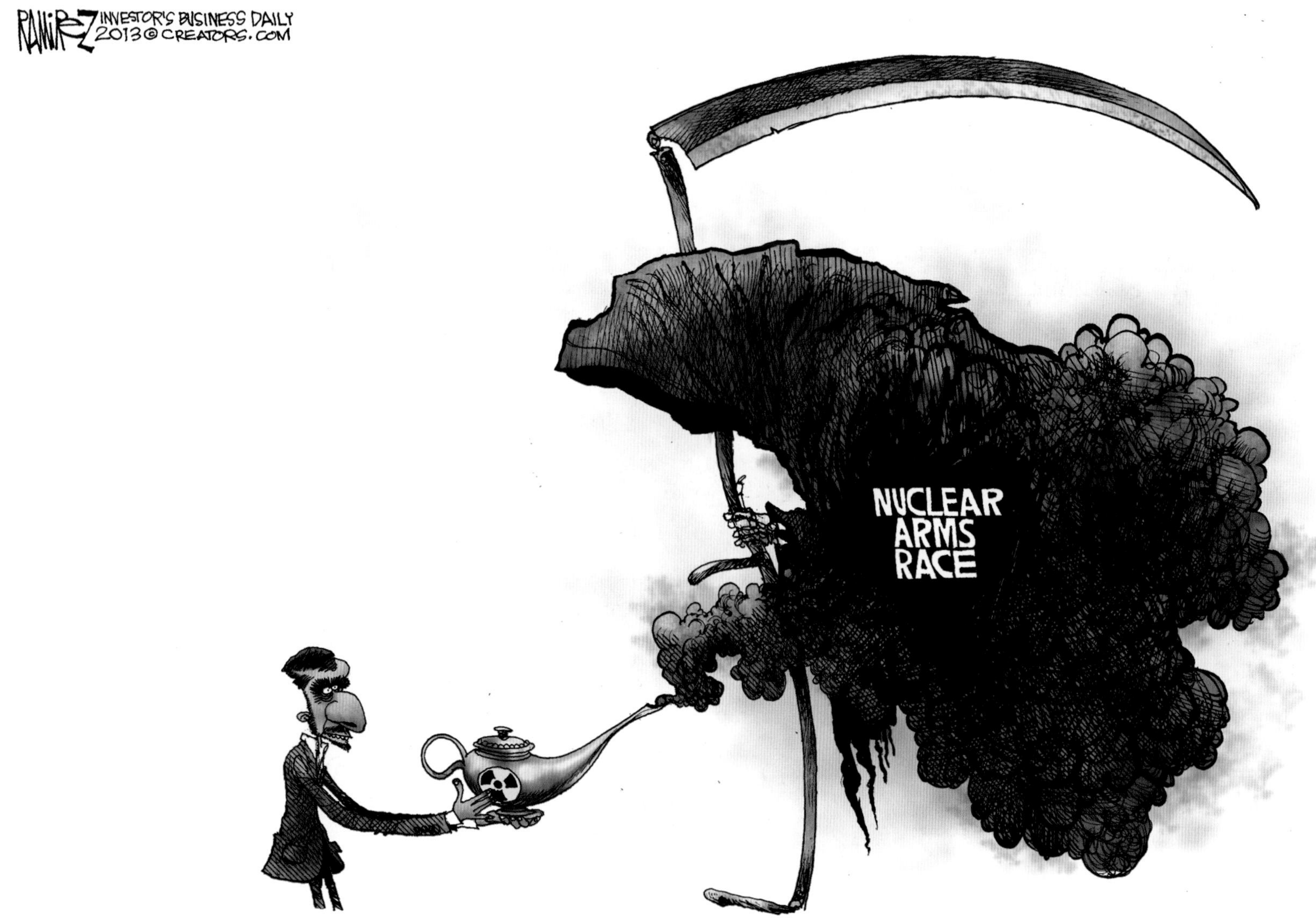
RAMIREZ INVESTOR'S BUSINESS DAILY
2013 © CREATORS.COM
NUCLEAR
ARMS
RACE

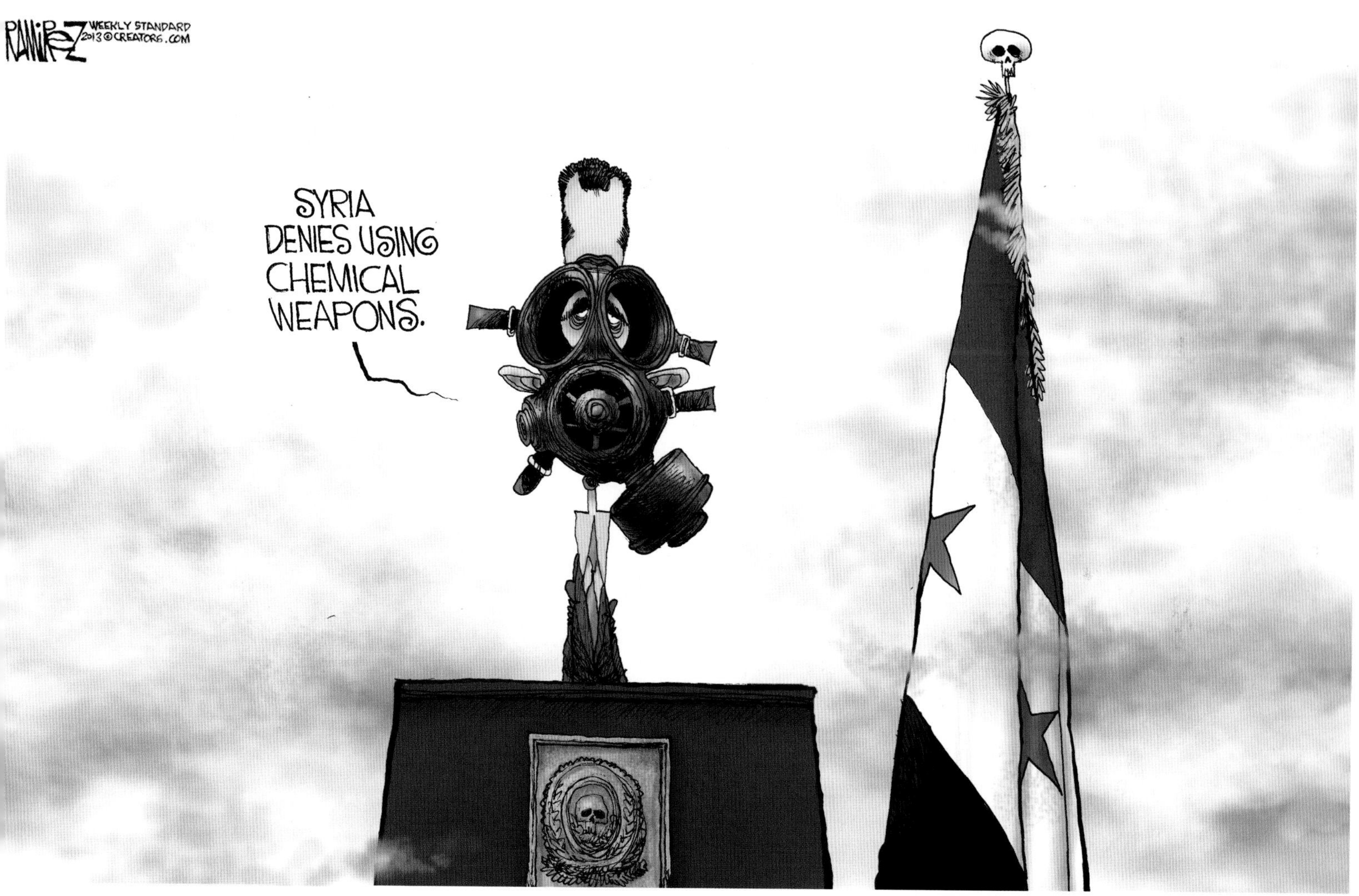
RAMIREZ WEEKLY STANDARD 2013 © CREATORS.COM
SYRIA DENIES USING CHEMICAL WEAPONS.

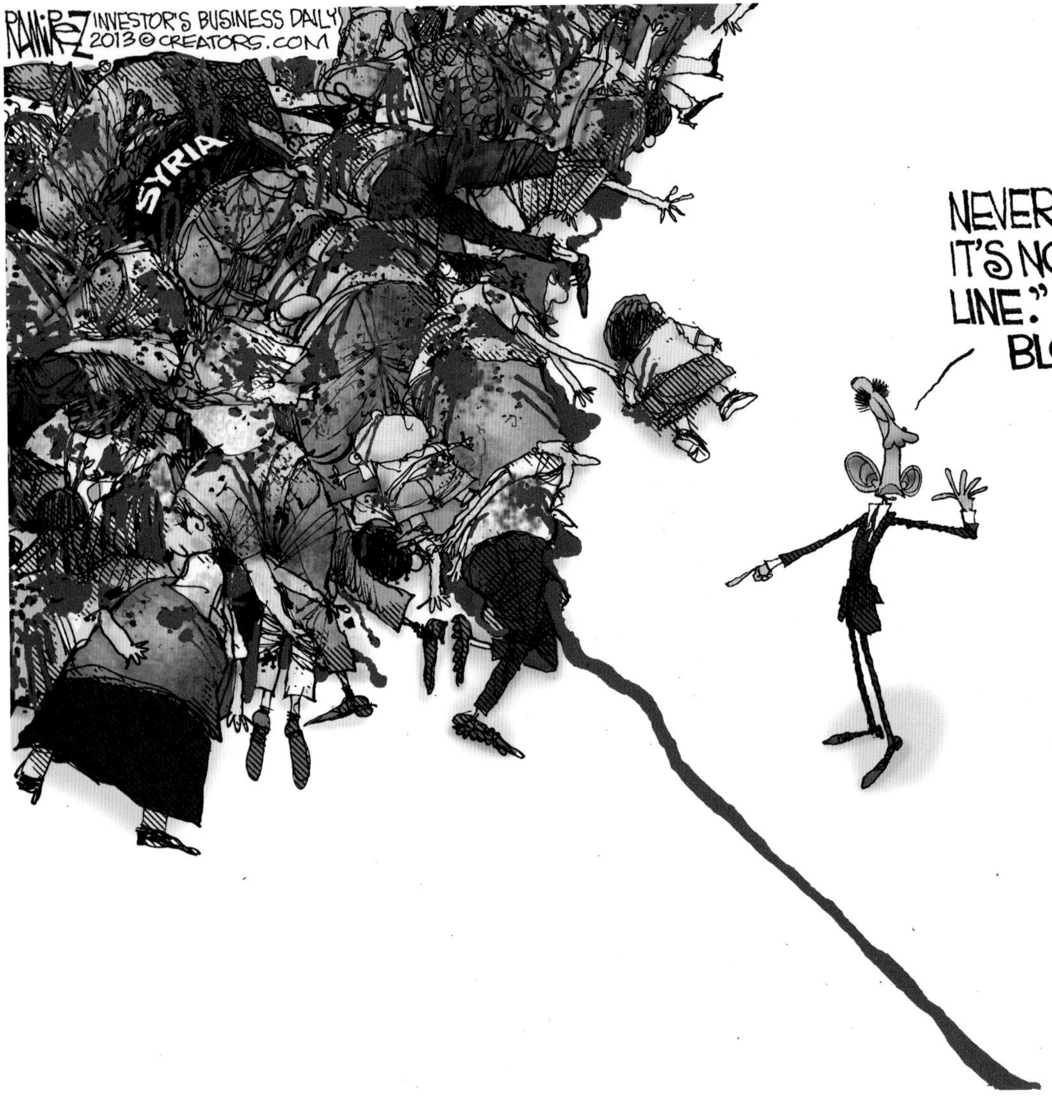
RAMIREZ INVESTOR'S BUSINESS DAILY 2013 © CREATORS.COM
SYRIA
NEVER MIND. IT'S NOT A "RED LINE." IT'S JUST BLOOD.

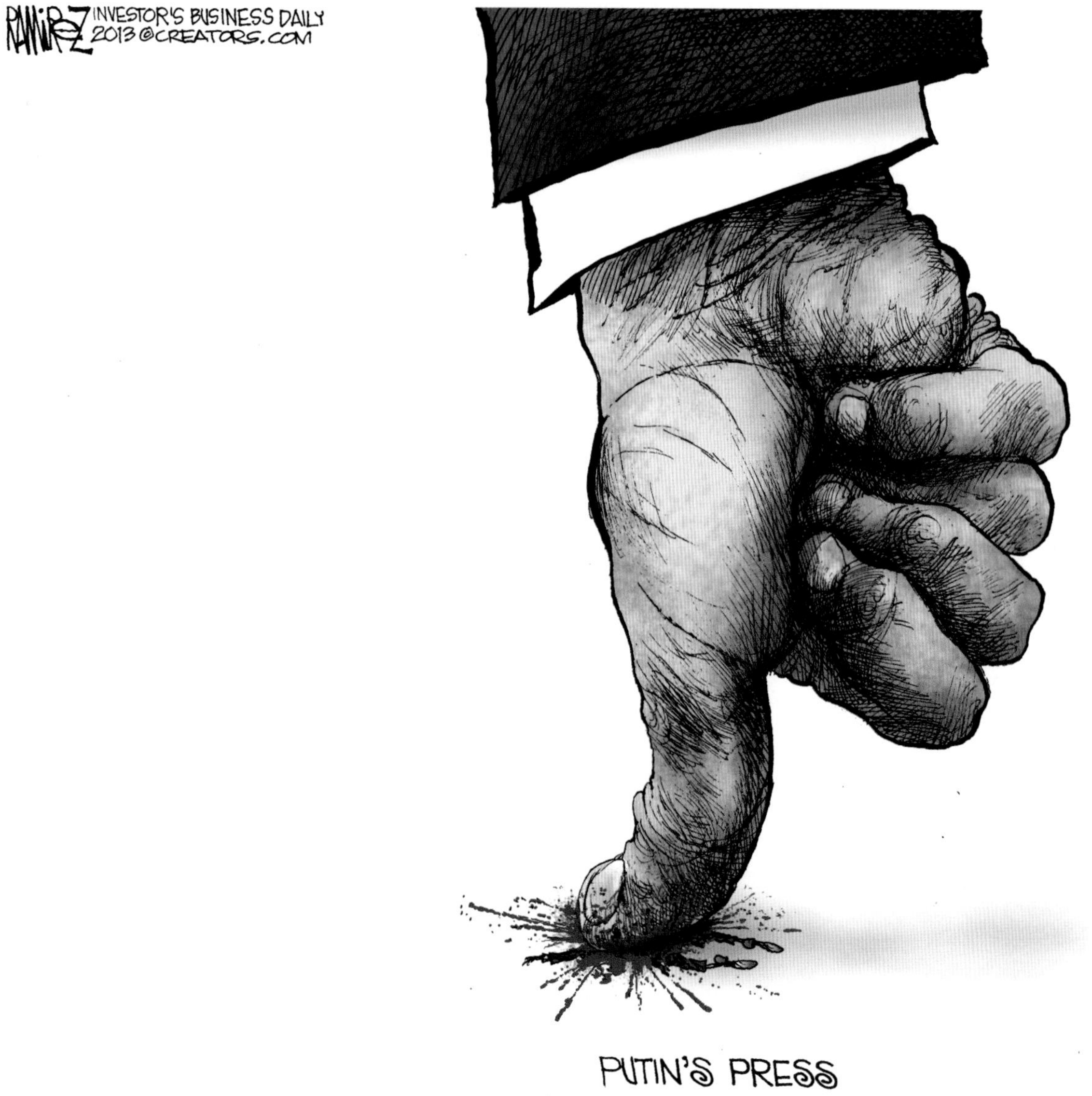
RAMIREZ INVESTOR'S BUSINESS DAILY
2013 ©CREATORS.COM
PUTIN'S PRESS

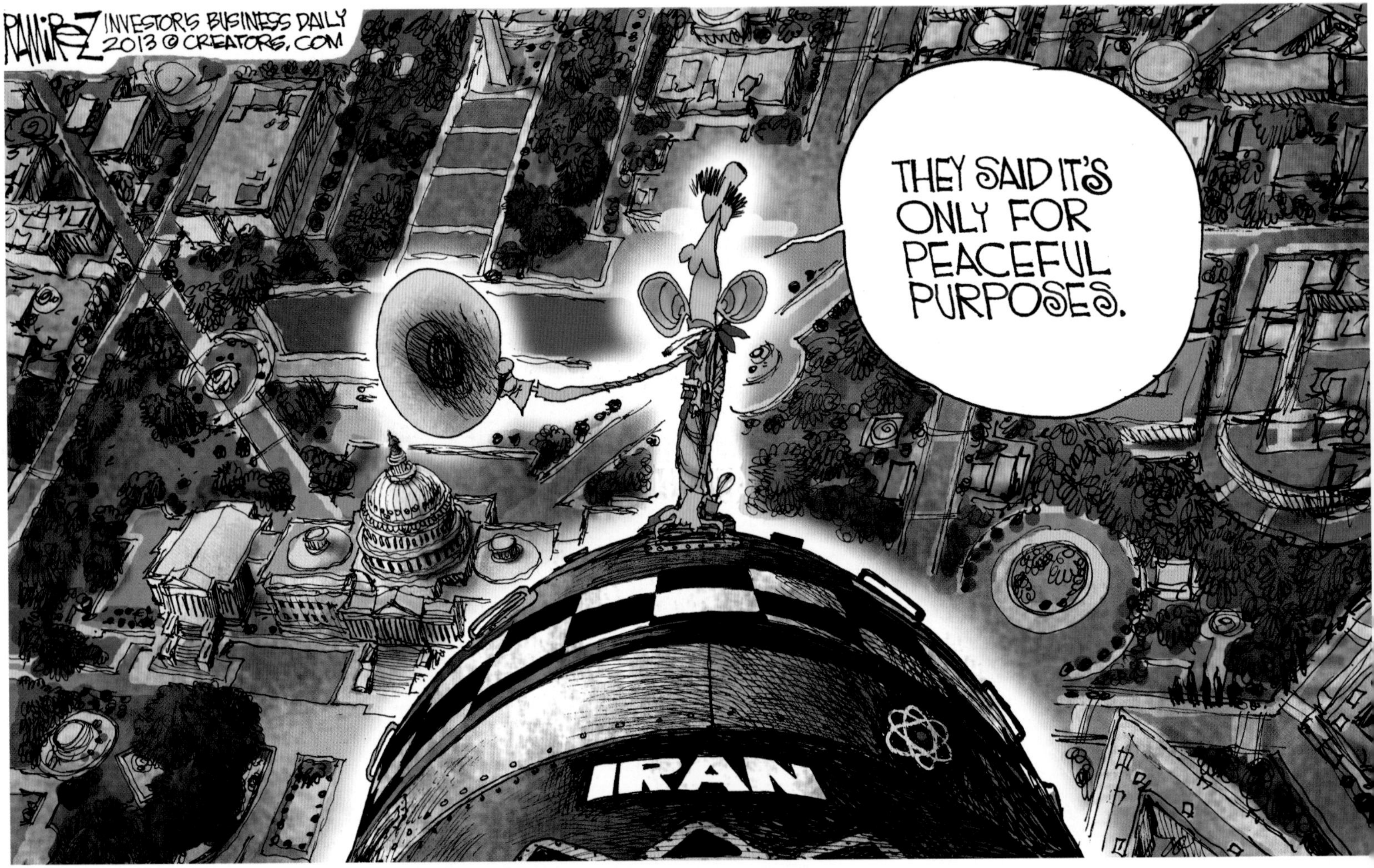
RAMIREZ INVESTOR'S BUSINESS DAILY 2013 © CREATORS.COM
THEY SAID IT'S ONLY FOR PEACEFUL PURPOSES.
IRAN

Dr. Strangepolicy

Or: How I Learned To STOP *Worrying* And LOVE The Iranian Bomb.

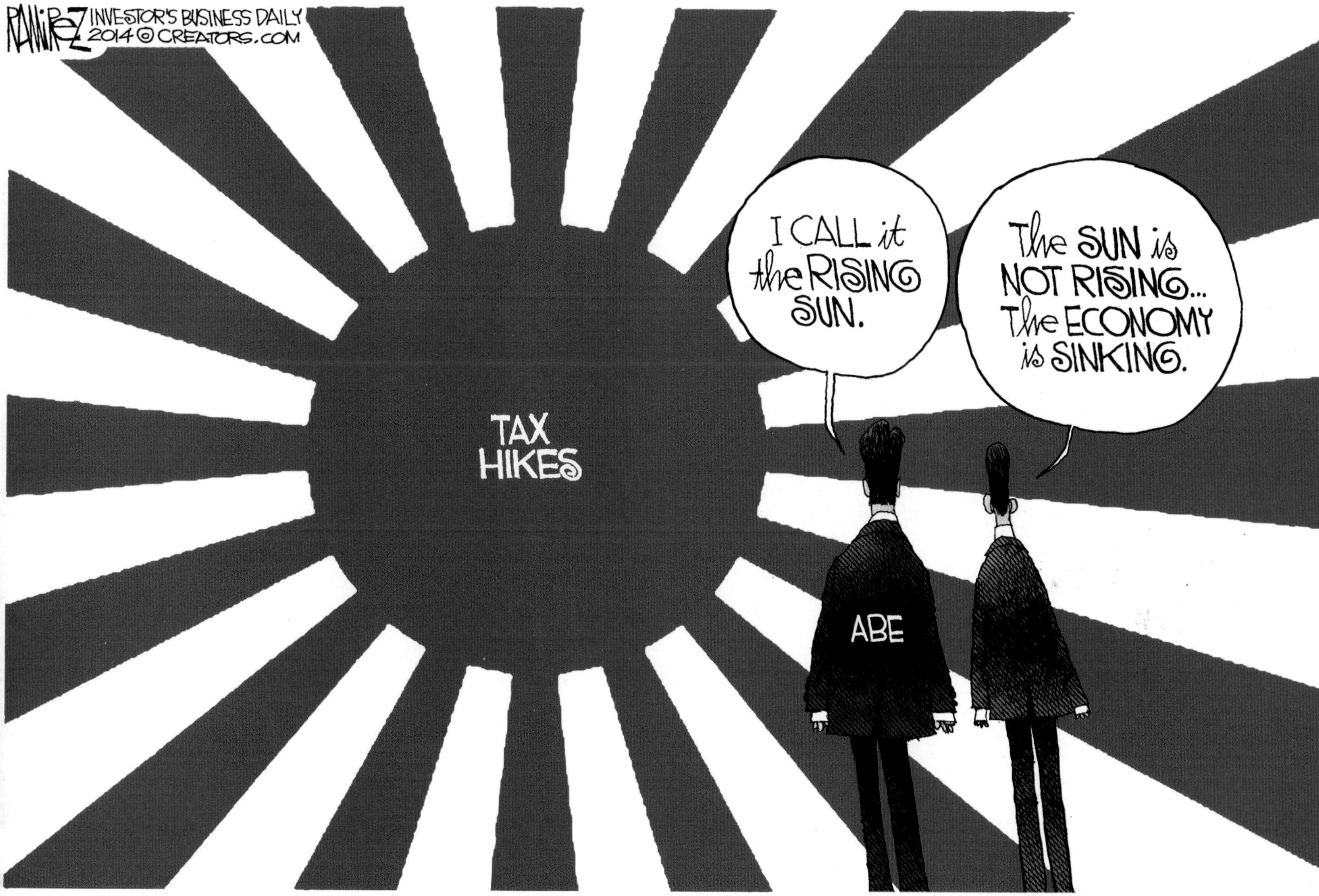
RAMIREZ INVESTOR'S BUSINESS DAILY
2014 © CREATORS.COM
TAX HIKES
I CALL it the RISING SUN.
The SUN is NOT RISING... The ECONOMY is SINKING.
ABE

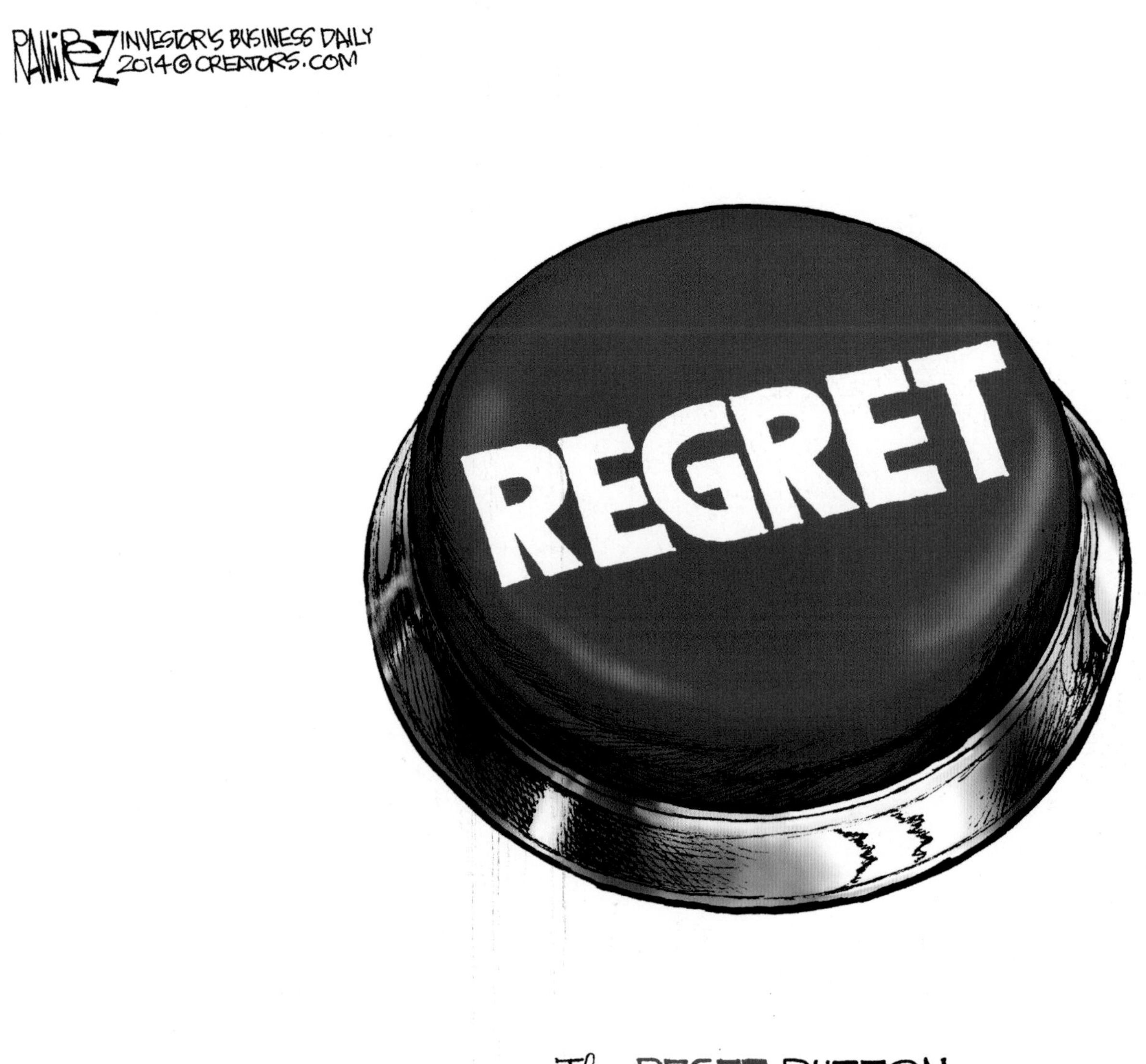
RAMIREZ
INVESTOR'S BUSINESS DAILY
2014 © CREATORS.COM
REGRET
The RESET BUTTON.

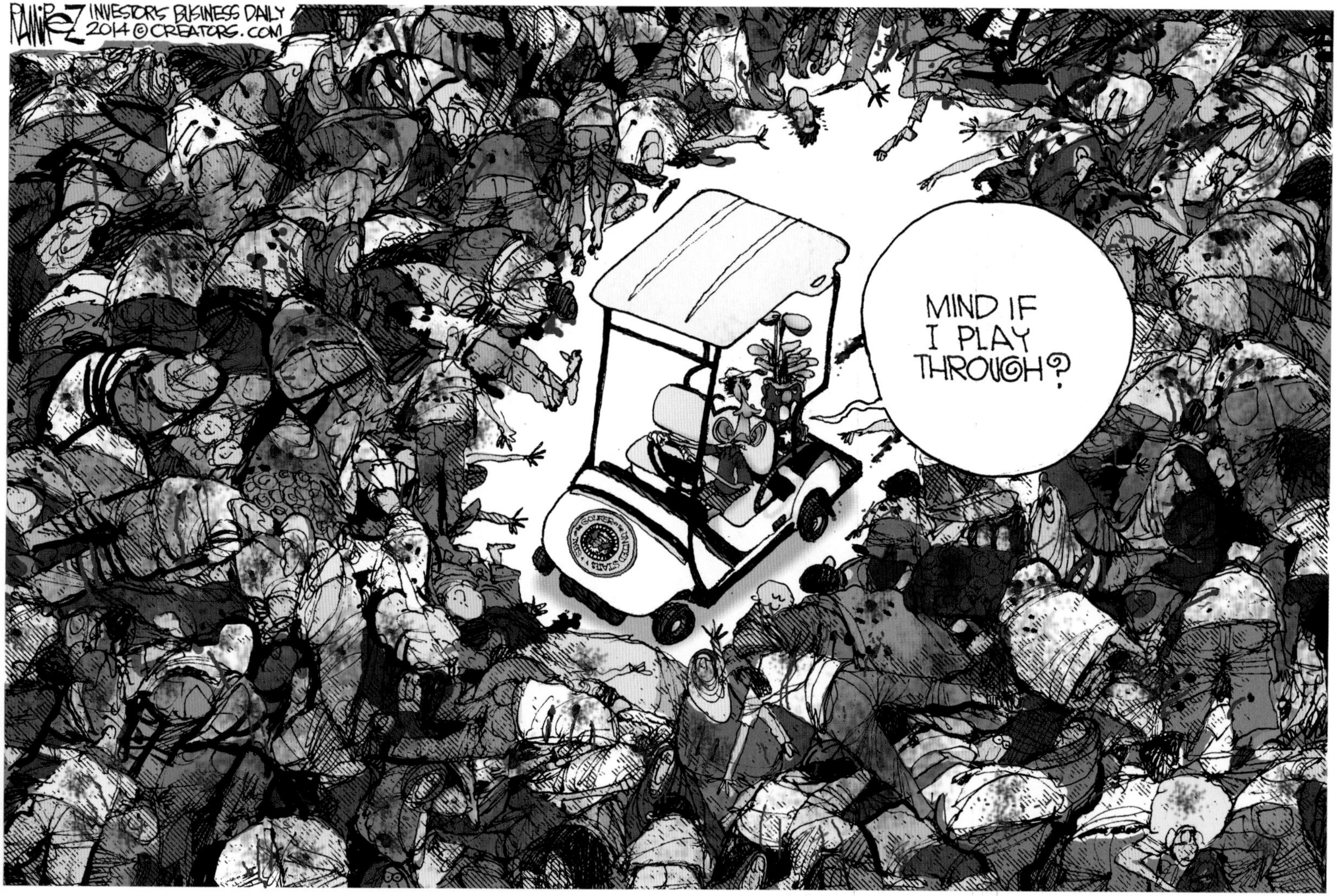
RAMIREZ INVESTOR'S BUSINESS DAILY
2014 © CREATORS.COM
MIND IF I PLAY THROUGH?

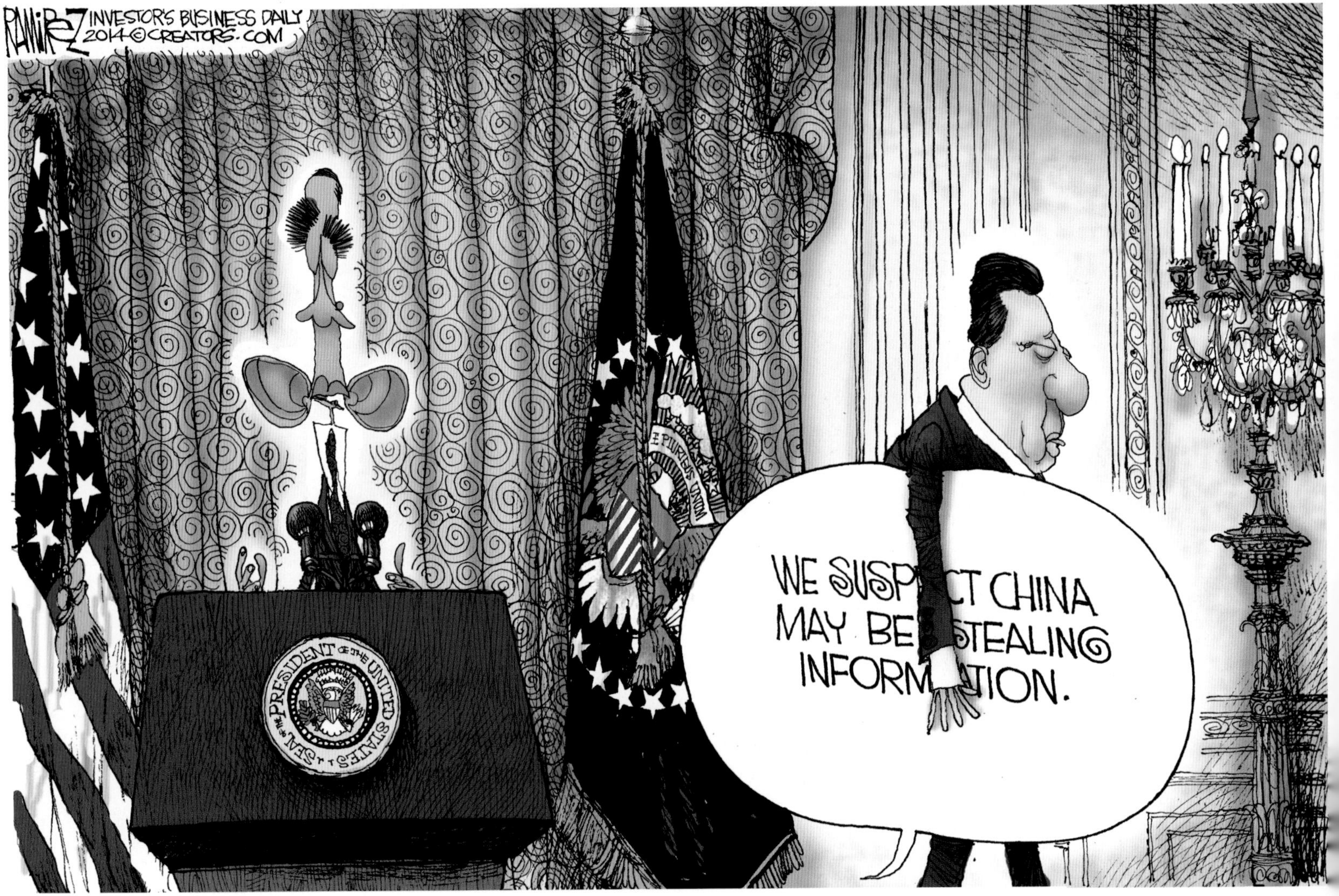
RAMIREZ INVESTOR'S BUSINESS DAILY
2014 © CREATORS.COM
WE SUSP CT CHINA
MAY BE STEALING
INFORM TION.
SEAL OF THE PRESIDENT OF THE UNITED STATES

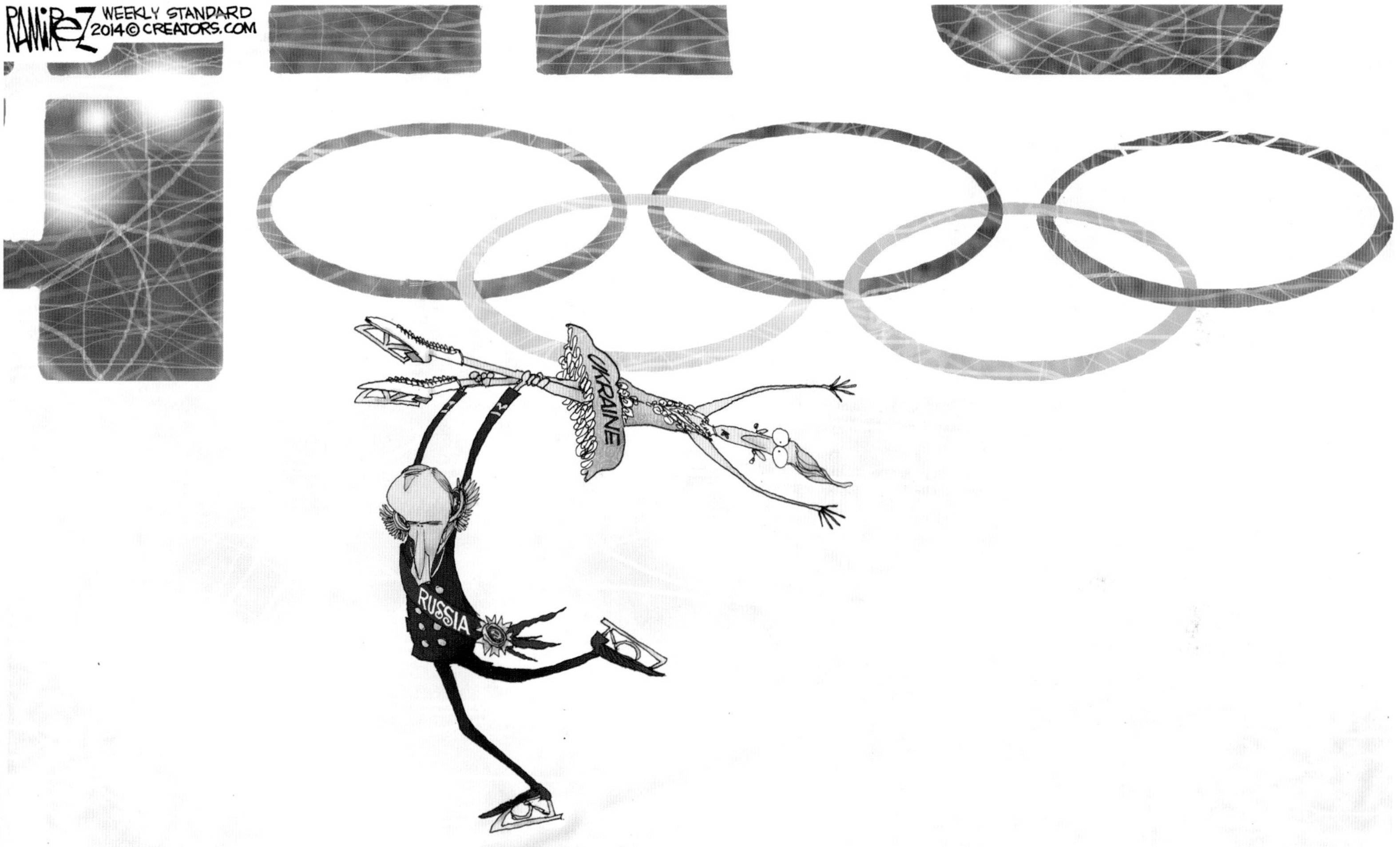
RAMIREZ WEEKLY STANDARD 2014 © CREATORS.COM
UKRAINE
RUSSIA

THE SHORT PROGRAM

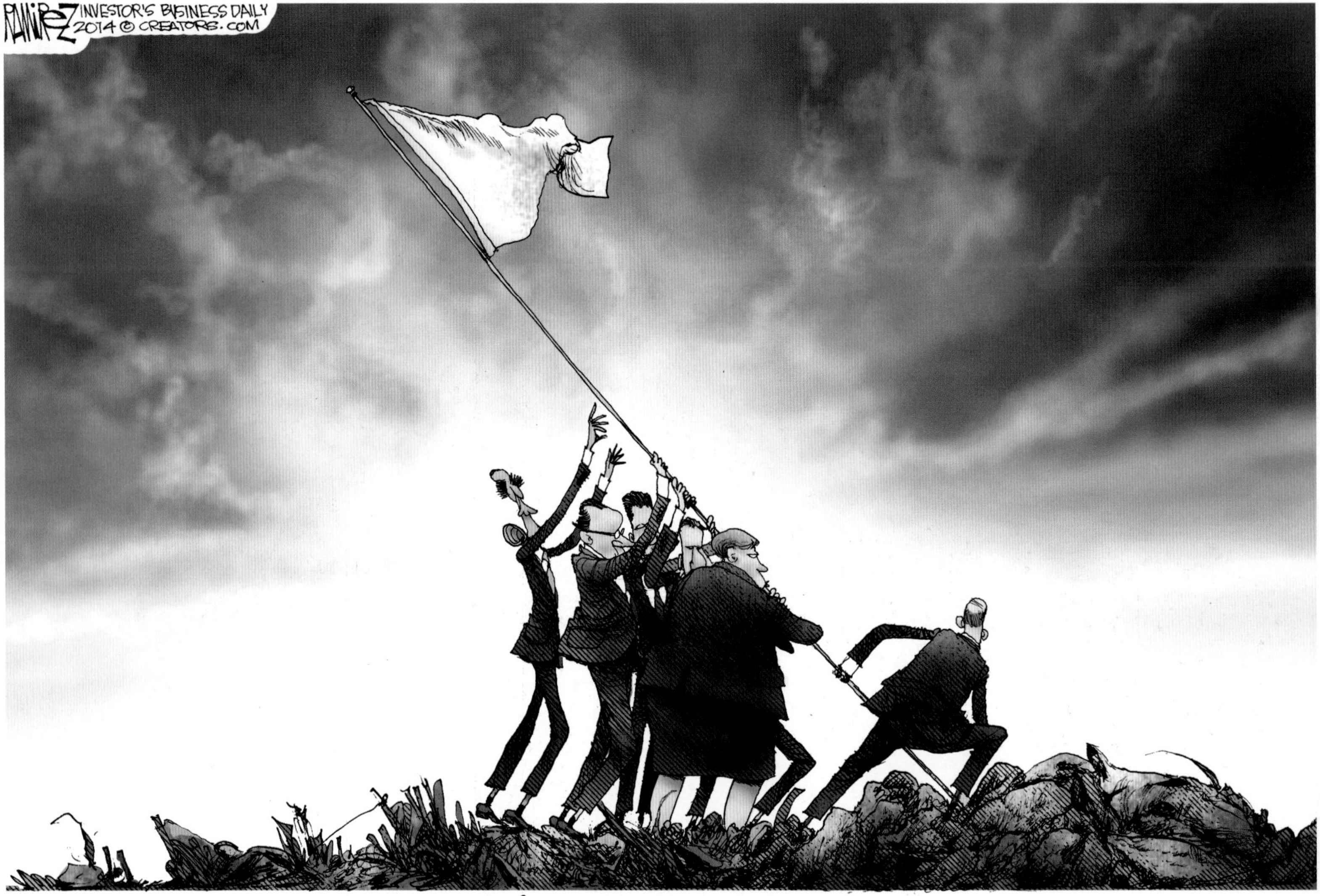
RAMIREZ
INVESTOR'S BUSINESS DAILY
2014 © CREATORS.COM

The IRAN NUCLEAR DEAL

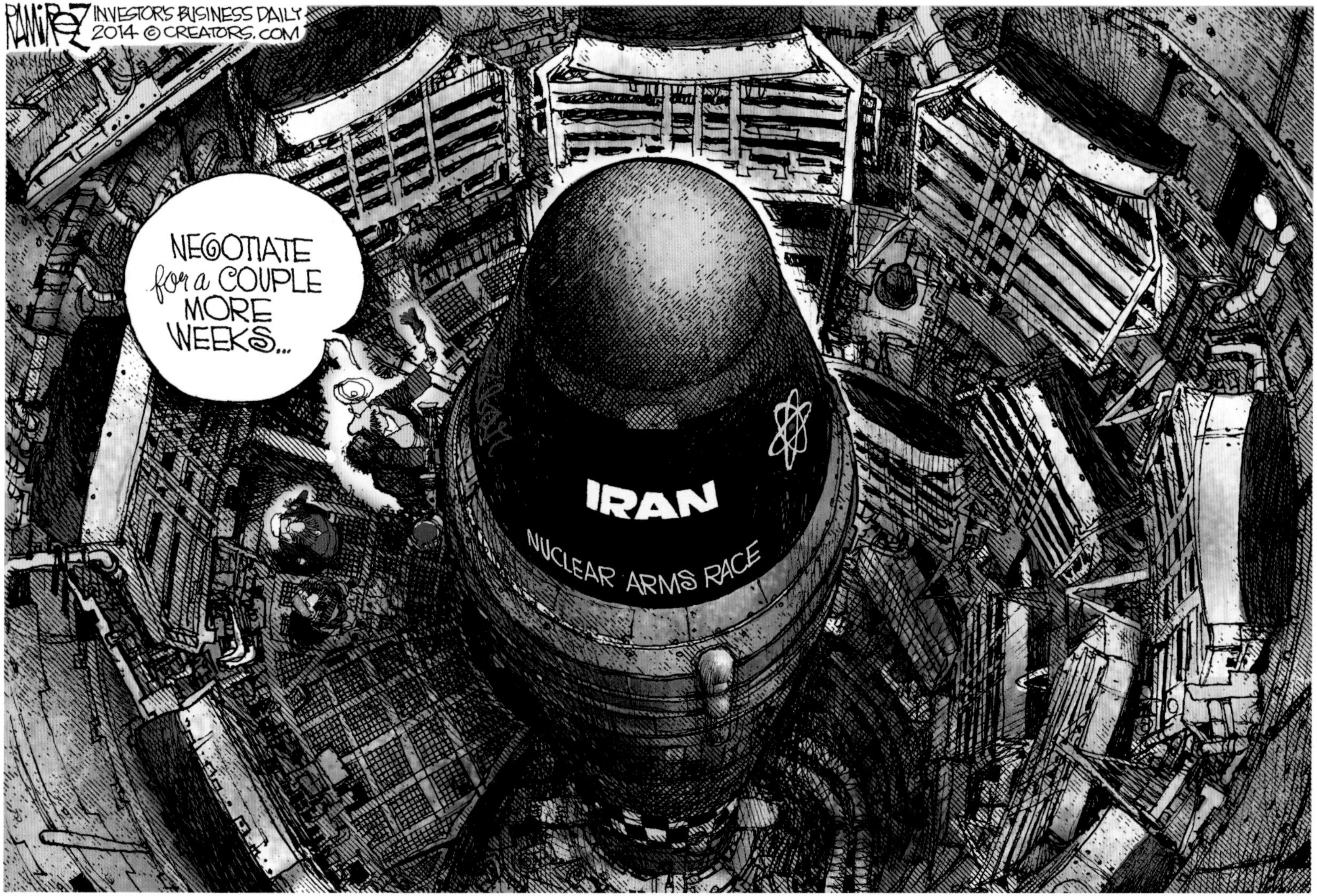
RAMIREZ INVESTOR'S BUSINESS DAILY 2014 © CREATORS.COM
NEGOTIATE for a COUPLE MORE WEEKS...
IRAN
NUCLEAR ARMS RACE

MEANWHILE...

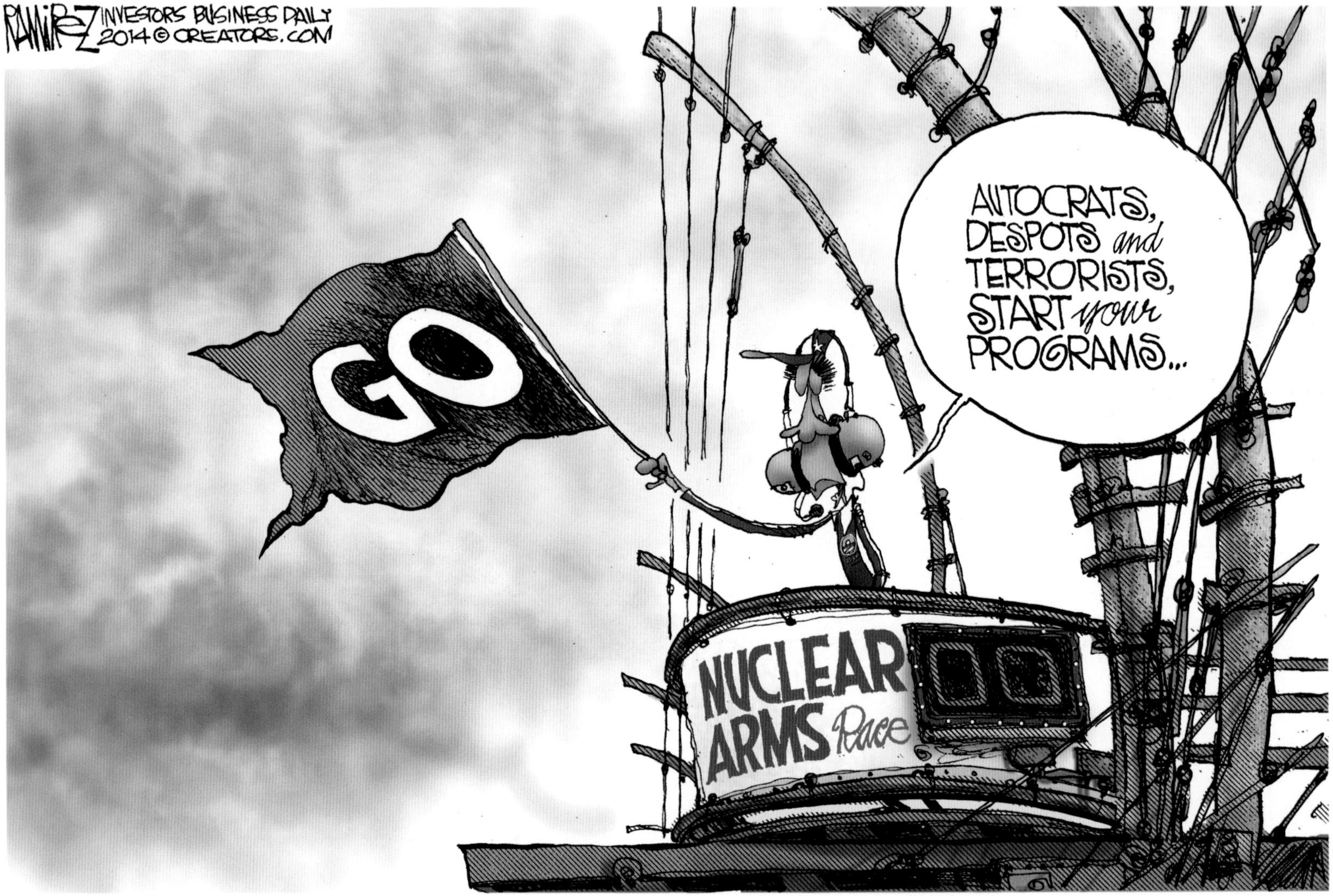
RAMIREZ INVESTORS BUSINESS DAILY 2014 © CREATORS.COM
GO
AUTOCRATS, DESPOTS and TERRORISTS, START your PROGRAMS...
NUCLEAR ARMS Race

The OBAMA ADMINISTRATION IRAN NUCLEAR POLICY.

WAR

"Four years ago, I promised to end the war in Iraq—and we did. I said we'd wind down the war in Afghanistan—and we are. And while a new tower rises above the New York skyline, al Qaeda is on the path to defeat, and Osama bin Laden is dead."

**—President Barack Obama,
Golden, Colorado, September 13, 2012**

President Obama boasted that he had ended wars, as did British general Cornwallis in 1781, Robert E. Lee in 1865, Gustav Bauer at the signing of the Treaty of Versailles in 1919, German general Alfred Jodl, and Emperor Hirohito of Japan in 1945. The Iraq War had been won and Afghanistan was contained, but President Obama still managed to snatch defeat out of the jaws of victory.

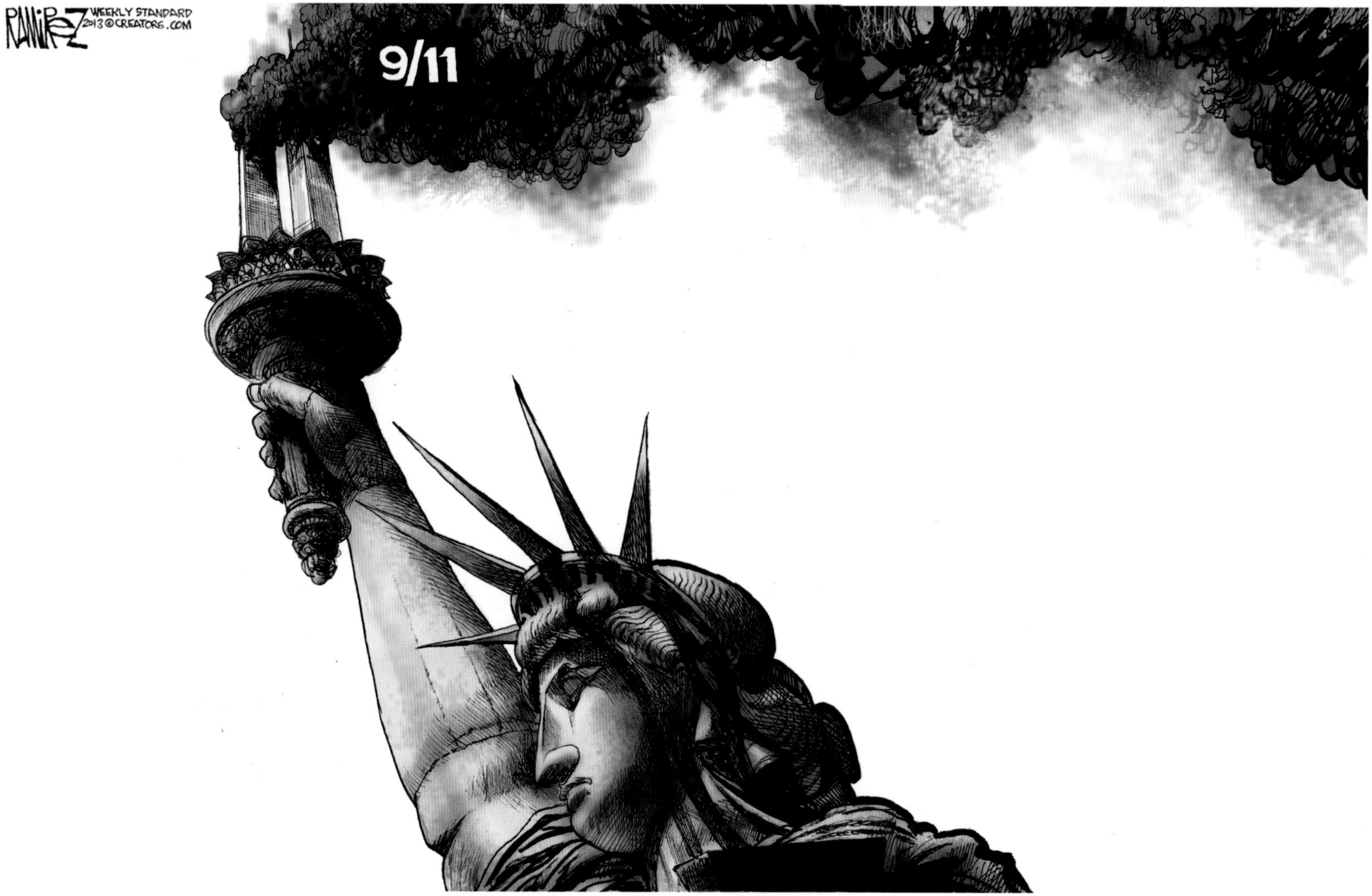
RAMIREZ WEEKLY STANDARD 2013 © CREATORS.COM
9/11
NEVER FORGET

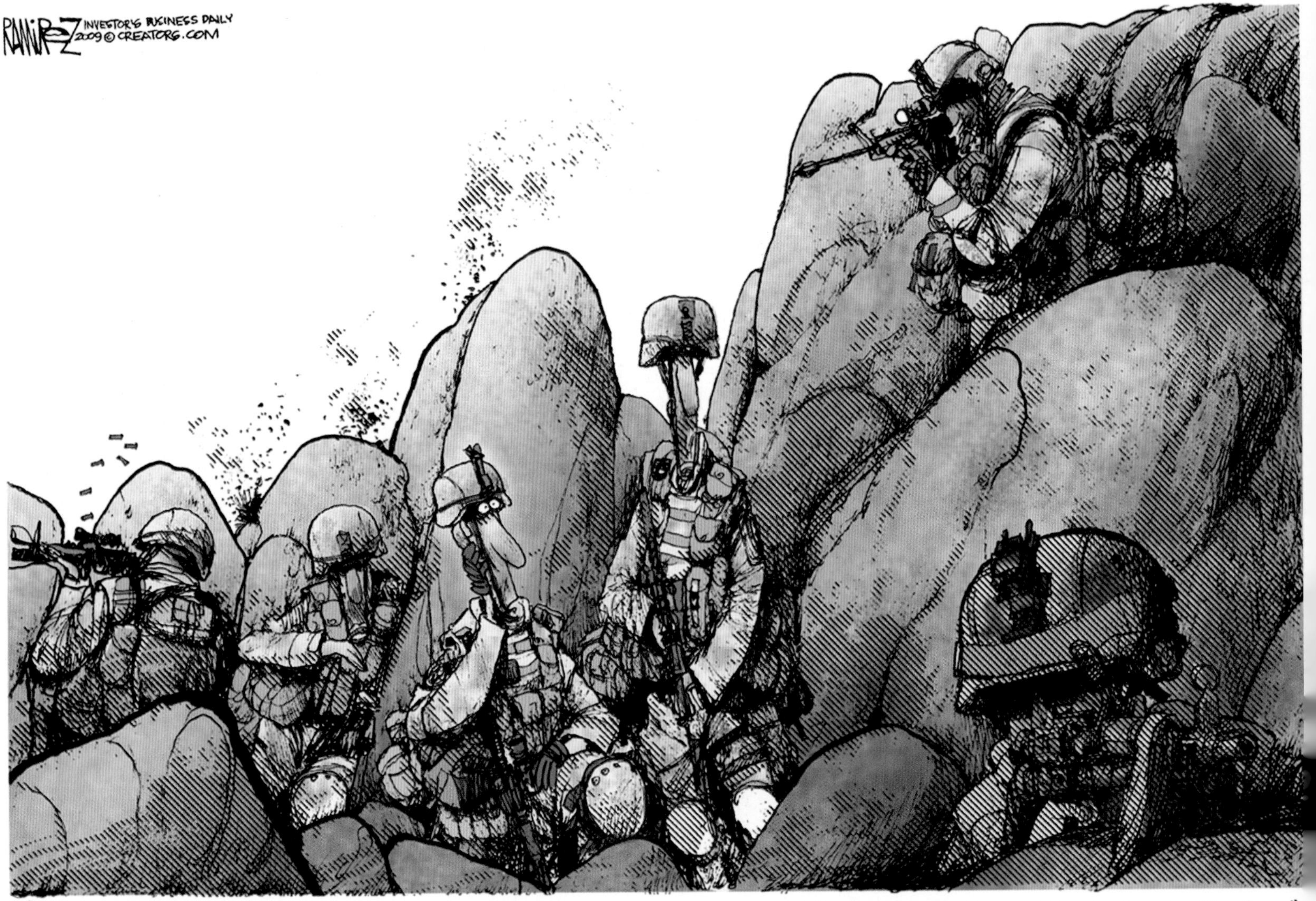
RAMIREZ INVESTOR'S BUSINESS DAILY
2009 © CREATORS.COM

"NO REINFORCEMENTS. THEY'VE ALLOCATED ALL AVAILABLE ASSETS TOWARDS ATTACKING FOX NEWS...."

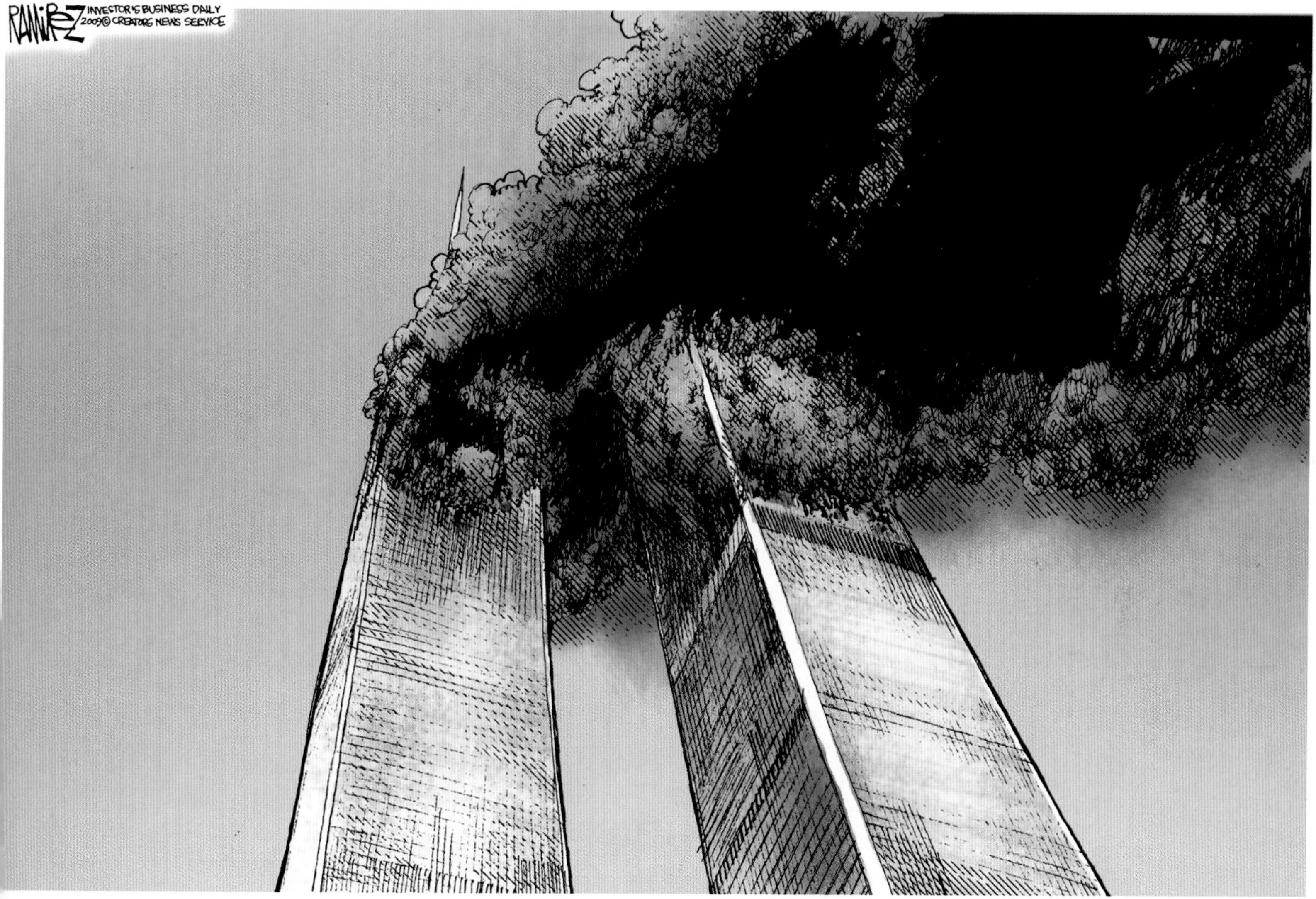
RAMIREZ
INVESTOR'S BUSINESS DAILY
2009 © CREATORS NEWS SERVICE

2,974 REASONS FOR SUPPORTING "ENHANCED INTERROGATION."

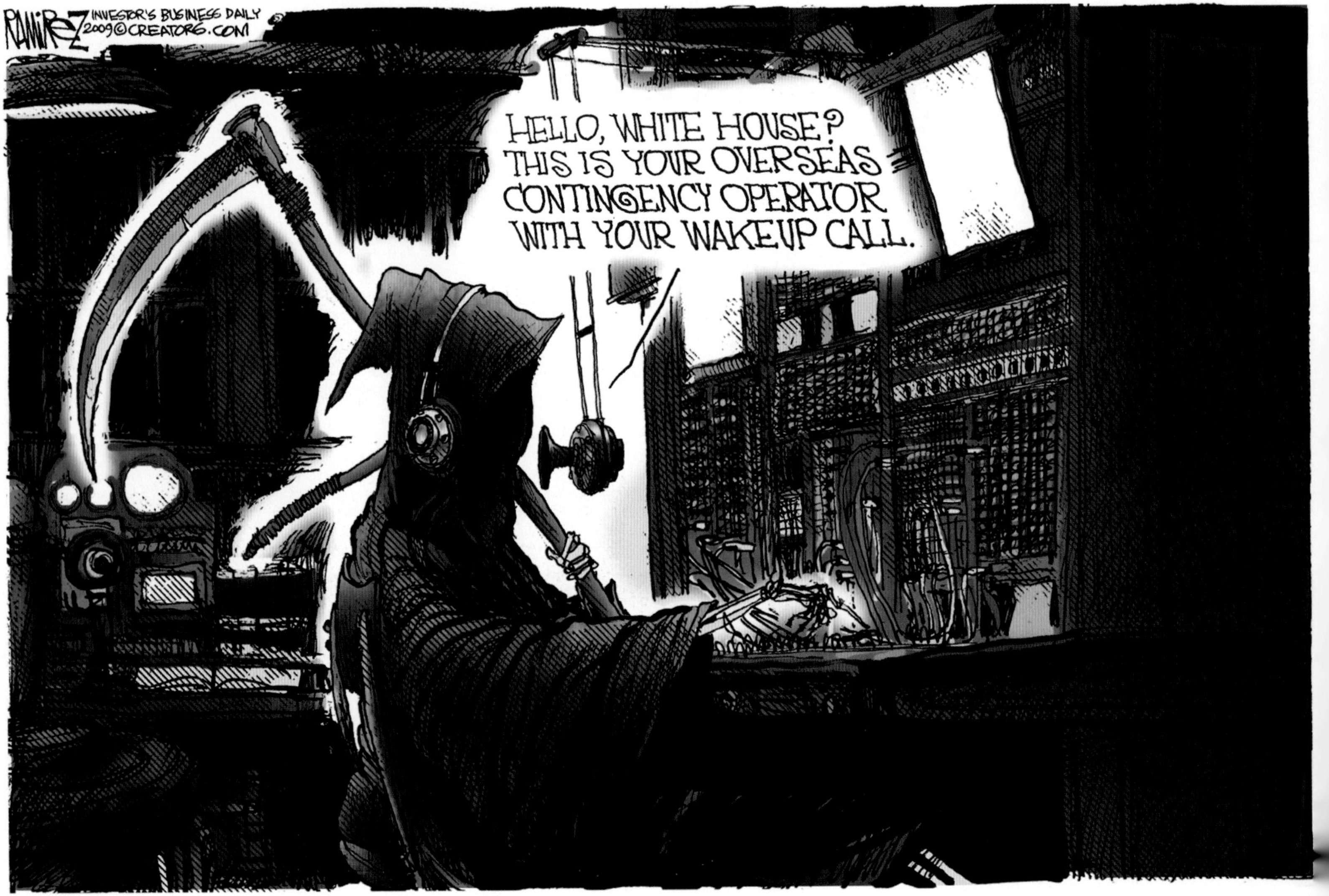
RAMIREZ INVESTOR'S BUSINESS DAILY 2009 © CREATORS.COM
HELLO, WHITE HOUSE? THIS IS YOUR OVERSEAS CONTINGENCY OPERATOR WITH YOUR WAKEUP CALL.

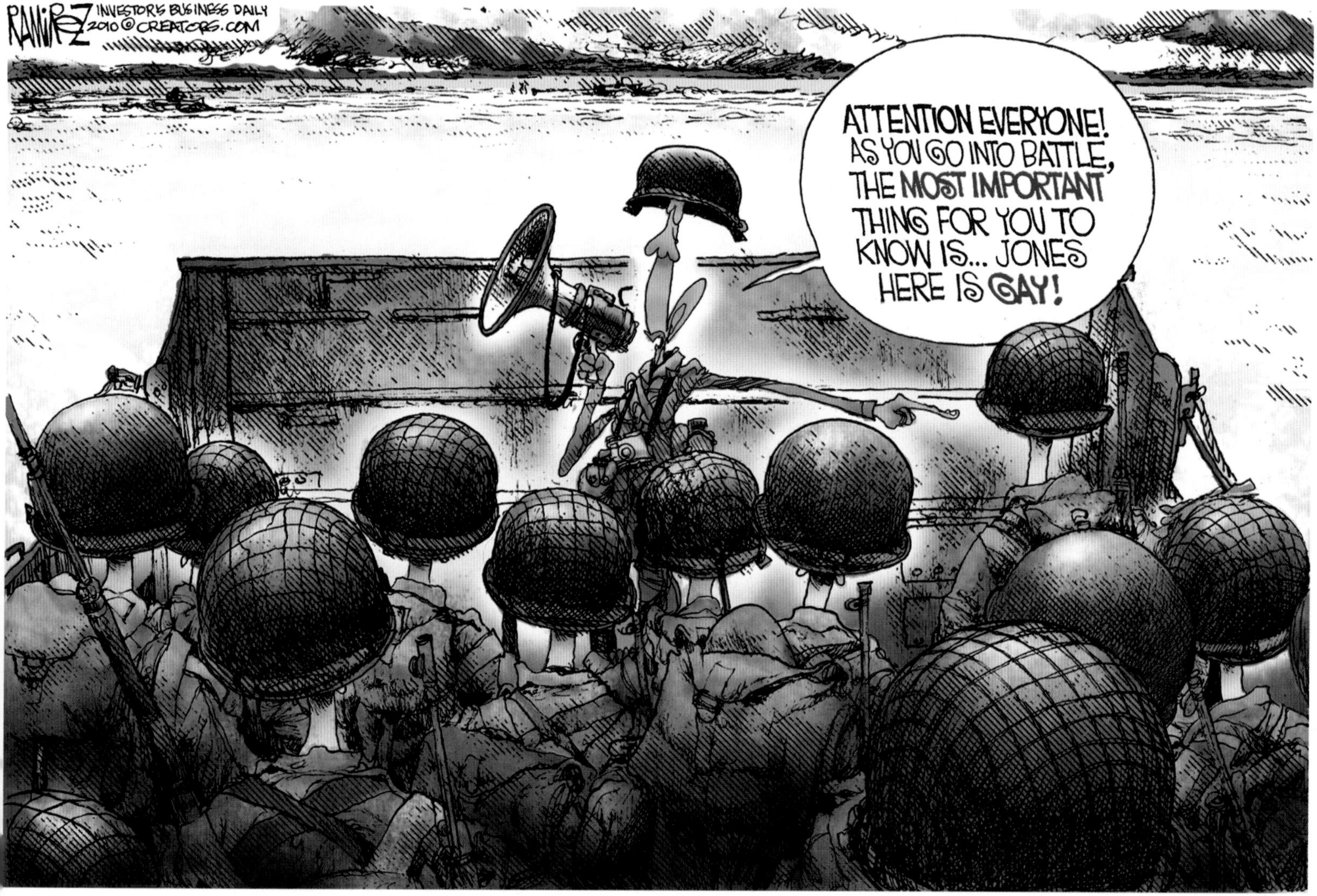
RAMIREZ INVESTOR'S BUSINESS DAILY 2010 © CREATORS.COM
ATTENTION EVERYONE! AS YOU GO INTO BATTLE, THE MOST IMPORTANT THING FOR YOU TO KNOW IS... JONES HERE IS GAY!

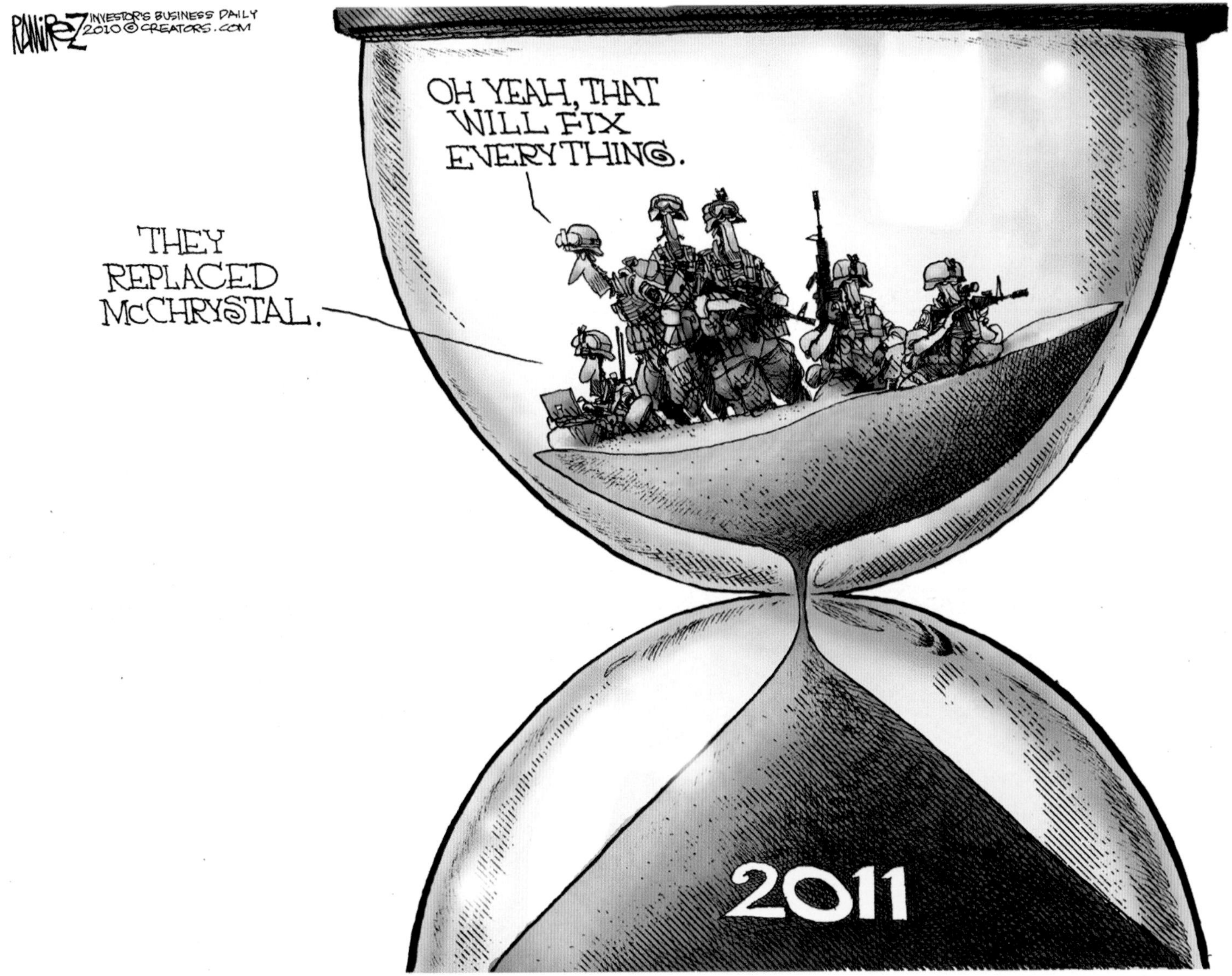
RAMIREZ INVESTOR'S BUSINESS DAILY 2010 © CREATORS.COM
OH YEAH, THAT WILL FIX EVERYTHING.
THEY REPLACED McCHRYSTAL.
2011

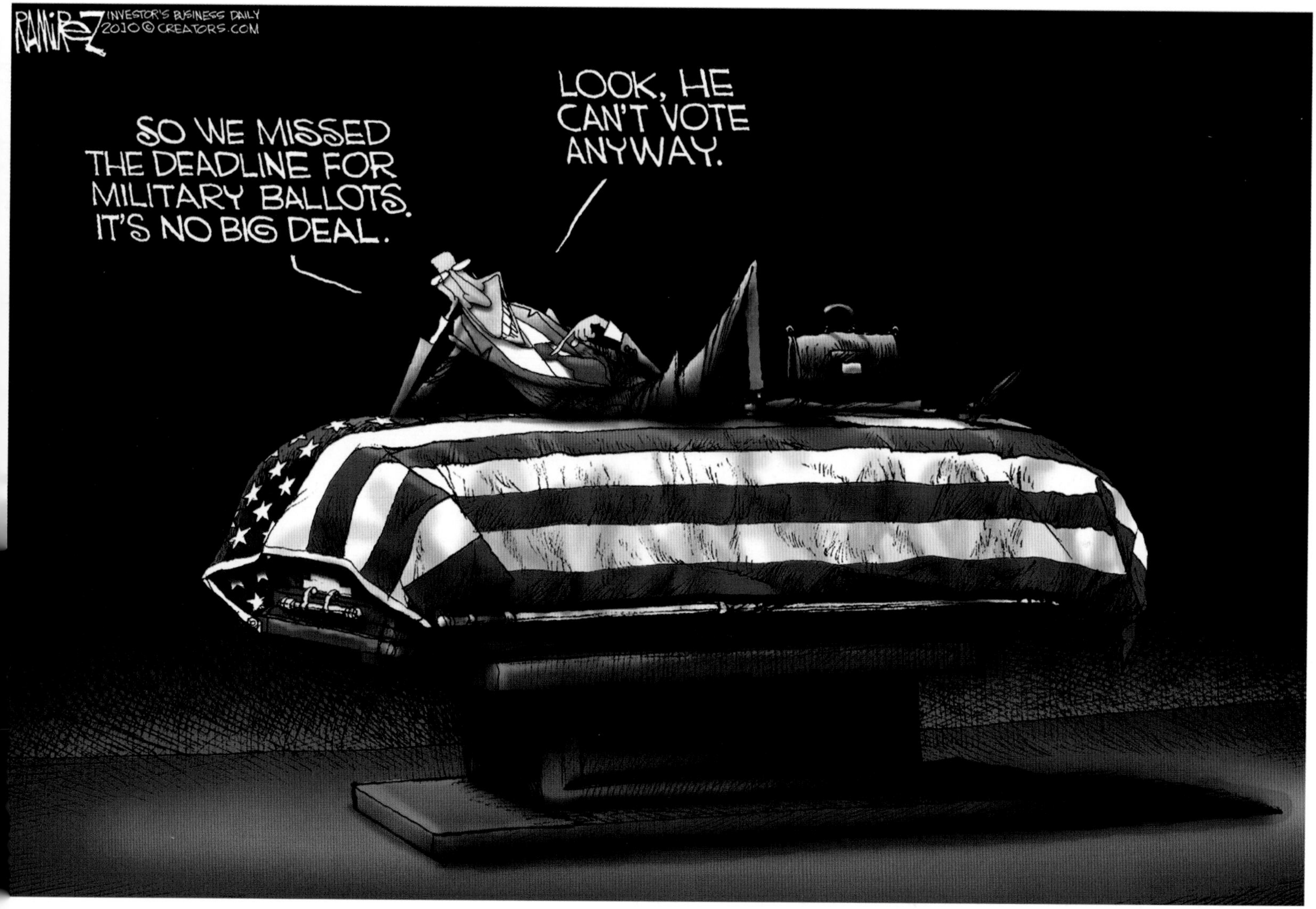
RAMIREZ INVESTOR'S BUSINESS DAILY 2010 © CREATORS.COM
SO WE MISSED THE DEADLINE FOR MILITARY BALLOTS. IT'S NO BIG DEAL.
LOOK, HE CAN'T VOTE ANYWAY.

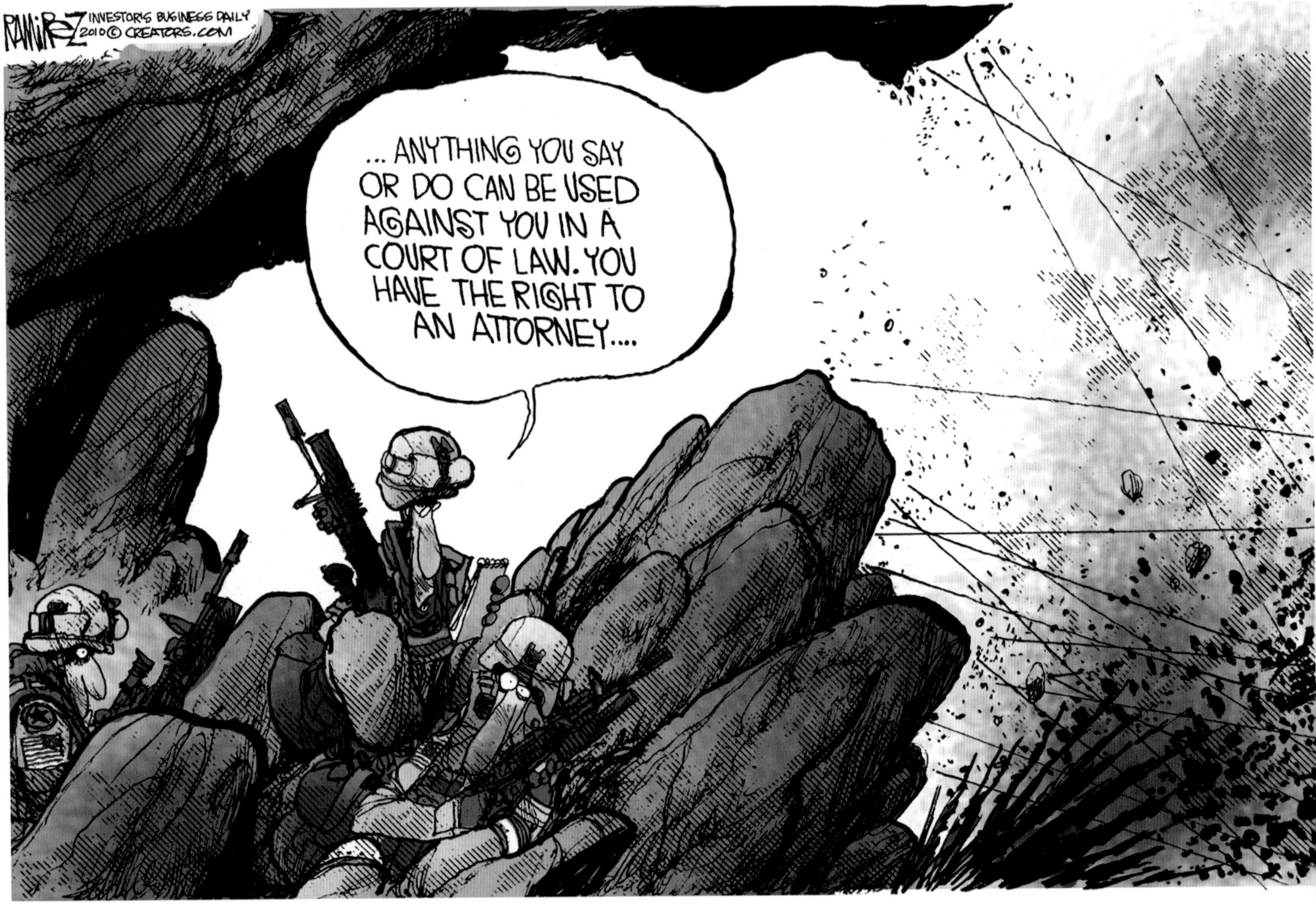
RAMIREZ INVESTOR'S BUSINESS DAILY 2010 © CREATORS.COM
... ANYTHING YOU SAY OR DO CAN BE USED AGAINST YOU IN A COURT OF LAW. YOU HAVE THE RIGHT TO AN ATTORNEY....

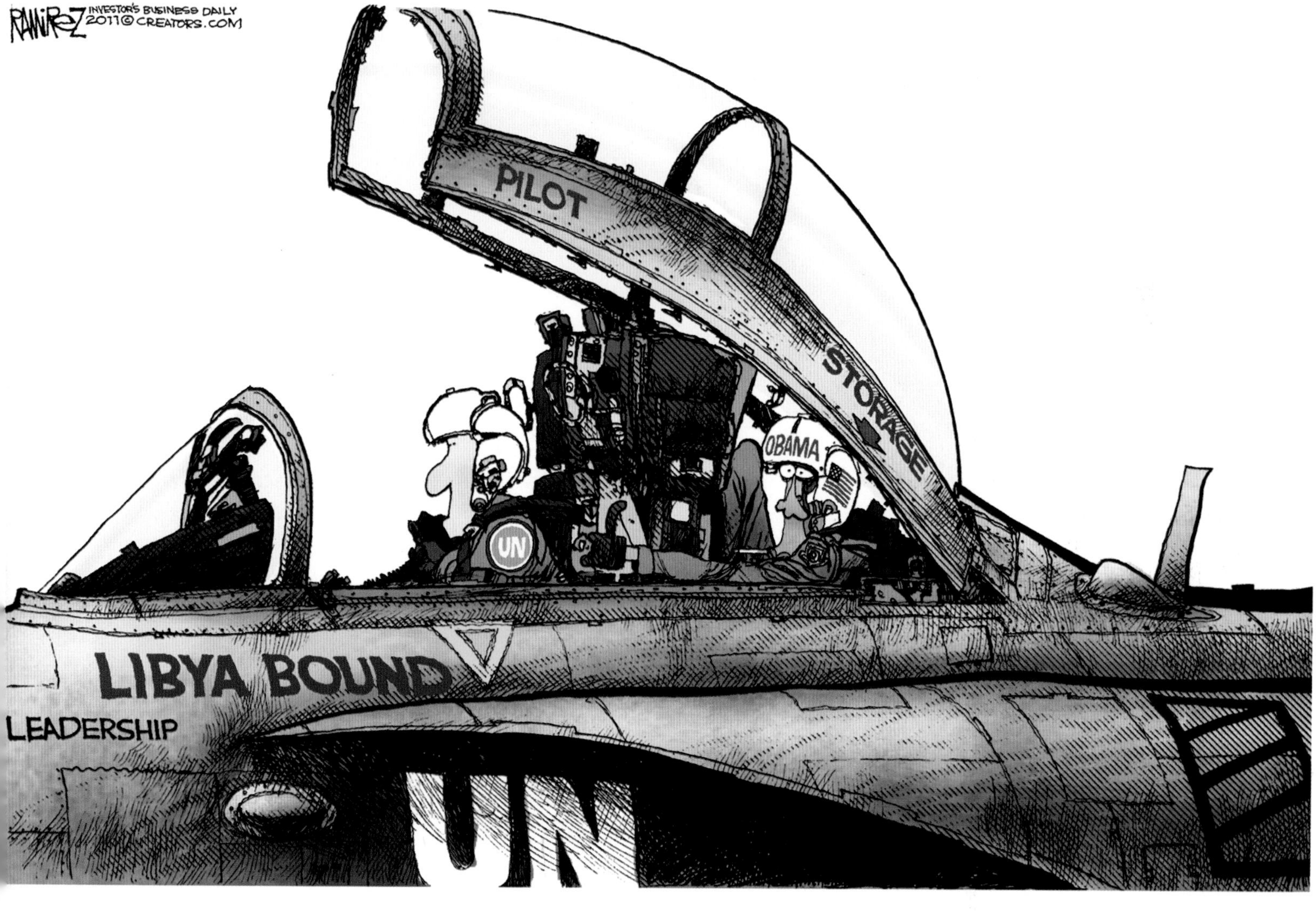
RAMIREZ INVESTOR'S BUSINESS DAILY 2011 © CREATORS.COM
PILOT
STORAGE
OBAMA
UN
LIBYA BOUND
LEADERSHIP
UN

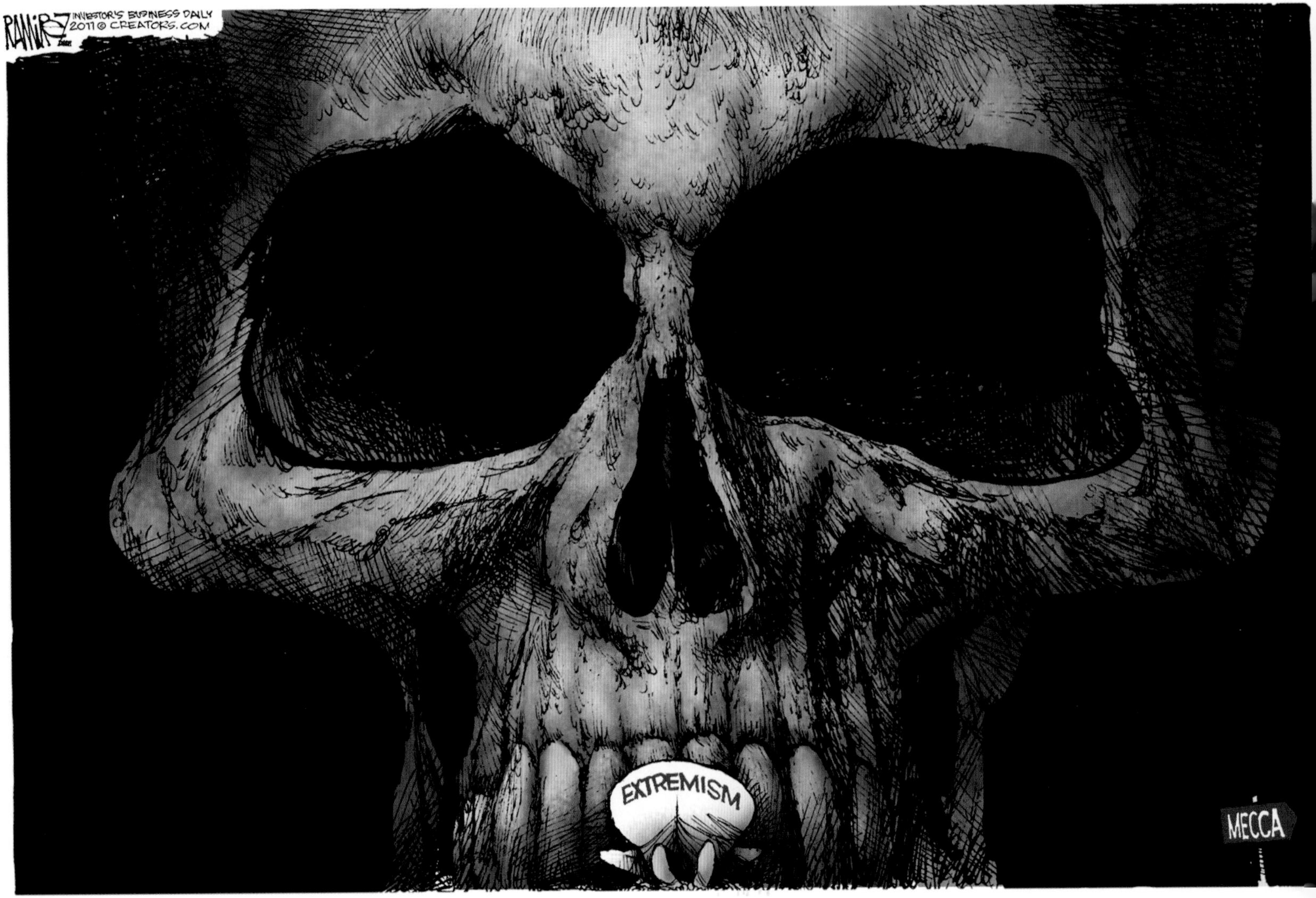
RAMIREZ
INVESTOR'S BUSINESS DAILY
2011 © CREATORS.COM
EXTREMISM
MECCA

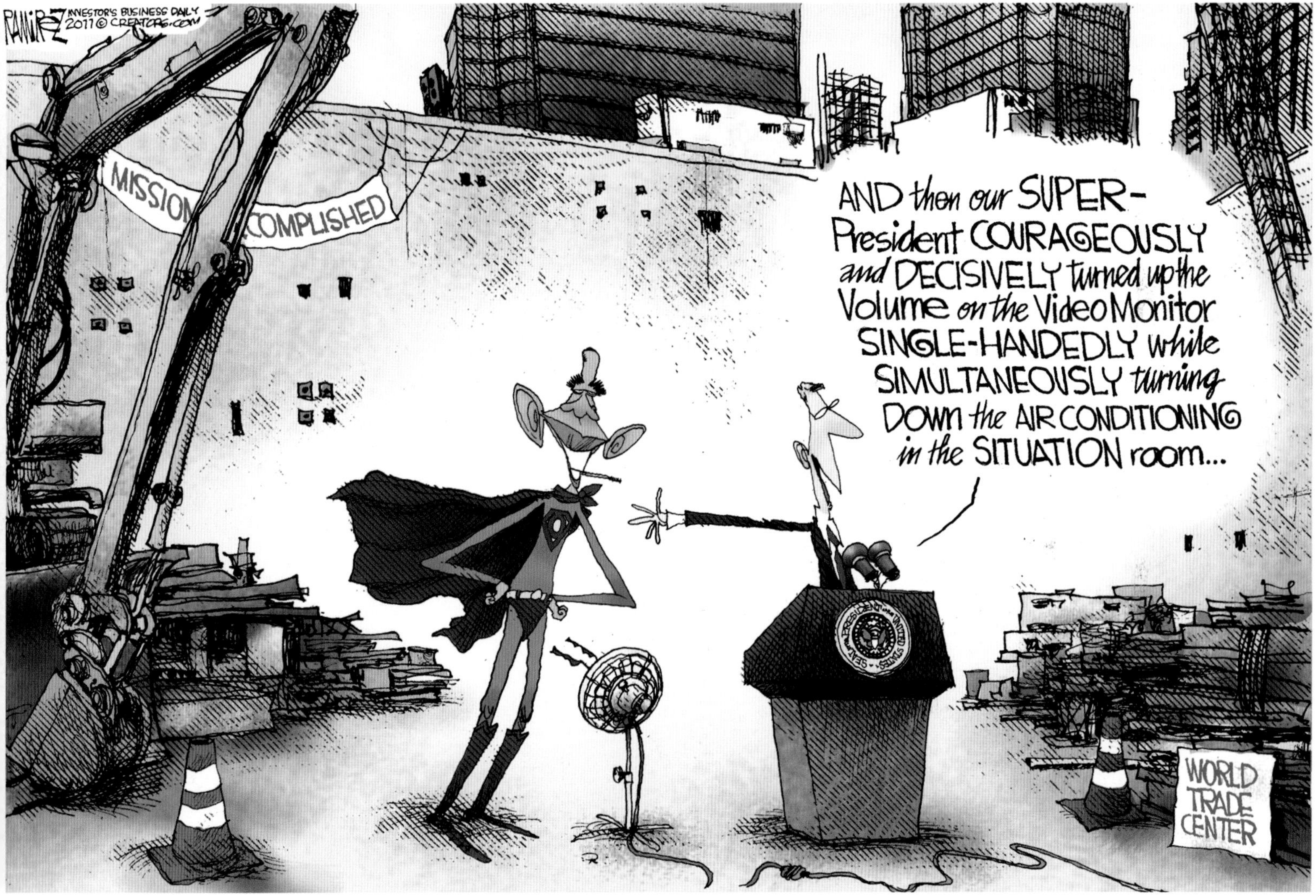
RAMIREZ INVESTOR'S BUSINESS DAILY 2011 © CREATORS.COM
MISSION ACCOMPLISHED
AND then our SUPER-President COURAGEOUSLY and DECISIVELY turned up the Volume on the Video Monitor SINGLE-HANDEDLY while SIMULTANEOUSLY turning Down the AIR CONDITIONING in the SITUATION room...
WORLD TRADE CENTER

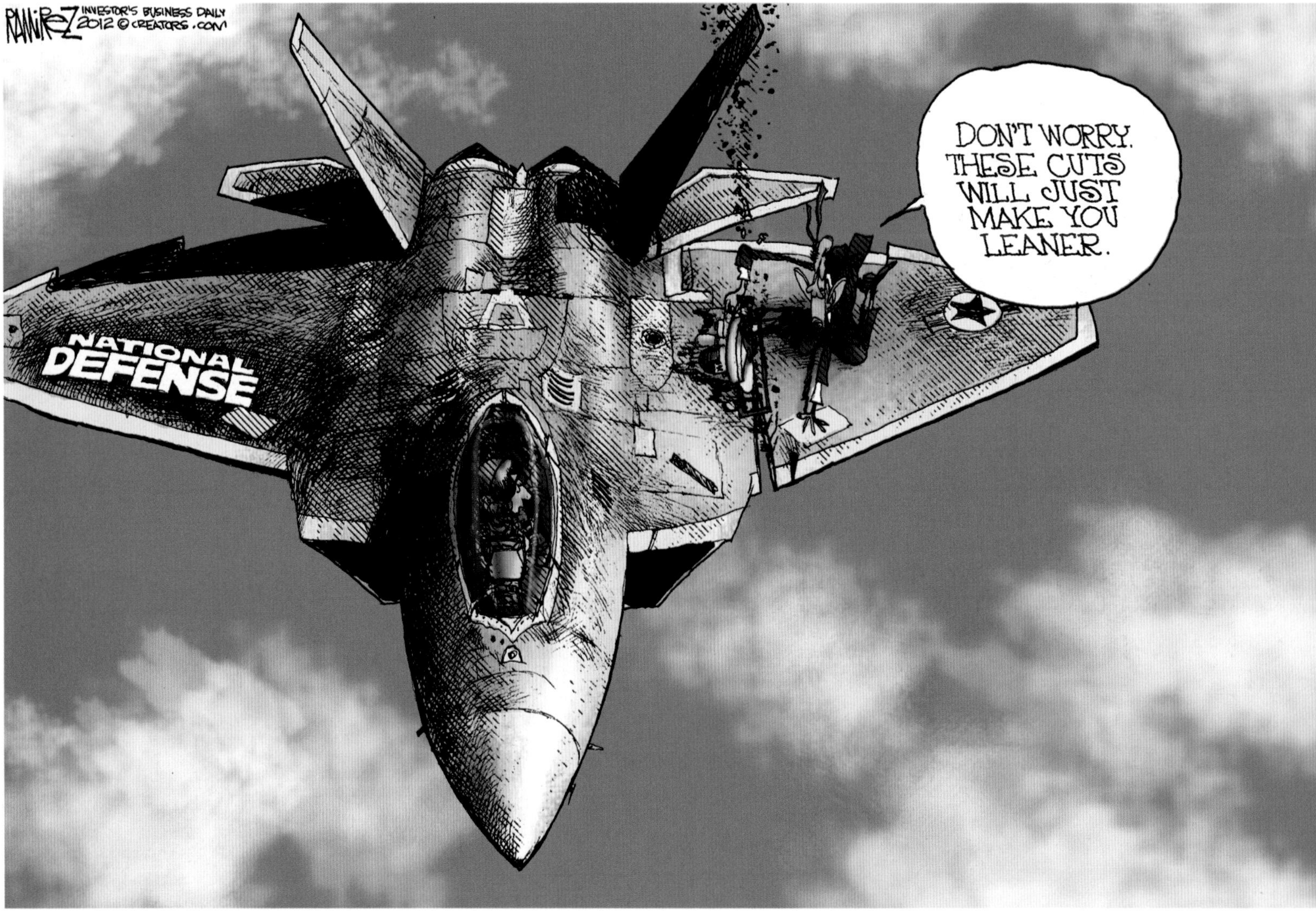
RAMIREZ INVESTOR'S BUSINESS DAILY 2012 © CREATORS.COM
NATIONAL DEFENSE
DON'T WORRY. THESE CUTS WILL JUST MAKE YOU LEANER.

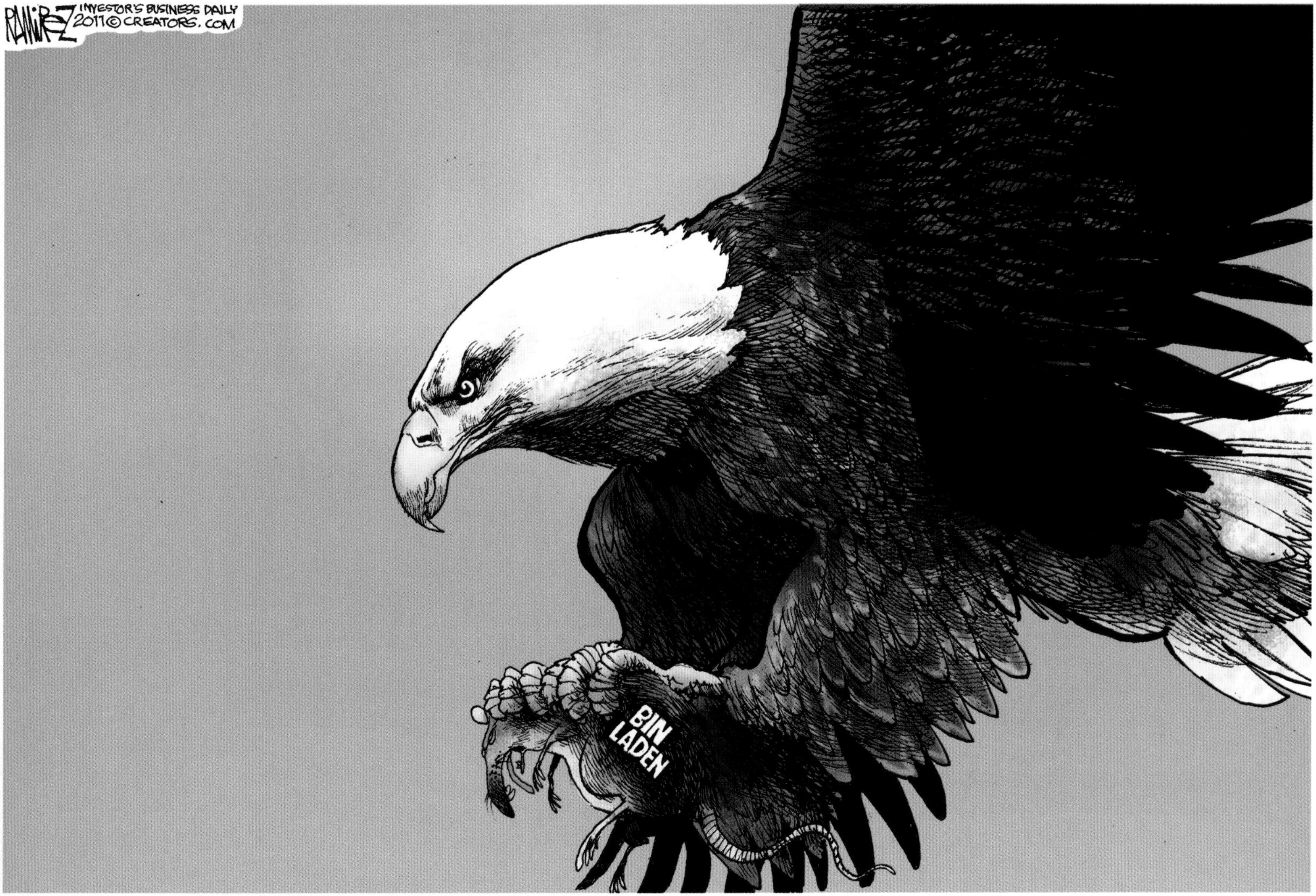
RAMIREZ
INVESTOR'S BUSINESS DAILY
2011 © CREATORS.COM
BIN LADEN

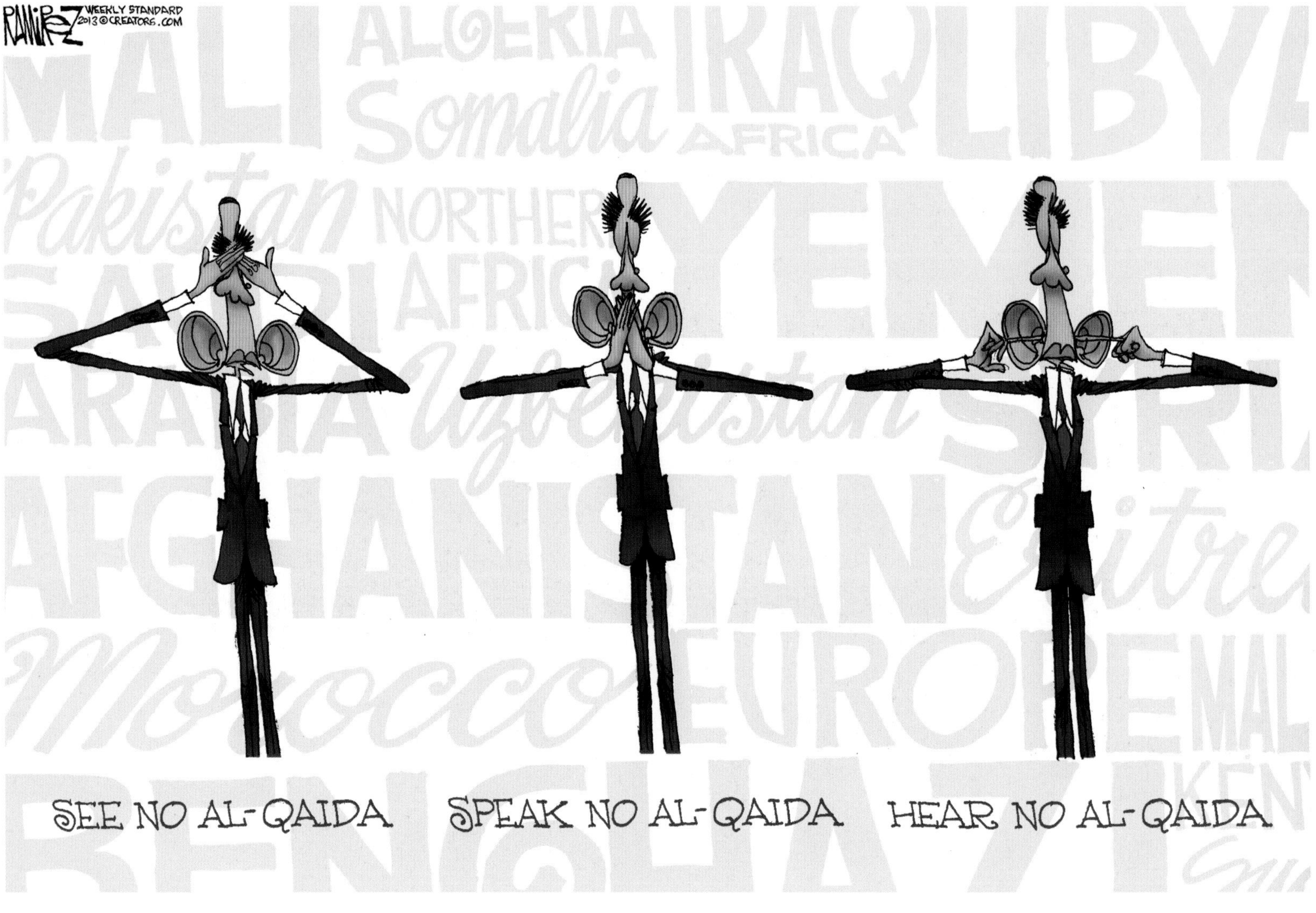
RAMIREZ
WEEKLY STANDARD
2013 © CREATORS.COM
MALI
Somalia
IRAQ
LIBYA
AFRICA
Pakistan
Uzbekistan
AFGHANISTAN
Morocco
EUROPE
SEE NO AL-QAIDA
SPEAK NO AL-QAIDA
HEAR NO AL-QAIDA

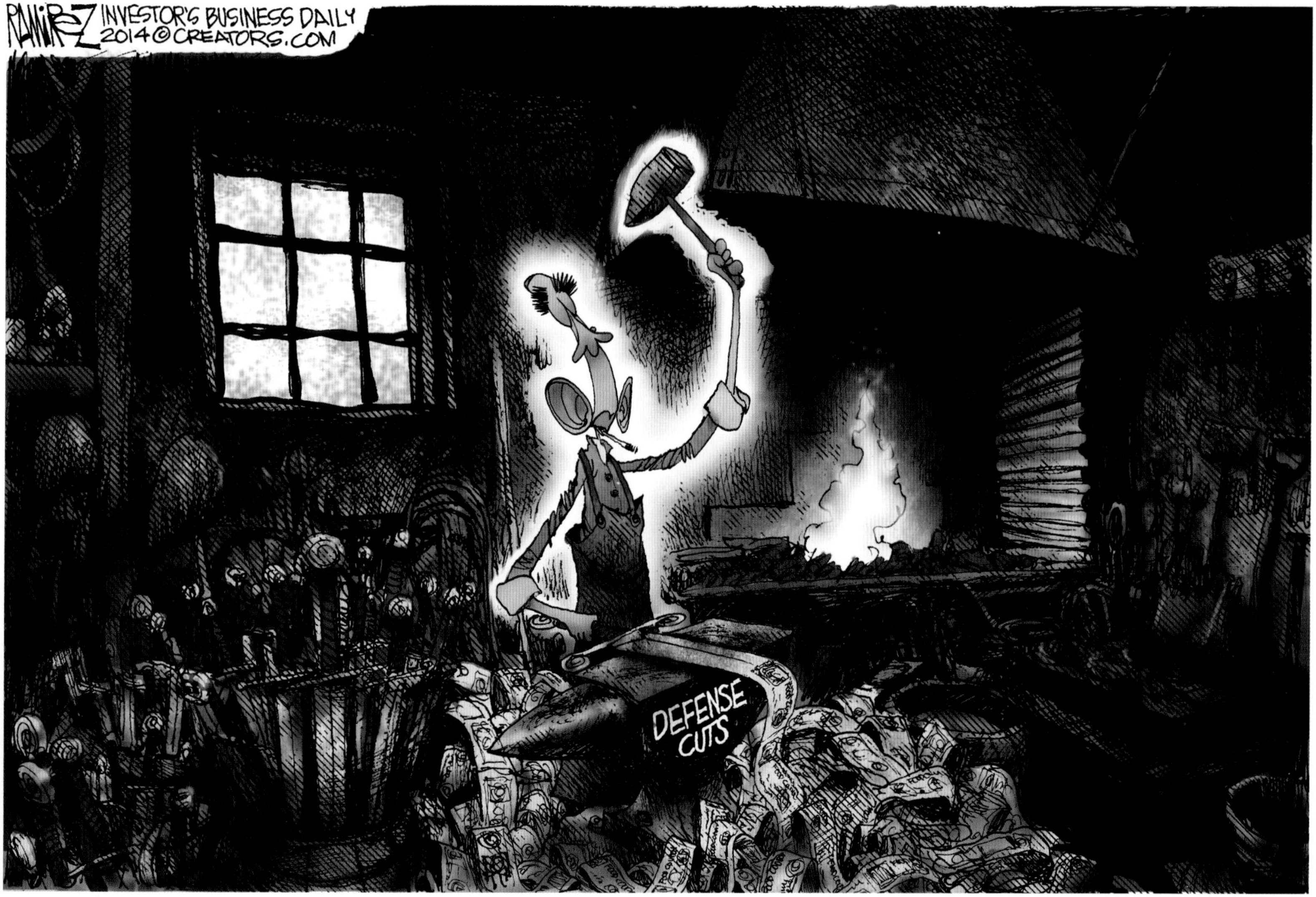
RAMIREZ INVESTOR'S BUSINESS DAILY
2014©CREATORS.COM
DEFENSE CUTS

BEATING SWORDS INTO FOOD STAMPS.

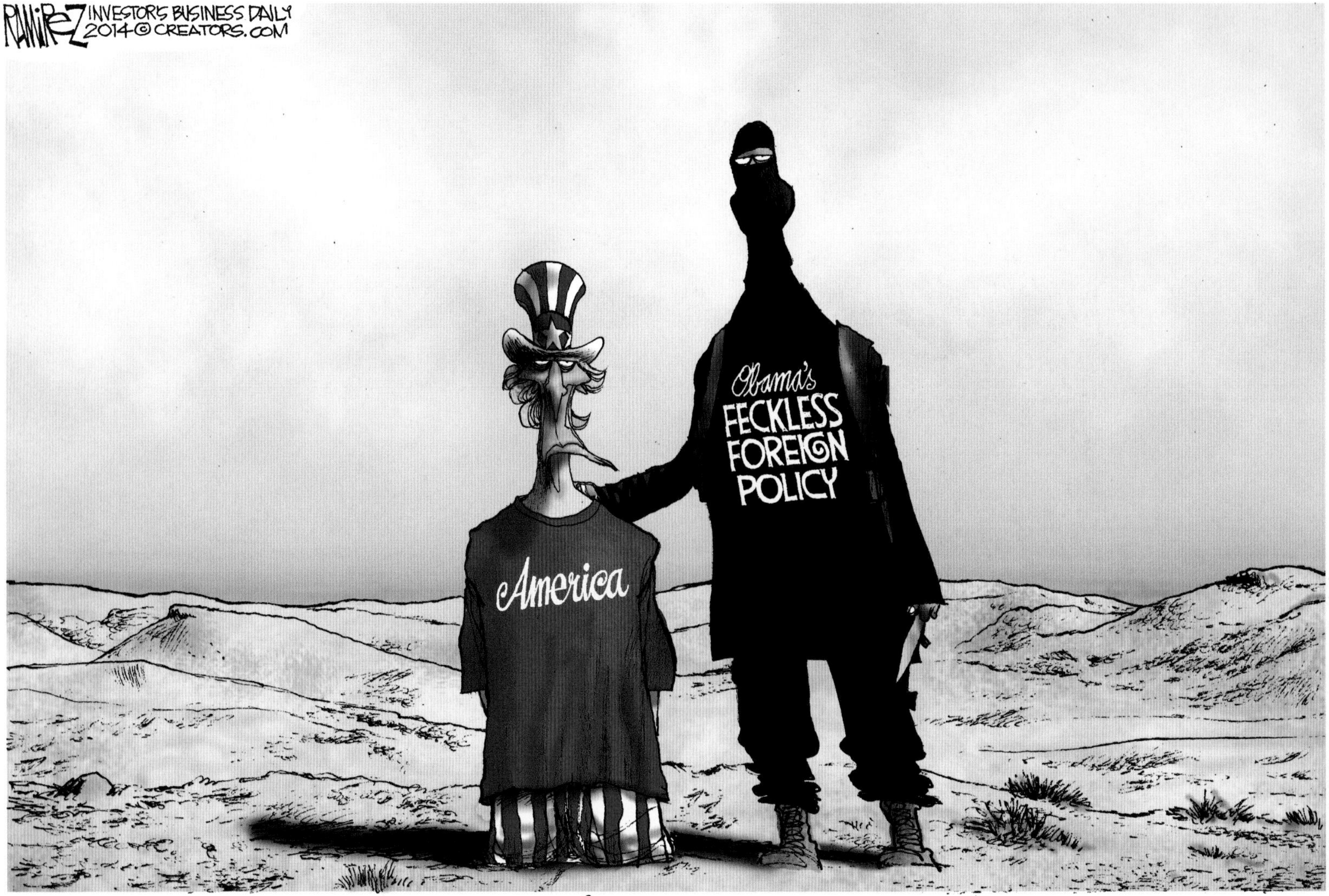
RAMIREZ INVESTOR'S BUSINESS DAILY
2014 © CREATORS.COM
Obama's
FECKLESS
FOREIGN
POLICY
America

The THREAT.

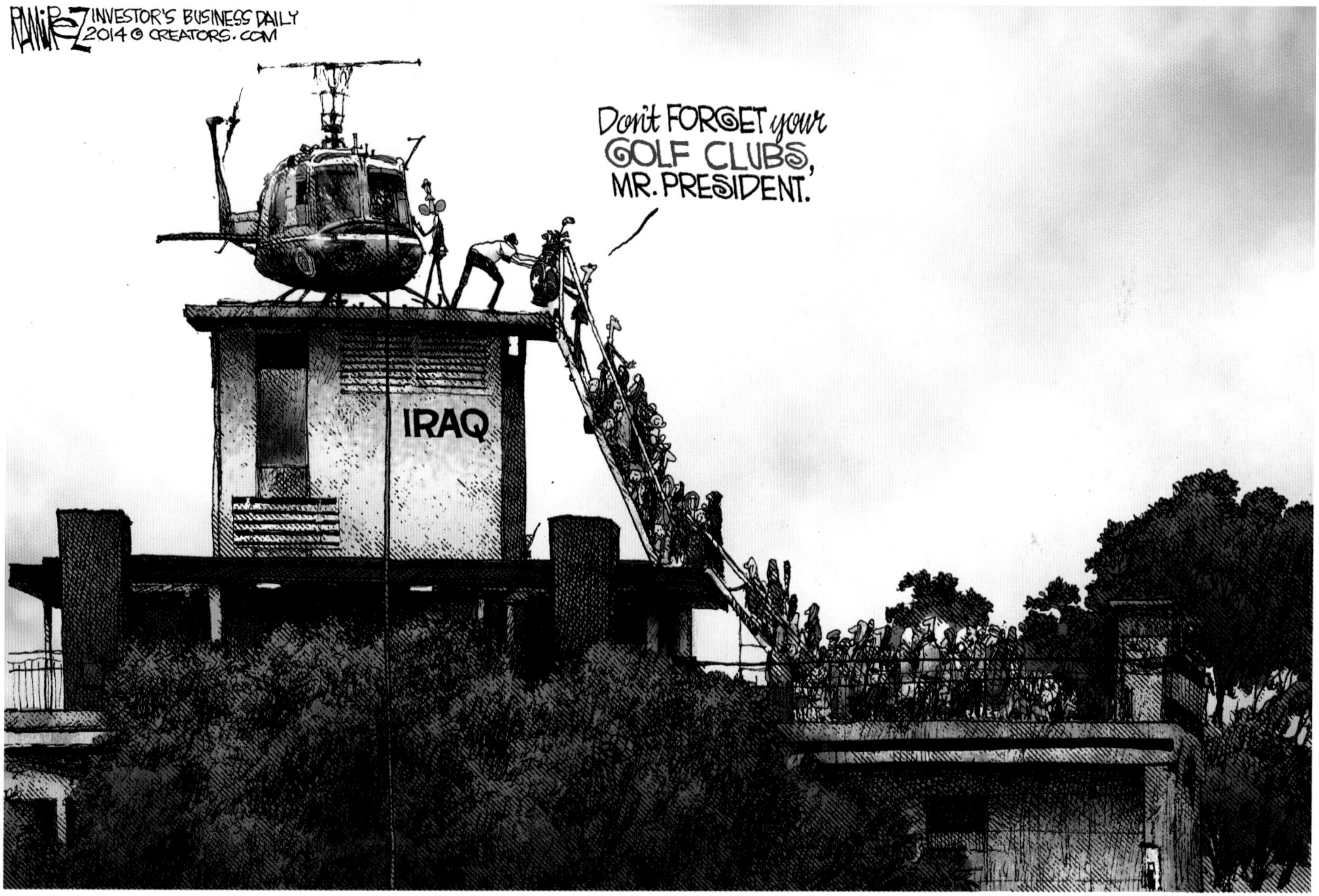
RAMIREZ INVESTOR'S BUSINESS DAILY
2014 © CREATORS.COM
Don't FORGET your GOLF CLUBS, MR. PRESIDENT.
IRAQ

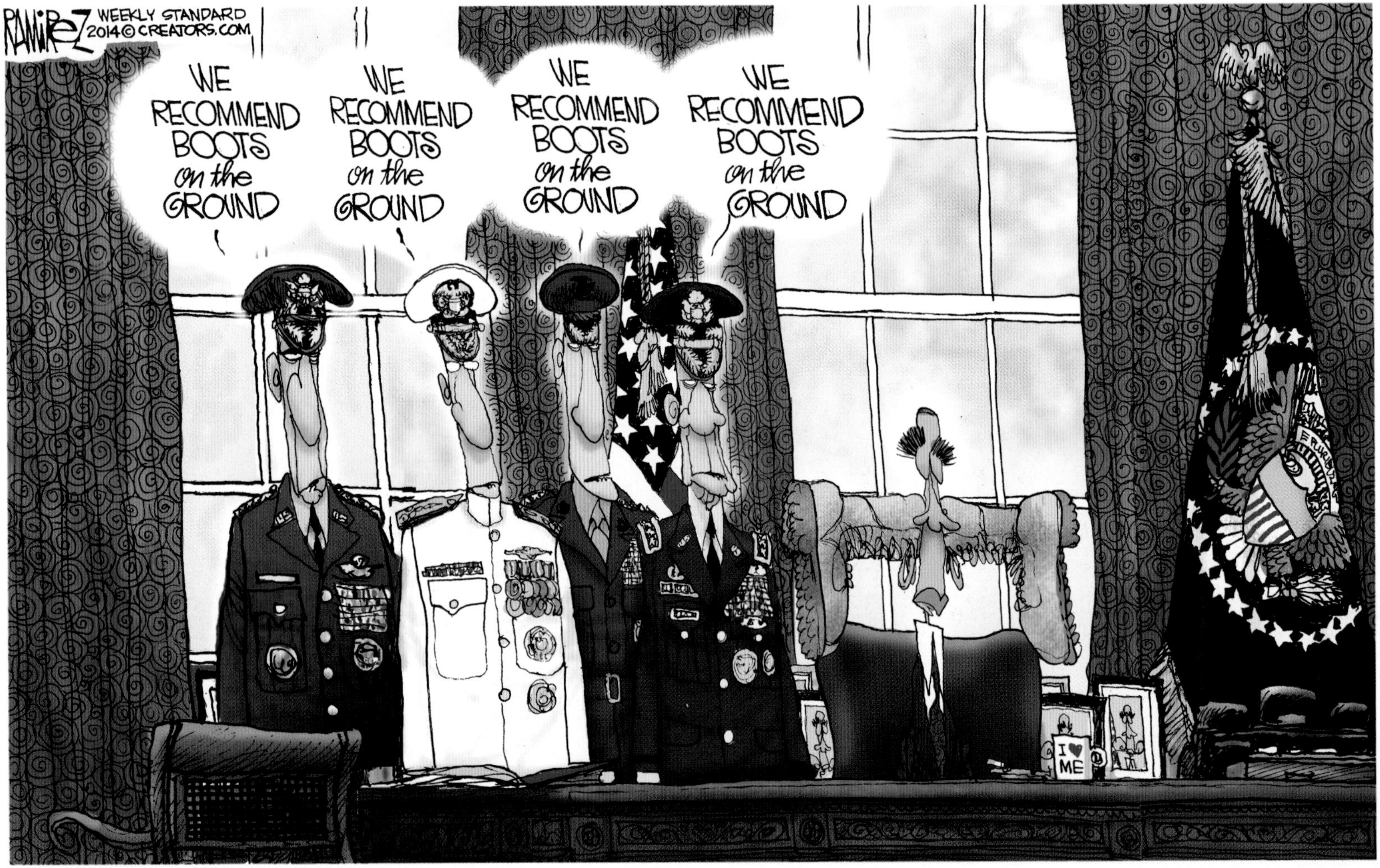
RAMIREZ WEEKLY STANDARD 2014 © CREATORS.COM
WE RECOMMEND BOOTS on the GROUND
WE RECOMMEND BOOTS on the GROUND
WE RECOMMEND BOOTS on the GROUND
WE RECOMMEND BOOTS on the GROUND
I ♥ ME

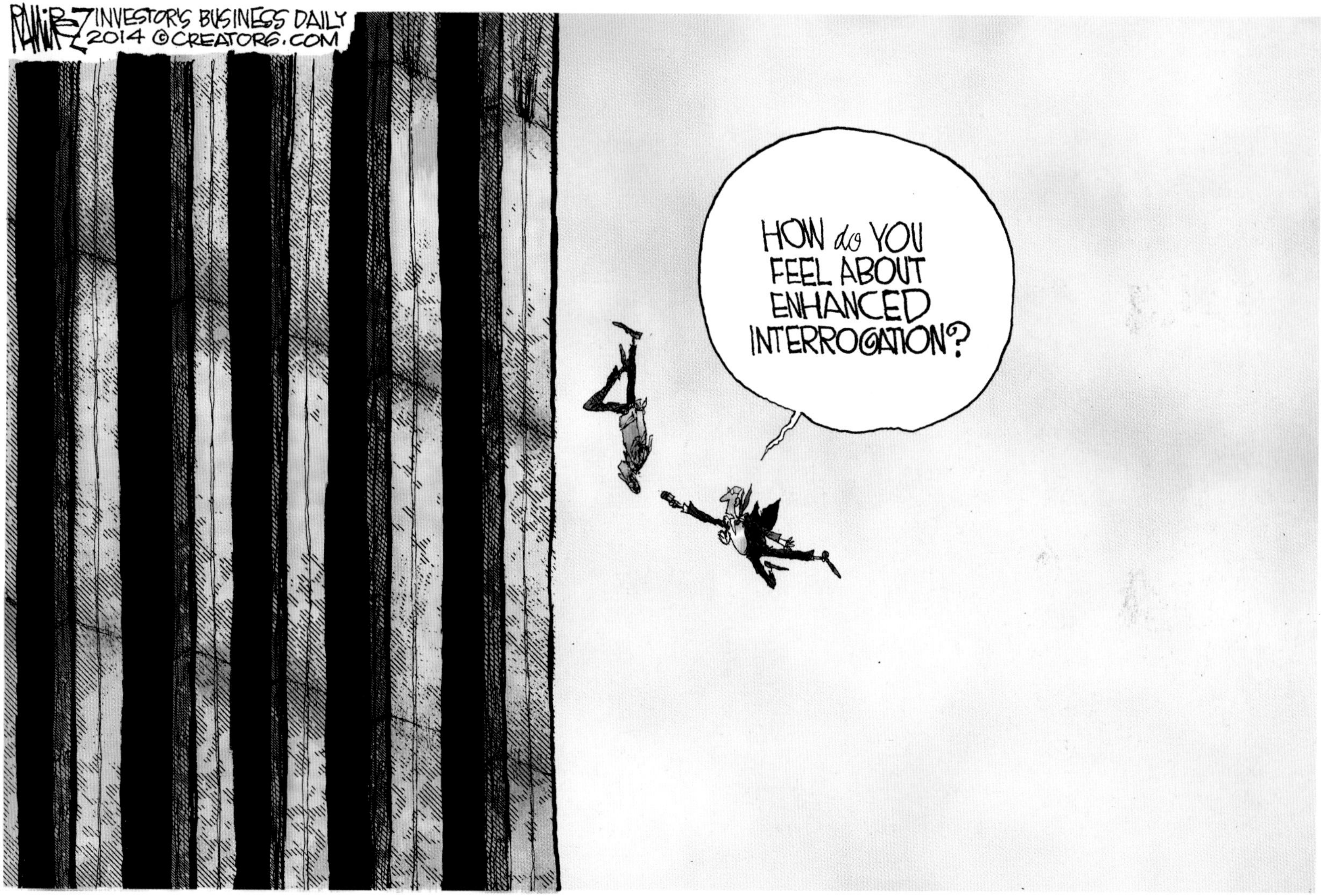
RAMIREZ INVESTOR'S BUSINESS DAILY
2014 ©CREATORS.COM
HOW do YOU FEEL ABOUT ENHANCED INTERROGATION?

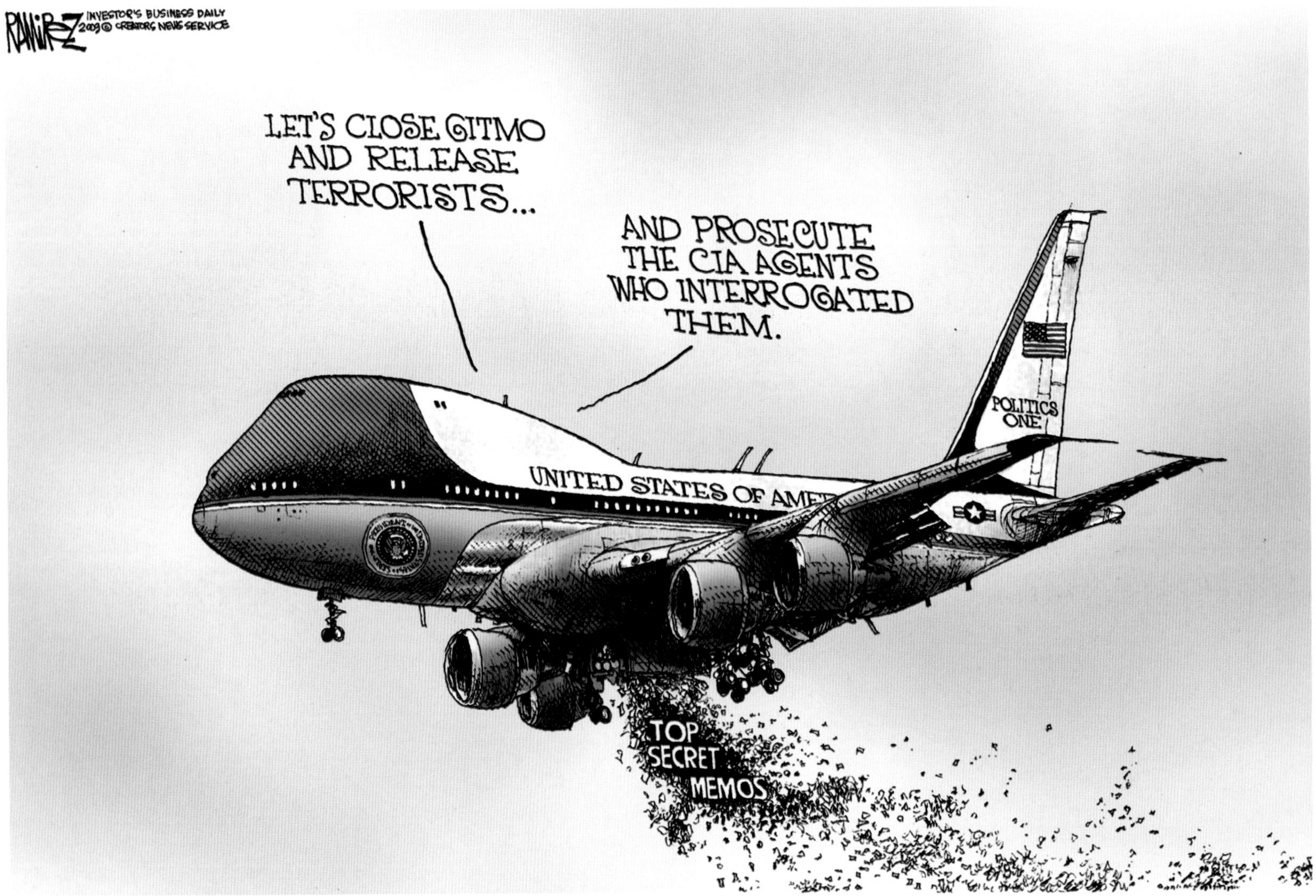
RAMIREZ INVESTOR'S BUSINESS DAILY 2009 © CREATORS NEWS SERVICE
LET'S CLOSE GITMO AND RELEASE TERRORISTS...
AND PROSECUTE THE CIA AGENTS WHO INTERROGATED THEM.
POLITICS ONE
UNITED STATES OF AME
TOP SECRET MEMOS

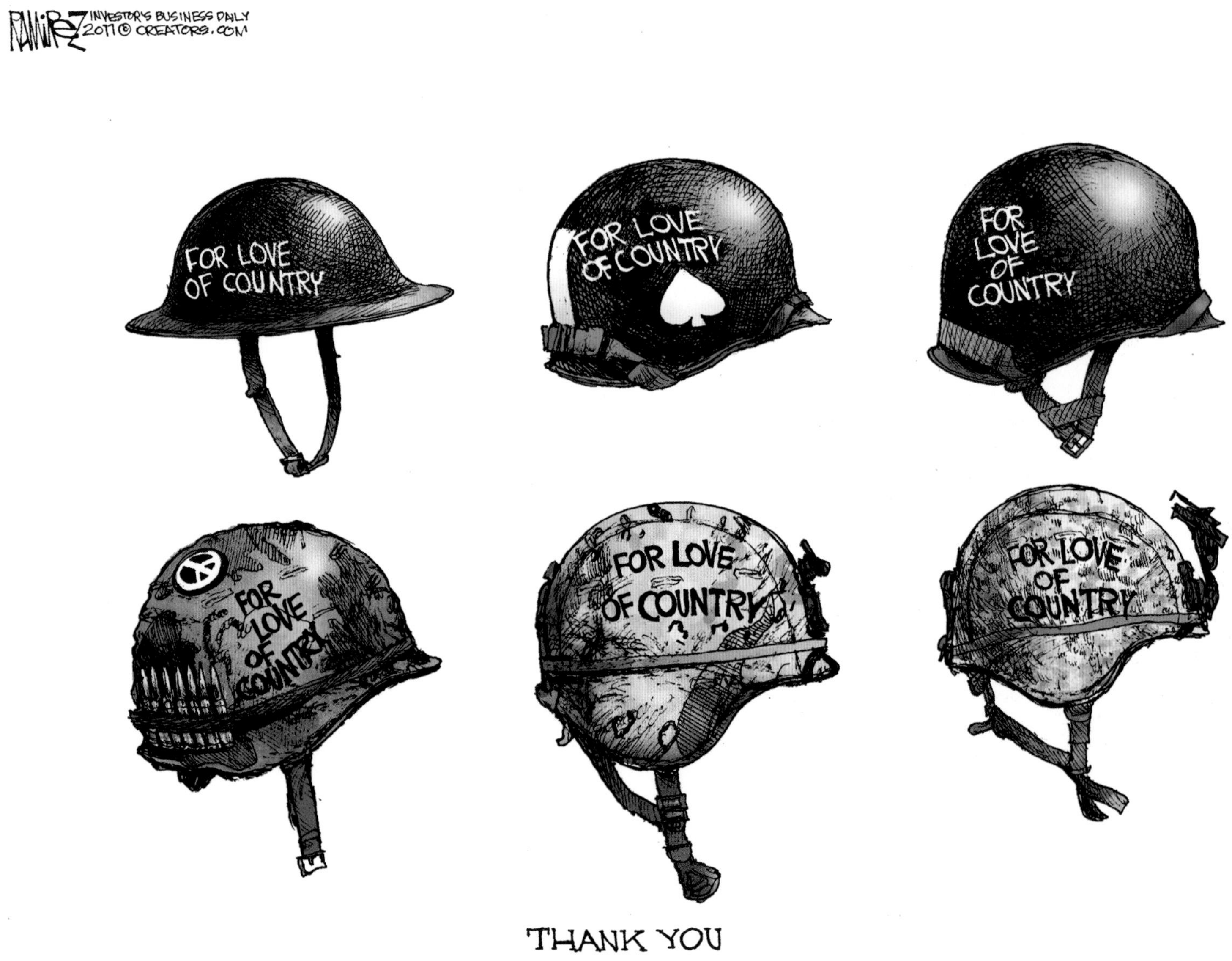
RAMIREZ INVESTOR'S BUSINESS DAILY 2011 © CREATORS.COM
FOR LOVE OF COUNTRY
FOR LOVE OF COUNTRY
FOR LOVE OF COUNTRY
FOR LOVE OF COUNTRY
FOR LOVE OF COUNTRY
FOR LOVE OF COUNTRY
THANK YOU

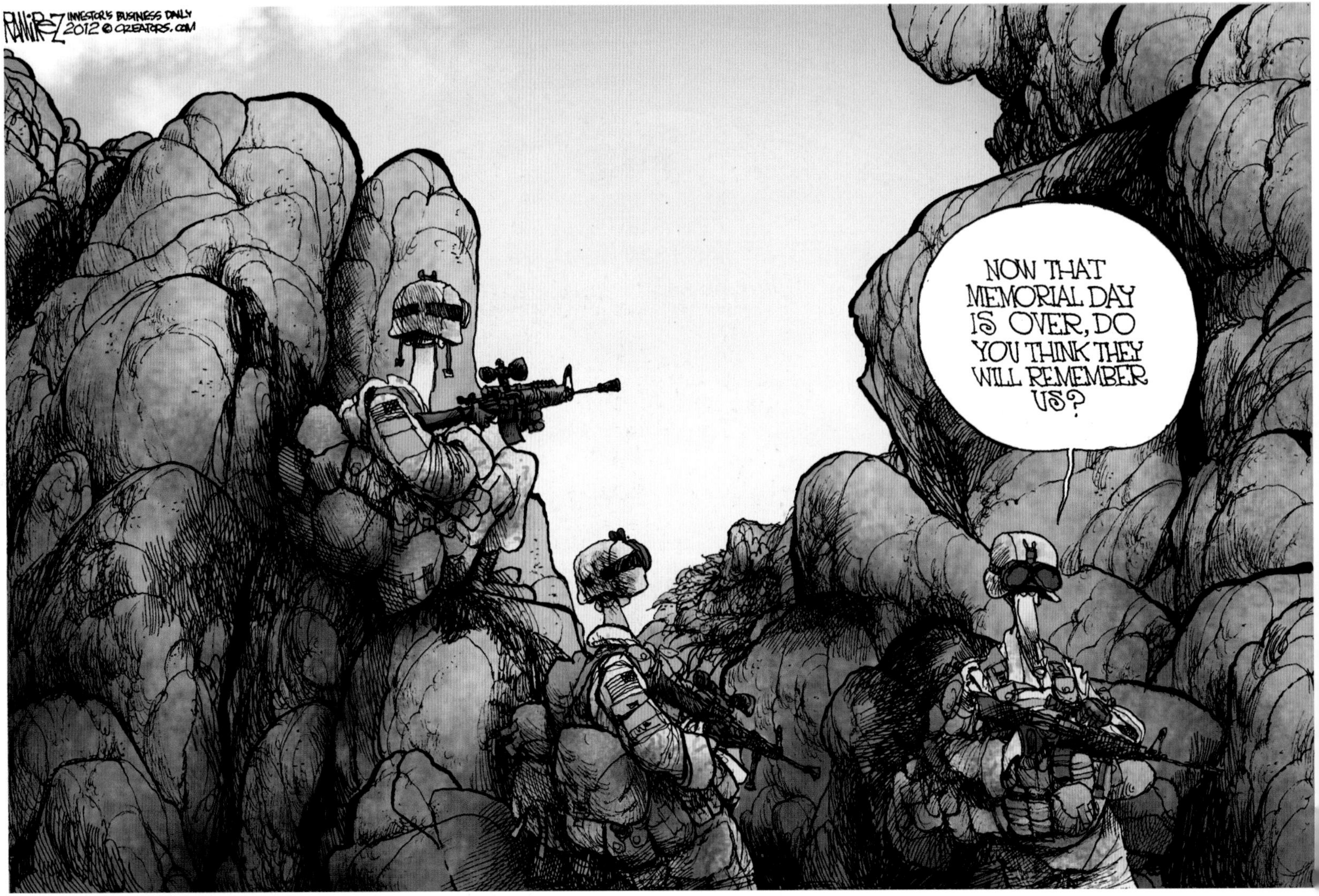
RAMIREZ INVESTOR'S BUSINESS DAILY 2012 © CREATORS.COM
NOW THAT MEMORIAL DAY IS OVER, DO YOU THINK THEY WILL REMEMBER US?

2012

"I would put our legislative and foreign policy accomplishments in our first two years against any president—with the possible exceptions of Johnson, F.D.R., and Lincoln."

—President Barack Obama,
***60 Minutes* interview, December 11, 2011**

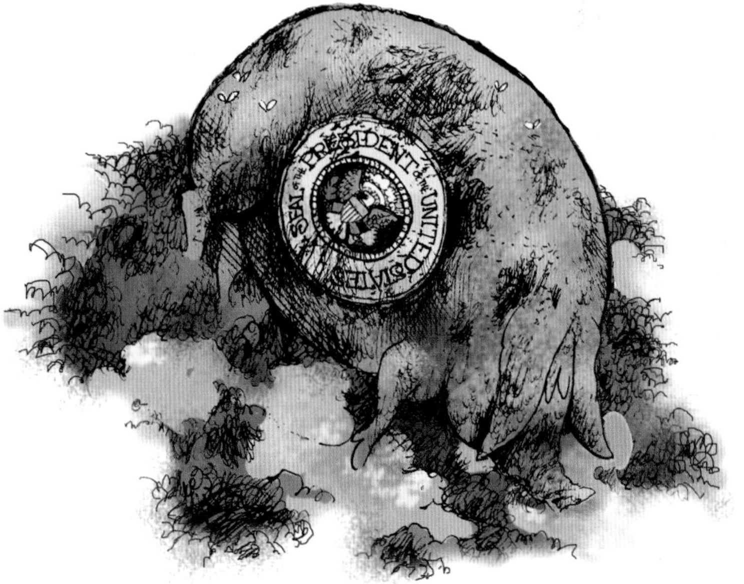
SEAL OF THE PRESIDENT OF THE UNITED STATES

Media bias played an overwhelming role in defining the candidates and their messages while insulating the president from his record. The media made the economy irrelevant, overlooked the president's other shortfalls, and defined Mitt Romney as a rich outsourcer out of touch with the average man. It was the first time an incumbent president won reelection with fewer votes than his first election.

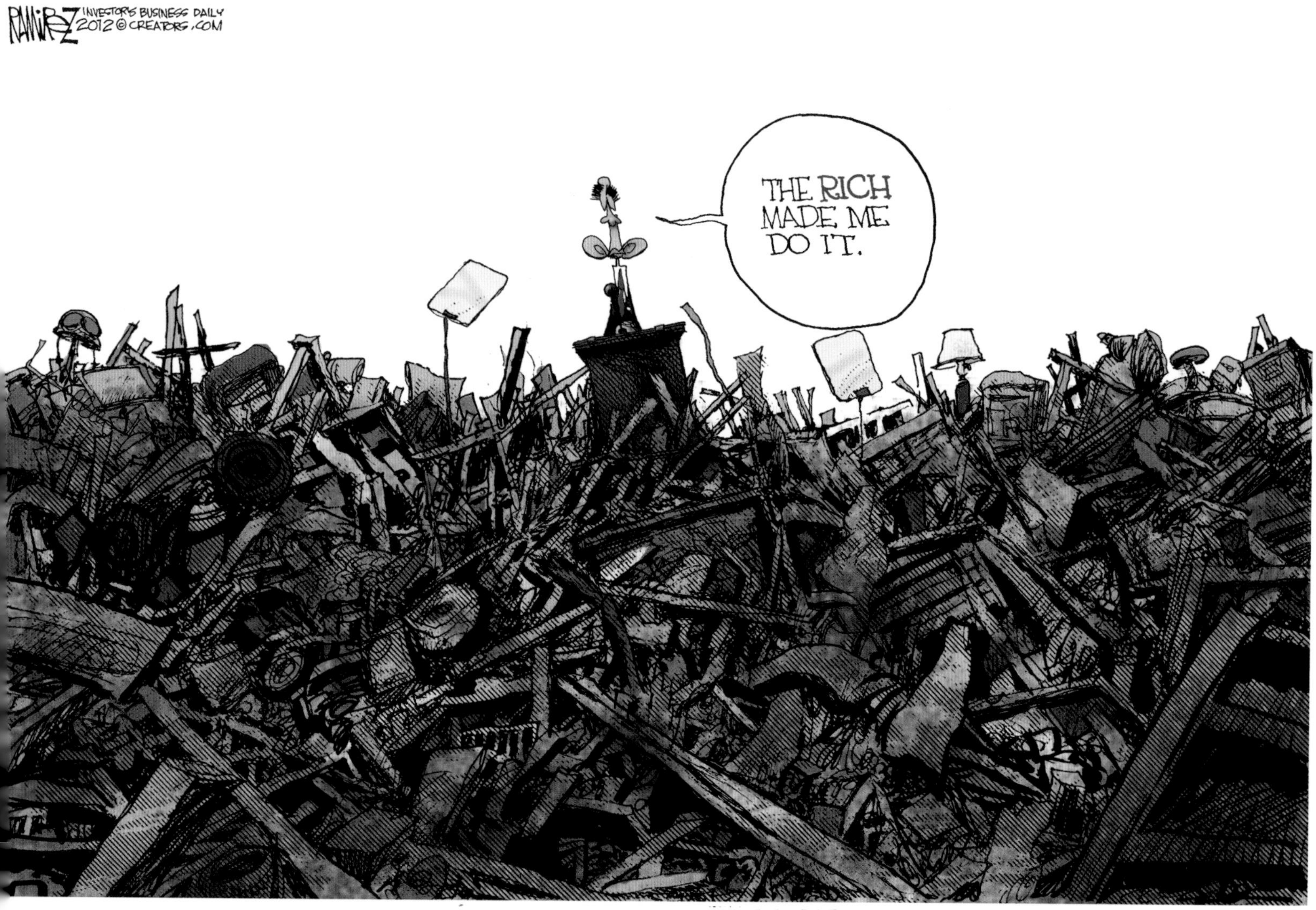
RAMIREZ INVESTOR'S BUSINESS DAILY 2012 © CREATORS.COM
THE RICH MADE ME DO IT.

THE STATE OF THE UNION

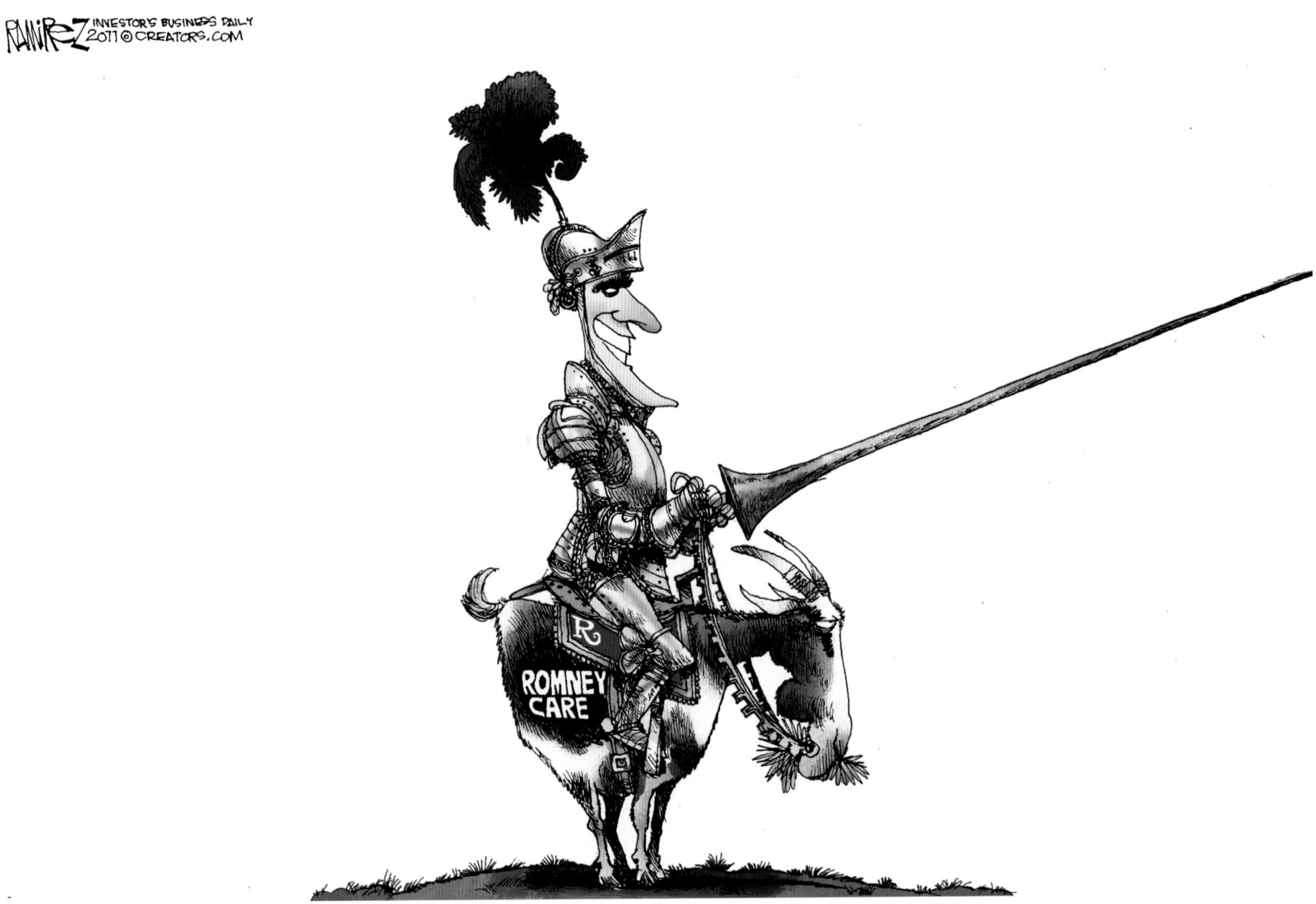
RAMIREZ INVESTOR'S BUSINESS DAILY 2011 © CREATORS.COM
R
ROMNEY CARE

THE KNIGHT IN SHINING ARMOR

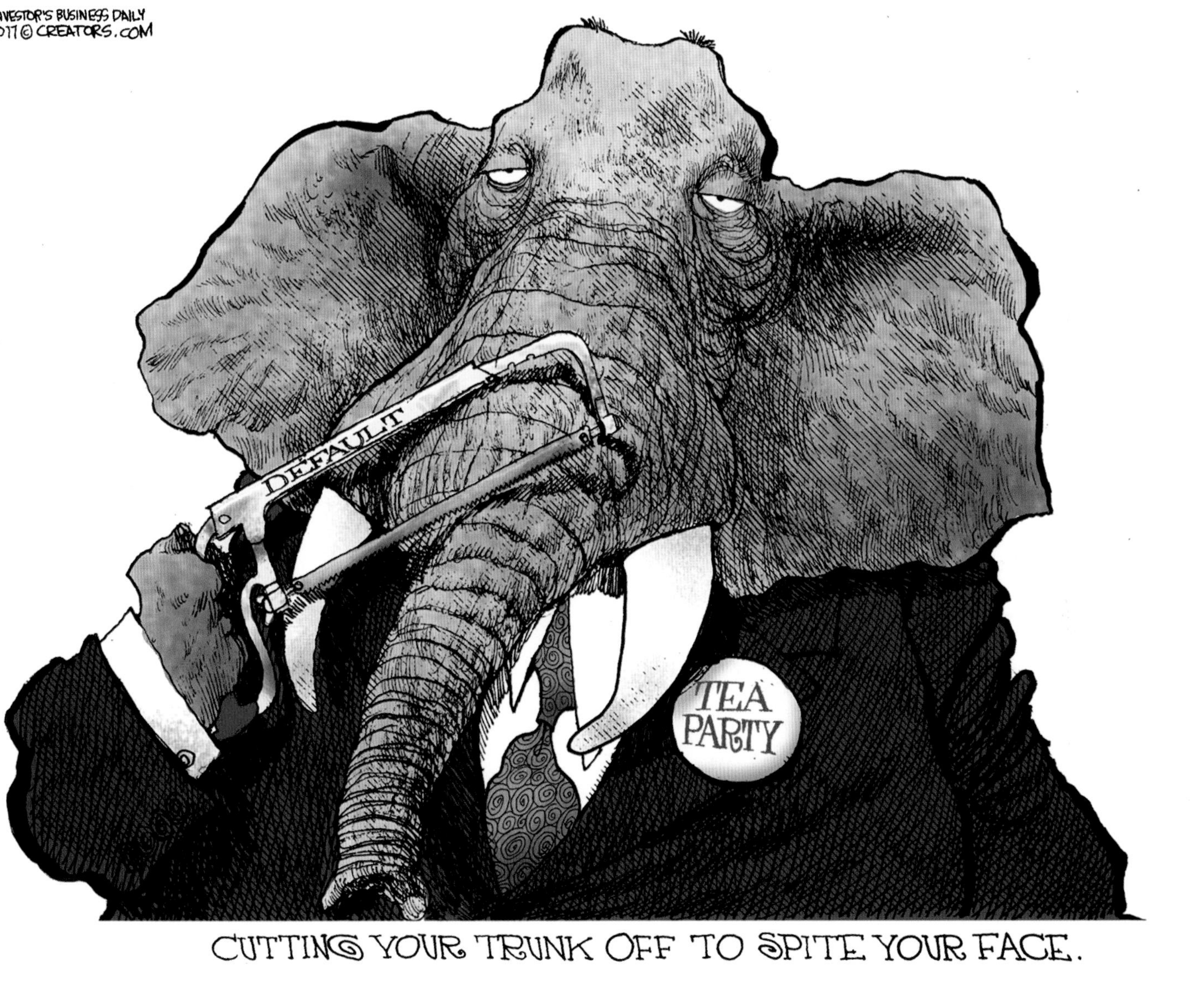
RAMIREZ INVESTOR'S BUSINESS DAILY 2011 © CREATORS.COM
DEFAULT
TEA PARTY
CUTTING YOUR TRUNK OFF TO SPITE YOUR FACE.

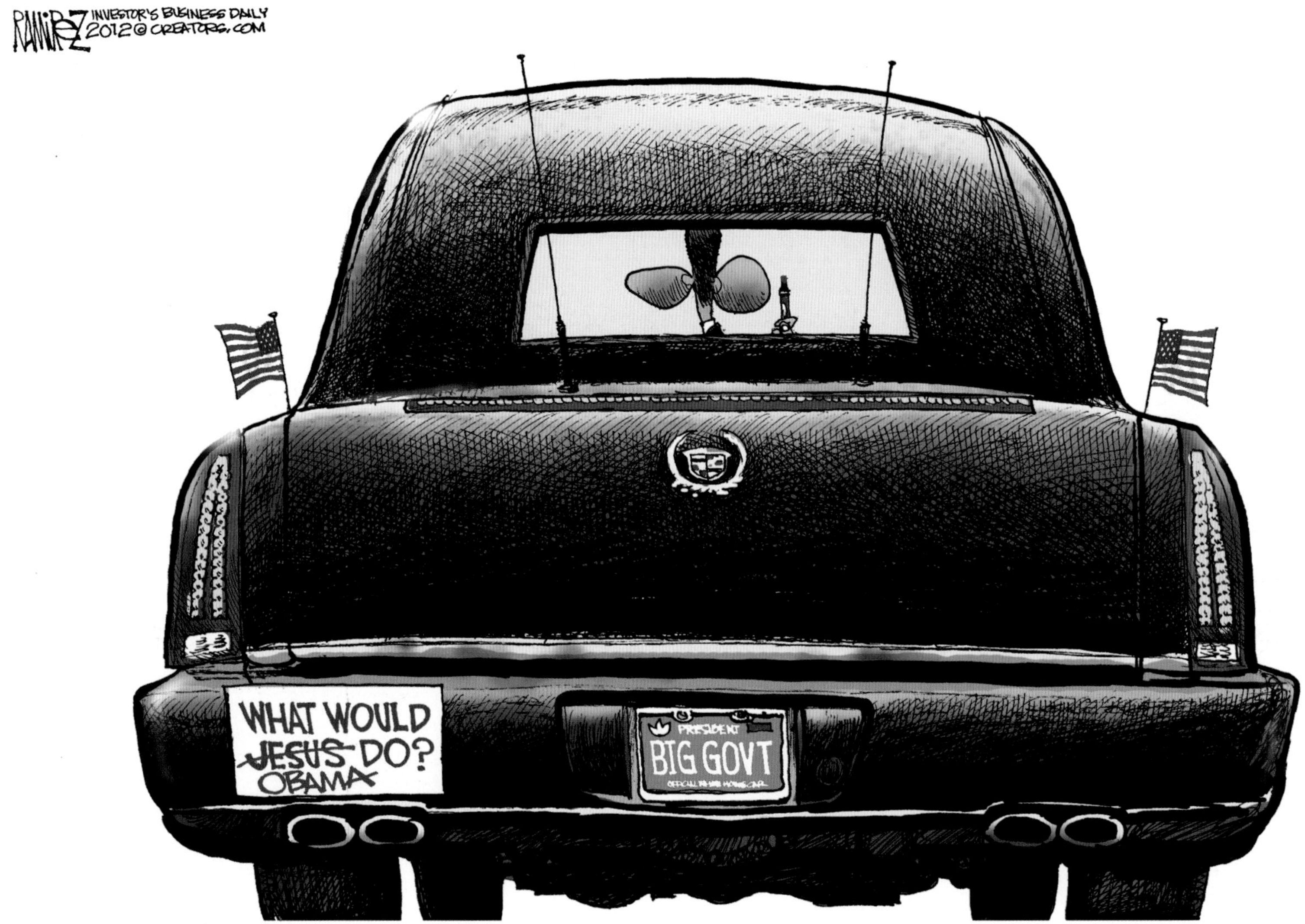
RAMIREZ
INVESTOR'S BUSINESS DAILY
2012 © CREATORS.COM
WHAT WOULD JESUS DO?
OBAMA
PRESIDENT
BIG GOVT

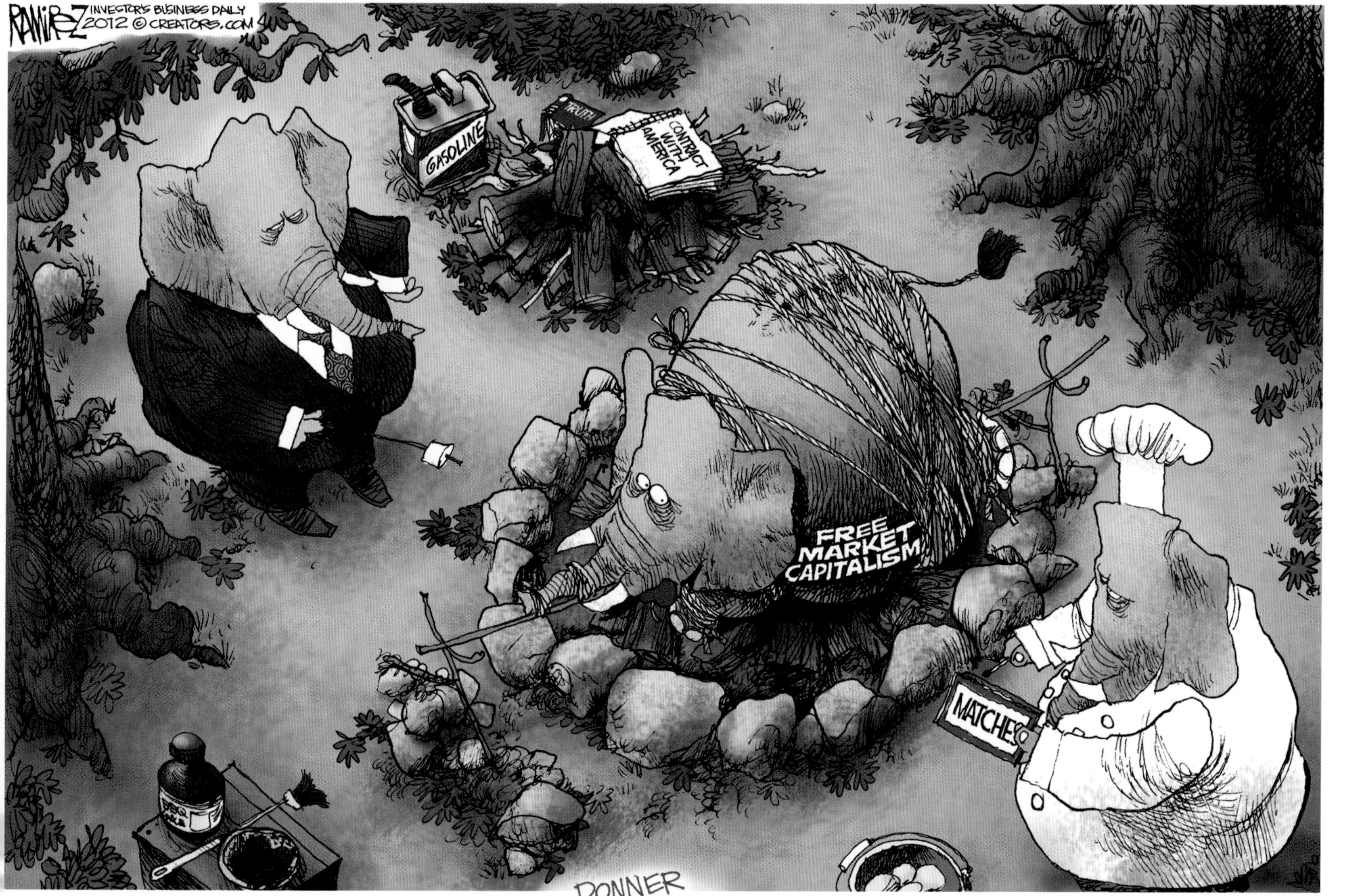
RAMIREZ
INVESTOR'S BUSINESS DAILY
2012 © CREATORS.COM
GASOLINE
TRUTH
CONTRACT WITH AMERICA
FREE MARKET CAPITALISM
MATCHES

THE ~~REPUBLICAN~~ DONNER PARTY

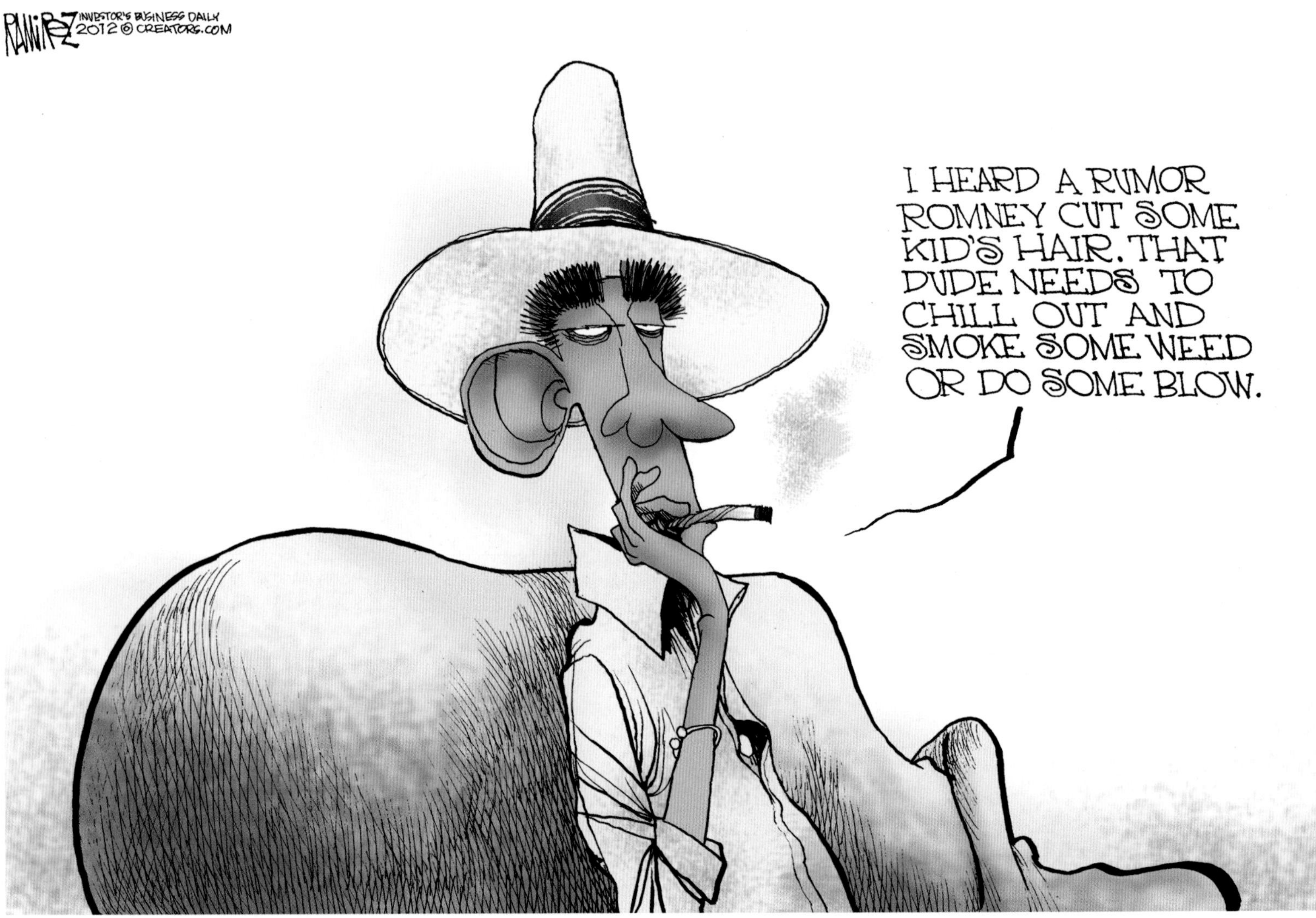
RAMIREZ INVESTOR'S BUSINESS DAILY 2012 © CREATORS.COM
I HEARD A RUMOR ROMNEY CUT SOME KID'S HAIR. THAT DUDE NEEDS TO CHILL OUT AND SMOKE SOME WEED OR DO SOME BLOW.

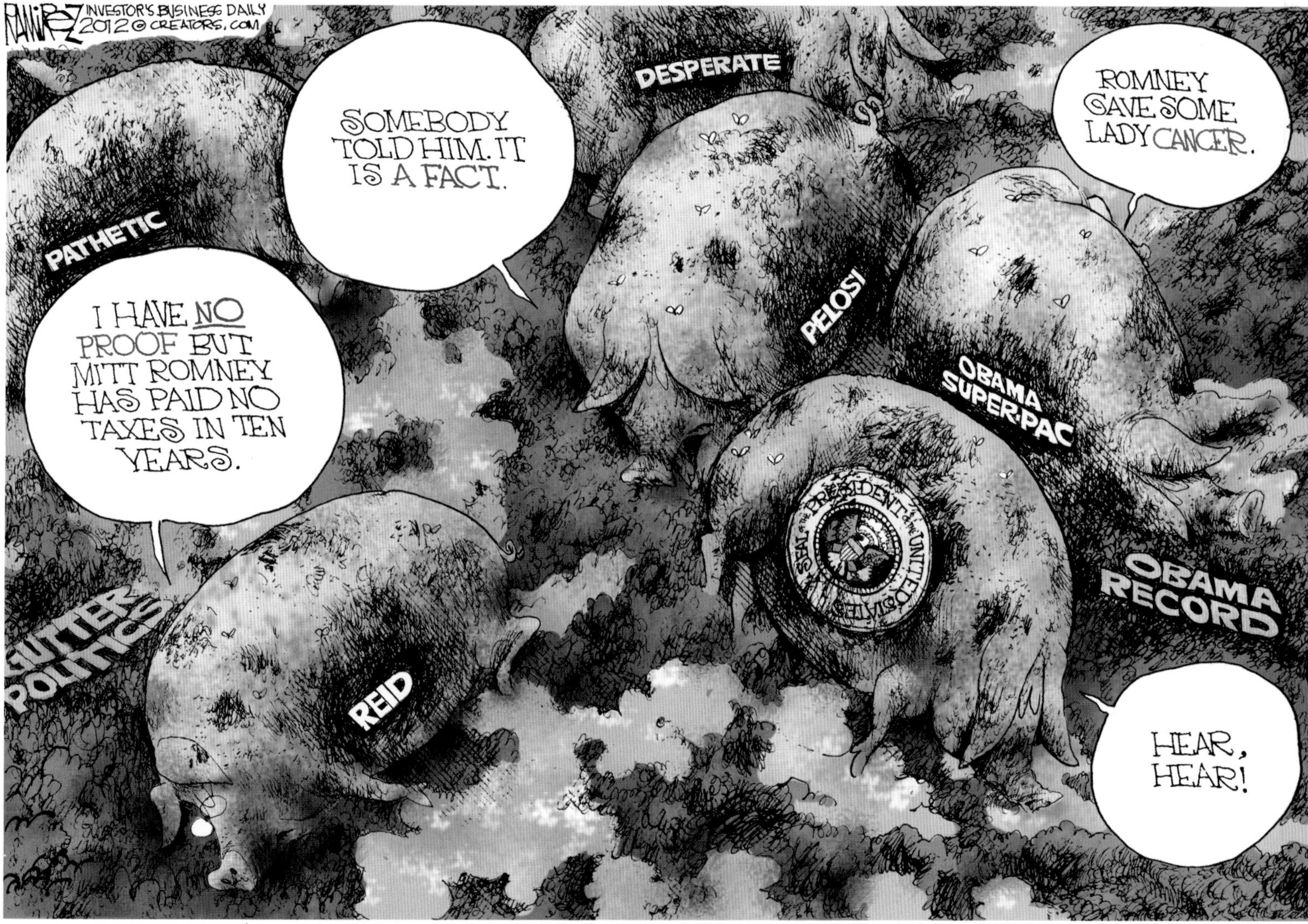
RAMIREZ INVESTOR'S BUSINESS DAILY 2012 © CREATORS.COM
PATHETIC
SOMEBODY TOLD HIM. IT IS A FACT.
DESPERATE
ROMNEY GAVE SOME LADY CANCER.
I HAVE NO PROOF BUT MITT ROMNEY HAS PAID NO TAXES IN TEN YEARS.
PELOSI
OBAMA SUPER-PAC
SEAL OF THE PRESIDENT OF THE UNITED STATES
OBAMA RECORD
GUTTER POLITICS
REID
HEAR, HEAR!

THE DEMOCRATIC LEADERSHIP

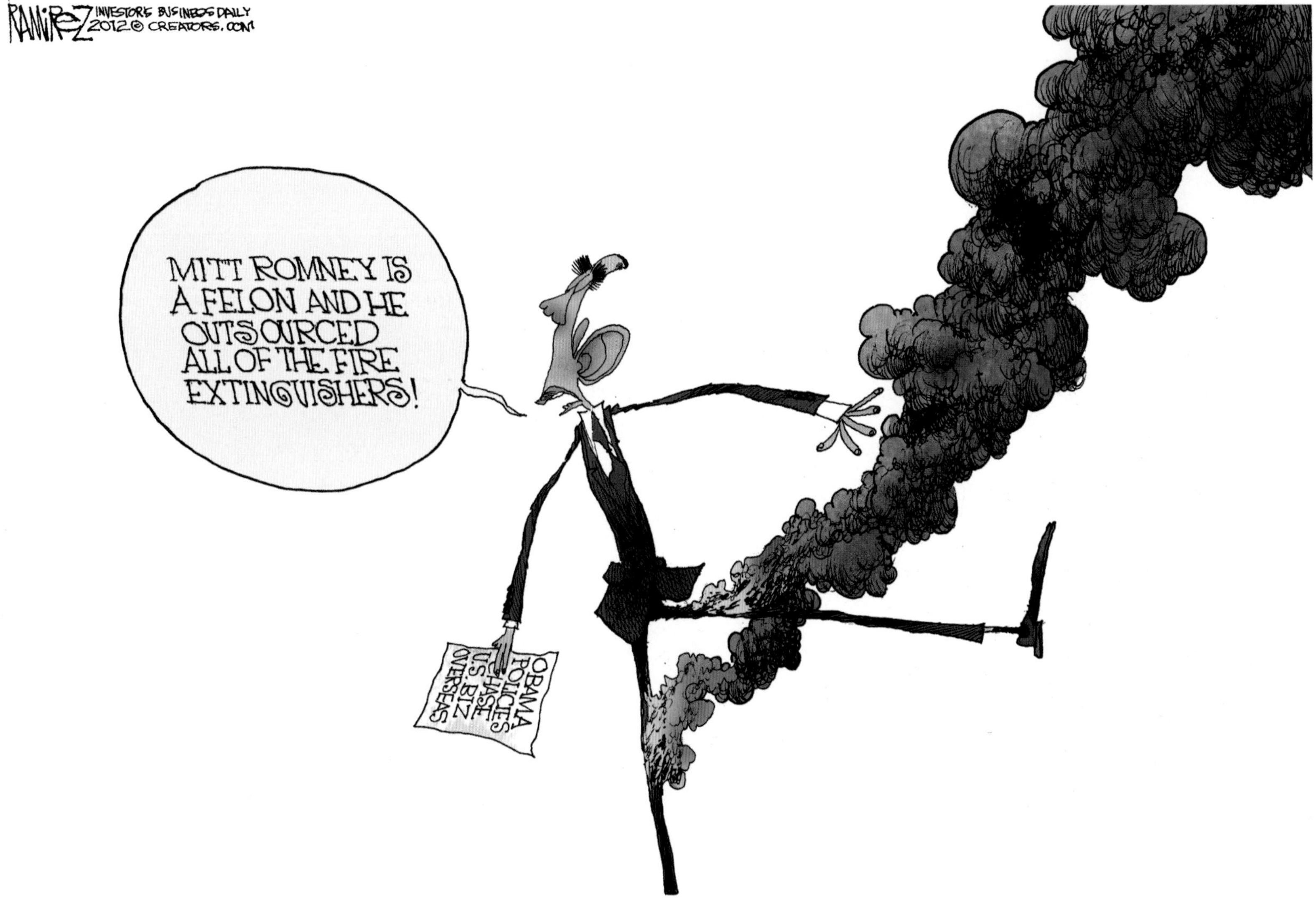
RAMIREZ INVESTOR'S BUSINESS DAILY 2012 © CREATORS.COM
MITT ROMNEY IS A FELON AND HE OUTSOURCED ALL OF THE FIRE EXTINGUISHERS!
OBAMA POLICIES CHASE U.S. BIZ OVERSEAS

LIAR, LIAR....

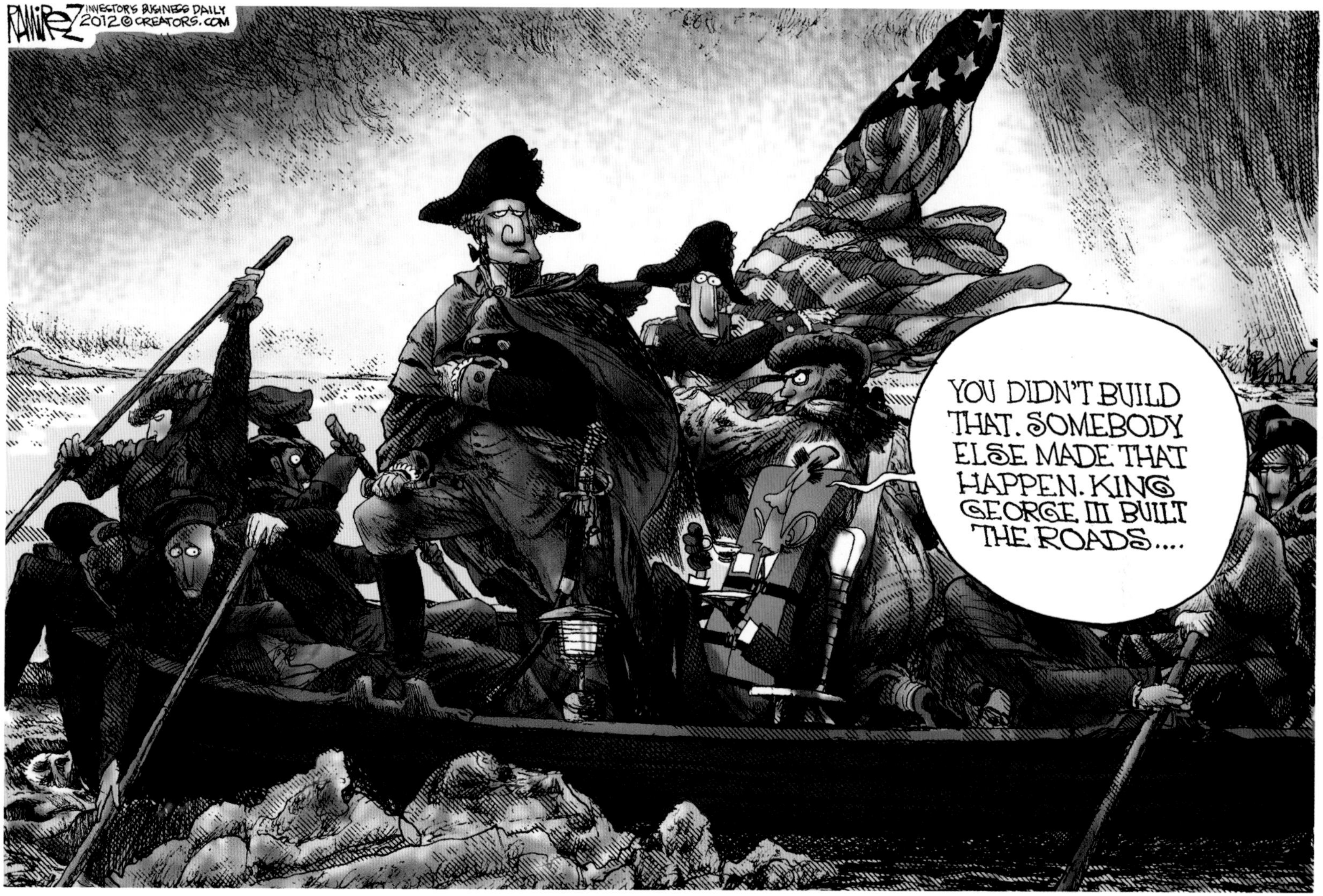
RAMIREZ INVESTOR'S BUSINESS DAILY 2012 © CREATORS.COM
YOU DIDN'T BUILD THAT. SOMEBODY ELSE MADE THAT HAPPEN. KING GEORGE III BUILT THE ROADS....

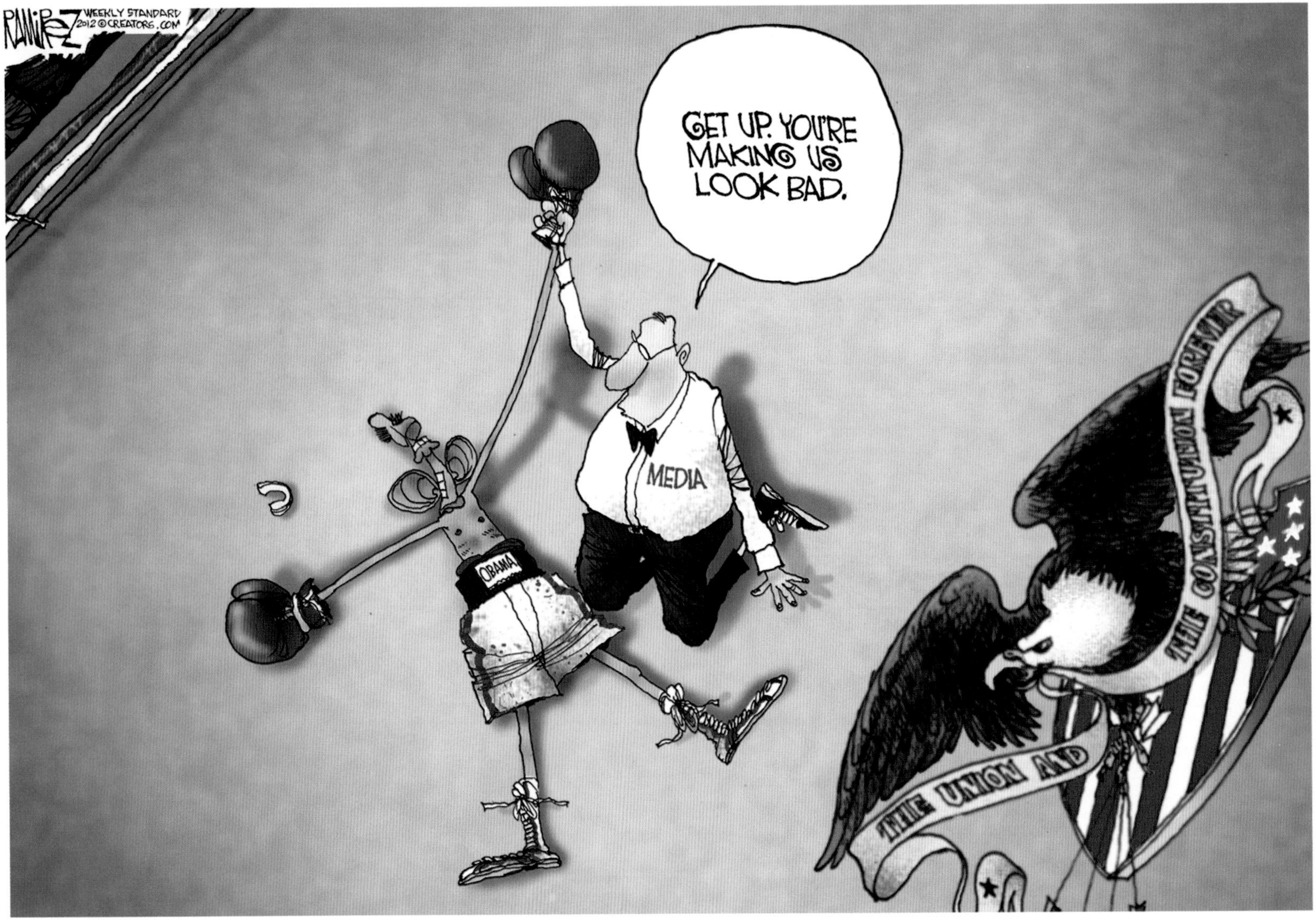
RAMIREZ
WEEKLY STANDARD
2012 © CREATORS.COM
GET UP. YOU'RE MAKING US LOOK BAD.
MEDIA
OBAMA
THE CONSTITUTION FOREVER
THE UNION AND

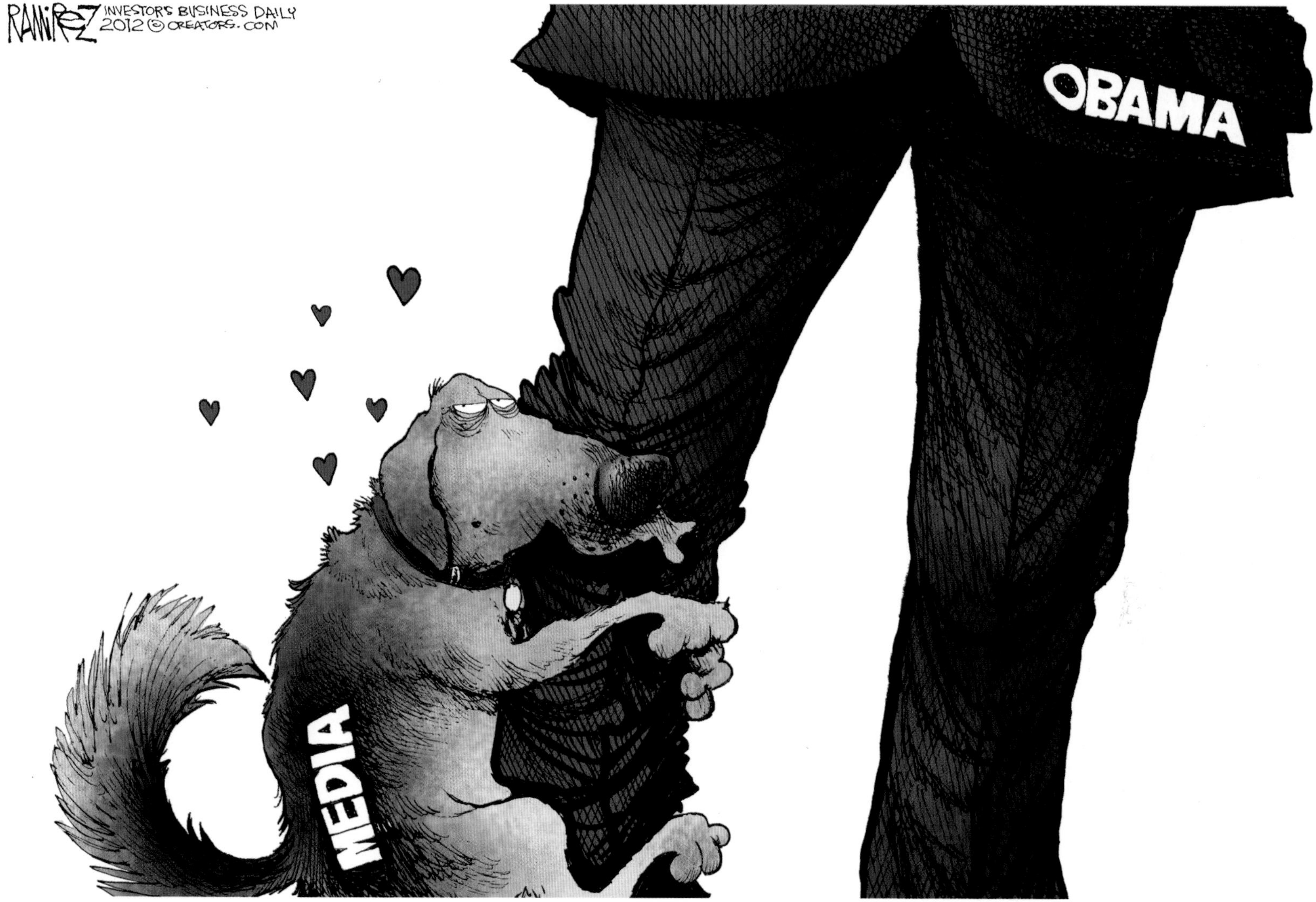
RAMIREZ INVESTOR'S BUSINESS DAILY
2012 © CREATORS.COM
OBAMA
MEDIA

THE LAP DOG.

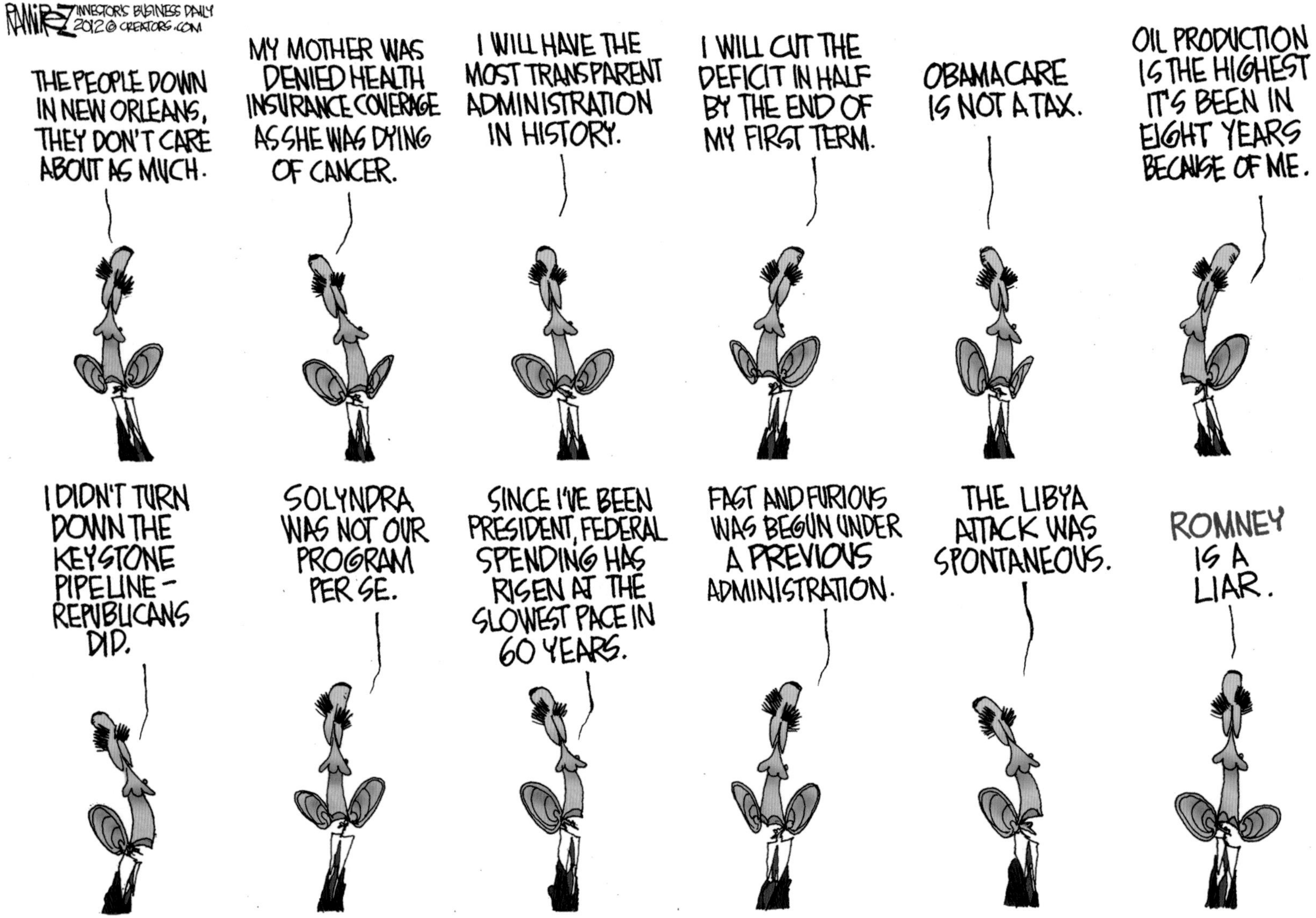
RAMIREZ INVESTOR'S BUSINESS DAILY 2012 © CREATORS.COM
THE PEOPLE DOWN IN NEW ORLEANS, THEY DON'T CARE ABOUT AS MUCH.
MY MOTHER WAS DENIED HEALTH INSURANCE COVERAGE AS SHE WAS DYING OF CANCER.
I WILL HAVE THE MOST TRANSPARENT ADMINISTRATION IN HISTORY.
I WILL CUT THE DEFICIT IN HALF BY THE END OF MY FIRST TERM.
OBAMACARE IS NOT A TAX.
OIL PRODUCTION IS THE HIGHEST IT'S BEEN IN EIGHT YEARS BECAUSE OF ME.
I DIDN'T TURN DOWN THE KEYSTONE PIPELINE - REPUBLICANS DID.
SOLYNDRA WAS NOT OUR PROGRAM PER SE.
SINCE I'VE BEEN PRESIDENT, FEDERAL SPENDING HAS RISEN AT THE SLOWEST PACE IN 60 YEARS.
FAST AND FURIOUS WAS BEGUN UNDER A PREVIOUS ADMINISTRATION.
THE LIBYA ATTACK WAS SPONTANEOUS.
ROMNEY IS A LIAR.

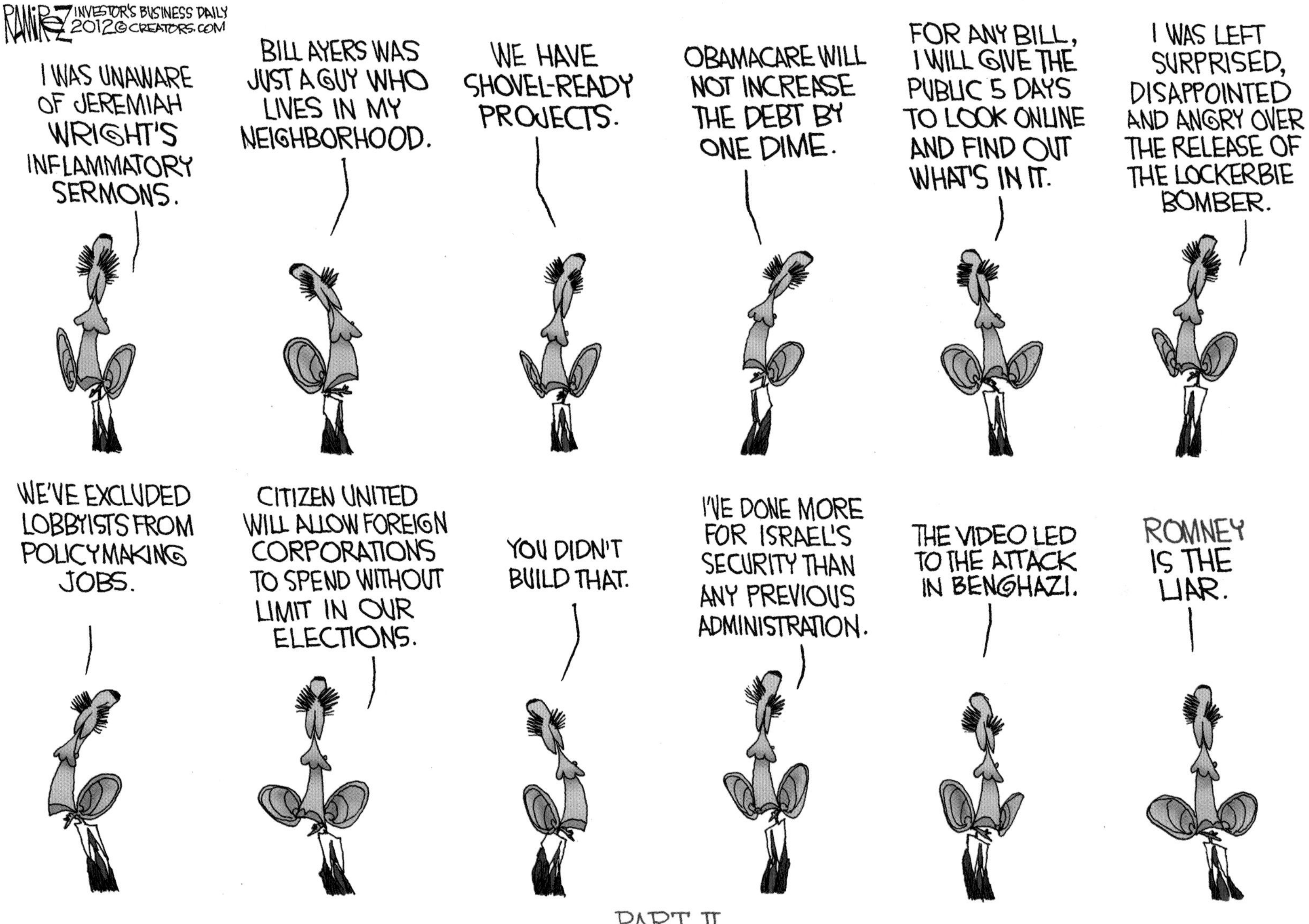
RAMIREZ INVESTOR'S BUSINESS DAILY 2012 © CREATORS.COM
I WAS UNAWARE OF JEREMIAH WRIGHT'S INFLAMMATORY SERMONS.
BILL AYERS WAS JUST A GUY WHO LIVES IN MY NEIGHBORHOOD.
WE HAVE SHOVEL-READY PROJECTS.
OBAMACARE WILL NOT INCREASE THE DEBT BY ONE DIME.
FOR ANY BILL, I WILL GIVE THE PUBLIC 5 DAYS TO LOOK ONLINE AND FIND OUT WHAT'S IN IT.
I WAS LEFT SURPRISED, DISAPPOINTED AND ANGRY OVER THE RELEASE OF THE LOCKERBIE BOMBER.
WE'VE EXCLUDED LOBBYISTS FROM POLICYMAKING JOBS.
CITIZEN UNITED WILL ALLOW FOREIGN CORPORATIONS TO SPEND WITHOUT LIMIT IN OUR ELECTIONS.
YOU DIDN'T BUILD THAT.
I'VE DONE MORE FOR ISRAEL'S SECURITY THAN ANY PREVIOUS ADMINISTRATION.
THE VIDEO LED TO THE ATTACK IN BENGHAZI.
ROMNEY IS THE LIAR.

PART II

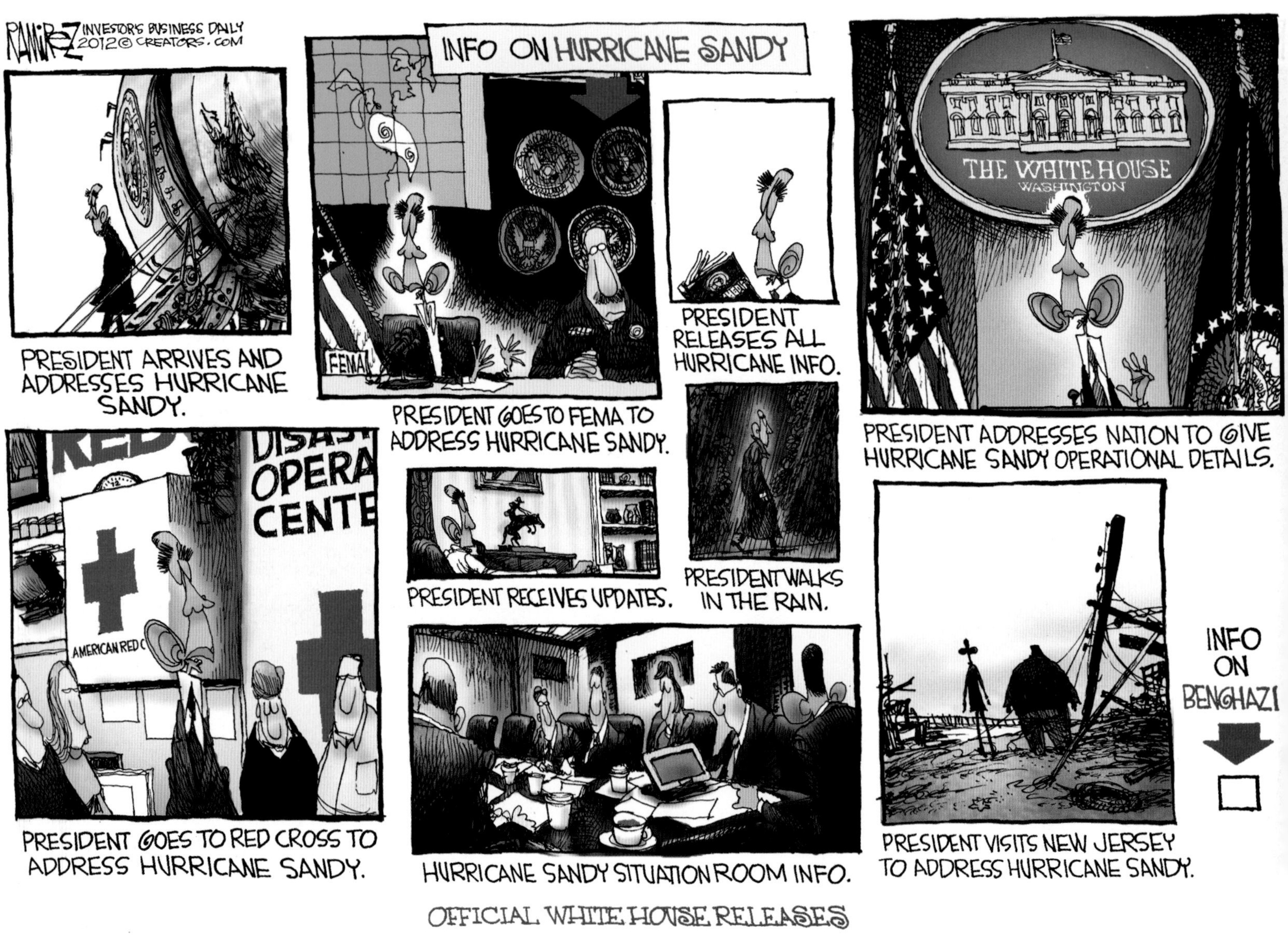
RAMIREZ INVESTOR'S BUSINESS DAILY 2012 © CREATORS.COM
INFO ON HURRICANE SANDY
PRESIDENT ARRIVES AND ADDRESSES HURRICANE SANDY.
FEMA
PRESIDENT GOES TO FEMA TO ADDRESS HURRICANE SANDY.
PRESIDENT RELEASES ALL HURRICANE INFO.
THE WHITE HOUSE
WASHINGTON
PRESIDENT ADDRESSES NATION TO GIVE HURRICANE SANDY OPERATIONAL DETAILS.
RED
DISAST
OPERA
CENTE
AMERICAN RED C
PRESIDENT RECEIVES UPDATES.
PRESIDENT WALKS IN THE RAIN.
PRESIDENT GOES TO RED CROSS TO ADDRESS HURRICANE SANDY.
HURRICANE SANDY SITUATION ROOM INFO.
PRESIDENT VISITS NEW JERSEY TO ADDRESS HURRICANE SANDY.
INFO ON BENGHAZI
OFFICIAL WHITE HOUSE RELEASES

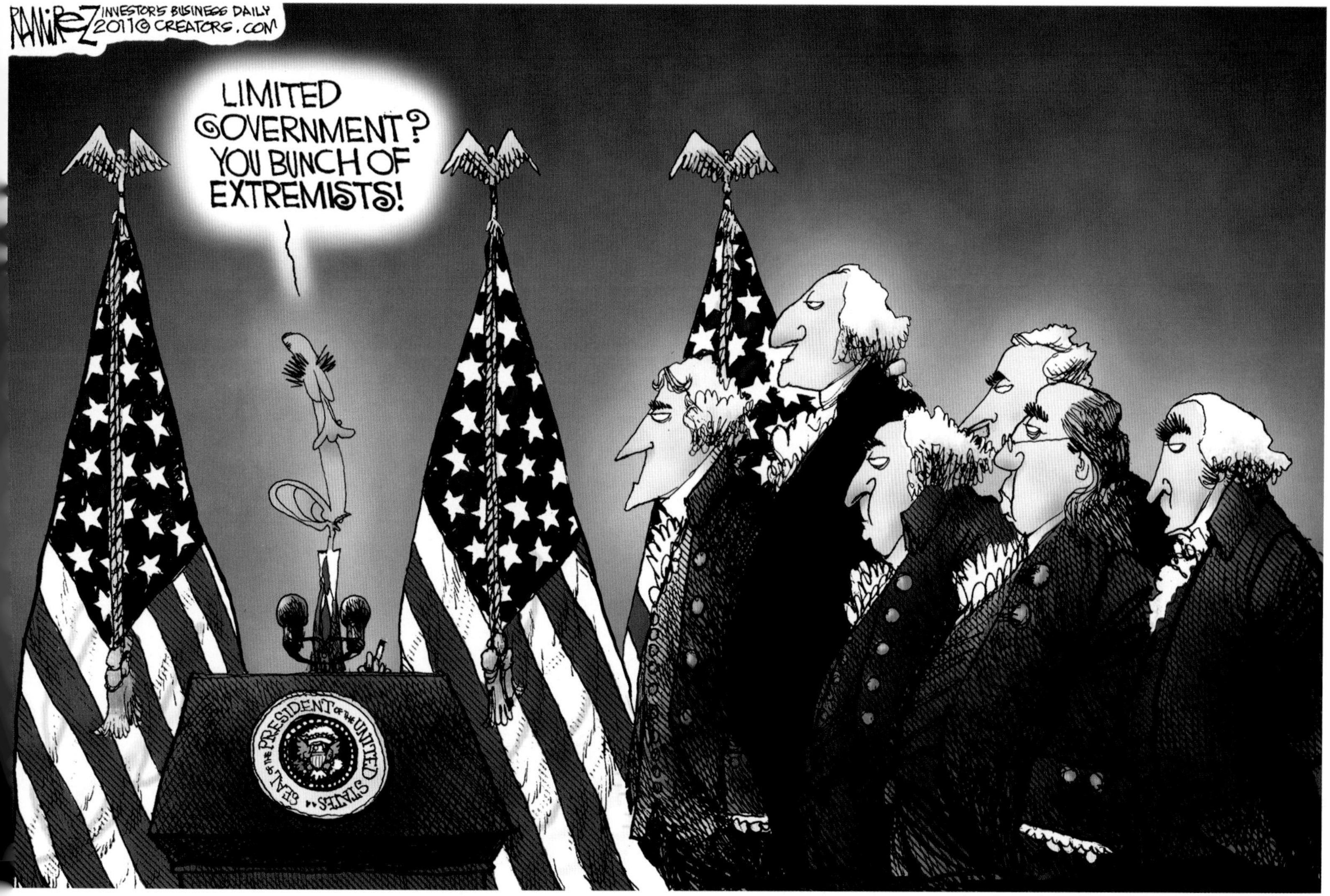
RAMIREZ INVESTOR'S BUSINESS DAILY 2011© CREATORS.COM
LIMITED GOVERNMENT? YOU BUNCH OF EXTREMISTS!
SEAL OF THE PRESIDENT OF THE UNITED STATES

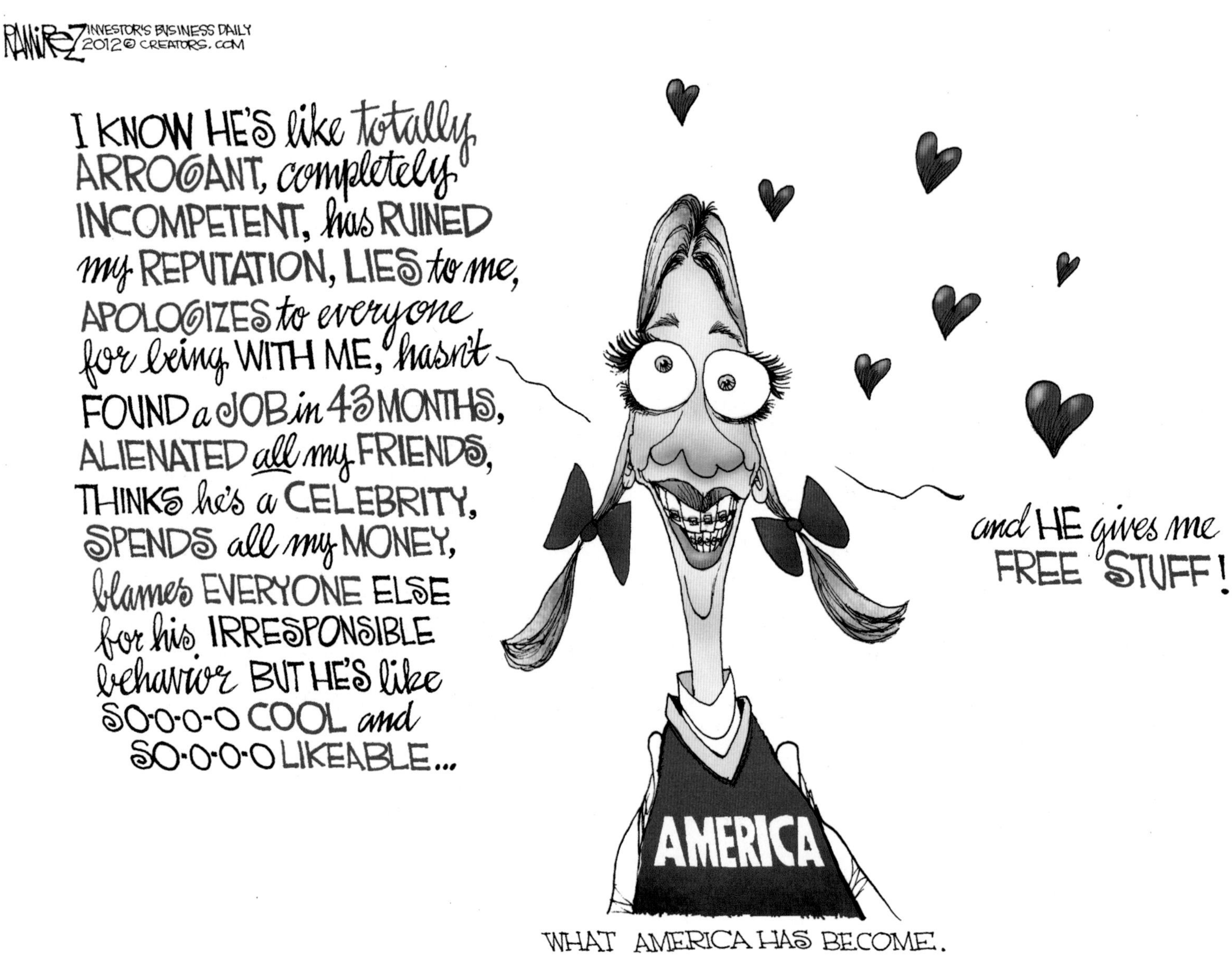
RAMIREZ INVESTOR'S BUSINESS DAILY 2012© CREATORS.COM
I KNOW HE'S like totally ARROGANT, completely INCOMPETENT, has RUINED my REPUTATION, LIES to me, APOLOGIZES to everyone for being WITH ME, hasn't FOUND a JOB in 43 MONTHS, ALIENATED all my FRIENDS, THINKS he's a CELEBRITY, SPENDS all my MONEY, blames EVERYONE ELSE for his IRRESPONSIBLE behavior BUT HE'S like SO-O-O-O COOL and SO-O-O-O LIKEABLE...
and HE gives me FREE STUFF!
AMERICA
WHAT AMERICA HAS BECOME.

REVELATION

"The problem is that I'm the president of the United States, I'm not the emperor of the United States. My job is to execute laws that are passed."

—President Barack Obama,
Google Hangout session, February 14, 2013

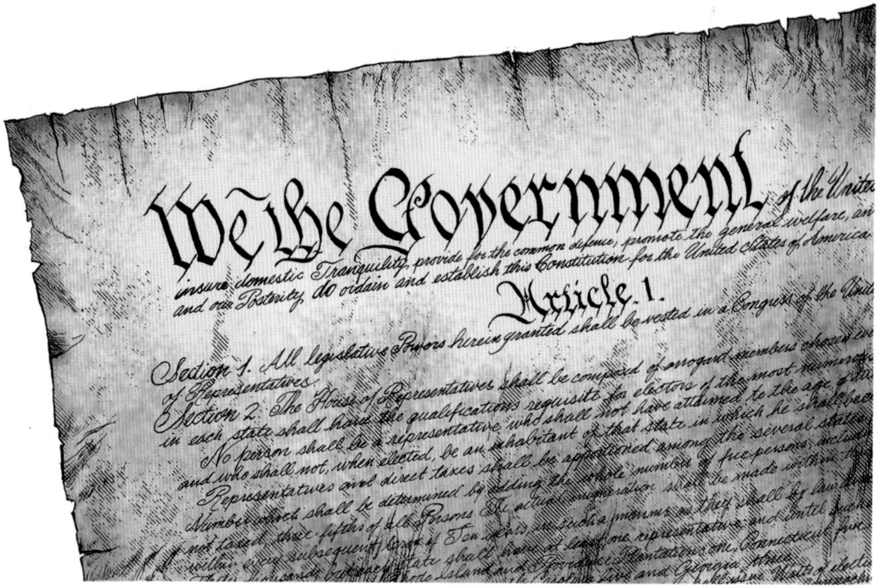
We the Government
Article. 1.

After two terms of President Obama, America is weaker, more divided, less respected, more in debt, and less consequential than any time in history. The president who promised to bring America together and heal our political and racial divide has instead polarized the country more than ever. The hope that was inspired by his historic election dissipated, but the damage from his failed policies will endure.

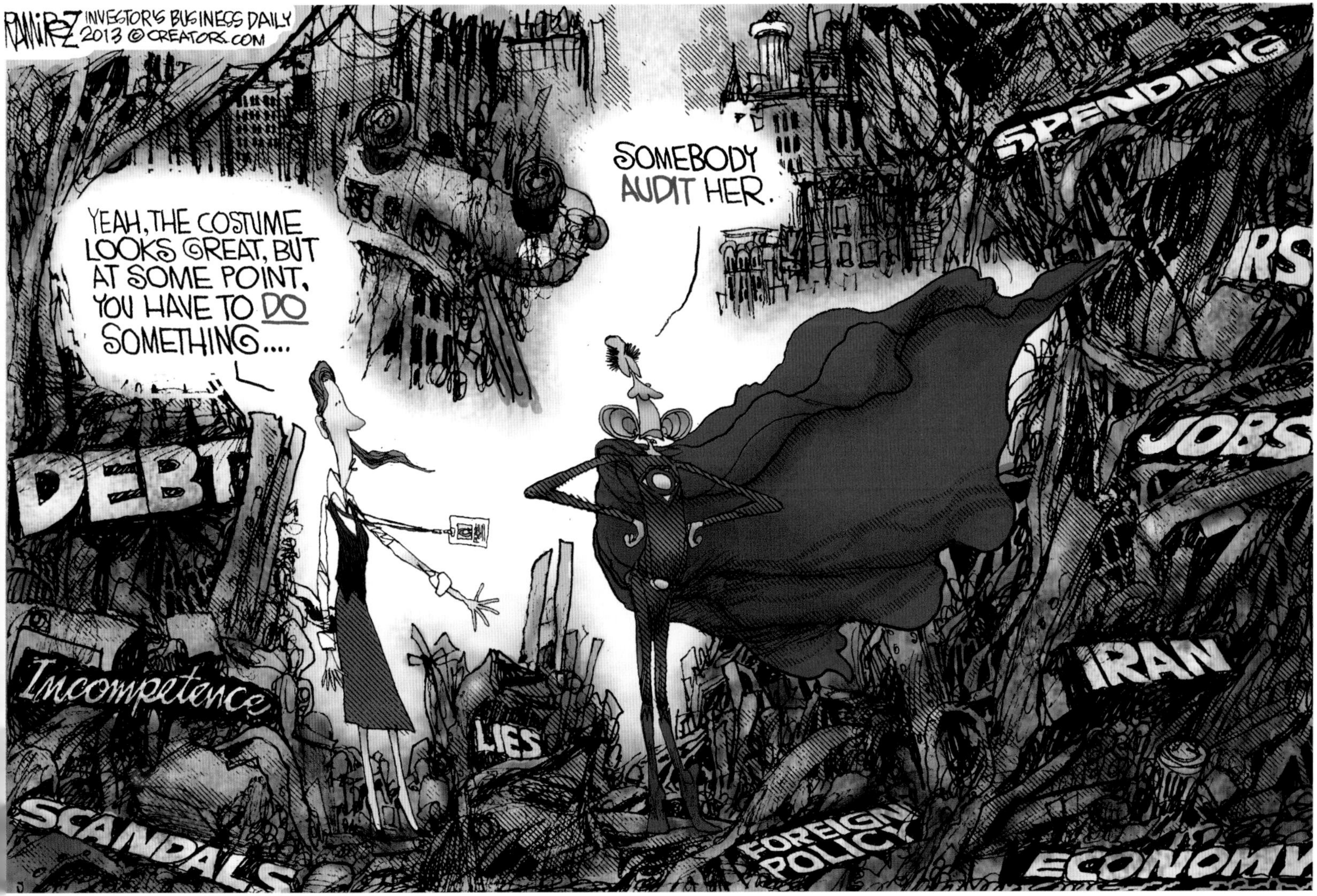
RAMIREZ INVESTOR'S BUSINESS DAILY 2013 © CREATORS.COM
YEAH, THE COSTUME LOOKS GREAT, BUT AT SOME POINT, YOU HAVE TO DO SOMETHING....
SOMEBODY AUDIT HER.
SPENDING
IRS
JOBS
DEBT
IRAN
Incompetence
LIES
SCANDALS
FOREIGN POLICY
ECONOMY

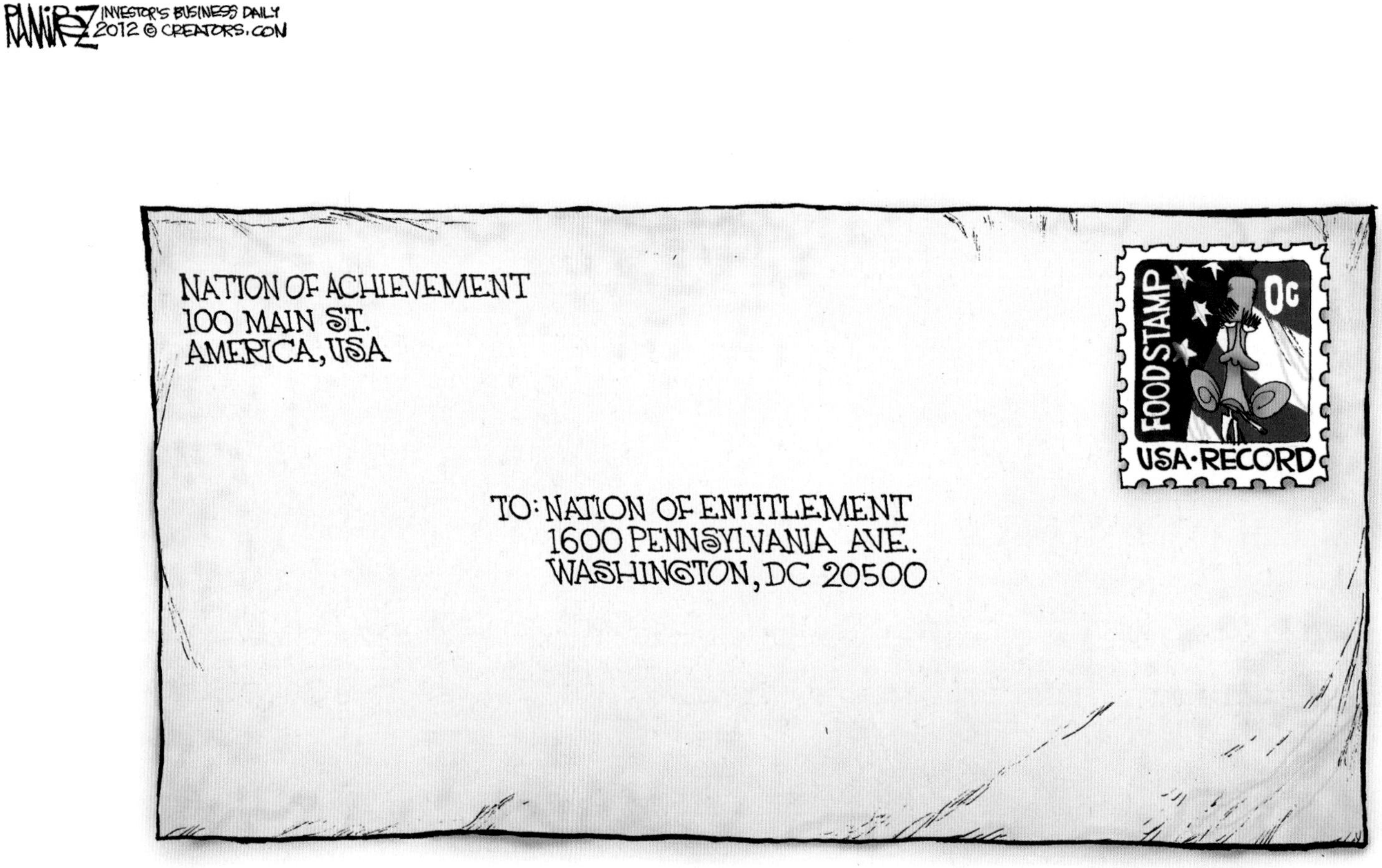
RAMIREZ INVESTOR'S BUSINESS DAILY 2012 © CREATORS.COM
NATION OF ACHIEVEMENT
100 MAIN ST.
AMERICA, USA
FOODSTAMP
0¢
USA·RECORD
TO: NATION OF ENTITLEMENT
1600 PENNSYLVANIA AVE.
WASHINGTON, DC 20500

LETTER OF INTENT

We the Government of the United... insure domestic Tranquility, provide for the common defence, promote the general welfare, and our Posterity, do ordain and establish this Constitution for the United States of America.

Article. 1.

Section. 1. All legislative Powers herein granted shall be vested in a Congress of the United... of Representatives.

Section. 2. The House of Representatives shall be composed of arrogant members chosen eve... in each state shall have the qualifications requisite for electors of the most numero...

No person shall be a representative, who shall not have attained to the age of...

and who shall not, when elected, be an inhabitant of that state in which he shall be...

Representatives and direct taxes shall be apportioned among the several state...

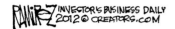
INVESTOR'S BUSINESS DAILY
2012 © creators.com

DISENGAGEMENT

CARTER 2.0

PROJECTING

American
WEAKNESS

FLAMMABLE

POLICY *of* APPEASEMENT

THE FUEL FOR THE FIRE

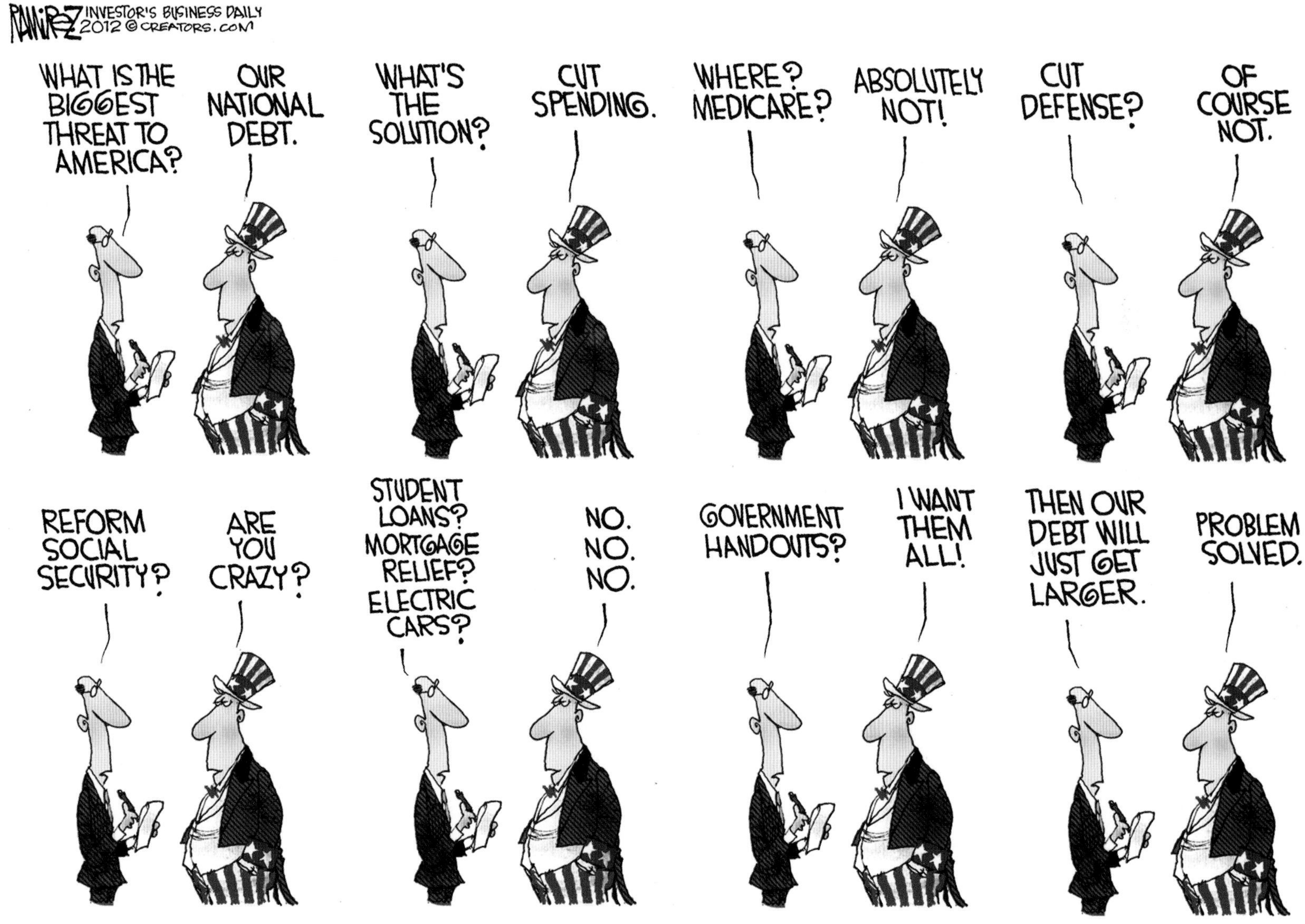
RAMIREZ INVESTOR'S BUSINESS DAILY 2012 © CREATORS.COM
WHAT IS THE BIGGEST THREAT TO AMERICA?
OUR NATIONAL DEBT.
WHAT'S THE SOLUTION?
CUT SPENDING.
WHERE? MEDICARE?
ABSOLUTELY NOT!
CUT DEFENSE?
OF COURSE NOT.
REFORM SOCIAL SECURITY?
ARE YOU CRAZY?
STUDENT LOANS? MORTGAGE RELIEF? ELECTRIC CARS?
NO. NO. NO.
GOVERNMENT HANDOUTS?
I WANT THEM ALL!
THEN OUR DEBT WILL JUST GET LARGER.
PROBLEM SOLVED.

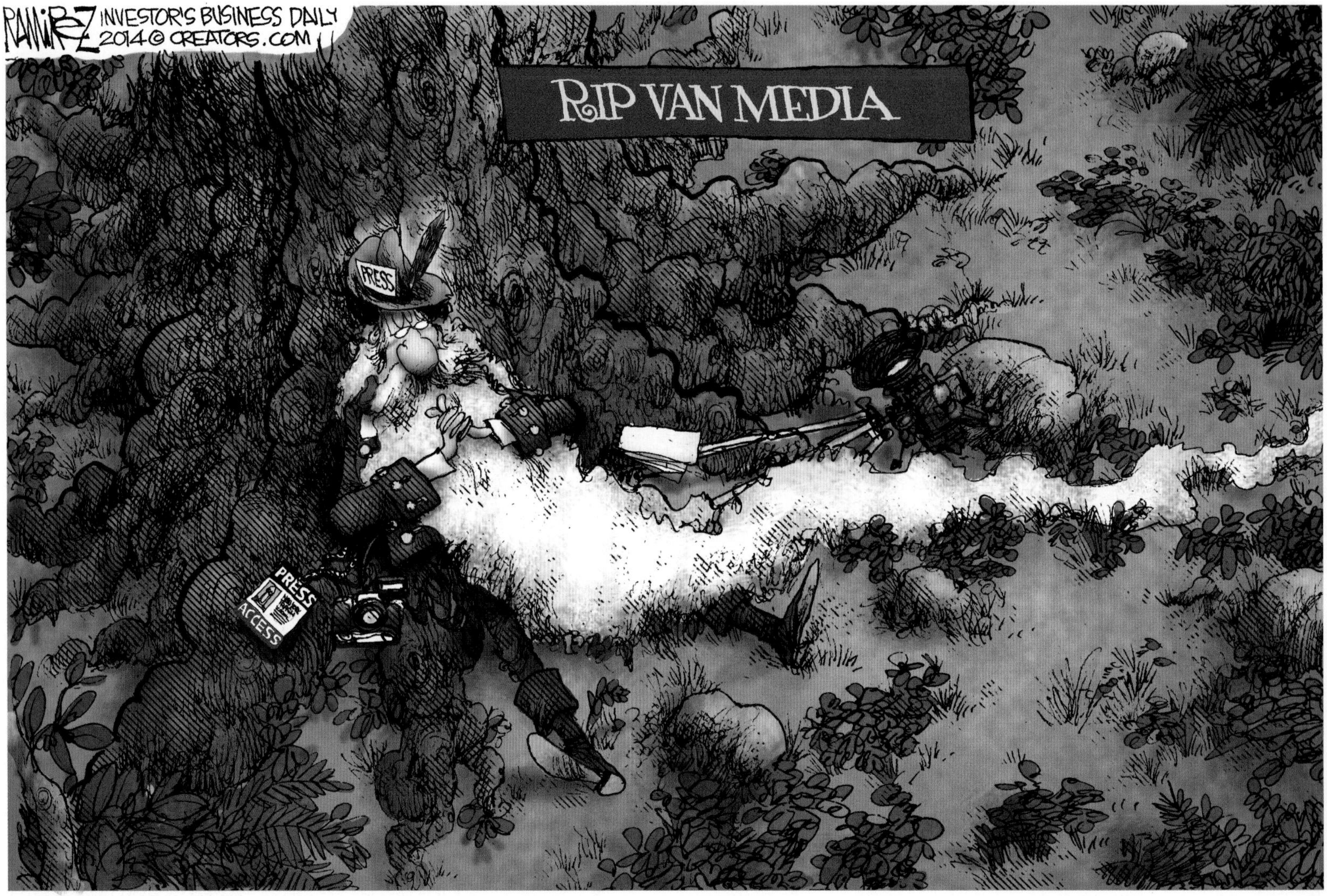
RAMIREZ INVESTOR'S BUSINESS DAILY
2014 © CREATORS.COM
RIP VAN MEDIA
PRESS
PRESS
ACCESS

And they SLEPT and SLEPT and SLEPT through ALL the SCANDALS...

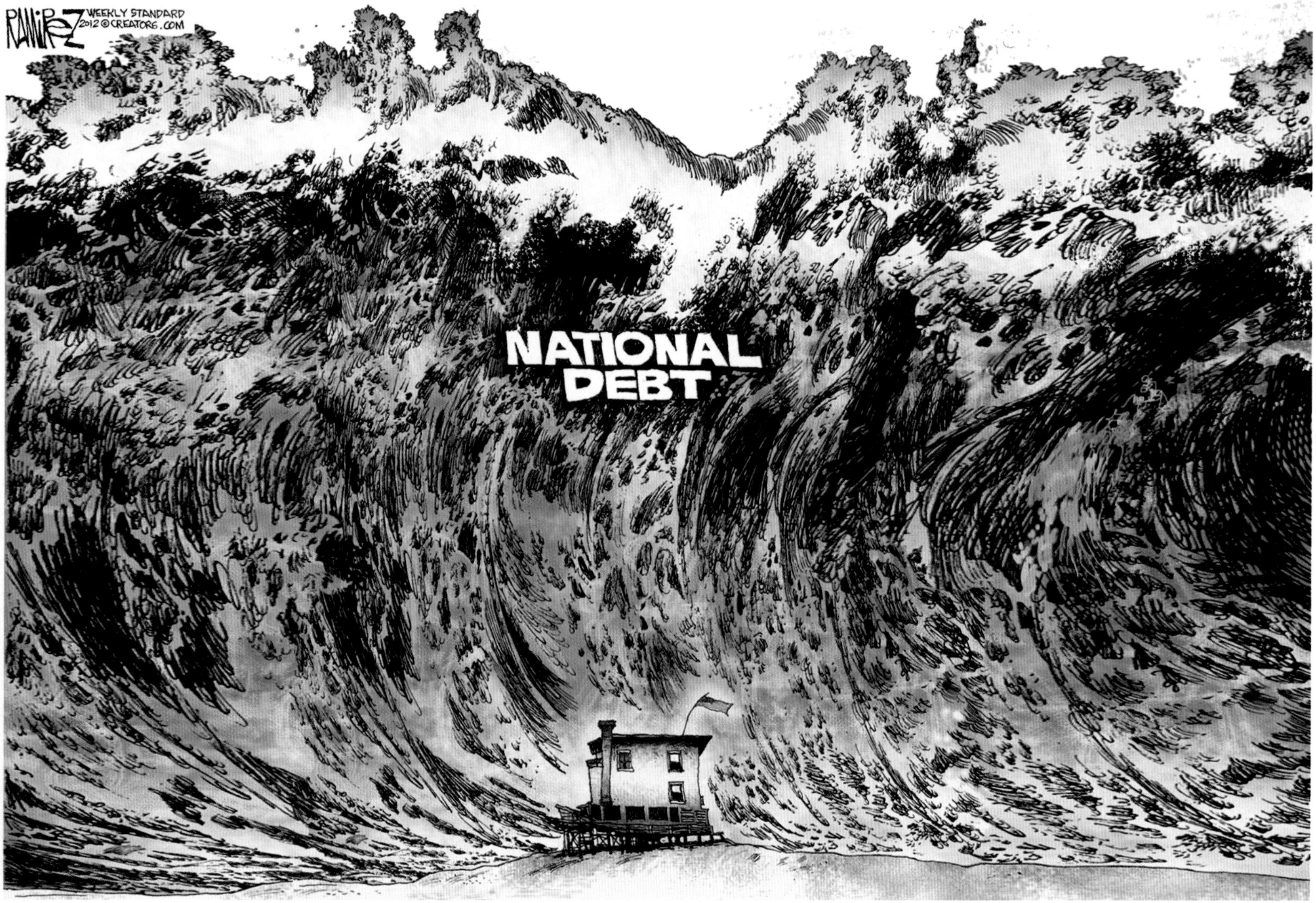
RAMIREZ WEEKLY STANDARD 2012 © CREATORS.COM
NATIONAL DEBT

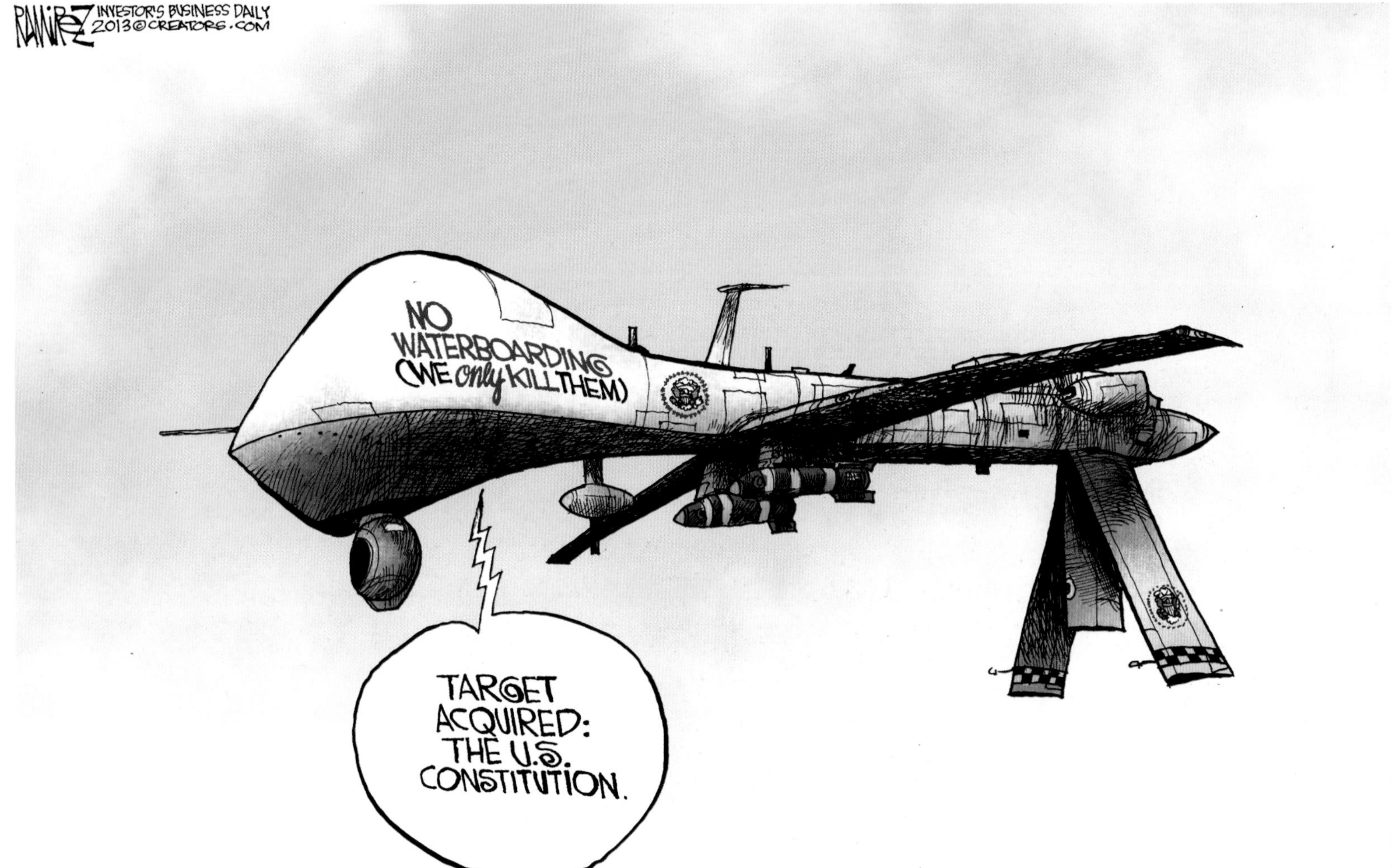
RAMIREZ INVESTOR'S BUSINESS DAILY 2013 © CREATORS.COM
NO WATERBOARDING (WE only KILL THEM)
TARGET ACQUIRED: THE U.S. CONSTITUTION.

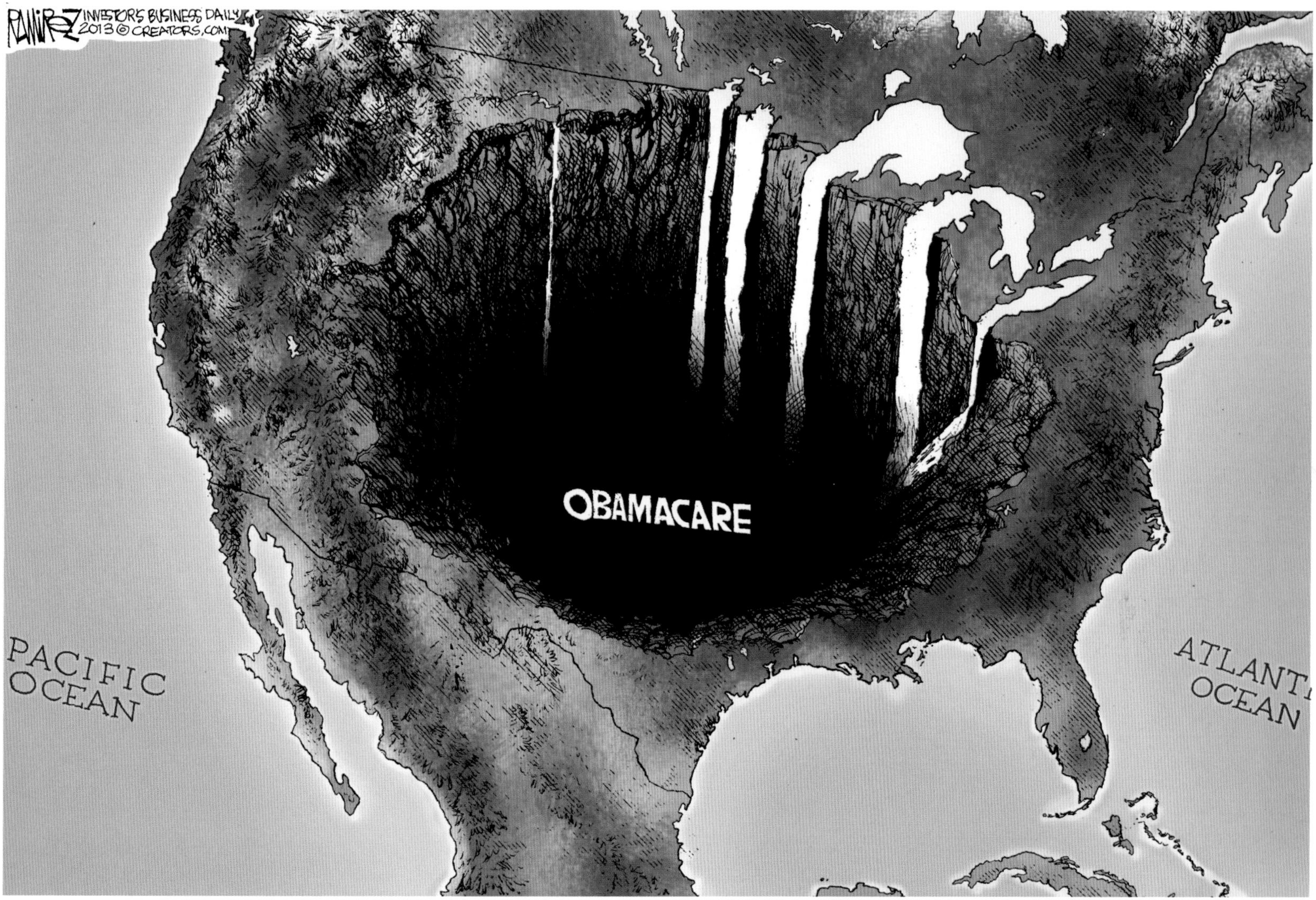
RAMIREZ INVESTOR'S BUSINESS DAILY 2013 © CREATORS.COM
OBAMACARE
PACIFIC OCEAN
ATLANTI OCEAN

THE SINK HOLE

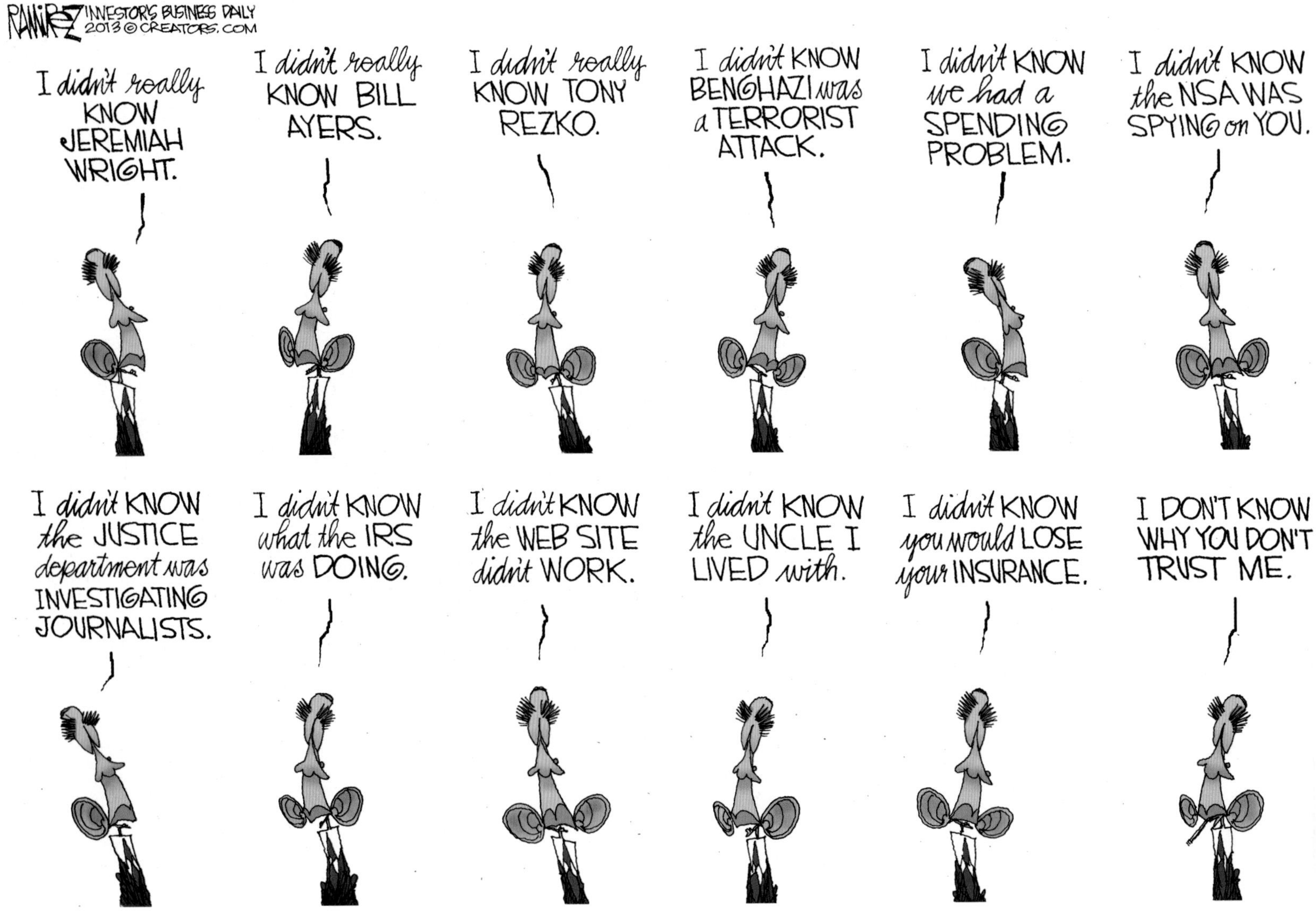
RAMIREZ INVESTOR'S BUSINESS DAILY 2013 © CREATORS.COM
I didn't really KNOW JEREMIAH WRIGHT.
I didn't really KNOW BILL AYERS.
I didn't really KNOW TONY REZKO.
I didn't KNOW BENGHAZI was a TERRORIST ATTACK.
I didn't KNOW we had a SPENDING PROBLEM.
I didn't KNOW the NSA WAS SPYING on YOU.
I didn't KNOW the JUSTICE department was INVESTIGATING JOURNALISTS.
I didn't KNOW what the IRS was DOING.
I didn't KNOW the WEB SITE didn't WORK.
I didn't KNOW the UNCLE I LIVED with.
I didn't KNOW you would LOSE your INSURANCE.
I DON'T KNOW WHY YOU DON'T TRUST ME.

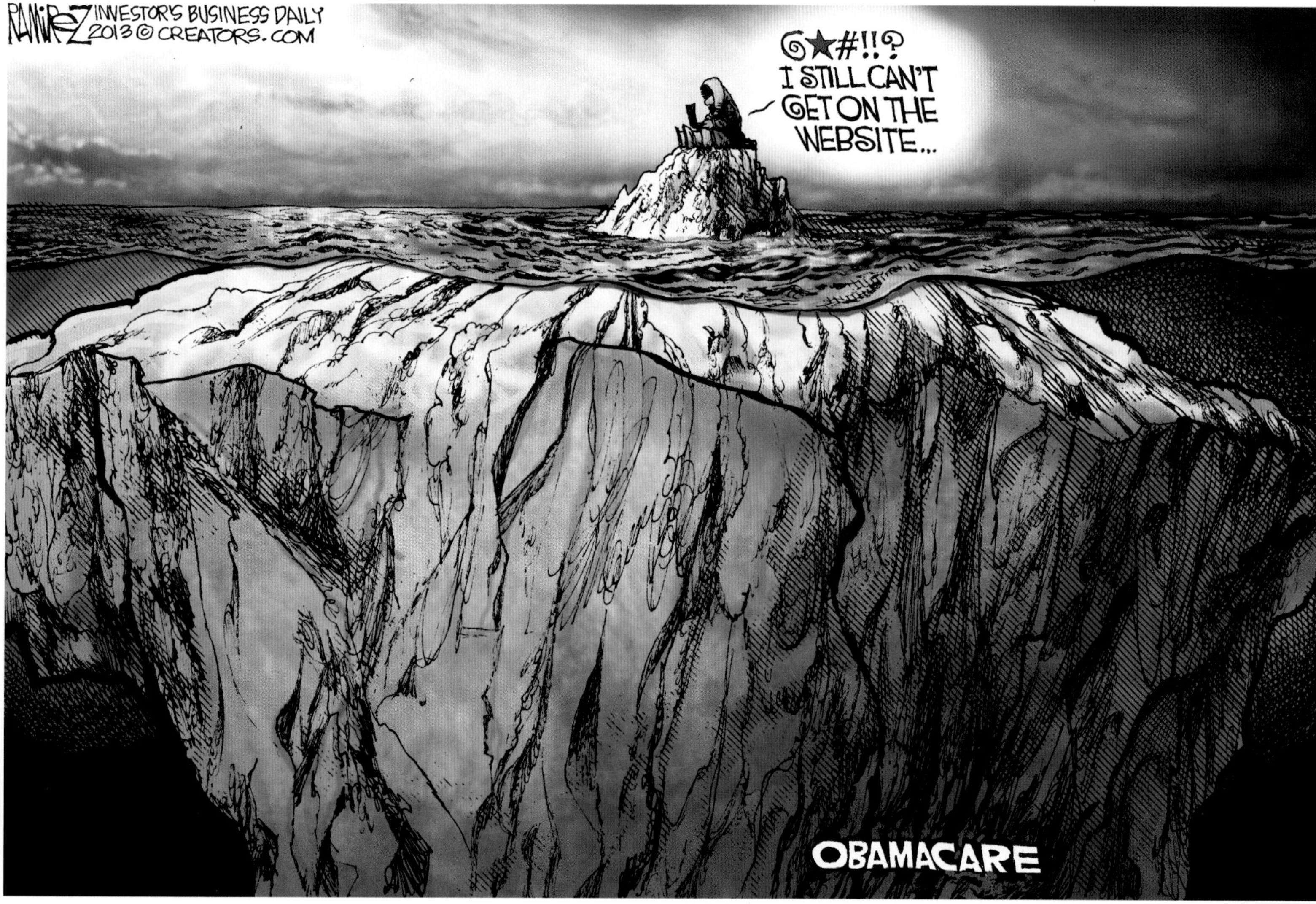
RAMIREZ INVESTOR'S BUSINESS DAILY 2013 © CREATORS.COM
@★#!!? I STILL CAN'T GET ON THE WEBSITE...
OBAMACARE

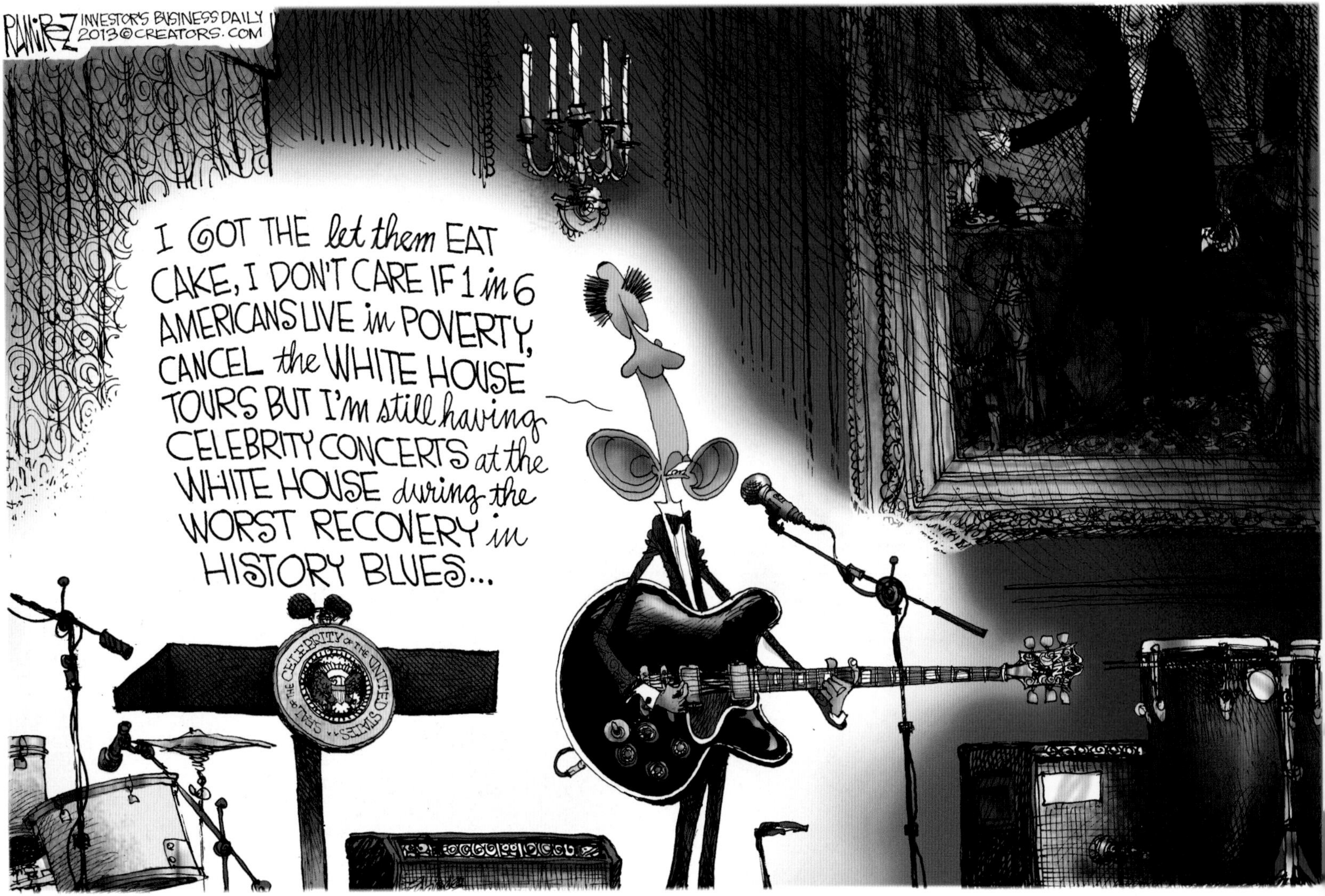
RAMIREZ INVESTOR'S BUSINESS DAILY 2013©CREATORS.COM
I GOT THE let them EAT CAKE, I DON'T CARE IF 1 in 6 AMERICANS LIVE in POVERTY, CANCEL the WHITE HOUSE TOURS BUT I'm still having CELEBRITY CONCERTS at the WHITE HOUSE during the WORST RECOVERY in HISTORY BLUES...
SEAL OF THE CELEBRITY OF THE UNITED STATES

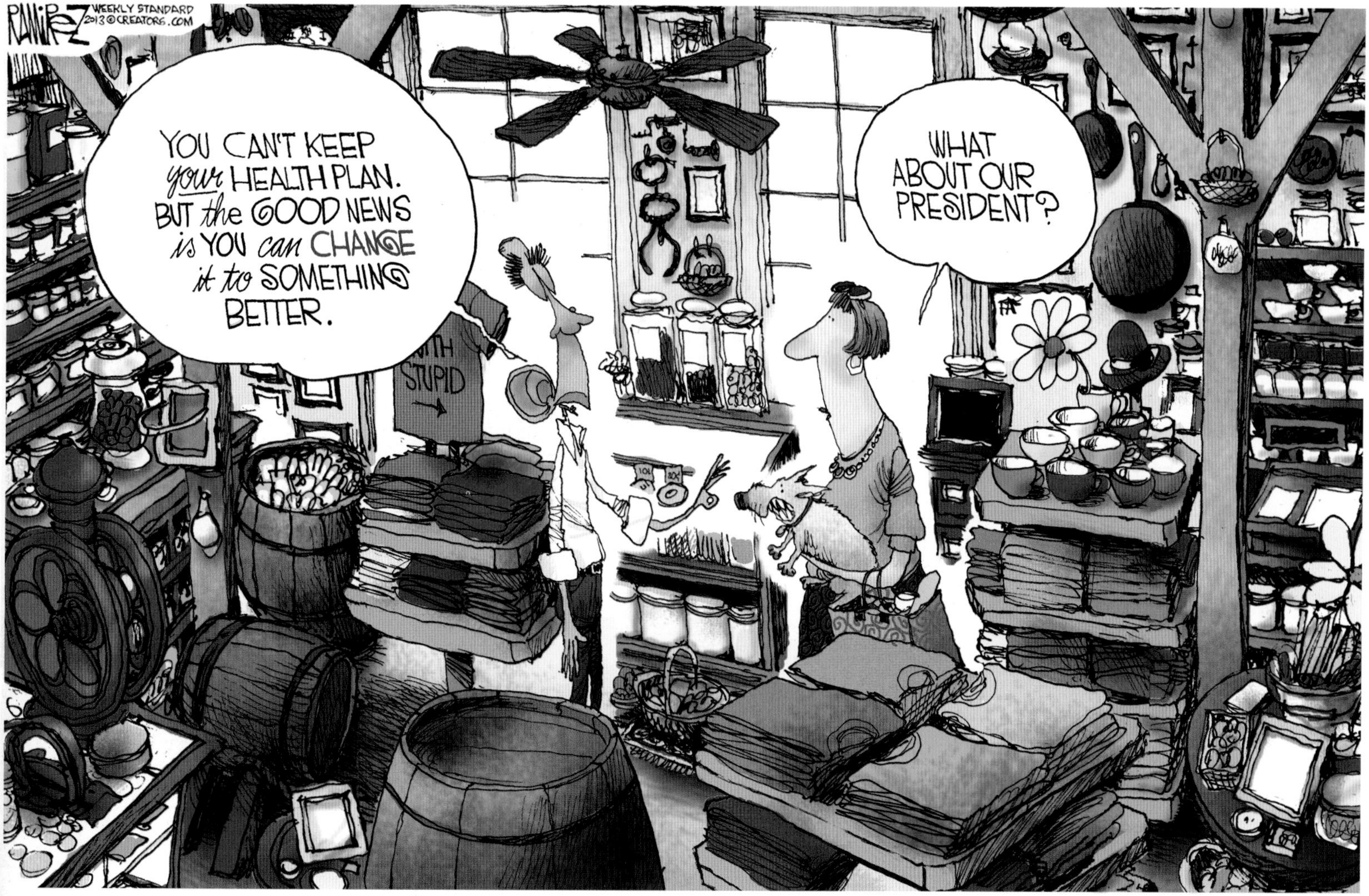
RAMIREZ WEEKLY STANDARD 2013 © CREATORS.COM
YOU CAN'T KEEP your HEALTH PLAN. BUT the GOOD NEWS is YOU can CHANGE it to SOMETHING BETTER.
WHAT ABOUT OUR PRESIDENT?
STUPID

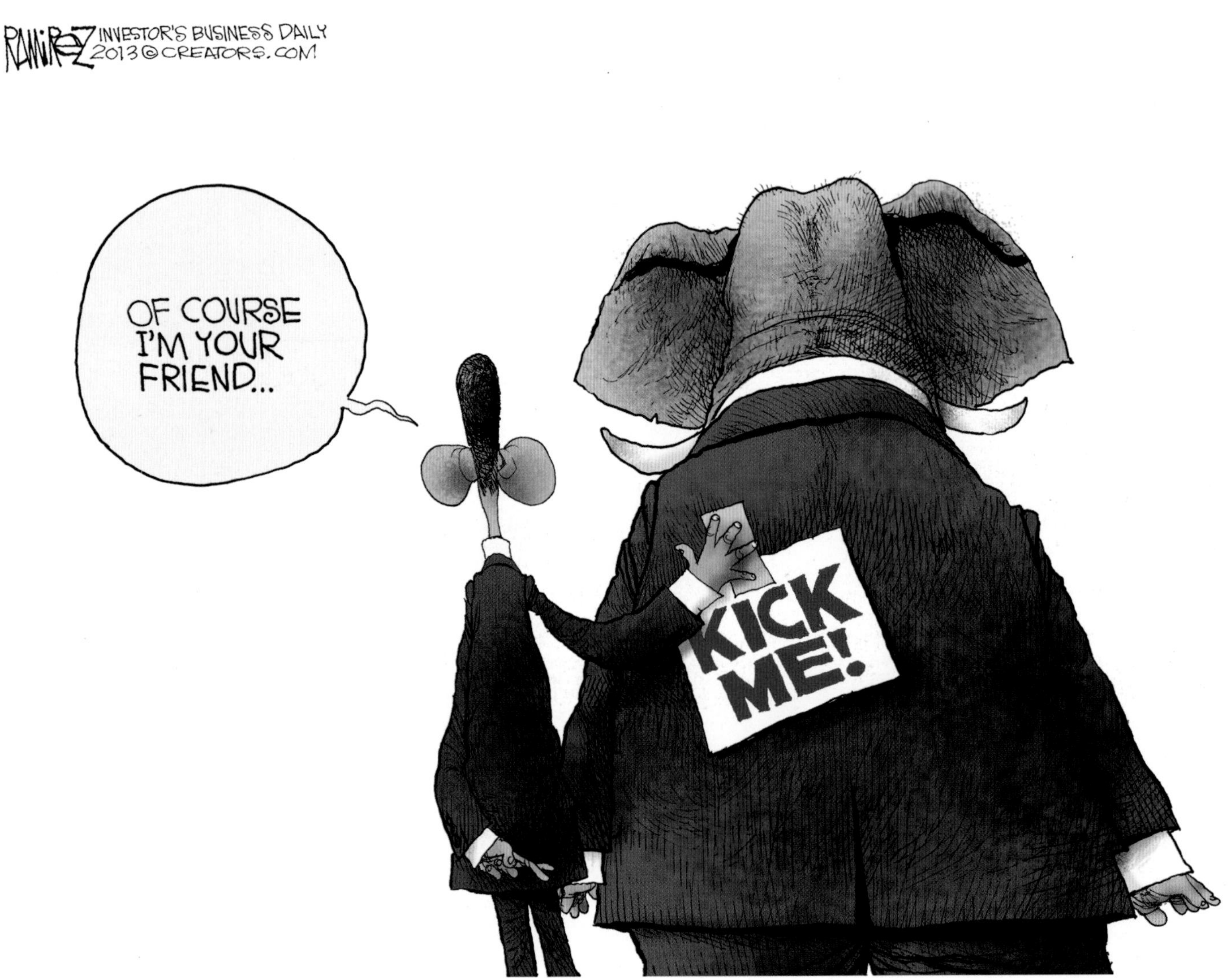
RAMIREZ INVESTOR'S BUSINESS DAILY 2013 © CREATORS.COM
OF COURSE I'M YOUR FRIEND...
KICK ME!

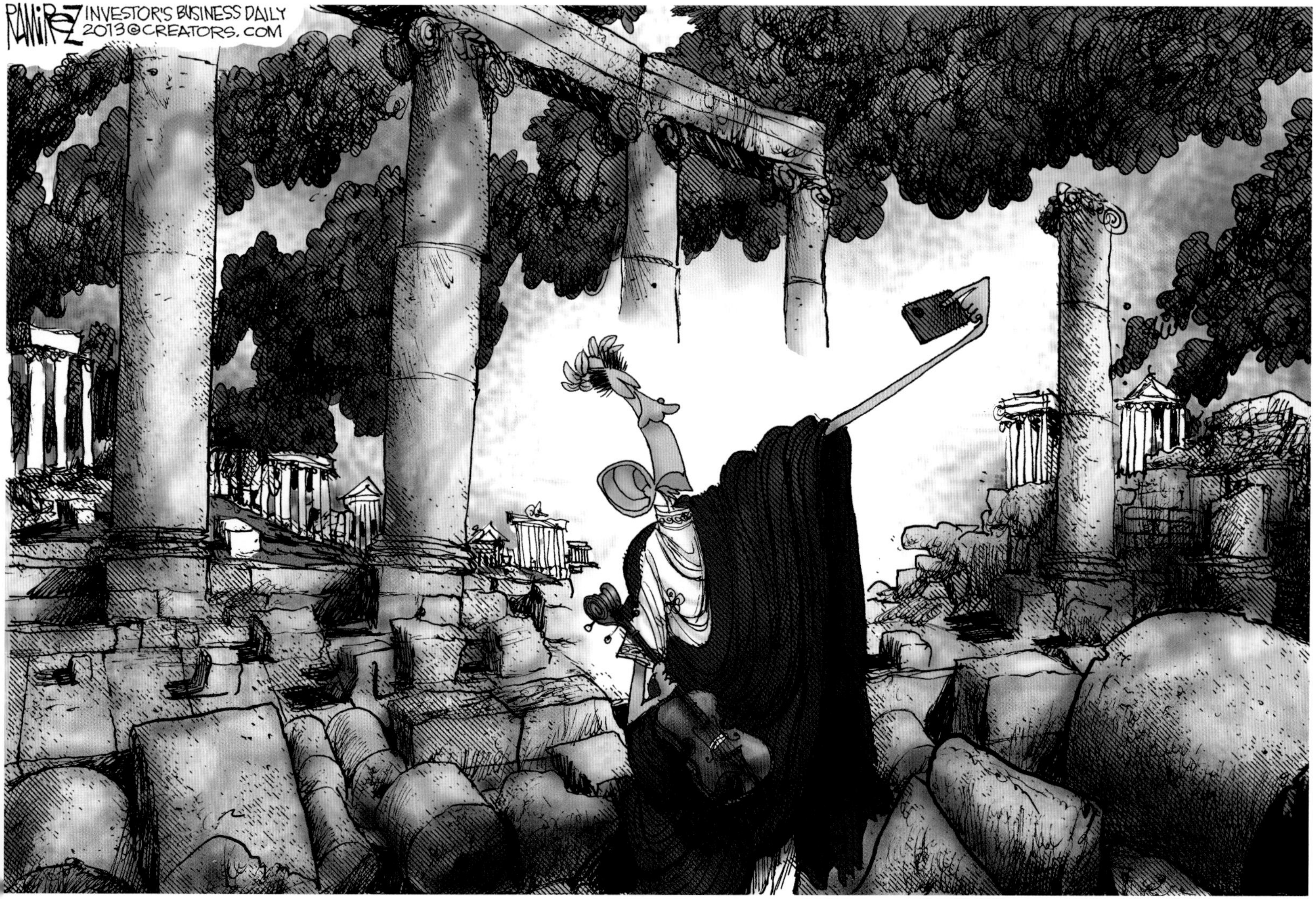
RAMIREZ INVESTOR'S BUSINESS DAILY
2013©CREATORS.COM

THE SELFIE.

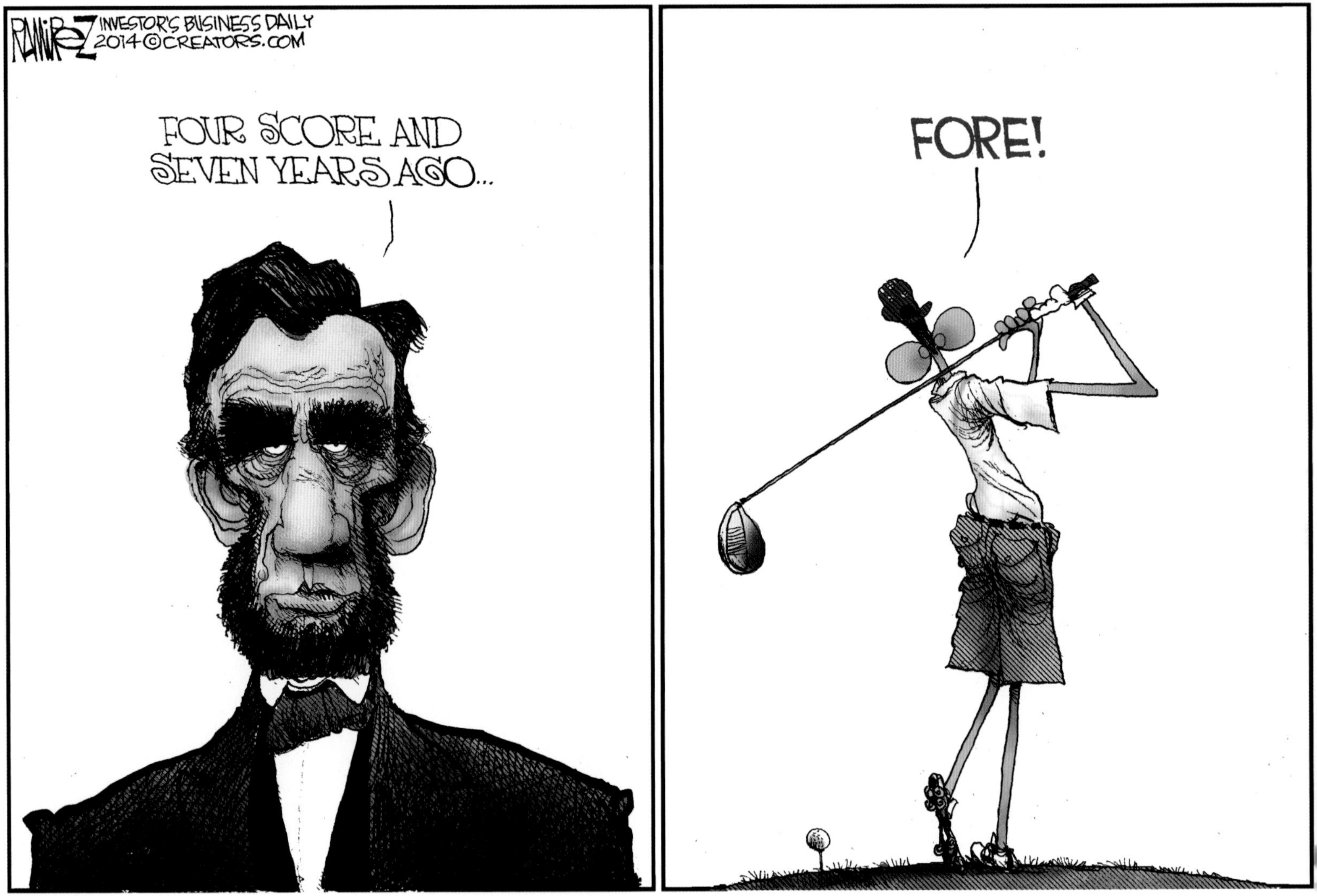
RAMIREZ INVESTOR'S BUSINESS DAILY 2014 ©CREATORS.COM
FOUR SCORE AND SEVEN YEARS AGO...
FORE!

PRESIDENTS DURING A CRISIS.

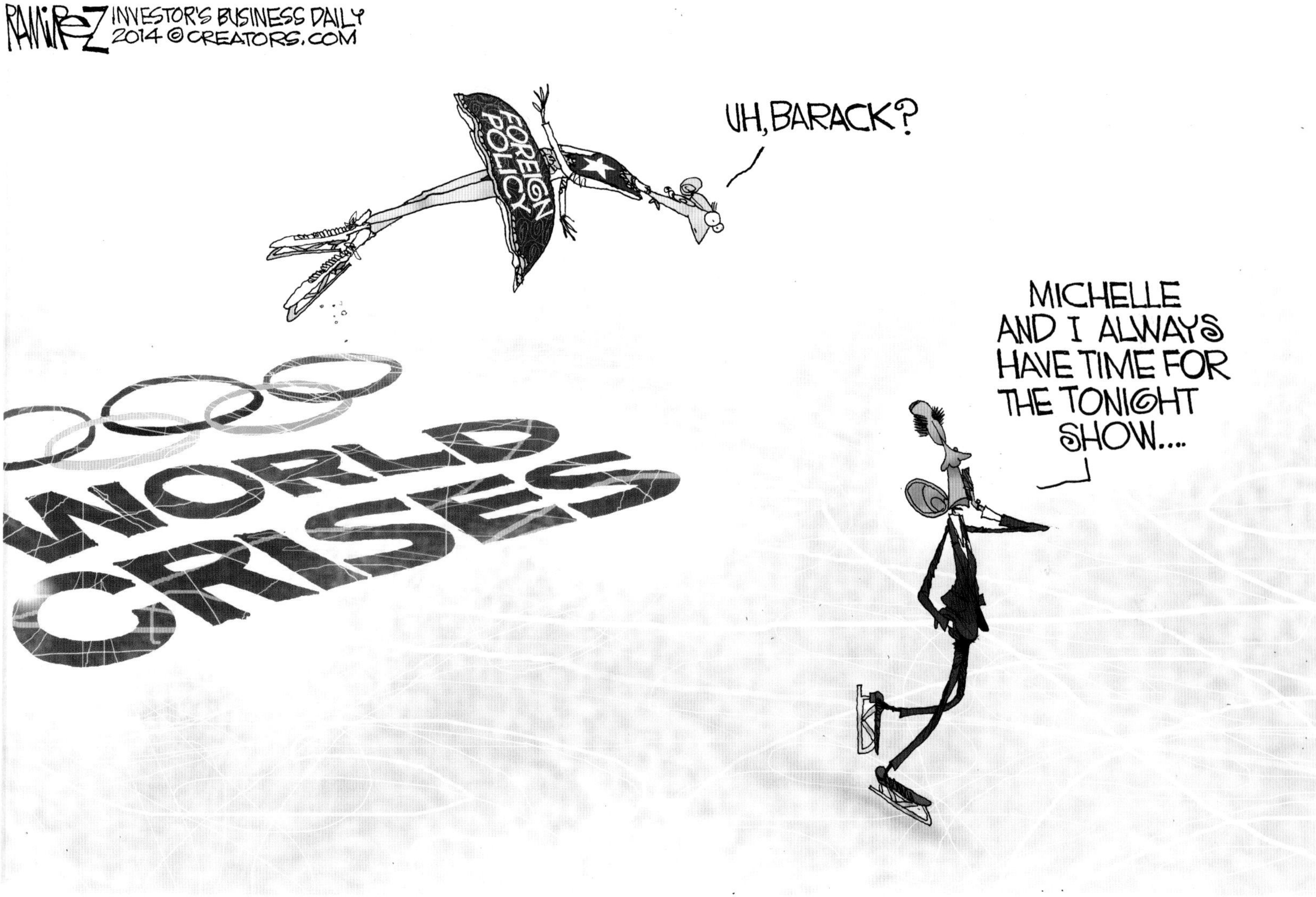
RAMIREZ INVESTOR'S BUSINESS DAILY
2014 © CREATORS.COM
FOREIGN POLICY
UH, BARACK?
WORLD CRISES
MICHELLE AND I ALWAYS HAVE TIME FOR THE TONIGHT SHOW....

LEADING FROM BEHIND.

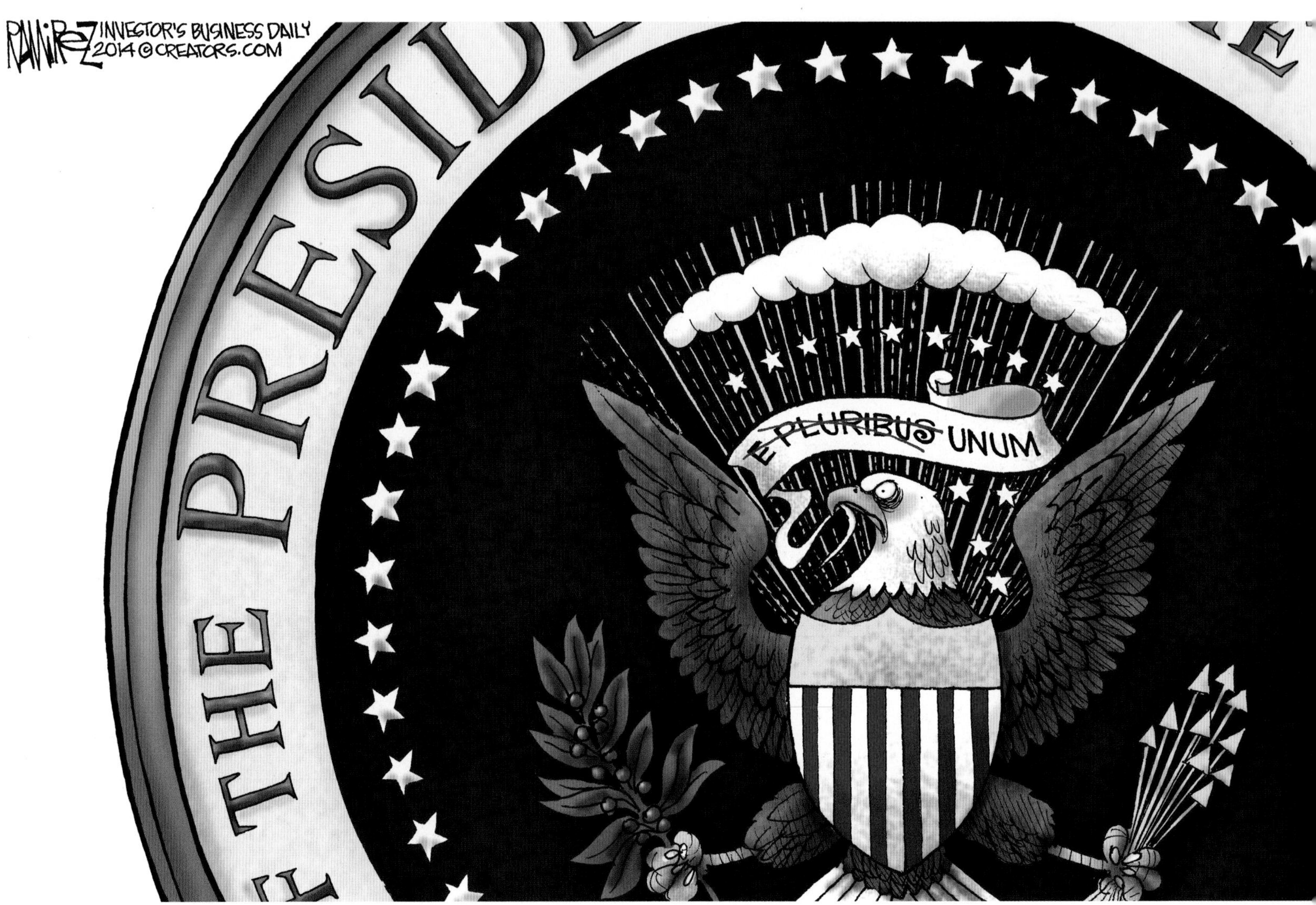
RAMIREZ INVESTOR'S BUSINESS DAILY
2014 © CREATORS.COM
THE PRESID
E PLURIBUS UNUM

The IMPERIAL PRESIDENT.

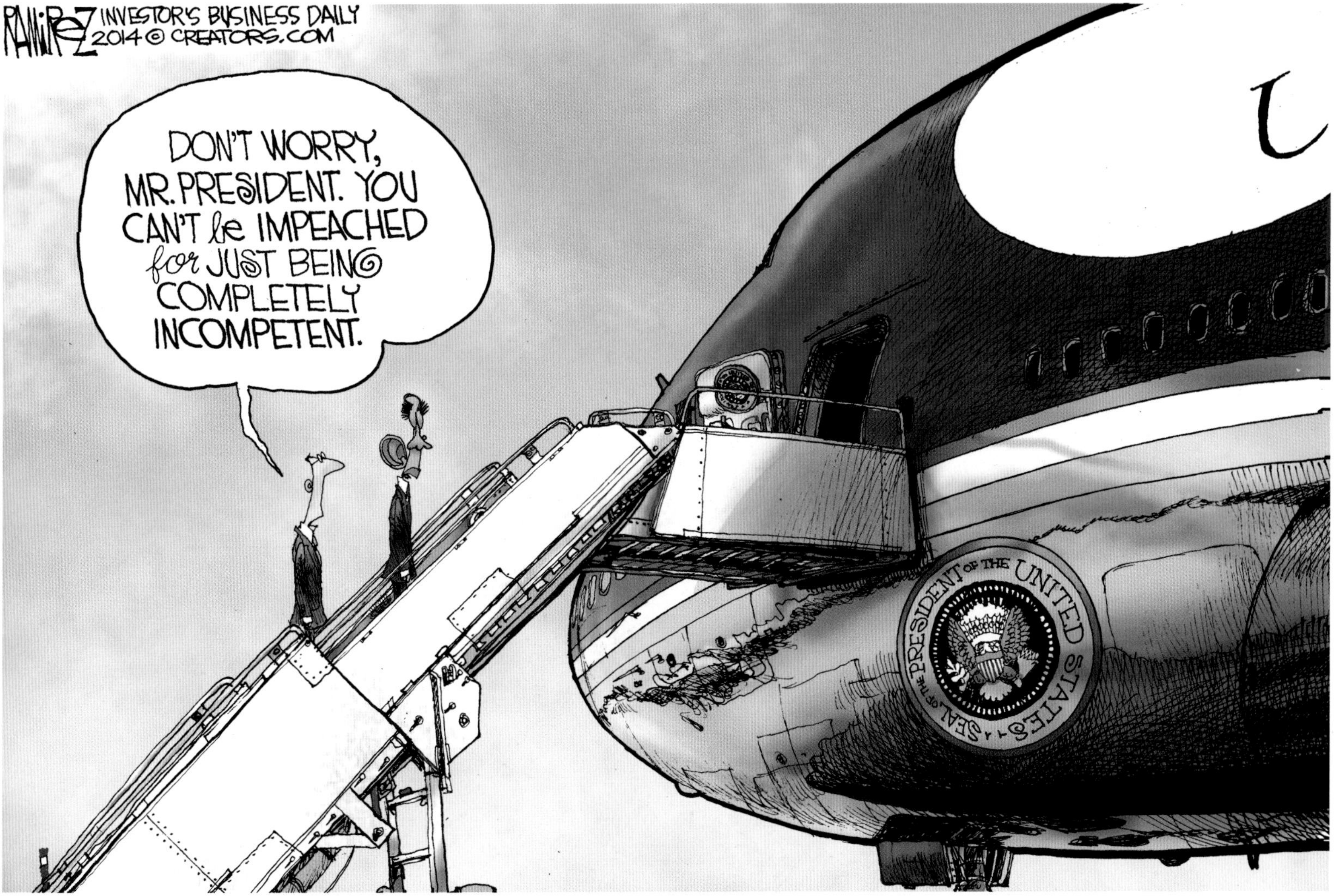
RAMIREZ INVESTOR'S BUSINESS DAILY 2014 © CREATORS.COM
DON'T WORRY, MR. PRESIDENT. YOU CAN'T be IMPEACHED for JUST BEING COMPLETELY INCOMPETENT.
SEAL OF THE PRESIDENT OF THE UNITED STATES

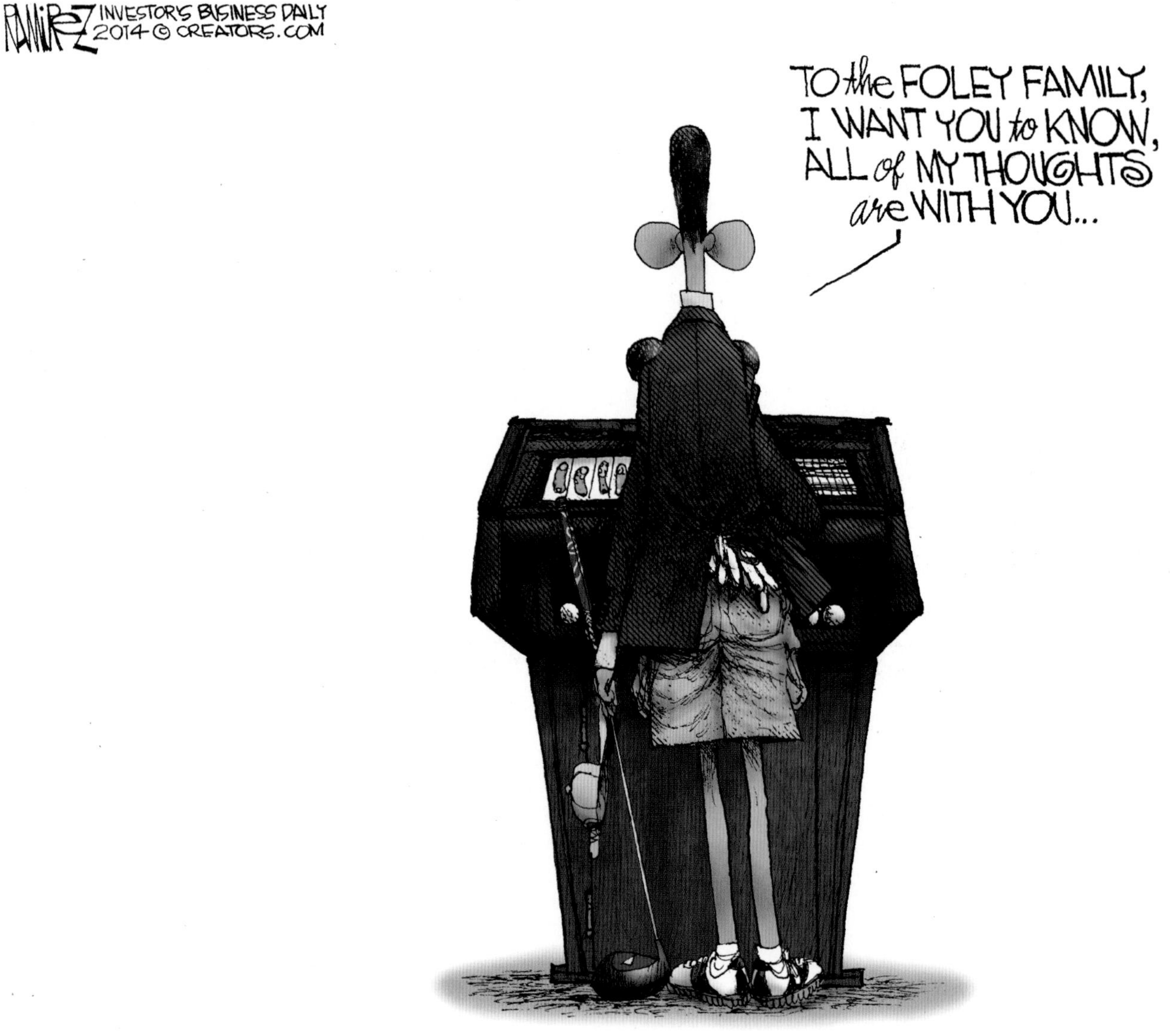
RAMIREZ INVESTOR'S BUSINESS DAILY 2014 © CREATORS.COM
TO the FOLEY FAMILY, I WANT YOU to KNOW, ALL of MY THOUGHTS are WITH YOU...

www.investors.com/cartoons

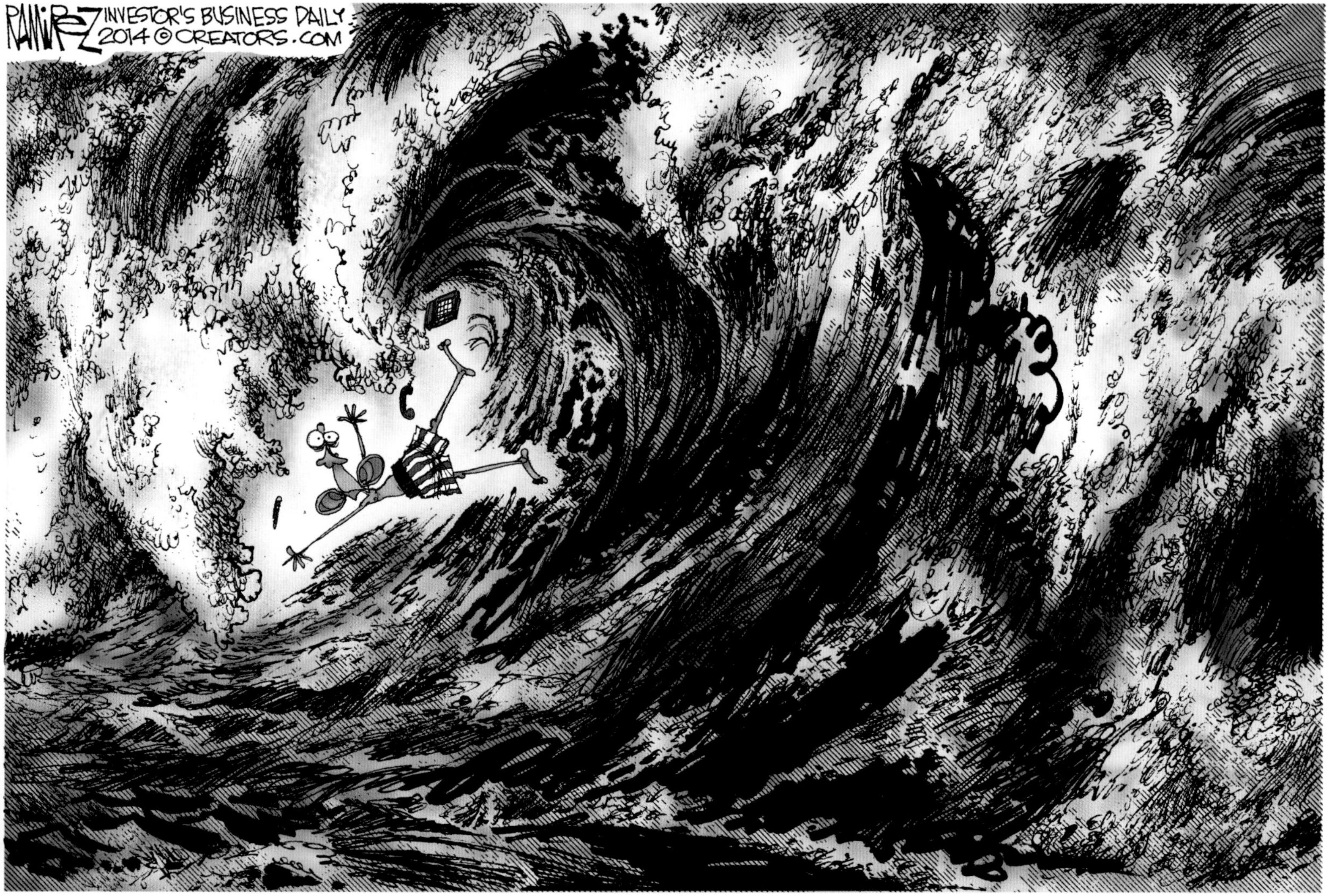
RAMIREZ
INVESTOR'S BUSINESS DAILY
2014 © CREATORS.COM

www.investors.com/cartoons

The WAVE

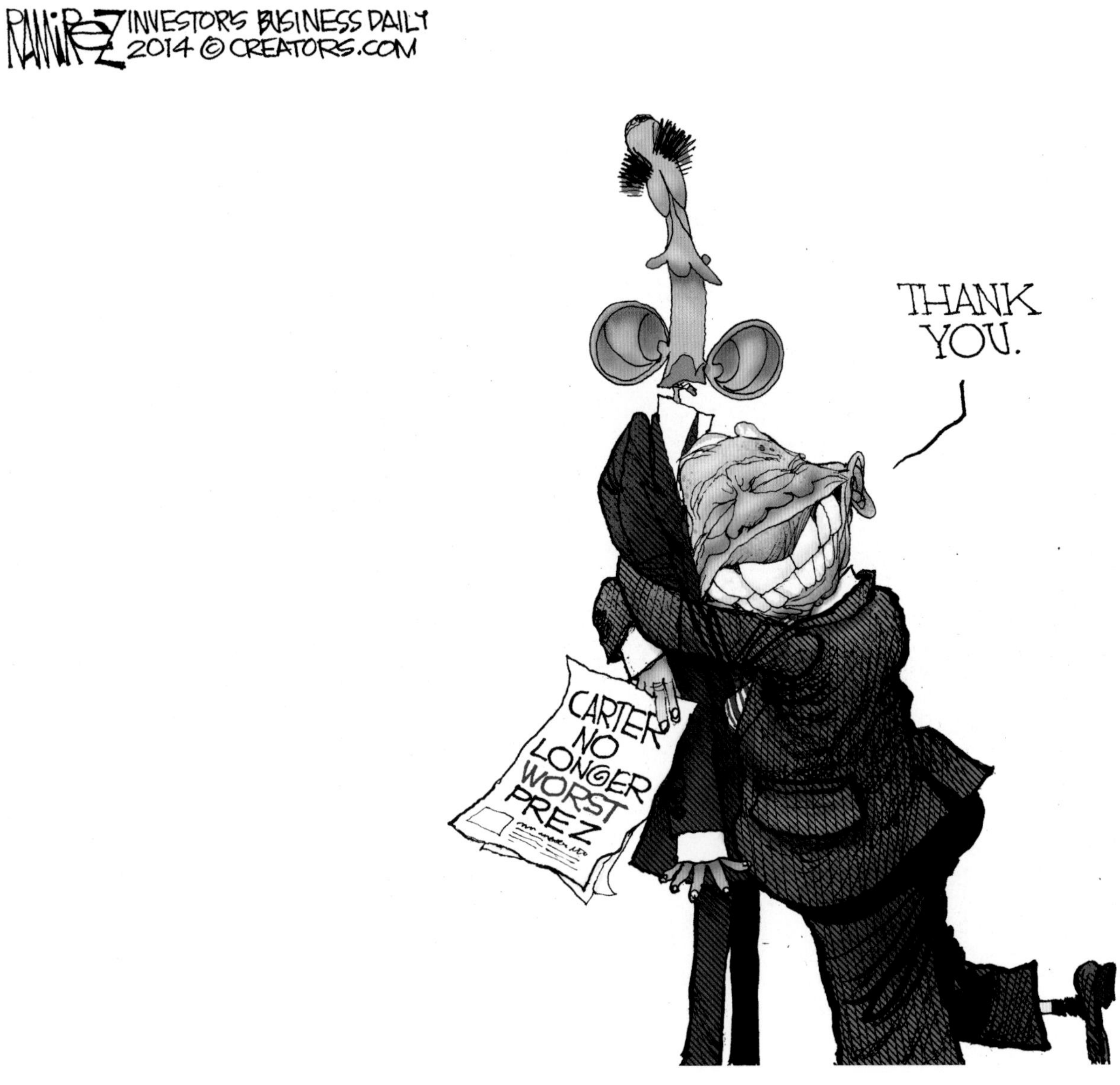
RAMIREZ INVESTOR'S BUSINESS DAILY
2014 © CREATORS.COM
THANK YOU.
CARTER NO LONGER WORST PREZ

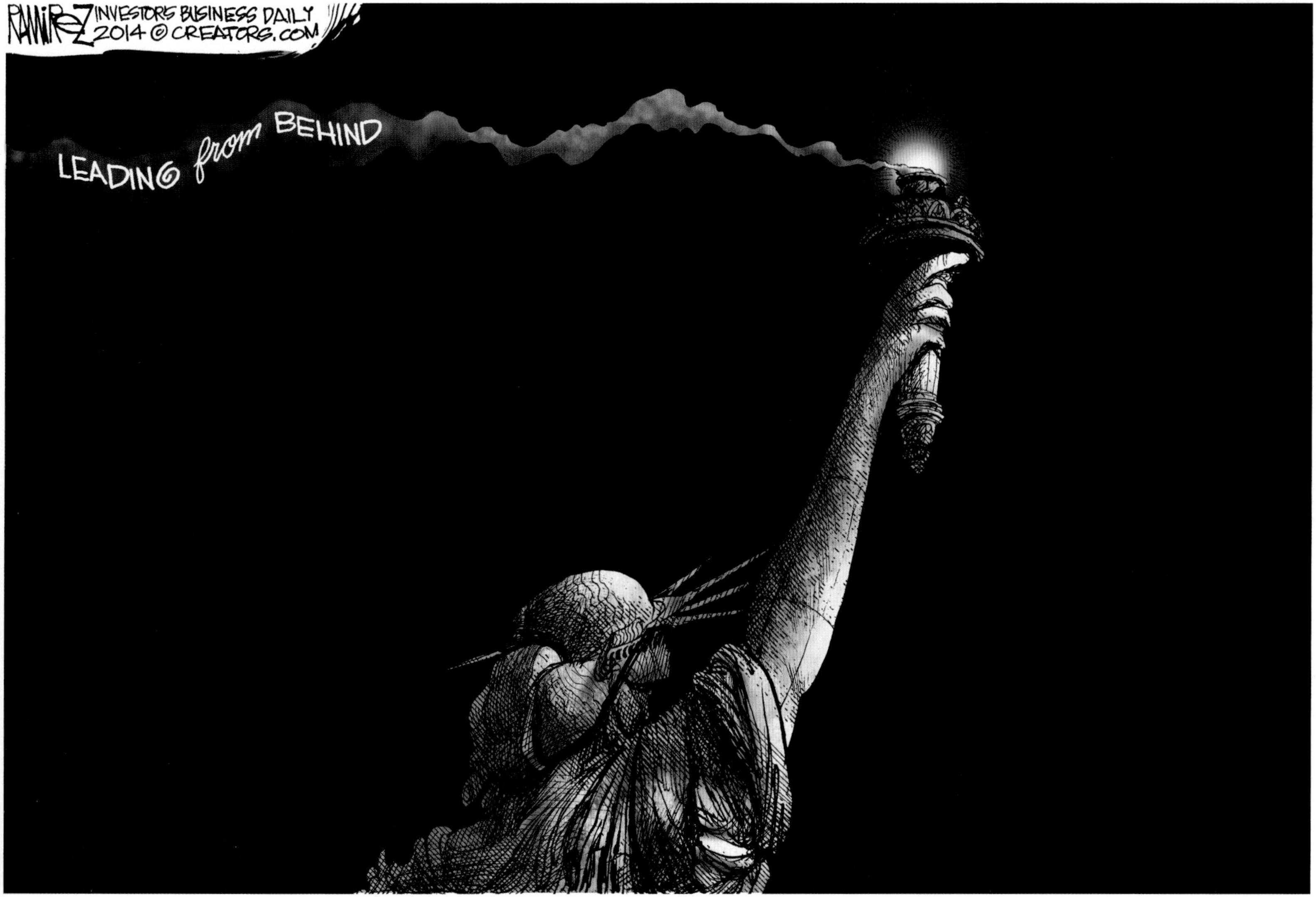
RAMIREZ INVESTOR'S BUSINESS DAILY 2014 © CREATORS.COM
LEADING from BEHIND

THE FADING LIGHT OF LIBERTY.

AFTERWORD

BY RUSH LIMBAUGH

Two Pulitzers and every cartooning award known to man. Not bad for the kid who was disqualified for not submitting an original work to a sixth-grade art contest. The teachers thought, "No kid could draw something this good!" But young Michael Ramirez did . . . and still does.

Mike and I have some things in common. It is why I have such profound respect and admiration for him. Mike was the black sheep of his family. While his siblings focused on the serious world of medicine (my family, the law), Mike was compulsively and literally covered in ink. He wanted to make statements, to be heard, to be influential. Mike had the rare ability to combine irreverent and sarcastic humor with serious commentary, simultaneously. Few in the world can do that, especially with the brevity and soul of wit he possesses. Nevertheless, his parents were unsure of exactly where he was headed, where this talent would take him. But they were confident he was going to get there and be a success.

His wide-ranging artistic abilities are from his mother, Fumico, while his wry sense of humor comes from his father, Edward, the career Army intelligence officer who schooled Mike in the world of politics.

He became serious about editorial cartooning while working for his college newspaper at the University of California, Irvine, when a man was pulled over by the Newport Beach Police and arrested for drunk driving and not allowed a phone call. As it turned out, he was a city council member who did not drink. Ramirez drew a cartoon with a man hogtied on the hood of a police car with a shoe wedged in his mouth. The arresting officer was explaining to his sergeant, "I was merely reinforcing his constitutional right to remain silent." The cartoonist was forced to appear before the Student Council and told he needed to be "educated." Mike Ramirez simply left the room, refusing the PC indoctrination. The police chief was so mad at the cartoon, he tried to find out where Ramirez lived. Talk about a Rush!

That was when Michael realized what a profound impact these drawings have, and fell in love with editorial cartooning.

A little about editorial cartooning: Information is the most necessary element in a self-governing republic. It is said that freedom cannot exist without the open exchange of ideas and truthful information. Very true, but how does one communicate truth in a persuasive manner? It's not enough to have the facts. It's not productive to get in another person's face and wag your finger at him, telling him he must believe, because that could convey the idea you think that person is an idiot. To be effective, one must assume and respect the intelligence of one's audience. The whole idea is to do things in such a way that your object convinces himself or herself of what you want them to believe, to see. Successful persuasion results in your target thinking he is brilliant, not that you are. And that is what Michael Ramirez has mastered. In panel after panel, Ramirez illuminates ideas, philosophies, and conclusions. His work opens eyes and minds, and does it with humor and laughter. None of it is intimidating, but it is all so penetrating. It is an axiom of great communication that the most powerful points are made with the fewest words possible. That's difficult enough. Now try it with one picture. It's like advertising. You have ten seconds to capture the audience's attention and another ten seconds to deliver the punch. Do all that, and what you have is Michael Ramirez.

It is also said, by me, that those who are great at what they do make it look easy. Effortless. In the example of Michael Ramirez, you might think it took him no longer to draw and write his cartoon than it took you to read it. This is another of his supreme talents. But like all hard work, Ramirez spends hours on each one and will not release it until it is perfect. He does everything he can . . . and then just a little bit more. This is why Michael Ramirez sits atop his profession.

Each Ramirez cartoon informs. Each one is a catalyst for thought. Each one influences the reader about the con-sequences of important decisions we are making today and what their impact will be on tomorrow. Each one delivers a serious message while at the same time being laugh-out-loud funny. Again, that rare combination of the serious and humorous that is so rare in commentary and entertainment today.

Today, Michael co-manages the editorial page at *Investor's Business Daily*, a role that I believe no other editorial cartoonist has in America. He was once introduced as one of the most influential minority journalists in America, apparently because of his Hispanic surname. He responded to the introduction by saying, "I am a member of the smallest minority in America today: I'm a conservative journalist."

Michael Ramirez. Making the complex understandable. Making you laugh at the same time.

I cannot tell you how honored I am to have been asked to write this afterword. It is comforting and encouraging to know that I am on the same team as Michael Ramirez.

Rush Limbaugh
Palm Beach, FL
August 2015

Free people, remember this maxim: we may acquire liberty, but it is never recovered if it is once lost.

—Jean-Jacques Rousseau